# Serial Communications:
# A C++ Developer's Guide

# Serial Communications:
# A C++ Developer's Guide

A comprehensive guide to writing serial communications applications using object-oriented techniques.

Mark Nelson

First published in 1992 in North America by M&T Publishing, Inc., 411 Borel Avenue, Suite 100, San Mateo, CA 94402, U.S.A., and co-published for sale outside North America by Prentice Hall International (UK) Limited, Campus 400, Marylands Avenue, Hemel Hempstead, Hertfordshire, HP2 7EZ, England, a division of Simon & Schuster International Group.

 © 1992 by M&T Publishing

All rights reserved. No part of this book may be reproduced or transmitted in any form or by any means, electronic or mechanical, including photocopying, recording, or by any information storage and retrieval system, without prior written permission from the Publisher. For permission within North America contact M&T Publishing, 411 Borel Avenue, Suite 100, San Mateo, CA 94402, U.S.A.

This edition may be sold only in those countries to which it is consigned by Prentice Hall International (UK) Limited. It is not to be re-exported, and is not for sale in North America.

The Author and Publisher make no warranty of any kind, expressed or implied, with regard to these programs or the documentation contained in this book. The Author and Publisher shall not be liable in any event for incidental or consequential damages in connection with, or arising out of, the furnishing, performance, or use of these programs.

All brand names, trademarks, and registered trademarks are the property of their respective holders.

British Library Cataloguing-in-Publication Data is available from the British Library.

**Developmental Editor:** Erica Liederman
**Copy Editor:** Heather Leitch
**Cover Design:** Lauren Smith Design
**Art Director:** Margaret Horoszko
**Layout:** Stacey L. Evans

*To Laura*

# Contents

**Why This Book Is for You** ......................................................................... 1

**Introduction** ................................................................................................ 3
    Why C++? ................................................................................................ 3
    No Dogma ................................................................................................ 4
    The Virtual Approach ............................................................................. 4
    Virtual Functions Everywhere ................................................................ 7
    The C Programmer .................................................................................. 8
    Compiler Support .................................................................................... 8
    Source Code ............................................................................................ 9

**Chapter 1: An Overview of RS-232** ......................................................... 11
    Who Should Read This Chapter ............................................................ 11
    The RS-232 Standard ............................................................................ 11
    Results of the Omissions ...................................................................... 12
    ASCII-Another RS-232-C? ................................................................... 13
    One from Column A, One from Column B .......................................... 14
    DTE and DCE ....................................................................................... 14
    RS-232: Let's Get Physical .................................................................. 15
    Signal Formats ...................................................................................... 18
    Data Lines ............................................................................................. 19
    Control Lines ........................................................................................ 21
        RTS/CTS ......................................................................................... 21
        DTR/DSR ....................................................................................... 22
        CD .................................................................................................. 22
        RI ................................................................................................... 23
        Electrical lines ............................................................................... 23

| | |
|---|---|
| Limitations | 23 |
| Cabling | 24 |
|     The null modem cable | 26 |
|     A more rational cable design | 27 |
| RS-2332 9- to25-Pin Adapters | 29 |
|     Home surgery for fun and profit | 31 |
|     Macintosh cabling | 31 |
|     Cabling conclusion | 32 |
| UARTS | 33 |
| Doomed to Repeat | 33 |
|     Electronic Darwinism | 34 |
| 8250 Functionality | 35 |
|     Data registers | 36 |
|     Control registers | 36 |
|     Status registers | 36 |
|     Interrupt functions | 36 |
| The 16550 Difference | 37 |
| Multiport Boards | 38 |
| The Multitasking Grail | 39 |
| Intelligent Multiport Boards | 39 |
| Modems | 41 |
|     Data rates | 42 |
|     Intelligence | 44 |
|     Handshaking | 46 |
| Hardware Flow Control | 47 |
| Software Flow Control | 48 |
|     Local versus pass through | 49 |
| File Transfers | 50 |
| Software and Hardware | 53 |
|     PC software | 53 |
|     BBS software | 54 |
|     On line information services | 55 |
|     Programming libraries | 55 |

Tools of the Trade ..................................................................................... 57
    Breakout boxes .................................................................................... 57
    Line monitors ....................................................................................... 59
Cable-Making Equipment ........................................................................ 61
    Gender changers/adapters .................................................................. 62
    Voltmeter .............................................................................................. 63
Summary ................................................................................................... 64

## Chapter 2: The RS232 Class ................................................................ 65

A Base Class? ........................................................................................... 65
Doing It in C .............................................................................................. 66
    Excess baggage ................................................................................... 66
    Function pointers ................................................................................. 67
    Function pointers as part of the RS232 structure ............................... 68
    So why C++? ....................................................................................... 69
Class RS232 .............................................................................................. 72
A Few Conventions .................................................................................. 75
    Function/element names ..................................................................... 75
    Function return values ......................................................................... 76
    Byte counts .......................................................................................... 78
    Elapsed time ........................................................................................ 78
Default Parameters .................................................................................. 79
    Mandatory and optional ...................................................................... 80
    Where is the constructor? .................................................................. 81
    The class, member by member .......................................................... 81
Protected Members ................................................................................. 81
Protected Member Functions .................................................................. 85
Public Data Members ............................................................................... 86
Mandatory Virtual Functions ................................................................... 87
Nonvirtual Functions ................................................................................ 92
A Very Short Program .............................................................................. 97
The Optional Functions ............................................................................ 98
The Code ................................................................................................... 109

**Chapter 3: The PC8250 Class** .................................................................. **133**
    The 8250 UART ................................................................................. 133
    8250 Register Set .............................................................................. 134
        Receive Buffer Register ............................................................. 135
        Transmit Holding Register ......................................................... 136
        Interrupt Enable Register ........................................................... 137
        Interrupt ID Register .................................................................. 139
        Line Control Register/Baud Rate Divisor .................................. 141
        Modem Control Register ........................................................... 144
        Line Status Register .................................................................. 146
        Modem Status Register ............................................................. 148
    8250 Look-alikes ............................................................................... 148
    8250 Oddities .................................................................................... 152
        Interrupt pulsing ........................................................................ 152
        Jump starting interrupts ............................................................ 152
        Extra modem status interrupts .................................................. 153
        Motherboard timing ................................................................... 153
    The Standard COM Card .................................................................. 154
        Laptop oddities .......................................................................... 154
        Upgrading to a 16550 ................................................................ 156
        The Hayes ESP card .................................................................. 157
    How Interrupts Work on the PC ........................................................ 157
        Hardware basics ........................................................................ 158
        Enter Micro Channel architecture ............................................. 160
    PC8250 Driver Structure ................................................................... 160
        The interrupt service routine ..................................................... 160
    The isr_data Structure ...................................................................... 165
    The ISR Code .................................................................................... 169
        The modem status interrupt handler ......................................... 178
        The TX interrupt handler .......................................................... 179
        The receive interrupt handler ................................................... 180
        The line status handler ............................................................. 181
        jump_start( ) .............................................................................. 181
    PC8250.CPP ...................................................................................... 182

Support Packages .................................................................................................. 224
    The Queue package ........................................................................................ 224
    The interrupt manager package .................................................................. 229
A Test Program ....................................................................................................... 240
Conclusion ............................................................................................................... 243

## Chapter 4: Shared Interrupt Devices ............................................................... 245

The Micro Channel Handler ................................................................................ 245
ISR Protocols ......................................................................................................... 246
The Micro Channel Handler Class ...................................................................... 248
The Handler Class .................................................................................................. 249
Testing the Micro Channel Code .......................................................................... 253
Nonintelligent Multiport Boards .......................................................................... 257
Hardware ................................................................................................................. 258
    Enter the status register ................................................................................ 259
    The BocaBoard handler ................................................................................ 260
    The constructor ............................................................................................. 261
    The destructor ............................................................................................... 265
Modifications to TEST232.EXE .......................................................................... 266
Multitasking Under MS-DOS ............................................................................... 268
    Sources for boards ........................................................................................ 269

## Chapter 5: Intelligent Multiport Boards ........................................................ 271

The Hardware ......................................................................................................... 271
    Design freedom .............................................................................................. 273
    Control programs ........................................................................................... 273
    Software interface ......................................................................................... 274
Drivers to the Rescue ............................................................................................ 275
    The DigiBoard API ....................................................................................... 275
Configuring Your DigiBoard ................................................................................ 295
    Configuring the ports .................................................................................... 296
    Implementing the DigiBoard class ............................................................... 298

  The Code ...................................................................................................298

  TEST232.EXE ............................................................................................319

  Summary ...................................................................................................322

## Chapter 6: The BIOS and EBIOS Drivers ...................................................323

  BIOS Details ..............................................................................................324

    Problems ............................................................................................328

    The code ............................................................................................330

    Inheritance .........................................................................................330

    Testing the BIOS classes ...................................................................352

## Chapter 7: The FOSSIL Driver .....................................................................355

  BBS Drivers ...............................................................................................355

    The solution ......................................................................................356

  The FOSSIL Specification .........................................................................356

    Sources...............................................................................................366

    Why bother? ......................................................................................366

  The Source Code .......................................................................................367

    Building TEST232.EXE ....................................................................382

    A test run ...........................................................................................383

## Chapter 8: The Microsoft Windows Driver .................................................385

  Windows Programming..............................................................................385

    The MS-Windows device driver........................................................386

    The communications API .................................................................386

    Putting it together ..............................................................................401

  A Test Program...........................................................................................424

    Building TEST232W.EXE ................................................................431

  Summary ....................................................................................................432

**Chapter 9: Making Modems Usable** ............................................................**433**
   The Hardware Standards ........................................................................434
   The Software Standards ..........................................................................435
      The Smartmodem 2400 command set ................................................436
      The S registers ...................................................................................442
   Today's Modems .....................................................................................444
      Modem capabilities............................................................................446
      Creating a capability entry................................................................449
      The Modem class..............................................................................450
      The public interface ..........................................................................452
      Protected members ...........................................................................456
   A Test Program........................................................................................468
      Making TSTMODEM.CPP ..............................................................472

**Chapter 10: File Transfers and ZMODEM** ..................................................**475**
   XMODEM and YMODEM......................................................................475
   Enter ZMODEM .....................................................................................476
      Why ZMODEM?...............................................................................477
      An overview of ZMODEM ..............................................................478
      ZMODEM frame types......................................................................479
      The data subpacket ...........................................................................483
      Header formats .................................................................................486
          *HEX headers* ..............................................................................487
          *16- and 32-bit CRC Binary headers* ..........................................488
   Data Subpacket Formats .........................................................................488
      Encoding...........................................................................................490
      Odds and ends...................................................................................491
      A file transfer....................................................................................492
      The FileTransfer class.......................................................................493
      The Zmodem class............................................................................496
   The Test Program ....................................................................................496
   The CRC Classes.....................................................................................499
   Source Code ............................................................................................503

**Chapter 11: Terminal Emulation** ............................................................. 543
    Escape Sequences ............................................................................. 544
    Terminal Intelligence Quotients ....................................................... 545
    Tower of Babel ................................................................................. 545
    ANSI.SYS ......................................................................................... 546
        ANSI.SYS Escape sequences ................................................ 546
        Keyboard sequences .............................................................. 552
    A Terminal Class .............................................................................. 553
    A Test Program ................................................................................. 555
    Class AnsiTerminal ........................................................................... 557
    Debugging Hooks ............................................................................. 579
        The TextWindow class .......................................................... 581
        Making the test program ........................................................ 607

**Appendix A: TEST232.EXE** ..................................................................... 609
    A General Purpose Test Program .................................................... 609
    Operations ......................................................................................... 609
    Function Descriptions ...................................................................... 611
    The Source Code .............................................................................. 616
    Building TEST232.EXE ................................................................... 625
    Conclusion ........................................................................................ 627

**Appendix B: Sources** .................................................................................. 629

**Appendix C: Source Code** ......................................................................... 635

**Glossary** ...................................................................................................... 643

**Index** ........................................................................................................... 649

# Acknowledgments

I owe a special thanks to my friends at Greenleaf Software.
Without them, this book would not have been possible. I wish them all the best.

# Why This Book Is for You

This valuable reference tool teaches C programmers how to create serial communications applications that are easily ported between different operating systems and hardware platforms. It covers all of the basics and presents the new object-oriented techniques offered by C++.

You will find this book particularly valuable if:

- You develop RS-232 applications for the IBM PC architecture. This book will help you write C and C+ programs that are portable across the majority of hardware and software platforms in use today.

- You are a C programmer who wants to start using C++, but aren't sure where to start. You can start using the code in this book without having to be a C++ guru.

- You are frustrated with C++ books that give ivory tower examples of classes, but don't help with real world functions. Books that show "class gorilla" derived from "class zoo-animal" might be interesting, but they don't help you transfer files between systems today.

- You want to know how to use a: DigiBoard, FOSSIL driver, Windows device driver, BIOS interface, ANSI Terminal Emulator, or Zmodem file transfer class. Full working examples are provided for all these types of applications and more.

# Introduction

This book teaches programmers how to use C++ to develop flexible communications programs. The sample code is targeted to the IBM PC but, by definition, is easy to port to other machines.

In the past, C programmers developing programs for RS-232 hardware found themselves locked into a "deadly embrace" with particular hardware. While their software may have worked properly in the given environment, changing any one of several variables, such as the hardware platform, the operating system, the C compiler, or the type of serial interface used often required an extensive rewrite of the program. This book shows how to avoid the limitations of serial programming using one of the most powerful tools available to a C programmer: C++.

This book focuses on writing programs that use the RS-232 ports; it doesn't go into detailed discussions of RS-232 hardware, applications software, BBS programs, and so on. Those topics have been discussed elsewhere. What the other RS-232 books don't cover are the intricacies involved in developing software to interface computers to RS-232 hardware.

## Why C++?

Five years ago, I would have written all the code in this book in C, the most popular language for software development at that time. C++ was still considered an oddity mostly confined to use by researchers, and certainly wasn't thought of as a suitable language for a production environment.

But C++ is moving rapidly toward replacing C as the most favored language of software developers. First of all, the language has evolved in a textbook case of cooperation between researchers, industry, and standards organizations. Second, as PC software projects have grown more complex, C has begun to show some weaknesses. And finally, competition among vendors has led to the availability of a number of excellent C++ compilers that are, in most cases, extensions of existing C compilers.

In terms of sales, the most popular vendors of C and C++ compilers today are probably Borland, Microsoft, and Zortech. Borland's and Zortech's compilers are pure C++, and have a C compiler as a subset. Microsoft's C++ compiler is that company's flagship product; only their entry-level compiler, Quick C, remains as a "C-only" product. Most serious C programmers now have a C++ compiler, even if they are only using it to compile C programs.

## No Dogma

Two schools of thought govern the use of the C++ programming language. The purist camp believes that to use C++ properly, the trappings of procedural programming used for writing C code must be left behind. These zealots favor adopting a "politically correct" object orientation towards programming, which means reworking the development process from the ground up.

Those who follow a more pragmatic approach to C++ programming use C++ as a better C. Instead of diving head-first into object-oriented programming, these people begin by testing the waters. Approaching C++ as an improved C means you can take advantage of C++ features, such as stronger typing, inline code, typesafe linkage, and default parameters immediately without worrying about more exotic items, such as virtual destructors or multiple inheritance.

My approach falls into the second camp. The code in this book does not require you to master conversation stoppers, such as "polymorphism" or "operator overloading." In fact, you can use this book with only a beginner's knowledge of C++. Using traditional C syntax, you can write programs that will make efficient use of the C++ interface code, giving you the best of both worlds.

## The Virtual Approach

No matter which approach you take, programming in C++ has quite a few benefits. One feature stands out above the others: virtual functions. When combined with the inheritance mechanism in C++, virtual functions let you write applications that are truly portable across different types of hardware, user interfaces, and operating systems.

# INTRODUCTION

If you are C programmer, think of a virtual function simply as a function pointer. When you call a function that has been defined as virtual, the compiler knows that you are not calling a function directly, but are instead calling a function via a pointer to a member of a class.

The code below illustrates how I will use virtual functions and the inheritance mechanism. At the very top level is a class called RS232. The RS232 class is an *"abstract class"* because it doesn't represent an actual thing; rather it represents an abstraction of what we expect to find in an RS232 object. The virtual function Read() indicates that any object derived from an RS232 object will have a function used to read bytes from an RS232 port.

```
class RS232
{
   public :
      virtual int Read( void );
};

class PC8250 : public RS232
{
   private :
      Queue RXQueue;
   public :
      virtual int Read( void );
};

int PC8250::Read( void )
{
   return ( RXQueue.Remove() );
}
```

The second class shown here is the PC8250 class, which is derived from the RS232 class. It also has a virtual function declared as Read(), which is defined immediately below the PC8250 class definition.

So far this may look like just another explanation of the C++ inheritance mechanism. However, we'll see an immediate payoff. Once this hierarchy is established, we can write high-level software that uses only `RS232` virtual functions when manipulating data. For example, a function might look like this:

```
int XModemReceive( RS232& port )
{
    .
    .
    .
    c = port.Read();
    .
    .
    .
}
```

In this case, our high-level function calls a virtual function from the base class since, through the use of function pointers, the derived class's function will be called instead. A user may write a program that looks like this:

```
int main()
{
    PC8250 port( COM1 );

    XmodemReceive( port );
}
```

Here, we can pass a `PC8250` object to the `XmodemReceive` function, even though it expects an `RS232` object. Since `PC8250` is derived directly from `RS232`, `XmodemReceive()` can count on all the member functions and data being represented properly in `PC8250`.

Later, we can modify the program to use a Windows port via the Microsoft Windows device driver. We would only have to change a single line of code so the program would look like this:

```
int main()
{
        WindowsPort port( COM1 );

        XmodemReceive( port );
}
```

So the immediate benefit we get from C++ is the ability to modify programs to support different types of communications hardware quickly without rewriting any high-level code. All we need is a new set of virtual functions for every device type we intend to use.

Of course, all of this could be done in C, but we would have to do a lot of the work manually that the C++ compiler does automatically for us. When creating an object of class `PC8250`, for example, the C++ compiler will initialize all of the virtual function pointers so that the correct functions are called by the `XmodemReceive()` function. In C, we would have to write initialization code to do this for every derived type, with plenty of extra opportunities for mistakes.

## Virtual Functions Everywhere

Elsewhere in this book, virtual functions will be used to great benefit. Virtualization of our keyboard and screen input and output will help a great deal when performing terminal emulation. By supporting classes designed specifically for MS-DOS, Windows, and intelligent multiport boards, we will once again be able to write programs that are easy to port. And file transfer protocols will also benefit from virtualization.

## The C Programmer

If you are a novice C++ programmer, but feel comfortable with C, the idea of virtual functions and classes can seem scary. But once the class is defined, you can write code that looks just like traditional C code for writing your own high-level functions. However, your function calls to access the RS-232 port will look slightly different under C++. A C function used to access a port might look like this:

```
WriteChar( port, c );
```

The same function in C++ will be turned around a bit to look like this:

```
port.Write(c);
```

This requires the C programmer to make a minor adjustment in syntax, but definitely doesn't require a major paradigm shift.

## Compiler Support

As the ANSI C committee worked its way toward the eventual C standard, it became increasingly easy for programmers to use more than one C compiler on the same piece of code. In the MS-DOS arena, each C compiler still has its own unique features, particularly in areas such as graphics libraries, which were left untouched by the standard. By avoiding these unique features, however, it was possible to write code that would compile and run under Microsoft, Borland, Zortech, and Watcom C compilers.

The C++ world has evolved a bit differently. While there is no C++ ANSI standard as of this writing, there is an unofficial standard; the AT&T C++ specification. The MS-DOS compiler vendors are trying to adhere strictly to this specification, so there is much more uniformity among products than there was in the early years of C.

# INTRODUCTION

This means that it is possible to write code for a book like this that can support every major C++ compiler available. The code you read in this book will have been compiled, and will work properly, with the current C++ releases from:

Borland
Zortech/Symantec
Microsoft

All code should compile cleanly with maximum warning levels set.

## Source Code

All of the source code presented here is found on the diskette that accompanies the book. Simple make files are provided that can be easily modified for any of the C++ compilers previously mentioned. Each chapter has specific instructions on how to build the demo programs that are used to illustrate the chapter.

In the event that you are using a compiler other than those specifically supported here, you should still be able to compile and run the test programs. Most compiler have a `make` program similar to those used here, and will work with the make files found on the source code disk.

CHAPTER 1

# An Overview of RS-232

Many of you may already have a good background in working with RS-232 hardware. If you are comfortable with modems, serial ports, cabling, and so on, you may want to skim this chapter or even skip it entirely for now and come back to it if needed.

## Who Should Read This Chapter

This chapter provides a concentrated overview of RS-232, some of the hardware used in serial communications, and tools of the trade. If you feel like you need a book devoted entirely to covering this material, several other good books are available.

By necessity, this chapter skips some of the topics that are tangential to programming. For example, it doesn't talk about the history of electronic communications. It doesn't describe the modulation schemes used by various modems, and it doesn't discuss how to log-on to CompuServe.

Rather, this chapter briefly covers topics that directly affect the creation and testing of the programs in this book. Such topics include the RS-232 standard, connectors and cables, Universal Asynchronous Receiver/Transmitters (UARTs) and serial boards, modems, handshaking, on-line services, and some basic debugging hardware.

## The RS-232 Standard

A well-written standard can become the framework around which developers build useful products. If such products carefully adhere to a standard, users count on them to perform predictably. For C programmers, ANSI C is such a standard, spelling out rules that a C compiler must follow to conform.

Because of the ANSI C standard, if I write a program that uses the `printf()` function call for output, I can count on finding that function in my compiler library. Thus, I can start to write software that is *portable*, meaning, in this case, that it can work with different compilers and even on different types of computers with different operating systems.

The RS-232 standard was developed in an attempt to ensure that computer *hardware* shared the same portability characteristics as computer software. In theory, computer equipment that adheres to this standard can communicate with other RS-232 equipment with little or no trouble. The official standard is published by the Electronic Industries Association (EIA), a trade organization in Washington, D.C.

In practice, the RS-232 standard (and its sister standard, CCITT Recommendation V.24) can be termed a limited success. The industry developed a de facto standard based on the published standard, so that devices adhering to the de facto standard can usually communicate.

The best-known version of the RS-232 standard, RS-232-C, is only a limited success because of what it leaves out, rather than what it contains. The standard concentrates on the electrical interface between two different types of equipment: Data Terminal Equipment (DTE) and Data Communications Equipment (DCE). Typically, a desktop computer or terminal is a DTE and a modem is a DCE. The standard spells out which circuits can connect these two pieces of equipment and what the electrical characteristics of these circuits should be.

Nowhere in the RS-232-C standard do we find items of major importance, such as: the size and shapes of connectors; the format of serial data being exchanged; types of codes used to exchange data; protocols used to exchange data; methods for connecting DTE to DTE or DCE to DCE; or rules regarding when and where particular circuits must be used or can be omitted.

Some of these issues have been addressed in later versions of the specification (the latest came in 1987), but because of the widespread dissemination of RS-232-C, later versions of the specification have largely been ignored.

## Results of the Omissions

Because the EIA left so much open area in the standard, designers of RS-232-C equipment have relied on an informal process of evolution to arrive at the de facto standard. Some portions of the specification have jelled very nicely, while others are still evolving.

The RS-232 connector is a good example of how the lack of definition has brought about duplication. The EIA elected not to define the RS-232 connector in the C specification. Since there were 25 circuits defined, designers began using the

# AN OVERVIEW OF RS-232

D-Subminiature 25-pin connector for their RS-232 interfaces. This quickly became part of the de facto standard. However, when IBM introduced the AT in 1984, it used a 9-pin D-Subminiature connector, presumably to save space on its card edges. Since IBM is big enough to set standards on its own, there are now two types of connectors in the de facto standard, and users have to deal with both.

## ASCII-Another RS-232-C?

Just as a hardware standard is needed, support of a universal standard for text-based information is required for proper development of serial communications. Without a standard for information interchange (the "II" in "ASCII"), serial communications would be limited to machines of similar architectures, creating an array of information universes that would be unconnected.

| NUL | SOH | STX | ETX | EOT | ENQ | ACK | BEL | BS | HT | LF | VT | FF | CR | SO | SI |
| --- | --- | --- | --- | --- | --- | --- | --- | --- | --- | --- | --- | --- | --- | --- | --- |
| 0 | 1 | 2 | 3 | 4 | 5 | 6 | 7 | 8 | 9 | 10 | 11 | 12 | 13 | 14 | 15 |
| DLE | DC1 | DC2 | DC3 | DC4 | NAK | SYN | ETB | CAN | EM | SUB | ESC | FS | GS | RS | US |
| 16 | 17 | 18 | 19 | 20 | 21 | 22 | 23 | 24 | 25 | 26 | 27 | 28 | 29 | 30 | 31 |
| SP | ! | " | # | $ | % | & | ' | ( | ) | * | + | , | - | . | / |
| 32 | 33 | 34 | 35 | 36 | 37 | 38 | 39 | 40 | 41 | 42 | 43 | 44 | 45 | 46 | 47 |
| 0 | 1 | 2 | 3 | 4 | 5 | 6 | 7 | 8 | 9 | : | ; | < | = | > | ? |
| 48 | 49 | 50 | 51 | 52 | 53 | 54 | 55 | 56 | 57 | 58 | 59 | 60 | 61 | 62 | 63 |
| @ | A | B | C | D | E | F | G | H | I | J | K | L | M | N | O |
| 64 | 65 | 66 | 67 | 68 | 69 | 70 | 71 | 72 | 73 | 74 | 75 | 76 | 77 | 78 | 79 |
| P | Q | R | S | T | U | V | W | X | Y | Z | [ | \ | ] | ^ | _ |
| 80 | 81 | 82 | 83 | 84 | 85 | 86 | 87 | 88 | 89 | 90 | 91 | 92 | 93 | 94 | 95 |
| ` | a | b | c | d | e | f | g | h | i | j | k | l | m | n | o |
| 96 | 97 | 98 | 99 | 100 | 101 | 102 | 103 | 104 | 105 | 106 | 107 | 108 | 109 | 110 | 111 |
| p | q | r | s | t | u | v | w | x | y | z | { | | | } | ~ | DEL |
| 112 | 113 | 114 | 115 | 116 | 117 | 118 | 119 | 120 | 121 | 122 | 123 | 124 | 125 | 126 | 127 |

Figure 1-1. The official ASCII chart

Because of ASCII, we can now use RS-232 connections to send files back and forth between UNIX systems, IBM PCs, Apples, and DEC VAX systems. Even recalcitrant systems like IBM 370s know enough to include conversion software for transportation of data outside their domain. All of the code in this book is written with the assumption that ASCII code is used for all tranasactions.

## One from Column A, One from Column B

There is, however, a major problem with 7-bit ASCII that is evident from its name: *American* Standard Code for Information Interchange. Foreign characters with their accents, umlauts, and tildes are not really welcome in the ASCII domain. However, the ASCII standard defines special operations that can be used to transmit some foreign characters.

Despite this provision, the standard still suffers from exactly the same problem as the RS-232 standard. That is, it has made these features optional, rather than required. Thus, the vast majority of devices transferring ASCII data via RS-232 lines are not able to translate alternate character sets.

The Unicode standard, developed by a consortium of companies, including IBM, Apple, and a number of UNIX vendors, uses a 16-bit encoding that encompasses all existing national character code standards, including those used in East Asia for ideographic characters. The International Organization for Standardization (ISO) adopted the Unicode standard as a superset of ISO 10646 in June 1992. ISO's adoption of the Unicode standard will encourage programmers worldwide to use a 16-bit encoding, although it may take some time before 16-bit serial transmission is in widespread use.

Most RS-232 communications is done either via transfer of raw binary data (which is generally tied to the architecture of a specific machine), or data encoded in ASCII format.

## DTE and DCE

The RS-232-C specification wasn't really designed to let computers talk to one another directly. The specification was laid out to let Data Terminal Equipment talk to Data Communications Equipment. In the classic definition, Data Terminal Equipment refers to either terminals or PCs acting as terminals (by using terminal emulation software). DCE usually refers to modems that communicate via telephone lines.

# AN OVERVIEW OF RS-232

Figure 1-2 shows a DTE/DCE session being carried out according to the RS-232-C specification. Two DTE devices (in this case a terminal and a UNIX computer) are communicating long distance via phone lines.

DCE modems move the data long distances over telephone wires. The two DTE devices and the two DCE devices communicate via the RS-232 specification.

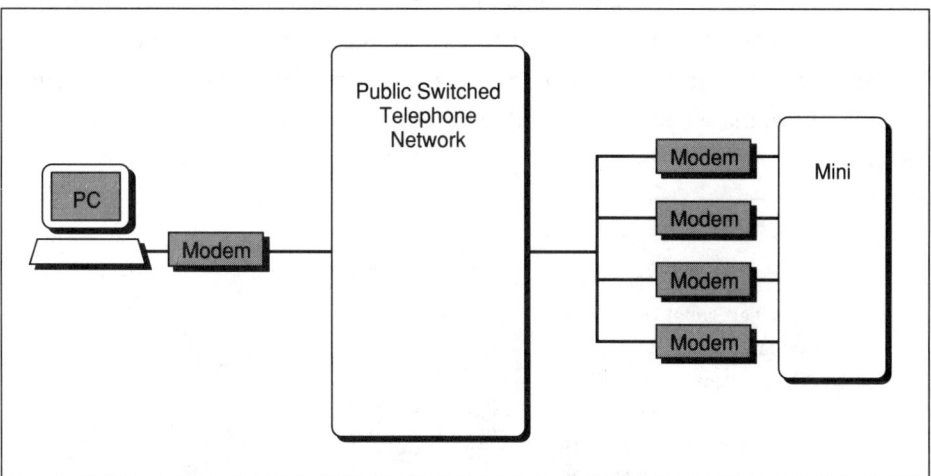

Figure 1-2. A communications session a la RS-232-C

The RS-232 control lines discussed in the next section were all clearly designed for the establishment and control of a communications session using a DTE and a DCE. This is one reason that RS-232 runs into some trouble when trying to communicate between two DTEs, for example. To connect two PCs directly without the use of a modem, we have to resort to such unusual devices as a null modem cable.

## RS-232: Let's Get Physical

The average user first encounters RS-232 at the mechanical and electrical level. For programmers, having even a basic understanding of RS-232 connections is enough to feel comfortable working with cables, connectors, cards, and wires.

As mentioned earlier, the RS-232-C standard does not specify a particular connector. Implementors were free to use any type of connector for RS-232 devices. Of course, this sort of freedom leads to the chaos that a good standard should prevent. Manufacturers came to a consensus during the 1970s that led to the acceptance of the D-Subminiature 25-pin connector as the standard RS-232 connector.

Another evolving part of the standard is related to the gender of connectors used in an RS-232 connection. Before the IBM PC, there wasn't much consistency in the use of male and female connectors for RS-232 equipment. IBM began using exclusively male connectors for their RS-232 ports, thereby implying that DCE equipment should use female connectors. Once again, by sheer power of inertia, most of the industry has followed this convention. Now regardless of whether a connector is 9-pin or 25-pin, we can reasonably expect that DTE devices such as PCs will have male connectors, and DCE equipment such as modems will have female connectors.

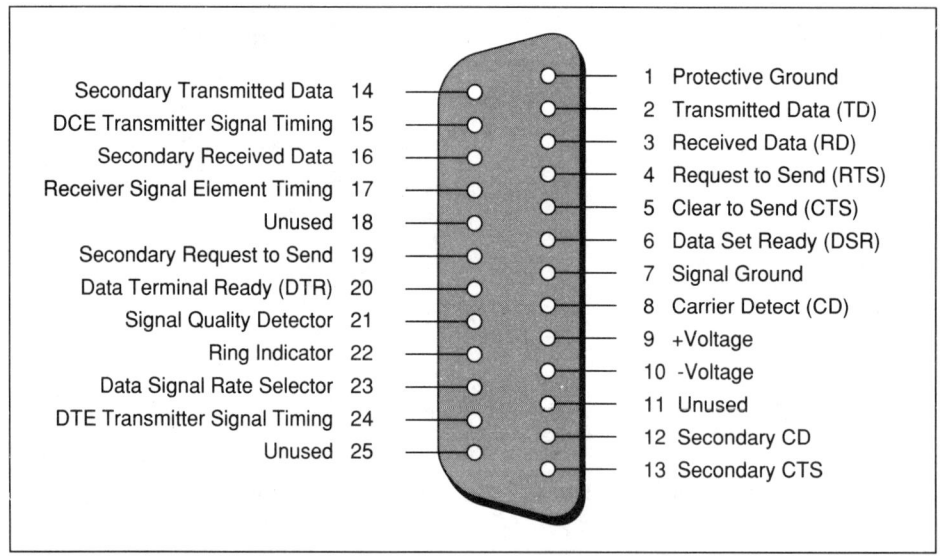

**Figure 1-3. Pinouts on a 25-pin connector**

Figure 1-3 shows the pinouts on the standard 25-pin D-Subminiature connector normally used for RS-232 connections. For someone unfamiliar with the interface, even 25 signals can seem like an overwhelming number. All of these signals have a purpose, but many are only used rarely.

Figure 1-4 shows the connectors as they are more commonly seen in the desktop world. The 25 pins used in a standard RS-232-C connection have been reduced to a more manageable nine. Some manufacturers are now using the space-saving 9-pin connector pioneered by IBM.

# AN OVERVIEW OF RS-232

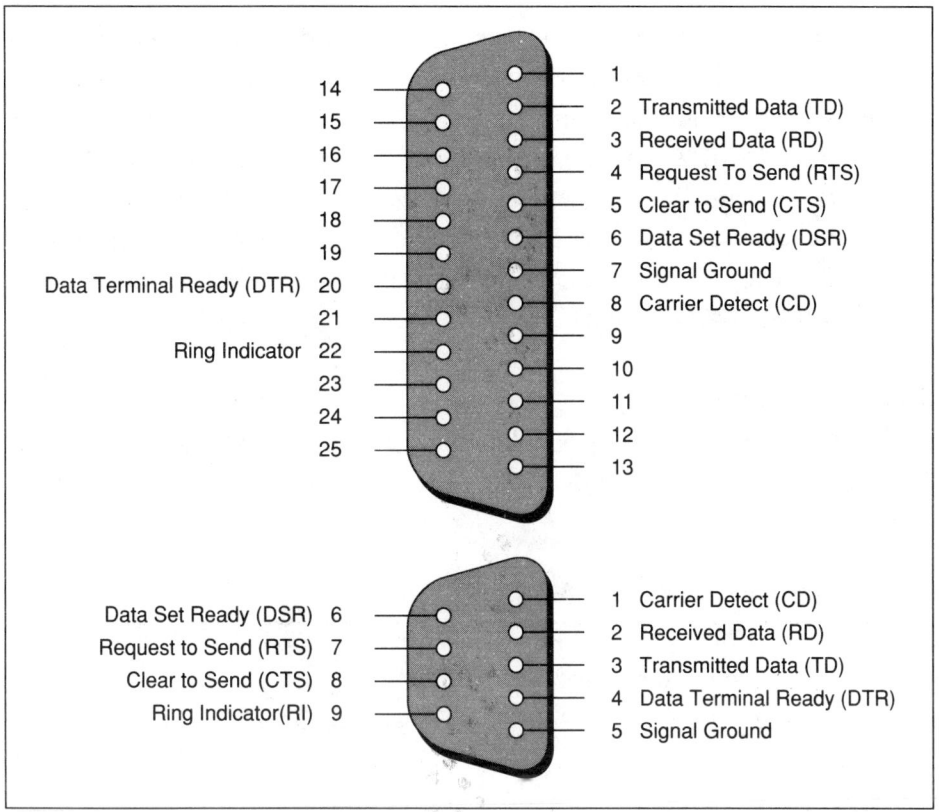

**Figure 1-4. Commonly used RS-232 signals ( 9 & 25 )**

With the exception of the two ground signals on the connector, all RS-232 connections have the same electrical characteristics. Normally, the digital electronics found in a PC use a single voltage (usually 5 volts) as a logical 1, and 0 volts, or ground, as a logical 0. This works fine when the circuit is confined to a well-behaved circuit board with solid copper traces and little or no noise.

RS-232 lines may have to send signals hundreds of feet over noisy lines. The normal 5-volt signals would suffer too much degradation when transmitted over longer distances. To assure successful transmission, RS-232 signals must produce outputs that range from +5 to +15 volts for a positive signal, and -5 to -15 volts for a negative signal. A valid input for an RS-232 receiver is defined as +3 volts or greater for a valid 1, and -3 volts or less for a valid 0.

This signaling method is complicated by undefined inputs. Because the standard specifies that input voltages in the range of -3 to +3 volts are undefined, we can't count on any logical behavior from unconnected or heavily loaded lines. For example, I often write software that tries to read the status of a modem via the Carrier Detect (CD) line. If no modem is connected to the CD input pin on my PC, I have no guarantee as to whether I will read in a 1 or a 0 on that line. Under some circumstances, my reading from that input line may jump back and forth between 0 and 1 as noise comes in from other lines.

## Signal Formats

The nine commonly used RS-232 lines can be broken down into three groups: data, control, and electrical lines. Table 1-1 shows the lines broken down into this format.

Table 1-1. The commonly used RS-232 lines

| Category | 9-Pin Connector | 25-Pin Connector | Signal Name | Abbreviation |
|---|---|---|---|---|
| Data | 3 | 2 | Transmitted Data | TD |
| | 2 | 3 | Received Data | RD |
| Control | 7 | 4 | Request To Send | RTS |
| | 8 | 5 | Clear To Send | CTS |
| | 6 | 6 | Data Set Ready | DSR |
| | 1 | 8 | Carrier Detect | CD |
| | 4 | 20 | Data Terminal Ready | DTR |
| | 9 | 22 | Ring Indicator | RI |
| Electrical | 5 | 7 | Signal Ground | |

Note that signal CD is formally referred to as RLSD, for Received Line Signal Detect. "CD" has come into more common usage, and it will be used consistently in this book.

The communications and control lines used in an RS-232 connection are all unidirectional, meaning that they are output by one side of the connection and input

# AN OVERVIEW OF RS-232

on the other. Each signal has a particular orientation that depends mostly on whether a device is a DCE or DTE. Figure 1-5 shows the normal directions for most of these signals.

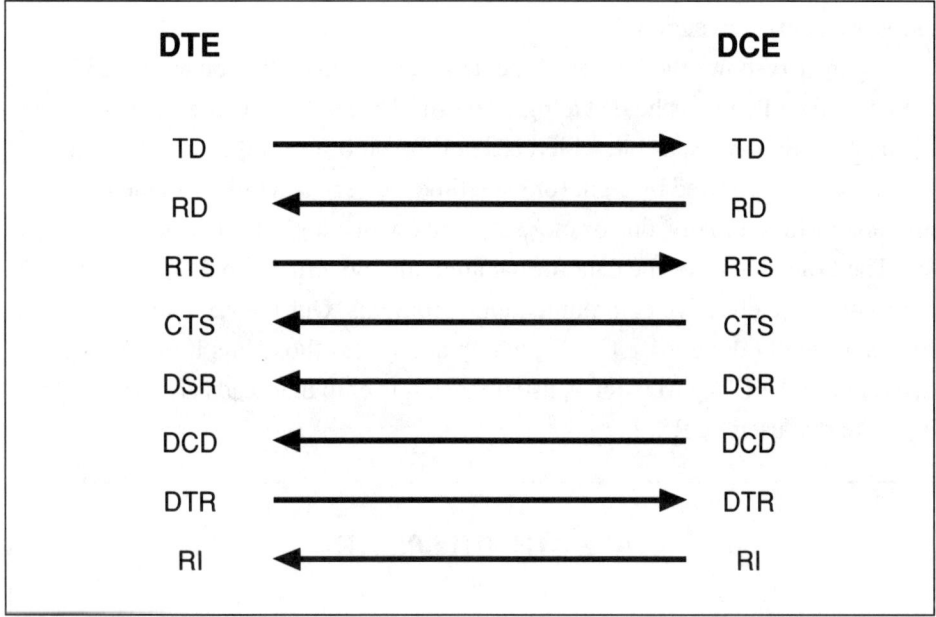

**Figure 1-5. Direction of RS-232 Lines**

It is difficult to remember the direction of the TD and RD lines. TD has the ambiguous name of Transmitted Data, which could refer to either side of the connection since both are transmitting data. For these lines (and many other RS-232 lines), you should always take the point of view of the DTE device, which is usually the terminal or PC you will be working on. So TD refers to data that is being *transmitted* from your PC. RD refers to data that is being *received* by your PC.

## Data Lines

The actual transmission of data between a DTE and a DCE takes place over the two RS-232 communication lines, RD and TD. The TD line handles data being transmitted from the PC (DTE device), and RD handles data being sent from the modem, or DCE device. In the world of desktop systems, TD and RD transmit asynchronous data at a fixed rate using start and stop bits for framing. One oddity associated with RS-232 data is that for the communications lines, a low voltage (less than -3 volts) is considered to be a logic 1 and a high voltage (greater than 3 volts) is considered to be a logic 0. All of the RS-232 control lines use the opposite (and more frequent) convention.

Figure 1-6 shows the format of the data being transmitted on an RS-232 line. Note that the idle line is held at a logic level 1. The start of a character is signified by the reception of a start bit, which is a normal bit 0 sent at the current baud rate. The start bit is followed by eight (or sometimes fewer) data bits, with the least significant bit first. Finally, one or more stop bits with a logic 1 are sent.

The exact details of the data format are really not crucial to the programmer's ability to write effective communications programs. Our interface to the RS-232 line is normally done via a UART, which assembles those bits into a byte to be delivered to the CPU. AUART is usually a single chip that reads and writes serial data like that used by RS-232.

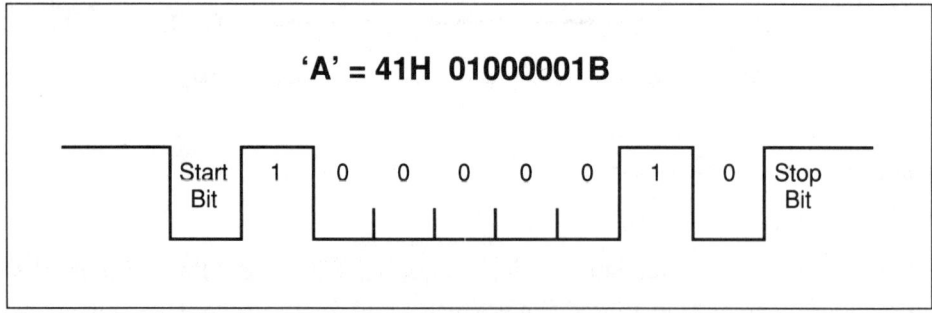

**Figure 1-6. A sample character sent via RS-232**

The duration of each bit sent across the channel determines the speed of the signal. The unit of speed is commonly referred to as either *Bits per second* or *baud*, with the two terms being used interchangably. Some sticklers for accuracy will point out that "baud" is not interchangeable with "bits per second"; however, for our purposes they are synonymous. That is, for normal RS-232 connections, we will consider them identical.

## Control Lines

Six commonly used control lines are shown in the subset of RS-232. Physically, these lines are all defined to be true, or logic "1" when a positive RS-232 voltage is asserted, and false, or logic "0" when a negative voltage is present. As I mentioned previously, a floating input is undefined, which can cause programmers some trouble.

The six lines discussed here are all supported on the PC by the 8250 family of UARTs, making them the most popular subset of control lines. However, many RS-232 connections are made without these lines, in some cases using only three: Transmit Data, Receive Data, and Signal Ground.

### RTS/CTS

In early implementations of RS-232 equipment, these lines were intended for use by half-duplex modems. Now, half-duplex modems are rarely used and, for the most part, RTS and CTS are used almost exclusively to implement hardware handshaking. A device connected to an RS-232 line uses handshaking to indicate when its input buffers are full. For example, if a PC is receiving data from a modem, it may have to suspend reading data from the RS-232 port while it performs a disk access. As more data comes in, the PC buffer may approach filling up. The PC alerts the modem of this condition by dropping the RTS line. When the buffer data has been read in, RTS can once again be asserted, which tells the modem the PC is ready to handle more data.

Some devices still emulate the traditional uses for RTS and CTS. For example, the IBM PC BIOS asserts RTS when it sends data out of one of its COM ports, and waits for CTS to be asserted before sending any of its characters. However, this traditional usage is the exception rather than the rule and is usually considered just a slightly less sophisticated form of handshaking.

Most high-speed modems today support handshaking of some sort. The modems' preferred method of handshaking will generally be RTS/CTS. Thus, understanding this sort of handshaking and knowing how to implement it is essential to the development of high-quality communications software.

### DTR/DSR

At one time, Data Terminal Ready (DTR) was used to cause a modem to go off hook and to attempt to connect to a remote modem. Data Set Ready (DSR) was used to indicate that the modem had made this connection. DTR would normally be low when the DTE equipment wasn't actually trying to make a connection, and DSR would be low when the modem was idle.

Today's modems generally keep DSR high whenever they are powered up. This is primarily because newer modems can accept commands via the RS-232 connection to the DTE at any time. The DTE device also usually keeps DTR high whenever it actually has an established connection to the modem.

In one instance, DTR is still used as a modem control line. Most modems will hang up when DTR is dropped, which could also indicate that no DTE is hooked up to the modem. Dropping DTR for one or two seconds is still a conventional way to disconnect a modem from a remote line.

To complicate matters even further, the occasional off-beat device will still insist on using DTR/DSR handshaking, although RTS/CTS is really the norm. The programmer should build in driver and software support for DTR/DSR handshaking, as well as for RTS/CTS handshaking.

Even worse, some machines use hybrids of the two forms of handshaking. The Apple Macintosh uses DTR and CTS as its two handshaking lines, which means you must either develop unusual communications software, buy an even more unusual cable, or both.

### CD

CD, or Carrier Detect, ought to be relatively unambiguous. This line should only be asserted by a DCE when it has established a connection with another DCE, usually over telephone lines. This lets the DTE device know that communications can now take place. Any time this line is low, the modem does not have a valid connection.

CD is frequently used by electronic bulletin board applications that have to wait for incoming calls. If a modem is programmed to auto answer an incoming phone line, the BBS software can simply scan the incoming control lines for assertion of CD. If CD goes high on a line, it means the modem has successfully answered an incoming call.

# AN OVERVIEW OF RS-232

Unfortunately, before the era of intelligent modems, some terminals or other DTE equipment were designed to treat a modem as unusable without CD. Devices such as these would not send or receive characters to a modem that had CD low. Because of these anachronisms, most modems built today can keep CD high at all times, whether or not a carrier has been established. Because this feature is sometimes the default mode of operation, using CD for accurate detection of carrier presence is somewhat risky. However, most users should be able to configure their modems so as to disable this troublesome behavior.

## RI

Ring Indicator (RI) is a signal originating from a DCE and is used solely to indicate that the incoming phone line is ringing. RI should rise and fall in lockstep with the ring cycle, which allows software not only to detect incoming calls, but also to count rings. RI is one of the few RS-232 control lines that has remained true to its roots. RI signals still behave much like they did 20 years ago.

In the future, RI may become even more useful. PBX manufacturers have been offering distinctive ringing features for years, and telephone companies are now starting to offer this service for business and residential customers. With these new services a phone line can serve multiple phone numbers, allowing users to share a single phone line between a FAX and modems, or between several different classes of incoming calls. To differentiate among types of calls, the communications software will have to determine the cadence of the incoming ring by monitoring RI.

### Electrical lines

Pin 7 on the 25-pin RS-232 connector is reserved for a signal ground line. Because computers connected using RS-232 links can be physically separated by significant distances, their reference grounds can easily be several volts apart. The sharing of a common signal ground line insures a common reference point for incoming data and control lines.

## Limitations

The RS-232 specification recommends that signals be limited to 20,000 bps. At high speeds, it also recommends that cable length not exceed 50 feet. These limitations are routinely ignored by RS-232 users. High-speed modems frequently are connected to PCs at 38,400 baud or 57,600 baud with little or no problem. And even high-speed signals such as these will frequently be routed hundreds of feet.

Unfortunately, while the speed and distance limits of RS-232 are routinely broken, it isn't easy to find anyone willing to speculate on what the *real* limitations are. Most manufacturers of driver chips and cables fall back on the standard when asked for recommendations. So for most of us, performance is determined empirically.

## Cabling

Over the years, no subject has caused more trouble and frustration for RS-232 users than that of cabling. Every RS-232 connection requires a cable, and every cable has 25 wires that can be routed incorrectly. The odds are against you every time you try to make a connection.

Once again, the IBM PC has helped resolve this problem, strictly because of its massive presence in the market. IBM defined what an RS-232 port was supposed to look like on a PC and what the equivalent connector should look like on a modem. By default, they then defined what the cable between the two should be.

| DTE | | | | DCE |
|---|---|---|---|---|
| TD | 2 | ⎯⎯⎯⎯⎯⎯ | 2 | TD |
| RD | 3 | ⎯⎯⎯⎯⎯⎯ | 3 | RD |
| RTS | 4 | ⎯⎯⎯⎯⎯⎯ | 4 | RTS |
| CTS | 5 | ⎯⎯⎯⎯⎯⎯ | 5 | CTS |
| DSR | 6 | ⎯⎯⎯⎯⎯⎯ | 6 | DSR |
| GND | 7 | ⎯⎯⎯⎯⎯⎯ | 7 | GND |
| DCD | 8 | ⎯⎯⎯⎯⎯⎯ | 8 | DCD |
| DTR | 20 | ⎯⎯⎯⎯⎯⎯ | 20 | DTR |
| RI | 22 | ⎯⎯⎯⎯⎯⎯ | 22 | RI |

**Figure 1-7. A "PC-to-modem" cable**

# AN OVERVIEW OF RS-232

Figure 1-7 shows the "PC to Modem" cable. This cable has a male D-Subminiature 25-pin connector on one end, and its female equivalent on the other. All of the signals are routed straight through, terminating on the same numbered pin where they began. Conceptually, the cable is easier to handle than one whose lines are routed back and forth between various pins. Don't belittle this advantage. Many manuals for older RS-232 devices are filled with different pinout and routing combinations for interfacing to various devices.

In addition to the 25-pin cable, there is also an equivalent cable for routing the 9-pin DTE connection on a PC to a 25-pin DCE device. Thus, even though there are now two "standard" cables, they are difficult to confuse since one is for a 9-pin connector and the other for a 25.

| DTE (9-Pin) | | | DCE (25-Pin) |
|---|---|---|---|
| TD | 3 | 2 | TD |
| RD | 2 | 3 | RD |
| RTS | 7 | 4 | RTS |
| CTS | 8 | 5 | CTS |
| DSR | 6 | 6 | DSR |
| GND | 5 | 7 | GND |
| DCD | 1 | 8 | DCD |
| DTR | 4 | 20 | DTR |
| RI | 9 | 22 | RI |

Figure 1-8. The standard cable for 9-Pin connectors

Mass production of molded cables has brought prices down tremendously and increased availability. You can purchase the typical PC/Modem cables off the shelf at any computer store for just a few dollars. In 1980, the same cable would likely have to be custom-made, and would have cost 10 times as much.

### The null modem cable

You are likely to get into more trouble with cabling when attempting to do something a little more unconventional. One common problem that arises is that the standard modem cable won't work when two PCs are connected via their serial ports. The standard modem cable fails here, for two reasons.

First, the modem cable has a problem with the gender of its connectors. Since both PCs will have male RS-232 connectors, you will need a cable with two female ends. Unfortunately, the standard modem cable has one male end and one female end.

However, solving the gender problem for this cable still won't allow the two PCs to communicate. Since both PCs consider themselves DTE devices, both will transmit on Pin 2 and receive on Pin 3 of their 25-pin connectors. Thus, a cable that routes all signals straight through will be connecting the output from one PC directly to the output of the other PC, and the RD line from one PC will be connected to the RD line of the other. With outputs connected to outputs and inputs connected to inputs, you are guaranteed failed communications.

The solution to this age-old dilemma: the "null modem" cable. Null modem refers to the fact that this cable takes the place of the pair of modems that should be connecting the two DTE devices. Remember that traditionally in the RS-232 specification, DTEs only communicate via a connection through DCEs.

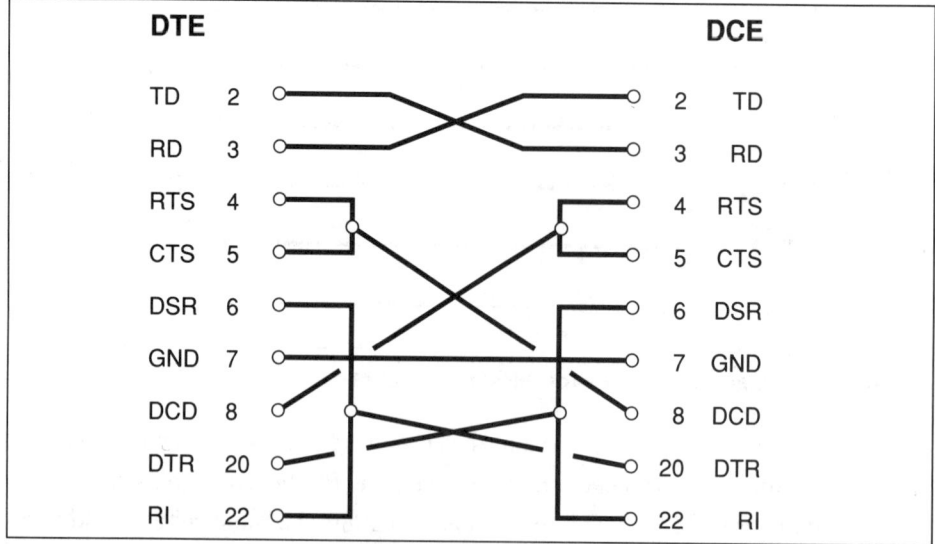

Figure 1-9. A traditional null modem cable

# AN OVERVIEW OF RS-232

If you go back to the neighborhood discount computer store and buy a null modem cable, you will generally get a cable with two female 25-pin connectors like the one in Figure 1-9. Probably the first thing you'll notice in the cabling diagram is that this cable doesn't seem to route any control or data lines straight through. Instead, they cross over, bend back on themselves, and generally seem to follow convoluted paths. The lone exception to this is the signal ground pin, which, just as before, is always connected straight through.

It makes sense that the TD and RD lines cross over as shown in Figure 1-9. With this method of wiring, the data output of each PC is connected directly to data input of the other PC, the way things ought to work. By simply crossing wires, you accomplish the same thing that a pair of modems does; routing data to the appropriate lines.

The rest of the connectors are wired as shown for reasons that may be a little more confusing. Each connector has RTS and CTS in a local loopback configuration. If a DTE is using RTS in the traditional fashion, it will automatically receive an assertion on CTS whenever it wants to transmit.

The logic behind the wiring of the remaining pins is even harder to understand. Both the CD and RI lines are routed to dubious destinations on the other side of the connector, presumably to be left on at all times. DTR and DSR are also connected through to the other side using wiring that may not seem logical.

More often than not, this version of a null modem cable accomplishes its purpose. If we write our application to be independent of the state of any control lines in the RS-232 connection, then this cable will work perfectly. Of course, we are giving up some of the functionality of the 9-wire connection, but this isn't usually a problem.

### A more rational cable design

If available, a properly designed null-modem cable would offer somewhat more functionality. Figure 1-10 shows the wiring diagram for a cable that attempts to handle the crisscrossing of control lines somewhat more rationally.

Like the traditional cable, the rational null modem cable simply swaps the TD and RD lines. It really wouldn't make sense to wire these two lines any other way.

The main difference between the traditional and rational cabling is in the way the two pairs of control lines match up. RTS and CTS are swapped across the cable, so that each PC's RTS output is routed in to the CTS input on the other machine. Likewise, DTR and DSR are swapped, so that the DTR output of one machine heads straight into the DSR on the other machine.

Such a wiring scheme makes much more sense than the traditional version shown in Figure 1-9. Typically, RTS/CTS on modern machines is used for hardware handshaking. Under the traditional cabling scheme, this would not be possible. With the rational cable, RTS/CTS handshaking is wired in directly and should work with no problem.

Likewise, DTR and DSR are typically used to check for a connection between the DTE and DCE. When the DTE opens up a port for use, it asserts DTR, so that the DCE knows it is being addressed. An active DSR tells the DTE that a DCE is connected. For example, by testing for an active incoming DSR line, communications software can determine that a modem is powered up and ready to communicate. The configuration in Figure 1-10 accomplishes this goal without any problem.

In any null modem cable, you must decide what to do with the RI and CD lines. In this configuration, Ring Indicator doesn't really have an equivalent and Carrier Detect probably ought to be on all the time. So the best thing to do seems to be to connect RI and CD across the line to the DTR line on the remote end. RI could just as easily be disconnected, but leaving it disconnected opens the port to sporadic modem status interrupts that may cause confusion later.

There is only one problem with the rational null modem cable: it is nearly impossible to find. This cable, or one nearly like it, is used in commercial communication products such as LapLink, but those cables generally ship with the product. The cables can be custom-made by several of the sources listed at the end of this book, but price can be prohibitive. The next section on RS-232 adapters describes my solution.

# AN OVERVIEW OF RS-232

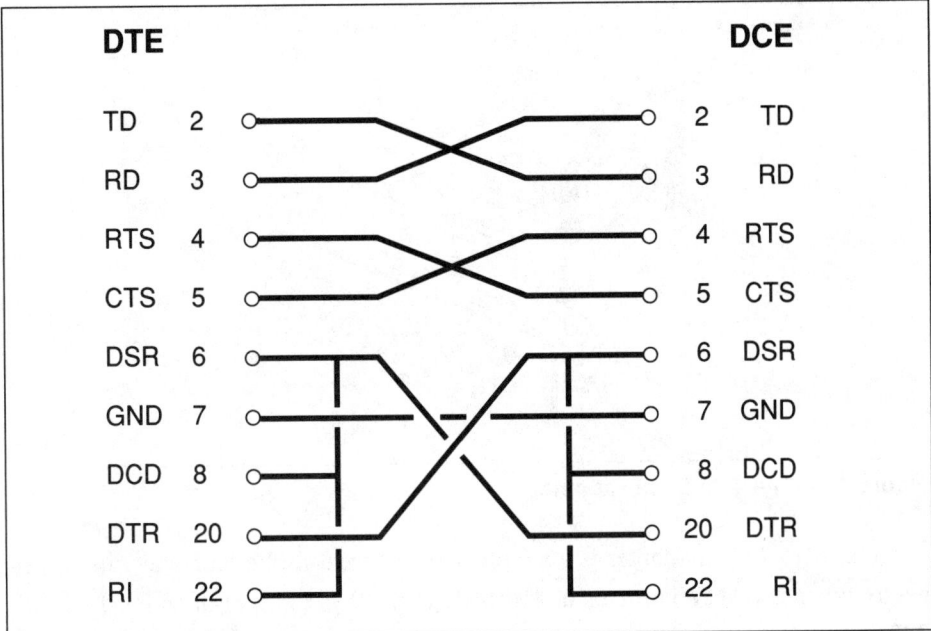

Figure 1-10. The Rational Null Modem Cable

## RS-232 9- to 25-Pin Adapters

The popularity of the IBM PC architecture led to the availability of inexpensive molded RS-232 cables, which are relatively easy to find. The advent of the AT architecture ushered in another piece of cabling hardware: the RS-232 9- to 25-pin adapter.

When IBM first introduced the AT, they began using a 9-pin D-Subminiature connector instead of the standard 25-pin connector. Users who bought an AT were now faced with the fact that no existing cables would work with their machines. This problem quickly established a market for the 9- to 25-pin adapter, shown in Figure 1-11.

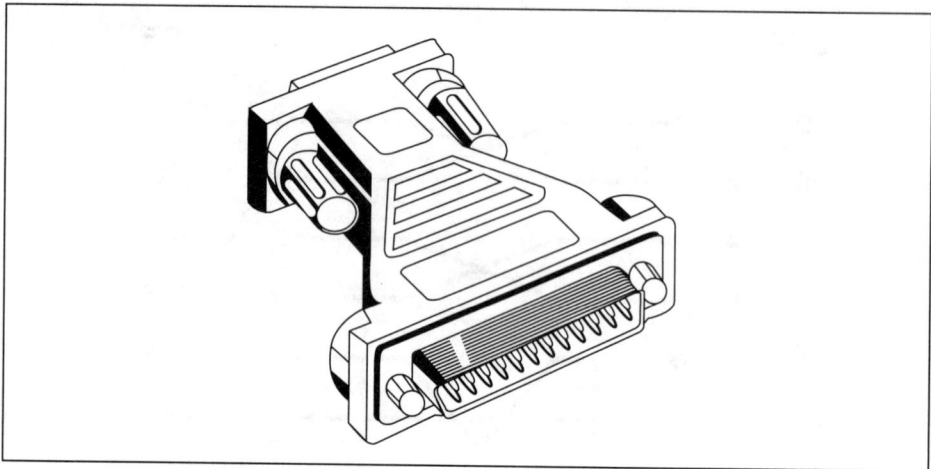

**Figure 1-11. The 9- to 25-pin adapter**

The 9- to 25-pin adapter is a simple piece of hard-molded plastic with a connector on each end. When attached directly to the 9-pin output of an IBM AT RS-232 port, it immediately made it possible to use that port with all existing 25-pin cables. Mass production techniques made this cable so inexpensive that it was usually given away with add-on interface cards.

This adapter quickly paved the way for new equipment: gender changers and null modem adapters. A gender changer is also a small piece of molded plastic with a 25-pin connector on each end. A cable mismatch can quickly be corrected by the addition of a gender changer. Again, mass production techniques keep the cost of these adapters down to just a few dollars, making them easily affordable for any devoted RS-232 user.

Last but not least is the null modem adapter. It simply performs all the internal wire swapping shown in Figure 1-9, which means that two PCs (or other DTE devices) can be directly connected without intervening modems. The low cost of these devices insures that no wiring diagrams or optional configurations are available. The only way to be sure about a null modem cable like this is to check all connections with a voltmeter.

# AN OVERVIEW OF RS-232

### Home surgery for fun and profit

Despite the lack of availability of the rational style null-modem adapter, all is not lost. Anyone handy with a soldering iron and a wire cutters can quickly convert a female-to-male gender changer to an effective null modem cable. In 15 minutes or so, the offending wires can be removed and replaced with more usable connections. The plastic cases for these adapters pop back together easily, leaving an adapter that looks and acts just as good as new.

### Macintosh cabling

While this book concentrates on the IBM architecture for desktop systems, more adventurous readers may want to tackle communications programming for the Macintosh. There are a couple of interesting problems that arise when using the Macintosh for serial communications. Instead of using RS-232 for an interface, the Mac uses RS-422. Like much on the Mac, RS-422 is a technically superior communications standard that has not yet achieved critical mass in the market place. Fortunately, the two standards are similar enough that a special cable can be used to connect a Macintosh to either a modem or a PC.

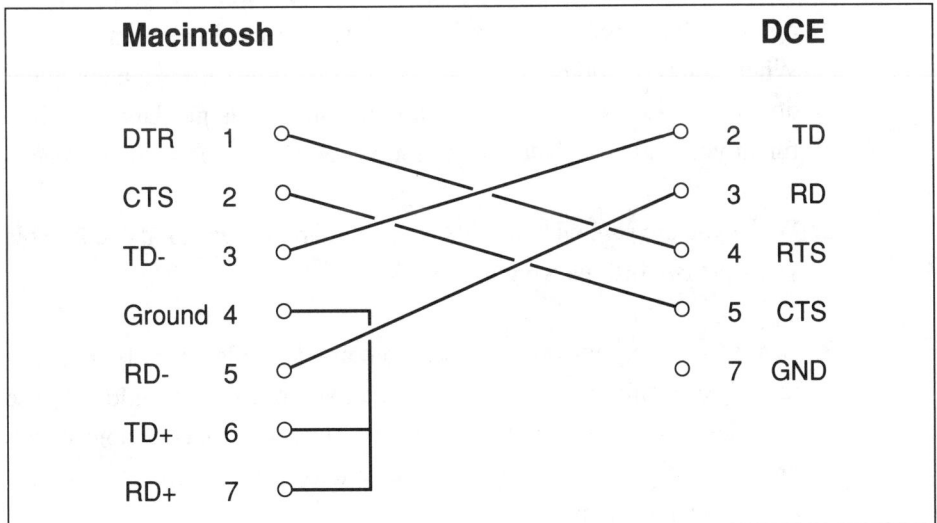

Figure 1-12. Macintosh/modem cables

Figure 1-12 shows a Macintosh/Modem cable. A couple of points are worth noting here. First, under RS-422, the TD and RD lines come in balanced pairs. Each data line having its own dual balanced driver lines increases the noise resistance of RS-422, allowing for faster transmission over longer distances. However, RS-232 only has a single line for both directions of data. Remember also that RS-232 transmits its data using an inverted line, so that a logical 1 is transmitted as a low voltage. This leads to the strange cabling configuration shown in Figure 1-12.

Figure 1-12 shows the newer Mini 8-pin connector used by Apple. Older Apple equipment used a 9-pin D-Subminiature connector with a slightly different pinout. The primary difference was that the older cable did not have the DTR line connected, which meant that hardware handshaking on older Macs was strictly a one-way affair.

**Cabling conclusion**

Unfortunately, this section on cabling will be confusing to newcomers. For what it's worth, I have developed a few rules for working with RS-232 cables:

1. Never trust a strange cable. Until you have tested it and verified its pinouts, don't assume that it is anything like what you want it to be. When your co-workers tell you that it worked just fine on a computer down the hall, assume that they are mistaken or is just having a little fun at your expense. These assumptions will save you a lot of time.

2. When you are sure what a cable is, label it and never modify it. A cable you trust is worth its weight in gold.

3. Learn to make your own cables. Homemade cables usually aren't as reliable as professionally built ones, and you probably should only use them for testing configurations. But when you need an odd cable at 5:00 on Friday afternoon, having your own cable, crimping tool, hoods, and pins will be a lifesaver.

Later in this chapter, I will discuss the ultimate cabling tool: the breakout box.

# AN OVERVIEW OF RS-232

## UARTS

The process of writing data out in a serial bit stream is labor intensive for a computer. Each bit has to be shifted into position, placed into the output stream, then timed for the proper bit width. Reading input bits is even more difficult. The input stream has to be sampled at a significantly higher rate than the serial bit rate. The processor has to look for start bits, screen out any invalid start bits caused by noise, then clock in each bit by sampling somewhere near the expected middle of the bit.

Because of the real-time nature of this task, a CPU that is trying to manage a disk-based operating system cannot do it very effectively. So virtually every desktop system performs serial data transfers via a UART chip. For users, the UART is essentially a black box that performs two very important functions. First, it converts bytes to serial data on the RS-232 line. Second, it reads in serial data and converts the data streams into bytes that can be read by the computer. This relieves the computer of all the time-critical jobs of shifting and timing data bits.

## Doomed to Repeat

There are literally dozens of different chips from different manufacturers being built into PCs every day, but they are all register compatible with the original 8250.

The reason for this is simply that when IBM and Microsoft collaborated on the design of a BIOS and operating system for the first IBM PCs, they completely left out support for interrupt-driven input from the serial port. By only supporting polled-mode input and output, they limited the functionality of MS-DOS. With polled-mode output, the operating system could handle writing to a serial printer pretty well and that would be about it. Some tightly written programs could manage terminal emulation at 300 baud using only BIOS function calls, but that avenue was closed by the advent of inexpensive 1,200-baud modems.

Any programmer wanting to support realistic baud rates for a communications program had to write an interrupt-driven driver for the 8250 UART. This meant programming the chip at the register level, which tied applications software to a particular piece of hardware.

Had IBM and Microsoft been wise enough to offer an interrupt-driven device driver for the 8250 UART (as they do now under OS/2 and MS-Windows), things would have been very different. Manufacturers would be free to choose whatever

UART they desired for their hardware. By then writing an MS-DOS device driver, they would immediately work with most application programs written for the IBM PC.

Instead, any new serial hardware that goes into a PC must be able to respond properly to commands designed to control an 8250 UART. The serial hardware can be enhanced; it just needs to be downward compatible with the original PC.

**Electronic Darwinism**

Because of this hardware straightjacket, 10 years of progress in CPUs and motherboards has not been matched by similar progress in RS-232 hardware on IBM PCs. While there are a wide variety of UARTs being used on PCs, all are essentially identical to the 8250, with one very minor exception. The 16550 UART, in use on some new systems, has 16-byte internal buffers for both the transmitter and receiver. Other than that, it is functionally identical to the 8250. Common UART types for the PC come in these variations:

> 8250: The original PC UART. This part has a few quirks that I will cover in Chapter 3. These quirks have all been replicated in later revisions so as not to upset the apple cart of compatibility.

> 16450: This version of the PC UART is designed for machines with faster I/O busses, such as the PC/AT. It is functionally identical to the 8250, as far as the communications programmer is concerned.

> 16550: This UART family has 16-byte buffers added to the transmit and receive data lines, so as to cut down on the CPU load required to service interrupts.

Many books and articles on PC-based communications discuss the difference between these UARTs, how to tell them apart, and so on. Fortunately, the differences are really nothing but window dressing. All three of these UARTs, as well as various clone chips, will respond properly if treated like the base part, the 8250.

In Chapter 3, I will present an interrupt-driven interface to the 8250 family UARTs. This driver attempts to determine if the UART is a 16550, only so it can take advan-

# AN OVERVIEW OF RS-232

tage of the 16-byte FIFOs on these parts. Even this is not really necessary, but it offers some low-cost performance enhancements that are hard to pass up.

## 8250 Functionality

The 8250 has most of the functions we need in a UART. In particular, it supports the nine RS-232 lines used in most common RS-232 connections. On the IBM PC, it is addressed via eight consecutive register locations on the I/O bus. On the PC ISA architecture, each UART gets its own interrupt line. The original designers of the PC allocated two interrupt lines for serial ports, effectively limiting the PC to COM1 and COM2.

The 8250 produces an asynchronous output bit stream that looks like that shown in Figure 1-13. Each output byte starts with a start bit, and is followed by 5, 6, 7, or 8 data bits. The output data is followed by either 1, 1.5, or 2 stop bits. The output stream can contain as its final bit a parity bit, which can use even, odd, mark, or space parity. Typical PC-based communications applications will only use 7 or 8 data bits, and even, odd, or no parity. Usually only one stop bit is used.

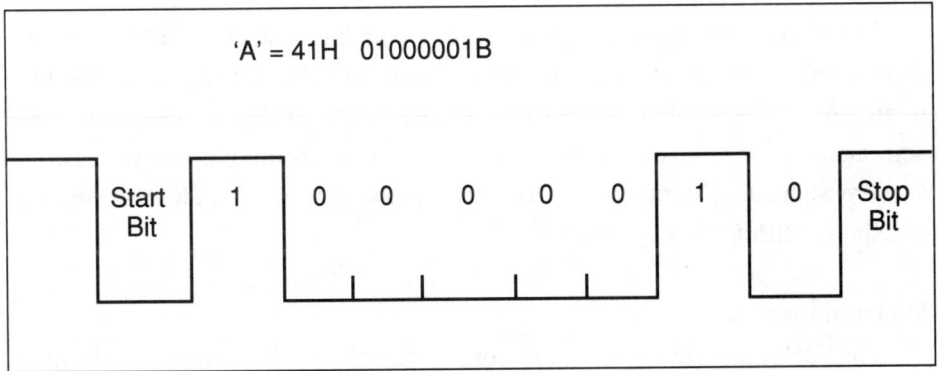

Figure 1-13. The character "A" with 8 bits, no parity

The 8250 has a built in baud-rate generator, which produces baud rates by dividing an input clock down by an integer. On the IBM PC, the baud rate generator uses a crystal that oscillates at 115,200 cycles per second. The baud rate generator divides the crystal output by a 16 bit integer ranging from 1 to 65535. Because of the way the 8250 is wired on an IBM COM card, the input and output baud rates must be the same.

## Data registers

The 8250 has a single byte-wide register for both the transmitted and received data. The programmer sends a byte by just writing out to the Transmit register using an output instruction. Likewise, reading in a byte from the Received Data register is all it takes to read in a byte that the UART has assembled from the incoming bit stream. The simplicity of these two operations is the primary reason for having a UART.

## Control registers

The 8250 has several control registers. The Line Control Register (LCR) is used to set up the word size, parity, and stop bits used in reading and writing the serial bit stream. The Modem Control Register (MCR) is used to control DTR and RTS, as well as two undedicated lines called OUT1 and OUT2. On the IBM PC, OUT2 is used to gate the UART interrupt line onto the PC bus, which is necessary before interrupts can take place.

## Status registers

Just as there are registers to control the modem lines and the serial data stream, there are also a pair of registers to read the status of the serial data stream and the input modem control lines. The Line Status Register (LSR) is used to read and detect parity, framing, and overrun errors, as well as incoming Break signals. The Modem Status Register (MSR) is used to read the state of the four incoming RS-232 lines: DSR, CTS, RI, and CD.

## Interrupt functions

The 8250 can generate interrupts for any one of four different types of events. First, it generates interrupts when a new character is read in from the RS-232 line. It also will generate an interrupt when the transmitter is done sending a character out on the line. The 8250 can generate an interrupt when any line status condition occurs, and it can also generate an interrupt when any of the four incoming modem status lines change.

Each of these four interrupts can be enabled or disabled independently. To achieve just a minimal interrupt-driven interface, you only have to turn on the Received Data interrupt. With this in place, the application program won't have to

# AN OVERVIEW OF RS-232

poll the input register once every millisecond in order to get every incoming data byte. You can then have a reliable and useful communications program.

More sophisticated applications require the use of the other three interrupt systems as well. Having the UART generate interrupts when RS-232 data is output as well as input takes a huge load off the CPU. Polled-mode output is reliable; you don't have to worry about missing characters. But it is CPU intensive since the processor has to sit in wait loops until the output buffer is ready for another character.

Changes in the incoming RS-232 control lines generate interrupts that allow effective hardware handshaking, and line status interrupts allow finer control over data errors.

Chapter 3 includes an interrupt service routine and explains in detail how to use them.

## The 16550 Difference

When the PC was first making its mark in the desktop world, communications applications typically operated at 1200 baud by modem, or perhaps 9600 baud when connected directly. Today, the V.32*bis* modem with V.42*bis* data compression is quickly becoming the desktop standard. This modem has a data throughput rate of 14.4K bps. V.42*bis* data compression can quadruple that throughput, meaning that to achieve maximum throughput, the RS-232 port has to operate at 57.6K baud. At this data rate, the UART will assemble a new character roughly every 175 microseconds, and the CPU will have to quickly read it in before the next character is done being assembled.

With data coming in at this rate, any operation that locks out interrupts for 175 microseconds or more can cause the CPU to lose at least one incoming byte. One leading candidate for causing this loss of data is mode switching. When an 80286 processor switches from protected mode to real mode, or vice versa (as it does frequently when running programs like Microsoft Windows), the processor can be prevented from receiving incoming interrupts for as long as 1,000 microseconds. In this length of time, six or seven characters could have been lost. This error is referred to as a "hardware overrun error."

The 16550 UART has extra hardware built into its chip designed to avoid this specific problem. It has a 16-byte buffer on the receiver, which can prevent this overrun error from occurring. If the buffer is enabled, the UART can be programmed to generate an interrupt as soon as a single character is stored in the buffer. The CPU then has 15 more character times to respond before the buffer fills up. This generally eliminates the problem of hardware overrun errors, even at exceptionally high baud rates. IBM now uses the 16550 as standard equipment on its top-of-the-line machines, and other manufacturers should begin following suit soon.

## Multiport Boards

Although DOS and the IBM ISA hardware design limit the PC to two COM ports, some applications need many more ports. To fill this void, a number of third-party manufacturers have developed Shared Interrupt Multiport Boards. This board takes a number of 8250 family UARTs, usually four or eight, and combines them on a board that contains some additional interrupt management circuitry.

These shared interrupt boards all have one feature in common: interrupt arbitration is done via a status register that indicates to the application which UART on the board needs servicing. The logic on the board takes care of generating an interrupt whenever any of the UARTs requests one, and letting the application software know which UART to service.

Since these boards use conventional 8250 family UARTs, existing programs can easily be modified to support multiple UARTs in this fashion. All that is needed is some "wrapper" code to go around the conventional interrupt service routine. The wrapper code simply sits in a loop, reading in the value from the status register, then dispatching the interrupt service routine for the correct UART, until the status register indicates that no more UARTs need servicing.

Different manufactures such as DigiBoard, Stargate, and Arnet all make these boards, with minor variations on the central theme. However, the shared interrupt boards remain similar enough that it is easy to design code that will work with virtually any of them.

The primary disadvantage to these boards is that although they are <u>nearly</u> compatible with standard IBM COM ports, they just don't quite make it. So any application that needs a multiport board will require new code. Most mass-market communications applications don't bother to try to take advantage of this small segment of the market, so popular communications programs don't work with these boards. Because of this, the boards tend to be used in specialized situations that can justify the expense of custom software.

# AN OVERVIEW OF RS-232

## The Multitasking Grail

The other reason that multiport boards don't take the market by storm is more of an operating system issue than anything else. Most of the applications that people would like to write in order to use multiport boards tend to be multitasking. For example, it would be natural to want to use an eight-port board on a 386 system to design a multiuser BBS, or a point-of-sale system for a supermarket. The hardware will work fine, but the desktop world has yet to embrace an operating system that can accommodate these ambitious goals.

Most board vendors do in fact supply drivers for their boards that will work with OS/2 and UNIX, so multitasking applications are possible. However, both OS/2 and UNIX have a lot of potential but very little market penetration. They tend to be used in vertical applications that are very specialized and can justify the expense of custom software and hardware.

As Microsoft Windows evolves more sophisticated multitasking features, and captures more of the desktop market, it may prove to be the platform of choice for multitasking communications applications.

## Intelligent Multiport Boards

The CPU timing requirements on multiport boards can be extremely difficult to manage. As I showed earlier in this chapter, some applications that run at high baud rates already require the CPU to service an interrupt as often as 7500 times per second. With a shared interrupt multiport board, that figure can easily be multiplied by 8 under worst-case conditions. Desktop machines simply don't have the power to keep up with that kind of a load. In fact, the whole notion of having a CPU running MS-DOS or Windows and frantically servicing 8250 interrupts at the same time is somewhat ludicrous. It seems wasteful to have an expensive processor spending so much time on such a mundane task. The solution is to move the interrupt servicing chores off the motherboard and onto a dedicated card.

These dedicated cards are called intelligent multiport boards. They are manufactured by the same companies who sell the shared interrupt multiport boards. The market for these boards is healthy because people are designing and building multiuser systems running on Intel x86 platforms, such as Xenix or UNIX. If the main CPUs were performing interrupt servicing, system performance would grow intolerably slow as the number of users increased.

An intelligent board starts off like a shared interrupt multiport board, by putting four or eight UARTs on the board. The similarities end there, however. The intelligent board then proceeds to build an entire standalone computer system on the same card. Typically, the intelligent board will contain a processor oriented towards real-time embedded applications, such as an Intel 80186. A control program will be present in EPROM on the board, along with a moderate amount of RAM, usually somewhere between 16KB and 64KB.

The processor on the intelligent board takes care of initializing the UARTs, servicing all their interrupts, reading characters in and sending characters out, taking care of handshaking, and reporting errors. It does all this based on commands it receives from the CPU running on the main machine. Generally, the communication between the main CPU and the intelligent board takes place via a block of shared memory. The main CPU places commands and data in the shared memory block, then lets the intelligent board know that data and commands are ready. Entire blocks of data can be transferred in one command via the shared memory, leading to much more efficient use of the main CPU.

The desktop CPU running UNIX, MS-DOS, or some other system, doesn't ever communicate directly with the UARTs on the intelligent board. Instead it controls the UARTs via a high-level API, much as it would have done had a decent device driver been developed for the COM ports under MS-DOS. Because of this, the board designer has some freedom in hardware design. As long as the command format and the shared memory operation remain the same, any processor can be designed into the intelligent board or any UARTS can be in operation there. This is why many other UARTs, besides the conventional 8250 family, reside on intelligent multiport boards. It also means we can expect to see continued improvements in intelligent board hardware with boards becoming more powerful as better and cheaper hardware becomes available.

Intelligent boards work very well for UNIX users, because their access to serial ports already has to go through a device driver. Once you design a good intelligent board, all you have to do is write a device driver (the serial device driver under UNIX is not particularly difficult to write), and you can start selling your board to every UNIX user of your hardware platform.

# AN OVERVIEW OF RS-232

MS-DOS is a completely different story. The code written to support the traditional 8250 family of UARTs is completely wasted on these intelligent boards. It usually requires a completely different approach than interrupt-driven RS-232 hardware. One of the reasons for writing this book is to demonstrate how an object-oriented approach can enable the easy implementation of new hardware without having complete rewrites of existing programs. Unfortunately, most real-world software was not written using object-oriented techniques, so intelligent multiport boards are for the most part locked out of the MS-DOS arena.

## Modems

When RS-232 was first formulated, the typical modem was a synchronous half-duplex device that operated at fairly slow speeds. Half-duplex operation meant that either end of the channel had to specifically request permission to transmit, via the RTS line, and wait for permission to be granted via CTS. Once the device had permission to transmit, the remote end of the connection was locked out until the first device was finished.

One obvious implication was that the remote character echo we take for granted when talking to another computer was simply not possible. Today, as I type characters into my local BBS via a modem connection, the BBS transmits my characters back to me as it receives them. This remote echoing lets me see that my data is being properly transmitted. Under the tyranny of the half-duplex regime, however, this wasn't possible. Instead, modems performed the echo function locally, transmitting the characters back to the DTE as they were transmitted. You would see characters echoed to your screen automatically, whether or not the other end was receiving them.

Now modems operate as full-duplex modems, and typically operate at 9,600 or 14,400 bits per second. With data compression and error control, actual throughputs on these modems can be as high as 57,600 baud. Standards groups are working on the next generation of modems, which may have a basic data rate as high as 28,800 bits per second. Modem designers feel this speed will approach the limits of throughput on analog phone lines.

**Data rates**

Historically, progress in modems has proceeded along two paths. First, modems have continually become faster. The data carrier used by most modems in the early 1970s had a capacity ranging from 110 to 300 bps. Todays most advanced modems can transmit up to 14.4K bps. At the same time, modems have grown progressively more intelligent. The 300 bps modems of the 1970s had virtually no intelligence and did nothing more than convert voltage levels to frequency outputs. Today, modems interact locally with the computers they service. They also maintain error-free communications over noisy lines and compress the data streams they transmit.

A brief look at the historical progression of modem transmission schemes follows. While there are many side branches off the main path, the vast majority of computer users have stayed more or less on this same road.

Bell 103: The first standard asynchronous modems to make a big splash in the world of computers were the Bell 103 family. They were capable of full duplex communications at data rates ranging from 110 to 300 bps.

Typically, Bell 103 modems were connected to the phone line via an acoustic coupler, a mechanical device that held the handset of a telephone up against the microphone and speaker for the modem.

Bell 212, V.22: The 212 and V.22 standards took a quantum leap forward, quadrupling Bell 103 by increasing throughput on the telephone line to 1,200 bps. Most 212-type modems produced also would fall back to supporting a 300-baud connection with older 103 devices, establishing a trend towards downward compatibility that is still with us today.

V.22*bis*: With this modem, the world was able to finally settle on a single standard! At 2,400 bps, this modem doubled the throughput of the previous generation. PC users in the early 1980s looked to this modem as the standard for high-speed communications. After 10 years of telecommunications for IBM users, the 2400 bps modem probably has the widest installed base of any modem.

# AN OVERVIEW OF RS-232

**V.32:** It took many years for the V.32 9,600-bps modem standard to be finalized. The technical difficulties involved in developing this new generation of modems were formidable, requiring much research and testing before the final version could be accepted. In the years leading up to V.32, several proprietary high-speed schemes were promulgated by modem manufacturers such as U.S. Robotics and Telebit. Without the backing of worldwide standardization, however, these unique methods were generally viewed as stopgap measures, and are slowly falling by the wayside.

**V.32*bis*:** This standard came close on the heels of the V.32 standard. V.32*bis* is not nearly as big a jump as we have encountered in the past, jumping from 9,600 bps to 14,400 bps However, the 50 percent increase in speed was viewed as relatively easy to accomplish, while still maintaining compatibility with the earlier V.32 standard. Given the public's hunger for ever increasing bandwidth, this standard was accepted quite quickly.

Hardware manufacturers learned a lot during the development of V.32 modems, which, in turn, has done a lot to lower the cost of V.32*bis* modems. Because of this, 14,400-bps modems are well on their way to being the standard for desktop communications applications. Now, 2,400-baud modems are used strictly for hobbyist and home applications, where they are still popular due to their low price. Business applications will almost always lean towards 9600- and 14,400-bps modems as more economical because they reduce the use of phone lines.

**V.fast:** The CCITT is working on the next generation of modems, which are expected to operate at 19,200 or 28,800 bps. This basic data rate will approach the theoretical limit of standard dial-up phone lines, so there is some question as to what will follow. Some manufacturers of V.32*bis* modems are already claiming that their existing units will be able to upgrade to this new standard, in some cases simply by modifying the firmware that drives their DSP chips. This remains to be tested.

## Intelligence

"Dumb" modems: While it isn't likely that any manufacturer ever referred to their modems as "dumb," virtually the entire generation of 110- and 300-bps modems have earned this moniker. "Dumb" refers to the fact that these modems don't have any on-board microprocessor to help with dialing, going on and off hook, or controlling the connection once it has been established.

Smart modems: Probably the first widely known "smart" modem (modem with microprocessor) was the Hayes Smartmodem. Hayes first put intelligence in their early 300-baud modems, then quickly followed with higher speed 1200- and 2,400-bps models. These smart modems communicated with the computer through the same RS-232 connection used to communicate with the remote end.

Initially, the smart modems didn't do much more than help set up the phone call. The user could type in a phone number using the now standard "AT" command set. A typical command might be ATD555-1212, which would cause the modem to go off hook and attempt to make a connection with another modem at 555-1212.

Smart modems have now evolved to the point where they not only establish connections, but also store phone numbers, interactively monitor the progress of a phone call, provide help screens, and much more.

MNP-4: Microcom, Inc. developed a protocol referred to as MNP which provided the next step in the evolution of modem intelligence. MNP is layered in "classes," with each class adding functionality to the modem. MNP features would be virtually impossible without the help of powerful on-board microprocessors.

The first three classes of MNP, MNP-1, 2, and 3, provide for slightly improved use of the phone line. By sending data using a synchronous protocol, these first three levels of MNP eliminate start and stop bits, adding about 20 percent to modem throughput. This feature alone was enough to assure the success of MNP.

But MNP-4 was where the real improvements began. MNP-4 is an error-detecting and correcting protocol that assures the user that the connection between two DTE devices will be 100 percent error free. Two modems connected using MNP-4 will add validation information to data and will retransmit any blocks with errors.

MNP-4 represents an enormous step forward in serial communications. By using MNP-4-class modems, applications programmers can stop worrying about data transmission and spend more time on more important concerns, such as on what to do with the data once it arrives.

**MNP-5:**

MNP-5 offers an even more tangible benefit. It compresses the data stream before transmitting it through the phone lines. MNP-5 uses an adaptive Huffman coding scheme that can compress highly redundant data by a factor of 2:1. This means that the owner of a 2,400-baud modem with MNP-5 data compression can perform like a 4,800-baud modem if connected to another MNP-5 modem at the remote end.

MNP-5 was an immediate success, although it did have drawbacks. The compression scheme used in MNP-5 actually caused performance to deteriorate if the data had already been compressed using more conventional methods. And MNP was a proprietary protocol. Anyone who wanted to add MNP protocols to their modem was at the mercy of Microcom, Inc., for licensing. Of course, Microcom acted in enlightened self-interest, realizing that licensing terms had to be attractive enough to help promote the standard. Apparently Microcom found a good balance, judging from the widespread adoption of MNP protocols.

V.42, V.42*bis*: MNP-4 and MNP-5 pioneered the use of error detection and data compression in asynchronous modems. However, just as the AT&T standards for data transmission gave way to CCITT international standards, the Microcom protocols soon gave way as well. The CCITT was reluctant to let a proprietary scheme be used as an international standard. Additionally, some technical improvements over MNP-4 and MNP-5 were suggested and eventually adopted. The result was V.42 and V.42*bis*.

V.42 is a standard that uses one of two methods to detect and retransmit erroneous data. The preferred method for this is to use the Link Access Protocol for Modems (LAPM). Microcom managed to incorporate MNP-4 as a fallback method for V.42. If a modem that supports V.42 calls an MNP-4 modem, the V.42 is supposed to fall back to MNP-4 link management.

V.42*bis* is a standard for data compression by the modem. This standard uses an LZW-based data compression algorithm that is considerably more powerful than MNP-5, allowing up to 4:1 data compression ratios for highly redundant data.

**Handshaking**

As I mentioned earlier in this chapter, one of the consequences of the progression in modems was the steadily increasing speed the modem uses to communicate with the computer. Modem manufacturers today support interface rates as high as 57,600 bps, and V. fast modems will push this rate even higher. These high baud rates, combined with error-correcting protocols, have created a basic need for local handshaking in modem communications.

Most high-speed modems now use a "locked DTE" method of communicating with the locally attached computer. This means that regardless of the rate at which a connection is established, the local connection with the computer remains at the same baud rate. For example, a V.32 modem will frequently suggest a connection of 38,400 baud with a computer. Even when the modem connects to a V.22*bis* modem at 2,400 bps, the local connection remains at 38.4Kbps. It is up to the modem to convert the 38,400 bps data stream coming from the computer to the 2,400 bps data stream going out over the telephone line.

Obviously, a few major difficulties can occur here. If the computer continues pumping data as fast as it can at 38,400 bps, and the modem is only transmitting at 2400 bps, data is backing up inside the modem at a rapid pace. The modem undoubtedly has to have some internal storage space, but it can't continue indefinitely storing data. The only solution to this problem is to implement flow control.

Flow control has been used in various forms with RS-232 connections since their inception. Flow control is simply an agreed-upon method of letting one end of the connection signal the other end to stop transmission while processing occurs. The two primary methods of flow control used in asynchronous RS-232 connections are RTS/CTS and XON/XOFF.

## Hardware Flow Control

RTS/CTS flow control is part of the family of flow-control methods collectively referred to as "hardware flow control." Hardware flow-control methods use RS-232 control lines to start and stop the flow of serial data. With RTS/CTS, the computer or other DTE uses RTS to start and stop the flow of data from the modem or other DCE device. The modem uses CTS to start and stop data from the computer.

In theory, RTS/CTS flow control is relatively simple to implement. The modem's input buffer is limited to a certain size. Every time a new character is read in, the modem processor checks to see how full the buffer is. Once it passes a certain point, referred to as the "high-water mark," it turns the CTS line off by telling the UART to apply a logic 0 voltage on that pin. When the DTE sees this line drop, it stops transmitting. The DTE generally won't be able to respond to the signal instantly, so there will almost always be a few characters that are transmitted even after the control line drops.Once the control line is brought down and the DTE stops transmitting, the modem can continue pulling characters out of its input buffer and processing them. Eventually, the modem will empty its input buffer past a point referred to as the "low-water mark". At this point the modem will reassert the CTS line, and the DTE will begin transmitting characters again.

Typical values for the low and high water marks would be 25 percent and 75 percent of the buffer capacity. We don't want to put the marks too much lower or higher than that. Setting the low-water mark too low creates the risk of emptying the buffer completely before the DTE resumes transmission, resulting in idle capacity. Setting the high-water mark too high risks input buffer overflow, when the sender doesn't stop transmitting in time.

This discussion of handshaking has concentrated on the modem's restraint of the DTE/computer. This handshaking operation is completely symmetrical and is applied in exactly the reverse fashion when the computer needs to restrain the modem. The only difference in this case would be that the computer uses RTS to restrain the modem.

Note that while RTS/CTS is a very common method of flow control, there are many variations of hardware flow control, and every modem will offer at least a few. First, other hardware lines can be used besides RTS and CTS, with the second most popular choice being DTR/DSR. Modems traditionally use DTR and DSR for other purposes, but many devices, such as printers, use one of these lines for hardware flow control.

In addition, I have discussed RTS/CTS as if it automatically paired both sides in flow control. This is frequently not the case. Often, the flow control will only operate in a single direction, as just RTS flow control, for example. The computer may not ever need to prevent the modem from transmitting data since it has such a large capacity that the buffer can't become full.

## Software Flow Control

There are plenty of reasons not to like hardware flow control. At the top of the list is the fact that hardware flow control requires a properly configured cable. Many cables don't have RTS and CTS routed through, instead they use only TD and RD. This is particularly true of a null-modem cable used to connect two similar devices. If hardware flow control isn't practical or desirable, the alternative is software flow control.

Traditionally software flow control is implemented via the XON/XOFF protocol. As before, the receiver will have a predetermined high water mark. When the receiver's input buffer fills beyond this high water mark, it will send an XOFF character to the remote end (Decimal 19 or Control-S). When the remote end receives this character, it knows that it has been requested to stop transmitting, and does so at once. Once the input buffer for the receiver falls below the low water mark, the receiver sends an XON to the other side (Decimal 17 or Control-Q). This character alerts the remote end to the fact that transmission can resume.

# AN OVERVIEW OF RS-232

Like hardware flow control, software flow control comes in several varieties. The start and stop characters used by the protocol can vary. There is nothing magical about XON and XOFF; these characters are just traditional. Second, the protocol can be unidirectional, with just one side obeying the flow control characters. In general, however, a link that uses software flow control will almost always use XON/XOFF signaling and will support flow control in both directions.

XON/XOFF has one major disadvantage compared with hardware flow control. When a computer attempts to send raw binary data, the flow control characters will inevitably show up in the data stream. When this happens, the remote end can get very confused. For example, if I am using XON/XOFF flow control with my V.32 modem, and I am trying to send a file to the remote end that contains numerous appearances of XON and XOFF, I am going to have a problem. My modem will think those characters are to be used for flow control, and it will strip them out of the data stream and try to respond to them. One of two things will happen: either the file will arrive at the remote end in a corrupted state, or my link will freeze up because the modem has received an inadvertent XOFF character.

**Local versus pass through**

Until now, my discussion of flow control has concentrated on local flow control. This is the flow control between a DTE and a DCE, generally consisting of a modem and a computer directly connected. However, at times I will want to exercise end-to-end flow control. For example, I might be using a modem to connect to a remote UNIX system. During the course of my session, I may be typing a file out to the screen. If my modems and computers are set up properly, I may not need local flow control because all four pieces of hardware are keeping up with the data stream. However, my brain can't keep up with the file pouring out on my screen, so I may want to manually stop the flow of data. If I press a Control-S on my keyboard, I want that character to go through my modem, pass through the remote modem, and be sent to the UNIX system.

In this scenario, if my modem is using XON/XOFF flow control for my local session, I will immediately run into trouble. My modem will stop transmitting data, but it will not pass the XOFF through to the remote end. So my UNIX system will continue spewing data out to its modem, not knowing that I don't particularly want to see any more. If the two modems don't have a V.42 or MNP-4 connection, the data will continue pouring into my local modem until its internal buffers overflow, resulting in loss of data.

This means that if I want flow control with the far end of my connection, both DTE devices should be set up for XON/XOFF flow control, but neither DCE should have it enabled. If I still need local flow control under these circumstances, it has to be done using hardware flow control such as RTS/CTS.

This setup of local versus end-to-end flow control, combined with the differences between hardware and software flow control, has made modem setup of modems a subject of consternation among desktop computer users. For one thing, not only do the modems and cables have to be configured properly, but the PC applications software needs to be properly set up as well.

Unfortunately, the problem is not likely to go away soon. I recommend that you *always* set up your local modem connection to use RTS/CTS flow control. It is important when doing this to test your flow control out early, to verify both that your cable works and that your modem has been properly configured. Once the hardware flow control is working properly, you can consider adding software flow control for end-to-end handshaking as needed.

## File Transfers

Once a system has been properly set up with modems and flow control, one of the most common activities a user will want to undertake is that of file transfers. This is another area that once again causes a lot of grief for users of communications software, whether they are novices or experienced users. As with RS-232 cabling, modems, and handshaking, for file transfers to work properly, both computers involved in the transaction have to be set up to do exactly the same thing.

One of the main problems with file transfers is that there are no clear-cut definitive standards for how to do things. Accordingly, when we want to move files from machine to machine, we have to examine the menu of protocols that are available to both machines. We then look for the protocols common to both machines and try to select the "best" one for the job. Usually, but not always, it is possible to find a match and get the job done.

Following is a brief overview of some of the more well-known protocols. Keep in mind that it is much easier to develop a new software file transfer protocol than it is to develop a new hardware interface, so new protocols seem to spring up weekly.

XMODEM: The XMODEM protocol was one of the first file transfer methods that achieved widespread use on the desktop. XMODEM is a relatively simple protocol that allows a user to perform a binary transfer of a single file. It requires a clear 8-bit channel with no software handshaking, which makes XMODEM somewhat difficult to implement on many mainframe and minicomputer platforms.

The XMODEM protocol is the lowest common denominator among the on-line community of electronic bulletin boards and information services. When all else fails, XMODEM can usually be relied on to work for both ends of the connection.

Many minor variants of XMODEM have sprung up over the years. The most universal is XMODEM-CRC, which uses a 16-bit CRC checksum instead of an 8-bit additive checksum for improved error detection. XMODEM-1K increases the block size from 128 to 1024 bytes, giving greater utilization of connection bandwidth. And XMODEM-1K-G can be used on channels using MNP-4 or V.42, since it assumes an error-free connection and does not require immediate acknowledgment of each packet. Despite its primitive roots, XMODEM-1K-G can transfer files using nearly 100 percent of the available bandwidth.

YMODEM: YMODEM is an enhancement of the XMODEM file transfer protocol. YMODEM adds a file information packet to the XMODEM protocol, so that it can send the file name, size, and date along with the file contents. Because of this extra layer in the protocol, YMODEM can also send batches of files instead of just one file at a time, leading to its often-used alias, "YMODEM-Batch."

YMODEM is a fairly simple addition to the XMODEM protocol, so that it is not too difficult to add to existing software that supports XMODEM. This ease of upgrading has led to the widespread dissemination of this protocol as well.

ZMODEM: XMODEM and YMODEM work well under certain circumstances, but they definitely suffer from limitations. They only work on 8-bit communication lines, and XON/XOFF or other forms of software handshaking give them fits. Packet-switched networks cause XMODEM performance to degrade horribly. Even under the best circumstances, XMODEM and YMODEM don't make very efficient use of their available bandwidth.

ZMODEM was designed to overcome all of these problems. First of all, ZMODEM was specifically designed to work well on packet-switched networks. ZMODEM is referred to as a "streaming" protocol, meaning that it sends data in a continuous fashion, without waiting for acknowledgment of individual blocks. Instead, ZMODEM only expects to see indications of erroneous data, which will interrupt the current block and cause a retransmission of the bad data.

ZMODEM was also designed to work in conjunction with software handshaking, such as XON/XOFF. Enhancments to ZMODEM will also allow it to work over 7-bit data channels, which still account for a certain amount of electronic data traffic.

Public domain ZMODEM source code is now available so ZMODEM has spread to many different types of systems. Unfortunately, ZMODEM is a relatively complex protocol to implement and, as such, has not spread quite as rapidly as proponents might like.

Kermit: Like ZMODEM, Kermit was developed in an attempt to let machines from various incompatible architectures communicate. Kermit is a carefully designed, well-layered protocol, with a detailed specification and public domain source code available.

Kermit is a packet-oriented protocol that avoids using characters that could conflict with software handshaking or other protocol characters. It can work on either 8-bit or 7-bit channels and offers built-in data compression and other advanced features.

Kermit has been implemented on a wider variety of computer systems than any other protocol. The Kermit community also maintains a

# AN OVERVIEW OF RS-232

very strong spirit of communication, with code, ideas, and implementation help being freely distributed.

As a result of its ease-of-use, one might expect Kermit to be the most widely used protocol. Although protocols such as YMODEM and ZMODEM aren't as easy to work with and implement as Kermit, they are much faster. Kermit has a lot of overhead in both packet formation and acknowledgment.

Enhancements to Kermit have been made to help address efficiency problems. However, these enhancements have generally met with the same fate as enhancements and supersets of other protocols: without mandatory implementation, optional features just aren't used often enough to generate a critical mass of users.

Others: Other contenders for the protocol limelight include less notable implementations such as CompuServe Quick-B, Bimodem, and proprietary protocols used in programs such as Blast and Crosstalk. At present there don't seem to be any protocols offering enough in the way of new features to knock any of the leaders off their perches, but a good new protocol can take off rapidly in today's environment.

## Software and Hardware

The last section of this chapter discusses software and hardware that can be useful to the communications programmer. Details on company names and other sources for these products are found in the Sources Directory at the end of this book.

### PC software

For those just getting started in the world of PC communications, an enormous variety of software is available. For the user, there are quite a few communications programs, ranging from inexpensive shareware programs like Telix to good commercial software, such as Procomm and Crosstalk.

Most users first encounter a communications package when they purchase their modems. Most intelligent modems sold today are accompanied by a communications package designed to work properly with that modem. For the most part, these manufacturer-supplied programs are sparse and just barely adequate. Experienced users generally discard them and move on to more powerful commercial and shareware packages.

A good communications package should be able to control your modem; handle all the tasks associated with calling on-line services and BBSs; have a scripting or macro capability for automating routine chores; and offer upload and download capability for files. Competition among these products has seen vendors going far beyond these basics, with lists of additional features too numerous to detail here.

**BBS software**

BBS systems started off as simple programs that let users exchange electronic messages and files. The best BBS systems have now moved far beyond that, with networked capability for worldwide messaging, on-line games and chat features, massive file libraries, and custom "door" software that lets BBS operators develop their own special features.

Arguably the most popular commercial BBS program is PCBoard, by Clark Development Company. PCBoard owes much of its popularity to the fact that it has kept pace with industry developments as far as BBS features go. For example, one of the most exciting developments in the world of BBS has been the growth of international message conferences that allow groups of users to participate in public forums, with hundreds of new messages generated every day.

Another commercial system that is doing well is Wildcat! by Mustang Software. While Wildcat! can't claim the market share of PCBoard, Mustang is doing a lot to improve their product as well. Mustang has purchased both the Qmodem communications program as well as a popular off-line mail reader, and is working on integrating them into the Wildcat! BBS.

Two noncommercial systems that still are doing very well are RBBS and Opus. RBBS is one of the earliest BBS systems available. Originally written in BASIC and distributed in source form, it could be executed under the IBM BASIC interpreter that came bundled with the IBM PC. While it is still written in BASIC, RBBS is now a much larger and more powerful package, so it naturally has moved on to using compiled BASIC. However, the source code for RBBS is still available, allowing adventurous systems operators to experiment .

Opus does not have the source code availability, but it provided a powerful BBS free of charge, enabling it to carve a relatively large niche in the BBS world.

# AN OVERVIEW OF RS-232

## On line information services

On-line information services are commercial ventures that provide many of the same functions as a BBS.

The leading on-line information service is probably CompuServe Information Service, or CIS. As this is being written, CompuServe should be passing the 1 million mark for total membership. Like most BBSs, CIS offers access to message and file areas. Many of these message and file areas are dedicated to support for commercial and shareware products. CIS also has access to news services, stock market quotes, various informative databases, an encyclopedia, and electronic shopping.

While CIS is a very capable service, it comes at a very high price. A typical connect time charge starts at $12.95 per hour. CompuServe has begun to come under pressure from some other services that are offering reduced rates, and in some cases, no connect time charges. CompuServe is now offering a limited set of features referred to as "Basic Services," which will be made available for a flat monthly fee.

The pressure on CompuServe to lower prices has come from two different competitors: Prodigy and GEnie. Prodigy is a joint venture of Sears and IBM, and offers a videotext-like service for a flat monthly fee. Unlike CompuServe or GEnie, Prodigy must be used with a specific access program provided as part of the membership. Prodigy attempts to reach a wider audience by providing an easy-to-use, handholding environment. Prodigy offers access to on-line games, mail, conferences, news services, and various databases. At this time, Prodigy doesn't offer any file transfers.

GEnie offers nearly identical service to that of CompuServe. GEnie is a product of General Electric Information Services. They pioneered the concept of basic services with an offer to their customers of flat-fee access to a limited set of services.

Other services that are jockeying for position at this time include America On Line, BIX, and Telepath. At the same time, various large BBS systems have been expanding into on-line information services.

## Programming libraries

This book should teach enough about RS-232 programming to allow you to develop good communications programs. While this book will start you down the road towards becoming an expert, you might want to take a short cut. If you decide not to develop your own communications programs from scratch, many excellent C libraries are available to help.

Regardless of how diligently you apply yourself, you are probably not going to be able to approach the level of testing that goes into one of these commercial libraries. Most have been available for several years, and have been purchased and used by hundreds or even thousands of programmers. Thus, they have been tested on a vast number of platforms and operating environments.

The economics of purchasing a library are generally very favorable, *as long as the library is reliable*. If you purchase a buggy product with poor support, you will often end up expending so much time and energy ironing out problems that your initial investment will be dwarfed. Accordingly, my suggestions for evaluating commercial libraries are:

1. Get working demos of applications built with the library. Most vendors have demo programs available. Test these programs using various hardware and other communications software. This should give you some insight into the quality and flexibility of the library.

2. Talk to the vendor's technical support department about problems you may have had with the demo programs. If you don't experience any problems, try to talk to the technical support person about questions you might have. The ability of the technical support person to help you solve problems quickly will probably be one of the most important factors in deciding whether the library saves you money.

3. Check over the features list of the library, but don't let the number of features be an overwhelming factor in your decision. It is easy to get carried away and make decisions based on the presence or absence of features you don't really need.

4. Check the quality of the documentation and source code of the library. If the library doesn't come with source code, don't buy it. To check these items, you may have to purchase the library on an evaluation basis, so this is usually the last part of the evaluation process. Most vendors offer unconditional warranties, and will gladly sell you a library on an evaluation basis.

# AN OVERVIEW OF RS-232

I suggest that you survey the entire market before you make a decision. There are two different sources of information: 1) programming magazines, and 2) mail order catalogs. Programming magazines such as *Dr. Dobb's Journal* and the *C User's Journal* will feature ads from many of the library vendors. A quick call to mail order software houses such as Programmer's Paradise or Programmer's Connection will usually yield a free catalog listing most of the available libraries.

Several shareware communications libraries are also available. The decision to purchase one of these libraries probably needs to be made for reasons other than those that would factor into choosing a commercial package. You will rarely if ever get the same quality of documentation and support with a shareware library. However, for much less money, you may get access to well-written source code. If you want to learn more about communications programming and incorporate good programming techniques into your own work, these libraries will usually provide good working material.

Shareware communications libraries are usually found on major BBSs, as well as services like CompuServe and GEnie.

## Tools of the Trade

One of the reasons that so many people shy away from communications programming is that it tends to be somewhat hardware intensive. You can feel more confident when faced with all this hardware if you have an adequate supply of tools. Most of these tools are relatively inexpensive, and will often pay for themselves the first time you use them.

### Breakout boxes

Figure 1-14 shows the Datatracker DT-5 (Datatran Corporation), a typical breakout box. A breakout box is simply a piece of diagnostic hardware that is inserted in line with a cable between two RS-232 devices. Usually a breakout box will have miniature switches that let you break open or shut individual lines on the 25-conductor cable. In addition, it will usually have some jumper wires so that individual signals can be routed to different destinations. These jumper wires can come in very handy. For example, if you determine that you have two DTE devices trying to talk over a straight cable, you can use two jumper wires to convert the straight cable to a three-wire null-modem cable.

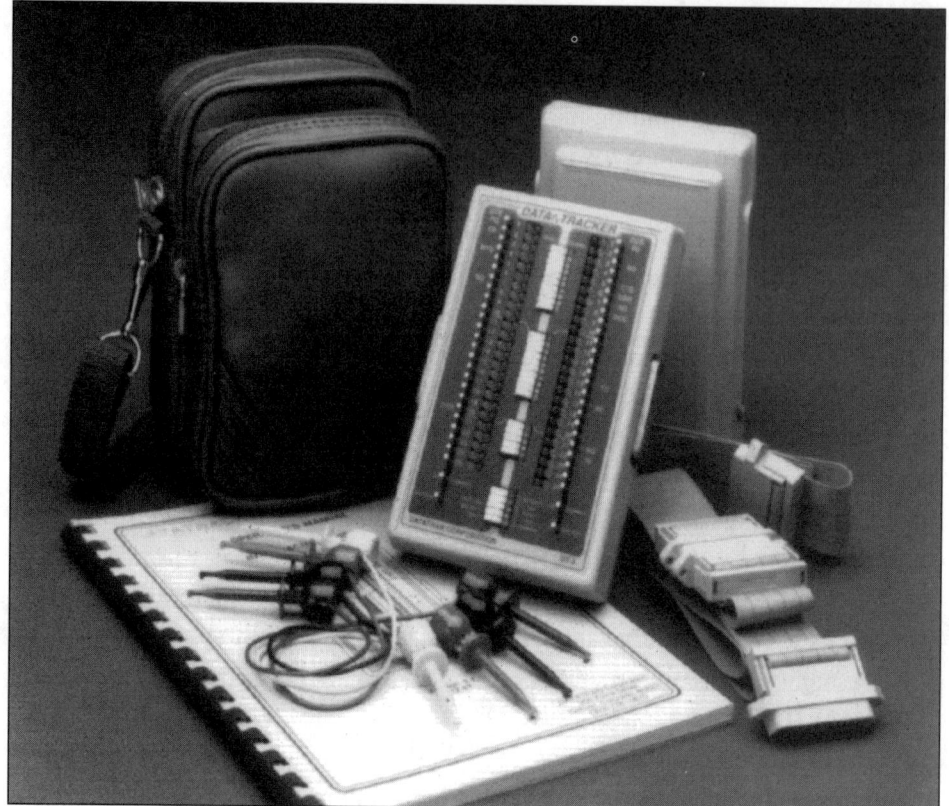

**Figure 1-14. A typical breakout box**

Perhaps the most useful features on a breakout box are the LEDs attached to most of the commonly used lines. With the aid of these LEDs, you can determine what sort of activity is happening on a given line. For example, if a PC and a modem are using RTS/CTS communications while transmitting, an LED monitor on the RTS and CTS lines should show the lines periodically changing back and forth between two states.

You should try to purchase a breakout box that has dual-state LEDs. Remember that RS-232 signals come in three varieties, not two: low, high, or invalid. A line that is not hooked up to a negative or positive voltage is considered invalid. Unfortunately, a normal red LED can only indicate two states: high or low. It usually can't distinguish between a CTS line that is low and a CTS line that isn't connected.

# AN OVERVIEW OF RS-232

To solve this problem, better breakout boxes employ an LED that shows three different states: low, high, and off. Usually red will indicate high, green will indicate low, and no color will indicate no signal. This way you can tell if a line is actually disconnected from an RS-232 driver. This information is very valuable when you are dealing with an unknown RS-232 device. For example, with a dual-state LED display, you can quickly determine which of pins 2 and 3 are inputs and which are outputs, which will help you properly cable your equipment. Inputs will show up as having no valid RS-232 signal, whereas outputs will always show up as high or low. Another valuable use for dual state LED is to determine when your device is actually transmitting data. At high baud rates it may not be possible to determine if a single LED is flickering off for brief periods of time, but if the LED changes color to become slightly more green than before, you will know the device is actually transmitting data.

As an alternative to an actual dual-state LED, many breakout boxes simply have a pair of LEDs on each line: one green and one red. This accomplishes exactly the same task, it just takes up slightly more space. The Datatracker shown in Figure 1-15 has a pair of LEDs on every signal on both the DTE and DCE sides of the connection. This may seem like overkill, but it is very helpful to never be in doubt as to the state of a given signal.

Breakout box prices can go as high as $300, but you can find very useful units for less than $100. In fact, a fully functional breakout box with 12 dual-state LEDs can be purchased for less than $30. If you are only working on desktop PCs, remember that breakout boxes that have switches and LEDs for all 25 RS-232 lines aren't going to be any more useful than those that have just nine lines. Your PCs are only going to be using 9 of those 25 signal lines, so there isn't much point to paying for any more. If you are wondering what features are most important, I would look first for dual-state or dual LEDs, second for the ability to jumper every pin.

### Line monitors

Breakout boxes do several useful things. They let you examine the state of individual RS-232 lines using an LED. They let you disconnect individual lines using switches, and they let you reconfigure your cable using jumper wires. Breakout boxes also let you observe whether or not data is being transmitted by letting you watch the LEDs attached to the TD and RD lines.

But just seeing if data is being transmitted often isn't enough to help you debug an application. Sometimes you need to know exactly what data is being transmitted. And most of us aren't skillful enough to decode the actual data by watching LEDs blink on and off several thousand times per second.

Fifteen years ago this problem would have been solved by the purchase of an RS-232 Data Line Analyzer. This multithousand-dollar piece of equipment would monitor the data and control lines on an RS-232 connection. It would display the actual data being passed in both directions on a screen. And it would log the data for later review, along with accurate time stamps showing when the data was sent. These machines were very nice, but unfortunately, they were also very expensive.

The advent of the inexpensive desktop PC created the possibility for an inexpensive version of the RS-232 Line Analyzer. By combining an existing PC with two serial ports, some custom software, and a special cable, you could have the equivalent of an expensive Line Analyzer for no more than the cost of the software.

Naturally, once this opportunity existed, several people began making products to take advantage of it. Now there are at least half a dozen PC-based line monitors. They share one characteristic: they require a special cable that taps into an RS-232 connection like a breakout box and routes the signals found there to two serial ports on the PC. Then they all manage the acquisition, display, and storage of that data via their custom software package. All of these packages retail for less than $500, so the cost of an RS-232 Data Line Analyzer has dropped dramatically.

Figure 1-15 shows a screen shot from a typical (hypothetical) monitor program. The main portion of the screen shows the RS-232 data from both sides of the connection being displayed in real time. The top of the screen has a set of pull-down menus to allow you to analyze the data, save it to disk, or reconfigure the program. A real-time monitor such as this can prove invaluable when debugging RS-232 applications. These products are sold in the same places I recommended earlier for C programming libraries. You should also consult the Sources appendix at the end of this book.

# AN OVERVIEW OF RS-232

```
┌─────────────────────────────────────────────────────────────────┐
│                     Hypothetical Datascope                       │
│ DTE: COM1   9600,N,8,1    152,122 Characters                    │
│ DCE: COM2   9600,N,8,1      334 Characters                      │
│ ──────────────────────── [ Data Captured ] ──────────────────── │
│  Please enter your command >         Do you really want to log off
│                           Quit [CR][CR]
│  ? You have 128 minutes left on line?      Thank you for calling
│                           Yes [CR][CR]
│
│  the Happy Camper BBS. You have been on line for 12 minutes. You have
│
│  128 minutes left today. [CR][LF] NO CARRIER       A T D T 1 8 0 0 5
│                                       [CR][CR] A T D T 1 8 0 0 5 5
│  5 5 1 2 1 2 [CR][LF] RINGING [CR][LF] CONNECT 38400[CR][LF][CR][LF]Wel
│    5 1 2 1 2 [CR]
└─────────────────────────────────────────────────────────────────┘
```

**Figure 1-15. An RS-232 monitor screen shot**

## Cable-Making Equipment

As I mentioned earlier in this chapter, RS-232 cables continue to be one of the biggest headaches for programmers working on serial applications. As long as your hardware only needs standard cables with 25-pin connectors, you should not have serious problems. However, anytime your needs stray from this, requiring custom cables, life suddenly becomes much more difficult. But there are several simple methods for making your own cables and I will discuss the basic idea behind three fairly simple methods.

One method that is fairly flexible, yet very easy to manage, involves buying premade cabling kits. These kits consist of a 9-conductor wire with connector pins already crimped on to the ends of the wires. All you need to buy in addition to the cables are connectors, hoods, strain reliefs, and an insertion tool. The insertion tool is a simple mechanical device that only costs a few dollars. In addition, you can purchase jumper wires that are used to loop back signals at the connector.

To make a cable using the cabling kit, you simply use the insertion tool to push the crimped pins into the appropriate locations on the connector. Once all the pins have been inserted, you complete the end of the cable by connecting the strain relief and the hood. After 5 or 10 minutes you have a complete cable. This very simple procedure doesn't require any expensive equipment.

Another relatively simple method involves the use of modular connectors. These connectors use RJ-45 8-conductor telephone cable to join connectors, instead of standard unshielded cable. As in the previous cable kits, you buy a hood and a connector, then insert the pins wherever you want. You don't need a strain relief because the RJ-45 connector fastens to the hood to provide strain relief. Perhaps the only major disadvantage to this cabling method is that the RJ-45 cable only has eight conductors, which means that on a standard PC you are going to have to leave one signal unconnected. This may not be as much of a problem as it sounds. Most applications can probably function quite well with the RI pin disconnected, since modems typically send an ASCII message when the phone is ringing. An application can simply watch for the ASCII "RING" message to determine when an incoming ring is detected.

The final method for making cables is completely do-it-yourself. You buy 10- or 12-conductor cable in bulk, then buy connector pins, a crimping tool, connectors, hoods, and strain reliefs. You cut your own cable to custom sizes, strip the wires and crimp on the pins to the wires. You then insert the pins into the connectors, attach the hoods and strain reliefs, and you have a cable.

This final method has the most flexibility, but with two big disadvantages. First, it is labor intensive, and will take a fairly long time. Second, the crimping tool generally costs about $100 (although cheaper models are available) so the initial outlay is high.

**Gender changers/adapters**

Along with whatever cabling kits you decide on, you should lay in a supply of several different sorts of adapters (discussed earlier in this chapter). An adapter looks like a normal RS-232 connector, except it has pins at both ends and no wire coming out of it. These adapters can be found at prices as low as five dollars.

# AN OVERVIEW OF RS-232

The adapters you will want to always have on hand are listed below:

9-pin female to 25-pin male - adapter for AT Serial port
25-pin null modem adapter
25-pin male-to-female gender changer
25-pin female-to-male gender changer

As I mentioned earlier in this chapter, you might want to get out the soldering iron and modify the null-modem adapter so that its connections are somewhat more useful than those in the pre-assembled connector. Since the adapter only costs a few dollars, you shouldn't feel inhibited about practicing soldering on it.

## Voltmeter

One final piece of equipment that will help you with your RS-232 hardware debugging is a low-cost voltmeter. You will want to use the voltmeter for two different things. First, using it either as an ohmmeter or a continuity checker (if it has that function), you can test cables for internal breaks and shorts. Unknown cables can be checked out for duplication.

If your voltmeter has a continuity setting, you usually can apply it to ends of a piece of wire and determine immediately if they are connected. If they are, the meter will beep. If your meter doesn't have a continuity setting, you can use the ohmmeter setting. A solid piece of wire should have a very low resistance, less than 100 ohms. An open wire should show a resistance in the Megohms.

Getting voltmeter probes onto RS-232 connectors can try your patience. Two pieces of equipment will help. The first is a set of probes with minihook clips at the end. You can purchase the minihook clips at Radio Shack and just attach them to your voltmeter probes. These clips are small enough that they can attach to a normal RS-232 pin. For getting your probe to make contact with the female connector, there is nothing better than an ordinary paper clip. Just straighten the paper clip out, hook the clip to it, then stick the other end of the paper clip in the socket.

Second, use the voltmeter to check the voltages on RS-232 pins. Remember that a valid RS-232 voltage should be at least plus or minus 3 volts. In practice, unless travelling over a very long cable, most RS-232 voltages will be around plus or minus 12 volts, normally standard for the RS-232 driver chips. All voltage measurements on an RS-232 connector should be made relative to pin 7, which is the signal ground. If you fail to connect the black lead of your voltmeter to pin 7, any measurements will be faulty and should be ignored.

## Summary

This chapter contains all the necessary background information on equipment and compilers for you to become proficient in writing code for RS-232 hardware. Chapter 2, The RS232 Class, provides information specific to programming for RS-232 in C++.

CHAPTER 2

# The RS232 Class

The `RS232` class is the base class for all the RS-232 drivers used in this book. This book is intended to be useful for people who have little or no C++ programming experience, so much of the explanation of this class will rely on C terminology. The `RS232` class gives a very straightforward and simple example of the reasons for using C++ instead of C, so ideally it will provide a bridge for C programmers to begin working in C++.

## A Base Class?

The reason for using C++ for the communications code in this book is to take advantage of virtual functions. In C terms, a virtual function is simply a function that is called via a pointer instead of directly. To the programmer, the fact that a virtual function is being called via a pointer is for the most part hidden behind C++ syntax.

Writing portable code that can work with various types of hardware means developing a base class called `RS232`. Class `RS232` contains the definition for a set of virtual functions that are intended to give you complete access to the usable interface to an RS-232 driver. For example, a typical virtual function we might define for class `RS232` might be called `Read()`. Using C++ syntax, a programmer uses this function to read in a byte from an RS-232 port of some kind. The important fact to remember about `Read()` is that when we call it, we don't actually call a function named `Read()`. Instead, we call a specific version of `Read()` that has been written for a particular driver. For example, the `Read()` coded for an 8250 interface on a standard PC will probably be very different from that coded for an intelligent DigiBoard plugged into the same PC. But either one can be called via the `Read()` virtual function.

## Doing It in C

To understand why I want to use virtual functions in C++, it might help to see how things would develop if I were to proceed using standard C. Remember that the goal is to be able to write applications that make calls to device-independent RS-232 function calls. The tried-and-true method for resolving this problem would probably be to write a routine that is a dispatcher for Read(). This function would be called with a function pointer to a structure, which would be tested to see what sort of port is being referenced. Then, the appropriate function can be invoked.

The code to implement this intelligent dispatcher is probably similar to code that any experienced programmer has written dozens of times for dozens of different applications. A simple version might look like this:

```
int Read( RS232 *port )
{
    switch( port->type ) {
        case PC8250       : return ReadPC8250( port );
        case INTELLIGENT  : return ReadIntelligent( port );
        case NASI         : return ReadNASI( port );
        case FOSSIL       : return ReadFossil( port );
        default           : return RS232_INVALID_PORT_TYPE;
    }
}
```

### Excess baggage

This code is easy to follow and will work reliably. However, as your library of RS-232 drivers is built up over time, a couple of things will become clear. First, your application is going to be linking in the code for every driver, regardless of whether it is used. So when you try to write a short little program that only writes a couple of bytes out to a PC COM port, you will be dragging along all the code to accomplish the same task over a network, an intelligent board, a FOSSIL driver, and so forth. This could easily double or triple the size of a small application.

# THE RS232 CLASS

Second, I will be paying a small price at runtime for every function call made this way. Every time I make a function call, I have to proceed through the same arbitration process, checking my port types against all the various types before proceeding.

From a programmer's point of view, the maintenance of this code is not that simple. Any time you decide to implement a new driver, you not only have to write all the supported functions for that particular sort of hardware, but you also have to implement the hooks in all of the dispatcher routines. This effectively doubles the amount of maintenance you have to do, which increases the chances for error.

**Function pointers**

One way to get around the problems of a dispatch function is to use function pointers. If we were to code Read() using Standard ANSI C, we would be able to write portable, device-independent code that used function pointers instead of direct calls to functions.

When operating in this mode, you would expect that at sometime during the opening of the port, a routine has been called that linked the appropriate functions to the function pointers you use to call them. A typical application might end up having a code fragment that looked something like this:

```
int (*Read)( RS232 *port );

int ReadLine( RS232 *port )
{
    int c;
    char buffer[ 81 ];

    for ( ; ; ) {
        c = Read( port );
        if ( c == '\r' )
            break;
        .
        .
        .
```

The method shown above for implementing a function pointer works very well with C, and is easy to read under ANSI C. The mechanism for calling a function via a pointer is syntactically identical to that for calling a function directly, so the programmer doesn't need to learn anything new.

One problem with the code shown above is that it doesn't really take into account the possibility that different ports in the same program may well need different versions of `Read()`. For example, in a given program I might be using COM1, COM2, and 4 ports from a shared interrupt multiport board. This means that I have two different types of hardware that are accessed by two different `Read()` routines. However, there is just one function pointer for that function. How do we resolve this?

### Function pointers as part of the RS232 structure

To manage multiple port types under ANSI C properly, your next step is to have a private set of function pointers for each port that you open. That way, you can open two different types of ports and still call the correct functions for each one in the same program. To support this, you will have to start carrying around these function pointers in a structure. A sample code fragment that defines this structure and then makes use of it might look something like this:

```
struct RS232 {
    int (*Read)( struct RS232 *port );
    int (*Write)( struct RS232 *port, int c );
         .
         .
         .
};

int ReadLine( struct RS232 *port )
{
    int c;
    char buffer[ 81 ];

    for ( ; ; ) {
        c = port->Read( port );
```

# THE RS232 CLASS

```
        if ( c == '\r' )
           break;
        .
        .
        .

    main()
    {
        struct RS232 *Port;
        int c;

        Port = OpenComPort( COM1, 9600 );
        ReadLine( Port );
```

At this point, two things have happened. First, the functions are now showing a little more flexibility. By allocating the functions on a port-by-port basis, you now have the flexibility you need to use various kinds of ports within the same program via indirect function calls. There is still some overhead associated with each function, but not nearly as much as there was. In this case, it is simply a matter of an extra pointer dereference required to indirectly call the function. With proper function calls to open the port, you won't be dragging in all the RS-232 drivers to support just one of them.

The second interesting thing that has happened is that the RS232 structure defined here now looks a lot like a C++ class. The function pointers shown here are acting exactly the way virtual functions work in C++. The only real difference is that the C functions have to pass an explicit pointer to the RS232 structure. In C++, this structure is passed implicitly.

### So why C++?

The code sample shown above illustrates that it is possible to implement virtual functions without switching to C++. The obvious question then comes up: Why switch to C++?

Virtual functions were designed as part of the C++ language: implementing them in C requires a lot of extra manual labor. In C++, the compiler takes care of most of the work. More importantly, in C++ the compiler also ensures that the derived classes built from the base class are implemented properly.

The C structure shown earlier had two function pointers defined that pointed to the C code used to read and write bytes. Presumably, a derived "class" (realizing that in ANSI C there is no such thing) had its own Open function that set up these function pointers to point to the proper low-level implementations. A driver that communicated with serial ports via BIOS function calls would be opened using a function that looked something like this:

```
struct RS232 *OpenBIOSPort( int port_number, int baud_rate )
{
    struct RS232 *port;

    port = calloc( 1, sizeof( struct RS232 ) );
    if ( port != 0 ) {
        port->Read = ReadBIOS;
        port->Write = WriteBIOS;
        .
        .
        .
```

When writing the code for the routine shown above, it would be easy to inadvertently neglect to initialize the Write() function pointer. When the caller first attempted to call Port->Write( Port, 'A' ), the most likely event would be a system lockup, since the function pointer was set to 0.

When implementing this scheme using true virtual functions under C++, a good compiler would immediately generate an error message. When defining a base class, any virtual function that *must* be implemented by a derived class can just be predefined as 0. This makes that function a *pure* function, and the class containing it is therefore an *abstract class*.

When we derive a class from the base class, in this case RS232, we have to define new functions for all the pure virtual functions, or the derived class will still be an abstract class. Any attempt to create an object from an abstract class will generate an error message.

A piece of the class definition for class RS232 (the base class used for all the serial classes in this book), looks like this:

## THE RS232 CLASS

```
class RS232
{
    protected :
        RS232PortName port_name;
        Settings saved_settings;
        Settings settings;
        RS232Error error_status;
        int debug_line_count;
        virtual int read_buffer( char *buffer,
                                 unsigned int count ) = 0;
        virtual int write_buffer( char *buffer,
                                  unsigned int count = -1 )
                                                        = 0;
        virtual int read_byte( void ) = 0;
        virtual int write_byte( int c ) = 0;
            .
            .
            .
```

With this definition of the RS232 class, any program that attempted to create an RS232 class would get an error message from the compiler. For example, Borland C++ gives the following error message:

`Error TEST.CPP 26: Cannot create instance of abstract class 'RS232'`

This is exactly what a compiler should do and only C++ does it. This sort of error checking just wouldn't be possible with standard ANSI C.

Additionally, C++ benefits us by offering the easy ability to continue the derivation process in our applications without requiring that we reverse-engineer the entire library. For example, many of the driver programs used to access modems across networks use an expanded version of the PC BIOS interface calls to simulate direct access of a modem. They generally add a few proprietary calls to the existing INT 14H interface, usually to allow more baud rates, block transfers, and the ability to make and break logical connections to modems.

71

It makes sense to create new classes for each of these interfaces that use an existing BIOS class as a starting place. For example, to use the Novell NASI interface, I would like to be able to derive a NASI class from a BIOS class, and just add a couple of new virtual functions. Instead, if I were to try to do this in the C version of the library, I would probably have to take the C code for the BIOS interface, and modify it directly to add my new port open code, and to set up function pointers to my new virtual functions. With C++, I can derive a new class, and count on the compiler to copy all the existing virtual functions from the BIOS class.

## Class RS232

At the heart of this book, lies the definition of `class RS232`. This is the abstract base class that gives birth to all of the serial interface classes used over the next few chapters. It is also the class used as an interface to all the related functions that work with serial ports, including the modem control, terminal emulation, and file transfer routines. Any code that uses `class RS232` objects as parameters will then be portable to all the other drivers developed in this book, as well as to any you derive. The definition for the `RS232` class is shown below.

The master header file for all of the `RS232` derived driver classes, `RS232.H` contains the class definition.

Initially, we can easily be tempted to include everything but the kitchen sink in a given class. For example, we might like to include a virtual function in class `RS232` to enable the synchronous communications capabilities on an Intel 82510 UART. This approach poses two major problems. First, such a large class will eventually become unwieldy. It becomes extremely tedious to derive new classes that must implement all of these new functions. Second, our derived classes tend to suffer from "exception-itis," when faced with many calls that they can't support. In every case, a mechanism must be established for handling exceptional functions.

Here is the definition of the `RS232` class:

```
class RS232
{
    protected :
        RS232PortName port_name;
        Settings saved_settings;
```

# THE RS232 CLASS

```
        Settings settings;
        RS232Error error_status;
        int debug_line_count;
// Mandatory protected functions
        virtual int read_buffer( char *buffer,
                                unsigned int count ) = 0;
        virtual int write_buffer( char *buffer,
                                unsigned int count = -1 ) = 0;
        virtual int read_byte( void ) = 0;
        virtual int write_byte( int c ) = 0;

    public :
        unsigned int ByteCount;
        long ElapsedTime;

// Mandatory functions. All derived classes must define these.

        virtual RS232Error Set( long baud_rate = UNCHANGED,
                                int parity = UNCHANGED,
                                int word_length = UNCHANGED,
                                int stop_bits = UNCHANGED ) = 0;
        virtual int TXSpaceFree( void ) = 0;
        virtual int RXSpaceUsed( void ) = 0;
        virtual int Cd( void ) = 0;
        virtual int Ri( void ) = 0;
        virtual int Cts( void ) = 0;
        virtual int Dsr( void ) = 0;
        virtual int ParityError( int clear = UNCHANGED ) = 0;
        virtual int BreakDetect( int clear = UNCHANGED ) = 0;
        virtual int FramingError( int clear = UNCHANGED ) = 0;
        virtual int HardwareOverrunError( int clear = UNCHANGED )
                                                            = 0;

// Optional Functions. Derived class are not required to support
   these.

        virtual ~RS232( void ){ ; }
        virtual int Break( long milliseconds = 300 );
```

```cpp
            virtual int SoftwareOverrunError( int clear = UNCHANGED );
            virtual int XonXoffHandshaking( int setting = UNCHANGED );
            virtual int RtsCtsHandshaking( int setting = UNCHANGED );
            virtual int DtrDsrHandshaking( int setting = UNCHANGED );
            virtual int Dtr( int setting = UNCHANGED );
            virtual int Rts( int setting = UNCHANGED );
            virtual int Peek( void *buffer, unsigned int count );
            virtual int RXSpaceFree( void );
            virtual int TXSpaceUsed( void );
            virtual int FlushRXBuffer( void );
            virtual int FlushTXBuffer( void );
            virtual char *ErrorName( int error );
            virtual int IdleFunction( void );
            virtual int FormatDebugOutput( char *buffer = 0,
                                           int line_number = -1 );

// Non virtual functions. These work the same for all classes.
            int Read( void *buffer,
                  unsigned int count,
                  long milliseconds = 0 );
            int Read( void *buffer,
                  unsigned int count,
                  long milliseconds,
                  char *terminator );
            int Write( void *buffer,
                   unsigned int count = 0,
                   long milliseconds = 0,
                   char *terminator = 0 );
            int Read( long milliseconds = 0 );
            int Write( int c, long milliseconds = 0 );
            int Peek( void );
            int ReadSettings( Settings &copy ) { copy = settings;
                                                 return RS232_SUCCESS; }
            RS232Error ErrorStatus( void ) { return error_status; }
            int DebugLineCount( void ) { return debug_line_count; }
};
```

# THE RS232 CLASS

The `RS232` class is very straightforward. There are no complex relationships between this class and other classes, no strange constructors or hidden classes. Nearly all the functions are public functions intended to be called by programmers using various RS-232 devices. As stated, this book is not attempting sleight-of-hand using C++. It simply demonstrates a way to improve portability using C++ instead of C. You should be able to tell what most of these functions do just by reading the names.

## A Few Conventions

Classes should always be designed with ease of use as a goal. Such a design goes beyond trying to write fast and efficient code. If a class, such as the `RS232` class, is to be effective, it needs to present a clear, easy to understand, and consistent interface to the programmer. It is usually fairly easy for the original author of a library or program to keep track of a long list of exceptions and oddities associated with his or her work, but pity the programmer who has to take over the project after a corporate reorganization.

### Function/element names

One of the best ways to make a library easy to use is to supply it with clear, descriptive names for all the functions, structures, and other objects that appear in the code. In the `RS232` class, I try to use multiple word names for all variables and functions. By convention, functions and elements to be used by the programmer mix upper and lower case, like this:

```
port.Read( buffer, 20 );
```

Data and functions used internally by the library are defined using all lower case, with names separated by underscores, like this:

```
port.write_byte( c );
```

While many people loathe the extra typing necessitated when using "wordy" function names like those used here, I feel that the advantages in terms of code readability overwhelmingly mandate the use of such function names.

## Function return values

Communications libraries always contain some potential for confusion over function returns. C and C++ work best when a function returns a single parameter. But any time multiple pieces of information come back from a function, there is room for confusion. For example, when reading in a buffer full of data from a serial port, we may want to get back the characters, the character count, any error indications, and the elapsed time. Many different strategies can be adopted for this, and each has good and bad points. However, most important is to establish consistent conventions and to stick with them.

With a single exception, all of the functions defined in the `RS232` class return an integer value. The exception is the `ErrorName()` function, which always returns a string. In the case of all the other functions, any error code is returned directly from the function. To determine if a function has returned an error, see if the returned value is less than 0. All the standard `RS232` error codes are defined as values less than 0, so a function like `Read()` can return a positive or zero value if things work properly, or a negative value if an error occurs. This same convention is used in the C standard library for functions such as `getc()`.

```
enum RS232Error {   RS232_SUCCESS                 = 0,

// Warning errors
                    RS232_WARNING                 = -100,
                    RS232_FUNCTION_NOT_SUPPORTED,
                    RS232_TIMEOUT,
                    RS232_ILLEGAL_BAUD_RATE,
                    RS232_ILLEGAL_PARITY_SETTING,
                    RS232_ILLEGAL_WORD_LENGTH,
                    RS232_ILLEGAL_STOP_BITS,
                    RS232_ILLEGAL_LINE_NUMBER,
                    RS232_NO_MODEM_RESPONSE,
                    RS232_NO_TERMINATOR,
                    RS232_DTR_NOT_SUPPORTED,
                    RS232_RTS_NOT_SUPPORTED,
                    RS232_RTS_CTS_NOT_SUPPORTED,
                    RS232_DTR_DSR_NOT_SUPPORTED,
                    RS232_XON_XOFF_NOT_SUPPORTED,
                    RS232_NEXT_FREE_WARNING,
```

## THE RS232 CLASS

```
// Fatal Errors
                RS232_ERROR                  = -200,
                RS232_IRQ_IN_USE,
                RS232_PORT_NOT_FOUND,
                RS232_PORT_IN_USE,
                RS232_ILLEGAL_IRQ,
                RS232_MEMORY_ALLOCATION_ERROR,
                RS232_NEXT_FREE_ERROR };
```

The code above shows the standard `class RS232` error codes. The `RS232_SUCCESS` code is defined as a 0, but all the actual error codes are defined as negative numbers. I defined the error codes as an enumerated type instead of as constants so that the codes will be more visible during debugging. Note that this list may not be complete. Derived classes will always define their own error codes.

The list of error codes is divided in two. The first section consists of warning errors. When a function generates a warning message, the program should be able to recover and continue operating without much trouble. The second section of error messages are fatal errors. When a port encounters a fatal error, things are in very bad shape and the program probably needs to halt.

When an error occurs in a function, it is returned directly to the programmer via the function return. You can tested for it with a simple numeric test, like this:

```
int result;

result = port.Write( buffer, 80 );
if ( result < RS232_SUCCESS )
    printf( "Error, Write Buffer returned %s\n",
            port.ErrorName( result ) );
```

Programmers are frequently annoyed by the boring job of having to check error codes after *every* function call. This can make both reading and writing the code a somewhat unpleasant chore.

But the `RS232` class maintains an internal error state at all times. If a fatal error occurs, the protected member `error_status` will retain that error code. If a subsequent function is called after a fatal error, the program will not crash or lockup. Ideally, it should just check the error state, see that a fatal error has occurred, and return an error code. So a program can make a few consecutive calls to `RS232` functions without worrying about major catastrophes in the event of an error.

**Byte counts**

Two of the functions called here need to return byte counts as well as error codes. For example, when calling the `Read()` routine with a buffer as the destination argument, the programmer gives a byte count to indicate how many bytes are going to be requested from the port. If `Read()` times out before reading the entire buffer, it returns the `RS232_TIMEOUT` warning error. It must also return a count of bytes actually read in.

The way this is accomplished by class `RS232` member functions is by consistently returning the actual count of bytes transferred in the public element `ByteCount`. After any function call that transfers data, `ByteCount` can be checked for an actual count of bytes transferred.

**Elapsed time**

Finally, the programmer may occasionally want to see the amount of time that has elapsed during the function call. Many of the functions in the `RS232` class have time parameters, which indicate how long the function should attempt to read or write before timing out. Occasionally, it is useful to know just how long the function took before it returned. For example, a BBS program might sit in a loop reading in strings while waiting to receive a "CONNECT 1200" message from a modem.

Some of the strings that come back are simply ignored, such as a message like "CONNECT" or "DIALING". By knowing how long each of those messages took to arrive, you can maintain an overall timeout counter.

The `ElapsedTime` member of the `RS232` class takes care of this. `ElapsedTime` will contain a count of the number of milliseconds that elapsed during the reception or transmission of the data. Note that even though the value is in milliseconds, the actual resolution of the timer is dependent on the host system's hardware and software. For MS-DOS, the granularity of the timer is 55 milliseconds. You can perform a few tricks under MS-DOS to get a timer with finer resolution, but most communications applications will work just fine with the 55 millisecond resolution.

## Default Parameters

The `RS232` class makes extensive use of default parameters in its member functions. Default parameters are another C++ feature that probably don't have much to do with object-oriented programming, but nonetheless are very useful. The exact use of default parameters varies from function to function, so there isn't a completely consistent pattern. However, there are some general rules of thumb:

milliseconds: Most of the functions that actually read or write data from the serial port have a time parameter. This indicates how long the function should take to complete its job. If the function is unable to read or write all of the bytes requested during the elapsed time, it will return an `RS232_TIMEOUT` error.

These functions, such as `Read()`, have a default value of 0 for the milliseconds parameter. This means that they will attempt to read or write as many bytes as requested one time, then return.

settings: Many of the functions in class `RS232` are used to set port parameters. For example, there is the general `Set()` command, used to set the baud rate, parity, word length, and stop bits. Other functions that set parameters include `Dtr()`, `Rts()`, and `XonXoffHandshaking()`.

For all of these functions, the default value of the settings is the constant UNCHANGED. When a function receives a value of UNCHANGED for a setting, it leaves that setting alone. This can be particularly useful when using the `Set()` command. There are probably many times when a programmer just wants to change the baud rate or one of the other parameters. With ANSI C, the function call would require that all the other parameters be set to legitimate values as well (not that you couldn't use the UNCHANGED parameter here as well). In this case, you can simply call `port.Set( 9600 )` to accomplish the same thing. The remaining three parameters in the function call default to UNCHANGED.

terminator: The `Read( void * )` and `Write( void * )` routines both have an optional string parameter that specifies a string terminator to use for input and output. By default, both of these strings are null pointers, meaning they are not used.

**Mandatory and optional**

Virtual functions help to define which functions are mandatory for a given driver and which are optional. When we declare a virtual function as being pure (by defining it as "0" in the class definition), a derived class *must* implement that function. However, some of the virtual functions are optional. For these functions we have implemented simple versions in the base class that usually just return a warning error. These base class implementations mean that a derived class can choose to implement or to ignore the function.

Some functions, such as `read_byte()` and `write_buffer()`, are fundamental to the operation of serial ports. Functions that operate on the base class expect that these have been implemented, so these functions are defined as pure in the class declaration.

Other functions may be difficult or impossible to implement in every derived class, so they are left as optional. For example, the base class has a definition for the `XonXoffHandshaking()` function, which means derived classes are not compelled to implement it. Keep this in mind when writing utility code that operates on the base class.

```
int RS232::XonXoffHandshaking( int enable )
{
    UNUSED( enable );
    return RS232_FUNCTION_NOT_SUPPORTED;
}
```

The code implementation of this function in the base class looks like the code shown above. The `UNUSED()` macro is there to avoid a compiler warning. It also helps to point out that I am deliberately not doing anything with the parameter. This function doesn't do anything except return the warning message to the calling routine. If a derived class can't make use of this function, it will exclude it from its class definition. By default, any code attempting to use this function will then revert to the base class, receiving this warning error.

### Where is the constructor?

Missing from the class definition for RS232 is a constructor. Generally, a C++ class has a constructor or two for creating objects of that class. However, as this class is an abstract base class, we cannot create an instance of it so there is no point in having a constructor. The compiler will provide a default constructor, which in this case just allocates and initializes the storage used by the base class.

The derived classes that we will eventually use must perform all initializations themselves. This makes sense, because the RS232 class doesn't recognize the hardware being used for the derived class, so its ability to initialize the class is limited.

### The class, member by member

Finally, to make sense of the RS232 class, we must define what each data element and function does. There are quite a few members in the class, but each member has a clearly defined function so these definitions should serve as a reference.

More importantly, you should know exactly what job each member performs so that you may create useful derived classes. While C++ is good at handling the syntax and clerical work associated with deriving classes, the compiler can do nothing to force derived classes to perform as expected. The compiler can ensure that a virtual function takes the right number and type of arguments, and that it returns the right type of data, but it cannot monitor the methods for transforming input to output.

## Protected Members

Class RS232 has several protected data members. In C++, a protected data element cannot be accessed by foreign functions. In order to read or modify a protected data element, a function has to either belong to the member's class, a class derived from the member class, or be a friend function or member of a friend class.

When writing application code, we cannot inadvertently modify a protected member. This helps avoid inadvertent errors and also clearly stakes out the territory that a class considers to be "off-limits."

One feature I would have liked to see in the language is the ability to make a data member "read-only." This would mean that a nonprivileged function could read the value of a data element, but not change it. You will find in C++ classes lots of one-line functions whose only purpose in life is to return the value of protected data elements to functions outside the class. Fortunately, these functions are usually inline functions, and the compiler can usually optimize them away, but just the fact that the function needs to be created in the first place can be annoying.

The protected members of `class RS232` are:

**RS232PortName port_name**

This data member is of the type `RS232PortName`, an enumerated type that contains `COM1`, `COM2`, etc. When first opened, a serial port is always given a port name, and the value is stored here. The constructor's job is to initialize this value. This data element is protected because it doesn't need to be changed throughout the life of the port.

**Settings saved_settings**

`Settings` is a class defined earlier in the `RS232.H` header file, as shown next. When a port is opened, the base class assumes that all of the settings in the class are available for the port. One of the jobs of the constructor in a derived class is to store all the saved settings in this data member. When the `RS232` object is eventually destroyed, the destructor must restore all the settings in the port to their original states.

```
class Settings
{
    public :
        long BaudRate;
        char Parity;
        int WordLength;
        int StopBits;
        int Dtr;
        int Rts;
        int XonXoff;
        int RtsCts;
```

# THE RS232 CLASS

```
        int DtrDsr;
        void Adjust( long baud_rate,
                     int parity,
                     int word_length,
                     int stop_bits,
                     int dtr,
                     int rts,
                     int xon_xoff,
                     int rts_cts,
                     int dtr_dsr );
    };
```

One implication of maintaining this data element is that a derived class is free to change the saved settings of a port. When the `RS232` port object is destroyed, a different group of settings could be applied to it. Sometimes a function such as this could be useful and could simply be accomplished through the creation of either a derived class or a friend function. However, access to this element is generally not needed, so the base class does not provide functions to access this data element.

Note that for both `saved_settings` and `settings`, there will be times when the state of a setting is either unknown or illogical. In these cases, all of the members of the class that are unknown will be set to -1. The lone exception is the parity character, which will be set to '?'.

**Settings settings**

This data element contains all of the current settings for the port. While a derived class may have additional settings to maintain for a port, this data member contains the basic list supported by most RS-232 hardware. The derived class maintains this list of settings. In particular, it must properly initialize the list in the constructor, then properly modify it upon execution of functions like `Set()`, `XonXoffHandshaking()`, and so on.

These settings are sometimes useful to other classes. For example, a file transfer class may need to check the baud rate of a connection in order to properly determine the best packet size. Protocols such as Kermit need to know whether the serial port is operating in 7-bit or 8-bit mode so that they can decide whether to use the special escape codes needed for transmitting 8-bit wide characters on a 7-bit channel.

The data elements in the `Settings` structure are protected because the settings of the serial port should only be modified via functions in or derived from the `RS232` class. However, certainly many functions want to be able to view these settings, so an access function is defined as a member of this class. The member function `ReadSettings()`, which will be explored in more detail later, allows a calling function to obtain a copy of the current settings of the port.

**RS232Error error_status**

Error handling is an important requirement of a library of functions that talk to hardware. Serial hardware is certainly no exception.

The first line of defense in the `RS232` class is the `error_status` element. This data element keeps track of any fatal error that has occurred somewhere in the life of the `RS232` object. Once the object has experienced a fatal error, by definition it should no longer be used. Thus, all derived functions should check for this error and simply return an error condition when called.

Again, the error status is stored away whenever a fatal error occurs, so the programmer doesn't have to slavishly check the error condition. Instead, the programmer can arrange a program to incorporate error checking so that it takes place at appropriate intervals.

Clearly we don't want to give easy access to this data element. The error status must be accurately maintained throughout the life of the object. Like so many other protected members, however, we would like to let any function read the error status whenever necessary, so the base class also contains an access function called `ErrorStatus()`.

**int debug_line_count**

One of the member functions of `class RS232` is called `FormatDebugOutput()`. This function provides a "snapshot" of the current state of the port. The programmer calls the function and asks for a line at a time of the debug output. The programmer is then free to do what she or he likes with the output, such as dumping it to a monitor screen or sending it to a file.

While you don't *have* to know in advance how many lines can be produced by

# THE RS232 CLASS

this virtual function, it can help. When the object is first created, this protected member is initialized with the correct number of lines for its specific class. The application program can then access that number and use it to size windows, buffers, or whatever else is necessary to properly display the debug output.

Since the only function that really can know how many lines this will take is the `FormatDebugOutput()` routine in the derived class, we want this data element to be protected. If a programmer were to inadvertently change it, he or she might get some scrambled output from the formatting function.

Often the application program needs to read this value. It does so by calling `FormatDebugOutput()` with a special 0 parameter in place of the buffer where the output is normally directed. The formatting function will then return the number of lines it needs, instead of doing its normal formatting job.

## Protected Member Functions

Class `RS232` has four protected virtual functions. These four functions are used to read and write both blocks and individual bytes of data. These low level virtual functions are called upon by the nonvirtual `Read()` and `Write()` functions to perform the low-level I/O functions.

These four functions are stripped of all the niceties and options found in the nonvirtual public functions used to transfer data. Each of the four attempts to do its task, and returns immediately with a count of bytes transferred, an error status value, and not much else.

```
int read_buffer( char *buffer, unsigned int count )
```

This function reads in as many bytes from the port as it can manage, up to the count specified in the second parameter. If the buffer was filled, a status of `RS232_SUCCESS` is returned, otherwise `RS232_TIMEOUT` is returned. This function is used by two different versions of the `Read()` function. The buffer has a null terminator appended to it when it returns. The actual count of bytes read in is stored in `ByteCount` before the function returns.

```
int write_buffer( char *buffer, unsigned int count = -1 )
```

This virtual function is used by the various `Write()` functions to send buffers and strings out the port. This function sends as many characters as it can without waiting, then returns to the calling program with either `RS232_SUCCESS` or `RS232_TIMEOUT`. Note that this function has a default parameter for the `count`. If no count is specified, the value of -1 signifies that the buffer is actually a string, and the byte count is the length of the string. The actual count of characters transferred is found in the `ByteCount` element after the function returns.

```
int write_byte( int c )
```

This function writes a single byte out if possible. It doesn't have to set the `ByteCount` element, because it returns that information to the calling routine by way of the return status, which is either `RS232_SUCCESS` or `RS232_TIMEOUT`. This function is used by the nonvirtual `Write()` functions to perform the virtualized low-level I/O.

```
int read_byte( int c )
```

This function performs the low level I/O for the nonvirtual `Read()` functions. It also doesn't set the `ByteCount` argument, which can easily be determined by checking the return value.

## Public Data Members

The RS232 class has two public data members. Any function in the program can access public data members without regard to class or friendship. You should be careful about which data members are fully exposed. In this case, the two data members declared as public are used only to provide information to calling routines. The member functions of class `RS232` don't depend on the values in these data members remaining consistent between function calls. Rather, they are provided to the calling function strictly for informational value.

## THE RS232 CLASS

`unsigned int ByteCount`

Earlier in this chapter, I mentioned that some of the functions in the `RS232` class need to return multiple pieces of information to the calling program. In particular, `Read()` and `Write()` have to return an actual count of bytes transferred. Both of these functions have options that could cause them to return before the entire buffer is transferred.

`ByteCount` is relatively safe as a public data member. The function calls that modify this byte don't depend on it remaining unchanged. They return it from a function after performing a transfer, and then forget about it. Because of this, it is relatively safe to allow public access of this member.

`long ElapsedTime`

All of the input and output functions have the option to be called with a timeout value. If a timeout value is specified, the routine will eventually return to the calling function, even though it has not completed the data transfer. If a complete buffer is transferred, the routines will return earlier. If a routine returns before the timeout value, the `ElapsedTime` data member will contain the amount of time that passed during the transfer. Since many communications applications are time dependent, this feature of the `RS232` class relieves the programmer of the burden of keeping track.

Like the `ByteCount` member, `ElapsedTime` is set by the function before it returns to the caller. Once the `RS232` function returns, it doesn't care what happens to the value afterwards so you can safely make this a public data member. `ElapsedTime` is measured in milliseconds, so this value needs to be a C long type. If it were a simple unsigned int, it would be limited to about 60 seconds, which could prove to be a limitation.

All of the timing values used in the RS232 class are platform dependent, so the values found in `ElapsedTime` will have a granularity that depends on system implementation. In the case of MS-DOS, the granularity of the system clock is roughly 55 milliseconds, so timer values of all kinds will only be accurate to that resolution.

## Mandatory Virtual Functions

The `RS232` class has 11 mandatory public virtual functions. When creating a useful class derived from the `RS232` class, I must create a constructor, 4 private virtual functions, and 11 public virtual functions. (Of course, many classes will probably implement quite a few more functions.)

You need to know which virtual functions are mandatory and which are optional. Later in this book, we will write utility code that operates strictly on objects of the `RS232` class. These general-purpose functions will perform useful jobs such as terminal emulation, modem control, and file transfers. Since utility functions operate on the `RS232` class, they cannot know in advance whether a particular driver supports certain virtual functions. Because of this, they need to be able to count on a certain set of functions.

In Chapter 3, you will see a complete implementation of all of these functions using the standard 8250 type UART on an IBM compatible PC. That particular class will probably be the most complex one in the entire book, largely because it has to be built from scratch; there is no operating system or device driver support for `class PC8250`.

For example, the Microsoft Windows operating environment provides a complete RS-232 API. The MS Windows class just has to implement a simple interface to that driver.

The best way to get a good handle on how serial communications work in the desktop environment is to understand how these virtual functions work. So, without further ado, here they are.

```
virtual int Set( long baud_rate = UNCHANGED,
                 char parity = UNCHANGED,
                 int word_length = UNCHANGED,
                 int stop_bits = UNCHANGED )
```

This function is used to set the transmission parameters for the UART. They are ordered in the same way as the MS-DOS MODE command so that they will be easier to remember. Note that while this function is mandatory for every driver, the specific baud rates and other parameters supported by the interface can vary among drivers. If an unsupported parameter is passed, one of the following four error messages is returned:

## THE RS232 CLASS

```
RS232_ILLEGAL_BAUD_RATE
RS232_ILLEGAL_PARITY_SETTING
RS232_ILLEGAL_WORD_LENGTH
RS232_ILLEGAL_STOP_BITS
```

Each of the parameters has a default value of UNCHANGED. This special parameter indicates to the Set function that the specified parameter should be left alone during the set operation. Because of the default parameters, a simple call like this:

```
port.Set( 9600 )
```

can be used to set the baud rate only. Other parameters can be added as necessary.

As another convenience to the programmer, the five parity settings are specified as easy-to-remember characters. For most MS-DOS implementations of serial drivers, the settings are:

| | |
|---|---|
| 'N' | No parity |
| 'E' | Even parity |
| 'O' | Odd parity |
| 'S' | Space parity |
| 'M' | Mark parity |

In this function call, you can specify the parity parameters in upper or lower case. Just as in the baud-rate parameter, various MS-DOS serial drivers will provide different levels of support for these parity settings. In general, every driver will support the first three: None, Even, and Odd. However, Space and Mark parity are not uniformly supported, so the programmer must be prepared to receive an RS232_ILLEGAL_PARITY_SETTING response when calling this function.

The word-length and stop-bit settings are fairly uniform across all MS-DOS serial drivers. The word length can be 5, 6, 7, or 8 bits. While some hardware supports the 5- and 6-bit settings, they are so rarely used that they are essentially historical oddities. Most hardware supports stop-bit settings of 1 and 2.

The four parameters used in this function are also generally used in the constructor for a serial object. Once again, the default value of all four parameters is UNCHANGED.

89

```
virtual int TXSpaceFree( void )
```

This function improves the operation of a serial driver. A utility routine written for the `RS232` class calls this function to determine if there is any space available for transmitting more characters. Without this function, a routine would have to blindly call the `Write()` routines without knowing in advance that it would succeed. This function helps applications utilities avoid this uncertainty.

It isn't always possible to know exactly how many bytes are free in the output buffer. If this is the case, the virtual implementation of `TXSpaceFree()` should return a 1 if *any* room is available, and a 0 if no space is free.

```
virtual int RXSpaceUsed( void )
```

Like the previous function, `RXSpaceUsed()` is an aid to the smooth operation of a serial driver. An application can determine if any characters are waiting to be read out of the input buffer. This information is often very useful to have in advance of calling the `Read()` function.

Just as with the previous function, a serial driver can't always know exactly how many bytes are available in the input buffer. This virtual routine should return a 1 if *any* bytes are available, and a 0 if none are. Of course, if an exact count is available it should be given.

```
virtual int Cd()
virtual int Ri()
virtual int Cts()
virtual int Dsr()
```

These four functions do essentially the same thing, which is to read in the current state of an input modem status line. In many communications programs, all four of these lines are read simultaneously into a bit mask that is returned to the calling function. While using a single bit mask cuts down on the number of calls in the API, it does require that the programmer learn and remember four equate masks used to extract the individual settings. The form used here is simple in that respect.

# THE RS232 CLASS

This family of functions reads in the instantaneous state of the control lines at the point where the function is called. Many times programmers need more control over these lines than is provided here. For example, it is frequently useful to have a function that will not only read the Carrier Detect line, but also report if it has dropped at any time since the previous call. This lets a BBS detect when a caller drops carrier by hanging up the phone line.

Unfortunately, implementation of these features is rather rare for MS-DOS serial interfaces. It doesn't really make sense to add these function calls to the `RS232` class set of virtual functions. Its best to add such calls to a derived class and restrict use to that class.

```
virtual int ParityError( int clear = UNCHANGED )
virtual int BreakDetect( int clear = UNCHANGED )
virtual int FramingError( int clear = UNCHANGED )
virtual int HardwareOverrunError( int clear = UNCHANGED )
```

These four functions correspond loosely to the four previous modem status line functions. Once again, these are frequently grouped together in many communications programs, with the individual settings being extracted via masking macros. For ease of programming, the alternate approach is used here.

Unlike the modem status functions, all four of these line status readings are permanently set once the condition occurs. For example, if an incoming break is detected, the `BreakDetect()` function will continue to return a true value every time it is called. The true setting will only go away if the optional default parameter is also set to true. In that case, the function will return the old state of the line status, then clear it.

Under certain circumstances, you might want to implement more sophisticated handling of line status errors. For example, you may want to call a C function in your program the instant the line status error occurs. However, just as with the modem status changes, this sort of functionality is generally not supported in most RS-232 drivers. If the programmer requires this functionality, he or she should develop a derived class with full support for the extended features.

## Nonvirtual Functions

There are 9 nonvirtual functions defined as part of class `RS232`. These functions all build on virtual functions defined earlier in the program to do their work.

```
int Read( long milliseconds = 0 )
```

This function is used to read in a byte from the serial interface. Like most of the other functions that perform I/O with a port, it has an optional timing parameter. The timing parameter, named `milliseconds`, gives the amount of time that the function should continue to wait for input before returning empty-handed. The default value is 0, which means the function will return immediately when no input is available. If no data is available, an error message of `RS232_TIMEOUT` is returned to the calling program.

The traditional approach to serial I/O on older operating systems such as UNIX has been for the program to request input of a certain amount of data (1 byte in this case), and then wait indefinitely for input. Options to timeout after a certain period were sometimes added, but almost as an afterthought. This sort of programming strategy might have been appropriate when your serial input consisted mostly of keystrokes from alphanumeric terminals, but it is definitely not optimal during file transfers from high-speed modems. Being able to set the time to any value desired is an improvement on this strategy.

If a valid character was input, the return value from this function will be greater than or equal to 0. If the return value from the function is less than 0, an error of some sort occurred, and the programmer needs to take action. Note that the `RS232_TIMEOUT` warning can probably be considered benign.

When this function returns, the two other public data members of the `RS232` class will also be set properly. The `ElapsedTime` data member will contain the number of milliseconds that elapsed while in the `Read()` function, and the `ByteCount` member will either contain a 0 or a 1, depending on whether a byte was read in or not.

If the `milliseconds` parameter is nonzero, the `Read()` function may have to wait for input. Under MS-DOS, what a program does while it is waiting for an event is not really important since usually no other programs are competing for system resources. However, under OS/2, MS-Windows, or some other multitask-

# THE RS232 CLASS

ing environment, other processes will want CPU time. This is particularly critical under MS-Windows, since the operating system will not preempt a process without the process's cooperation.

Because of these considerations, all of the I/O functions that may spend time waiting make a call to an environment-specific virtual function called `IdleFunction()`. The default MS-DOS version of `RS232::IdleFunction()` is found in the file `MSDOS.CPP`. It does absolutely nothing except execute an immediate return. So that while waiting for input, `Read()` sits in a polling loop that consumes all of the CPU time on the system.

Note that if the milliseconds parameter is not specified in a function call, it defaults to a value of 0. This means that `Read()` will try one time to read a character in, and if it doesn't receive one, it will return with an `RS232_TIMEOUT` warning message. In addition, there is a special integer parameter called FOREVER which means exactly that. If you specify FOREVER for the `milliseconds` parameter, the function will wait forever for an input byte.

This function calls the virtual version of `read_byte()` to actually do the low-level I/O associated with the port.

```
int Read(   void *buffer,
            unsigned int count,
            long milliseconds = 0 )

int Read(   void *buffer,
            unsigned int count,
            long milliseconds = 0,
            char *terminator )
```

The two `Read()` functions are a little bit more complicated than their single-byte relative. Like `Read(long)`, each has a buffer to fill, and a timer parameter indicating how long the function can take to perform the output. The second version of the buffer versions of `Read()` adds a new parameter, `terminator`. The first function reads in a block of fixed length, the second attempts to read in a string with a specific terminator.

These two functions could have been combined into one by using a default parameter for the `terminator`, but logically they are quite different. Since they will be implemented separately, it makes sense to have two completely different functions as opposed to one long function that could easily be broken in half.

When not using the terminator, `Read()` does exactly what you might expect, which is to attempt to read in the number of bytes specified in `count`. However, if the `terminator` parameter is in use, the function will attempt to match it during input. In this mode, the routine reads in bytes until one of three things happens. First, it will terminate if the buffer fills up, returning an `RS232_NO_TERMINATOR` error code. However, if it reads in an exact match for the termination string, it will return an `RS232_SUCCESS` message. In either case, the resulting buffer will be terminated with a `"\0"` character, meaning that it can be treated as a standard C string. Finally, it will return times out before either of the other two conditions is met.

The two most commonly used `terminator` parameters are `"\r"` and `"\r\n."` When entering input from the keyboard, a user typically terminates lines with a single carriage return. When data is being received from a computer and is intended for display, it usually ends with a carriage return-line feed pair, which means you would want to use the second choice of terminators.

Note that with a string terminator, the terminator is *not* included when the function returns. However, the input buffer must be able to hold the input string plus the termination characters. Once the terminator is read in, a `"\0"` byte is written over the first character of the terminator resident in the buffer.

In the buffered version of `Read()`, there is no terminator. In this mode, the routine is just trying to read in an entire buffer of data before the specified time elapses. Like the other routines, the time can be as short as 0 milliseconds, or as long as `FOREVER`. When the parameter is set to 0, the routine will just try to read in as many bytes as possible until it either completes, or runs out of characters and returns.

When these functions return, they will always give an accurate rendering of the elapsed time in the `ElapsedTime` public data member. The `ByteCount` member will contain the number of bytes being returned to the calling function. This means that the characters read in as part of the terminator will not be counted in the total returned to the calling program.

## THE RS232 CLASS

```
int Write( int c, long milliseconds = 0 )
```

    `Write(int, long)` performs the opposite function of `Read(long)`, by writing a single byte out to the serial port. Like the other I/O functions, `Write()` has an optional parameter that specifies a minimum number of milliseconds that the function will wait for a successful output. If it isn't specified, the `milliseconds` parameter defaults to a value of 0. A parameter of 0 means the function will attempt to perform the output one time only, returning the warning message `RS232_TIMEOUT` if unsuccessful.

    `Write()` sets the two public data members used by the other I/O functions. `ByteCount` will be set to either a 1 or a 0, depending on whether the output was successful or not. The `ElapsedTime` data element will contain the count of elapsed milliseconds that the function waited while trying to output the single character.

    `Write()` will call the virtual function `IdleFunction()` while it is waiting to perform output. This function is operating system dependent, and can be redefined by a derived class. In addition, the idle function can abort the I/O function by returning an error code when it is called.

```
int Write( void *buffer,
           unsigned int count = 0,
           long milliseconds = 0,
           char *terminator = 0 )
```

    The `Write( void *buffer )` routine manages to become even more complicated than `Read( void *buffer )`. It has the same list of parameters, which features the addition of the `count` and `terminator` parameters. Unlike the previous function, however, in this case the `count` parameter has a default value as well.

    The reason for the addition of these new parameters and defaults is the same as in `Read()`. This function has a split personality, with the ability to output both raw buffers of data and formatted strings with termination. When the count parameter is set to a positive integer, it means that the function is performing a traditional buffer output. In this case, the `count` parameter is relied upon for an accurate count of the number of characters to be sent.

    If the `count` parameter is set to 0, the function is operating on what is expected to be a string. In this case, the `count` parameter is ignored, and the length of the string is determined by looking for a "\0" string termination character. Once the character is found, the function then outputs the bytes in the string.

As in the previous function, the two most commonly used termination strings will be "\r" and "\r\n". Which is appropriate depends on what sort of data the receiving end expects.

This function returns one of the standard error codes based on how well it managed to output the entire buffer. A return of `RS232_SUCCESS` means that the entire buffer as well as the optional termination string made it out. A return of `RS232_TIMEOUT` means that the routine ran out of time before completing its task. This usually occurs because of a blocked condition due to handshaking.

The `ElapsedTime` and `ByteCount` public data members are set up to work much as you would expect. `ElapsedTime` returns a count of the number of milliseconds that the function spent waiting to send the data. `ByteCount` returns the count of characters actually transmitted, which includes the termination string, when used.

```
int Peek( void )
```

This function is simply a front-end that sends a function call to `Peek( void *)`, with a request for just one byte of data. It is included as a convenience for the programmer. The end of this chapter includes a listing of the actual function in `RS232.CPP`. Note that this function will return `RS232_TIMEOUT` if no character is available. It will also return with a valid count in `ByteCount`.

```
int ReadSettings( Settings &settings )
```

This short function provides access to the private data member `Settings`. As a safeguard, the `settings` data member is kept privately, so we need to have an access function that will return the values.

```
RS232Error ErrorStatus( void )
```

This is another access function that returns the value of the private data member `error_status`. Because the data member can't be changed by functions outside the class, we required an access function.

## THE RS232 CLASS

`int DebugLineCount( void )`

Another access function that allows an outside function to determine the number of lines of debug output produced by this class. This is simply a way to read the value of `debug_line_count`, which is a private data member.

## A Very Short Program

With just a few of the mandatory and nonvirtual functions from the RS232 class, you can easily build a simple terminal program. By simple, I mean a program whose sole purpose is to route serial input to the screen and keyboard input to the serial port. In addition to the mandatory functions shown earlier, we need only a derived class that can open a port on our PC. The listing below shows this type of simple program.

```
#include <stdio.h>
#include <conio.h>
#include "rs232.h"

int main()
{
   int c;
   Comport port( COM1, 9600, 'N', 8, 1 );

   for ( ; ; ) {
      if ( port.RXSpaceUsed() > 0 )
         if ( (c = port.Read()) >= RS232_SUCCESS )
            putc( c, stdout );
      if ( kbhit() ) {
         c = getch();
         if ( c == 27 )
            break;
         port.Write( c );
      }
   }
}
```

As I stated earlier in this chapter, you could easily use the C++ driver code developed in this book and still continue programming as if you were working with C. In the preceding example, the only real oddity from a C perspective is the constructor for the `Comport` object. Other than that, the code is more or less ANSI C. Admittedly, the member function calls (`port.Write()`) look somewhat strange, but they are still legitimate C. Even if your C experience is very limited, you should be able to read this code and modify it without too much difficulty.

## The Optional Functions

There are 16 optional functions defined in the RS232 class. I have made these optional mainly because the functions aren't supported by nearly as many drivers as the mandatory functions.

While the optional functions may be somewhat more rare than the mandatory functions, good drivers will still support them, and application programmers should feel free to use them. The code that uses these functions, however, has to be ready to receive an `RS232_NOT_SUPPORTED` message when calling any of them.

```
virtual ~RS232( void )
```

The destructor for class `RS232` is virtual. This has an advantage over a non-virtual destructor in that the utility code can destroy port objects without knowing anything about their class. Note that in the header file `RS232.H`, an empty function is created to be the destructor for the base class. When destroying a derived class, the destructor for the base class will be called first. It just happens that we don't need to do anything in the base destructor.

```
virtual int Break( long milliseconds = 300 )
```

The ability to send a line break is not available in every serial driver, so I have included it here as an optional feature. Remember that a break signal is not an actual character being sent out. When a UART sends a break, it actually changes the line to a spacing condition and holds it there for a long time. In this way, it will be recognized as a break signal regardless of the baud rate and other settings of the two receivers. This is used, for example, on UNIX systems. When a caller first connects to a UNIX system, the two ends are frequently set to different baud rates. The break signal provides an unambiguous message to the remote end, letting it know the baud rate must be changed.

The default length of the break is 300 milliseconds, long enough to provide a usable break on just about any system. However, the programmer can override this setting if needed. Note that the time spent while waiting for the break to finish is spent in the virtual `IdleFunction()`, doing whatever is recommended for that particular operating environment. Under MS-DOS, this consists of doing nothing at all.

```
virtual int SoftwareOverrunError( int clear = UNCHANGED )
```

This optional function manages a diagnostic function. A software overrun error occurs when an incoming character is received and there is no room for it in the buffer. The interrupt service routine has no choice but to throw the character away. In this situation, many drivers set a flag so that the application program can respond appropriately.

This function simply returns the state of the overrun flag. If the optional argument is set to be true, the flag is also cleared after it has been read. If the parameter is false, or no parameter is given, then the flag remains set.

Note that the overrun flag is not present in the RS232 class definition, since it is an optional feature. However, as with all optional features, there must be a base class implementation of the function. In this case, the base class implementation just returns the RS232_NOT_SUPPORTED error to the calling program.

```
virtual int XonXoffHandshaking( int setting = UNCHANGED )
virtual int RtsCtsHandshaking( int setting = UNCHANGED )
virtual int DtrDsrHandshaking( int setting = UNCHANGED )
```

These three functions do essentially the same thing. Each one has a dual purpose. Each function can be used to just read the current setting of the handshaking for a port, or it can be used to turn handshaking on or off.

When the function is called with no arguments, or with UNCHANGED as the argument, all it does is return the current state of the handshaking. If the new setting is something other than UNCHANGED (ENABLE and DISABLE being the recommended alternatives), the current state of that form of handshaking is either enabled or disabled. The function will return the previous state of the handshaking for that mode.

The function returns the state of the handshaking *before* the new control takes place, so that a programmer can set the handshaking mode and save the previous mode with one function call. If the function call returned the new setting of the handshake mode, two calls would be need to be made to store the old value and one to set the new one. Also, it would be redundant to set it and then return the value that was just set.

Certainly not every driver will support these optional functions. Worse, complications will accompany support of these features. For example, some drivers only allow one handshaking mode to be set at a time, so setting one might clear the others. Other drivers will support one of the modes, but not the others. These peculiarities go with the territory.

The base class versions of these functions can be found in RS232.CPP, and they do nothing more than return the warning message RS232_ NOT_SUPPORTED. If a derived class doesn't support these functions, the base class version will return the error flag to the program.

```
virtual int Dtr( int setting = UNCHANGED )
virtual int Rts( int setting = UNCHANGED )
```

These two functions are used to either read or control the state of the two RS-232 output lines normally supported on a PC. When not being used for handshaking, DTR and RTS have many other uses, according to the needs of the application programmer.

To read the current state of these control lines, the programmer simply calls either of these functions with no parameters or the single argument set to UNCHANGED. If the argument is some other value besides UNCHANGED, it will be interpreted as a boolean, and the control line will either be set or cleared depending on its value. It is recommended that the constants SET and CLEAR be used for readability

When the argument is used and the function sets the output line to a new value,

# THE RS232 CLASS

it still returns a value indicating the previous state of the line. This is done so that the programmer can set the line to a new state and store the old state with a single function call.

Most drivers will support these functions. If for some reason a driver doesn't support this function, the default virtual function for the base class will be called. The base class versions of these functions simply return the RS232_NOT_SUPPORTED warning error to the programmer.

```
virtual int Peek( void *buffer, unsigned int count )
```

There are many times when it is useful to be able to look ahead and see what is coming up in the input buffer without actually extracting any data. Many drivers implement various forms of a "peek" function, with the majority at least supporting the ability to peek ahead one character into the buffer. This virtual function lets the caller peek ahead an arbitrary number of characters into the input buffer, stuffing the results into the user-supplied data area.

The value returned by this function indicates how many bytes were actually read into the buffer. A count lower than the number requested by the caller doesn't necessarily mean there are only that many bytes in the buffer. Instead, it may well mean that the driver can only look ahead that far into the buffer. As with all the other functions, a value less than zero means an error occurred.

The base class implementation of this function does nothing more than return the RS232_NOT_SUPPORTED error message.

```
virtual int RXSpaceFree( void )
virtual int TXSpaceUsed( void )
```

These two functions correspond to the two buffer size functions found in the mandatory support area. These functions are not mandatory, and are generally not quite as useful as the mandatory ones. For example, we may have a pressing need to know how much space is free in the transmit buffer. If a program has data to go out, it needs to know if it is going to be able to send it. However, the knowledge about how much space is still in use in the transmit buffer is not as pressing.

The TXSpaceUsed() function still can be useful. For example, when preparing to exit a communications program, it is usually a good idea to wait until the transmit buffer has finished sending all its data. If it was in the middle of sending a screen full of logout data to a user when the program exited, the odds are the data stream would be cut off.

Likewise, `RXSpaceFree()` is not as urgently needed as `RXSpaceUsed()`. The space used function tells the programmer whether it is time to service the input data. The space free function can alert us to an overflow condition, but we usually leave that up to the driver anyway.

Both of these functions are defined in the base class with the typical return of `RS232_NOT_SUPPORTED`. If a derived class supports these functions, it needs to supply virtual implementations, so that they get called instead of the base version.

```
virtual int FlushTXBuffer( void )
virtual int FlushRXBuffer( void )
```

`FlushTXBuffer()` and `FlushRXBuffer()` are another pair of useful functions that aren't supported in every driver. This function throws away all the data queued up for output in the transmit buffer. For example, this function would be useful when a system has dumped out a few screenfuls of data in the process of being transmitted, and the user at the other end hits the break key. Rather than making the remote end wait through the lengthy process of dumping all the data, a simple call to `FlushTXBuffer()` will discard all that data in the output buffer

Although these functions are not always supported, it is relatively easy to implement. Most systems use a simple buffering system for storing data pending transmission. To flush the buffer, you would simply move the head pointer back to where the tail pointer is. Usually interrupts must be disabled, but other than that it isn't particularly difficult.

The base class implementation of this function is a one-line function that just returns the `RS232_NOT_SUPPORTED` error message.

```
virtual char *ErrorName( RS232Error error )
```

The `ErrorName()` function translates an error code from the `RS232Error` enumerated type into a readable ASCII string. This lets the error be presented to

## THE RS232 CLASS

the user of the program in a reasonable manner.

Traditionally, errors are implemented via a master list of error codes that could be accessed anywhere in the program. But when implementing a traditional error system like this for the RS232 class, it is fairly difficult to extend the list to include new errors introduced from derived classes. Under C++, we would like to be able to leave our base class definition alone, even when we add a new derived class. However, to add a new error under the traditional system, we would have to edit the header file with the error definitions, (RS232.H in this program), and then edit the function that translates the error names.

Here, a new system accomplishes this goal without too much trouble. The implementation of ErrorName() in the base class can translate all of the predefined error codes. The error names are assigned sequentially, with the first warning message starting at RS232_WARNING, (with a value of -100), and working up to RS232_NEXT_FREE_WARNING. The fatal errors start with RS232_ERROR, (with a value of -200), and work up to RS232_NEXT_FREE_ERROR. The base implementation of ErrorName() knows how to translate this predefined list of errors.

A derived class that wants to implement its own errors can start assigning them as its own enumerated class. The first warning defined by the derived class would be assigned a value of RS232_NEXT_FREE_WARNING, and the first fatal error would be assigned a value of RS232_NEXT_FREE_ERROR. The derived class would then be free to assign as many new error names as it wanted.

To properly translate an error code, the derived class would then need to implement its own virtual function ErrorName(). The derived version of Error-Name() would check the error code to see whether it was defined by the base class or the derived class. If the derived class was responsible for the error code, it would return the translated version to the caller. If the error code was one defined by the base class, the base version of ErrorName() would be called.

This system of "passing it up the line" allows for essentially never-ending chains of error codes to be defined by nested derived classes. To clear up any confusion over this operation, lets look at an actual example. A code fragment from the PC8250 class which will be developed in Chapter 3 is shown below. This fragment shows how PC8250 would support the addition of a single new error code, called PC8250_UART_NOT_FOUND.

First, when developing a new list of errors, we must define the new enumerated type. The new type `PC8250Error` does this, presumably somewhere in a header file. It defines the first error in the fatal error list as being defined by `RS232_NEXT_FREE_ERROR`. If there were a warning message being added as well, it would be defined as having the value `RS232_NEXT_FREE_WARNING`.

```
enum PC8250Error {
      PC8250_UART_NOT_FOUND = RS232_NEXT_FREE_ERROR,
      PC8250_NEXT_FREE_ERROR,
      PC8250_NEXT_FREE_WARNING = RS232_NEXT_FREE_WARNING };

char * PC8250::ErrorName( RS232Error error )
{
   if ( error < RS232_NEXT_FREE_ERROR && error >=
                                    RS232_ERROR )
      return RS232::ErrorName( error );
   if ( error < RS232_NEXT_FREE_WARNING &&
        error >= RS232_WARNING )
      return RS232::ErrorName( error );
   if ( error >= RS232_SUCCESS )
      return RS232::ErrorName( error );
   switch ( error ) {
     case PC8250_UART_NOT_FOUND : return( "UART not found" );
     default                    : return( "Undefined error" );
   }
}
```

Once the error messages have been defined, the definition of the `ErrorName()` function for the derived class is fairly simple. The version of this function for the `PC8250` class demonstrates this clearly. The code first checks to see if the error message is in the range of predefined fatal errors. If it is, the base class version of `ErrorName()` should be able to do the translation, so the parameters are passed along. The scoping operator `::` lets us pass the function call up the line.

Next, the routine checks to see if the error message is a predefined warning message from the base class, or the predefined success message. Again, if it is, the call is passed up the line to the base class.

If the routine falls through these tests, it can then translate the error code on its own by checking against the list of errors it knows about. The translation is made, and the correct ASCII string is returned to the calling function.

If another function were derived from `class PC8250`, the same sort of linkage could be achieved. The new class would have to start its new list of messages, starting at `PC8250_NEXT_FREE_ERROR` and `PC8250_NEXT_ FREE_WARNING`. When the derived version of `ErrorName()` was called, it would check to see if the error message belonged to the new class. If not, the error number would just be passed up the line to `PC8250::ErrorName()`, where the same process would be repeated until someone performed a translation.

The ability to add to the library without having to modify the existing code strengthens the case for C++. Once again, these features could be developed using ANSI C, but a thorough implementation would involve fairly significant overhead and some rigorous gymnastics.

```
virtual int IdleFunction( void )
```

The idle function is a virtual function that is called while one of the data input or output routines waits for data. Although this is a virtual function, a derived class does not necessarily need to implement it. The function has two important properties. First, it can yield control to other processes so as to be a good citizen in a multitasking environment. Second, it detects an abort condition and passes it back to the input routine.

The base version of `IdleFunction()` for MS-DOS only returns an `RS232_SUCCESS` to the calling function. Under MS-DOS, there generally isn't any penalty for hogging the CPU as long as interrupts are enabled, and this implementation does just that. Later in this book, I will develop versions of `IdleFunction()` for other environments. These will tend to be somewhat more sophisticated when cooperating with other processes.

Even though the base version of `IdleFunction()` doesn't check for any abort conditions, a derived class may want to do so. Reasons for aborting an input or output function include loss of carrier or a user-initiated break, among others.

```
virtual int FormatDebugOutput( char *buffer = 0,
                               int line_number = -1 )
```

This virtual function is similar to `ErrorName()` in that it depends on sharing the work load with classes farther up the hierarchy. The basic concept behind `FormatDebugOutput()` is that for any given class of serial port, there should be a descriptive set of output data to assist in diagnosing any problems with the port, or perhaps just in assessing operations.

When working with a class hierarchy, we can assume that the base class and each derived class have a certain amount of data to print out. How do we then coordinate the output from each of these functions?

The system developed here allows each class to contribute a few lines to the debug output, which all combines for a complete picture of the state of the port. This works if each class can recognize two things about its formatted output. First, the class must know how many lines it will contribute to the formatted debug output and, second, it must know on which line its output begins.

A user function uses `FormatDebugOutput()` in a relatively simple way. The output from this function consists of a number of lines. The actual number is determined by calling the member function `DebugLineCount()`, which just returns the value in the private data member, `debug_line_count`. Once this information is known, the user application can just call the formatting routine repeatedly, once for each line, and print out the buffer after it has been formatted. The sample code shown below would do this.

```
char buffer[ 81 ];
int i;

printf( "\n" );
for ( i = 0 ; i < port1.DebugLineCount() ; i++ ) {
    port1.FormatDebugOutput( buffer, i );
    puts( buffer );
}
```

## THE RS232 CLASS

When the virtual function for a derived class such as PC8250 is called, it will handle some of the lines of debug output itself and pass other ones up the line to the parent classes from which it is derived. A special feature of the FormatDebugOutput() function makes this bookkeeping relatively easy. When called with no arguments, instead of returning an RS232_SUCCESS value, this function instead returns the number of lines that it will take up. In its present implementation, the base class of RS232 takes up three lines. Thus, a derived version of FormatDebugOutput() would pass the function call up to RS232::FormatDebugOutput() when called with a line number of 0, 1, or 2. When the number is greater than that, the derived class will begin printing out its own data.

The line numbers used by the formatting routine in a derived class are determined when a member of the class is constructed. In the class PC8250, developed in the next chapter, an additional private data member is initialized in the constructor. This private data member is named first_debug_output_line. The constructor calling the formatting function in the base class (with no arguments) is responsible for initializing it. The total number of debug output lines are then stored in the private data member debug_line_counter. The code below shows a portion of the constructor.

```
PC8250::PC8250( enum RS232PortName port,
                long baud_rate,
                char parity,
                int word_length,
                int stop_bits )
{
   port_name = port;
   first_debug_output_line = RS232::FormatDebugOutput();
   debug_line_count = FormatDebugOutput();
   error_status = RS232_SUCCESS;
      .
      .
      .
```

The constructor determines the first line of output for the derived class. This is done by calling the base class version of the formatting routine with no argu-

107

ments: `RS232::FormatDebugOutput()`. The number returned tells how many lines the base class will be using; therefore, this is the number of the first line to be printed.

The constructor next determines the total number of output lines. This is done by calling the version of `FormatDebugOutput()` for this class. That function will add the number of lines it needs to print to the number required for the base class, and return the total.

The listing below shows how the formatting routine actually manages this data. The actual process looks a lot like the algorithm used by the `ErrorName()` function. First, if the buffer parameter is null, the formatting routine was called with no arguments and the caller wants to know how many lines can be produced by this routine. If this is the case, the actual count is returned, which consists of all the lines produced by the base class, plus two additional lines for this class.

```
int PC8250::FormatDebugOutput( char *buffer, int line_number )
{
    if ( buffer == 0 )
        return( first_debug_output_line +  2 );
    if ( line_number < first_debug_output_line )
        return RS232::FormatDebugOutput
                ( buffer, line_number );
    switch( line_number   first_debug_output_line ) {
        case 0 :
            sprintf( buffer, "Derived class: PC8250 Line 0" );
            break;
        case 1 :
            sprintf( buffer, "Line 1" );
            break;
        default :
            return RS232_ILLEGAL_LINE_NUMBER;
    }
    return RS232_SUCCESS;
}
```

If the line number passed to this routine happens to be less than the first line of debug output used by this class, the function call is passed up the line to the base

# THE RS232 CLASS

class for processing. Finally, if the line happens to be greater than the first line of output used by the derived class, it is managed locally.

Just like the `ErrorName()` function, this nesting concept can be extended indefinitely, with each derived class contributing its lines of debug output. Most importantly, you can achieve this extendibility without modifying the base class.

## The Code

The code for the class definitions used in this chapter are found in four files, consisting of two header files and two C++ source files. Following are explanations of the general content of these files.

PORTABLE.H   This file contains macros and definitions that are strictly compiler-dependent. In this early section of the book, the only macro that is actually used from PORTABLE.H is the UNUSED() macro, which fends off compiler warning messages.

RS232.H   This file contains the complete definition of the base RS232 class. Every file that is going to be developing serial classes for the derived classes in this book must include this header file.

RS232.CPP   The default virtual function definitions are found in this file. These are relatively uninspiring since all they do is return error messages. Two of the exceptions to this are `FormatDebugOutput()` and `ErrorName()`. Both of these virtual functions were explained earlier in this chapter. The `Read()` and `Write()` functions are all there as well.

MSDOS.H   This file is used as in internal routine to define prototypes for functions found in MSDOS.CPP.

MSDOS.CPP   This file contains two operating system specific functions. `IdleFunction()` was discussed earlier in this section. The other function, `ReadTime()` will be discussed in subsequent chapters.

109

```c
// ********************* START OF PORTABLE.H *********************
//
// This header file contains the macro definitions needed to
// provide portability across various compilers.
//

#ifndef _PORTABLE_DOT_H
#define _PORTABLE_DOT_H

#if defined(__TURBOC__) && (__TURBOC__ < 0x400 )
#define COMPILER            "Borland C++ 2.0/Turbo C++ 1.0"
#define INPUT( port )       inp( port )
#define OUTPUT( port, data ) (void) outp( port, data )
#define CLI()               disable()
#define STI()               enable()
#define UNUSED( a )         if ( a != a ) a = 0
#define INTERRUPT           far interrupt
#define FAR                 far
#ifdef __cplusplus
#include <iostream.h>
#endif  // #ifdef __cplusplus
#endif  // #ifdef __BORLANDC__

#if defined(__TURBOC__) && (__TURBOC__ >= 0x400 )
#define COMPILER            "Borland C++ 3.0/Turbo C++ 3.0"
#define INPUT( port )       inp( port )
#define OUTPUT( port, data ) (void) outp( port, data )
#define CLI()               disable()
#define STI()               enable()
#define UNUSED( a )         (void) a
#define INTERRUPT           _far _interrupt
#define FAR                 _far
#define DELETE_ARRAY
#ifdef __cplusplus
#include <iostream.h>
#endif  // #ifdef __cplusplus
#endif  // #ifdef __BORLANDC__

#if defined(__TSC__)
```

# THE RS232 CLASS

```
#define COMPILER            "Topspeed C++"
#define INPUT( port )       inp( port )
#define OUTPUT( port, data ) (void) outp( port, data )
#define CLI()               disable()
#define STI()               enable()
#define UNUSED( a )         if ( a != a ) a = 0
#define INTERRUPT           far interrupt
#define FAR                 far
#ifdef __cplusplus
#include <iostream.h>
#endif  // #ifdef __cplusplus
#endif  // #ifdef __TSC__

#ifdef __ZTC__
#if ( __ZTC__ < 0x300 )
#define COMPILER            "Zortech C++ 2.x"
#else
#define COMPILER            "Zortech C++ 3.x"
#endif
#define INPUT( port )       inp( port )
#define OUTPUT( port, data ) outp( port, data )
#define CLI()               int_off()
#define STI()               int_on()
#define UNUSED( a )
#define INTERRUPT           _cdecl
#define FAR                 _far
#ifdef __cplusplus
#if ( __ZTC__ < 0x300 )
#include <stream.hpp>
#else
#include <iostream.hpp>
#endif
#endif  // #ifdef __cplusplus
#include <int.h>
#endif  // #ifdef __ZTC__

#ifdef _MSC_VER
#define COMPILER            "Microsoft C/C++"
#define INPUT( port )       _inp( port )
```

111

# SERIAL COMMUNICATIONS: A C++ DEVELOPER'S GUIDE

```
#define OUTPUT( port, data )   (void) _outp( port, data )
#define CLI()                  _disable()
#define STI()                  _enable()
#define UNUSED( a )            (void) a
#define INTERRUPT              __ far __ interrupt
#define FAR                    __ far
#define DELETE_ARRAY
#pragma check_stack( off )
#pragma warning( disable : 4505 )
#ifdef __cplusplus
#include <iostream.h>
#endif  // #ifdef __ cplusplus
#include <conio.h>
#endif  // #ifdef _MSC_VER


#endif  // #ifndef _PORTABLE_DOT_H

// *********************** END OF PORTABLE.H ********************
```

**Listing 2-1. PORTABLE.H**


```
// *********************** START OF RS232.H *********************
//
// This header file contains the definitions for the base class
// RS232.
//
#ifndef _RS232_DOT_H
#define _RS232_DOT_H

#include "portable.h"
#include <conio.h>

enum RS232PortName { COM1 = 0, COM2,   COM3,   COM4,
                     COM5,     COM6,   COM7,   COM8 };

enum RS232Error {   RS232_SUCCESS                   = 0,

// Warning errors
                    RS232_WARNING                   = -100,
```

## THE RS232 CLASS

```
                RS232_FUNCTION_NOT_SUPPORTED,
                RS232_TIMEOUT,
                RS232_ILLEGAL_BAUD_RATE,
                RS232_ILLEGAL_PARITY_SETTING,
                RS232_ILLEGAL_WORD_LENGTH,
                RS232_ILLEGAL_STOP_BITS,
                RS232_ILLEGAL_LINE_NUMBER,
                RS232_NO_MODEM_RESPONSE,
                RS232_NO_TERMINATOR,
                RS232_DTR_NOT_SUPPORTED,
                RS232_RTS_NOT_SUPPORTED,
                RS232_RTS_CTS_NOT_SUPPORTED,
                RS232_DTR_DSR_NOT_SUPPORTED,
                RS232_XON_XOFF_NOT_SUPPORTED,
                RS232_NEXT_FREE_WARNING,

// Fatal Errors
                RS232_ERROR                  = -200,
                RS232_IRQ_IN_USE,
                RS232_PORT_NOT_FOUND,
                RS232_PORT_IN_USE,
                RS232_ILLEGAL_IRQ,
                RS232_MEMORY_ALLOCATION_ERROR,
                RS232_NEXT_FREE_ERROR };

//
// These constants are used as parameters to RS232 member
// functions.
//

const int UNCHANGED = -1;
const int FOREVER = -1;
const int DISABLE = 0;
const int CLEAR = 0;
const int ENABLE = 1;
const int SET = 1;
const int RESET = 1;
const int REMOTE_CONTROL = -1;
```

```cpp
//
// The Settings class provides a convenient mechanism for saving or
// assigning the state of a port.
//

class Settings
{
    public :
        long BaudRate;
        char Parity;
        int WordLength;
        int StopBits;
        int Dtr;
        int Rts;
        int XonXoff;
        int RtsCts;
        int DtrDsr;
        void Adjust( long baud_rate,
                     int parity,
                     int word_length,
                     int stop_bits,
                     int dtr,
                     int rts,
                     int xon_xoff,
                     int rts_cts,
                     int dtr_dsr );
};

//
// Class RS232 is the abstract base class used for any serial port
// class. RS232 cannot be instantiated. Only fully defined classes
// derived from RS232 can actually be created and used.
//

class RS232
{
    protected :
        RS232PortName port_name;
        Settings saved_settings;
```

## THE RS232 CLASS

```
        Settings settings;
        RS232Error error_status;
        int debug_line_count;

// Mandatory protected functions

        virtual int read_buffer( char *buffer,
                                 unsigned int count ) = 0;
        virtual int write_buffer( char *buffer,
                                  unsigned int count = -1 ) = 0;
        virtual int read_byte( void ) = 0;
        virtual int write_byte( int c ) = 0;

    public :
        unsigned int ByteCount;
        long ElapsedTime;

//  Mandatory functions. All derived classes must define these.

        virtual RS232Error Set( long baud_rate = UNCHANGED,
                                int parity = UNCHANGED,
                                int word_length = UNCHANGED,
                                int stop_bits = UNCHANGED ) = 0;
        virtual int TXSpaceFree( void ) = 0;
        virtual int RXSpaceUsed( void ) = 0;
        virtual int Cd( void ) = 0;
        virtual int Ri( void ) = 0;
        virtual int Cts( void ) = 0;
        virtual int Dsr( void ) = 0;
        virtual int ParityError( int clear = UNCHANGED ) = 0;
        virtual int BreakDetect( int clear = UNCHANGED ) = 0;
        virtual int FramingError( int clear = UNCHANGED ) = 0;
        virtual int HardwareOverrunError( int clear = UNCHANGED ) = 0;

// Optional Functions. Derived class are not required to support
// these.

        virtual ~RS232( void ){ ; }
        virtual int Break( long milliseconds = 300 );
```

```
        virtual int SoftwareOverrunError( int clear = UNCHANGED );
        virtual int XonXoffHandshaking( int setting = UNCHANGED );
        virtual int RtsCtsHandshaking( int setting = UNCHANGED );
        virtual int DtrDsrHandshaking( int setting = UNCHANGED );
        virtual int Dtr( int setting = UNCHANGED );
        virtual int Rts( int setting = UNCHANGED );
        virtual int Peek( void *buffer, unsigned int count );
        virtual int RXSpaceFree( void );
        virtual int TXSpaceUsed( void );
        virtual int FlushRXBuffer( void );
        virtual int FlushTXBuffer( void );
        virtual char *ErrorName( int error );
        virtual int IdleFunction( void );
        virtual int FormatDebugOutput( char *buffer = 0,
                                      int line_number = -1 );

// Nonvirtual functions. These work the same for all classes.

        int Read( void *buffer,
                  unsigned int count,
                  long milliseconds = 0 );
        int Read( void *buffer,
                  unsigned int count,
                  long milliseconds,
                  char *terminator );
        int Write( void *buffer,
                   unsigned int count = 0,
                   long milliseconds = 0,
                   char *terminator = 0 );
        int Read( long milliseconds = 0 );
        int Write( int c, long milliseconds = 0 );
        int Peek( void );
        int ReadSettings( Settings &copy ) { copy = settings;
                                             return RS232_SUCCESS; }
        RS232Error ErrorStatus( void ) { return error_status; }
        int DebugLineCount( void ) { return debug_line_count; }
};
// A miscellaneous support function. This may be implemented
// differently by different environments.
```

## THE RS232 CLASS

```
long ReadTime( void );

#endif   // #ifndef _RS232_DOT_H

// *********************** END OF RS232.H ***********************
```
**Listing 2-2. RS232.H**

```
// ********************* START OF RS232.CPP *********************
//
// This C++ file contains the definitions for all functions defined
// for the base class. Most of these are dummy functions that only
// return a warning message to the calling routine. A well-defined
// derived class will usually define new versions of these virtual
// functions, which means they will never be called.
//

#include "portable.h"
#include <stdio.h>
#include <string.h>
#include <ctype.h>
#include "rs232.h"

// FlushRXBuffer() doesn't have to be defined for every
// derived class. This default function should be able to flush
// the buffer using the mandatory read_buffer() function.
// Classes such as PC8250 that have direct access to their
// receive buffer can implement more efficient versions than this
// if they want.

int RS232::FlushRXBuffer( void )
{
    char buf[ 32 ];

    for ( ; ; ) {
        if ( error_status != RS232_SUCCESS )
            return error_status;
        read_buffer( buf, 32 );
        if ( ByteCount == 0 )
```

```
            break;
    }
    return RS232_SUCCESS;
}

// Peek( void ) isn't a virtual function. This is one of the
// few normal member functions in class RS232. It peeks at a
// single byte using the Peek( char *, int ) function.

int RS232::Peek( void )
{
    char c;
    int status;

    if ( error_status < RS232_SUCCESS )
        return error_status;
    if ( ( status = Peek( &c, 1 ) ) < RS232_SUCCESS )
        return status;
    if ( ByteCount < 1 )
        return RS232_TIMEOUT;
    return (int) c;
}

//
// This member function returns the character translation for one
// of the error codes defined in the base class. It is called by
// the ErrorName() function for a derived class after checking to
// see if the error code is not a new one defined by the derived
// class.

char * RS232::ErrorName( int error )
{
    switch ( error ) {
        case RS232_SUCCESS                  :
            return( "Success" );

        case RS232_WARNING                  :
            return( "General Warning" );
        case RS232_FUNCTION_NOT_SUPPORTED   :
```

# THE RS232 CLASS

```
            return( "Function not supported" );
        case RS232_TIMEOUT                  :
            return( "Timeout" );
        case RS232_ILLEGAL_BAUD_RATE        :
            return( "Illegal baud rate" );
        case RS232_ILLEGAL_PARITY_SETTING   :
            return( "Illegal parity setting" );
        case RS232_ILLEGAL_WORD_LENGTH      :
            return( "Illegal word length" );
        case RS232_ILLEGAL_STOP_BITS        :
            return( "Illegal stop bits" );
        case RS232_ILLEGAL_LINE_NUMBER      :
            return( "Illegal line number" );
        case RS232_NO_TERMINATOR            :
            return( "No terminator" );
        case RS232_NO_MODEM_RESPONSE        :
            return( "No modem response" );
        case RS232_DTR_NOT_SUPPORTED        :
            return( "DTR control not supported" );
        case RS232_RTS_NOT_SUPPORTED        :
            return( "RTS control not supported" );
        case RS232_RTS_CTS_NOT_SUPPORTED    :
            return( "RTS/CTS handshaking not supported" );
        case RS232_DTR_DSR_NOT_SUPPORTED    :
            return( "DTR/DSR handshaking not supported" );
        case RS232_XON_XOFF_NOT_SUPPORTED   :
            return( "XON/XOFF handshaking not supported" );

        case RS232_ERROR                    :
            return( "General Error" );
        case RS232_IRQ_IN_USE               :
            return( "IRQ line in use" );
        case RS232_PORT_NOT_FOUND           :
            return( "Port not found" );
        case RS232_PORT_IN_USE              :
            return( "Port in use" );
        case RS232_ILLEGAL_IRQ              :
            return( "Illegal IRQ" );
        case RS232_MEMORY_ALLOCATION_ERROR  :
```

```
                    return( "Memory allocation error" );

        default                                 :
            return( "???" );
    }
}

//
// The base class contributes four lines of output to the Debug
// output. Note that it returns the number 4 if called with a
// null buffer, to pass this information on. The four lines of
// output contain everything the base class knows about the port,
// which are its current settings, saved settings, port name, and
// error status. For line numbers greater than three, the derived
// class provides additional lines of debug output. Note that
// this function is called by the version of FormatDebugOutput()
// defined for the derived class.

int RS232::FormatDebugOutput( char *buffer, int line_number )
{
    if ( buffer == 0 )
        return 4;

    switch( line_number ) {

        case 0 :
            sprintf( buffer, "Base class: RS232   "
                             "COM%-2d  "
                             "Status: %-35.35s",
                             port_name + 1,
                             ErrorName( error_status ) );
            return RS232_SUCCESS;
        case 1 :
            sprintf( buffer, "Byte count: %5u  "
                             "Elapsed time: %9ld  "
                             "TX Free: %5u  "
                             "RX Used: %5u",
                             ByteCount,
                             ElapsedTime,
```

## THE RS232 CLASS

```
                        TXSpaceFree(),
                        RXSpaceUsed() );
            return RS232_SUCCESS;
        case 2 :
            sprintf( buffer,
                    "Saved port: %6ld,%c,%2d,%2d "
                    "DTR,RTS: %2d,%2d "
                    "XON/OFF,RTS/CTS,DTR/DSR: %2d,%2d,%2d",
                    saved_settings.BaudRate,
                    saved_settings.Parity,
                    saved_settings.WordLength,
                    saved_settings.StopBits,
                    saved_settings.Dtr,
                    saved_settings.Rts,
                    saved_settings.XonXoff,
                    saved_settings.RtsCts,
                    saved_settings.DtrDsr );
            return RS232_SUCCESS;

        case 3 :
            sprintf( buffer,
                    "Current port: %6ld,%c,%1d,%1d "
                    "DTR,RTS: %2d,%2d "
                    "XON/OFF,RTS/CTS,DTR/DSR: %2d,%2d,%2d",
                    settings.BaudRate,
                    settings.Parity,
                    settings.WordLength,
                    settings.StopBits,
                    settings.Dtr,
                    settings.Rts,
                    settings.XonXoff,
                    settings.RtsCts,
                    settings.DtrDsr );
            return RS232_SUCCESS;

        default :
            return RS232_ILLEGAL_LINE_NUMBER;
    }
}
```

# SERIAL COMMUNICATIONS: A C++ DEVELOPER'S GUIDE

```cpp
// This nonvirtual member function operates by repeatedly
// calling the read_byte() function for the derived class. It
// handles the optional milliseconds parameter, which determines
// how long the function will wait for input before returning a
// timeout. The idle function is called while waiting.

int RS232::Read( long milliseconds )
{
    int c;
    long start_time;
    int idle_status = RS232_SUCCESS;

    ElapsedTime = 0;
    ByteCount = 0;
    if ( error_status < RS232_SUCCESS )
        return error_status;
    start_time = ReadTime();
    for ( ; ; ) {
        c = read_byte();
        if ( c >= 0 )
            break;
        if ( milliseconds != FOREVER &&
            ( ReadTime() - start_time ) >= milliseconds )
            break;
        if ( ( idle_status = IdleFunction() ) < RS232_SUCCESS )
            break;
    }
    ElapsedTime = ReadTime() - start_time;
    if ( idle_status < RS232_SUCCESS )
        return idle_status;
    if ( c >= 0 ) {
        ByteCount = 1;
        return c;
    }
    return RS232_TIMEOUT;
}
```

## THE RS232 CLASS

```
// This nonvirtual member function of class RS232 operates by
// repeatedly calling the virtual function write_byte() for the
// derived class. The milliseconds parameter defines how long
// the function will keep trying before giving up. While
// waiting, the idle function is called.

int RS232::Write( int c, long milliseconds )
{
    int write_status;
    int idle_status = RS232_SUCCESS;
    long start_time;

    ElapsedTime = 0;
    ByteCount = 0;
    if ( error_status < 0 )
        return error_status;
    start_time = ReadTime();
    for ( ; ; ) {
        write_status = write_byte( c );
        if ( write_status != RS232_TIMEOUT )
            break;
        if ( milliseconds != FOREVER &&
             ( ReadTime() - start_time ) >= milliseconds )
            break;
        if ( ( idle_status = IdleFunction() ) < RS232_SUCCESS )
            break;
    }
    ElapsedTime = ReadTime() - start_time;
    if ( idle_status < RS232_SUCCESS )
        return idle_status;
    if ( write_status < RS232_SUCCESS )
        return write_status;
    ByteCount = 1;
    return RS232_SUCCESS;
}

// This nonvirtual member function of class RS232 writes out
// a buffer using the virtual write_buffer() routine. It has
// two additional parameters beyond those used by write_buffer(),
```

# SERIAL COMMUNICATIONS: A C++ DEVELOPER'S GUIDE

```
// which are a timeout value and a terminator. The terminator
// can be used to automatically append a CR/LF pair to output
// strings.

int RS232::Write( void *buffer,
                  unsigned int count,
                  long milliseconds,
                  char *terminator )
{
    char *b = ( char * ) buffer;
    long start_time;
    unsigned int byte_count;
    int idle_status = RS232_SUCCESS;
    int write_status;

    ElapsedTime = 0;
    ByteCount = 0;
    if ( error_status < 0 )
        return error_status;

    byte_count = 0;
    start_time = ReadTime();
    if ( count == 0 )
        count = strlen( b );
    for ( ; ; ) {
        write_status = write_buffer( b, count );
        byte_count += ByteCount;
        b += ByteCount;
        count -= ByteCount;
        if ( count == 0 && terminator != 0 ) {
            count += strlen( terminator );
            b = terminator;
            terminator = 0;
            continue;
        }
        if ( write_status != RS232_TIMEOUT || count == 0 )
            break;
        if ( milliseconds != FOREVER &&
             ( ReadTime() - start_time ) >= milliseconds )
```

```
            break;
        if ( ( idle_status == IdleFunction() ) < RS232_SUCCESS )
            break;
    }
    ElapsedTime = ReadTime() - start_time;
    ByteCount = byte_count;
    if ( idle_status < RS232_SUCCESS )
        return idle_status;
    if ( write_status < RS232_SUCCESS )
        return write_status;
    else if ( count > 0 )
        return RS232_TIMEOUT;
    else
        return RS232_SUCCESS;
}


// There are two versions of the nonvirtual ReadBuffer()
// function defined for the base class. They differ only in what
// causes their normal termination. This version terminates only
// when it reads in a full buffer of data, or times out. The
// next version stops when it sees the terminator string
// specified as a parameter.

int RS232::Read( void *buffer, unsigned int count,
                              long milliseconds )
{
    long start_time;
    unsigned int byte_count;
    char *b = (char *) buffer;
    int read_status;
    int idle_status = RS232_SUCCESS;

    ElapsedTime = 0;
    ByteCount = 0;
    if ( error_status < 0 )
         return error_status;
    start_time = ReadTime();
    byte_count = 0;
    for ( ; ; ) {
```

```
            read_status = read_buffer( b, count );
            byte_count += ByteCount;
            count -= ByteCount;
            b += ByteCount;
            if ( read_status != RS232_TIMEOUT || count == 0 )
                break;
            if ( milliseconds != FOREVER &&
                ( ReadTime() - start_time ) >= milliseconds )
                break;
            if ( ( idle_status = IdleFunction() ) < RS232_SUCCESS )
                break;
        }
        *b = '\0';
        ElapsedTime = ReadTime() - start_time;
        ByteCount = byte_count;
        if ( idle_status < RS232_SUCCESS )
            return idle_status;
        else
            return read_status;
}


// This version of ReadBuffer() looks for a termination string
// in the incoming data stream. Because of this, it has to read
// in characters one at a time instead of in blocks. It looks
// for the terminator by doing a strncmp() after every new
// character is read in, which is probably not the most efficient
// way of doing it.

int RS232::Read( void *buffer,
                 unsigned int count,
                 long milliseconds,
                 char *terminator )
{
    long start_time;
    unsigned int byte_count;
    char *b = (char *) buffer;
    int idle_status = RS232_SUCCESS;
    int c;
    int term_len;
```

```c
        term_len = strlen( terminator );
        ElapsedTime = 0;
        ByteCount = 0;
        if ( error_status < 0 )
            return error_status;
        start_time = ReadTime();
        byte_count = 0;
        for ( ; ; ) {
            c = read_byte();
            if ( c >= 0 ) {
                byte_count++;
                count--;
                *b++ = (char) c;
                if ( byte_count >= (unsigned int) term_len ) {
                    if ( strncmp( b - term_len,terminator,term_len)
                                                        == 0 ) {
                        b -= term_len;
                        c = RS232_SUCCESS;
                        byte_count -= term_len;
                        break;
                    }
                }
                if ( count == 0 )
                    break;
            } else {
                if ( c != RS232_TIMEOUT )
                    break;
                if ( milliseconds != FOREVER &&
                    ( ReadTime() - start_time ) >= milliseconds )
                    break;
                if ( ( idle_status = IdleFunction() ) < RS232_SUCCESS )
                    break;
            }
        }
        *b = '\0';
        ElapsedTime = ReadTime() - start_time;
        ByteCount = byte_count;
        if ( idle_status < RS232_SUCCESS )
            return idle_status;
```

```c++
        else if ( c < RS232_SUCCESS )
            return c;
        else
            return RS232_SUCCESS;
}

// All of the remaining functions defined here are optional
// functions that won't be defined for every class. The default
// versions of these virtual functions just return an error
// message.

int RS232::Break( long duration )
{
    UNUSED( duration );
    return RS232_FUNCTION_NOT_SUPPORTED;
}

int RS232::SoftwareOverrunError( int clear )
{
    UNUSED( clear );
    return RS232_FUNCTION_NOT_SUPPORTED;
}

int RS232::FlushTXBuffer( void )
{
    return RS232_FUNCTION_NOT_SUPPORTED;
}

int RS232::RXSpaceFree( void )
{
    return RS232_FUNCTION_NOT_SUPPORTED;
}

int RS232::TXSpaceUsed( void )
{
    return RS232_FUNCTION_NOT_SUPPORTED;
}

int RS232::XonXoffHandshaking( int enable )
```

```cpp
{
    UNUSED( enable );
    return RS232_FUNCTION_NOT_SUPPORTED;
}

int RS232::RtsCtsHandshaking( int enable )
{
    UNUSED( enable );
    return RS232_FUNCTION_NOT_SUPPORTED;
}

int RS232::DtrDsrHandshaking( int enable )
{
    UNUSED( enable );
    return RS232_FUNCTION_NOT_SUPPORTED;
}

int RS232::Dtr( int setting )
{
    UNUSED( setting );
    return RS232_FUNCTION_NOT_SUPPORTED;
}

int RS232::Rts( int setting )
{
    UNUSED( setting );
    return RS232_FUNCTION_NOT_SUPPORTED;
}

int RS232::Peek( void *buffer, unsigned int count )
{
    UNUSED( buffer );
    UNUSED( count );
    return RS232_FUNCTION_NOT_SUPPORTED;
}

void Settings::Adjust( long baud_rate,
                       int parity,
                       int word_length,
```

# SERIAL COMMUNICATIONS: A C++ DEVELOPER'S GUIDE

```cpp
                        int stop_bits,
                        int dtr,
                        int rts,
                        int xon_xoff,
                        int rts_cts,
                        int dtr_dsr )
{
    if ( baud_rate != UNCHANGED )
          BaudRate = baud_rate;
    if ( parity != UNCHANGED )
        Parity = (char) toupper( parity );
    if ( word_length != UNCHANGED )
        WordLength = word_length;
    if ( stop_bits != UNCHANGED )
        StopBits = stop_bits;
    if ( dtr != UNCHANGED )
        Dtr = dtr;
    if ( rts != UNCHANGED )
        Rts = rts;
    if ( xon_xoff != UNCHANGED )
        XonXoff = xon_xoff;
    if ( rts_cts != UNCHANGED )
        RtsCts = rts_cts;
    if ( dtr_dsr != UNCHANGED )
        DtrDsr = dtr_dsr;
}

// ********************* END OF RS232.CPP *********************
```

**Listing 2-3. RS232.CPP**

```cpp
// ********************* START OF _MSDOS.H *********************
//
// This file contains header files used to call MS-DOS
// specific support routines. The only one defined at this
// time is the Bus() function, which determines whether an ISA or
// Microchannel bus is in use on the target machine.

#ifndef __MSDOS_DOT_H
```

```
#define __MSDOS_DOT_H

enum BusType { ISA_BUS, MCA_BUS };
BusType Bus( void );

#endif   // #ifndef __MSDOS_DOT_H

// ********************* END OF _MSDOS.H ***********************
```

**Listing 2-4. _MSDOS.H**

```
// ********************* START OF MSDOS.CPP *********************
//
// This module contains OS specific routines. These routines are
// all defined for MS-DOS. When the target OS is OS/2, Windows, or
// UNIX, different versions of these routines must be linked in.
//

#include <dos.h>
#include "rs232.h"
#include "_msdos.h"

// The default idle function for MS-DOS does nothing.

int RS232::IdleFunction( void )
{
    return RS232_SUCCESS;
}

//
// ReadTime() returns the current time of day in milliseconds.
//

long ReadTime( void )
{
    union REGS r;
    long milliseconds;

    r.h.ah = 0x2c;
```

```cpp
        int86( 0x21, &r, &r );
        milliseconds = (long) r.h.dl * 10;          // dl : hundredths
        milliseconds += (long) r.h.dh * 1000;       // dh : seconds
        milliseconds += (long) r.h.cl * 60000L;     // cl : minutes
        milliseconds += (long) r.h.ch * 3600000L;   // ch : hours
        return( milliseconds );
}

// This function determines whether we are on a Microchannel
// or ISA machine.

BusType Bus( void )
{
        union REGS r;
        struct SREGS s = { 0, 0, 0, 0 };
        char FAR *system_data;

        r.h.ah = 0xc0;
        int86x( 0x15, &r, &r, &s );
        if ( r.x.cflag )
                return ISA_BUS;
        system_data = ( char FAR *) ( ( (long) s.es << 16 ) + r.x.bx );
        if ( system_data[ 5 ] & 0x02 )
                return MCA_BUS;
        else
                return ISA_BUS;
}

// ********************* END OF MSDOS.CPP *********************
```

**Listing 2-5. MSDOS.CPP**

CHAPTER 3

# The PC8250 Class

In this chapter, I will present a fully functional interface to the IBM PC standard communications ports derived from the `RS232` class. This driver will support all of the standard and optional virtual functions from this class, meaning it will be fully compatible with any software written to use the `RS232 class`..

The `PC8250` class will also play a key role in working with the nonintelligent multiport board drivers from the next chapter. Object-oriented programming should enable properly written code to be reused for new applications.

## The 8250 UART

In Chapter 1, I went over the history of the venerable 8250 UART family as it relates to the IBM PC. Certainly IBMs choice of the Intel 8088 as the CPU for the PC is one of the most influential hardware decisions in history. While the choice of the National Semiconductor 8250 as the UART on the PC COM card may seem like a footnote in comparison, it has had a considerable impact as well.

Because the IBM PC BIOS as well as MS-DOS itself, left out any significant driver support for RS-232 interface cards, communications software developers have had to work directly with the hardware. Over the years, thousands of communications programs have been written to access the 8250 registers directly, ranging from top-quality professional software down to inexpensive shareware. The installed base of communications software users with 8250 UARTs has grown so much that it is difficult to support anything else.

Because communications code talks directly to the 8250 hardware, PC and peripheral manufacturers have not had too many choices regarding UARTs for the PC ISA. Basically, if a UART is not completely 8250 compatible, it isn't going to sell. Any nonstandard hardware will require custom software to work, and most reasonable people just aren't interested in replacing off-the-shelf software with custom implementations.

This is really more of a problem to the end user than it is to the programmer. The 8250 is not a particularly high-powered chip, so "power users" are finding that their existing hardware is running out of gas. Programmers can't do much to squeeze more performance out of existing parts, so they continue writing code that works with the standard until something better comes along. The techniques developed in this book will help you ensure that your software will be ready for the change when it happens.

## 8250 Register Set

The 8250 family and its close derivatives are controlled by approximately 11 (the exact number depends on how you view things) hardware registers. On the IBM PC standard COM cards, these registers are mapped into a block of eight consecutive I/O ports. In general, hardware designed to work with Intel CPU architectures usually maps to the I/O bus, leaving the higher speed memory bus to peripherals that have large blocks of shared memory, such as video cards.

The I/O bus on the PC is an 8-bit bus that operates at a slower speed than the memory bus, usually 8 MHz. Unlike conventional memory, the I/O bus has only a couple of different machine instructions for accessing hardware. The 8088 instruction set only has four output and four input instructions, and two from each set can't be used on the PC ISA Bus because the I/O bus is only 8 bits wide. But this RISC-like implementation doesn't seem to cause any particular hardship to systems level programming. Most of the difficulties implementing communications software are timing and hardware related, and are not related to an anemic instruction set.

The registers found in the 8250 family are:

**Table 3-1. 8250 family register definitions.**

| Register Name | Offset | Abbreviation | Access Type |
|---|---|---|---|
| Receiver Buffer Register | 0 | RBR | Read Only |
| Transmit Holding Register | 0 | THR | Write Only |
| Interrupt Enable Register | 1 | IER | Read/Write |
| Interrupt Identification Register | 2 | IIR | Read Only |
| FIFO Control Register (16550) | 2 | FCR | Write Only |
| Line Control Register | 3 | LCR | Read/Write |
| Modem Control Register | 4 | MCR | Read/Write |

## THE PC8250 CLASS

**Table 3-1,** *Continued*

| Register Name | Offset | Abbreviation | Access Type |
|---|---|---|---|
| Line Status Register | 5 | LSR | Read Only |
| Modem Status Register | 6 | MSR | Read Only |
| Scratch Register (16450/550) | 7 | SCR | Read/Write |
| Divisor Latch (16 bits) | 0/1 | DL | Read/Write |

Each of these registers has its own well-defined role to play in the proper operation of an 8250-type UART. The offsets listed in the preceding table refer to the offsets from the base address of the UART on the I/O bus. For example, COM1 on an IBM PC is normally configured to be at 3F8. Since the Scratch Register is defined as having an offset of 7, it will appear at address 3FF and can be accessed with an input or output instruction. Note that the addresses on the UART could be mapped differently if necessary; IBM simply mapped the UART the conventional way.

The next few sections discuss each of the UART's registers in greater detail.

### Receive Buffer Register

The Receive Buffer Register (RBR) is the address where data that the UART has received from an RS-232 line can be read into the computer. The CPU actually gets the data from the UART by executing an input instruction at an offset of 0 past the base address of the UART. This means that on COM1, we can read in a byte from the UART by executing a piece of assembly code that looks like this:

```
INPUT:      MOV     DX,3F8H
            IN      AL,DX
```

The 8250 uses a technique for its input and output registers known as double buffering. This means that internal to the chip are a pair of registers for input and a pair for output. On the input side, the UART uses one register as a temporary holding area for a byte coming down the RS-232 line. As each bit comes in, it is shifted into this holding register. After 7 or 8 bits have come in, the UART decides that it has assembled a complete data word. At this point, the word is dumped from the receiver holding register to the RBR. The holding register can then begin assembling the next RS-232 byte coming down the line, while the last word rests comfortably in the buffer register.

Thus, the programmer has a minimum of one data word time to read the byte from the RBR before the next word is assembled. As soon as the next word is completely assembled, it is written out into the RBR, obliterating the current contents. So response time is critical to the accurate reception of the input data.

Not long ago, this amount of time was more than adequate. A 300-baud modem only transmits a maximum of 30 bytes per second, so each data word has a maximum response time of around 33 milliseconds. But today, not too many applications exist for 300-baud modems  The standard interface is probably 19,200 bps, and many modems are working at 38,400 bps. At 19,200 bps, characters arrive at the UART twice a millisecond. Even on today's fast machines, 500 microseconds is a very brief interval.

The 16550 UART was the most practical solution to this problem. It has a 16-byte receiver buffer, allowing for significantly longer durations between servicing the chip. The 16550 UART can be configured to generate an interrupt when the very first character enters the FIFO, which then leaves 15 more data word times before loss of data. This can cause a dramatic increase in performance, even on a very fast machine.

**Transmit Holding Register**

Just like on the receive side of the UART, the transmit side is double buffered. The character actually being shifted out on to the RS-232 line is contained in the Transmitter Buffer. The next character to be sent is placed in the Transmit Holding Register (THR). When the transmitter completes shifting out the last bit from the current output byte, it immediately moves the byte from the THR into the transmit register. At that point, the UART lets the CPU know by way of a data bit or an interrupt that it is ready to accept another character. If the processor can write a new data byte to the THR before the next character is done shifting out, a continuous stream of  RS-232 characters will be sent.

The transmitter's response time is not nearly as critical as the receivers. If the CPU is a little slow moving the next character into the transmit buffer, the RS-232 line will suffer some dead air when nothing is being transmitted. The computer will be wasting some of its data bandwidth on nothing, but no data will be lost.

Nonetheless, when the 16550 was designed, it incorporated a 16-byte FIFO buffer on the transmitter side as well. Once the CPU knows that the transmit buffer is empty, it can immediately load up the TX FIFO with 16 data words ready to be sent. The CPU won't be bothered again for 16 more data word times, allowing for much less overhead when transmitting blocks of data.

**Interrupt Enable Register**

The 8250 family of UARTs can generate interrupts based on four classes of events. These events are:

- Receive Data Available
- Transmit Holding Register Empty
- Modem Status Line Change
- Line Status Event

Depending on the type of interface to the 8250, one or more of these interrupts may be in use at any time. As I have already stated, the BIOS talks to the 8250 without using any of the interrupt types, which renders it nearly useless for any serious work.

The four types of interrupts are enabled via individual bits in the Interrupt Enable Register (IER). Figure 3-1 shows the bit map of the IER. Writing a one to the bit in the register enables that particular interrupt. Note that the IER is a read/write register, which means that the programmer can read the bits back out of the register at any time. This is convenient when programming the register, because you can set or clear an individual bit.

When developing the device driver for the 8250, we must ask which of the four interrupts to enable and when. Clearly the most important interrupt to support in any driver software is the Receive Data Available (RDA) interrupt. With any real world application running on conventional RS-232 hardware, it is simply not possible to poll the UART fast enough to read in all incoming data. The only solution is the RDA interrupt. But then you must ensure that your code can respond to the interrupt rapidly enough to not lose any data.

The Transmit Holding Register Empty (THRE) interrupt is also useful, but it can be safely ignored under certain circumstances. In a single-tasking environment, with the right type of application, polled-mode output will prove more than satisfactory to the task at hand. When transmitting data, the CPU simply sits in a polling loop, waiting for the THRE to become empty before sending each character. The CPU wastes an awful lot of time doing nothing but waiting, but often this is still the best approach.

| 7 | 6 | 5 | 4 | 3 | 2 | 1 | 0 |
|---|---|---|---|---|---|---|---|
| Not Used | Not Used | Not Used | Not Used | Modem Status | Line Status | Transmit Holding Register Empty | Received Data Available |

**Figure 3-1. The Interrupt Enable Register.**

A modem status interrupt is generated any time one of the four incoming modem status lines to the UART changes state. The 8250 family has four incoming modem status lines that are normally connected to CTS, DSR, CD, and RI.

The 8250 driver developed in this chapter will have modem status interrupts enabled at all times. Many applications can get by without enabling these interrupts, but having them on makes it particularly easy to manage hardware flow control. When one of the two modes of hardware flow control is enabled, we want our driver to be able to either start or stop interrupts when an incoming CTS or DSR line changes state.

If the modem status interrupts weren't turned on, there would be a polling problem. When the 8250 driver was in a blocked state while waiting for CTS or DSR to go high, our driver would have to be polling the state of the modem status lines. Otherwise, when the line went high again we would have no way of knowing it was time to begin transmission again.

There is a down side to enabling modem status interrupts, however. First, as I mentioned in Chapter 1, if a cable leaves some of the modem status lines unconnected, they can pick up noise from adjacent data lines in the cable. This can result in massive floods of modem status interrupts, with an interrupt being generated for literally every bit that is input or output.

Even if the modem status lines are properly connected on the cable, most of the modem status interrupts just waste CPU cycles. If hardware handshaking isn't being used, most applications would work properly by just polling the input lines. But with the 8250 architecture being what it is, we have to accept the necessity of leaving these interrupts turned on.

The final interrupt that can be turned on in the 8250 is the Line Status Interrupt (LSI). There are four line status conditions that can generate an interrupt. Parity errors occur when an incoming character doesn't obey the parity that the part has been programmed to expect. A Framing Error occurs when an incoming character doesn't appear to have a valid stop bit. A Break Detect occurs when the incoming RS-232 line stays at the logic 0 state for an entire character, time, including start, stop, and data bits. The final line status interrupt condition occurs when the CPU fails to service an 8250 interrupt rapidly enough, resulting in the loss of a character. The 8250 terminology for this condition is an Overrun Error. In this book, I will refer to this particular error as a Hardware Overrun Error to clearly differentiate it from a buffer overflow in the interrupt service routine.

The 8250 driver developed in this chapter will run with line status interrupts enabled at all times. However, no real time action will be taken when a line status interrupt occurs. Instead, the line status bits will just be ORed into a cumulative register that keeps track of cumulative line status errors.

For general-purpose software, it isn't always clear how to respond to a line status interrupt. For example, when performing terminal emulation, there usually isn't any way to retry a transmission, so errors cannot be corrected. File transfer protocols detect errors that occur during a file transfer, so the line status bits become redundant.

If an error-free connection is of paramount importance, I would probably rewrite this driver to respond differently to line-status interrupts. When the interrupt occurs, the application program could be alerted immediately, allowing it to take whatever action the programmer deems necessary.

### Interrupt ID Register

When an interrupt does occur, the CPU will respond by entering an Interrupt Service Routine (ISR). This is a special piece of code designed to handle the incoming hardware event rapidly and efficiently. Once it takes control of the machine, the ISR needs to decide what action to take. For the 8250, this means reading in the Interrupt ID Register (IIR). This 8-bit register has five valid states, shown in Table 3-2.

**Table 3-2. The Interrupt ID Register values.**

| IIR Contents | Interrupt Type | Priority |
|---|---|---|
| 0 | Modem Status Interrupt | Lowest |
| 2 | Transmit Holding Register Empty | Third |
| 4 | Received Data Available | Second |
| 6 | Line Status | Highest |
| 1 | No Interrupt Pending | N/A |

When the ISR takes control, it normally sits in a loop reading in the contents of the IIR. If the IIR contents indicate that an interrupt needs to be serviced, the appropriate handler routine can be dispatched. If the value 1 is read out of the IIR, no interrupts are pending and the routine can exit, returning control to the main program.

With most variations of the 8250, the interrupt service routine doesn't have to sit in a loop polling the IIR.

A common approach is to simply read in the IIR, dispatch a handler, then exit. However, there are a couple of problems with that approach. First, if the 8250 is in a very active state, managing a high number of interrupts, it is much more efficient for the CPU to handle as much activity as is possible while in the ISR.

Second, a few variations of the 8250 will fail to correctly interrupt 80x86 processors if only one interrupt at a time is serviced. Later in this chapter, I will offer details about this particular problem.

The four interrupt types in the 8250 have specific actions that must be taken to clear the interrupt state. If these actions aren't properly taken after reading the IIR, the UART could get into a hang state, unable to generate further interrupts until the last one is cleared.

Line Status Interrupt: Clearing this interrupt just requires that the CPU read the Line Status Register.

Modem Status Interrupt: Reading the Modem Status Register clears this interrupt.

# THE PC8250 CLASS

Received Data Available:     Reading the data from the Receiver Buffer Register clears this interrupt.

Transmit Holding Register:     When the Transmit Holding Register goes empty, there are two ways to clear the interrupt. Just reading the Interrupt ID Register will clear it, as will sending a byte to the transmitter.

The THRE interrupt is particularly important. If the interrupt service routine fails to reload the transmit register when it is empty, no further interrupts will occur. Thus, the program might be ready to send out data to the transmitter, but it may never receive an interrupt to let it know it can.

## Line Control Register / Baud Rate Divisor

The Line Control Register (LCR) is used to set up the data transmission parameters for the 8250 UART. An additional parameter, the baud rate, is indirectly controlled by this register. The LCR is divided into five different fields which are controlled with nonintuitive bit field values. Figure 3-2 shows how the fields are broken out across the 8-bit register.

| 7 | 6 | 5 | 4 | 3 | 2 | 1 | 0 |
|---|---|---|---|---|---|---|---|
| Divisor Latch Access Bit | Break Control | Parity Control Bits | | | Number of Stop Bits | Word Length Select | |

**Figure 3-2. The Line Control Register bit settings.**

The two least significant bits in the LCR are used to control the number of bits in a word transmitted by the UART. The 8250 has the capability to transmit words of 5, 6, 7, or 8 bits. There aren't many applications that use words of a length other than 7 or 8, but they could. Table 3-3 details the four possible settings of this bit field.

Table 3-3. The word length bit field in the LCR.

| Bit Field Value | Resulting Word Length |
|---|---|
| 00 | 5 bits |
| 01 | 6 bits |
| 10 | 7 bits |
| 11 | 8 bits |

The stop bits setting is merely a binary flag. A value of 1 indicates that two stop bits should be used, 0 means a single stop bit is used. For most applications, the slightly faster throughput afforded by using just a single stop bit is usually the desired setting. However, on a noisy line with continuous data flow, two stop bits may be required to quickly recover synchronization when an error occurs.

Decoding the functions of the three parity bits can be difficult at first. For one thing, there are 3 bits, which allow for eight different settings. However, the UART only actually has five different parity settings. The reason for this is that the 3 bits operate somewhat independently, so that each one controls a different aspect of the parity settings. The actual binary decoding of the parity bits is shown in Table 3-4.

The least significant bit in the parity select field is the parity enable bit. When this bit is clear, no parity is generated or checked under any conditions. If this bit is set, the next two bits determine what sort of parity is actually generated. The second bit in the field is the even parity select bit. Usually, if this bit is set, even parity is used, and if it is clear, odd parity is used. However, the setting of the third bit, the stick parity control, can overrule this bit. If the stick parity bit is set, an extra bit is appended to the data word. If a stick parity of 1 is selected, the extra bit is always 1; if a stick parity of 0 is selected, the extra bit is always a 0. The previous bit, the even parity select bit, controls the setting of the extra bit.

The stick parity setting is rarely used, but is still available, and many drivers will at least support it. Using a 0 bit for stick parity is referred to as Space parity, a 1 is referred to as Mark parity.

# THE PC8250 CLASS

**Table 3-4. The Parity Bit field in the LCR.**

| Stick Parity Bit | Even Parity Bit | Parity Enable Bit | Effect |
|---|---|---|---|
| 0 | 0 | 0 | No parity |
| 0 | 0 | 1 | Odd Parity |
| 0 | 1 | 0 | No Parity |
| 0 | 1 | 1 | Even Parity |
| 1 | 0 | 0 | No Parity |
| 1 | 0 | 1 | Mark Parity |
| 1 | 1 | 0 | No Parity |
| 1 | 1 | 1 | Space Pariyt |

Calculating exactly what the parity settings do for each bit field can be somewhat confusing. But you can create a switch statement one time for setting the parity and forget about it after that. That is the approach we will take.

The break bit in the LCR is used to send a break signal on the outgoing RS-232 line. A break signal is not a properly formatted character like the ones normally sent on the outbound line. Rather, a break signal is created when the UART forces the transmit line to a logic 0 and holds it there for significantly longer than a single character time. Generally a break signal should last at least 250 milliseconds. Using a long time guarantees that a break will be interpreted correctly even at very low baud rates.

The 8250 has no built-in break timer, so sending a break becomes a manual operation. Asserting the break bit in the LCR puts the line into a spacing condition. The line has to be held there while the main program counts off enough CPU ticks to amount to a significant fraction of a second. After that, the bit is cleared and the UART goes back to normal operations.

The final bit in the LCR is the Baud Rate Divisor Latch Access Bit (DLAB). The LCR directly controls all of the RS-232 transmission parameters for the UART, except for the baud rate. The 8250 has a flexible baud rate generator that is configured by loading a 16-bit divisor with a value determined by the program. The 8250 designers at National Semiconductor apparently were unhappy with the idea of having a register map with more than eight entries, so they mapped the two 8-byte components of the baud rate divisor into the same locations as the transmit

143

register and the interrupt enable register (register offsets of 0 and 1). A single bit, the DLAB, determines which set of registers is actually mapped at any given moment.

To write to the baud-rate divisor, the programmer just asserts the DLAB in the LCR, then writes out the two bytes of the divisor to register positions 0 and 1. Register 0 gets the least significant byte, register 1 gets the most significant. After the baud rate is set, the DLAB is cleared and register positions 0 and 1 revert to their normal mode of operation.

Problems can arise if an interrupt occurs while the DLAB is in an unknown state. If the ISR thinks it is reading in data from the Receiver Buffer Register, but is actually reading in the LSB of the baud-rate divisor, it will not be able to communicate.

One way to handle this problem is for the ISR to save and restore the state of the DLAB bit at the entry and exit of the ISR. A simpler method, which I will use here, is to disable interrupts while changing the baud rate.

On the IBM PC, the transmitter and receiver both derive their clock from a 115,200 Hz fundamental clock that is divided by the baud-rate divisor. This sets the maximum baud rate to 115,200 bps (except for the undefined case when the divisor is 0). The rate was set to 115,200 Hz because that rate divides down nicely to frequently used rates such as 9,600 and 2,400 baud.

The design of the IBM COM port hardware also prohibits the use of split baud rates, where the transmitter and receiver are operating at different speeds. The 8250 could operate in this mode with a different hardware setup. However, few applications require this feature.

### Modem Control Register

The Modem Control Register (MCR) sets or clears the four output lines from the 8250 UART. The UART lines are conventionally labeled as DTR, RTS, OUT1, and OUT2. Figure 3-3 details the bit settings used in the MCR, and Table 3-5 shows what function the control bits perform on an IBM PC COM card.

OUT1 and OUT2 are undedicated lines that hardware designers can use for whatever purposes they wish. For an IBM PC COM card, OUT1 is not connected to anything. OUT2 enables or disables the interrupt line to the PC bus. When OUT2 is low, the interrupt output from the 8250 UART is electrically disconnected from the bus, so that other peripheral cards are free to use the interrupt line. When OUT2

# THE PC8250 CLASS

is high, the 8250 interrupt line will be driving the interrupt line either high or low, depending on its current state.

| 7 | 6 | 5 | 4 | 3 | 2 | 1 | 0 |
|---|---|---|---|---|---|---|---|
| | Unused | | Loopback | OUT2 | OUT1 | RTS | DTR |

**Figure 3-3. The bit settings in the MCR.**

The DTR and RTS lines are used just as you would expect them to be. On the IBM COM card, they directly control the RTS and DTR output lines to the RS-232 connector. The UART doesn't have any automatic modes of operation that can change either of these control lines. Instead, the lines have to be controlled by the driver software. If you want to implement RTS/CTS flow control, for example, the ISR will have to toggle these bits at the correct trigger points in the buffer state.

**Table 3-5. Functions of the MCR bits on the PC COM card.**

| Control Bit | Function |
|---|---|
| Loopback | Loops back data and control lines |
| OUT2 | Enabled interrupts on PC COM card |
| OUT1 | Not connected, does nothing on PC COM card |
| RTS | Conventional modem control line |
| DTR | Conventional modem control line |

The final bit in the MCR of concern is the Loopback bit. This bit can be used to place the UART into internal Loopback mode for testing. When this bit is set, the output of the transmitter is internally routed to the input of the receiver. This means that if you write out a character to the THR, you should see the same character appear in there RBR immediately after.

While Loopback mode sounds like a useful thing to have in the UART, in practice it has one small flaw. As soon as the part is placed into Loopback mode, the four output bits, OUT1, OUT2, RTS, and DTR, are all disconnected from the UART output pins and instead are routed back internally to connect to the four modem inputs. The modem control outputs are dropped to logic 0 states for the duration of the output tests. Because of this, the low OUT2 pin on the UART disables any PC interrupts from taking place. If you want to test the UART in Loopback mode, you will need to write code that uses polled-mode input.

The MCR is another read/write register. This is convenient for programmers, since they can determine the actual state of the output lines at any time. Additionally, they can easily modify the state of a single output line by reading in the MCR, changing the state of a single bit, then writing the contents back out.

**Line Status Register**

The Line Status Register (LSR) is a read-only register that has seven bits of information regarding the state of the RS-232 data transmission. Figure 3-4 shows the value of the actual bits in question. Four of the bits in the LSR are used to flag incoming data errors or conditions. The other three bits give the status of the transmit and receive buffers.

| 7 | 6 | 5 | 4 | 3 | 2 | 1 | 0 |
|---|---|---|---|---|---|---|---|
| Not Used | Transmitter Empty | Transmit Holding Register Empty | Break Detected | Framing Error | Parity Error | Overrun Error | Data Ready |

**Figure 3-4. The Line Status Register.**

The four error status bits are used to signal events, not conditions. As such, they will be cleared as soon as they are read. This means that if the programmer wants to keep track of these error conditions, it is critical that the four error bits be recorded *every* time the LSR is read in. For example, the LSR may be polled in the interrupt service routine to determine if the Transmitter is ready to accept a new byte. If the LSR is read in during the polling, the contents of the four error bits will then be cleared. Accordingly, the status of those four bits needs to be updated after the LSR is read.

# THE PC8250 CLASS

The definition and use of the seven bits in the LSR is shown below.

Data Ready: This bit is used to indicate that a new byte has been read in from the RS-232 line, and is ready to read out of the Receiver Buffer Register. Once the character is read in, Data Ready is cleared.

Overrun Error: A Hardware Overrun Error occurs when a new byte is read in from the RS-232 line before the last one was read out. This bit is set to indicate that at least one character was lost.

Parity Error: If an incoming character does not have a parity setting that the UART is expecting, this bit is set.

Framing Error: If an incoming character doesn't have a valid stop bit, the Framing Error bit is set. This condition usually indicates either a noisy line or mismatched baud rates between the sender and the receiver.

Break Detect: A break consists of an incoming RS-232 line in the logical "0" state for at least one entire character time, including start and stop bits. Most breaks will actually remain in the logic 0 state for much longer, but one character time is the minimum.

Transmit Holding
Register Empty: When the Transmit Holding Register is empty, it means the UART is ready for the CPU to load another character for transmission. If the Transmit Holding Register is loaded before the Transmitter itself becomes empty, transmission will continue with no gap between the characters except the stop and start bits. This allows for maximum use of the RS-232 bandwidth.

Transmitter Empty: This bit is used to signal that the transmitter is empty. Probably the most important time this bit is used is when closing a port. If a programmer wants to be sure that every byte that is supposed to be sent has actually gone out on the line, this bit must be polled.

### Modem Status Register

The Modem Status Register (MSR) has two matched sets of four bits each. The first set of bits indicates the current *states* of the four incoming modem control lines. The next set of four bits record *events*, namely a change in any one of the four lines. Just like in the Line Status Register, the status bits will always reflect the current state of the incoming line, but the event bits will be cleared once they are read in for the first time.

| 7 | 6 | 5 | 4 | 3 | 2 | 1 | 0 |
|---|---|---|---|---|---|---|---|
| Carrier Detect | Ring Indicator | Data Ready Set | Clear to Send | Change in CD | Change in RI | Change in DSR | Change in CTS |

**Figure 3-5. The Modem Status Register.**

In our implementation of the 8250 driver, any time one of the four modem status lines changes state, an interrupt will be generated. In the interrupt service routine, we read in the MSR, and check to see which bits have changed by looking at bits 0 through 3. In our implementation, the two bits that matter are the DSR and CTS bits. Event flags in either of these bits can trigger either a stop or start of transmitter interrupts, if hardware handshaking is turned on.

## 8250 Look-alikes

Most of the UARTs found in the PC family today are compatible with the 8250 family. However, there are a couple of exceptions that are worth noting, and one that will receive some additional support from the device interface developed here.

## THE PC8250 CLASS

For many years, Intel has been making a chip labeled the 82510. The 82510 powers up in a default state with a fully compatible 8250 register set. However, the 82510 has additional register banks that can be accessed by writing a control word to register offset 2. On the 8250, register offset 2 is the IIR register, which is a read-only register. Since no standard communications software is going to be writing to register 2, this is a good choice for adding normally hidden features.

By selecting alternate register banks with this hidden register, the 82510 can have many useful features turned on. The feature list includes valuable items such as hardware handshaking, synchronous operation, input FIFO buffering, and higher baud rates.

Unfortunately, there really aren't enough 82510s installed in desktop machines to justify writing code to support them, unless a special requirement justifies it. Intel has kept the price of these parts fairly high in relationship to the 8250 family, and there haven't been too many design wins for the 82510. Not surprisingly, you will find these parts on the Intel line of Above Board EMS cards and on Intel-made PC motherboards. Other than that, they don't show up too often anywhere else.

An 8250 variant that is showing up in quite a few places is the 16550. The 16550, like the 82510, is compatible with the 8250 at the register level. All those IBM PC applications that write directly to the 8250 chips will work properly with the 16550. And, like the 82510, the 16550 has additional features that can be accessed via a hidden register. The 16550 has the added feature of a 16-byte FIFO (first in, first out) buffer on both the transmit and receive sides. The FIFOs are enabled and controlled by way of the FIFO Control Register (FCR). The FCR is a write-only register located at offset 2, which is shared by the read-only IIR.

The 16550 is electrically compatible with the 8250 as well. The 16550 UART can be plugged into an existing 8250 socket, and it will work without code changes. This not only enables end users to replace their 16450 (the faster twin of the 8250) and 8250 UARTs with a better performing one, but also gives manufacturers of PCs and interface boards the capability to upgrade their designs by simply replacing one part. The 16550 is now becoming standard equipment on high-speed machines designed for multitasking.

| 7 | 6 | 5 | 4 | 3 | 2 | 1 | 0 |
|---|---|---|---|---|---|---|---|
| RX Trigger Interrupt Level | | Unused | Unused | DMA Mode | TX FIFO Reset | RX FIFO Reset | FIFO Enable |

**Figure 3-6. The 16550 FIFO Control Register.**

Figure 3-6 shows the bit settings in the 16550 FIFO Control Register. To use the Transmit and Receive FIFOs, the FIFO Enable bit in position 0 needs to be set. Once this bit is set, the input and output buffers on the UART are no longer just double buffered; instead they have a 16-byte buffer.

The 16-byte FIFO on the receive side cures a major problem for many PC users. When the serial port is operating at relatively high speeds, say 19200 bps or greater, users will frequently find that they are getting large numbers of hardware overrun errors. Many activities on a PC can disable interrupts for significant periods of time. Chief among them is the processor switching back and forth between protected mode and real mode, as it does constantly under MS-Windows.

The 16-byte RX FIFO can be set up to generate an interrupt when it has only a single character in it. When it has just one character buffered up, the part can then generate an interrupt and know that it has 15 more character times left before the processor has to respond. This will nearly always cure the problem of hardware overruns.

The interrupt trigger level is set by bits 7 and 6, the RX Trigger Level bits. These two bits have four possible settings, which determine how full the FIFO has to be before generating an interrupt: When a system is having problems with hardware overruns, the earliest possible setting can be used, giving the maximum time allowance for interrupts to be disabled before an error occurs.

**Table 3-6. The Trigger Level Bits in the 16550 FIFO Control Register**

| Bit Setting | Trigger Level |
|---|---|
| 0 | 1 Character in the FIFO |
| 1 | 4 Characters in the FIFO |
| 2 | 8 Characters in the FIFO |
| 3 | 14 Characters in the FIFO |

If a system isn't plagued with hardware overruns, the maximum setting can be selected, which will not generate an interrupt until the FIFO is nearly full. This drastically reduces the number of interrupts on a busy system, which results in more efficient operation.

If characters are not streaming in continuously, the 16550 won't continue waiting indefinitely before generating an interrupt. Regardless of the FIFO count, if no new characters come in for three character times, the 16550 will generate an interrupt if any characters are waiting in the FIFO.

The transmit FIFO is a little less complicated. It generates an interrupt only when empty. When the transmit holding register empty interrupt occurs, the ISR can simply stuff 16 characters into the transmitter, whereas on a normal 8250 it can only send one.

The two reset bits in the FCR are used when initializing. They simply take care of properly resetting the transmit and receive FIFOs.

The DMA bit in the FCR is used to control DMA transfers on the part of the UART. Unfortunately, to take advantage of this part of the UART's feature set, you must modify the COM card, and the hardware required is not readily available.

Detecting the presence of a 16550 is relatively simple. During the initialization phase of the UART, the FIFOs can be enabled by writing the correct control word to the FCR. The 16550 has an additional two bits in the bit positions 6 and 7 of the Interrupt ID Register. If the FIFOs are properly enabled, both of these bits will be set, and the program can begin using both the transmit and receive FIFOs.

If both bits aren't set, a word with all zeros should immediately be written out to the FCR. Two problems can arise if the programmer doesn't do this. First, some early versions of the 16550 had bugs that prevented the FIFOs from working properly. These versions of the part only had one of the two bits set. Since the FIFOs won't work on these parts, they need to be disabled. Second, if the part is actually an Intel 82510, writing out the FIFO setup byte to the FCR will perform a bank select operation, rendering the 82510 essentially unusable. Writing a 0 back to the FCR will reset the 82510 to 8250 compatibility mode.

## 8250 Oddities

Just reading the data sheet for the 8250 parts can give a programmer a false sense of security. Writing programs that conform strictly to the specifications of the part has often led to nonfunctional code. You should know about a few bugs and operational problems with the 8250 family.

### Interrupt pulsing

One 8250 bug was particularly useful to IBM PC programmers. The designers of the first IBM PC hardware and BIOS elected to operate the 8259 interrupt controller in edge-triggered mode, instead of using the more conventional level triggering. This means that to generate a new interrupt, a device has to actually take the interrupt line from a logic 0 to a logic 1. Once an interrupt has been serviced, the device in question has to lower its interrupt line and raise it again to get more service.

In theory, the 8250 should keep its interrupt line asserted as long as interrupts are pending. This could cause trouble. If a programmer finished servicing interrupts on an 8250 and exited the ISR at the same time another incoming character arrived, the 8259 interrupt controller might not recognize that another interrupt occurred. In practice, however, the initial 8250 design pulsed the interrupt line low after each interrupt condition was cleared. Because of this, the hardware worked properly with an edge-triggered interrupt controller. This bug is now considered a feature and is required for proper operation with most communications software.

### Jump starting interrupts

Another "feature" of the early 8250 family UARTs gave programmers an easy way to jump start transmit interrupts. As specified, an 8250 should only generate a TX interrupt when the THR goes empty. This register goes empty when a character is moved into the Transmit Register and starts being shifted out to the RS-232 data line.

In practice, however, programmers found that just enabling TX interrupts when the THR was empty was enough to generate a TX interrupt. Programmers could take a convenient shortcut when sending the very first character out the UART. All a programmer had to do was load the character into the buffer used by the ISR, then

# THE PC8250 CLASS

enable TX interrupts. At that point, an interrupt would automatically be generated, and the ISR could take care of the details of transmitting the character.

Unfortunately, some later versions of the 8250 family fixed this bug, so that TX interrupts only occurred when they should. This had the unexpected effect of suddenly causing lots of working application software to break, much to the consternation of the owners of new brand-name computers. Since many of these chips are still in circulation, communications programmers have had to adjust.

The solution to this problem is actually quite simple and should be a standard part of every programmers communications software. If TX interrupts aren't presently running, and a character needs to be transmitted, the programmer needs to manually write the first character out to the THR as if in polled mode operation, and *then* enable TX interrupts. The first character will "prime the pump" by generating an interrupt when it is shifted to the transmitter. After that, interrupts will run in the traditional manner, with a new one following the transmission of each character.

### Extra modem status interrupts

One annoying bug found both in original National Semiconductor chips as well as some clone chips is the false modem status interrupt. The IIR can report a modem status interrupt when none has occurred. This could easily lead to trouble with the ISR code.

The best solution to the false modem status interrupt is to always check the "changed" bits in the MSR when servicing this interrupt. By checking these bits, the ISR will take action only on a particular modem status line if a change in state has actually occurred on that line.

### Motherboard timing

When IBM first introduced the AT, they published a Technical Reference Manual that included a complete listing of the BIOS for this machine. If you look at the INT 14H service routines that access the COM ports for the AT, you probably noticed some sequences of 8086 assembly language that looked like this:

```
LOOP:       IN      AL,DX
            JMP     $+2
            JNZ     LOOP
```

The exact purpose of the "`JMP $+2`" code wasn't spelled out clearly at all in the code listings, so the reader had to dig in the Technical Reference Manual. Eventually, if you looked hard enough, you would find a statement from IBM to the effect that the I/O Bus had some timing problems. If the 8086 processor executed back-to-back I/O instructions, bus timing could cause a read or write error. Thus, the inserted delays.

The use of the "`JMP $+2`" instruction had a few further implications. Any one of the jump instructions on this processor would flush the instruction prefetch queue on the processor, resulting in an inordinately long delay. Apparently, IBM did not feel that a simple `NOP` instruction would use up enough cycles for everything to work properly.

Communications programmers everywhere have taken the hint, and all of our programs are now liberally salted with "`JMP $+2`" sequences. However, some nagging doubts remain. For example, as future generations of processors run faster, will the current sequences ever become too short? Will future processors find ways of maintaining a valid prefetch queue even through `JMP` instructions? The answers to these questions appear to be somewhat murky.

## The Standard COM Card

The standard IBM-compatible communications card has few surprises. The original card developed by IBM was an exercise in minimalism, offering as little supporting functionality as possible in order to let the 8250 do its job. The card supported the standard RS-232 input and output lines, an 8-bit interface between the AT I/O bus and the UART registers, and added support for an interrupt line.

For various reasons (discussed in Chapter 1), the IBM COM card design has not changed for 10 years or so. The COM card in most systems sold today is electrically identical to the one used in 1982. The only real improvements have been in reduced manufacturing costs.

### Laptop oddities

Makers of notebook and laptop computers have had major difficulties with the standard COM card. For the designers of these machines, the sun rises and sets around power consumption. Because of this, most of the parts used in portable computers are of the CMOS variety, known for very low power consumption. However, early designers of portable computers did not have CMOS versions of 8250-

## THE PC8250 CLASS

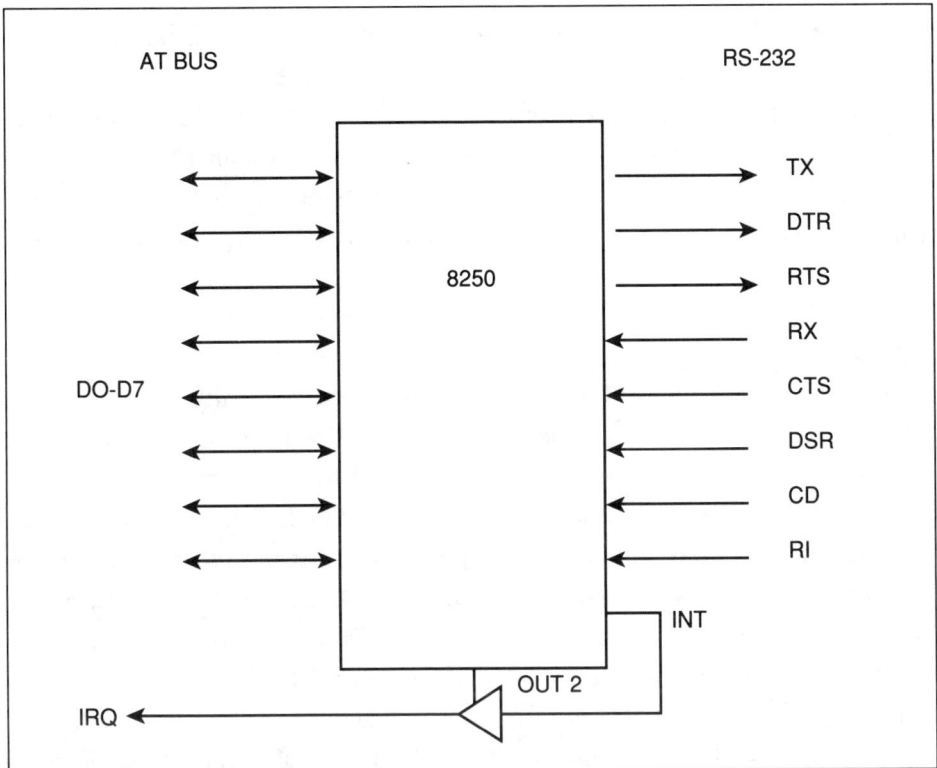

**Figure 3-7. The IBM COM card.**

compatible UARTS available. Some portable machine designers, such as those at Data General, were brave enough to use nonstandard UARTs. Needless to say, these machines are no longer being manufactured.

The next best alternative was to include circuitry that kept the COM card in a powered-down state most of the time, only turning on power to the UART when given special commands. All users had to do to use their existing communications software was to issue a special MS-DOS MODE command before starting the program. This compromise seems to have been effective.

Today, laptop designers do have CMOS versions of 8250-compatible UARTs available, but they seem to be leaving the power management features in place on their COM ports. This is probably because driving the RS-232 line still consumes more power than they feel comfortable with, even after power consumption of the chips in the COM interface has been minimized.

To the COM programmer, this presents something of a dilemma. No standard commands exist to universally power up and turn off these laptop COM cards. This means users have to be savvy enough to encapsulate their COM programs with batch files or other software that manages the power. Unfortunately, for most laptop users this is out of the question. So COM software frequently runs into difficulties on laptops. Until more standardization arrives, the situation probably will not change.

- **Upgrading to a 16550**

One of the best things PC users can do to upgrade the quality of com-munications on their systems is to upgrade to a 16550 UART on their COM cards. As both operating system software and communications hardware become more powerful, the 8250 UART stands in the way as a bottleneck to high-speed communications.

Inexpensive clones are usually shipped with inexpensive clone I/O cards and, as a rule, these will be equipped with 8250 class chips. There are a couple of different approaches to upgrading the UARTs in these systems. The inexpensive approach is to buy a 16550 UART and replace the 8250 UART(s) on the I/O card. This is a quick, easy solution and should cost less than $20.

Replacing the UART is only possible if it is first of all a pin-compatible 8250 clone and is not soldered in place. This is usually simple enough to check. Most I/O cards will have two identical 40 pin IC positions. If the card is only populated with one 40-pin part and the other position has an empty socket, you have located an 8250-compatible UART. You should be able to tell quickly if the 40-pin part(s) are soldered in place or just pushed into sockets. If they are socketed, you are in luck and can replace them with 16550s.

If instead of a 40-pin part, you have a square package with 80 or so narrowly spaced pins, you have purchased a card that has a slightly less expensive electronic equivalent of the 8250, or possibly two 8250s. While this is good for the manufacturer, as the price is lower, it is bad for you because you can't replace the UART chip.

If you can't replace just the chip, you will need to purchase a 16550-equipped COM card. Fortunately, you have several choices, and while the cost is more than a standard COM card, it shouldn't ruin your budget. The added performance will offset the pain in your wallet. See the Sources appendix at the end of this book for information on pricing and availability.

### The Hayes ESP card

If you want to move a step higher on the communications ladder, a board such as the Hayes ESP card might be right for you. This board is compatible with standard COM cards, and comes already equipped with 16550 UARTs on board. This is good news because you will not only be compatible with existing communications software, but you can use any software that takes advantage of the 16550 FIFO buffers.

However, the Hayes ESP goes a step further in sophistication. In addition to the 16-byte FIFOs on the 16550 UARTs, the ESP card comes equipped with up to 1K of RAM per port of on-board buffering, along with hardware and software handshaking controlled by an 8051 class microcontroller. In addition, the ESP is capable of performing DMA transfers of data to and from the on-board buffers. You now have a board that can move massive amounts of data with minimal processor overhead.

The only drawback to the ESP card is a noticeable lack of support. Hayes neglected to ship an MS-DOS driver with the card so any software vendors that wanted to support the card would need to write low-level driver software to take advantage of the advanced features. So far, this does not seem to be happening. Armed with the techniques in this book, you could conceivably tackle this job yourself, and perhaps help Hayes bootstrap their way into a more viable market position.

## How Interrupts Work on the PC

Probably the single greatest fear that keeps people from working with PC communications software is that of interrupts. Writing an ISR takes a programmer a step deeper than normal applications programming. An ISR has to work directly with hardware in an environment very unforgiving of mistakes.

Despite these obstacles, *every* PC programmer can write and use a simple ISR to service 8250 UARTs. The ISR developed in the last half of this chapter will be somewhat more complex than the ISR you would write the first time around, but it is still relatively straightforward. And while any programmer can make mistakes, virtually nothing can go wrong in this ISR that can't be fixed by judicious application of the front panel reset switch. As long as you save your source frequently, you have nothing to fear from working with an ISR.

## Hardware basics

Like most microprocessors, the Intel 80x86 family has built-in support for interrupts. If you look at the hardware data sheet for the 8088 (the IBM world's first brush with Intel), you will see a pair of pins labeled INTR and INTA. These two pins are more properly referred to as "Interrupt Request" and "Interrupt Acknowledge." With the proper hardware in place, these two pins allow an external piece of hardware to interrupt the processor and so to save its current state and go off to manage some time-critical task.

However, most computers must manage more than a single source of interrupts. The IBM PC family started with support for eight external interrupt sources and expanded that number to sixteen with the introduction of the AT. Even before adding any external peripherals, many of these interrupt sources are taken up by standard equipment: the timer tick, keyboard interrupt, floppy and hard disk controller, etc.

The addition of a part known as the 8259 Programmable Interrupt Controller (PIC) lends support to these various interrupt sources. This part accepts up to eight external interrupt sources and manages them so that the 80x86 CPU doesn't have to. The 8259 takes care of prioritizing external interrupts and presenting them to the processor in an orderly fashion. The 8259 won't let lower priority interrupts interfere with higher priority ones, and it won't let an interrupt interrupt itself.

The 8259 was developed well before the 8088 began its quest to take over the world. It supports several different modes of operation, designed to support different families of CPUs. The original designers of the hardware and BIOS for the IBM PC had to choose from several possible implementations of interrupts on their machines. Unfortunately for all of us, they elected to use edge-triggered interrupts.

Edge-triggered interrupts differ from conventional level-triggered interrupts in precisely the way their names imply. On the IBM PC, the 8259 operates in edge-triggered mode. This means that the PIC will only consider an interrupt to be valid when the interrupt line makes the transition from a logic 0 to a logic 1. In level-triggered mode, the 8259 is considered to have a valid interrupt any time the interrupt line is asserted.

I find the choice of edge-triggered interrupts less than desirable, because it essentially mandates against the use of shared interrupt lines on the standard PC architecture. There is a relatively simple solution for the electrical problem of having multiple cards all driving the same line. Using an "open collector" configuration,

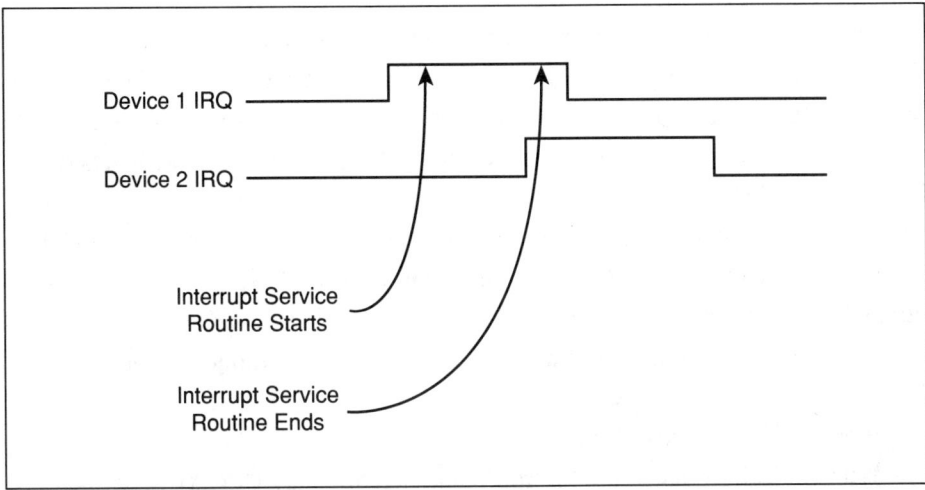

**Figure 3-8. Why Interrupt Sharing won't work.**

any number of cards can drive the same interrupt line. In this configuration, sometimes referred to as a "wired OR," *any* card that tries to assert the interrupt line will bring it high. The cards that are not driving the line high will not try to pull the interrupt line low.

In the open collector scheme, the interrupt controller would simply generate an interrupt any time the interrupt line was active. One card might be trying to interrupt the CPU or five cards might. The BIOS and the interrupt servers must check every device attached to the line for service requirements.

In edge-triggered mode, the wired-OR configuration simply won't work. Figure 3-8 gives a graphical description of the problem. Imagine that two devices were connected to the same IRQ line on the PC bus, using an open collector configuration. If the first device initiated an interrupt, it would raise its interrupt line, and the CPU would initiate the interrupt service routine. So far things would be working properly.

During the course of servicing the first device, the second device might try to initiate another interrupt. Unfortunately, the interrupt line is already high, so when the second device raises the line, it just remains high. Since the 8259 on the PC requires a transition from low to high in order to generate an interrupt, nothing happens.

Of course, on the PC, we never come this close to sharing interrupts anyway. Peripheral cards designed for the PC don't use open collector drivers, they use standard TTL outputs to drive the bus. Because of this, if two devices were trying to use the same line as in Figure 3-9, they would clash, and the voltage levels on the bus would probably be invalid, leading to unpredictable results.

This most affects communications programmers when working with COM1 and COM3 or COM2 and COM4 simultaneously. The only way to get this to work on the PC is to operate one of the ports in polled mode. It just can't be done properly with both cards in interrupt mode, despite occasional reports to the contrary.

### Enter MicroChannel architecture

When IBM introduced the Micro Channel architecture (MCA), they reworked the interrupt system so that the 8259 responded to level-triggered interrupts instead of edge-triggered ones. The PS/2 systems will support up to eight COM ports on the system board, with COM2 through COM8 all sharing IRQ3.

On Micro Channel machines, the BIOS developers created a simple system for sharing interrupt lines. As each new device enables an interrupt service routine for a device on the MCA bus, it simply adds itself to the chain of devices present on that IRQ. When an interrupt occurs, each device checks to see if it has an active interrupt, then passes control to the next device in the chain. This system lets you share interrupts even among disparate cards.

## PC8250 Driver Structure

The remainder of this chapter discusses the implementation of the PC8250 class. PC8250 is a class derived from RS232 and is designed to work with various types of hardware that use this UART. In this chapter, the PC8250 class will interface with standard IBM COM cards. In the next chapter, we will use the same class to interface with non-intelligent multiport boards.

### The interrupt service routine

A fairly sizable body of code makes up the PC8250 class. It is a fully featured class derived from RS232 so it supports quite a few virtual functions. However, to really understand this class, you must understand the ISR.

As I stated earlier in this chapter, the 8250 class of UARTs has four different

# THE PC8250 CLASS

interrupts. This particular class will be using all four types of interrupts: the Transmit Holding Register Empty interrupt, the Receive Data interrupt, the Modem Status interrupt, and the Line Status Interrupt.

The ISR is essentially four tightly packed subroutines, each handling its own interrupt. These routines will need to run and terminate in the shortest possible time, so as not to tie up the system with a lot of interrupt overhead. Most of the work done during the interrupt service routine consists of modifying elements in a data structure that is a subset of the `PC8250` class.

Listing 3-1 shows the header file that contains the definitions for the `PC8250` class. To understand how this class operates, you must understand the `struct isr_data` definition. This conventional C structure contains the information used by the interrupt service routine when processing an interrupt for a given port. Once you understand how the interrupt service routine manipulates the data in that structure, you will be able to follow the rest of the support code for this particular class.

```
// ******************** START OF PC8250.H ********************

// This header file has all of the definitions and prototypes
// needed to use the PC8250 class.  This file should be included
// by any code that needs to access this class.

#ifndef _PC8250_DOT_H
#define _PC8250_DOT_H

#include "rs232.h"
#include "queue.h"
#include "pcirq.h"
#include "_8250.h"

// A few type definitions used with this class.

enum PC8250Error {
        PC8250_UART_NOT_FOUND           = RS232_NEXT_FREE_ERROR,
        PC8250_NEXT_FREE_ERROR,
        PC8250_HANDSHAKE_LINE_IN_USE = RS232_NEXT_FREE_WARNING,
        PC8250_NEXT_FREE_WARNING };
```

# SERIAL COMMUNICATIONS: A C++ DEVELOPER'S GUIDE

```cpp
enum UARTType { UART_8250, UART_16550, UART_UNKNOWN };

enum handshaking_bits {  dtr_dsr = 1, rts_cts = 2, xon_xoff = 4 };

class PC8250;

// The ISR data is contained in a conventional C structure instead
// of a class.  The ISR is much easier to work with as a normal C
// function instead of a member function, and as such it wants to
// work with structures instead of classes.

struct isr_data_block {
    int uart;
    UARTType uart_type;
    volatile int overflow;
    volatile int tx_running;
    volatile unsigned int rx_int_count;
    volatile unsigned int tx_int_count;
    volatile unsigned int ms_int_count;
    volatile unsigned int ls_int_count;
    volatile unsigned int line_status;
    unsigned int handshaking;
    volatile unsigned int blocking;
    volatile unsigned int blocked;
    volatile int send_handshake_char;
    volatile unsigned int modem_status;
    Queue TXQueue;
    Queue RXQueue;
};

// The Handler class is used when multiple ports share an
// interrupt, such as on a multiport board or a Microchannel bus.

class Handler {
    public :
        virtual RS232Error AddPort( RS232PortName port_name,
                                    struct isr_data_block *data )
                                                            = 0;
```

# THE PC8250 CLASS

```cpp
        virtual void DeletePort( RS232PortName port_name ) = 0;
};

class PC8250 : public RS232
{
    private :
        struct isr_data_block *isr_data;
        enum irq_name irq;
        int interrupt_number;
        int first_debug_output_line;
        int fifo_setting;
        Handler *interrupt_handler;

        void check_uart( void );
        void read_settings( void );
        RS232Error write_settings( void );
        void set_uart_address_and_irq( Handler *handler,
                                       int uart_address,
                                       irq_name irq_line );
        virtual int read_buffer( char *buffer,
                                 unsigned int count );
        virtual int write_buffer( char *buffer,
                                  unsigned int count = -1 );
        virtual int read_byte( void );
        virtual int write_byte( int c );
        void check_rx_handshaking( void );

    public :
        PC8250( enum RS232PortName port_name,
                long baud_rate = UNCHANGED,
                char parity = UNCHANGED,
                int word_length = UNCHANGED,
                int stop_bits = UNCHANGED,
                int dtr = SET,
                int rts = SET,
                int xon_xoff = DISABLE,
                int rts_cts = DISABLE,
                int dtr_dsr = DISABLE,
                Handler *handler = 0,
```

```
                    int uart_address = 0,
                    irq_name irq_line = ILLEGAL_IRQ );
        virtual ~PC8250( void );
        virtual RS232Error Set( long baud_rate = UNCHANGED,
                                int parity = UNCHANGED,
                                int word_length = UNCHANGED,
                                int stop_bits = UNCHANGED );
        virtual int TXSpaceFree( void );
        virtual int RXSpaceUsed( void );
        virtual int Break( long milliseconds = 300 );
        virtual int Cd( void );
        virtual int Ri( void );
        virtual int Cts( void );
        virtual int Dsr( void );
        virtual int ParityError( int clear = UNCHANGED );
        virtual int BreakDetect( int clear = UNCHANGED );
        virtual int FramingError( int clear = UNCHANGED );
        virtual int HardwareOverrunError( int clear = UNCHANGED );
        virtual int SoftwareOverrunError( int clear = UNCHANGED );
        virtual int XonXoffHandshaking( int setting = UNCHANGED );
        virtual int RtsCtsHandshaking( int setting = UNCHANGED );
        virtual int DtrDsrHandshaking( int setting = UNCHANGED );
        virtual int Dtr( int setting = UNCHANGED );
        virtual int Rts( int setting = UNCHANGED );
        virtual int PeekBuffer( void *buffer, unsigned int count );
        virtual int RXSpaceFree( void );
        virtual int TXSpaceUsed( void );
        virtual int FlushRXBuffer( void );
        virtual int FlushTXBuffer( void );
        virtual char * ErrorName( int error );
        virtual int FormatDebugOutput( char *buffer = 0,
                                       int line_number = -1 );
};

#endif // #ifndef _PC8250_DOT_H

// ********************** END OF PC8250.H **********************
```

**Listing 3-1. PC8250.H**

## THE PC8250 CLASS

It may seem odd that I have gone to all the trouble of creating a `PC8250` class and I then packed all the ISR data into its own structure. However, I have good reasons for doing so. To have access to all of the protected elements of the `PC8250` class, a function needs to be a member function of class `PC8250`, or a member function of a friend class. With our current implementations of C++, it just isn't easy to have an interrupt service routine operate as member function, since it doesn't have access to the `this` pointer. An even more important concern is that of interfacing to assembly language. One of the natural steps in the refinement of an interrupt service routine is rewriting it in assembly language for speed. By keeping all the data the ISR needs to access in a conventional C structure, it becomes much easier to write assembly language code to access it.

### The isr_data Structure

The `isr_data` structure has 17 data members, which completely define the state of the UART as far as the ISR is concerned. A list of these member definitions follows.

`uart:` — This is the address of the 8250 family UART. The ISR and other class member functions need this address to access the UART.

`uart_type:` — The UART can either be an 8250 or 16550 family. The ISR needs to know what type the UART is so it can try to use the receive FIFO if it is available.

`overflow:` — This flag is set if a software overflow of the RX buffer occurs.

`tx_running:` — This flag is set when a character is loaded into the Transmitter. It lets the ISR know that it can expect a TX interrupt to occur in the future. Once the last character has been transmitted, no more TX interrupts will occur, and this flag is cleared.

`rx_int_count:` — This counter keeps track of how many RX interrupts have occurred. This is useful for debugging.

`tx_int_count:` A count of how many TX interrupts have occurred.

`ms_int_count:` A count of how many modem status interrupts have occurred.

`ls_int_count:` A count of line status interrupts.

`line_status:` Every time a line status interrupt occurs, the status bits are ORed into this word. It can be checked at any time for a cumulative look at the line status bits.

`handshaking:` This word has three bits that can be set for the three different types of handshaking. The bits are defined in `enum handshaking_bits`. They are packed into a word like this so they can be tested as a group to see if any form of handshaking is in effect.

`blocking:` This word uses the same bits as the `handshaking` data member to indicate when a particular form of handshaking has been invoked to stop transmission from the remote end.

`blocked:` This word uses the same bits as the `handshaking` data member to indicate when a handshake signal has been received from the remote end blocking us from transmitting.

`send_handshake_char:` When an XON or XOFF character needs to be sent, the traditional approach is to either wait for the 8250 to be ready to accept another character, or to stuff the XON or XOFF at the head of the queue. Both of these approaches have problems, so instead the PC8250 class has a special flag word used to indicate when an XON or XOFF needs to be sent. The

## THE PC8250 CLASS

word is set to -1 when no special protocol characters need to be set, and to the protocol character when one is ready to be transmitted. The TX interrupt handler looks at this word first so as to transmit the handshake character ahead of any active data in the TX buffer.

`modem_status:` Every time a modem status interrupt occurs, the modem status data is read into this word. When one of the member functions needs to know the state of the modem status word, it can just check this data member.

`TXQueue:` This `QUEUE` object contains all of the characters queued up for transmission.

`RXQueue:` This `QUEUE` object contains all of the characters that have been received but not yet read in by the application program.

Note that we do use C++ objects in the ISR to manipulate the TX and RX Queues. Even though the ISR can't be a member function, it has no problem manipulating C++ objects, and this is an example of it. Since most of the member functions for the `QUEUE` class are defined as inline functions, we should see a good improvement in performance by using C++ instead of C for the ISR.

Most of the data in the `isr_data` is labeled with the C keyword `volatile`. This lets the compiler know that those values may be modified by another process, so the compiler can be careful not to count on data being constant. This prevents the compiler from performing certain optimizations that could cause this code not to work.

The remainder of the data members of class `PC8250` are defined in the `PC8250` class, and are not accessed by the ISR. None of them is publicly accessible, so they can only be manipulated by members of class `PC8250`. They are defined on the next page.

`isr_data:` — This is a pointer to the `isr_data` structure discussed previously. Each `PC8250` objects has a single `isr_data` structure allocated for it, and keeps a pointer to the data here.

`irq:` — The IRQ line the port is attached to.

`interrupt_number:` — The actual interrupt number used on the PC by the IRQ line.

`first_debug_output_line:` — The first line of debug output that is output by the member function of class `PC8250`. All of the lines smaller than this one will be passed up to class `RS232` for definition.

`fifo_setting:` — The trigger level used for the UART if it was a 16550. The default is 14, but heavily loaded systems may want to lower the number.

`handler:` — 8250 UARTs that are sharing an interrupt, such as those on a multiport board, will have a command interrupt handler that dispatches the handlers for individual UARTs. This pointer points to the handler this UART belongs to. If it is a standalone UART that isn't sharing interrupts with any other device, this will be NULL.

Listing 3-2 is a listing of the ISR, found in file `ISR_8250.CPP`. The main entry point for the ISR is near the top of the file, at function `isr_8250()`. This function takes a single argument, which is a pointer to the data structure defined in the PC8250 class header file. Note that the ISR is called by an ISR manager found in file `PCIRQ.CPP`, which will be discussed later in this chapter.

By itself, `isr_8250()` is a very simple function. All it does is sit in a loop, reading the Interrupt ID Register from the UART. As long as a valid interrupt ID is read out of the register, it is processed by one of the four handlers. When the loop finally processes all of the interrupts, the 8250 should drop its interrupt request line, which means the PC's 8259 interrupt controller will recognize the next interrupt as a new one.

One comment in the source code that deserves some attention relates to stack overflow checking. Most C compilers have an option that allows the compiler to generate code at the entry of every routine to check for stack overflow. This works well for the most part, and prevents many problems, but it most emphatically won't work for code inside an ISR. The stack being used while in the ISR is different from what the compiler expects, and this will cause the overflow checking code to get confused. If the error checking causes the program to abort while in the middle of an interrupt, the results are usually catastrophic.

Microsoft is one of the few compilers that turns on stack checking by default, but fortunately, we can turn off Microsoft's stack checking with the application of a pragma. Borland and Zortech only turn on stack checking if the default compiler settings are overridden, so there is less danger of this happening for them. However, neither one of these other compilers provides a pragma to disable it should it inadvertently be enabled. This means you need to check your make files, project files, and command-line options carefully.

## The ISR Code

Listingss 3-2 through 3-5 are the source listings for files `ISR_8250.CPP`, `_PC8250.H`, `_8250.H`, and `ASCII.H`, respectively. The first file contains all the source code used in the interrupt service routine for the `PC8250` class. The second header file, `_PC8250.H`, is a private header file used by both the main body of the `PC8250` class and the `ISR`. `_8250.H` contains a set of constants that define all of the registers and bit masks used when communicating with an 8250 class UART. These are stored in a separate file because they are used by many of the other classes developed in this book. Finally, `ASCII.H` contains the definitions for many commonly used ASCII characters. The ISR needs these for the definitions of XON and XOFF, used with software handshaking.

# SERIAL COMMUNICATIONS: A C++ DEVELOPER'S GUIDE

```cpp
// ******************* START OF ISR_8250.CPP *******************
//
// All of the code used in the 8250 interrupt service
// routine is found in this file.  The Queue class inline
// functions are pulled in from QUEUE.H

// Microsoft has a pragma that lets us disable stack
// checking in the ISR, which is absolutely a must.  Using
// the pragma here helps to prevent bad side effects that
// result from bad command line or PWB option settings.

#include <dos.h>
#include "pc8250.h"
#include "_pc8250.h"
#include "ascii.h"

// Prototypes for the internal handlers called by the ISR.

void handle_modem_status_interrupt( struct isr_data_block *data );
void handle_tx_interrupt( struct isr_data_block *data );
void handle_rx_interrupt( struct isr_data_block *data );

// This is the main body of the 8250 interrupt handler.  It
// sits in a loop, repeatedly reading the Interrupt ID Register,
// and dispatching a handler based on the
// interrupt type.  The line status interrupt is so simple
// that it doesn't merit its own handler.

void isr_8250( struct isr_data_block * data )
{
    STI();
    for ( ; ; ) {
        switch( INPUT( data->uart + INTERRUPT_ID_REGISTER ) & 7 ) {
            case IIR_MODEM_STATUS_INTERRUPT :
                handle_modem_status_interrupt( data );
                break;
            case IIR_TX_HOLDING_REGISTER_INTERRUPT :
                handle_tx_interrupt( data );
                break;
```

# THE PC8250 CLASS

```
            case IIR_RX_DATA_READY_INTERRUPT :
                handle_rx_interrupt( data );
                break;
            case IIR_LINE_STATUS_INTERRUPT :
                data->ls_int_count++;
                data->line_status |=
                    INPUT(data->uart + LINE_STATUS_REGISTER);
                break;
            default :
                return;
        }
    }
}

// The modem status interrupt handler has to do three
// things.  It has to handle RTS/CTS handshaking, it has
// to handle DTR/DSR handshaking, and it has to update the
// modem_status member of the isr_data structure.

void handle_modem_status_interrupt( struct isr_data_block *data )
{
    data->ms_int_count++;
        data->modem_status =
            (unsigned int)
                INPUT( data->uart + MODEM_STATUS_REGISTER );
    if ( data->handshaking & rts_cts )
        if ( data->modem_status & MSR_DELTA_CTS ) // Has CTS changed?
            if ( data->modem_status & MSR_CTS ) {
                if ( data->blocked & rts_cts ) {
                    data->blocked &= ~rts_cts;
                    jump_start( data );
                }
            } else {
                if ( !( data->blocked & rts_cts ) )
                    data->blocked |= rts_cts;
            }
    if ( data->handshaking & dtr_dsr )
        if ( data->modem_status & MSR_DELTA_DSR )
            if ( data->modem_status & MSR_DSR ) {
```

```c
                if ( data->blocked & dtr_dsr ) {
                    data->blocked &= ~dtr_dsr;
                    jump_start( data );
                }
            } else {
                if ( !( data->blocked & dtr_dsr ) )
                    data->blocked |= dtr_dsr;
            }
}

// The TX interrupt is fairly simple.  All it has to do is
// transmit the next character, if one is available.  Depending
// on whether or not a character is available, it will set or
// clear the tx_running member.  Note that here and in
// jump_start(), the handshake_char gets first shot at going
// out.  This is normally an XON or XOFF.

void handle_tx_interrupt( struct isr_data_block *data )
{
    int c;

    data->tx_int_count++;
    if ( data->send_handshake_char >= 0 ) {
        OUTPUT( data->uart + TRANSMIT_HOLDING_REGISTER,
            data->send_handshake_char );
        data->send_handshake_char = -1;
    } else if ( data->blocked ) {
        data->tx_running = 0;
    } else {
        c = data->TXQueue.Remove();
        if ( c >= 0 )
            OUTPUT( data->uart + TRANSMIT_HOLDING_REGISTER, c );
        else
            data->tx_running = 0;
    }
}

// The RX interrupt handler is divided into two nearly
// independent sections.  The first section just reads in the
```

# THE PC8250 CLASS

```
// character that has just been received and stores it in a
// buffer.  If the UART type is a 16550, up to 16 characters
// might be read in.  The next section of code handles the
// possibility that a handshaking trigger has just occurred,
// modifies any control lines or sends an XOFF as needed.

void handle_rx_interrupt( struct isr_data_block *data )
{
    int c;
    int mcr;
    int lsr;

    data->rx_int_count++;
// The receive data section
    for ( ; ; ) {
        c = INPUT( data->uart + RECEIVE_BUFFER_REGISTER );
        if ( data->handshaking & xon_xoff ) {
            if ( c == XON ) {
                data->blocked &= ~xon_xoff;
                jump_start( data );
                return;
            } else if ( c == XOFF ) {
                data->blocked |= xon_xoff;
                return;
            }
        }
        if ( !data->RXQueue.Insert( (char) c ) )
            data->overflow = 1;
        if ( data->uart_type == UART_8250 )
            break;
        lsr = INPUT( data->uart + LINE_STATUS_REGISTER );
        data->line_status |= lsr;
        if ( ( lsr & LSR_DATA_READY ) == 0 )
            break;
    }

// The handshaking section

    if ( data->handshaking ) {
```

# SERIAL COMMUNICATIONS: A C++ DEVELOPER'S GUIDE

```cpp
            if ( data->RXQueue.InUseCount() > HighWaterMark ) {
                if ( ( data->handshaking & rts_cts ) &&
                    !( data->blocking & rts_cts ) ) {
                    mcr = INPUT( data->uart + MODEM_CONTROL_REGISTER );
                    mcr &= ~MCR_RTS;
                    OUTPUT( data->uart + MODEM_CONTROL_REGISTER, mcr );
                    data->blocking |= rts_cts;
                }
                if ( ( data->handshaking & dtr_dsr ) &&
                    !( data->blocking & dtr_dsr ) ) {
                    mcr = INPUT( data->uart + MODEM_CONTROL_REGISTER );
                    mcr &= ~MCR_DTR;
                    OUTPUT( data->uart + MODEM_CONTROL_REGISTER, mcr );
                    data->blocking |= dtr_dsr;
                }
                if ( ( data->handshaking & xon_xoff ) &&
                    !( data->blocking & xon_xoff ) ) {
                    data->blocking |= xon_xoff;
                    if ( data->send_handshake_char == XON ) {
                        data->send_handshake_char = -1;
                    } else {
                        data->send_handshake_char = XOFF;
                        jump_start( data );
                    }
                }
            }
        }
    }
}


// Any time transmit interrupts need to be restarted, this
// routine is called to do the job.  It gets the interrupts
// running again by sending a single character out the TX
// register manually.  When that character is done
// transmitting, the next TX interrupt will start.  The
// tx_running member of the class keeps track of when we can
// expect another TX interrupt and when we can't.

void jump_start( struct isr_data_block *data )
```

# THE PC8250 CLASS

```
{
    int c;

// Both tx_running and blocked can change behind my back in the
// ISR, so I have to disable interrupts if I want to be able to
// count on them.

    CLI();
    if ( !data->tx_running ) {
        if ( ( c = data->send_handshake_char ) != -1 )
            data->send_handshake_char = -1;
        else if ( !data->blocked )
            c = data->TXQueue.Remove();
        if ( c >= 0 ) {
            OUTPUT( data->uart, c );
            data->tx_running = 1;
        }
    }
    STI();
}

// ******************** END OF ISR_8250.CPP ********************
```

**Listing 3-2. ISR_8250.CPP**

```
// ******************** START OF _PC8250.H ********************
//
// This header file provides prototypes for functions that are shared
// between the PC8250 class and the PC8250 ISR routines. This header
// file is only for use by the PC8250 class, not the end user of the
// class.
//

#ifndef __PC8250_DOT_H
#define __PC8250_DOT_H

void jump_start( struct isr_data_block *data );
void isr_8250( struct isr_data_block * data );
```

```
#endif  // #ifndef __PC8250_DOT_H

// ********************** END OF _PC8250.H **********************
```

**Listing 3-3. _PC8250.H**

```
// ********************** START OF _8250.H **********************

#ifndef __8250_DOT_H
#define __8250_DOT_H

//
// These are the definitions for the 8250 and 16550 UART
// registers.  They are used in both the ISR and the main
// class functions.
//

const int TRANSMIT_HOLDING_REGISTER      = 0x00;
const int RECEIVE_BUFFER_REGISTER        = 0x00;
const int INTERRUPT_ENABLE_REGISTER      = 0x01;
const int   IER_RX_DATA_READY            = 0x01;
const int   IER_TX_HOLDING_REGISTER_EMPTY = 0x02;
const int   IER_LINE_STATUS              = 0x04;
const int   IER_MODEM_STATUS             = 0x08;
const int INTERRUPT_ID_REGISTER          = 0x02;
const int   IIR_MODEM_STATUS_INTERRUPT   = 0x00;
const int   IIR_TX_HOLDING_REGISTER_INTERRUPT = 0x02;
const int   IIR_RX_DATA_READY_INTERRUPT  = 0x04;
const int   IIR_LINE_STATUS_INTERRUPT    = 0x06;
const int FIFO_CONTROL_REGISTER          = 0x02;
const int   FCR_FIFO_ENABLE              = 0x01;
const int   FCR_RCVR_FIFO_RESET          = 0x02;
const int   FCR_XMIT_FIFO_RESET          = 0x04;
const int   FCR_RCVR_TRIGGER_LSB         = 0x40;
const int   FCR_RCVR_TRIGGER_MSB         = 0x80;
const int   FCR_TRIGGER_01               = 0x00;
const int   FCR_TRIGGER_04               = 0x40;
```

## THE PC8250 CLASS

```
const int     FCR_TRIGGER_08              = 0x80;
const int     FCR_TRIGGER_14              = 0xc0;
const int   LINE_CONTROL_REGISTER         = 0x03;
const int     LCR_WORD_LENGTH_MASK        = 0x03;
const int     LCR_WORD_LENGTH_SELECT_0    = 0x01;
const int     LCR_WORD_LENGTH_SELECT_1    = 0x02;
const int     LCR_STOP_BITS               = 0x04;
const int     LCR_PARITY_MASK             = 0x38;
const int     LCR_PARITY_ENABLE           = 0x08;
const int     LCR_EVEN_PARITY_SELECT      = 0x10;
const int     LCR_STICK_PARITY            = 0x20;
const int     LCR_SET_BREAK               = 0x40;
const int     LCR_DLAB                    = 0x80;
const int   MODEM_CONTROL_REGISTER        = 0x04;
const int     MCR_DTR                     = 0x01;
const int     MCR_RTS                     = 0x02;
const int     MCR_OUT1                    = 0x04;
const int     MCR_OUT2                    = 0x08;
const int     MCR_LOOPBACK                = 0x10;
const int   LINE_STATUS_REGISTER          = 0x05;
const int     LSR_DATA_READY              = 0x01;
const int     LSR_OVERRUN_ERROR           = 0x02;
const int     LSR_PARITY_ERROR            = 0x04;
const int     LSR_FRAMING_ERROR           = 0x08;
const int     LSR_BREAK_DETECT            = 0x10;
const int     LSR_THRE                    = 0x20;
const int   MODEM_STATUS_REGISTER         = 0x06;
const int     MSR_DELTA_CTS               = 0x01;
const int     MSR_DELTA_DSR               = 0x02;
const int     MSR_TERI                    = 0x04;
const int     MSR_DELTA_CD                = 0x08;
const int     MSR_CTS                     = 0x10;
const int     MSR_DSR                     = 0x20;
const int     MSR_RI                      = 0x40;
const int     MSR_CD                      = 0x80;
const int   DIVISOR_LATCH_LOW             = 0x00;
const int   DIVISOR_LATCH_HIGH            = 0x01;
```

```
#endif // #ifndef _8250_DOT_H

// *********************** END OF _8250.H ***********************
```

**Listing 3-4. _8250.H**

```
// ******************* START OF ASCII.H *******************

#ifndef _ASCII_DOT_H
#define _ASCII_DOT_H

const int BS   = 8;
const int LF   = 10;
const int CR   = 13;
const int DLE  = 16;
const int XON  = 17;
const int XOFF = 19;
const int CAN  = 24;
const int ESC  = 27;

#endif // #ifndef _ASCII_DOT_H

// ******************* END OF ASCII.H *******************
```

**Listing 3-5. ASCII.H**


**The modem status interrupt handler**

The code that is invoked to handle this type of interrupt is found in routine `handle_modem_status_interrupt()`. The easy work in this routine is done right away. The MSI counter is incremented, and the current value of the MSR is read in and stored in the `isr_data` structure used throughout the ISR.

Once that job has been done, the routine can work on the more difficult portion of its job: managing handshaking lines. If either DTR/DSR or RTS/CTS handshaking is in effect, a change in state of those control lines means that the transmitter of the UART is either going to be blocked or unblocked.

The CTS and DSR code handlers are identical, except for the specific bits that

# THE PC8250 CLASS

they manipulate. Each routine first checks whether a specific control line has changed by looking at the delta bit in the MSR.

If the appropriate delta bit hasn't changed, the ISR skips over the rest of the handshaking code. If the appropriate line has changed, the next step is to look for a change in state.

If the transmitter is already in a blocked state, and the status line has just gone high, a change of state has occurred. To go from blocked to unblocked, the ISR must do two things. First, it needs to clear the appropriate bit in the `blocked` data member. Second, it must call the `jump_start()` routine. If conditions are right, `jump_start()` restarts transmit interrupts, meaning no blocking states exist and there is data to be transmitted.

If the transmitter isn't blocked, and the status line goes low, the state has changed in the opposite direction. The routine only has set the appropriate bit in the `blocked` data member. The next time a transmit interrupt occurs, the transmit routine takes note of the blocked state, and shuts down interrupts.

### The TX interrupt handler

The TX interrupt handler has only a few decisions to make. First, it checks to see if a handshake character needs to be sent. Any time another routine in either the main class or the ISR needs to send a handshake character, it stuffs the character into the `send_handshake_char` data element. When the TX interrupt handler executes, it checks to see if `send_handshake_char` contains a character (a value of -1 means no character). If a character is found there, the TX interrupt handler sends it out immediately, and the handler exits.

If there is no handshake character to be sent, the transmit handler next checks to see if it is in a blocked state. If so, transmit interrupts are shut down, signified by the `tx_running` data member being set to 0, and an exit is taken.

If the `blocked` data member is clear, none of the three handshaking modes is in effect, and the transmitter is free to send any available characters. The `Remove()` member function of the `TXQueue` object is called to remove any characters that are waiting for transmission. If one is successfully removed from the queue, it is transmitted, and the routine exits. If there aren't any characters waiting to be transmitted, the `tx_running` element is cleared to indicate that no more Transmit Interrupts can be expected, and the handler exits.

The important thing to remember about the transmitter interrupt is that although it is always enabled, it becomes quiescent if a TX interrupt occurs and the transmitter is not reloaded with a new character. This state is indicated by the `tx_running` data member being set to 0. Once this is set to 0, starting interrupts up again requires a call to `jump_start()` to get things going again (`jump_start()` is very similar in structure to the transmit interrupt handler).

**The receive interrupt handler**

The receive interrupt handler is the longest of the four handlers. It has chores to handle for both directions of handshaking in addition to receiving the data, so it ends up occupying more lines of code than any of the other interrupt routines.

After incrementing its interrupt counter, the receive handler first goes into a loop where it reads in all of the characters pending in the UART. For a normal 8250, this means just reading in a single character. For a 16550, the FIFO could contain as many as 16 characters. If the UART is a 16550, the routine checks the Line Status Register at the end of the loop to see if the `LSR_DATA_READY` bit is still set. If it is, another character is read in from the Receive Buffer Register.

While in the receive loop, the interrupt handler has to perform a couple of additional chores. If the incoming character is an XON or an XOFF, and XON/XOFF handshaking has been enabled, the handler may have to either block or unblock transmission. In addition, nonhandshaking characters must all be placed into the receive buffer, and the overflow flag set if this insertion fails.

Once all the available characters have been read in and acted on, the receive interrupt handler then has to manage all three types of handshaking. If handshaking is enabled, and if the receive buffer is above the high-water mark, each of the three handshaking methods is checked. For the two hardware handshaking methods (RTS/CTS and DTR/DSR), the routine checks to see if that type of handshaking is enabled, and then checks to see if it is not currently blocking. If not, the appropriate modem control line is lowered. Next, the XON/XOFF status is checked. If an XOFF needs to be sent, the blocking bit is set, and the handshake character is set to XOFF. Finally, `jump_start()` needs to be called to get transmit interrupts running again, in case they are presently off, and to send the XOFF character, if it was set.

One thing to note about the `send_handshake_char` data member is that it is at least remotely possible that when our receive routine wants to send an

# THE PC8250 CLASS

XOFF, there is still an XON waiting to be sent. If so, we assume that the remote end is still blocked from a previous XOFF and we don't send another one. A similar test is performed by the receive interrupt handler when it is time to send an XON during the process of reading characters out of the receive buffer.

### The line status handler

The final one of the four interrupt handlers is so short that it doesn't even need its own routine. When an LSI occurs, the current value in the line status register is read out and ORed in with the `line_status` member of the `isr_data` structure. This means that any line status error that occurs will remain set until it is cleared by a call to the appropriate `RS232` member function call.

### jump_start()

One additional important piece of code in the ISR routines is the `jump_start()` routine. Both in the ISR and the `PC8250` member functions call `jump_start()` when they need to restart transmit interrupts. It is safe to call `jump_start()` even with transmit interrupts already running, as the routine will simply return.

The `jump_start()` routine only has to check if the `tx_running` member is already set to be true. If not, that TX interrupt needs to be restarted. To do so, the next character to be transmitted needs to be pushed into the UART transmitter. If a handshake character needs to go out, `jump_start()` sends it immediately. If no handshake character needs to go out, the routine first checks to be sure none of the three `blocked` bits is set, then it tries to pull a character out of the Transmit buffer. If a character is available, it is stuffed into the transmitter, and the `tx_running` member is set.

All of this must be done under the cover of disabled interrupts. If a member function were to call `jump_start()` and find that `tx_running` was not set, it would be possible to begin the process of restarting interrupts, only to have an incoming modem status interrupt start up the process for you. This could lead to a character being stuffed out into the transmit buffer when it shouldn't be. Wrapping up all the code inside disabled interrupts prevents this from happening. This routine should be able to execute quickly, so having interrupts disabled won't adversely affect system performance.

# SERIAL COMMUNICATIONS: A C++ DEVELOPER'S GUIDE

## PC8250.CPP

The source file `PC8250.CPP` contains all of the source code to support the use of class `PC8250`. The only code for this class that doesn't show up in this file is the interrupt service routine code that is found in `ISR_8250.CPP`. This source file is relatively long, but most of the code in it is used to develop the small member functions for this class.

```cpp
// ******************* START OF PC8250.CPP *******************
//
// This file contains most of the code used in the PC8250
// class.  The remainder of the code can be found in
// ISR_8250.CPP, which has the ISR and its support code.

#include <stdio.h>
#include <dos.h>
#include <ctype.h>
#include "rs232.h"
#include "pc8250.h"
#include "_pc8250.h"
#include "_msdos.h"
#include "ascii.h"

// Data used to initialize UART addresses and IRQ lines.

static int ISA_uarts[]         = { 0x3f8, 0x2f8, 0x3e8, 0x2e8 };
static enum irq_name ISA_IRQs[] = { IRQ4,  IRQ3,  IRQ4,  IRQ3 };
static int MCA_uarts[]         = { 0x03f8, 0x02f8, 0x3220, 0x3228,
                                   0x4220, 0x4228, 0x5220, 0x5228 };
static enum irq_name MCA_IRQs[] = { IRQ4,  IRQ3,  IRQ3,  IRQ3,
                                    IRQ3,  IRQ3,  IRQ3,  IRQ3 };


// This is the one and only constructor for an object of class
// PC8250.  A quick look at PC8250.H will show you that all of
// the parameters in the list except the port have default
// values, so the list isn't as overwhelming as it might look.
```

# THE PC8250 CLASS

```cpp
PC8250::PC8250( RS232PortName port,
                long baud_rate,
                char parity,
                int word_length,
                int stop_bits,
                int dtr,
                int rts,
                int xon_xoff,
                int rts_cts,
                int dtr_dsr,
                Handler *handler,
                int uart_address,
                irq_name irq_line )
{
    int mcr;

    interrupt_handler = handler;
    port_name = port;
    error_status = RS232_SUCCESS;

// This section of code initializes most of the items in the
// isr_data structure, which contains all of the items used in
// the ISR.

    isr_data = new isr_data_block;
    if ( isr_data == 0 ) {
        error_status = RS232_MEMORY_ALLOCATION_ERROR;
        return;
    }
    set_uart_address_and_irq( handler, uart_address, irq_line );
    if ( error_status < RS232_SUCCESS )
        return;
    isr_data->overflow = 0;
    isr_data->tx_running = 0;
    isr_data->tx_int_count = 0;
    isr_data->rx_int_count = 0;
    isr_data->ls_int_count = 0;
    isr_data->ms_int_count = 0;
    isr_data->line_status = 0;
```

```
        isr_data->handshaking = 0;
        isr_data->blocking = 0;
        isr_data->blocked = 0;
        isr_data->send_handshake_char = -1;

// PC8250 has to share the debug output with the parent
// class.  To determine where our first line starts, we call the
// FormatDebugOutput() function from our parent class.

        first_debug_output_line = RS232::FormatDebugOutput();
        debug_line_count = FormatDebugOutput();

// Determine whether the UART is there and what type it is.

        check_uart();
        if ( error_status < RS232_SUCCESS )
            return;

//   Save all of the old UART settings, and then set it to the
//   new ones passed to the constructor.

        read_settings();
        saved_settings = settings;
        settings.Adjust( baud_rate,
                         parity,
                         word_length,
                         stop_bits,
                         dtr,
                         rts,
                         xon_xoff,
                         rts_cts,
                         dtr_dsr );
        write_settings();

// Here we set up the interrupt handler, then turn on
// interrupts.  After this code is done the UART will be
// running.

        OUTPUT( isr_data->uart + INTERRUPT_ENABLE_REGISTER, 0 );
        mcr = INPUT( isr_data->uart + MODEM_CONTROL_REGISTER );
```

# THE PC8250 CLASS

```c
        mcr |= MCR_OUT2;
        mcr &= ~MCR_LOOPBACK;
        OUTPUT( isr_data->uart + MODEM_CONTROL_REGISTER, mcr );
        if ( interrupt_handler == 0 ) {
            error_status = ConnectToIrq( irq,
                                    isr_data, (void (*)(void *))
                                    isr_8250 );
            if ( error_status < RS232_SUCCESS ) {
                OUTPUT( isr_data->uart + MODEM_CONTROL_REGISTER, 0 );
                OUTPUT( isr_data->uart + INTERRUPT_ENABLE_REGISTER,
                                                            0 );

                return;
            }
        } else {
            error_status = interrupt_handler->AddPort( port_name,
                                                    isr_data );
            if ( error_status < RS232_SUCCESS )
                return;
        }
        INPUT( isr_data->uart );   // Clear any pending interrupts
        INPUT( isr_data->uart + INTERRUPT_ID_REGISTER );
        CLI();
        isr_data->modem_status -
            (unsigned int)
                INPUT( isr_data->uart + MODEM_STATUS_REGISTER );
        OUTPUT( isr_data->uart + INTERRUPT_ENABLE_REGISTER,
                IER_RX_DATA_READY + IER_TX_HOLDING_REGISTER_EMPTY +
                IER_MODEM_STATUS + IER_LINE_STATUS );
        OUTPUT( 0x20, 0xc0 + IRQ3 - 1 );
        STI();
// Finally, set up the last few parameters and exit.

        Dtr( settings.Dtr );
        Rts( settings.Rts );
        XonXoffHandshaking( settings.XonXoff );
        RtsCtsHandshaking( settings.RtsCts );
        DtrDsrHandshaking( settings.DtrDsr );
    }
```

# SERIAL COMMUNICATIONS: A C++ DEVELOPER'S GUIDE

```cpp
void PC8250::set_uart_address_and_irq( Handler *handler,
                                       int uart_address,
                                       irq_name irq_line )
{
// If I have a handler or have a defined irq_line, I won't
// use the default IRQs.  If I have a uart_address, I won't
// use the default UART address.

    if ( handler == 0 && irq_line == ILLEGAL_IRQ ) {
        if ( Bus() == ISA_BUS ) {
            if ( port_name > COM4 )
                error_status = RS232_PORT_NOT_FOUND;
            else
                irq = ISA_IRQs[ port_name ];
        } else {
            if ( port_name > COM8 )
                error_status = RS232_PORT_NOT_FOUND;
            else
                irq = MCA_IRQs[ port_name ];
        }
    } else
        irq = irq_line;

    if ( uart_address == 0 ) {
        if ( Bus() == ISA_BUS ) {
            if ( port_name > COM4 )
                error_status = RS232_PORT_NOT_FOUND;
            else
                isr_data->uart = ISA_uarts[ port_name ];
        } else {
            if ( port_name > COM8 )
                error_status = RS232_PORT_NOT_FOUND;
            else
                isr_data->uart = MCA_uarts[ port_name ];
        }
    } else
        isr_data->uart = uart_address;
}

// The destructor has a much easier time of it than the
```

# THE PC8250 CLASS

```c
// constructor.  It disables interrupts, then restores the line
// settings of the UART.
PC8250::~PC8250( void )
{
    if ( error_status == RS232_SUCCESS ) {
        OUTPUT( isr_data->uart + INTERRUPT_ENABLE_REGISTER, 0 );
        OUTPUT( isr_data->uart + MODEM_CONTROL_REGISTER, 0 );
        if ( interrupt_handler == 0 )
            DisconnectFromIRQ( irq );
        else
            interrupt_handler->DeletePort( port_name );
        settings = saved_settings;
        write_settings();
        Dtr( settings.Dtr );
        Rts( settings.Rts );
    }
    if ( isr_data != 0 )
        delete isr_data;
}

// This routine determines if a UART is present, and if so,
// whether or not it is a 16550.  If it is a 16550, the FIFO is
// enabled with a trigger at 14 bytes.

void PC8250::check_uart( void )
{
    int temp;

    OUTPUT( isr_data->uart + FIFO_CONTROL_REGISTER, 0 );
    temp = INPUT( isr_data->uart + INTERRUPT_ID_REGISTER );
    if ( ( temp & 0xf8 ) != 0 ) {
        isr_data->uart_type = UART_UNKNOWN;
        error_status = RS232_PORT_NOT_FOUND;
        return;
    }
    OUTPUT( isr_data->uart + FIFO_CONTROL_REGISTER,
            FCR_FIFO_ENABLE + FCR_TRIGGER_14 );
    temp = INPUT( isr_data->uart + INTERRUPT_ID_REGISTER );
    if ( ( temp & 0xf8 ) == 0xc0 ) {
        isr_data->uart_type = UART_16550;
```

# SERIAL COMMUNICATIONS: A C++ DEVELOPER'S GUIDE

```
            fifo_setting = 14;
        } else {
            isr_data->uart_type = UART_8250;
            fifo_setting = 0;
            OUTPUT( isr_data->uart + FIFO_CONTROL_REGISTER, 0 );
        }
    }

// After any function that reads data from the ISR buffers,
// this routine is called.  If the read operation dropped us
// below a handshaking trigger point, this routine will figure
// out what action to take.

void PC8250::check_rx_handshaking()
{
    int mcr;

// Take a quick exit if we aren't handshaking, blocking, or if
// the RX Queue is not below the low-water mark.

        if ( !isr_data->handshaking || !isr_data->blocking )
            return;
        if ( isr_data->RXQueue.InUseCount() > LowWaterMark )
            return;

// If RTS/CTS handshaking is in effect, I raise RTS.

        if ( ( isr_data->handshaking & rts_cts ) &&
             ( isr_data->blocking & rts_cts ) ) {
            CLI();
            mcr = INPUT( isr_data->uart + MODEM_CONTROL_REGISTER );
            mcr |= MCR_RTS;
            OUTPUT( isr_data->uart + MODEM_CONTROL_REGISTER, mcr );
            isr_data->blocking &= ~rts_cts;
            STI();
        }

// If DTR/DSR handshaking is in effect, I raise DTR.
```

## THE PC8250 CLASS

```
    if ( ( isr_data->handshaking & dtr_dsr ) &&
         ( isr_data->blocking & dtr_dsr ) ) {
        CLI();
        mcr = INPUT( isr_data->uart + MODEM_CONTROL_REGISTER );
        mcr |= MCR_DTR;
        OUTPUT( isr_data->uart + MODEM_CONTROL_REGISTER, mcr );
        isr_data->blocking &= ~dtr_dsr;
        STI();
    }

// If XON/XOFF is in effect, I send an XON.  Note that if
// there is a pending XOFF that never made it out, I cancel it
// and don't send anything else.

    if ( ( isr_data->handshaking & xon_xoff ) &&
         ( isr_data->blocking & xon_xoff ) ) {
        CLI();
        isr_data->blocking &= ~xon_xoff;
        if ( isr_data->send_handshake_char == XOFF )
            isr_data->send_handshake_char = -1;
        else {
            isr_data->send_handshake_char = XON;
            jump_start( isr_data );
        }
        STI();
    }
}

// This routine just pulls out a byte and checks for
// handshaking activity.

int PC8250::read_byte( void )
{
    int c;

    if ( error_status < 0 )
        return error_status;
    c = isr_data->RXQueue.Remove();
    if ( c < 0 )
        return RS232_TIMEOUT;
```

```cpp
        check_rx_handshaking();
        return c;
}
// When sending a byte to the output buffer, I have to check
// to see if the TX interrupt system needs to be restarted.

int PC8250::write_byte( int c )
{
    if ( error_status < 0 )
        return error_status;
    if ( !isr_data->TXQueue.Insert( (unsigned char) c ) )
        return RS232_TIMEOUT;
    if ( !isr_data->tx_running && !isr_data->blocked )
        jump_start( isr_data );
    return RS232_SUCCESS;
}


// read_buffer() pulls in only as many bytes as are
// immediately available.  Any high-level functions such as
// timing out or looking for a terminator are handled by one of
// the higher level Read() routines from class RS232.

int PC8250::read_buffer( char *buffer, unsigned int count )
{
    ByteCount = 0;
    if ( error_status < 0 )
        return error_status;
    while ( isr_data->RXQueue.InUseCount() ) {
        if ( count <= 0 )
            break;
        *buffer++ = (char) isr_data->RXQueue.Remove();
        count--;
        ByteCount++;
    }
    *buffer = '\0';
    if ( ByteCount > 0 )
        check_rx_handshaking();
    if ( count > 0 )
        return RS232_TIMEOUT;
    else
```

## THE PC8250 CLASS

```
        return RS232_SUCCESS;
}

// write_buffer() sends as many characters as the buffer can
// immediately manage.  Like read_buffer(), it relies on higher
// level routines from class RS232 to perform the nicer functions
// such as adding termination, timing, etc.

int PC8250::write_buffer( char *buffer, unsigned int count )
{
    ByteCount = 0;
    if ( error_status < 0 )
        return error_status;
    for ( ; ; ) {
        if ( count == 0 )
            break;
        if ( !isr_data->TXQueue.Insert( *buffer ) )
            break;
        buffer++;
        count--;
        ByteCount++;
    }
    if ( !isr_data->tx_running && !isr_data->blocked )
        jump_start( isr_data );
    if ( count > 0 )
        return RS232_TIMEOUT;
    else
        return RS232_SUCCESS;
}

// The Queue functions make it easy to flush the RX queue.
// After emptying it all, we need to be sure that handshaking
// gets managed.

int PC8250::FlushRXBuffer( void )
{
    if ( error_status < RS232_SUCCESS )
        return error_status;
    CLI();
```

# SERIAL COMMUNICATIONS: A C++ DEVELOPER'S GUIDE

```cpp
    isr_data->RXQueue.Clear();
    STI();
    check_rx_handshaking();
    return RS232_SUCCESS;

}


// write_settings() is a protected routine called by the
// constructor and the public Set() function.  It is long and
// stringy, mostly because setting up the UART is just a long
// case of setting or clearing bits in control registers.  It
// might be possible to modularize this code, but it wouldn't be
// particularly useful.

RS232Error PC8250::write_settings( void )
{
    int lcr;
    int divisor_high;
    int divisor_low;
    RS232Error status = RS232_SUCCESS;
    long result_baud;

    if ( settings.BaudRate <= 0 || settings.BaudRate > 115200L ) {
        settings.BaudRate = 9600;
        status = RS232_ILLEGAL_BAUD_RATE;
    }
    divisor_low = (int) ( ( 115200L / settings.BaudRate ) & 0xff );
    divisor_high = (int) ( ( 115200L / settings.BaudRate ) >> 8 );
    result_baud = 115200L / ( 115200L / settings.BaudRate );
    if ( result_baud != settings.BaudRate ) {
        settings.BaudRate = result_baud;
        status = RS232_ILLEGAL_BAUD_RATE;
    }
    lcr = INPUT( isr_data->uart + LINE_CONTROL_REGISTER );
    lcr |= LCR_DLAB;
    CLI();
    OUTPUT( isr_data->uart + LINE_CONTROL_REGISTER, lcr );
    OUTPUT( isr_data->uart + DIVISOR_LATCH_LOW, divisor_low );
    OUTPUT( isr_data->uart + DIVISOR_LATCH_HIGH, divisor_high );
```

```
    lcr &= ~LCR_DLAB;
    OUTPUT( isr_data->uart + LINE_CONTROL_REGISTER, lcr );
    STI();
    lcr &= ~LCR_PARITY_MASK;
    switch ( toupper( settings.Parity ) ) {
        case 'O' :
            lcr |= LCR_PARITY_ENABLE;
            break;
        case 'E' :
            lcr |= LCR_PARITY_ENABLE + LCR_EVEN_PARITY_SELECT;
            break;
        case 'M' :
            lcr |= LCR_PARITY_ENABLE + LCR_STICK_PARITY;
            break;
        case 'S' :
            lcr |= LCR_PARITY_ENABLE +
                   LCR_EVEN_PARITY_SELECT +
                   LCR_STICK_PARITY;
            break;
        default :
            settings.Parity = 'N';
            status = RS232_ILLEGAL_PARITY_SETTING;
        case 'N' :
            break;
    }
    lcr &= ~LCR_WORD_LENGTH_MASK;
    switch ( settings.WordLength ) {
        case 5 :
            break;
        case 6 :
            lcr |= LCR_WORD_LENGTH_SELECT_0;
            break;
        case 7 :
            lcr |= LCR_WORD_LENGTH_SELECT_1;
            break;
        default :
            settings.WordLength = 8;
            status = RS232_ILLEGAL_WORD_LENGTH;
        case 8 :
```

```
            lcr |= LCR_WORD_LENGTH_SELECT_0 +
                   LCR_WORD_LENGTH_SELECT_1;
            break;
    }
    lcr &= ~LCR_STOP_BITS;
    switch ( settings.StopBits ) {
        default :
            settings.StopBits = 1;
            status = RS232_ILLEGAL_STOP_BITS;
        case 1 :
            break;
        case 2 :
            lcr |= LCR_STOP_BITS;
            break;
    }
    OUTPUT( isr_data->uart + LINE_CONTROL_REGISTER, lcr );
    return status;
}

// read_settings() is the protected inverse of
// write_settings().  This routine just reads in the state of the
// UART into a settings object.  This is done when the routine
// starts up, so that the RS232 class will always have the saved
// settings available for restoration when the RS232 port is
// closed.

void PC8250::read_settings( void )
{
    int lcr;
    int mcr;
    int divisor_low;
    int divisor_high;

    lcr = INPUT( isr_data->uart + LINE_CONTROL_REGISTER );
    lcr |= LCR_DLAB;
    CLI();
    OUTPUT( isr_data->uart + LINE_CONTROL_REGISTER, lcr );
    divisor_low = INPUT( isr_data->uart + DIVISOR_LATCH_LOW );
    divisor_high = INPUT( isr_data->uart + DIVISOR_LATCH_HIGH );
    lcr &= ~LCR_DLAB;
```

# THE PC8250 CLASS

```
    OUTPUT( isr_data->uart + LINE_CONTROL_REGISTER, lcr );
    STI();

    if ( divisor_high | divisor_low )
        settings.BaudRate = 115200L / ( ( divisor_high << 8 ) +
                                        divisor_low );
                                                else
        settings.BaudRate = -1;

    switch ( lcr & LCR_PARITY_MASK ) {
        case LCR_PARITY_ENABLE :
            settings.Parity = 'O';
            break;
        case LCR_PARITY_ENABLE + LCR_EVEN_PARITY_SELECT :
            settings.Parity = 'E';
            break;
        case LCR_PARITY_ENABLE + LCR_STICK_PARITY :
            settings.Parity = 'M';
            break;
        case LCR_PARITY_ENABLE +
             LCR_EVEN_PARITY_SELECT +
             LCR_STICK_PARITY :
            settings.Parity = 'S';
            break;
        default :
            settings.Parity = 'N';
            break;
    }
    switch ( lcr & LCR_WORD_LENGTH_MASK ) {
        case 0 :
            settings.WordLength = 5;
            break;
        case LCR_WORD_LENGTH_SELECT_0 :
            settings.WordLength = 6;
            break;
        case LCR_WORD_LENGTH_SELECT_1 :
            settings.WordLength = 7;
            break;
        case LCR_WORD_LENGTH_SELECT_0 + LCR_WORD_LENGTH_SELECT_1 :
```

```
                settings.WordLength = 8;
                break;
        }
        switch ( lcr & LCR_STOP_BITS ) {
            case 0 :
                settings.StopBits = 1;
                break;
            default :
                settings.StopBits = 2;
                break;
        }
        mcr = INPUT( isr_data->uart + MODEM_CONTROL_REGISTER );
        settings.Dtr = ( mcr & MCR_DTR ) != 0;
        settings.Rts = ( mcr & MCR_RTS ) != 0;
        settings.XonXoff = -1;
        settings.RtsCts = -1;
        settings.DtrDsr = -1;
}


// Set() takes advantage of code used by the constructor to
// set up some of the UART parameters.

RS232Error PC8250::Set( long baud_rate,
                       int parity,
                       int word_length,
                       int stop_bits )
{
    settings.Adjust( baud_rate,
                     parity,
                     word_length,
                     stop_bits,
                     UNCHANGED,
                     UNCHANGED,
                     UNCHANGED,
                     UNCHANGED,
                     UNCHANGED );
    return write_settings();
}
```

# THE PC8250 CLASS

```
// This virtual routine is easily handled by a Queue member
// function.

int PC8250::TXSpaceFree( void )
{
    if ( error_status < RS232_SUCCESS )
        return error_status;
    return isr_data->TXQueue.FreeCount();
}

// The same thing is true here.

int PC8250::RXSpaceUsed( void )
{
    if ( error_status < RS232_SUCCESS )
        return error_status;
    return isr_data->RXQueue.InUseCount();
}

// The 8250 UART doesn't have an intelligent BREAK function,
// so we have to just sit on the line while the BREAK goes out.
// Hopefully the IdleFunction() can do something useful while
// this takes place.

int PC8250::Break( long milliseconds )
{
    int lcr;
    long timer;

    if ( error_status < RS232_SUCCESS )
        return error_status;
    timer = ReadTime() + milliseconds;
    lcr = INPUT( isr_data->uart + LINE_CONTROL_REGISTER);
    lcr |= LCR_SET_BREAK;
    OUTPUT( isr_data->uart + LINE_CONTROL_REGISTER, lcr );
    while ( ReadTime() < timer )
        IdleFunction();
    lcr &= ~LCR_SET_BREAK;
    OUTPUT( isr_data->uart + LINE_CONTROL_REGISTER, lcr );
    return RS232_SUCCESS;
}
```

```
// The four modem status functions just check the bits that
// were read in the last time a modem status interrupt took
// place, and return them to the calling routine.

int PC8250::Cd( void )
{
    if ( error_status < RS232_SUCCESS )
        return error_status;
    return ( isr_data->modem_status & MSR_CD ) ? 1 : 0;
}

int PC8250::Ri( void )
{
    if ( error_status < RS232_SUCCESS )
        return error_status;
    return ( isr_data->modem_status & MSR_RI ) ? 1 : 0;
}

int PC8250::Cts( void )
{
    if ( error_status < RS232_SUCCESS )
        return error_status;
    return ( isr_data->modem_status & MSR_CTS ) ? 1 : 0;
}

int PC8250::Dsr( void )
{
    if ( error_status < RS232_SUCCESS )
        return error_status;
    return ( isr_data->modem_status & MSR_DSR ) ? 1 : 0;
}

// The four line status routines are similar to the modem
// status routines in that they just check a bit in a data
// member.  However, they also have an optional parameter that
// can be used to clear the error flag.  This is just a matter of
// clearing the same bit.

int PC8250::ParityError( int reset )
```

# THE PC8250 CLASS

```cpp
{
    int return_value;

    if ( error_status < RS232_SUCCESS )
        return error_status;
    return_value =
            ( isr_data->line_status & LSR_PARITY_ERROR ) ? 1 : 0;
    if ( reset != UNCHANGED && reset != 0 ) {
        CLI();
        isr_data->line_status &= ~LSR_PARITY_ERROR;
        STI();
    }
    return return_value;
}

int PC8250::BreakDetect( int reset )
{
    int return_value;

    if ( error_status < RS232_SUCCESS )
        return error_status;
    return_value =
        ( isr_data->line_status & LSR_BREAK_DETECT ) ? 1 : 0;
    if ( reset != UNCHANGED && reset != 0 ) {
        CLI();
        isr_data->line_status &= ~LSR_BREAK_DETECT;
        STI();
    }
    return return_value;
}

int PC8250::FramingError( int reset )
{
    int return_value;

    if ( error_status < RS232_SUCCESS )
        return error_status;
    return_value =
            ( isr_data->line_status & LSR_FRAMING_ERROR ) ? 1 : 0;
```

```cpp
    if ( reset != UNCHANGED && reset != 0 ) {
        CLI();
        isr_data->line_status &= ~LSR_FRAMING_ERROR;
        STI();
    }
    return return_value;
}

int PC8250::HardwareOverrunError( int reset )
{
    int return_value;

    if ( error_status < RS232_SUCCESS )
        return error_status;
    return_value =
          ( isr_data->line_status & LSR_OVERRUN_ERROR ) ? 1 : 0;
    if ( reset != UNCHANGED && reset != 0 ) {
        CLI();
        isr_data->line_status &= ~LSR_OVERRUN_ERROR;
        STI();
    }
    return return_value;
}

// This just reads in the status bit from the isr_data
// structure, and optionally clears it.

int PC8250::SoftwareOverrunError( int clear )
{
    int temp = isr_data->overflow;
    if ( clear )
        isr_data->overflow = 0;
    return temp;
}

// The three handshaking functions all have approximately the
// same mode of operation.  If the setting parameter is set to
// UNCHANGED, they just return a boolean indicating whether or
// not handshaking is in effect.  If handshaking is being turned
```

# THE PC8250 CLASS

```cpp
// on or off, things become a little more complicated.  The
// major complication is that after setting the bits needed by
// the ISR to handshake, they also have to take action to make
// sure the control lines and XON/XOFF output are where they need
// to be to accurately get things started.

int PC8250::XonXoffHandshaking( int setting )
{
    if ( setting != UNCHANGED ) {
        if ( setting )
            isr_data->handshaking |= xon_xoff;
        else {
            isr_data->handshaking &= ~xon_xoff;
            isr_data->blocked &= ~xon_xoff;
// If blocking, I need to send an XON
            if ( isr_data->blocking & xon_xoff ) {
                CLI();
                if ( isr_data->send_handshake_char == -1 )
                    isr_data->send_handshake_char = XON;
                else
                    isr_data->send_handshake_char = -1;
                STI();
            }
            // Restart TX if I was blocked, or have to send and XON
            jump_start( isr_data );
            isr_data->blocking &= ~xon_xoff;
        }
        settings.XonXoff = ( setting != 0 );
    }
    return( ( isr_data->handshaking & xon_xoff ) != 0 );
}

int PC8250::RtsCtsHandshaking( int setting )
{
    int old_setting;

    if ( setting != UNCHANGED ) {
        old_setting = isr_data->handshaking & rts_cts;
        isr_data->handshaking &= ~rts_cts;
```

```cpp
            isr_data->blocking &= ~rts_cts;
            isr_data->blocked &= ~rts_cts;
            if ( setting ) {
                Rts( 1 );
                CLI();
                if ( ( isr_data->modem_status & MSR_CTS ) == 0 )
                    isr_data->blocked |= rts_cts;
                isr_data->handshaking |= rts_cts;
                STI();
                settings.Rts = REMOTE_CONTROL;
            } else {
                if ( old_setting )
                    Rts( 1 );  //If turning handshaking off,
                               //                set RTS high
                if ( isr_data->blocked == 0 )
                    jump_start( isr_data );
            }
            settings.RtsCts = ( setting != 0 );
        }
        return( ( isr_data->handshaking & rts_cts ) != 0 );
}

int PC8250::DtrDsrHandshaking( int setting )
{
    int old_setting;

    if ( setting != UNCHANGED ) {
        old_setting = isr_data->handshaking & dtr_dsr;
        isr_data->handshaking &= ~dtr_dsr;
        isr_data->blocking &= ~dtr_dsr;
        isr_data->blocked &= ~dtr_dsr;
        if ( setting ) {
            Dtr( 1 );
            CLI();
            if ( ( isr_data->modem_status & MSR_DSR ) == 0 )
                isr_data->blocked |= dtr_dsr;
            isr_data->handshaking |= dtr_dsr;
            STI();
            settings.Dtr = REMOTE_CONTROL;
```

## THE PC8250 CLASS

```c
        } else {
            if ( old_setting )
                Dtr( 1 ); //If turning handshaking off,
                                        set RTS high
            if ( isr_data->blocked == 0 )
                jump_start( isr_data );
        }
        settings.DtrDsr = ( setting != 0 );
    }
    return( ( isr_data->handshaking & dtr_dsr ) != 0 );
}

// Just reading the state of the control line is relatively
// easy.  The setting returned is just the stored value in the
// settings element.  However, both of the next two routines have
// to handle setting or clearing the line as well.  This only
// gets complicated if handshaking is turned on.  If it is, these
// routines refuse to play with the control lines.

int PC8250::Dtr( int setting )
{
    int mcr;

    if ( setting != UNCHANGED ) {
        if ( isr_data->handshaking & dtr_dsr )
            return PC8250_HANDSHAKE_LINE_IN_USE;
        else {
            settings.Dtr = setting;
            CLI();
            mcr = INPUT( isr_data->uart + MODEM_CONTROL_REGISTER );
            if ( setting )
                mcr |= MCR_DTR;
            else
                mcr &= ~MCR_DTR;
            OUTPUT( isr_data->uart + MODEM_CONTROL_REGISTER, mcr );
            STI();
        }
    }
    return settings.Dtr;
}
```

```
int PC8250::Rts( int setting )
{
    int mcr;

    if ( setting != UNCHANGED ) {
        if ( isr_data->handshaking & rts_cts )
            return PC8250_HANDSHAKE_LINE_IN_USE;
        else {
            settings.Rts = setting;
            CLI();
            mcr = INPUT( isr_data->uart + MODEM_CONTROL_REGISTER );
            if ( setting )
                mcr |= MCR_RTS;
            else
                mcr &= ~MCR_RTS;
            OUTPUT( isr_data->uart + MODEM_CONTROL_REGISTER, mcr );
            STI();
        }
    }
    return settings.Rts;
}


// PeekBuffer uses the class Queue function to read as many
// bytes as possible from the RXBuffer.

int PC8250::PeekBuffer( void *buffer, unsigned int count )
{
    if ( error_status < RS232_SUCCESS )
        return error_status;
    ByteCount =
            isr_data->RXQueue.Peek( (unsigned char *) buffer, count );
    ( (char *) buffer )[ ByteCount ] = '\0';
    return RS232_SUCCESS;
}

// The next two functions just return a count using a Queue
// class primitive function.
```

# THE PC8250 CLASS

```cpp
int PC8250::RXSpaceFree( void )
{
    if ( error_status < RS232_SUCCESS )
        return error_status;
    return isr_data->RXQueue.FreeCount();
}

int PC8250::TXSpaceUsed( void )
{
    if ( error_status < RS232_SUCCESS )
        return error_status;
    return isr_data->TXQueue.InUseCount();
}

// Flushing the TX buffer is easy when using the Queue class
// primitive.

int PC8250::FlushTXBuffer( void )
{
    if ( error_status < RS232_SUCCESS )
        return error_status;
    CLI();
    isr_data->TXQueue.Clear();
    STI();
    return RS232_SUCCESS;
}


// The debug output routine has three possible modes.  If the
// buffer passed to it is a null, it means it should just return
// the total number of lines used by the the output, which is 6
// plus the number used by the base class.  If the line number
// requested is less than where we start, the request is passed
// up the line to the base class.  Finally, if it is one of our
// lines, the buffer is formatted and returned to the calling
// routine.

int PC8250::FormatDebugOutput( char *buffer, int line_number )
{
    if ( buffer == 0 )
```

```cpp
            return( first_debug_output_line +  6 );
    if ( line_number < first_debug_output_line )
        return RS232::FormatDebugOutput( buffer, line_number );
    switch( line_number - first_debug_output_line ) {
        case 0 :
            sprintf( buffer,
                     "Derived class: PC8250   "
                     "UART: %04x  "
                     "Overflow: %1d  "
                     "TX Running: %1d  "
                     "Line Status: %02x",
                     isr_data->uart,
                     ( isr_data->overflow ) ? 1 : 0,
                     ( isr_data->tx_running ) ? 1 : 0,
                     isr_data->line_status );
            break;
        case 1 :
            sprintf( buffer,
                     "TX Head, Tail, Count %4d %4d %4d  "
                     "RX Head,Tail,Count %4d %4d %4d",
                     isr_data->TXQueue.Head(),
                     isr_data->TXQueue.Tail(),
                     isr_data->TXQueue.InUseCount(),
                     isr_data->RXQueue.Head(),
                     isr_data->RXQueue.Tail(),
                     isr_data->RXQueue.InUseCount() );
            break;
        case 2 :
            sprintf( buffer,
                     "Counts: TX: %5u  RX: %5u  MS: %5u  LS: %5u  "
                     "CTS/DSR/RI/CD: %d%d%d%d",
                     isr_data->tx_int_count,
                     isr_data->rx_int_count,
                     isr_data->ms_int_count,
                     isr_data->ls_int_count,
                     ( isr_data->modem_status & MSR_CTS ) ? 1 : 0,
                     ( isr_data->modem_status & MSR_DSR ) ? 1 : 0,
                     ( isr_data->modem_status & MSR_RI ) ? 1 : 0,
                     ( isr_data->modem_status & MSR_CD ) ? 1 : 0 );
```

# THE PC8250 CLASS

```c
            break;
    case 3 :
        sprintf( buffer,
                "Handshake DTR/RTS/XON : %d%d%d  "
                "Blocking: %d%d%d  "
                "Blocked: %d%d%d  "
                "Handshake char: %04x",
                ( isr_data->handshaking & dtr_dsr ) ? 1 : 0,
                ( isr_data->handshaking & rts_cts ) ? 1 : 0,
                ( isr_data->handshaking & xon_xoff ) ? 1 : 0,
                ( isr_data->blocking & dtr_dsr ) ? 1 : 0,
                ( isr_data->blocking & rts_cts ) ? 1 : 0,
                ( isr_data->blocking & xon_xoff ) ? 1 : 0,
                ( isr_data->blocked & dtr_dsr ) ? 1 : 0,
                ( isr_data->blocked & rts_cts ) ? 1 : 0,
                ( isr_data->blocked & xon_xoff ) ? 1 : 0,
                isr_data->send_handshake_char );
            break;
    case 4 :
        sprintf( buffer,
                "Parity Err: %d  "
                "Break Det: %d  "
                "Overrun Err: %d  "
                "Framing Err: %d  "
                "FIFO Setting: %2d",
                ( isr_data->line_status & LSR_PARITY_ERROR )
                                                    ? 1 : 0,
                ( isr_data->line_status & LSR_BREAK_DETECT )
                                                    ? 1 : 0,
                ( isr_data->line_status & LSR_OVERRUN_ERROR )
                                                    ? 1 : 0,
                ( isr_data->line_status & LSR_FRAMING_ERROR )
                                                    ? 1 : 0,
                fifo_setting );
            break;
    case 5 :
        char *uart_name;
        switch( isr_data->uart_type ) {
            case UART_8250  : uart_name = "8250";     break;
```

```cpp
                    case UART_16550 : uart_name = "16550";   break;
                    default         : uart_name = "Unknown"; break;
                }
                sprintf( buffer,
                        "Uart type: %-7s",
                        uart_name );
                break;
            default :
                return RS232_ILLEGAL_LINE_NUMBER;
    }
    return RS232_SUCCESS;
}

// Just like the debug format routine, ErrorName has to pass
// most requests up the line to the base class, saving only a few
// to which it responds.

char * PC8250::ErrorName( int error )
{
    if ( error < RS232_NEXT_FREE_ERROR && error >= RS232_ERROR )
        return RS232::ErrorName( error );
    if ( error < RS232_NEXT_FREE_WARNING && error
                              >= RS232_WARNING )
        return RS232::ErrorName( error );
    if ( error >= RS232_SUCCESS )
        return RS232::ErrorName( error );
    switch ( error ) {
        case PC8250_UART_NOT_FOUND        : return( "UART not"
                                                    "found" );
        case PC8250_HANDSHAKE_LINE_IN_USE: return( "Handshake line"
                                                    "in use" );
        default                           : return( "Undefined"
                                                    "error" );
    }
}
```

**Listing 3-6. PC8250.CPP**

## THE PC8250 CLASS

**PC8250::PC8250()**

This class only has a single constructor. This constructor has a formidable argument list, but every argument except the port number has a default value, so the function can actually be used fairly easily. The first argument is the port name, which is found in the enumerated set `RS232PortName`, defined in `RS232.H`. The next four arguments are used to set up the initial line state for the UART: `baud_rate`, `parity`, `word_length`, and `stop_bits`. In each case, these arguments default to the `UNCHANGED` value, meaning the current setting will not be changed.

The next two arguments determine the initial setting of DTR and RTS. Normally, most programs will want to set these two lines high, so the default setting for these two parameters is `SET`. If some program has a reason for wanting to open the port with either of these two parameters `UNCHANGED` or `CLEAR`, the parameter can be specified as part of the constructor.

The next three arguments allow for the three different handshaking modes to be initialized to a defined setting. The default values for XON/XOFF, RTS/CTS, and DTR/DSR handshaking is for all three values to be disabled initially.

The last three arguments are used to specify nonstandard UARTs. A handler is an object of a class `Handler`. A handler is used when multiple ports are sharing a single interrupt, such as when a multiport board is in use. If no handler is specified, the parameter defaults to a value of 0, and control is automatically routed to that port whenever an interrupt occurs. The next chapter of this book will look at some handlers used in different situations.

The `uart_address` and `irq_line` parameters should be self-explanatory. They are only needed when a port doesn't adhere to the standard addresses and IRQ lines defined for the IBM PC.

Most of the body of `PC8250::PC8250()` is concerned with initialization of all the data members of both `RS232` and `PC8250`. The first section of code allocates the `isr_data` structure that is used by the ISR. The various members of this structure are all initialized, with a few opportunities for failures coming into play. The initialization code identifies whether the system is running on an ISA system or a MicroChannel machine, and selects port and IRQ addresses based on that.

The debug output parameters are determined dynamically. The first line of output for the `PC8250` class depends on what the last number for the `RS232` class will be. This is calculated by calling the base class version of the `FormatDebugOutput()` routine, using the scoping operator to override the virtual function selection. Once you know the first line number for this class, you can calculate the total number for the derived class by calling the `FormatDebugOutput()` routine for this class.

The next section of code performs all of the initialization of the UART. First you must identify the UART type by calling `check_uart()`. If no UART is detected, an error exit is taken. To store the current UART settings in the `saved_setting` data member, `read_settings()` is called. The new settings are initialized to the same state, then the parameters passed to the constructor help set up new settings. The new settings are then applied to the UART using the `set_uart_state()` protected member function. And the line parameters are set to those requested when the constructor was called, but the handshaking parameters and control lines are still in an unknown state.

The UART is then hooked to an interrupt handler. By default, `isr_8250()` will handle interrupts for the UART. If another handler was specified, it will be used instead. The `PC8250` object gets passed to the `Handler` object via the virtual `AddPort()` member function. It is up to the `Handler()` routine to establish its own interrupt handler at that point.

All four interrupts in the 8250 UART are enabled, the `modem_status` data member is initialized, and the UART is up and running. A single output to the 8259 interrupt controller is made to lower the priority of the keyboard interrupt. (The default for the PC is to have keyboard interrupts set at a higher priority than the communications ports, exactly the opposite of the way it should be.) Finally, before the constructor exits, DTR and RTS are set appropriately and the three handshaking types are set to their initialized values.

Since a constructor doesn't return a value, we depend on the `error_status` data member to convey a fatal error back to the calling program. Various errors can occur during initialization, rendering an `RS232` object unusable. By setting `error_status` to an error code, we not only let the calling program know that the constructor failed, but we also insure that none of the member functions will try to access an invalid port.

## THE PC8250 CLASS

### PC8250::set_uart_address_and_irq()

This private member function is called to do two things. First, it needs to determine the address of the UART, as well as the IRQ line on which the UART will generate interrupts. These two parameters can either be specified (from the constructor), or default values will be chose.

Second, this routine needs to assign the interrupt to a handler. The default handler will always be used for standard PC comm ports, but special hardware such as multiport boards will need special handlers as well.

### PC8250::~PC8250

The code for the destructor is considerably more simple than that for the constructor. It first disables interrupts in the UART, then calls the interrupt disconnect routine. If a Handler object owns the port, then the Handler::DeletePort() routine is called to disconnect the port from the interrupt service routine. Otherwise, the DisconnectFromIRQ() routine is called to do the job.

The saved settings are then applied to the UART so that its baud rate, parity, etc., are all set back to their values before the port was opened. Finally, the isr_data member is deleted, and the destructor can exit.

### PC8250::check_uart()

This routine is called by the constructor to determine if a valid UART is present at the address stored in the isr_data->uart data member. The simple check done here just looks at the IIR and verifies that the upper 6 bits are all set to 0. Before doing this, the FIFO Control Register is set to 0, since the two FIFO enabled bits could show up in the Interrupt ID Register.

Once the presence of the UART is established, the routine checks whether it is a 16550 UART. If so, the FIFOs are enabled, and the RX trigger level is set to 14 bytes. An interrupt will be generated when the FIFO has 14 bytes, doubling the time available to process the interrupt when compared to that available on a conventional 8250 UART.

If this function doesn't find a UART at the specified address, it sets the error_status to a fatal error flag, which shuts down all the other member functions in an attempt to minimize any trouble caused by continued use of the object.

### PC8250::check_rx_handshaking()

This routine is called after any member function that reads data from the RX buffer. If the RX buffer has passed below the low-water mark, and handshaking is in effect, it may be necessary to either raise a handshaking line or send an XON.

Each of the three possible handshaking conditions is handled individually. The DTR/DSR and RTS/CTS code is essentially identical, except for the actual control lines involved. Each checks to see if the particular mode of handshaking is in effect and if blocking is in effect. If so and the RX count has dropped below the low water mark, the appropriate control line is raised and the blocking flag is cleared.

The software handshaking code is nearly identical. The major difference is that instead of raising a control line, this code has to issue an XON, which means setting the `send_handshake_character` data member, then calling `jump_start()` to actually cause the transmission.

Note that all three of these routines have to momentarily disable interrupts in order to do their job properly. Both the interrupt service routine and this function are actively manipulating much of the same handshaking data, so you must block interference while critical changes are made.

### PC8250::read_byte()

This protected member function is the fundamental read function that is used whenever bytes need to be read in one at a time instead of in block mode. This is necessary any time the single character version of `RS232::Read()` is called, as well as the mode of `RS232::Read()` that scans for a terminator string while reading.

This function only takes up a few lines of code because all the hard work necessary to accomplish the read function has already been done elsewhere. Pulling the data out of the RX buffer is done with the `Queue::Remove()` function (discussed later in this chapter), with an error return if no characters are available. Once the character has been read in, a quick call to `PC8250::check_rx_handshaking()` will handle any handshaking generated by this call. Once that is done, the character that has just been read is returned to the calling program.

This is a protected function, and is intended to only be available to functions like `RS232::Read()`. It is a little more terse than the public functions available

## THE PC8250 CLASS

to the programmer. In particular, it doesn't support any of the timing options, and doesn't set the `ElapsedTime` or `ByteCount` data members. These high-level niceties are handled by other functions.

### PC8250::write_byte()

Like `read_byte()`, this is a protected function that is not intended for direct access by the application programmer. Instead, this virtual function is called by high-level functions in the base class such as `RS232::Write(int)`, which also support some of the niceties such as timing information in `ElapsedTime`. All this function does is check to see if it can successfully insert the character into the transmit queue using the inline `Queue` class member function `Queue::Insert()`. If successful, the routine then checks to see if transmit interrupts must be restarted. If interrupts appear to be stopped, `jump_start()` is called to get them going again.

### PC8250::read_buffer()

This is the block-oriented equivalent to `read_byte()`. This protected member function is not intended for direct use by the applications programmer. Instead, it is for the use of the high-level functions in class `RS232` such as `Read(void*)`. The `read_buffer()` function reads in bytes repeatedly into the user specified buffer until one of two things happens: either the RX buffer goes empty or the user buffer fills up. In either case, the actual number of characters read in is returned to the calling program in the `ByteCount` data member. The actual return from the function is either `RS232_SUCCESS` if all of the bytes requested were found, or `RS232_TIMEOUT` if only an incomplete read was accomplished.

In keeping with a convention used with the `RS232` class, the user buffer is terminated with a `'\0'` character after the characters have all been read in. This is done as a convenience to the programmer, and it comes in handy for many programs. For example, a terminal emulation program can have a code sequence that looks like this:

```
Port->ReadBuffer( buffer, 81 );
cout << buffer;
```

This is a little more efficient than a polling loop where a single character at a time is read in, then echoed out to some output stream. The major implication this has for the programmer is that any read request for *n* bytes must always be directed towards a buffer that has room for *n + 1* bytes.

Once `read_buffer()` has finished reading in bytes, it has to check for RX handshaking conditions. This is all managed by `PC8250::check_rx_handshaking`, so it can be accomplished with a single function call.

The routine then returns the data to the calling routine. Note that the `ElapsedTime` data member is not set here. It would be somewhat redundant, since this function will never wait for more data after the buffer is empty. The higher level functions that have a timing parameter are in more urgent need of returning an accurate time value.

### PC8250::write_buffer()

This is a virtual protected routine that is used by the high-level block-oriented write routines from class RS232. Like the previous three functions, it isn't intended for use directly by an application programmer, instead it is a support routine for other functions.

This function doesn't have any timing constraints so it simply stuffs characters from the user buffer into the TX Queue until one of two things happens: either the TX Queue fills up and can't handle any more data, or the entire user buffer is sent.

Once the routine is done stuffing characters into the TX Queue, it checks to see if transmit interrupts are actively running. If not, a quick call to `jump_start()` should get things started again.

After interrupts have been started, one of two values is returned to the calling program. `RS232_SUCCESS` is returned if all of the buffer was successfully transmitted. If only some of the buffer was sent, `RS232_TIMEOUT` is sent instead. The calling routine can then check the byte count in `ByteCount` to see how many characters were sent.

### PC8250::FlushRXBuffer()

This is an optional virtual function defined in class `RS232`. It is optional because it is already implemented in the base class. `RS232::FlushRXBuffer()` can

## THE PC8250 CLASS

empty the RX buffer by simply calling `read_buffer()` repeatedly until a `Byte-Count` of 0 is returned. At that point, you can assume that the RX buffer is empty.

The `PC8250` class implements its own version of this function simply for efficiency. Because of the implementation of the `Queue` class, emptying a queue is simply a matter of making a single call to an inline function which sets the head and tail pointers to be equal. This is definitely more fast and efficient than making numerous calls to `read_buffer()`, with all of its associated overhead.

After `FlushRXBuffer()` is done clearing the RX Queue, it naturally has to make a call to `PC8250::check_rx_handshaking()` to update any of the handshaking parameters. After clearing the buffer, any handshake conditions will have to be cleared as well.

You are pretty much guaranteed that this function will return `RS232_SUCCESS` that is, unless the port is in a fatal error state.

**PC8250::write_settings()**
**PC8250::read_settings()**

These two functions are grouped together here and in the source code because they are perfectly symmetrical. Both operate on the `settings` member of the class. One function reads in all the line settings from the UART and stores them in the `settings` object, the other reads the data from the `settings` object and stores them in the UART. And the code they use is very similar.

Both functions are protected and are used only by other member functions, not by the programmer. The `read_settings()` function is called in the constructor of the `PC8250` object and nowhere else. Its `settings` object is eventually transferred to the `saved_settings` member of the base `RS232` class. The `write_settings()` function is called in three different places. First, it is called in the constructor to establish the initial settings of the UART. It is also called in the destructor to restore the old settings of the UART to their original state. Finally, it is the engine for the `PC8250::Set()` function, which modifies one or more of the UART's line setting conditions.

These functions aren't available to the end user at least in part because of their lack of error detection. All data passed to `write_settings()` is already assumed to be valid. In our present definition of the `PC8250` class this is true, since all settings get passed through `Settings::Adjust()` before being used by

215

write_settings(). The read_settings() function does not verify that the UART it is being told to read is valid or that it, in fact, exists.

Both of these functions set parameters in the UART one by one. While there may be some benefit to breaking these routines into smaller individual modules (such as, one for setting the baud rate, one for the parity, etc.), this system works well and confines debugging to a single potential point of failure.

Note that for class PC8250, no attempt is made by read_settings() to save or restore any of the handshaking states. In a class interfacing to an O/S device driver that supports handshaking, it makes sense it makes sense to try and preserve the state. However, there is no DOS driver in use with the PC8250 class, so no default handshaking parameters exist.

**PC8250::Set()**

This function takes advantage of a couple of functions developed earlier to support the constructor. A single call to Settings::Adjust() parses through all the passed parameters, making sure they are valid, then updates their values into the settings object in the base class. Next, a single call to write_settings() writes all these new parameters out to the UART, performing a wholesale conversion of parameters.

This routine can, in fact, return with an error code. If any of the parameters passed to Settings::Adjust() looks invalid, Set() passes the appropriate error code back to the calling application program.

**PC8250::TXSpaceFree()**
**PC8250::RXSpaceUsed()**
**PC8250::TXSpaceUsed()**
**PC8250::RXSpaceFree()**

These four functions are grouped because they operate in nearly identical fashions. Two are mandatory virtual functions, while the other two are optional. However, since the space free and space used for both the TX Queue and RX Queues are readily available to member functions of class PC8250, all four functions are implemented.

## THE PC8250 CLASS

Every function just calls one of two inline functions from class `Queue` for either the RX Queue or the TX Queue. `Queue::FreeCount()` returns the space free in a queue, and `Queue::InUseCount()` returns the space in use.

**PC8250::Break()**

This function generates a break signal on the line. The 8250 class of UART has only minimal support for hardware breaks. To actually transmit a break, a bit in the LCR has to be set. The LCR is then held in that state for as long as necessary for the given break. Once time has expired, the break bit in the LCR is lifted, and the UART returns to normal operation.

This mode of operation is clearly problematic in a multitasking operating system. Obviously, we don't want to tie up an entire system while we wait for a break signal to complete. The `PC8250` class won't generally have to deal with this problem, since MS-DOS is a single tasking operating system. However, this class could be used in a specialized environment such as DESQView. When this is the case, the `IdleFunction()` used by the `RS232` class can be replaced with a function that yields time to the operating system.

**PC8250::Cd()**
**PC8250::Ri()**
**PC8250::Cts()**
**PC8250::Dsr()**

These four functions are nearly identical in implementation. Each function just picks a bit up out of the `modem_status` data member of the ISR data structure. The `modem_status` data member gets updated each time there is a modem status interrupt, so it always has the most recent status of all incoming control lines.

Following the general convention of this library, these functions only return a 1 or a 0. While any nonzero value is an acceptable boolean under C and C++, programmers will want to store the state of control lines in bit fields or similar C++ classes. Since they return only a single bit value, these functions can easily be used in this manner.

Although it wouldn't be possible to implement in every class derived from the `RS232` class, a useful enhancement to these functions would be to not just keep track of modem status *states*, but modem status *events* as well. For example, since the 8250 generates an interrupt any time a modem status line changes state, you could set a flag if CD drops low so that a BBS program could avoid the problem of missing a momentary drop in carrier. Even more useful would be the ability to detect ring pulses, which can easily be missed when a program is just polling the line with calls to Ri().

**PC8250::ParityError()**
**PC8250::BreakDetect()**
**PC8250::FramingError()**
**PC8250::HardwareOverrunError()**

These four functions are similar to the previous four modem status functions. Each of them just checks the state of a bit in the line_status word. Whenever a line status interrupt occurs, line_status is ORed with the contents of the UART's LSR. This means that the bits in line_status contain a cumulative record of all of the line status events that have occurred while the system has been running.

Although it is helpful to know that a software overrun error has occurred without missing a momentary state, these functions must also safely clear the flags so that a program can detect the next occurrence of an event. These functions differ from the four modem status functions in that the optional reset parameter for each can clear the line status bit.

Because the ISR can modify the line_status word while these routines are in the process of modifying it, the modification has to be made while interrupts are disabled. Since the only thing that happens while interrupts are disabled is the modification of a flag in memory, it isn't likely to have any impact on system performance.

Like the modem status functions, these functions also only return a 1 or a 0 for the state value, although presumably any boolean value would do.

**PC8250::SoftwareOverrunError()**

Like the hardware line status function, this function returns the state of an event, in this case the overflow of the receive buffer. However, this event is strictly a soft-

## THE PC8250 CLASS

ware matter, unlike the UART line status events. When the ISR receives a character and has no room for it in the RX buffer, it sets the `overflow` flag in the `isr_data` structure. This function just returns the value of that flag.

This function also has an optional parameter that can be used to clear the software overrun flag. Unlike the `line_status` word, interrupts don't have to be disabled to clear this flag. All that needs to be done to clear the overflow flag is to write a 0 to an integer, which is an atomic operation on the 80x86 processor architecture. It can be down without risking an interruption halfway through the operation.

### `PC8250::XonXoffHandshaking()`

This function also has a dual purpose. When called without any arguments, it just returns a boolean value to indicate whether handshaking is enabled. To do so, it checks the setting of the `xon_xoff` bit in the `isr_data->handshaking` word. If it is set, handshaking is enabled, and the function returns a 1. If it is clear, that form of handshaking is disabled, and a 0 is returned.

Turning handshaking on is relatively simple: All the routine has to do is set the `xon_xoff` bit in the handshaking status word. This doesn't even have to be done with interrupts disabled, since the ISR doesn't ever modify the handshaking status word. Once this bit is set, the next incoming data byte will automatically trigger the ISR to send an XOFF if the receive buffer is past the high-water mark. That way we don't have to worry about manually putting the port into a blocking state.

However, when turning off handshaking, you have to take some extra things into consideration. Since the port may have previously been in handshaking mode, the transmitter could be in a blocked state, and the port may have at some time issued an XOFF and gone into a blocking state. To manage this, the routine first clears the `xon_xoff` bit in the handshaking status word. Once this is done, the blocked and blocking states won't change unless we do so manually. If the port is in the blocked state, it received an XOFF from the remote end at some time and is still waiting for an XON. Clearing the `xon_xoff` bit in the `isr_data->blocked` word will solve half the problem. But clearing the status bit won't start the transmitter up again. You can resume the transmission of interrupts later in the routine. A call to `jump_start()` will begin transmit interrupts again by pulling the next available character out of the

TXQueue and sending it out the transmitter if and only if the other blocked bits are clear.

If the `xon_xoff` bit is set in the `isr_data->blocking` word, an XOFF was sent to the remote end to block it from further transmission. Since handshaking is turned off, the remote end won't ever receive an XON to get it started again unless it is sent out now. This routine takes care of that by checking the blocking bit and setting the `send_handshake_char` bit to XON. If the `send_handshake_char` character still has the last XOFF character in it, `send_handshake_char` is canceled and nothing is sent.

Once all this work is done and the call to `jump_start()` has been made, the `XonXoff` flag in the `settings` data member of the base class is set to the appropriate value, and the function returns.

`PC8250::RtsCtsHandshaking()`
`PC8250::DtrDsrHandshaking()`

These two functions do exactly the same thing as the previous function does, which is to report on a handshaking state and, optionally, change it. However, these functions perform their handshaking using the modem control lines, instead of by transmitting XON and XOFF characters, so they have to operate somewhat differently. The code for these two functions is nearly identical, with the only difference being which of the control lines they read and write.

Like the XON/XOFF function, when called with no arguments these functions just return their current handshaking status. A 1 means handshaking is enabled, and a 0 means it is disabled. As with the previous function, when the parameter is set to a 1 or a 0, a new handshaking mode is selected and requires a bit more effort to handle.

When either RTS/CTS or DTR/DSR handshaking is being enabled, the appropriate control line (RTS or DTR) is first set to a logic 1, so that the remote end won't initially be blocked. Then, with interrupts disabled, the state of the corresponding input control line is checked via the `modem_status` word. If CTS or DSR is low, the appropriate blocked bit is set. No other characters will be sent because the next TX interrupt will detect the blocked state. Finally, the `rts_cts` bit in the `handshaking` member is set, and interrupts are enabled. The remote end isn't blocked, but if the RX Queue is past the high water mark, the next RX interrupt will cause a blocking event

# THE PC8250 CLASS

and the appropriate modem control line will be lowered.

When handshaking is being enabled, the `Settings.Rts` and/or `Settings.Dtr` bits are also set to the somewhat odd value of `REMOTE_CONTROL`. This special value is used to indicate that the line is being used for handshaking and can be expected to change on a regular basis.

The sequence of events that takes place when hardware handshaking is being disabled is much simpler. If hardware handshaking was previously enabled, the appropriate control line is raised to a level 1, to make sure any blocking status is cleared. After raising the line and clearing the appropriate bits in the `handshaking`, `blocked`, and `blocking members`, a call to `jump_start()` is made. If the transmitter was previously in a blocked state, this will get it restarted.

When the routine exits, its final task is to return the current setting of the appropriate type of handshaking, which it does simply by testing the appropriate bit in the `isr_data->handshaking` word.

**PC8250::Dtr()**
**PC8250::Rts()**

These two functions also have two purposes. When called without any parameters, they simply return the current setting of the output modem control line. When called with a parameter other than UNCHANGED, they also set the output of the control line either high or low.

The control line might already be in use as a handshaking line. If this is the case, the request to change the output is rejected with a return code of `PC8250_HANDSHAKE_LINE_IN_USE`. If the line is not in use for handshaking, its setting is modified as its control bit in the 8250 modem control register is modified. Since the interrupt service routine could also modify the MCR, `Rts()` and `Cts()` have to write to the control lines with interrupts disabled.

The `settings.Rts` or `settings.Dsr` bits in the base class are also modified when the line is changed. The correct way to examine the settings of these control lines is to read back the settings structure, so these values need to be kept up-to-date.

### PC8250::PeekBuffer()

Since the interrupt service routine maintains its receive buffer as a data member of the derived class `PC8250`, it should be easy to peek into that receive buffer. In this case, it was made even easier by the fact that the `Queue` class has a member function that will perform the equivalent of the peek buffer on request.

Because of these convenient facts, the `PeekBuffer()` routine only takes up a few lines of code. A single call to the `Queue::Peek()` function reads in as many bytes as possible from the RX Queue and returns the count to be stored in the `ByteCount` data member. The only thing to do at this point is to terminate the buffer with a `'\0'` character and return to the calling program.

### PC8250::FlushTXBuffer()

Flushing the transmit buffer is an optional virtual functions. Not every driver will have the easy access to the output buffer that `class PC8250` has. In this class, a single call to a member function of `class Queue` for the TX Queue object takes care of clearing the buffer out. This member function is an inline function that just has to set the head and tail pointers of the queue to the same value.

The only complication is that interrupts must be disabled during the clearing operation, because the ISR can modify the queue pointers in the middle of the operation, leading to unexpected results.

### PC8250::FormatDebugOutput()

As I described in Chapter 2, the debug output function has to work in cooperation with the same function in the base class. Each class in a hierarchy of derived classes is free to contribute its own lines of output, as many or as few as necessary. By definition, this function returns a total line count it will need when it is called with no arguments. In the constructor for the `PC8250` object, we call `RS232::FormatDebugOutput()` to determine how many lines of output the base class will contribute. We then know which line our first line output will appear on.

As presently coded, the `PC8250` class contributes six lines to the debug output. When this routine is called with a buffer pointer set to 0, the caller is asking

# THE PC8250 CLASS

how many lines total can be expected from us. In this case, we return the total contribution of the base class plus six, for a total of eight.

If this routine is called with a valid buffer pointer, we need to format a line of output and return it to the caller. If the line number requested was less than the total contribution of the base class, the function call is passed up the line to the base class for processing. If, instead, the line number is one of the lines designated for class `PC8250`, this routine formats it with pertinent data and returns it to the calling function.

```
Base class: RS232  COM1    Error status: Success
Saved Settings:      2400,N,8,1  DTR,RTS:  0, 0  XON/OFF,RTS/CTS,DTR/DSR: 0,0,0
Current Settings:    2400,N,8,1  DTR,RTS:  1, 1  XON/OFF,RTS/CTS,DTR/DSR: 0,0,0
Derived class: PC8250    UART: 03f8  Overflow: 0  TX Running: 0  Line Status: 00
TX Head, Tail, Count    6    6    0  RX Head,Tail,Count  330  330    0
Counts: TX:    6  RX:    330  MS:    0  LS:    0  CTS/DSR/RI/CD: 1100
Handshake DTR/RTS/XON : 000  Blocking: 000  Blocked: 000  Handshake char: ffff
Parity Err: 0  Break Det: 0  Overrun Err: 0  Framing Err: 0  FIFO Setting:  0
```

**Figure 3-9. PC8250::FormatDebugOutput() results.**

Figure 3-9 shows the output from this routine when called for every line possible. This version of the debug output just attempts to show all of the member data, so that a programmer or user can attempt to interpret the current state of the port. While this type of display may not be particularly useful to the end user of an application, it can be invaluable to a programmer during development.

One other nice feature about the debug output is that it is easily extensible. It would be relatively easy to derive a new class from `PC8250` that retained all the same functionality, but added a few new lines of output to the FormatDebugOutput() routine. This feature demonstrates the strength of C++ in making it easy to add on to existing work.

## `PC8250::ErrorName()`

Like the previous function, the `ErrorName()` function works by extending the same function in the base class. Each derived class is free to create its own error codes. If they do not overlap with the error codes in the base class, they can be properly translated into ASCII.

Here, three ranges of error codes are defined by the base class. They are the fatal errors, warning errors, and success messages. If the error code passed to this function appears to belong to the base class, the code is passed up to RS232::ErrorName() for translation. Otherwise, this routine does its best to translate the error code as one of the ones defined for this class.

## Support Packages

Two different support packages are needed to implement the PC8250 class. The first is the Queue class, which is used to support the transmit and receive queues. The second package is the interrupt manager, which is a set of general-purpose code that sets up interrupt handlers. Both packages are rather generic, and could easily prove useful elsewhere.

### The Queue package

The Queue package consists of the Queue class definition, along with nine member functions, including the constructor. All but one of the functions are defined as inline functions, for two reasons. First, these functions are used when efficiency is important, such as in the ISR. Execution speed is at an absolute premium in such frequently called routinesideal applications for inline code. Second, the inline functions are generally very short and, in some cases, inline code may not take much more code space than a separately compiled function combined with calling overhead.

Because most of the functions are inline, most of the code is found in the header file QUEUE.H. QUEUE.CPP only contains the lone compiled function, Queue::Peek().

```
// ********************* START OF QUEUE.H *********************
//
// This header file contains the definitions needed to use the
// Queue class.  This class is used for both the input and
// output queues used by class PC8250.  Most of the functions
// in this class are defined as inline, as speed is essential
```

# THE PC8250 CLASS

```
// in the interrupt service routine.  Those that aren't can
// be found in QUEUE.CPP
//

#ifndef _QUEUE_DOT_H
#define _QUEUE_DOT_H

const unsigned int QueueSize = 1024;
const unsigned int HighWaterMark = ( QueueSize * 3 ) / 4;
const unsigned int LowWaterMark = QueueSize / 4;

class Queue
{
    private :
        volatile unsigned int head_index;
        volatile unsigned int tail_index;
        volatile unsigned char buffer[ QueueSize ];
    public :
        Queue( void );
        int Insert( unsigned char c );
        int Remove( void );
        int Peek( unsigned char *buffer, int count );
        int InUseCount( void );
        int FreeCount( void );
        int Head( void ) { return head_index; }
        int Tail( void ) { return tail_index; }
        void Clear( void );
};

inline Queue::Queue( void )
{
    head_index = 0;
    tail_index = 0;
}

inline int Queue::Insert( unsigned char c )
{
    unsigned int temp_head = head_index;
```

```cpp
    buffer[ temp_head++ ] = c;
    if ( temp_head >= QueueSize )
        temp_head = 0;
    if ( temp_head == tail_index )
        return 0;
    head_index = temp_head;
    return 1;
}

inline int Queue::Remove( void )
{
    unsigned char c;
    if ( head_index == tail_index )
        return( -1 );
    c = buffer[ tail_index++ ];
    if ( tail_index >= QueueSize )
        tail_index = 0;
    return c;
}

inline int Queue::InUseCount( void )
{
    if ( head_index >= tail_index )
        return head_index - tail_index;
    else
        return head_index + QueueSize - tail_index;
}

inline int Queue::FreeCount( void )
{
    return QueueSize - 1 - InUseCount();
}

inline void Queue::Clear( void )
{
    tail_index = head_index;
}
```

# THE PC8250 CLASS

```
#endif   // #ifndef _QUEUE_DOT_H

// ********************* END OF QUEUE.H *********************
```

**Listing 3-7. QUEUE.H**

```cpp
// ******************* START OF QUEUE.CPP *******************
//
// Most of the queue class functions are defined in QUEUE.H as
// inline for speed.  This routine probably won't generate inline
// code with most compilers, and it is not used in the ISR, so
// speed is not as critical.  Thus, it gets defined normally.

#include "portable.h"
#include "queue.h"

int Queue::Peek( unsigned char *buf, int count )
{
    unsigned int index = tail_index;
    int total = 0;

    while ( total < count && index != head_index ) {
        *buf++ = buffer[ index++ ];
        if ( index >= QueueSize )
            index = 0;
        total++;
    }
    return total;
}
// ********************* END OF QUEUE.CPP *********************
```

**Listing 3-8. QUEUE.CPP**

227

The Queue class functions are used in various places throughout the PC8250 class code. The functions are described below.

Queue::Queue()           The constructor for the queue sets the head and tail indices to 0. The buffer is allocated automatically as a data member of the queue.

Queue::Insert()          The insertion routine tries to stuff a character into the buffer, advancing the head index. If the buffer is full, the function returns a 0, indicating failure. Otherwise a 1 is returned, indicating success.

Queue::Remove()          This function tries to remove a character from the buffer, advancing the tail index if successful. If a character can't be removed, a -1 is returned, otherwise the character is removed and returned.

Queue::Peek()            This is the only function in the package that isn't defined as an inline function. It tries to pull as many characters out of the receive buffer as requested, without advancing the tail pointer. The actual count of characters removed is returned.

Queue::InUseCount()      This function returns the number of characters presently stored in the Queue.

Queue::FreeCount()       This function returns the number of spaces available in the Queue.

# THE PC8250 CLASS

Queue::Head()        This function returns the current head index for the queue. The only place this is presently used is in the debug display output. Ideally, the head index would be a read-only element, but there is no such thing in C++.

Queue::Tail()        This function returns the current tail index for the queue. Like the Head() function, this is only presently used in the debug output dump.

Queue::Clear()       This function sets the tail index to the same value as the head index, effectively emptying the queue.

## The interrupt manager package

This package is a set of functions that connect and disconnect interrupt routines to and from interrupt vectors. This package has two function calls that are used in the PC8250 class. The ConnectToIRQ() function is used to connect a function to an interrupt vector, and the DisconnectFromIrq() function removes that connection. When a function is connected to an interrupt vector, the connect routine also accepts a parameter specifying a pointer to a data item that is passed to the function when the interrupt occurs. For the PC8250 class, the function is always isr_8250(), and the data item is a pointer to the isr_data structure for the given port.

The interrupt manager works by keeping a separate stub routine for each of the usable IRQs on the PC. When an interrupt is connected to a particular IRQ, a DOS function call is made to connect the interrupt vector for that IRQ to the stub function. When control passes to that stub function, it immediately calls the user-specified function with a pointer to the user-specified data area.

This package has to deal with a compiler-induced complication as well. Microsoft and Borland both support the _interrupt function type modifier, which lets a

C function be branched to directly as an interrupt service routine. To use an `_inter-rupt` function as an ISR, MS-DOS functions 0x25 and 0x35 are called to replace the old interrupt vector with a pointer to a C function. Unfortunately, Zortech has a completely different method of hooking into interrupts, so the code is blemished with a few occurrences of "`#ifdef`" code.

```
// ********************* START OF PCIRQ.H *********************
//
// This header file has the prototypes and definitions used with the
// IRQ manager routines.  The three public functions have their
// prototypes here.  All the code for the IRQ manager is found in
// PCIRQ.CPP.

#ifndef _PCIRQ_DOT_H
#define _PCIRQ_DOT_H

#include "rs232.h"

enum irq_name { IRQ0=0, IRQ1,   IRQ2,   IRQ3,   IRQ4,   IRQ5,   IRQ6,
                                                                IRQ7,
                IRQ8,   IRQ9,   IRQ10,  IRQ11,  IRQ12,  IRQ13,  IRQ14,
                                                                IRQ15,
                ILLEGAL_IRQ = -1 };

RS232Error ConnectToIrq( irq_name irq,
                         void *isr_data_block,
                         void ( *isr_routine )
                             ( void *isr_data_block ) );
int DisconnectFromIRQ( enum irq_name irq );

#endif // #ifndef _PCIRQ_DOT_H

// ********************* END OF PCIRQ.H *********************
```

**Listing 3-9. PCIRQ.H**

# THE PC8250 CLASS

```cpp
// ******************* START OF PCIRQ.CPP *******************
//
// This module contains the interrupt management code.
// ConnectToIRQ() is called to establish an interrupt handler
// function, DisconnectFromIRQ() is called to break the
// connection.  The funny parameter passed to all of the isr
// routines is there because of the way Zortech calls interrupt
// handlers.  There are several places in this module where you
// may see casts to type NEW_HANDLER that appear unnecessary.
// They are there strictly to mollify Turbo C++ 1.0.


#include <dos.h>
#include "portable.h"
#include "pcirq.h"

#ifndef __ZTC__

struct INT_DATA {
    void *dummy;
};

#endif

typedef void ( INTERRUPT *OLD_HANDLER )( void );
typedef int ( INTERRUPT *NEW_HANDLER )( struct INT_DATA *pd );

// Prototypes for all the handlers defined here

int INTERRUPT isr2( struct INT_DATA *pd );
int INTERRUPT isr3( struct INT_DATA *pd );
int INTERRUPT isr4( struct INT_DATA *pd );
int INTERRUPT isr5( struct INT_DATA *pd );
int INTERRUPT isr7( struct INT_DATA *pd );
int INTERRUPT isr10( struct INT_DATA *pd );
int INTERRUPT isr11( struct INT_DATA *pd );
int INTERRUPT isr15( struct INT_DATA *pd );
int INTERRUPT int1b( struct INT_DATA *pd );
int INTERRUPT int23( struct INT_DATA *pd );
```

# SERIAL COMMUNICATIONS: A C++ DEVELOPER'S GUIDE

```cpp
// When any IRQs are hooked by one of our routines, the IRQ
// code disables control-break termination by taking over the two
// control-break vectors.  The saved control-break state is
// stored in the following three variables.

static OLD_HANDLER old_int1b;
static OLD_HANDLER old_int23;
static unsigned char old_dos_break_state;

// A count of the number of handlers currently in use.

static int count = 0;

// This structure keeps track of the state of each of the
// eight possible IRQ lines our program can take over.  This
// includes the address of the new handler, the old handler, and
// most importantly, the data pointer passed to the new handler
// when it is invoked.

struct {
    enum irq_name irq;
    void *isr_data;
    void ( *isr_routine)( void *isr_data );
    NEW_HANDLER handler;
    OLD_HANDLER old_isr;
    int old_pic_enable_bit;
} irq_data[] = { { IRQ2,  0, 0, (NEW_HANDLER) isr2,  0, 0 },
                 { IRQ3,  0, 0, (NEW_HANDLER) isr3,  0, 0 },
                 { IRQ4,  0, 0, (NEW_HANDLER) isr4,  0, 0 },
                 { IRQ5,  0, 0, (NEW_HANDLER) isr5,  0, 0 },
                 { IRQ7,  0, 0, (NEW_HANDLER) isr7,  0, 0 },
                 { IRQ10, 0, 0, (NEW_HANDLER) isr10, 0, 0 },
                 { IRQ11, 0, 0, (NEW_HANDLER) isr11, 0, 0 },
                 { IRQ15, 0, 0, (NEW_HANDLER) isr15, 0, 0 }
               };

// All of the new ISR handlers are called when the interrupt
// occurs.  All they do is call the hooked routine, passing it a
// pointer to the data block it asked for in the ConnectToIRQ()
```

## THE PC8250 CLASS

```c
// routine.  When this is done, they take care of issuing the EOI
// instruction and then exiting.  The "return 1" is necessary for
// Zortech's interrupt handlers.  If a "return 0" is used, the
// handler will then chain to the old interrupt, which we don't
// want.

int INTERRUPT isr2( struct INT_DATA *pd )
{
    UNUSED( pd );
    irq_data[ 0 ].isr_routine( irq_data[ 0 ].isr_data );
    CLI();
    OUTPUT( 0x20, 0x20 );
    return 1;
}

int INTERRUPT isr3( struct INT_DATA *pd )
{
    UNUSED( pd );
    irq_data[ 1 ].isr_routine( irq_data[ 1 ].isr_data );
    CLI();
    OUTPUT( 0x20, 0x20 );
    return 1;
}

int INTERRUPT isr4( struct INT_DATA *pd )
{
    UNUSED( pd );
    irq_data[ 2 ].isr_routine( irq_data[ 2 ].isr_data );
    CLI();
    OUTPUT( 0x20, 0x20 );
    return 1;
}

int INTERRUPT isr5( struct INT_DATA *pd )
{
    UNUSED( pd );
    irq_data[ 3 ].isr_routine( irq_data[ 3 ].isr_data );
    CLI();
    OUTPUT( 0x20, 0x20 );
```

```
        return 1;
}

int INTERRUPT isr7( struct INT_DATA *pd )
{
    UNUSED( pd );
    irq_data[ 4 ].isr_routine( irq_data[ 4 ].isr_data );
    CLI();
    OUTPUT( 0x20, 0x20 );
    return 1;
}


// These routines have to send an EOI to the second 8250 PIC
// as well as the first.

int INTERRUPT isr10( struct INT_DATA *pd )
{
    UNUSED( pd );
    irq_data[ 5 ].isr_routine( irq_data[ 5 ].isr_data );
    CLI();
    OUTPUT( 0xa0, 0x20 );
    OUTPUT( 0x20, 0x20 );
    return 1;
}

int INTERRUPT isr11( struct INT_DATA *pd )
{
    UNUSED( pd );
    irq_data[ 6 ].isr_routine( irq_data[ 6 ].isr_data );
    CLI();
    OUTPUT( 0xa0, 0x20 );
    OUTPUT( 0x20, 0x20 );
    return 1;
}

int INTERRUPT isr15( struct INT_DATA *pd )
{
    UNUSED( pd );
```

## THE PC8250 CLASS

```
    irq_data[ 7 ].isr_routine( irq_data[ 7 ].isr_data );
    CLI();
    OUTPUT( 0xa0, 0x20 );
    OUTPUT( 0x20, 0x20 );
    return 1;
}

// The two control-break vectors do nothing, so that Control-C
// and Contrl-Break both have no effect on our program.

int INTERRUPT int1b( struct INT_DATA *pd )
{
    UNUSED( pd );
    return 1;
}

int INTERRUPT int23( struct INT_DATA *pd )
{
    UNUSED( pd );
    return 1;
}

// This utility routine is only used internally to these
// routines.  It sets control of the given interrupt number to
// the handler specified as a parameter.  It returns the
// address of the old handler to the caller, so it can be stored
// for later restoration.  Note that Zortech stores the old
// handler internally, so we just return a 0.

OLD_HANDLER HookVector( int interrupt_number,
                        NEW_HANDLER new_handler )
{
#ifdef __ZTC__
    int_intercept( interrupt_number, new_handler, 0 );
    return 0;
#else  // #ifdef __ZTC__
    union REGS r;
    struct SREGS s = { 0, 0, 0, 0 };
    OLD_HANDLER old_handler = 0;
```

235

```c
        r.h.al = (unsigned char) interrupt_number;
        r.h.ah = 0x35;
        int86x( 0x21, &r, &r, &s );
        *( (unsigned FAR *) old_handler + 1 ) = s.es;
        *( (unsigned FAR *) old_handler ) = r.x.bx;
        s.ds = FP_SEG( new_handler );
        r.x.dx = FP_OFF( new_handler );
        r.h.al = (unsigned char) interrupt_number;
        r.h.ah = 0x25;
        int86x( 0x21, &r, &r, &s );
        return old_handler;
#endif // #ifdef __ZTC__ ... #else
}

// When we are done with an IRQ, we restore the old handler
// here.  Note once again that Zortech does this internally, so
// we don't have to.

void UnHookVector( int interrupt_number, OLD_HANDLER old_handler )
{
#ifdef __ZTC__
    int_restore( interrupt_number );
#else // #ifdef __ZTC__
    union REGS r;
    struct SREGS s = { 0, 0, 0, 0 };

    s.ds = FP_SEG( old_handler );
    r.x.dx = FP_OFF( old_handler );
    r.h.al = (unsigned char) interrupt_number;
    r.h.ah = 0x25;
    int86x( 0x21, &r, &r, &s );
#endif // #ifdef __ZTC__ ... #else
}
```

// When we have taken over an interrupt, we don't want
// keyboard breaks to cause us to exit without properly restoring
// vectors.  This routine takes over the DOS and BIOS
// control-break routines, and sets the DOS BREAK flag to 0.  The
// old state of all these variables is saved off so it can be

# THE PC8250 CLASS

```c
// restored when the last interrupt routine is restored.

void TrapKeyboardBreak( void )
{
    union REGS r;

    old_int1b = HookVector( 0x1b, (NEW_HANDLER) int1b );
    old_int23 = HookVector( 0x23, (NEW_HANDLER) int23 );
    r.h.ah = 0x33;
    r.h.al = 0;
    int86( 0x21, &r, &r );
    old_dos_break_state = r.h.dl;
    r.h.ah = 0x33;
    r.h.al = 1;
    r.h.dl = 0;
    int86( 0x21, &r, &r );
}

// When the last interrupt is restored, we can set the
// control-break vectors back where they belong, and restore the
// old setting of the DOS break flag.

void RestoreKeyboardBreak( void )
{
    union REGS r;

    UnHookVector( 0x1b, old_int1b );
    UnHookVector( 0x23, old_int23 );
    r.h.ah = 0x33;
    r.h.al = 1;
    r.h.dl = old_dos_break_state;
    int86( 0x21, &r, &r );
}

// When connecting to an IRQ, I pass it an IRQ number, plus a
// pointer to a function that will handle the interrupt.  The
// function gets passed a pointer to a data block of its choice,
// which will vary depending on what type of interrupt is being
// handled.
```

```c
RS232Error ConnectToIrq( enum irq_name irq,
                        void *isr_data,
                        void ( *isr_routine )( void *isr_data ) )
{
    int i;
    int pic_mask;
    int pic_address;
    int interrupt_number;
    int temp;

    for ( i = 0 ; ; i++ ) {
        if ( irq_data[ i ].irq == irq )
            break;
        if ( irq_data[ i ].irq == IRQ15 )
            return RS232_ILLEGAL_IRQ;
    }
    if ( irq_data[ i ].isr_routine != 0 )
        return RS232_IRQ_IN_USE;
    if ( count++ == 0 )
        TrapKeyboardBreak();
    irq_data[ i ].isr_data = isr_data;
    irq_data[ i ].isr_routine = isr_routine;

    pic_mask = 1 << ( irq % 8 );
    if ( irq < IRQ8 ) {
        pic_address = 0x20;
        interrupt_number = irq + 8;
    } else {
        interrupt_number = irq + 104;
        pic_address = 0xa0;
    }
    irq_data[ i ].old_isr = HookVector( interrupt_number,
                                        irq_data[ i ].handler );

    temp = INPUT( pic_address + 1 );
    irq_data[ i ].old_pic_enable_bit = temp & pic_mask;
    OUTPUT( pic_address + 1, temp & ~pic_mask );
    return RS232_SUCCESS;
}
```

# THE PC8250 CLASS

```c
// This routine restores an old interrupt vector.

int DisconnectFromIRQ( enum irq_name irq )
{
    int i;
    int pic_mask;
    int pic_address;
    int interrupt_number;
    int temp;

    for ( i = 0 ; ; i++ ) {
        if ( irq_data[ i ].irq == irq )
            break;
        if ( irq_data[ i ].irq == IRQ15 )
            return 0;
    }
    if ( irq_data[ i ].isr_routine == 0 )
        return 0;

    irq_data[ i ].isr_data = 0;
    irq_data[ i ].isr_routine = 0;

    pic_mask = 1 << ( irq % 8 );
    if ( irq < IRQ8 ) {
        pic_address = 0x20;
        interrupt_number = irq + 8;
    } else {
        interrupt_number = irq + 104;
        pic_address = 0xa0;
    }

    temp = INPUT( pic_address + 1 );
    temp &= ~pic_mask;
    temp |= irq_data[ i ].old_pic_enable_bit;
    OUTPUT( pic_address + 1, temp );

    UnHookVector( interrupt_number, irq_data[ i ].old_isr );

    if ( --count == 0 )
```

**239**

```
        RestoreKeyboardBreak();
    return 1;
}
// ********************* END OF PCIRQ.CPP *********************
```

**Listing 3-10. PCIRQ.CPP**

`ConnectToIrq()`

This function takes three arguments: an IRQ number, a function name, and a data pointer. It attempts to set up the interrupt vectors so that when the interrupt defined for that IRQ takes place, a call is made to the C function specified as an argument with a pointer to the data item.

When the connect routine is called, it also saves off the present status of the 8259 PIC controller for that particular line. When the function is finally disconnected from the interrupt vector, the 8259 state is restored.

When the first port is connected to an interrupt vector, the IRQ manager package also does its best to disable the ability of the user to break out of the program from the keyboard with either Control-C or Control-Break. It does this by taking over INT 23H and INT 1BH, both of which can be invoked when one of these events occur. When the last IRQ is restored to its original state, the break vectors are restored to their original settings, which will allow the user to break.

`int DisconnectFromIRQ()`

This function takes a single argument, which is an IRQ number. The disconnect function attempts to restore both the old interrupt vector and the enable/disable bit for that IRQ in the 8259 PIC. In the event that there isn't a stored vector for this IRQ, an error value of 0 is returned.

## A Test Program

Appendix A describes in detail a general-purpose test program that can be used with the `RS232` class. `TEST232.CPP` is a general-purpose program that lets you test most of the functionality of any of the classes that will be developed in this and following chapters. Figure 3-10 shows a screen shot from the program as config-

```
OK
ATDT250-3778
CARRIER 9600
PROTOCOL: LAP-M
COMPRESSION: V.42BIS
CONNECT 9600




F1  Help Toggle        ALT F1  Toggle XON/XOFF
F2  Next port          ALT F2  Toggle RTS/CTS
F3  Spew Toggle        ALT F3  Toggle DTR/DSR
F4  Reading Toggle     ALT F4  Toggle RTS
F5  Set baud rate      ALT F5  Toggle DTR
F6  Set parity         ALT F6  Flush RX Buffer
F7  Set word length    ALT F7  Flush TX Buffer
F8  Set stop bits      ALT F8  Peek at 1 byte
F9  Send break         ALT F9  Read a byte
F10 Exit               ALT F10 Send 1K block
```

**Figure 3-10. TEST232.EXE with the help screen.**

sion between the keyboard and the `PC8250 port`. In this case, the port has been attached to a Practical Peripherals V.32*bis* modem and is engaged in an on-line session. The bottom half of the screen has a description of the function keys that can be pressed for quick testing of many of the features of the class. Plenty of room is left for further customization of the function keys.

Figure 3-11 shows the same program with the help screen turned off. In this mode, the bottom half of the screen shows a port dump, with all the available information that the debug output functions supply. Watching this information while the program runs and function keys are pressed can give you an excellent feel for how the class operates.

The actual process of building a custom program requires small modifications to two files. First, the actual source file for the test program, `TEST232.CPP` has to be changed. When testing different classes, we will have to make very minor adjustments to the main program.

```
    Last caller  : MARK NELSON
    08/14/1992   10:02pm
    _____

    What is your first name? Mark Nelson
    Looking up "MARK NELSON". Please wait...
    Welcome MARK NELSON from Greenleaf World HQ.
    Password? *****



Base class: RS232  COM1   Status: Success
Byte count:       0  Elapsed time:        0  TX Free: 1023  RX Used:     0
Saved port:    2400,N, 8, 1  DTR,RTS: 0, 0  XON/OFF,RTS/CTS,DTR/DSR: -1,-1,-1
Current port:  9600,N,8,1    DTR,RTS: 1, 1  XON/OFF,RTS/CTS,DTR/DSR:  0, 0, 0
Derived class: PC8250  UART: 03f8  Overflow: 0  TX Running: 0  Line Status: 6b
TX Head, Tail, Count    48    48    0  RX Head,Tail,Count  748   748    0
Counts: TX:      49  RX:   748  MS:      1  LS:      1  CTS/DSR/RI/CD: 1101
Handshake DTR/RTS/XON : 000  Blocking: 000  Blocked: 000  Handshake char: ffff
Parity Err: 0  Break Det: 0  Overrun Err: 1  Framing Err: 1  FIFO Setting: 0
Uart type: 8250
```

**Figure 3-11. TEST232.EXE with the debug display.**

The first thing we have to do is include the header file needed to define the PC8250 class. I just append this to the normal list of header files at the top of the program, so that it looks like this:

```
#include "portable.h"
#include <stdio.h>
#include <stdlib.h>
#include <string.h>
#include <conio.h>
#include <ctype.h>
#include "rs232.h"
#include "textwind.h"
#include "pc8250.h"
```

For this particular program, I was only testing a single port. In order to give myself a little extra screen space, I simply changed the window count to 1. The program automatically reconfigures the size of the window to take advantage of the extra space:

## THE PC8250 CLASS

```
#define WINDOW_COUNT 1
```

Finally, I modified the loop that opens the ports and windows, so it will open a `PC8250` port:

```
for ( i = 0 ; i < 1 ; i++ ) {
    switch ( i ) {
        default :
            Ports[ i ] = new PC8250( port_names[ i ],
                                    9600, 'N', 8, 1 );
    }
}
```

The make file that builds the test program also needs to be slightly modified, since each class will require different files to be linked in. These implementation dependent files are defined in a single line in the makefile with the symbol `FILES`. The line looks like this:

```
FILES = pc8250.obj pcirq.obj isr_8250.obj queue.obj
```

Finally, the executable can be built and tested following the instructions in Appendix A.

### Conclusion

The `PC8250` class is one of the most fully featured classes that we will use in this book. While the amount of code to digest in this chapter is fairly long, it provides an excellent reference we can use time and time again when developing other classes.

CHAPTER 4

# Shared Interrupt Devices

In this chapter, I will give this book's first demonstration of actual code reuse. The basic `PC8250` class developed in the previous chapter works with standard IBM compatible Comm ports. By developing some new derivatives of the `Handler` class, all the code in class PC8250 will work properly with shared interrupt ports of several different varieties. In the first part of the chapter, the Microchannel handler will be used to manage up to seven Comm ports sharing a single interrupt on a MicroChannel architecture computer. A somewhat more complicated approach will be needed to work with unintelligent multiport boards. The `Multiport` class developed for use with the standard multiport boards from Boca Research is easily adapted or modified to work with boards from nearly any manufacturer.

## The MicroChannel Handler

As was discussed earlier in this book, when IBM developed the MicroChannel bus, they made several improvements over the ISA bus used in their earlier PCs. For our discussion, the most significant modification was to the IRQ lines on the bus. The IRQ lines on the ISA bus were directly driven by TTL output lines from individual cards, and the 8259 interrupt controller was programmed to generate interrupts when the IRQ line changed from the idle state to the active state. This made it impossible for more than one device at a time to use an IRQ line.

Under the MicroChannel Architecture (MCA), the 8259 interrupt controller is level-triggered instead of edge-triggered. This is an improvement because multiple devices can share the same interrupt line. Because of IRQ conflicts, it is difficult if not impossible to use more than two COM ports on a standard PC. Applications that need to use three or four ports need to use multiport boards, which generally cost quite a bit more per port.

IBM defined the PS/2 line as supporting up to eight RS-232 ports, designated as COM1 through COM8. COM1 and COM2 are defined identically to their counterparts on the ISA PCs, with COM1 residing on IRQ4 and COM2 using IRQ3. Because of the MicroChannel bus, IBM was able to define COM3 through COM8 as all using IRQ3. Table 4-1 shows a map of the I/O addresses and IRQ lines for PS/2 COM ports.

Table 4-1. MicroChannel UART parameters.

| Port | I/O Address | IRQ Line |
|------|-------------|----------|
| COM1 | 0x3f8 | IRQ4 |
| COM2 | 0x2f8 | IRQ3 |
| COM3 | 0x3220 | IRQ3 |
| COM4 | 0x3228 | IRQ3 |
| COM5 | 0x4220 | IRQ3 |
| COM6 | 0x4228 | IRQ3 |
| COM7 | 0x5220 | IRQ3 |
| COM8 | 0x5228 | IRQ3 |

The UART addressing plan in the preceding Table has the advantage of working properly with existing communications software. Applications that just use COM1 and/or COM2 will still work without modification on MicroChannel machines. But it is now possible to write new applications that use COM3 through COM8 simultaneously and still work properly on the MicroChannel bus.

## ISR Protocols

There are two equally valid approaches towards sharing the IRQ lines on the MicroChannel BUS. The first approach is known as interrupt chaining and it has the official blessing of IBM's Technical Reference Manual. With this technique, each device that has an ISR for a MicroChannel device keeps track of any previously installed interrupt handler. When it comes time to service an interrupt on the given IRQ line, the interrupt handler first checks to see if its device needs servicing. If so, the normal interrupt handling routine is invoked. Once the handler routine is done, instead of returning control to the interrupted process via the IRET instruction, the interrupt routine chains to the previously installed handler.

# SHARED INTERRUPT DEVICES

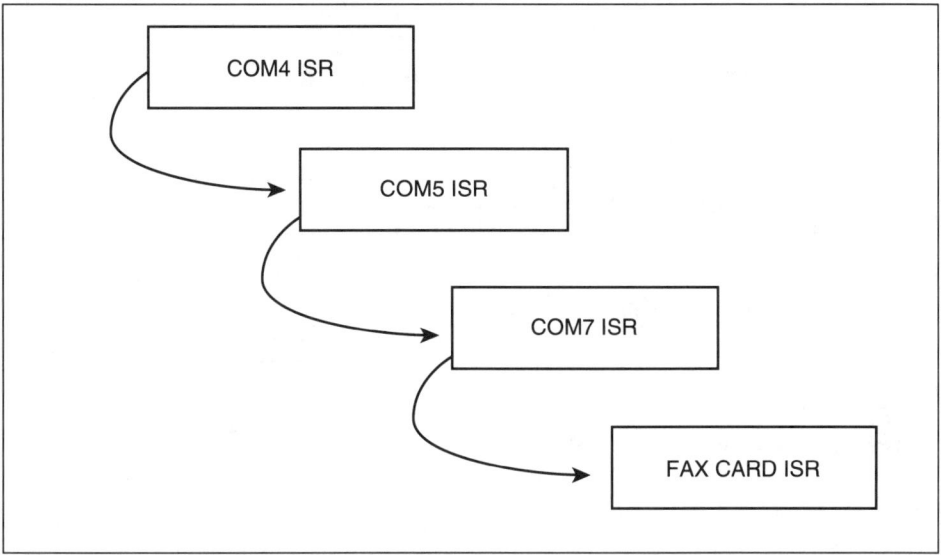

Figure 4-1. The MicroChannel interrupt chain.

Figure 4-1 shows a sample of what this might look like in a heavily populated MicroChannel computer. The full complement of eight COM ports reside on the same IRQ line, as well as a FAX card. A single process has opened three of the COM ports, and a device driver is managing the FAX card.

When an interrupt occurs on IRQ3 on this system, control first passes to the handler that was most recently installed. In this case, that is COM4, but it could just as easily have been any other port. The COM4 ISR completes and then passes control to the COM5 ISR, which in turn passes control to the COM7 ISR, which ends the chain by passing control to the FAX card ISR.

While this chaining mechanism works well, there is one major problem with it: lack of support. The number of MicroChannel machines in service is dwarfed by the number of ISA machines, and so MicroChannel specific support is not a very high priority item for most software developers. This is particularly true in light of the fact that in most cases, existing code will work fine on the MicroChannel machines without even bothering to support interrupt chaining. And no hardware manufacturer is going to be willing to produce a board whose ISR depends on interrupt chaining to work.

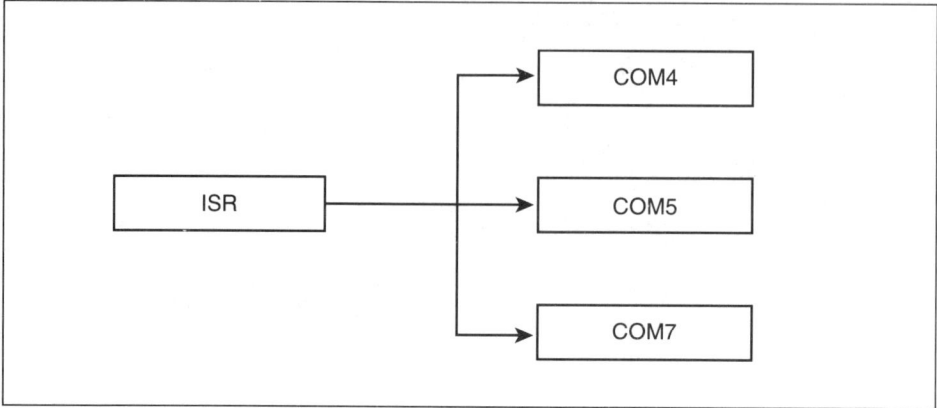

**Figure 4-2. Servicing from a single ISR**

So instead of relying on interrupt chaining, most COM drivers written specifically for the MicroChannel rely instead on internal UART scanning techniques. Rather than generating a single ISR for each port that has been opened, these techniques instead use a single ISR that scans each open port for activity.

Figure 4-2 shows the operation of a more conventional ISR on a MicroChannel machine. In this view, a single ISR polls three different UARTs to determine which ones need service.

In this chapter, the sample code for the MicroChannel architecture uses the second method of interrupt handling for two reasons: first, while interrupt chaining is an interesting technique, it is essentially a dead-end, largely because of the lack of support. Second, polling multiple UARTs in a single interrupt provides a good introduction to the multiport board support that will be used later in this chapter.

## The MicroChannelHandler Class

As you probably recall from Chapter 3, the PC8250 class had an additional class referenced in its header file named Handler. This class was listed as an optional parameter that could be specified in the PC8250 constructor. While it wasn't used in Chapter 3, the handler class was specified if and when a handler needed to be used to support multiple UARTs per interrupt service routine. Since multiport boards have such a wide variety of architectures, it makes sense to not try to integrate support for all of the various systems into the standard interrupt handler.

# SHARED INTERRUPT DEVICES

As it happens, we can make use of the handler class as an interrupt manager for the shared ports on the MicroChannel bus. Its function in this case will be nearly identical to that of the handler for a multiport shared interrupt board. The only difference is that the multiport board handler has to read in a status register to determine which ports need servicing, the MicroChannel handler has to blindly try every port on the IRQ line to properly service all of them.

## The Handler Class

Class `Handler` is an abstract base class that is defined as having nothing more than a pair of virtual functions. The two functions are used to add a `PC8250` port to the handler when opening the port, and to delete it when closing the port. It is the handler's job to intercept the interrupt, determine which ports need servicing, and invoke the appropriate hardware servicing routines. Since every type of hardware is going to have different ways of handling this task, the base class makes no assumptions whatsoever about data members or other member functions.

A handler is attached to a port during the execution of the `PC8250` constructor. The constructor takes a single argument of a pointer to type `Handler`, which defaults to a value of 0. When a normal Comm port is opened, the handler argument is set to 0, and the constructor calls `ConnectToIrq()` to attach the port to the default interrupt service routine, `isr_8250()`. If a handler is specified, the virtual function `AddPort()` is called instead. `AddPort()` is a member function of the handler, which is an instance of a class derived from class `Handler`.

Listing 4-1 is a listing of `MCA.H`, which contains the definition of the `MicroChannelHandler` class. In addition to the standard `AddPort()` and `DeletePort()` functions defined in the base class, there is naturally a constructor and a destructor. The only other thing needed for this class to be complete is a pair of data members, used internally.

```
// ********************* START OF MCA.H *********************
// This header file has all of the definitions and prototypes
// needed to use the MicroChannel handler class;
#ifndef _MCA_DOT_H
#define _MCA_DOT_H

#include "rs232.h"
```

```
#include "pc8250.h"

class MicroChannelHandler : public Handler {
    private :
        static int initialized;
        static struct isr_data_block *data_pointers[ 8 ];
    public :
        MicroChannelHandler( void );
        ~MicroChannelHandler( void );
        virtual RS232Error AddPort( RS232PortName port_name,
                                    struct isr_data_block *data );
        virtual void DeletePort( RS232PortName port_name );
};

#endif // #ifndef _MCA_DOT_H
// *********************** END OF MCA.H ***********************
```

**Listing 4-1. The MicroChannelHandler class definition.**


To use shared interrupts on the MicroChannel bus, the programmer has to first create a `MicroChannelHandler` object to manage the ports that will be sharing an interrupt. In this case, that is fairly simple as the constructor doesn't take any arguments. Since we are using hardware whose parameters have been predefined by IBM, there aren't any options left to the user. The primary argument that will be used with other handlers is an IRQ line number. For the MicroChannel shared interrupt Comm ports, the IRQ line will always be IRQ3.

After creating the handler, the ports need to be opened. Each port that uses the shared interrupt line needs to pass a pointer to the handler to the `PC8250` constructor when it is opened. This causes the `PC8250` constructor to call the `AddPort()` virtual function for the handler in order to connect the port to an interrupt service routine.

```
// *********************** START OF MCA.CPP ***********************
#include "rs232.h"
#include "pc8250.h"
#include "_pc8250.h"
#include "pcirq.h"
```

# SHARED INTERRUPT DEVICES

```c
#include "mca.h"
#include "_msdos.h"

struct isr_data_block *MicroChannelHandler::data_pointers[ 8 ];
int MicroChannelHandler::initialized = 0;

void mca_isr( struct isr_data_block *data[ 8 ] )
{
    int i;
    for ( i = 0 ; i < 8 ; i++ )
        if ( data[ i ] )
            isr_8250( data[ i ] );
}

MicroChannelHandler::MicroChannelHandler( void )
{
    int i;
    if ( !initialized ) {
        if ( Bus() != MCA_BUS ) {
            initialized = -1;
            return;
        }
        for ( i = 0; i < 8 ; i++ )
            data_pointers[ i ] = 0;
        initialized = 1;
        if ( ConnectToIrq(
                IRQ3,
                data_pointers,
                (void (*)( void *)) mca_isr ) < RS232_SUCCESS )
            return;
    }
}

MicroChannelHandler::~MicroChannelHandler( void )
{
    if ( initialized > 0 ) {
        DisconnectFromIRQ( IRQ3 );
        initialized = 0;
    }
}
```

```
RS232Error MicroChannelHandler::AddPort( RS232PortName port_name,
                                        struct isr_data_block *data )
{
    if ( initialized <= 0 )
        return RS232_ERROR;
    if ( data_pointers[ port_name ] )
        return RS232_PORT_IN_USE;
    data_pointers[ port_name ] = data;
    return RS232_SUCCESS;
}


void MicroChannelHandler::DeletePort( RS232PortName port_name )
{
    data_pointers[ port_name ] = 0;
}


// ********************* END OF MCA.CPP *********************
```

**Listing 4-2. The code for the MicroChannelHandler member functions**

Listing 4-2 shows MCA.CPP, which contains all of the member functions and data for the MicroChannelHandler class. When the constructor is executed, it first attempts to see if this class has already been initialized elsewhere. Since all ports will always be sharing a single IRQ line, the data members are static and can actually be shared by several instances of the MicroChannel handler.

During initialization, an array of pointers to isr_data_block structures is initialized to all zeros. As ports are opened up and added, the pointers to each port's isr_data_block will be added to the array. When an interrupt occurs, mca_isr() checks each element of the data array to see if it has a pointer to a valid data block. If the element does indeed have a valid pointer, the standard PC8250 ISR is called with a pointer to the isr_data_block for the given port.

One question that crops up repeatedly in C++ is how to deal with constructors that fail. In this case, when the constructor for the MicroChannelHandler fails, the static member initialized is set to a -1. When the AddPort() function is called, it checks the value of initialized, and if it finds a -1, returns an error code. This protects the application code from trying to use improperly constructed handler.

Only two things can prevent the handler object from being properly constructed.

## SHARED INTERRUPT DEVICES

First, the functions will fail if the target machine turns out to be an ISA bus machine. Second, if the `ConnectToIRQ()` function call fails, the error is noted and the constructor "fails." `ConnectToIRQ()` can fail if one of the ports in the range COM2 through COM8 has already been opened with no interrupt handler specified.

Once all of the MicroChannel shared interrupt ports have been opened, you can expect interrupts. Whenever an interrupt occurs, the IRQ package will route it to `mca_isr()`. This routine simply calls `isr_8250()`, the default interrupt handler, for each Comm port that has been opened and added to the handler. It is up to `isr_8250()` to determine whether the port actually needs servicing. While this polling system is probably not the optimal way of managing interrupts, its simplicity helps make it fast and at least fairly efficient.

When the program is complete, the `PC8250` destructors will be called as the ports are closed. The destructor code checks to see if the port has been assigned to a handler and, if it has, calls the `DeletePort()` function. `DeletePort()` just zeros out the entry in the static data table that previously pointed to the `isr_data_block` structure for the particular port. This insures that no attempt will be made to service the port when interrupts occur.

Finally, the `MicroChannelHandler` destructor is called for the handler object. Then, the `DisconnectFromIRQ()` routine is called. Calling this routine first restores the previous interrupt vector to its rightful position as owner of the IRQ. Then, the routine disables interrupts at the 8259, ensuring that no more interrupts will come in now that the vector no longer points to a valid address.

### Testing the MicroChannel Code

To properly test this code, I modified `TEST232.CPP` to support four simultaneous ports, with three of the ports opened on a shared interrupt line. This requires a couple of modifications to the test program. The PS/2 system I was testing on has four comm ports, with COM2 through COM4 all on a common IRQ line.

The first modification to `TEST232.EXE` was simply to change the `WINDOW_COUNT` constant to 4, so I can display all the ports. Note that this will have the effect of forcing the output screen into 43 line mode, or 50 line mode on a VGA. If your monitor is monochrome or CGA you will have to modify `TEST232.CPP` for smaller windows.

```
#define WINDOW_COUNT 4
```

The list of header files now has to include the header file that defines the MicroChannel handler, MCA.H. The resulting list looks like this:

```
#include "portable.h"
#include <stdio.h>
#include <stdlib.h>
#include <string.h>
#include <conio.h>
#include <ctype.h>
#include "rs232.h"
#include "textwind.h"
#include "pc8250.h"
#include "mca.h"
```

In the main body of the program, I declare an object of type `MicroChannelHandler`, using the only constructor for objects of this type. The constructor will automatically hook into the IRQ3 interrupt, and be ready to handle interrupts for any comm ports as soon as they are opened. The opening few lines of `main()` now look like this:

```
int main()
{
    int i;
    int c;
    char buffer[ 81 ];
    MicroChannelHandler handler;
```

Finally, when opening the ports, I need to modify the PC8250 constructor call. One of the last arguments to the constructor is a pointer to an interrupt handler. Normally we use the default value for this argument, which causes the PC8250 constructor to use its own internal handler. In this case, I assign the special `MicroChannelHandler` to do the job for COM2 through COM4. The resulting code in `main()` looks like this:

## SHARED INTERRUPT DEVICES

```
for ( i = 0 ; i < WINDOW_COUNT ; i++ ) {
    switch ( i ) {
        case COM1 :
            Ports[ i ] = new PC8250( port_names[ i ],
                                     9600, 'N', 8, 1 );
            break;
        default :
            Ports[ i ] = new PC8250( port_names[ i ],
                                     9600, 'N', 8, 1,
                                     1,1,          // DTR, RTS
                                     UNCHANGED,    // XON/XOFF
                                     UNCHANGED,    // RTS/CTS
                                     UNCHANGED,    // DTR/DSR
                                     &handler );
    }
```

Finally, to build this version of TEST232.EXE, you will need to add MCA.OBJ to the list of files in TEST232.MAK. The resulting line of file names should look like this:

```
FILES = pc8250.obj pcirq.obj isr_8250.obj queue.obj mca.obj
```

As each of the four ports is opened in main(), a test is made to see if that port passed its constructor properly. If so, a text window is opened for the port. That window will display any characters that are read in from the UART during the process. After being opened, I manually turned on XON/XOFF handshaking for each port, relying on it as the most successful form of handshaking in most circumstances.

Once the ports were configured, I connected pairs of ports to one another using null modem cables, and then began using the "Spew" function of TEST232.EXE to exercise the ports. Turning on spewing for a port results in the port continually sending out messages that look something like this:

```
Spewing Packet XXX from port XX
```

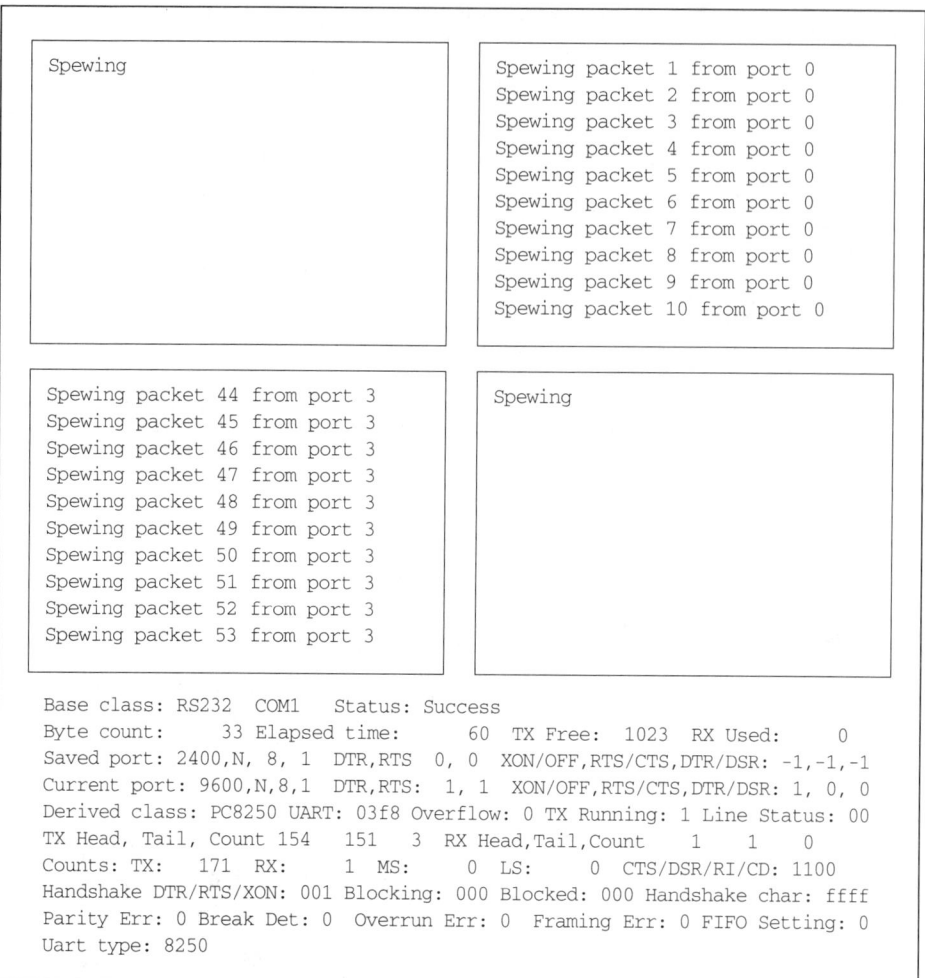

**Figure 4-3. A screen shot from TEST232.EXE**

By hooking up the input of one port to the output of another with a null modem cable, we can watch the spew output from one port show up on the input screen of another. If all four ports are spewing, and all four ports are looped back to one another, the ISR will be getting a good deal of exercise. Figure 4-3 shows the output screen of `TEST232.EXE` after spewing has been started on two ports.

In conclusion, the `MicroChannelHandler` class is nice and simple to implement, and does its job effectively. It also does a good job of fulfilling one of our

# SHARED INTERRUPT DEVICES

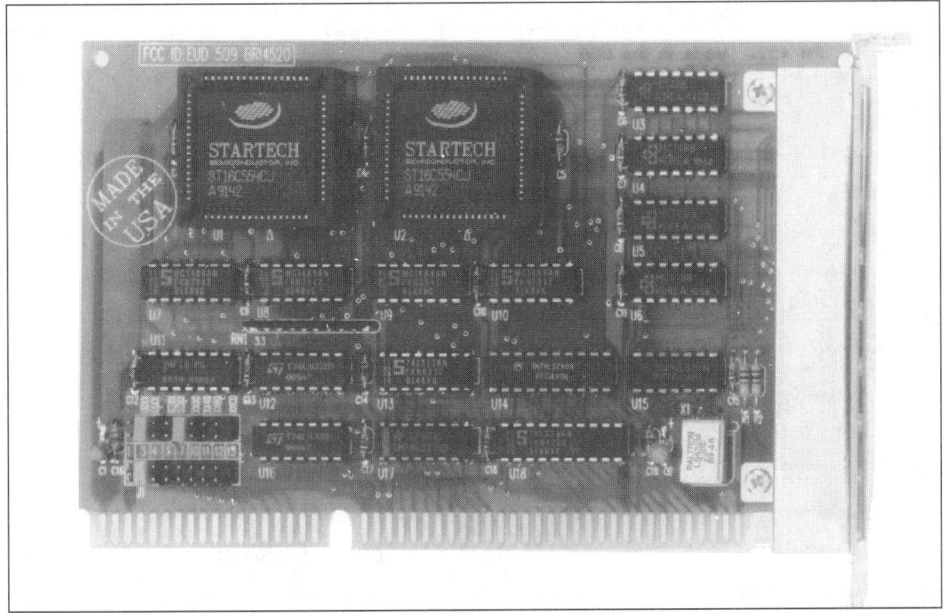

Figure 4-4. The BocaBoard.

programming goals in using C++, which is to re-use as much code as is practical. In this case, the `PC8250` class is used almost in its entirety to handler MicroChannel interrupts. The `mca_isr()` interrupt handler acts as a front-end only to the base class of the 8250 handler.

## Nonintelligent Multiport Boards

Taking a small step up in complexity from the MicroChannel architecture approach to handling shared interrupts brings you to nonintelligent multiport boards. Multiport boards are made to work on ISA bus machines, which means each board is only able to support a single interrupt line. Since most of these boards support 4, 8, or 16 UARTs, this means there must be logic on the board to handle arbitration of the individual UARTs.

Figure 4-4 shows a typical multiport board. This board is manufactured by Boca Research, Boca Raton, Florida. The BocaBoard can be configured with a 4-port or 8-port board. The two large chips on the top of the board are ASICs which each emulate four 16550 UARTs. The board can be configured with either one or two of these chips. Most multiport board makers are still using standard UARTs on their boards. Boca's approach helps them reduce the cost of the board.

Unfortunately, there are no standard ways to bring out the RS-232 connections from the card edge, and every manufacturer improvises when they design a new board. Boca has elected to use RJ-11 six-conductor telephone wire connectors for their connections. This is convenient, because an RJ-11 connector is just wide enough to fit in the space allocated to the card edge on an IBM compatible PC. RJ-45 connectors wouldn't fit in this space, and would have to be turned sideways, leaving room for only six or so.

Boca supplies RJ-11 cables and modular DB-25 connectors along with the board. Extra cabling equipment can be bought from several sources (listed in Appendix B.) One of the nice things about the cabling system used with the BocaBoard is that it allows you to connect two ports in a test configuration by connecting one end of the RJ-11 cable to each of two ports. The TX and RX lines are then connected between the two lines, so a program like `TEST232.EXE` can be run without having to resort to unusual cabling.

## Hardware

Multiport boards work by combining the various interrupt lines on the board into a single interrupt that can be effectively presented to the ISA bus. Boards like the BocaBoard perform a logical OR of the eight UART lines to create a single interrupt signal. If any of the ports are requesting an interrupt, the interrupt line on the bus will be high. This defines one of the basic functions that the BocaBoard ISR must perform. Once an interrupt is detected, all UARTs have to be serviced until no UART is requesting service. If the ISR exits while one of the UARTS on the board still has an interrupt request active, the 8259 PIC on the ISA bus will think that the previous interrupt has not been serviced and it will ignore the interrupt from the BocaBoard.

When the BocaBoard generates an interrupt, an ISR like the `MicroChannelHandler` could handle things fairly well. It would do this by polling each of the eight UARTs on the board, and performing the appropriate routines for those requesting service. While this is an effective general-purpose solution, it is fairly inefficient. For every port on the board, we have to call `isr_8250()` with a pointer

# SHARED INTERRUPT DEVICES

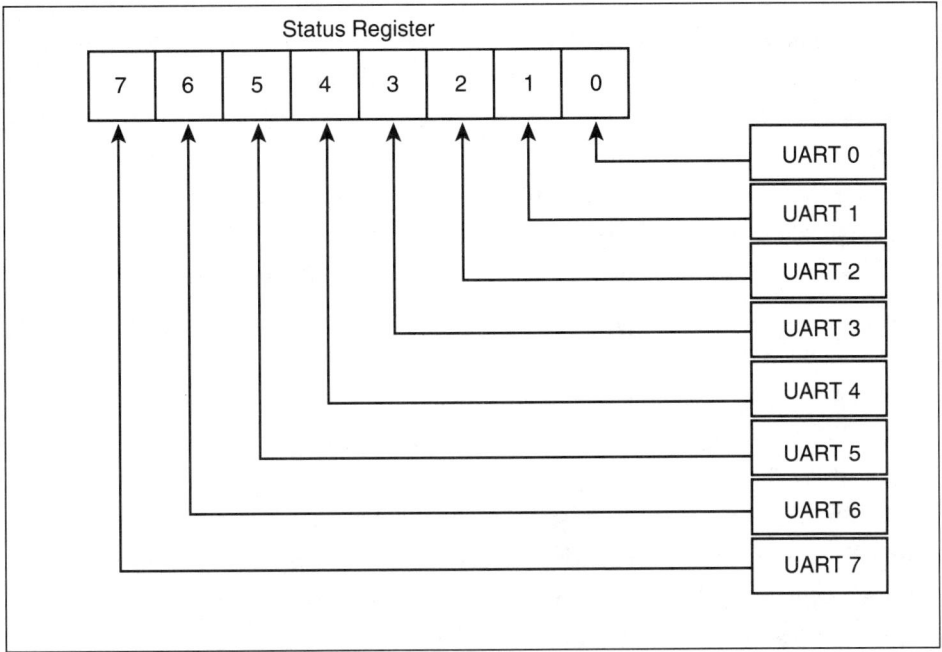

Figure 4-5. The Status Register on the BocaBoard

to the ISR data block for that board. If the UART isn't active at that time, this is a waste of CPU cycles. And wasting CPU cycles during an ISR is something we want to avoid wherever possible.

**Enter the status register**

The solution to this problem is to use a status register with a single bit corresponding to each UART on the multiport board. On the BocaBoard, this status register can be read at any time to determine which ports are presently requesting interrupt servicing. Figure 4-5 shows the layout of this status port.

The details of the status register vary quite a bit from board to board, but in principle they all do the same thing. On the BocaBoard, reading the status register gives the ISR a "snapshot" look at the state of the interrupt request states for each of the UARTs. If the bit for a given UART is set, it means that it presently is signaling an interrupt. If the bit is clear, it isn't.

For the BocaBoard, this means that the ISR has to read in the status register, then call `isr_8250()` for every port that has a bit set. Once that is complete, the ISR has to go back and read the status register again, repeating the process until finally the status register reads all zeros. Once the register reads in all zeros, it means no port is requesting an interrupt, so the IRQ line on the PC bus can safely be assumed to be low. The 8259 PIC will recognize the next incoming interrupt as a new one.

Many other multiport boards, such as those made by StarGate, use this same system for defining the bits of the status register. Some others, for example Arnet, use the same system but invert the sense of the bits in the status register, so that a 0 means an interrupt is pending and a 1 means no interrupt.

Boards made by DigiBoard (probably the leading supplier of ISA multiport boards) use a different scheme entirely. The status register contains a single binary number indicating which port is presently waiting for service. After reading in the number, the port can be serviced immediately. On the DigiBoard, the act of reading the status register also pulses the IRQ line low, so that instead of continually polling the status register, the routine can return immediately.

The actual address of the status register on the I/O bus also varies quite a bit among boards. The BocaBoard tries to handle this unobtrusively: the status register is at offset 7 from the base address of any of the UARTs on the board. Since offset 7 is reserved for the UART scratch register, this location can't conflict with any other hardware on the system bus. And since the status register isn't really useful to most PC programmers, this is a safe place for it.

For their status registers, most other multiport boards use a dedicated address, which is usually determined by setting DIP switches or jumpers. I favor the BocaBoard approach, since it reduces a single point of error for the board installer. By forcing the status register to be in a predefined location, there isn't as much opportunity to misconfigure the software, which can result in total failure of communications. In addition, there is a minor decrease in the chance of having an addressing conflict between the status register and some other piece of hardware on the board.

### The BocaBoard handler

Opening and using ports on the BocaBoard is nearly identical to the process of opening MicroChannel ports. Before any port can be opened, an object of `class`

# SHARED INTERRUPT DEVICES

`Handler` needs to be created to handle interrupts generated by those ports. Since the handler has to be tailored to the specific type of shared interrupt hardware, we need to create a new handler class, in this case the `BocaHandler`.

## The constructor

The `MicroChannelHandler` had a constructor that didn't take any arguments because we already knew the hardware configuration for all shared serial ports on a MicroChannel computer. Not so with the BocaBoard. The board can be placed on any one of nine different IRQ lines, including four of the upper eight lines. The status register for the board can range all over the I/O address map. And of course, there can be several different BocaBoards in the system (as long as their hardware parameters don't overlap).

The constructor for the Boca Board has to have a pair of parameters to be set up properly. The class definition and constructor prototype in Listing 4-3 show that the constructor takes as parameters the value of the IRQ line used by the board, and the address of the board's status registers.

```
// ********************* START OF BOCA.H *********************
// This header file has all of the definitions and prototypes
// needed to use the BocaHandler class.
#ifndef _BOCA_DOT_H
#define _BOCA_DOT_H
#include "rs232.h"
#include "pc8250.h"

struct boca_data {
    int status_register;
    struct isr_data_block *data_pointers[ 8 ];
};

class BocaHandler : public Handler {
    private :
        struct boca_data isr_info;
        irq_name irq;
        RS232Error connected;
    public :
```

```
        BocaHandler( irq_name irq_line,
                     int status_register_address );
        ~BocaHandler( void );
        virtual RS232Error AddPort( RS232PortName port_name,
                                    struct isr_data_block *data );
        virtual void DeletePort( RS232PortName port_name );
};
#endif  // #ifndef _BOCA_DOT_H

// ********************* END OF BOCA.H *************************
```

**Listing 4-3. The class definitions in BOCA.H**

The `BocaHandler` constructor clearly has to have the IRQ line for the board. When the handler is created, one of the few things that it actually has to do besides initialize its data members is to connect an ISR to the IRQ line. The location of the status register could conceivably not be defined until one of the ports was added to the handler, but doing it in the handler constructor probably helps clarify the code. A programmer not familiar with the BocaBoard could look at this code and understand what has happened more quickly than if the status register definition was not shown until its implicit use in the ISR.

```
// ********************* START OF BOCA.CPP *********************
#include <dos.h>
#include "rs232.h"
#include "pc8250.h"
#include "_pc8250.h"
#include "pcirq.h"
#include "boca.h"
#include "_msdos.h"

void boca_isr( struct boca_data *isr_info )
{
    int mask;
    int i;

    STI();
    for ( ; ; ) {
```

## SHARED INTERRUPT DEVICES

```
        mask = INPUT( isr_info->status_register );
        if ( ( mask & 0xff ) == 0 )
            break;
        for ( i = 0 ; i < 7 ; i++ ) {
            if ( mask & 1 )
                if ( isr_info->data_pointers[ i ] )
                    isr_8250( isr_info->data_pointers[ i ] );
            mask >>= 1;
        }
    }
}

BocaHandler::BocaHandler( irq_name irq_line,
                          int status_register_address )

{
    int i;

    isr_info.status_register = status_register_address;
    for ( i = 0 ; i < 8 ; i++ )
        isr_info.data_pointers[ i ] = 0;
    irq = irq_line;
    connected = ConnectToIrq( irq,
                              &isr_info,
                              (void (*)( void *)) boca_isr );
}

BocaHandler::~BocaHandler( void )

{
    if ( connected == RS232_SUCCESS )
        DisconnectFromIRQ( irq );
}

RS232Error BocaHandler::AddPort( RS232PortName port_name,
                                 struct isr_data_block *data )

{
    if ( connected != RS232_SUCCESS )
        return connected;
    if ( isr_info.data_pointers[ port_name ] )
```

```
         return RS232_PORT_IN_USE;
    isr_info.data_pointers[ port_name ] = data;
    return RS232_SUCCESS;
}
void BocaHandler::DeletePort( RS232PortName port_name )
{
    isr_info.data_pointers[ port_name ] = 0;

}

// ********************* END OF BOCA.CPP *********************
```

**Listing 4-4. The class functions in BOCA.CPP**

Listing 4-4 shows all of the BocaBoard specific class code. The constructor takes care of storing the IRQ line and status register addresses, and then initializes the data pointers to the eight ports that can be attached to the handler. Finally, the handler attaches the `boca_isr()` routine to the specified interrupt handler.

Interestingly, as in the `MicroChannelHandler()`, this ISR cannot be a member function. Interrupt routines don't have access to the *this* pointer, so they work much better when operating on conventional C structures. Because of this, all of the data needed in the ISR is packed into a C structure, defined in BOCA.H as `struct boca_data`. This structure has pointers to the `isr_data_block` structures for every port that gets added to the handler, as well as the status register address for the given board.

There is an interesting error-handling mechanism in the `BocaBoard` handler. The one place where there is potential for a failed constructor is in the `Connect-ToIRQ()` call. If some other port has already taken over that IRQ, an error return will come back to this routine. As usual, since a constructor has no return value, we need to improvise to come up with a method of returning an error.

We store the result of the `ConnectToIRQ()` statement in a member of type `RS232Error` called `connected`. Later, when one of the ports attempts to connect to the handler, the value of `connected` is checked and, if an error occurred, the add operation is aborted and the error code in `connected` is returned.

# SHARED INTERRUPT DEVICES

## The destructor

The destructor for `BocaHandler` only has to disconnect the `boca_isr()` from the interrupt specified in the constructor. This is done only if the `connected` member indicates that the connection took place properly. You should note that if any of the UARTs connected to the BocaBoard handler are still generating interrupts, the system will become unstable. The programmer must be sure that all of the ports have been properly closed before destroying the handler. Just as in the constructor however, it is difficult to handle errors in the destructor so I will leave this issue to the discretion of the application programmer.

The two virtual functions that have to be supported by an object derived from `class Handler` are the `AddPort()` and `DeletePort()` functions. These virtual functions are called in the `PC8250` constructor if a handler argument is specified.

## AddPort()

The `AddPort()` function has to set up all of the information needed by the `boca_isr()` routine to properly handle interrupts for the given port. Two items are important here. First, like all the other interrupt handlers, `boca_isr()` will need a pointer to the `isr_data_block` for the port. All of the data needed to process the interrupt by `isr_8250()` is contained in that data block.

Second, `boca_isr()` needs to know what port number this is relative to the BocaBoard. The `AddPort()` function has the port name as one of its parameters, so this does get passed to the handler. The actual port number parameter can be somewhat confusing, because the numbers seem to conflict with existing DOS port numbers. Remember that when a port is added to a board handler, the port number is relative to the board. The eight ports on a BocaBoard will be numbered COM1 through COM8. Even if a BocaBoard is using a port named COM1, your program can still use the standard IBM comm port COM1, and there won't be any problem.

The reason `boca_isr()` needs to know the port number is that in the interrupt service routine, each bit in the status register corresponds to a particular port. For example, bit 0 in the status register will be set if COM1 on the BocaBoard has an active interrupt. Without the `port_name` parameter passed in `AddPort()`, the BocaBoard handler would have no way of knowing which port corresponds to which bit in the status register. The `isr_data_block` pointer is stored away in an array of pointers for use by the ISR, with the index into the array determined by the `port_name` parameter.

`DeletePort()`

This routine doesn't do anything except to zero out the appropriate element in the array of pointers to `isr_data_block` elements. That way, a new port can be added later with a function call to `AddPort()`. The `PC8250` constructor calls this routine after it has shut down interrupts for the specified port, so there should be no possibility of an inadvertent interrupt occurring after the call to `DeletePort()`.

`boca_isr()`

All the work done in the other routines comes to fruition in the ISR for this handler. This routine will be invoked when an interrupt occurs on the IRQ line specified by the constructor to `BocaHandler`. This routine is related to the MicroChannel handler in that it keeps an array of pointers to the data block needed by `isr_8250()` to process a port. However, there are two critical differences. This routine reads in the status of the status registers before doing anything else. It sits in a loop checking each bit of the status register to determine which ports need servicing, and only calls those that are actively requesting an interrupt.

Second, this routine keeps running through its main loop until it reads in a status register value of zero. Once it does so, the board does not have any ports that are asserting their interrupt lines, which should mean that the IRQ line on the ISA bus is de-asserted. The ISR can now be safely exited, secure in the knowledge that the next incoming interrupt will properly trigger the 8259 PIC.

If the main loop in this `boca_isr()` didn't repeatedly read the mask, interrupts for all four ports would quit running as soon as a second interrupt occurred while the first one was still being processed.

## Modifications to TEST232.EXE

Only a few simple modifications need to be made to `TEST232.CPP` to test the BocaBoard. As before, the `WINDOW_COUNT` macro should be set to 4 so that we can test all four ports on the BocaBoard.

```
#define WINDOW_COUNT 4
```

## SHARED INTERRUPT DEVICES

Instead of including MCA.H as you did earlier in this chapter, you need to modify TEST232.CPP to include BOCA.H. The resulting list of include files should look like this:

```
#include "portable.h"
#include <stdio.h>
#include <stdlib.h>
#include <string.h>
#include <conio.h>
#include <ctype.h>
#include "rs232.h"
#include "textwind.h"
#include "pc8250.h"
#include "boca.h"
```

Instead of having a constructor for MicroChannelHandler, the entry for main() will create a BocaHandler object. When testing on my system, I set up the BocaBoard to use IRQ4, with the first UART address starting at location 100H. The appropriate constructor for those parameters is shown here:

```
int main()
{
    int i;
    int c;
    char buffer[ 81 ];
    BocaHandler handler( IRQ4, 0x107 );
```

Finally, the PC8250 constructor used in this program has two extra parameters that are normally not used. The handler parameter specifies the BocaHandler as the interrupt handler for the port. The UART address is calculated based on the port number, assuming my board is configured with UART addresses starting at location 100H.

```
for ( i = 0 ; i < WINDOW_COUNT ; i++ ) {
    switch ( i ) {
        default :
            Ports[ i ] = new PC8250( port_names[ i ],
                                     9600, 'N', 8, 1,
                                     1,           // DTR
                                     1,           // RTS
                                     UNCHANGED,   // XON/XOFF
                                     UNCHANGED,   // RTS/CTS
                                     UNCHANGED,   // DTR/DSR
                                     &handler,
                                     0x100 + ( i * 8 ) );
}
```

To build this version of `TEST232.EXE`, modify the list of files in `TEST232.MAK` to include all of the files needed for `PC8250` support, as well as the BocaBoard support file:

```
FILES = pc8250.obj pcirq.obj isr_8250.obj queue.obj boca.obj
```

Operation of the test program should proceed just as was discussed for the MicroChannel port example earlier in this Chapter. Note that the BocaBoard ports can be looped back to one another by just plugging the manufacturer-supplied RJ-11 cables from one port to another. The usual null modem cables aren't needed in this case.

## Multitasking Under MS-DOS

Earlier in this book I discussed the fact that people frequently want to use multiport boards under MS-DOS in a multitasking configuration. After seeing how the code in this chapter works, I hope you have an idea of why this is difficult to accomplish. It isn't easy to have the interrupt handler reside in one task, and have the `PC8250` objects reside in various other tasks running on the same system.

Probably the best way to accomplish multitasking with this setup is to create a device driver or a task that functions as one. The ISR and all of the open port objects would reside in a single task. Other tasks would then ask the driver for blocks of data and would send it data via some OS-dependent communications mechanism. Under pure MS-DOS, the most general way to do this would be using 80x86 interrupts. Other environments such as DESQview have specific function calls in their API to accomplish this.

**Sources for boards**

There are dozens of different multiport board suppliers making boards for the IBM compatible market. While the largest consumers of these boards have been in the UNIX and XENIX communities, MS-DOS users are steadily gravitating toward these boards. The best place to begin a search for suppliers of these boards would be UNIX-based magazines such as UNIX Review and UNIXWorld. Not only do they have plenty of advertisements for these boards, they also run occasional product roundup articles.

The Sources appendix at the end of this book lists some of the better known suppliers.

CHAPTER 5

# Intelligent Multiport Boards

The intelligent multiport board brings with it a host of new advantages and disadvantages. For comparatively large data transfers via RS-232 lines, it is vastly superior to its unintelligent cousin (discussed in Chapter 4). Despite the extra power they can bring to bear on an RS-232 problem, intelligent boards have been frequently overlooked by programmers. Programmers who had written applications using conventional RS-232 ports would have to completely rewrite their applications to convert to this type of board.

Fortunately, object-oriented programming techniques minimize the amount of rewriting necessary to convert to one of these boards. By developing drivers that are derived from a carefully constructed base class, such as the `RS232` class, applications can switch between different types of hardware with a minimum of trouble. This chapter develops a derived class `DigiBoard` to illustrate how you can develop an intelligent board interface.

## The Hardware

Dozens of different intelligent multiport boards are available for the PC-compatible bus, but most follow the same basic design. Figure 5-1 shows a block diagram of the major components of the board and its interface with the PC.

We are most familiar with the left side of Figure 5-1, the PC motherboard. The CPU, whether it is an 8088, 80386, or 80486, has direct connections to various components on the motherboard, such as RAM and BIOS chips. The CPU connects to plug-in cards and other devices via the ISA bus, which provides a standard interface.

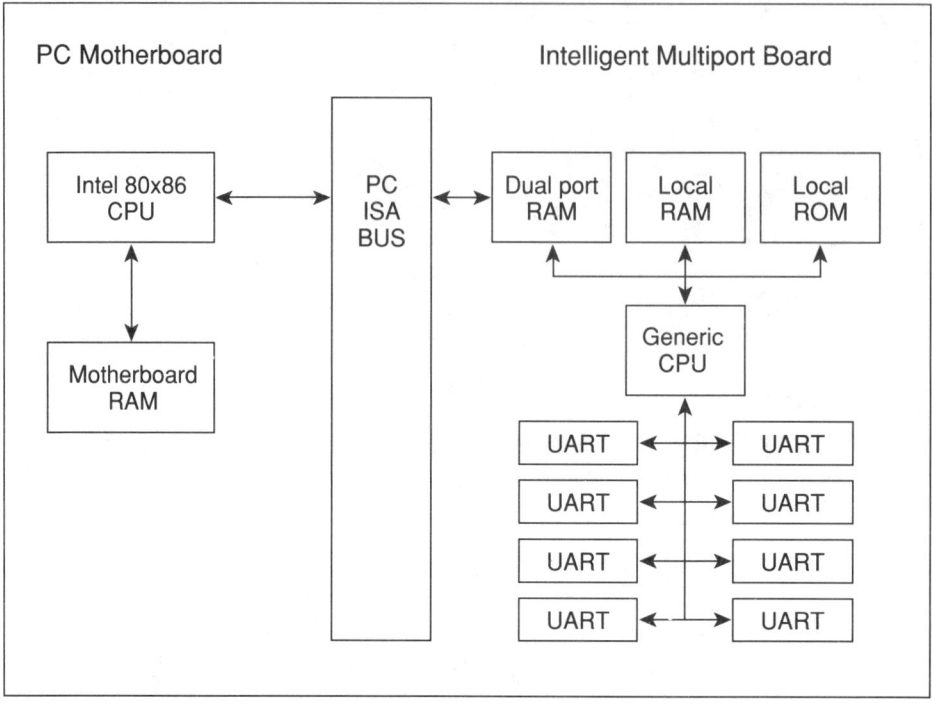

Figure 5-1. Intelligent board hardware design.

The ISA bus provides several mechanisms for communicating with the processor, including the I/O bus, memory bus, and interrupt lines. For transferring large amounts of data at relatively high speeds, the optimal solution is to use the memory bus. Multiport boards do this using standard RAM chips, with special control circuitry collectively referred to as "dual-port RAM."

Dual-port RAM is simply RAM that has control circuitry, allowing it to be accessed by two processors (or other devices) simultaneously. Most PCs already have dual-port RAM in their video frame buffer. The video data can be read or written to by the PC BIOS, while a CRT controller is simultaneously reading the data and forming dots on a raster.

The dual port RAM on the multiport board provides the connection between the ISA bus and the rest of the multiport board. The dual port RAM is read and written to by the controller CPU on the card. This CPU is the heart of the multiport card. It has direct access to the UARTs on the card, as well as local RAM and ROM.

# INTELLIGENT MULTIPORT BOARDS

**Design freedom**

From a hardware designer's perspective, a multiport board provides a level of freedom uncharacteristic of PC communications equipment. Because the UARTs and CPU are physically separated from the PC, communications is performed using a high-level API, not via direct hardware control. Thus, the 8250 compatibility restrictions that dog hardware and software designers alike can be thrown out, and a completely new system can be created. More importantly, the board's CPU does not have to maintain 8088 binary compatibility. This means that a processor can be selected strictly for its functionality.

Multiport boards, then, have a broad selection of CPUs ranging from lowly 8051 microcontrollers, through conventional 80186 CPUs, to custom RISC machines. UARTs include 16450 chips, Z80 DUARTs, and various other chips rarely seen elsewhere. Typically, the hardware on the board isn't a factor in programming considerations.

**Control programs**

Clearly, the CPU on the multiport card has to execute a program of its own. The question is, who writes that program? What operating system is the card using? What control do we have over it?

In nearly every case, an application programmer or end user doesn't have to know anything about the program running on the multiport board. The hardware developer creates the software and provides a way for us to load it onto the card. While end users can customize their hardware, most programmers do not feel it is worth customizing their software to support such a small segment of the market.

Most boards have loader software and perhaps an O/S kernel on EPROM or ROM on the multiport card. Software provided by the manufacturer usually downloads the control program when the PC boots. While some vendors are courageous enough to put the entire control program on EPROM, most like to retain the flexibility implied by downloading the code.

Once the control program is downloaded and running, it takes control of the UARTs and begins managing their traffic. This traffic includes initialization, interrupt handling, and communications with the PC CPU. Since signals to the keyboard, MS-DOS interrupts, and video modes do not affect the card, communications can proceed unimpeded. Using a real-time kernel or O/S instead of MS-DOS helps considerably as well.

## Software interface

Once the control program has been downloaded and is running, we need to establish an interface for sending data and control information back and forth between the PC and the card. No standard has been established for communications protocols; vendors have gone their own direction.

Two computers communicate via a shared block of memory using procedures that are relatively easy to work out. For most of these boards, communications are established through the use of control blocks. A control block is simply an area in memory that two CPUs use to communicate. One CPU signifies that a block is ready for the other CPU to take by way of a semaphore byte. The second CPU signals that it has read in the control block via another semaphore byte. With a carefully controlled protocol, both sides can communicate without memory conflicts.

```
PC::WriteControlBlock( block *data )
{
    while ( semaphore == BLOCK_FULL )
        ;
    *control_block =  *data;
    semaphore = BLOCK_FULL;
}

MultiPortBoard::ReadControlBlock( block *data )
{
    while ( semaphore == BLOCK_EMPTY )
        ;
    *data = *control_block;
    semaphore = BLOCK_EMPTY;
}
```

**Listing 5-1. Reading and writing control blocks with shared memory.**

Listing 5-1 shows sample routines that the PC and the multiport board might use to exchange a control block using shared memory. In this case, there is a single semaphore byte. The PC uses the semaphore to set a `BLOCK_FULL` flag when it has written a new block out. The multiport board uses the same semaphore to write a `BLOCK_EMPTY` flag after the block has been successfully transferred.

# INTELLIGENT MULTIPORT BOARDS

An algorithm like the one shown here must be written to avoid conflicts between the CPUs. Normally, only a single CPU should have write access to any given block of memory at a time. If both CPUs could write to a single byte at once, it would never be clear which data were actually be used.

## Drivers to the Rescue

Fortunately, most programmers don't have to deal with multiprocessing issues like these. Most board makers supply driver software that provides a more convenient interface to their boards (Stargate is the notable exception).

The board manufacturer supplies software loaded as a DOS device driver. The driver will usually provide at least one of two standard interfaces: a DOS device interface and the INT 14H BIOS interface. Some boards provide both, and a few go it alone with a completely nonstandard interface.

The driver I develop in this chapter uses the DigiBoard interface, so I present the API for their device driver. Because there isn't enough space in this chapter (or this book) to discuss the interfaces for all boards, I concentrate on today's market leader. If you learn how to work with the interface to one board's device driver, working with a different interface will be that much easier.

### The DigiBoard API

DigiBoard makes quite a few intelligent boards. Figure 5-2 shows a typical example. As new boards were developed, custom device drivers were developed on the fly. And as the product line fleshed out, the confusion grew. Programmers had to deal with functions that worked differently depending on whether the board was a COM/8i, a PC/4e, or a PC/16i.

By moving to a universal device driver, DigiBoard recently managed to restore some order. The new universal device driver, XIDOS5.SYS, has an API based on the INT 14H BIOS interface to PC Comm ports. The device driver is loaded upon system bootup and communicates with the intelligent DigiBoard via a block of shared memory. Programmers can then communicate with the device driver using the same INT 14H API for all boards in the product line.

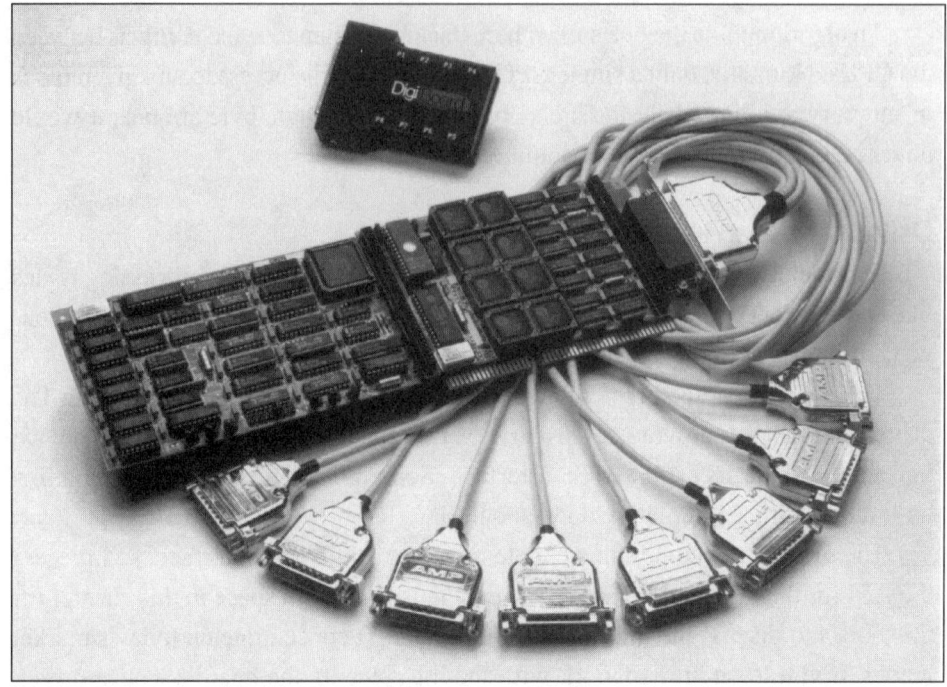

Figure 5-2. An Intelligent DigiBoard.

The interface to the DigiBoard is based on the INT 14H standard used by the IBM PC ROM BIOS to communicate with serial ports. As we've discussed, the ROM BIOS has an anemic feature set and isn't practical for "real world" communications applications. However, a few applications, such as programs that support serial printers, use INT 14H for all their serial port work. Such programs work with unmodified DigiBoards.

Programs such as those you will be developing need more features than are available with the standard BIOS set, and DigiBoard has provided them. The extensions to the BIOS found in the XIDOS5.SYS driver set make it possible to implement most of the virtual features found in the RS232 class.

All the functions in the DigiBoard API are accessed using the int86() and int86x() function calls in all MS-DOS C and C++ compilers. These functions take register structures as arguments, and let us set up the 80x86 registers with any values we choose. The following API listing details the usage of the registers.

# INTELLIGENT MULTIPORT BOARDS

One confusing point is the port number that is passed in register DX for every API function call. Under MS-DOS, DX can have a value between 0 and 3 on ISA machines for COM1-COM4, and 0-7 on MCA machines, for COM1-COM8. The DigiBoard device driver customarily sets up the ports on the DigiBoard as starting at COM5 on ISA machines and COM9 on MCA computers. However, these port numbers are entirely arbitrary, and can be changed at any time by running the `XICONFIG.EXE` program. The programs in this book assume that the DigiBoard is set up starting at COM5, but they could easily be set at other numbers.

### Function 0 : Initialize Port (BIOS compatible)

This is the standard INT 14H function used to set up a port's parameters. If a baud rate or parity setting isn't available here, the driver has other initialization functions that can be used.

*Input registers:*

    AH :    Set to 0, the function value
    AL :    Broken down into four bit fields, shown below
    DX :    The DigiBoard port number, where COM5 is 4

*Return values:*

    AH :    Set to 0xff if an error occurred, otherwise set to the line status value.
    AL :    Set to the reflect the modem status value.

The bit settings for the input values of AL follow:

| AL Bit Field Definitions ||||||||
|---|---|---|---|---|---|---|---|
| 7 | 6 | 5 | 4 | 3 | 2 | 1 | 0 |
| Baud Rate ||| Parity || Stop Bits | Word Length ||

**Note:** The DigiBoard driver can be set up to emulate either the BIOS or the Extended BIOS used on PS/2 machines. The Extended BIOS supports a baud rate of 19200, standard BIOS does not.

| CL : | Baud rate: |
|---|---|
| 0 | 110 baud |
| 1 | 150 baud |
| 2 | 300 baud |
| 3 | 600 baud |
| 4 | 1200 baud |
| 5 | 2400 baud |
| 6 | 4800 baud |
| 7 | 9600 baud |
| 8 | 19200 baud |
| 9 | 38400 baud |
| 10 | 57600 baud |
| 11 | 76800 baud |
| 12 | 115200 baud |
| 13 | 50 baud |
| 14 | 75 baud |
| 15 | 134 baud |
| 16 | 200 baud |
| 17 | 1800 baud |

DX :  The DigiBoard port number

*Return values:*
AH :  0xff on error, otherwise the port line status
AL :  The port modem status

### *Function 1 : Output a single character  (BIOS compatible)*
A single character is placed in the output buffer.

# INTELLIGENT MULTIPORT BOARDS

*Input registers:*
- AH : Set to 1, the function value
- AL : The character to be output
- DX : The DigiBoard port number

*Return values:*
- AH : Set to the line status value.
- AL : Set to the reflect the modem status value.

### Function 2 : Input a single character  (BIOS compatible)

A single character is read in from the input buffer. Like the BIOS, this function will wait indefinitely for a character to become available.

*Input registers:*
- AH : Set to 2, the function value
- DX : The DigiBoard port number

*Return values:*
- AH : Set to the line status value.
- AL : The character read in

**Note:** that this function will wait indefinitely for a character before returning.

### Function 3 : Read line and modem status  (BIOS compatible)

This function reads in the line and modem status settings for the UART. It is compatible with the BIOS function that does the same thing.

*Input registers:*
- AH : Set to 3, the function value
- DX : The DigiBoard port number

*Return values:*
- AH : The port line status
- AL : The port modem status

### Function 4 : Extended port initialization (EBIOS compatible)

The EBIOS was first made available with the PC Convertible and PS/2 lines. It provides for more initialization options the function 0, particularly in the area of extended baud rates.

*Input registers:*

| | | | |
|---|---|---|---|
| AH : | Set to 4, the function value | | |
| AL : | Break flag, 1 for break on, 0 for break off | | |
| BH : | Parity setting: | 0 | No parity |
| | | 1 | Odd parity |
| | | 2 | Even parity |
| BL : | Stop bits: | 0 | 1 stop bit |
| | | 1 | 2 stop bits |
| CH : | Word length: | 0 | 5 bits |
| | | 1 | 6 bits |
| | | 2 | 7 bits |
| | | 3 | 8 bits |
| CL : | Baud rate: | 0 | 110 baud |
| | | 1 | 150 baud |
| | | 2 | 300 baud |
| | | 3 | 600 baud |
| | | 4 | 1200 baud |
| | | 5 | 2400 baud |
| | | 6 | 4800 baud |
| | | 7 | 9600 baud |
| | | 8 | 19200 baud |
| | | 9 | 38400 baud |

## INTELLIGENT MULTIPORT BOARDS

| | |
|---|---|
| 10 | 57600 baud |
| 11 | 76800 baud |
| 12 | 115200 baud |
| 13 | 50 baud |
| 14 | 75 baud |
| 15 | 134 baud |
| 16 | 200 baud |
| 17 | 1800 baud |

DX : The DigiBoard port number

*Return values:*
    AH : 0xff on error, otherwise the port line status
    AL : The port modem status

### Function 5 : Extended port control (EBIOS compatible)

The EBIOS added a feature sorely missing from the BIOS: the ability to set and clear DTR and RTS.

*Input registers:*
    AH : Set to 5, the function value
    AL : A value of 0 is used to read the modem control lines
          A value of 1 is used to write the modem control lines.
    BL : If writing modem control, bit 0 sets DTR and bit 1 sets RTS
    DX : The DigiBoard port number

*Return values:*
    AH : The port line status
    AL : The port modem status
    BL : If reading modem control, bit 0 returns DTR, bit 1 returns RTS

### Function 6, Subfunction 0 : Get port name

This function serves two useful purposes. First, it tells you whether the DigiBoard device driver is actually in place and supports a particular port. Second, it lets us know if the DigiBoard driver has DOS support turned on. This means that a device with a name like COM5 has been installed.

*Input registers:*
    AH :     Set to 6, the function value
    AL :     Set to 0, the subfunction value
    DX :     The DigiBoard port number

*Return values:*
    AH :     Set to 0xff on error
    AL :     If no error, set to the highest INT 14H function supported
    ES:BX :     A pointer to an eight byte string, containing the port's DOS name (in the format "COMx"). If the driver does not have DOS support, the string "NoDriver."

**Function 6, Subfunction 1 : *Get driver information***

This function won't be used in the class found in this book, but it can provide useful information. For example, it can be used as a "sanity check" at the beginning of a program to determine if the DigiBoard driver is in place and, if so, what capabilities it has.

*Input registers:*
    AH :     Set to 6, the function value
    AL :     Set to 1, the subfunction value
    DX :     The DigiBoard port number

*Return values:*
    AH :     Set to 0xff on error
    AL :     If no error, set to the total number of channels supported
    BX :     The driver version
    CX :     Total number of boards controlled by this driver
    DX :     The first port number supported by the driver

### INTELLIGENT MULTIPORT BOARDS

***Function 6, Subfunction 2 : Get board information***

This function is also not used in the `DigiBoard` class, but can be useful in a configuration or test program.

*Input registers:*
- AH : Set to 6, the function value
- AL : Set to 2, the subfunction value
- BX : The board number, with 0 being the first board
- DX : Any valid DigiBoard port number

*Return values:*
- AH : Set to 0xff on error, otherwise set to the IRQ number
- AL : Board type :  1  COM/Xi
  -  2  MC/Xi
  -  3  PC/Xe
  -  4  PC/Xi
  -  5  PC/Xm
- BX : The memory segment of the board's dual ported RAM.
- CX : Number of channels on the board
- DX : The board's I/O port address
- SI : Port number for the first channel on the board

***Function 6, Subfunction 0xff : Get driver name***

This function could be used to make sure that the DigiBoard INT 14H support in place is coming from the Universal DigiBoard driver, and not an earlier, incompatible driver.

*Input registers:*
- AH : Set to 6, the function value
- AL : Set to 0xff, the subfunction value
- DX : Any valid DigiBoard port number

*Return values:*
- AX : Driver version number
- CX : Number of channels supported
- ES:BX : Pointer to the driver's name, an eight byte unterminated string. This should normally be "DIGIFEP5."

**Function 7 : Send break**

The class will use this function to send a break signal. This function is a major improvement over the break functions used in many other drivers in this book because it doesn't require that the driver sit in a hot idle loop waiting for the break time to expire.

*Input registers:*
- AH : Set to 7, the function value
- AL : A value of 0 indicates that the default break time should be used
  A value of 1 indicates that BX contains the break time
- BX : If AL is 1, BX contains the break time in 10 millisecond ticks
- DX : The port number

*Return values:*
- AH : 0xff indicates an error, 0 indicates success

**Function 8 : Alternate status check**

This function performs a peek, and also returns the current line status.

*Input registers:*
- AH : Set to 8, the function value
- DX : The port number

*Return values:*
- AH : 0xff is used to indicate no character was ready to be read
  If AH is not 0xff, it contains the port's line status
- AL : Next input character, if AH is not 0xff

### Function 9 : Clear a port's buffers

This function performs a reset of the port by flushing both the input and output buffers. It is used when the port is initialized.

*Input registers:*
- AH : Set to 9, the function value
- DX : The port number

*Return values:*
- AH : 0xff if an error occurred, otherwise 0

### Function 0x0a: Input buffer count

This function returns a count of the characters presently in the input buffer. It is used as one of the virtual functions inherited from the RS232 class.

*Input registers:*
- AH : Set to 0x0a, the function value
- DX : The port number

*Return values:*
- DH : Set to 0xff if an error occurred
- AX : Number of characters in input buffer if DH is not set to 0xff

### Function 0x0b : Drop a port's handshake lines

This function drops DTR and RTS, even if handshaking is enabled. Usually the DigiBoard driver ignores requests to change the modem status lines if handshaking is being used on a particular line. With this function, a blocking action could be forced, even if the input buffers haven't passed the high-water mark.

*Input registers:*
- AH : Set to 0x0b, the function value
- DX : The port number

*Return values:*
    AH :    Set to 0xff if an error occurred, otherwise set to 0

**Function 0x0c : Get a port's parameters**
This function reads back the current operating parameters of a given port, including the baud rate, parity, word length, and handshaking settings.

*Input registers:*
    AH :    Set to 0x0c, the function value
    DX :    The port number

*Return values:*
    AH :    Set to 0xff if an error occurred, otherwise set to 0
    AH :    If not 0xff, software flow control flags
                bit 0 :    XON/XOFF TX flow control
                bit 1 :    XON/XOFF RX flow control
    AL :    Hardware flow control flags
                bit 0 :    DTR RX flow control
                bit 1 :    RTS RX flow control
                bit 4 :    CTS TX flow control
                bit 5 :    DSR TX flow control
                bit 7 :    CD TX flow control

    BH :    Parity setting
                0 :    No parity
                1 :    Odd parity
                2 :    Even parity

    BL :    Stop bits
                0 :    1 stop bit
                1 :    2 stop bits

    CH :    Word length

## INTELLIGENT MULTIPORT BOARDS

        0 :    5 bits
        1 :    6 bits
        2 :    7 bits
        3 :    8 bits

CL :    Baud rate :
        0 :    110 baud
        1 :    150 baud
        2 :    300 baud
        3 :    600 baud
        4 :    1200 baud
        5 :    2400 baud
        6 :    4800 baud
        7 :    9600 baud
        8 :    19200 baud
        9 :    38400 baud
        10 :    57400 baud
        11 :    75600 baud
        12 :    115200 baud
        13 :    50 baud
        14 :    75 baud
        15 :    134 baud
        16 :    200 baud
        17 :    1800 baud

### Function 0x0d: Get pointer to character ready flag

The DigiBoard driver has a character ready flag that can be used to test if any characters are ready to be read in. The `Digiboard` class in this book uses this function.

*Input registers:*
    AH :    Set to 0x0d, the function value
    DX :    The port number

*Return values:*

> ES:BX : A far pointer to the character ready flag. The flag will contain a 0 if the input buffer for the port is empty, a 0xff if any characters are available.

### Function 0x0e : Write a buffer

This function is used to implement the `write_buffer()` private function for the `DigiBoard` class. It simply writes out a buffer full of characters to the intelligent board.

*Input registers:*

> AH : Set to 0x0e, the function value
> DX : The port number
> CX : The number of characters in the buffer
> ES:BX: A far pointer to the buffer

*Return values:*

> DH : If an error occurred, DH is set to 0xff.
> AX : The actual number of characters transmitted to the intelligent board.

### Function 0x0f : Read a buffer

This function is used to implement the `read_buffer()` private function for the `DigiBoard` class. It simply writes out a buffer full of characters to the intelligent board.

*Input registers:*

> AH : Set to 0x0f, the function value
> DX : The port number
> CX : The number of characters in the buffer
> ES:BX : A far pointer to the buffer

*Return values:*

> DH : If an error occurred, DH is set to 0xff.
> AX : The actual number of characters read from the intelligent board.

# INTELLIGENT MULTIPORT BOARDS

### Function 0x10 : Clear RX buffer

This function is used to clear the RX buffer for a particular port. Any and all characters that were pending in the buffer are discarded.

*Input registers:*
- AH : Set to 0x10, the function value
- DX : The port number

*Return values:*
- AH : Set to 0xff if an error occurred, otherwise 0

### Function 0x11 : Clear TX buffer

This function is used to clear the TX buffer for a particular port. Any and all characters that were pending in the buffer are discarded.

*Input registers:*
- AH : Set to 0x11, the function value
- DX : The port number

*Return values:*
- AH : Set to 0xff if an error occurred, otherwise 0

### Function 0x12 :  Get free space in the TX buffer

This function tells how many bytes are available in the TX buffer. This is used to implement one of the virtual functions derived from the RS232 class.

*Input registers:*
- AH : Set to 0x12, the function value
- DX : The port number

*Return values:*
- AX : Number of free bytes

### Function 0x13 : Raise a port's handshake lines

This function raises DTR and RTS, even if handshaking is enabled. Normally the DigiBoard driver ignores requests to change the modem status lines if handshaking is being used on a particular line. With this function, a blocking action could be cleared, even if the input buffers haven't passed below the low-water mark.

*Input registers:*

    AH :    Set to 0x13, the function value
    DX :    The port number

*Return values:*

    AH :    Set of 0xff if an error occurred, otherwise set to 0

### Function 0x14 : Peek at character

The DigiBoard driver only lets us peek a single character ahead. This function is used to perform the actual peeking.

*Input registers:*

    AH :    Set to 0x14, the function value
    DX :    The port number

*Return values:*

    AH :    If AH is not 0xff, it contains the port's line status
    AL :    Next input character, if AH is not 0xff

### Function 0x15 : Get free used in the RX buffer

This function tells how many bytes are present in the RX buffer. This is used to implement one of the virtual functions derived from the RS232 class.

## INTELLIGENT MULTIPORT BOARDS

*Input registers:*
- AH : Set to 0x15, the function value
- DX : The port number

*Return values:*
- AX : Number of bytes in use

### Function 0x1b : Get buffer sizes and water marks

This function retrieves the levels of the two water marks and the size of the two buffers.

*Input registers:*
- AH : Set to 0x1b, the function value
- AL : The subcommand, indicating which value is to be returned
  - 0 : Get the TX low-water mark
  - 1 : Get the RX low-water mark
  - 2 : Get the RX high-water mark
- DX : The port number

*Return values:*
- AX : The requested water mark
- BX : TX buffer size if AL was set to 0, otherwise the RX buffer size
- DH: Set to 0xff on error

### Function 0x1c : Set handshaking water marks

This function is used to set the high- and low-water marks used by the receiver when performing handshaking.

*Input registers:*

- AH : Set to 0x1c, the function value
- AL : The subcommand, indicating which water mark is to be set
    - 0 : Set the TX low-water mark
    - 1 : Set the RX low-water mark
    - 2 : Set the RX high-water mark
- BX : The water mark value
- DX : The port number

*Return values:*

- AH : 0xff on error, 0 on success

### Function 0x1e: Set handshaking

This function is used to establish the form of handshaking used for the given port.

*Input registers:*

- AH : Set to 0x1e, the function value
- BH : Software flow control flags
    - bit 0 : XON/XOFF TX flow control
    - bit 1 : XON/XOFF RX flow control
    - bit 2 : Flow control characters are in CX
- BL : Hardware flow control flags
    - bit 0 : DTR RX flow control
    - bit 1 : RTS RX flow control
    - bit 4 : CTS TX flow control
    - bit 5 : DSR TX flow control
    - bit 7 : DC TX flow control

## INTELLIGENT MULTIPORT BOARDS

    CH :    New XOFF character, if specified in BH
    CL :    New XON character, if specified in BH
    DX :    The DigiBoard port number

*Return values:*
    AH :    0xff on error, 0 on success

### Function 0x20 : Enable/Disable BIOS pacing

In order to emulate the BIOS, the DigiBoard emulates the BIOS pacing on the read and write functions. When trying to write, the BIOS checks for both CTS and DSR to be asserted, and will wait for up to 500 milliseconds before returning. We don't want to have to handle this with the current driver, so these functions are disabled.

*Input registers:*
    AH :    Set to 0x20, the function value
    AL :    Set to 1 to enable BIOS pacing, 0 to clear the pacing function
    DX :    The port number

*Return values:*
    AH :    0xff on error, 0 on success

### Function 0xfd : Get buffer counts

This function is used to retrieve the number of characters in the transmit or receive buffers.

*Input registers:*
    AH :    Set to 0xfd, the function value
    AL :    Set to 1 to get the TX buffer count, 2 to get the RX buffer count
    DX :    The port number

*Return values:*
    CX :    The buffer count

Table 5-1 is a quick reference chart of the Digiboard API. You might want to refer to this chart when looking at the code that implements the `DigiBoard` class.

**Table 5-1. The DigiBoard INT 14H interface.**

| Function | Description |
|---|---|
| 0 | BIOS compatible port parameter initialization |
| 1 | BIOS compatible single character output |
| 2 | BIOS compatible single character input |
| 3 | BIOS compatible read line status and modem status registers |
| 4 | EBIOS compatible extended port initialization |
| 5 | EBIOS compatible modem line control |
| 6 | Get driver information |
| 7 | Send break |
| 8 | Check line status and peek at character buffer |
| 9 | Clear buffers |
| 0x0a | Input buffer count |
| 0x0b | Drop handshaking lines |
| 0x0c | Read operating port parameters |
| 0x0d | Get pointer to the character ready flag |
| 0x0e | Write a buffer to a port |
| 0x0f | Read a buffer from a port |
| 0x10 | Clear the RX buffer |
| 0x11 | Clear the TX buffer |
| 0x12 | Get the TX buffer free space count |
| 0x13 | Raise a port's handshake lines |
| 0x14 | Peek at the next input character |
| 0x15 | Get the count of space used in the RX buffer |
| 0x1b | Get buffer sizes and handshaking water marks |
| 0x1c | Set the handshaking water marks |
| 0x1e | Set the type of handshaking |
| 0x20 | Enable/Disable BIOS pacing |
| 0xfd | Get buffer counts |

## Configuring Your DigiBoard

The DigiBoard device driver that interfaces with class DigiBoard is named XIDOS5.SYS. This file is normally shipped with the DigiBoard, along with printed documentation on how to configure the board. If you purchased a DigiBoard before this driver was developed, you may need to download the new driver from DigiBoard's BBS.

A configuration program named XIDOSCFG.EXE accompanies the device driver. This program lets you set up the board and port parameters to which the DigiBoard will be set when the system boots. You will need to run XIDOSCFG.EXE at least once to set up the board to work with this class.

Figure 5-3 shows the opening screen from the XICONFIG.EXE program. When you first run the configuration program, it asks you for the pertinent information that defines the interface with the board. You need to be fairly comfortable with PC hardware to make it past this stage unscathed, unless you are fortunate enough to have a MicroChannel machine. The ISA architecture boards require you to specify the shared RAM memory address, I/O port address, number of ports, and so on.

The Board Type, Memory Window, and I/O Port parameters are all just reflections of the way you have set up your board. You need to enter values in these fields that show how you have configured the board. The memory address and I/O port are both defined by jumpers or DIP switches on the board. The biggest difficulty with these is making sure that the values you choose don't conflict with existing hardware. In particular, the memory map setting has to coexist with 386 memory managers, hardware RAM caching, video and network boards, and 8/16 bit addressing conflicts.

The DigiBoard has an IRQ that can generate interrupts on certain events that take place on the board. This driver will not take advantage of those events so the IRQ should be disabled by setting it to a value of 0. Note that MicroChannel machines do not offer a choice about the IRQ number; the setup program configures it automatically.

The number of channels on the board should match your actual hardware. DigiBoard sells most of their boards in various port sizes, with 4-, 8-, and 16-port configurations available.

```
               DiGiCHANNEL CONFIGURATIONS PARAMETERS
Board    Type    Memory    I/O     IRQ     # Brd    Start      Driver
#                Window    Port    #       Chnls    Support
---------------------------------------------------------------------
1        COM/Xi  C000h     0100    0       8        4          EBIOS
---------------------------------------------------------------------
Configuration Selections:                   Use Arrow Keys

Q)uit       C)hannel Parameters     O)ptions   A)dd Board   R)emove Board

Enter Selection
```

**Figure 5-3.** The XICONFIG.EXE board configuration screen.

The starting channel parameter is somewhat arbitrary. By default, the port numbers start at COM5 on ISA machines, and COM9 on MCA computers. However, the actual value only really matters in the applications that talk to the ports. The value used in XICONFIG.EXE is the same value that will be loaded into the DX register before making an INT 14H function call. Remember that the value for COM5 is 4, since IBM defined COM1 as being 0 to the INT 14H BIOS.

The final parameter listed for the Board definition is "Driver Support". This simply defines which function calls the driver will accept. If DOS support is requested, an MS-DOS device called COMx will be defined for each port. This means that a program could conceivably open up COM15 and send output via the DigiBoard without having any special knowledge of how the DigiBoard works. EBIOS support means that the driver will accept the standard EBIOS function calls as well as the BIOS calls. For the DigiBoard class used here, EBIOS support is required. DOS support can be included, but the Digiboard class won't use it directly. It sometimes comes in handy when testing your configuration.

### Configuring the ports

Ports are configured using XICONFIG.EXE as well. Fortunately, the port configuration is not particularly critical to the successful operation of the board. The

## INTELLIGENT MULTIPORT BOARDS

```
                    BOARD 1 PARAMETERS
         CHANL    BAUD      MODE       RX FLOW    TX FLOW
         ---------------------------------------------------
          4       9600      8,N,1      NONE       NONE
          5       9600      8,N,1      NONE       NONE
          6       9600      8,N,1      NONE       NONE
          7       9600      8,N,1      NONE       NONE
          8      19200      7,E,1      XON        XON
          9      19200      7,E,1      DRT        DSR
         10      38400      7,E,2      RTS        CTS
         11      57600      7,E,1      XON        XON

A) 5,N,1  B) 6,N,1  C) 7,N,1  D) 8,N,1  E) 8,N,2  F) 6,N,2  G) 7,N,2  H) 8,N,2
I) 5,0,1  J) 6,0,1  K) 7,0,1  L) 8,0,1  M) 5,0,2  N) 6,0,2  O) 7,0,2  P) 8,0,2
Q) 5,E,1  R) 6,E,1  S) 7,E,1  T) 8,E,1  U) 8,E,2  V) 6,E,2  W) 7,E,2  X) 8,E,2
```

**Figure 5-4. The port configuration screen.**

parameters entered here define the settings of the individual ports at system startup, but any parameter can be overridden when the constructor for a `DigiBoard` object is first called.

The handshaking parameters may be the only thing in the configuration menu that ends up being important. While most programs will initialize the handshaking values when the port is opened, they are not required to do so. By leaving the handshaking parameters out of the constructor, the port will be opened with handshaking set to UNCHANGED. In this case, a port could be opened in a blocking state due to a low or missing handshake line.

To avoid this problem, I set all my ports to boot up with no handshaking. Then they can transmit immediately, even if I neglect to set up handshaking.

Additionally, if handshaking is not enabled immediately, during the debug phase, I can dump data out of the COM ports with the simple MS-DOS command line:

```
C> ECHO This is a test > COM5
```

If I have another device hooked up to monitor the connection, or even just a breakout box, I can see some activity on the TX lines, which lets me know that things are at least partly working. Note that this test will only work if you configured the driver to include DOS support.

### Implementing the DigiBoard class

Although getting the DigiBoard hardware to work properly can be difficult, interfacing with the `XIDOS5.SYS` device driver is fairly simple. This driver doesn't have to worry about interrupt handling. Any interrupts that occur as a result of incoming or outgoing data are handled directly on the DigiBoard by a dedicated processor.

Unlike the drivers we developed previously to work with the `PC8250` class UARTs, this class doesn't do too much low-level work. For example, when we want to read a buffer full of data in the `PC8250` class, the `read_byte()` routine has to check the input queue for data, extract as much as it can, then manage the incoming handshaking lines. In the `DigiBoard` class, we just have to ask the `XIDOS5.SYS` driver for the data and it does all the work.

## The Code

Listings 5-2 and 5-3 contain the listings for `DIGI.H` and `DIGI.CPP`, the two files that together implement `class DigiBoard`. One of the first things to take note of in `DIGI.H` is that it has a full implementation of the virtual functions defined in the base class RS232. DigiBoard designed an API flexible and complete enough to do the job.

`DIGI.H` extends the range of errors defined in `RS232.H` by only a single new error, which is `DIGIBOARD_DRIVER_NOT_FOUND`. This fatal error is returned when an attempt is made to open a port that isn't controlled by the DigiBoard device driver. Other than that, the header file for class `DigiBoard` is pretty much directly derived from `class RS232`.

## INTELLIGENT MULTIPORT BOARDS

```cpp
// ********************* START OF DIGI.H *********************

// This header file has the definitions and prototypes needed
// to use the Digiboard classes.

#ifndef _DIGI_DOT_H
#define _DIGI_DOT_H

#include <dos.h>
#include "rs232.h"

// A few type definitions used with this class.

enum DigiBoardError {
    DIGIBOARD_DRIVER_NOT_FOUND      = RS232_NEXT_FREE_ERROR,
    DIGIBOARD_NEXT_FREE_ERROR,
    DIGIBOARD_NEXT_FREE_WARNING     = RS232_NEXT_FREE_WARNING };

class DigiBoard : public RS232
{
    private :
        int line_status;
        int first_debug_output_line;
        void read_settings( void );
        RS232Error write_settings( void );
        int valid_port( void );
        virtual int read_buffer( char *buffer,
                            unsigned int count );
        virtual int write_buffer( char *buffer,
                            unsigned int count = -1 );
        virtual int read_byte( void );
        virtual int write_byte( int c );

    public :
        DigiBoard( enum RS232PortName port_name,
                long baud_rate = UNCHANGED,
                char parity = UNCHANGED,
                int word_length = UNCHANGED,
                int stop_bits = UNCHANGED,
                int dtr = SET,
```

```cpp
                    int rts = SET,
                    int xon_xoff = DISABLE,
                    int rts_cts = DISABLE,
                    int dtr_dsr = DISABLE );
    virtual ~DigiBoard( void );
    virtual RS232Error Set( long baud_rate = UNCHANGED,
                    char parity = UNCHANGED,
                    int word_length = UNCHANGED,
                    int stop_bits = UNCHANGED );
    virtual int TXSpaceFree( void );
    virtual int RXSpaceUsed( void );
    virtual int Break( long milliseconds = 300 );
    virtual int Cd( void );
    virtual int Ri( void );
    virtual int Cts( void );
    virtual int Dsr( void );
    virtual int ParityError( int clear = UNCHANGED );
    virtual int BreakDetect( int clear = UNCHANGED );
    virtual int FramingError( int clear = UNCHANGED );
    virtual int HardwareOverrunError( int clear = UNCHANGED );
    virtual int XonXoffHandshaking( int setting = UNCHANGED );
    virtual int RtsCtsHandshaking( int setting = UNCHANGED );
    virtual int DtrDsrHandshaking( int setting = UNCHANGED );
    virtual int Dtr( int setting = UNCHANGED );
    virtual int Rts( int setting = UNCHANGED );
    virtual int PeekBuffer( void *buffer, unsigned int count );
    virtual int RXSpaceFree( void );
    virtual int TXSpaceUsed( void );
    virtual int FlushRXBuffer( void );
    virtual int FlushTXBuffer( void );
    virtual char * ErrorName( int error );
    virtual int FormatDebugOutput( char *buffer = 0,
                                   int line_number = -1 );
};

#endif // #ifndef _DIGI_DOT_H

// ********************** END OF DIGI.H **********************
```

**Listing 5-2. The class definition in DIGI.H**

# INTELLIGENT MULTIPORT BOARDS

Most of the code in `DIGI.CPP` should be fairly simple to follow, given the documentation on the `XIDOS5.SYS` API earlier in this chapter. Most of the functions just make one or two calls via the INT 14H interface and return to the calling routine. Note that the `line_status` private member of class DigiBoard is updated after most of the function calls. This allows us to keep track of any line status events on a cumulative basis.

```cpp
// ******************* START OF DIGI.CPP *******************
//
// This file contains all of the code used by the DigiBoard class.
// All access of the DigiBoard is done via the INT 14H interface
// described in the DOC file available from DigiBoard.
//

#include <stdio.h>
#include <ctype.h>
#include "pc8250.h"
#include "rs232.h"
#include "digi.h"

// The DigiBoard constructor is nice and simple.  It has to read
// in the old settings to save them, then set the new ones according
// to the parameters passed in the constructor.  The only private
// member exclusive to the derived class is the line_status flag,
// which is initialized to 0.  The call to function 0x20 is used
// to disable BIOS timing emulation.

DigiBoard::DigiBoard( RS232PortName port,
                      long baud_rate,
                      char parity,
                      int word_length,
                      int stop_bits,
                      int dtr,
                      int rts,
                      int xon_xoff,
                      int rts_cts,
                      int dtr_dsr )
```

```cpp
{
    union REGS r;

    port_name = port;
    error_status = RS232_SUCCESS;

    first_debug_output_line = RS232::FormatDebugOutput();
    debug_line_count = FormatDebugOutput();
    if ( !valid_port() ) {
        error_status = (RS232Error) DIGIBOARD_DRIVER_NOT_FOUND;
        return;
    }
    read_settings();
    saved_settings = settings;
    settings.Adjust( baud_rate,
                     parity,
                     word_length,
                     stop_bits,
                     dtr,
                     rts,
                     xon_xoff,
                     rts_cts,
                     dtr_dsr );
    write_settings();
    r.h.ah = 0x20;
    r.h.al = 0;
    r.x.dx = port_name;
    int86( 0x14, &r, &r );
    line_status = 0;
}

// The destructor just restores the old state, nothing more.

DigiBoard::~DigiBoard( void )
{
    settings = saved_settings;
    write_settings();
}
```

# INTELLIGENT MULTIPORT BOARDS

```c
//
// A call to function 0x0c and 0x05 is needed to read all the
// parameters found in the Settings class.  All that is
// needed after that is a bunch of switch statements to convert
// the enumerated results that come back from the driver to
// settings usable by programmers.
//

void DigiBoard::read_settings( void )
{
    union REGS r;

    settings.BaudRate = -1L;
    settings.Parity = '?';
    settings.WordLength = -1;
    settings.StopBits = -1;
    settings.Dtr = -1;
    settings.Rts = -1;
    settings.XonXoff = -1;
    settings.RtsCts = -1;
    settings.DtrDsr = -1;
    r.h.ah = 0xc;
    r.x.dx = port_name;
    int86( 0x14, &r, &r );
    if ( r.h.ah == 0xff )
        return;
    switch ( r.h.cl ) {
        case 0x00 : settings.BaudRate = 110L;   break;
        case 0x01 : settings.BaudRate = 150L;   break;
        case 0x02 : settings.BaudRate = 300L;   break;
        case 0x03 : settings.BaudRate = 600L;   break;
        case 0x04 : settings.BaudRate = 1200L;  break;
        case 0x05 : settings.BaudRate = 2400L;  break;
        case 0x06 : settings.BaudRate = 4800L;  break;
        case 0x07 : settings.BaudRate = 9600L;  break;
        case 0x08 : settings.BaudRate = 19200L; break;
        case 0x09 : settings.BaudRate = 38400L; break;
        case 0x0a : settings.BaudRate = 57600L; break;
        case 0x0b : settings.BaudRate = 75600L; break;
```

```cpp
            case 0x0c : settings.BaudRate = 115200L; break;
            case 0x0d : settings.BaudRate = 50L;     break;
            case 0x0e : settings.BaudRate = 75L;     break;
            case 0x0f : settings.BaudRate = 134L;    break;
            case 0x10 : settings.BaudRate = 200L;    break;
            case 0x11 : settings.BaudRate = 1800L;   break;
        }
        switch ( r.h.bh ) {
            case 0 : settings.Parity = 'N'; break;
            case 1 : settings.Parity = 'O'; break;
            case 2 : settings.Parity = 'E'; break;
        }
        switch ( r.h.ch ) {
             case 0 : settings.WordLength = 5; break;
            case 1 : settings.WordLength = 6; break;
            case 2 : settings.WordLength = 7; break;
            case 3 : settings.WordLength = 8; break;
        }
        switch ( r.h.bl ) {
            case 0 : settings.StopBits = 1; break;
            case 1 : settings.StopBits = 2; break;
        }
        settings.XonXoff = ( r.h.ah & 3 ) ? 1: 0;
        settings.DtrDsr = ( r.h.al & 0x21 ) ? 1 : 0;
        settings.RtsCts = ( r.h.al & 0x12 ) ? 1 : 0;
        r.x.dx = port_name;
        r.h.ah = 5;
        r.h.al = 0;
        int86( 0x14, &r, &r );
        settings.Dtr = ( r.h.bl & MCR_DTR ) ? 1 : 0;
        settings.Rts = ( r.h.bl & MCR_RTS ) ? 1 : 0;
}

// Setting the Digiboard up with all the parameters found in the
// Settings class requires three INT 14H calls.  Function 4
// sets the standard communications parameters, Function 5 sets
// the modem control lines, and function 0x1e sets up handshaking.
//
```

# INTELLIGENT MULTIPORT BOARDS

```cpp
RS232Error DigiBoard::write_settings( void )
{
    union REGS r;
    RS232Error status = RS232_SUCCESS;

    r.x.dx = port_name;
    r.h.ah = 4;
    r.h.al = 0;
    switch ( toupper( settings.Parity ) ) {
        case 'E' : r.h.bh = 1; break;
        case 'O' : r.h.bh = 2; break;
        default  : settings.Parity = 'N';
                   status = RS232_ILLEGAL_PARITY_SETTING;
        case 'N' : r.h.bh = 0; break;
    }
    switch ( settings.StopBits ) {
        default : settings.StopBits = 1;
                  status = RS232_ILLEGAL_STOP_BITS;
        case 1 : r.h.bl = 0; break;
        case 2 : r.h.bl = 1; break;
    }
    switch ( settings.WordLength ) {
        case 5   : r.h.ch = 0; break;
        case 6   : r.h.ch = 1; break;
        case 7   : r.h.ch = 2; break;
         default : settings.WordLength = 8;
                   status = RS232_ILLEGAL_WORD_LENGTH;
        case 8   : r.h.ch = 3; break;
    }
    switch ( settings.BaudRate ) {
        case 110L    : r.h.cl = 0x00; break;
        case 150L    : r.h.cl = 0x01; break;
        case 300L    : r.h.cl = 0x02; break;
        case 600L    : r.h.cl = 0x03; break;
        case 1200L   : r.h.cl = 0x04; break;
        case 2400L   : r.h.cl = 0x05; break;
        case 4800L   : r.h.cl = 0x06; break;
        default      : settings.BaudRate = 9600L;
                       status = RS232_ILLEGAL_BAUD_RATE;
```

```
            case 9600L    : r.h.cl = 0x07; break;
            case 19200L   : r.h.cl = 0x08; break;
            case 38400L   : r.h.cl = 0x09; break;
            case 57600L   : r.h.cl = 0x0a; break;
            case 76800L   : r.h.cl = 0x0b; break;
            case 115200L  : r.h.cl = 0x0c; break;
            case 50L      : r.h.cl = 0x0d; break;
            case 75L      : r.h.cl = 0x0e; break;
            case 134L     : r.h.cl = 0x0f; break;
            case 200L     : r.h.cl = 0x10; break;
            case 1800L    : r.h.cl = 0x11; break;
        }
        int86( 0x14, &r, &r );
        r.x.dx = port_name;
        r.h.ah = 0x1e;
        r.h.bh = (unsigned char) ( ( settings.XonXoff ) ? 3: 0 );
        r.h.bl = (unsigned char) ( ( settings.RtsCts ) ? 0x12 : 0 );
        r.h.bl |= ( settings.DtrDsr ) ? 0x21 : 0;
        int86( 0x14, &r, &r );
        r.x.dx = port_name;
        r.h.ah = 5;
        r.h.al = 1;
        r.h.bl = (unsigned char) ( ( settings.Dtr ) ? 1 : 0 );
        r.h.bl |= ( settings.Rts ) ? 2 : 0;
        int86( 0x14, &r, &r );
        return status;
}

// Function 6 is called to return the name of the port, but
// it also functions effectively to check if the
// DigiBoard considers the port to be valid.

int DigiBoard::valid_port( void )
{
    union REGS r;

    r.x.dx = port_name;
    r.h.ah = 6;
     r.h.al = 0;
```

## INTELLIGENT MULTIPORT BOARDS

```c
        int86( 0x14, &r, &r );
        return ( r.h.ah != 0xff );
}

// Reading a byte uses the two BIOS emulation functions, one to
// read in the modem status, and the other to read the character.
// This function, like many of the other ones, updates the
// line status flags with the result read back from the board.

int DigiBoard::read_byte( void )
{
    union REGS r;

    if ( error_status < 0 )
        return error_status;
    r.h.ah = 3;
    r.x.dx = port_name;
    int86( 0x14, &r, &r );
    line_status |= r.h.ah;
    if ( r.h.ah & LSR_DATA_READY ) {
        r.h.ah = 2;
        r.x.dx = port_name;
        int86( 0x14, &r, &r );
        line_status |= r.h.ah;
        return( r.h.al );
    }
    return( RS232_TIMEOUT );
}

// This function also uses a standard BIOS function call.

int DigiBoard::write_byte( int c )
{
    union REGS r;

    if ( error_status < 0 )
        return error_status;
    r.x.dx = port_name;
    r.h.ah = 0x01;
```

```c++
    r.h.al = (char) c;
    int86( 0x14, &r, &r );
    line_status |= r.h.ah;
    if ( r.h.ah & 0x80 )
        return RS232_TIMEOUT;
    return RS232_SUCCESS;
}

// DigiBoard has two private functions, 14 and 15, that are
// used to read or write blocks of data.  They both transfer
// as much data as possible, then return a count.

int DigiBoard::read_buffer( char *buffer, unsigned int count )
{
    union REGS r;
    struct SREGS s;

    if ( error_status < 0 )
        return error_status;
    r.x.dx = port_name;
    r.x.cx = count;
    r.h.ah = 0x0f;
    s.es = (unsigned int) ( (long) (void FAR *) buffer >> 16 );
    r.x.bx = (unsigned int) (long) (void FAR *) buffer;
    int86x( 0x14, &r, &r, &s );
    ByteCount = r.x.ax;
    buffer[ ByteCount ] = '\0';
    if ( ByteCount != count )
        return RS232_TIMEOUT;
    return( RS232_SUCCESS );
}

int DigiBoard::write_buffer( char *buffer, unsigned int count )
{
    union REGS r;
    struct SREGS s;

    if ( error_status < RS232_SUCCESS )
        return error_status;
```

## INTELLIGENT MULTIPORT BOARDS

```c
    r.x.dx = port_name;
    r.x.cx = count;
    r.h.ah = 0x0e;
    s.es = (unsigned int) ( (long) (void FAR *) buffer >> 16 );
    r.x.bx = (unsigned int) (long) (void FAR *) buffer;
    int86x( 0x14, &r, &r, &s );
    ByteCount = r.x.ax;
    if ( ByteCount != count )
        return RS232_TIMEOUT;
    return RS232_SUCCESS;
}

// This function does no work on its own.  Instead, it uses
// the adjust function to change the settings member, then
// calls the write_settings() function to do the job.

int DigiBoard::Set( long baud_rate,
                    char parity,
                    int word_length,
                    int stop_bits )
{

    settings.Adjust( baud_rate,
                     parity,
                     word_length,
                     stop_bits,
                     UNCHANGED,
                     UNCHANGED,
                     UNCHANGED,
                     UNCHANGED,
                     UNCHANGED );
    return write_settings();
}

// DigiBoard function 7 sets a break of a variable time in 10
// millisecond ticks.

int DigiBoard::Break( long milliseconds )
```

```cpp
{
    union REGS r;

    if ( error_status < RS232_SUCCESS )
        return error_status;
    r.x.dx = port_name;
    r.h.ah = 7;
    r.h.al = 1;
    r.x.bx = (int) ( milliseconds / 10 );
    int86( 0x14, &r, &r );
    return RS232_SUCCESS;
}

// All four of the modem status functions just use BIOS function
// 3 to read in the MSR of the UART.  They then just mask off
// the appropriate bit from the MSR and return a boolean value
// to the calling program.

int DigiBoard::Cd( void )
{
    union REGS r;

    if ( error_status < RS232_SUCCESS )
        return error_status;
     r.x.dx = port_name;
    r.h.ah = 3;
    int86( 0x14, &r, &r );
    line_status |= r.h.ah;
    return ( r.h.al & MSR_CD ) != 0;
}

int DigiBoard::Ri( void )
{
    union REGS r;

    if ( error_status < RS232_SUCCESS )
        return error_status;
    r.x.dx = port_name;
    r.h.ah = 3;
```

```c
    int86( 0x14, &r, &r );
    line_status |= r.h.ah;
    return ( r.h.al & MSR_RI ) != 0;
}

int DigiBoard::Cts( void )
{
    union REGS r;

    if ( error_status < RS232_SUCCESS )
        return error_status;
    r.x.dx = port_name;
    r.h.ah = 3;
    int86( 0x14, &r, &r );
    line_status |= r.h.ah;
    return ( r.h.al & MSR_CTS ) != 0;
}

int DigiBoard::Dsr( void )
{
    union REGS r;

    if ( error_status < RS232_SUCCESS )
        return error_status;
    r.x.dx = port_name;
    r.h.ah = 3;
    int86( 0x14, &r, &r );
    line_status |= r.h.ah;
    return ( r.h.al & MSR_DSR ) != 0;
}

// Like the modem status functions, the four-line status functions
// use BIOS function 3 to read the LSR from the UART, then mask
// off the appropriate bits and return a logical true or false to
// the calling program.

int DigiBoard::ParityError( int reset )
{
    union REGS r;
```

```cpp
    int status;

    if ( error_status < RS232_SUCCESS )
        return error_status;
     r.x.dx = port_name;
    r.h.ah = 3;
    int86( 0x14, &r, &r );
    line_status |= r.h.ah;
    status = ( line_status & LSR_PARITY_ERROR ) != 0;
    if ( reset != UNCHANGED && reset != 0 )
        line_status &= ~LSR_PARITY_ERROR;
    return status;
}

int DigiBoard::BreakDetect( int reset )
{
    union REGS r;
    int status;

    if ( error_status < RS232_SUCCESS )
        return error_status;
    r.x.dx = port_name;
    r.h.ah = 3;
    int86( 0x14, &r, &r );
    line_status |= r.h.ah;
    status = ( line_status & LSR_BREAK_DETECT ) != 0;
    if ( reset != UNCHANGED && reset != 0 )
        line_status &= ~LSR_BREAK_DETECT;
    return status;
}

int DigiBoard::FramingError( int reset )
{
    union REGS r;
    int status;

    if ( error_status < RS232_SUCCESS )
        return error_status;
    r.x.dx = port_name;
```

# INTELLIGENT MULTIPORT BOARDS

```cpp
    r.h.ah = 3;
    int86( 0x14, &r, &r );
    line_status |= r.h.ah;
    status = ( line_status & LSR_FRAMING_ERROR ) != 0;
    if ( reset != UNCHANGED && reset != 0 )
        line_status &= ~LSR_FRAMING_ERROR;
    return status;
}

int DigiBoard::HardwareOverrunError( int reset )
{
    union REGS r;
    int status;

    if ( error_status < RS232_SUCCESS )
        return error_status;
    r.x.dx = port_name;
    r.h.ah = 3;
    int86( 0x14, &r, &r );
    line_status |= r.h.ah;
    status = ( line_status & LSR_OVERRUN_ERROR ) != 0;
    if ( reset != UNCHANGED && reset != 0 )
        line_status &= ~LSR_OVERRUN_ERROR;
    return status;
}

// The five handshaking and modem control functions are all
// basically lazy. They modify a the appropriate value in
// the settings member, then call write_settings() to do the
// real work.

int DigiBoard::XonXoffHandshaking( int setting )
{
    if ( setting != UNCHANGED ) {
        settings.XonXoff = ( setting != 0 );
        write_settings();
    }
    return settings.XonXoff;
}
```

```cpp
int DigiBoard::RtsCtsHandshaking( int setting )
{
    if ( setting != UNCHANGED ) {
        settings.RtsCts = ( setting != 0 );
        write_settings();
    }
    return settings.RtsCts;
}

int DigiBoard::DtrDsrHandshaking( int setting )
{
    if ( setting != UNCHANGED ) {
        settings.DtrDsr = ( setting != 0 );
        write_settings();
    }
    return settings.DtrDsr;
}

int DigiBoard::Dtr( int setting )
{
    if ( setting != UNCHANGED ) {
        settings.Dtr = ( setting != 0 );
        write_settings();
    }
    return ( settings.Dtr != 0 );
}

int DigiBoard::Rts( int setting )
{
    if ( setting != UNCHANGED ) {
        settings.Rts = ( setting != 0 );
        write_settings();
    }
    return ( settings.Rts != 0 );
}

// DigiBoard only lets you peek ahead by one byte into the
// input buffer.  If there is a character there, this function
// reads it in and stores it in the appropriate place.
```

# INTELLIGENT MULTIPORT BOARDS

```c
int DigiBoard::PeekBuffer( void *buffer, unsigned int count )
{
    union REGS r;

    if ( count ) {
        r.h.ah = 3;
        r.x.dx = port_name;
        int86( 0x14, &r, &r );
        line_status |= r.h.ah;
        if ( r.h.ah & 0x80 )
            return RS232_ERROR;
        if ( r.h.ah & 1 ) {
            r.h.ah = 0x14;
            r.x.dx = port_name;
            int86( 0x14, &r, &r );
            line_status |= r.h.ah;
            *( (char *) buffer ) = r.h.al;
            ByteCount = 1;
        } else
            ByteCount = 0;
    }
    return RS232_SUCCESS;
}

// These functions all use private digiboard INT 14 calls to
// return buffer counts.  The only complication is that there
// is no direct way to determine the RX space free.  It has to
// be calculated indirectly as the RX buffer size minus the buffer
// space used.

int DigiBoard::TXSpaceUsed( void )
{
    union REGS r;

    if ( error_status < RS232_SUCCESS )
        return error_status;
    r.x.dx = port_name;
    r.h.ah = 0xfd;
```

```c
    r.h.al = 1;
    int86( 0x14, &r, &r );
    return( r.x.cx );
}

int DigiBoard::TXSpaceFree( void )
{
    union REGS r;

    if ( error_status < RS232_SUCCESS )
        return error_status;
    r.x.dx = port_name;
    r.h.ah = 0x12;
    int86( 0x14, &r, &r );
    return r.x.ax;
}

int DigiBoard::RXSpaceUsed( void )
{
    union REGS r;

    if ( error_status < RS232_SUCCESS )
        return error_status;
    r.x.dx = port_name;
    r.h.ah = 0x0a;
    int86( 0x14, &r, &r );
    return r.x.ax;
}

int DigiBoard::RXSpaceFree( void )
{
    union REGS r;
    int buffer_size;

    if ( error_status < RS232_SUCCESS )
        return error_status;

    r.x.dx = port_name;
    r.h.ah = 0x1b;
```

## INTELLIGENT MULTIPORT BOARDS

```c
    r.h.al = 1;
    int86( 0x14, &r, &r );
    buffer_size = r.x.bx;
    r.h.ah = 10;
    r.x.dx = port_name;
    int86( 0x14, &r, &r );
    return( buffer_size - r.x.ax );
}

// DigiBoard provides two private INT 14 calls to handle flushing
// the TX and RX buffers.

int DigiBoard::FlushRXBuffer( void )
{
    union REGS r;

    if ( error_status < RS232_SUCCESS )
        return error_status;
    r.x.dx = port_name;
    r.h.ah = 0x10;
    int86( 0x14, &r, &r );
    return RS232_SUCCESS;
}

int DigiBoard::FlushTXBuffer( void )
{
    union REGS r;

    if ( error_status < RS232_SUCCESS )
        return error_status;
    r.x.dx = port_name;
    r.h.ah = 0x11;
    int86( 0x14, &r, &r );
    return RS232_SUCCESS;
}

int DigiBoard::FormatDebugOutput( char *buffer, int line_number )
{
    union REGS r;
```

```cpp
    if ( buffer == 0 )
        return( first_debug_output_line +  4 );
    if ( line_number < first_debug_output_line )
        return RS232::FormatDebugOutput( buffer, line_number );
    switch( line_number - first_debug_output_line ) {
        case 0 :
            r.x.dx = port_name;
            r.h.ah = 6;
            r.h.al = 1;
            int86( 0x14, &r, &r );
            sprintf( buffer,
                    "Derived class: DigiBoard  Boards/Channels:"
                    "%2d/%2d"
                    "Ver: %2x.%02x   1st Port: COM%-2d",
                    r.x.cx,
                    r.x.ax,
                    r.h.bh, r.h.bl,
                    r.x.dx + 1 );
            break;
        case 1 :
            ParityError( UNCHANGED );
            sprintf( buffer,
                    "Parity Err: %d  "
                    "Break Det: %d  "
                    "Overrun Err: %d  "
                    "Framing Err: %d  ",
                    ( line_status & LSR_PARITY_ERROR ) ? 1 : 0,
                    ( line_status & LSR_BREAK_DETECT ) ? 1 : 0,
                    ( line_status & LSR_OVERRUN_ERROR ) ? 1 : 0,
                    ( line_status & LSR_FRAMING_ERROR ) ? 1 : 0 );
            break;
        case 2 :
            sprintf( buffer,
                    "Buffer Counts: RX Used/Free: %5u/%5u  "
                    "TX Used/Free: %5u/%5u",
                    RXSpaceUsed(),
                    RXSpaceFree(),
                    TXSpaceUsed(),
                    TXSpaceFree() );
```

```
                break;
            case 3 :
                sprintf( buffer,
                        "RI: %2d  CD: %2d  CTS: %2d  DSR: %2d",
                        Ri(), Cd(), Cts(), Dsr() );
                break;
            default :
                return RS232_ILLEGAL_LINE_NUMBER;
        }
        return RS232_SUCCESS;
    }

    char * DigiBoard::ErrorName( int error )
    {
        if ( error < RS232_NEXT_FREE_ERROR && error >= RS232_ERROR )
            return RS232::ErrorName( error );
        if ( error < RS232_NEXT_FREE_WARNING && error >= RS232_WARNING )
            return RS232::ErrorName( error );
        if ( error >= RS232_SUCCESS )
            return RS232::ErrorName( error );
        switch ( error ) {
            case DIGIBOARD_DRIVER_NOT_FOUND   : return( "Driver not
                                                                found" );
            default                           : return( "Undefined
                                                                error" );
        }
    }
```

**Listing 5-3. The DigiBoard class implementation in DIGI.CPP.**

## TEST232.EXE

Modifying `TEST232.EXE` to work properly with the `DigiBoard` class is fairly simple. First, I modified the list of include files to pull in `DIGI.H`, the header file that contains the class definitions. Note that the header files used in the previous two chapters, including `PC8250.H`, are all gone now. Additionally, I set the `WINDOW_COUNT` constant to 4. I could open as many as 8 ports on the DigiBoard, but the screen management begins to become a little unruly.

# SERIAL COMMUNICATIONS: A C++ DEVELOPER'S GUIDE

```
#include "portable.h"
#include <stdio.h>
#include <stdlib.h>
#include <string.h>
#include <conio.h>
#include <ctype.h>
#include "rs232.h"
#include "textwind.h"
#include "digi.h"

// The window count can range from 1 to 4. The window_parms
// array will be modified depending on the value of
// WINDOW_COUNT.

#define WINDOW_COUNT 4
```

For the DigiBoard, I need to redefine the port names used in `TEST232.EXE`. I configured my DigiBoard to start at COM5, and go up from there:

```
RS232PortName port_names[ 4 ] = { COM5, COM6, COM7, COM7 };
```

The final change to be make to `TEST232.CPP` is to change the loop that opens all the ports. The port type needs to be changed to `DigiBoard`:

```
for ( i = 0 ; i < WINDOW_COUNT ; i++ ) {
    switch ( i ) {
        default :
            Ports[ i ] = new DigiBoard( port_names[ i ],
                                9600, 'N', 8, 1, 1, 1 );
    }
}
```

To build this program, you need to change the definition of the `FILES` in `TEST232.MAK` to only include the DigiBoard class definition file:

```
FILES = digi.obj
```

# INTELLIGENT MULTIPORT BOARDS

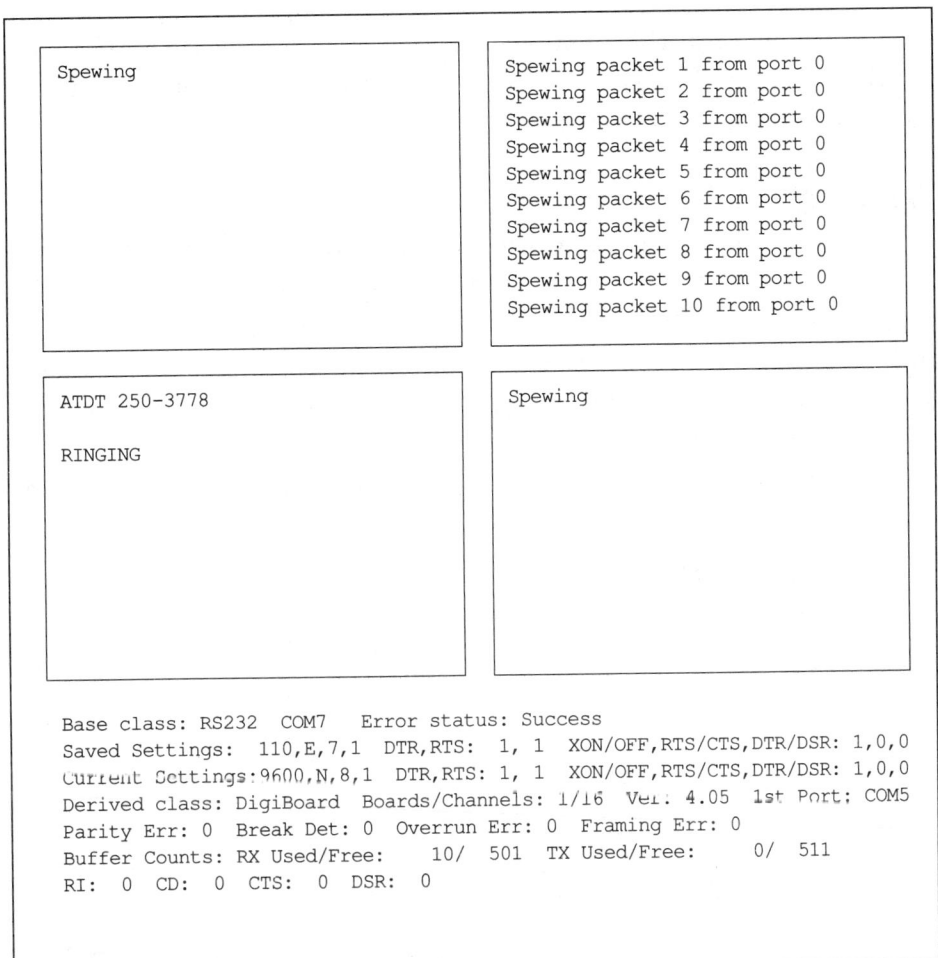

Figure 5-5. TEST232.EXE configured for the DigiBoard class.

After you make the new version of TEST232.EXE, you should then be able to talk to an intelligent DigiBoard. Assuming you are successful in installing the DigiBoard hardware on your system, you should see a screen shot such as that shown in Figure 5-5.

Due to the fact that the DigiBoard offloads much of the processing requirements from the PC to the card, you can easily put all ports in Spew mode with TEST232 and keep up with the load at high baud rates. This just wouldn't be possible with a nonintelligent multiport card. Unfortunately, the DOS driver for the

DigiBoard is not compatible with multitasking environments such as MS-Windows or DESQview. DigiBoard does supply a driver for OS/2, so the long-desired multitasking capability for a serial driver can in fact be realized.

## Summary

It's not too difficult to implement the class to support DigiBoards, although other boards might be more complicated. Each intelligent board manufacturer has a proprietary interface with its own virtues and drawbacks. Most are based on the INT 14H BIOS calls, but their similarities all end there. Some, like StarGate, don't even have a driver, requiring a developer to need an even more detailed understanding of the interface.

As the desktop world moves on to operating systems that are more sophisticated than MS-DOS, we can expect to start finding standardization. Until then, we have to contend with the current Tower of Babel.

CHAPTER 6

# The BIOS and EBIOS Drivers

According to its original design, the IBM PC was supposed to allow developers to write hardware-independent code. All system hardware was supposed to be accessed via a standardized BIOS interface. For some services, such as access to the hard disk, this method has been fairly successful. When developers want to read to or write from the hard disk on a PC, they either use the BIOS indirectly by making MS-DOS function calls or they use it directly via the INT 13H interface. However, the BIOS designers did not provide interrupt-driven support for the COM ports, which forced programmers to bypass the BIOS and write programs that directly accessed the hardware.

When writing code for standard comm ports on the IBM PC, the developer will usually use code such as that shown in Chapter 3 that implements the `PC8250` class, to be more efficient. However, there are good reasons for supporting the `BIOS` and `EBIOS` classes as well:

- You can interface with hardware that is not 8250 compatible. Over the years, some computers have used nonstandard hardware and provided support by replacing the standard BIOS routines with custom implementations.

- The INT 14H API is used as an interface for several different network access protocols. There are many competing systems for accessing modems across a network, such as Novell's NASI. Most of these systems support INT 14H access, with proprietary extensions.

- Some BBS "Door Programs" need to talk to serial ports on a PC via a FOSSIL driver, which is an extension of the IBM PC BIOS. The FOSSIL driver will be discussed later in chapter 7.

- Intelligent boards, such as the DigiBoard, usually support a BIOS or EBIOS interface. The `BIOSPort` driver I will present in this chapter will work well with an intelligent DigiBoard.

## BIOS Details

The BIOS designers provided a set of services for access to the serial ports on the PC, collectively accessed via 80x86 interrupt 14H. The original IBM PC BIOS provided four functions, which gave very limited support for polled mode I/O via the two system COM ports. The PS/2 introduced two additional function calls as part of the *Extended BIOS*. Descriptions of the six functions follow.

### Function 0 : Initialize port (BIOS)

This function is used to initialize the transmission parameters for the port. Some software that uses the INT 14H API interprets function 0 as the equivalent of opening a port. However, there is no equivalent function defined for the BIOS that closes a port.

*Input registers:*
- AH : Set to 0, the function value
- AL : Broken down into four bit fields, shown below
- DX : The port number, starting at 0 for COM1

*Return values:*
- AH : The current line status
- AL : Set to the reflect the modem status value.

## THE BIOS AND EBIOS DRIVERS

The bit settings for the input values of AL are shown below:

| AL Bit Field Definitions | | | | | | | | |
|---|---|---|---|---|---|---|---|---|
| 7 | 6 | 5 | 4 | 3 | 2 | | 1 | 0 |
| Baud Rate | | | Parity | | Stop Bits | | Word Length | |

Baud Rate Values :

| | |
|---|---|
| 000 | 110 |
| 001 | 150 |
| 010 | 300 |
| 011 | 600 |
| 100 | 1200 |
| 101 | 2400 |
| 110 | 4800 |
| 111 | 9600 |

Parity values:

| | |
|---|---|
| 00 | None |
| 01 | Odd |
| 10 | None |
| 11 | Even |

Stop bits:

| | |
|---|---|
| 0 | 1 Stop bit |
| 1 | 2 Stop bits |

Word length:

| | |
|---|---|
| 00 | 5 bits |
| 01 | 6 bits |
| 10 | 7 bits |
| 11 | 8 bits |

### Function 1 : Output a single character (BIOS)

This function sends a single character out the port. When using the actual BIOS, this function obeys IBM's version of half duplex transmission. DTR and RTS are asserted before the character is sent. The BIOS routine then waits for CTS and DSR to be asserted before sending the character. If the control lines don't ever go high, a timeout error is returned after a nominal wait, usually on the order of a second.

*Input registers:*
    AH :    Set to 1, the function value
    AL :    The character to be output
    DX :    The port number, starting at 0 for COM1

*Return values:*
    AH :    Timeout error if bit 7 is set, else the current line status

### Function 2 : Input a single character (BIOS)

This function also obeys IBM's version of RS-232 half-duplex signaling. When the function is called, DTR is first asserted, then the routine waits for DSR to come high. If DSR doesn't come high after the nominal timeout of one to two seconds, an error is returned. If DSR does come high, the routine waits again for a character to be ready in the RX buffer. A timeout error is returned if no character arrives, otherwise the character is returned.

*Input registers:*
    AH :    Set to 2, the function value
    DX :    The port number, starting at 0 for COM1

*Return values:*
    AH :    Timeout error if bit 7 is set, else the current line status
    AL :    The character read in

### Function 3 : Read line and modem status (BIOS)

This routine is nice and simple. It just reads in the two status register values, and returns them in AH and AL. While the IBM documentation indicates that this return could return a timeout bit in position 7 of AH, the BIOS cannot actually generate a timeout error for this function.

*Input registers:*
    AH :    Set to 3, the function value
    DX :    The port number, starting at 0 for COM1

*Return values:*

    AH :     The port line status
    AL :     The port modem status

**Function 4 : Extended port initialization (Extended BIOS)**

This function was added with the PS/2 line, in order to support a few more line settings.

*Input registers:*

| | | | |
|---|---|---|---|
| AH : | Set to 4, the function value | | |
| AL : | Break flag, 1 for break on, 0 for break off | | |
| BH : | Parity setting: | 0 | No parity |
| | | 1 | Odd parity |
| | | 2 | Even parity |
| | | 3 | Mark parity |
| | | 4 | Space parity |
| BL : | Stop bits: | 0 | 1 stop bit |
| | | 1 | 2 stop bits |
| CH : | Word length: | 0 | 5 bits |
| | | 1 | 6 bits |
| | | 2 | 7 bits |
| | | 3 | 8 bits |
| CL : | Baud rate: | 0 | 110 baud |
| | | 1 | 150 baud |
| | | 2 | 300 baud |
| | | 3 | 600 baud |
| | | 4 | 1200 baud |
| | | 5 | 2400 baud |
| | | 6 | 4800 baud |
| | | 7 | 9600 baud |
| | | 8 | 19200 baud |
| DX : | The port number, starting at 0 for COM1 | | |

*Return values:*

| | |
|---|---|
| AH : | The port line status |
| AL : | The port modem status |

### Function 5, Subfunction 0 : Read modem control register (extended BIOS)

Function 5 added the ability to read in the current settings for DTR and RTS, and to set them to any desired values.

*Input registers:*

| | |
|---|---|
| AH : | Set to 5, the function value |
| AL : | Set to 0, the subfunction value |
| DX : | The port number, starting at 0 for COM1 |

*Return values:*

| | |
|---|---|
| AH : | The port line status |
| AL : | The port modem status |
| BL : | The modem control register contents |

### Function 5, Subfunction 1 : Write modem control register (extended BIOS)

*Input registers:*

| | |
|---|---|
| AH : | Set to 5, the function value |
| AL : | Set to 1, the subfunction value |
| BL : | Bit 0 controls DTR, bit 1 controls RTS |
| DX : | The port number, starting at 0 for COM1 |

*Return values:*

| | |
|---|---|
| AH : | The port line status |
| AL : | The port modem status |

## Problems

Looking over the BIOS and EBIOS functions, we spot a number of problem areas. While we can implement a BIOS class, there are quite a few missing pieces.

## THE BIOS AND EBIOS DRIVERS

The INT 14H API does not support advanced features, such as handshaking. In addition, the following points will cause various degrees of trouble:

- No error codes are returned from the BIOS calls. This is a major problem if you are trying to open the port since there is no way to determine whether a port even exists.

- BIOS ports require the use of IBM's version of RS-232 control. If an attempt is made to read or write when the appropriate input control lines are low, the BIOS will delay for many hundreds of milliseconds before returning. But if the routines returned immediately, our code could manage the delay. It would be even better if the control line management could be disabled.

- There is no BIOS function to close a port. This missing feature in the BIOS API causes trouble for software that attempts to emulate the INT 14H functions, such as modem access software that works on networks.

- The selection of available baud rates is very limited. There is no practical reason for this restriction, it's really just a result of laziness on the part of the BIOS designers.

- There is no handshaking of any kind. This would be tough to implement properly in a polled environment, but it would have been useful as a BIOS extension.

- No function is provided to read in the current settings of the UART. The Extended BIOS offers a minor improvement here, by letting us read in the state of the Modem Control Register, giving us the settings of DTR and RTS.

Because of these problems, the BIOS interface should only be used when absolutely necessary. Probably the best use of `class BIOSPort` is as a base for a derived class with a better level of functionality.

# SERIAL COMMUNICATIONS: A C++ DEVELOPER'S GUIDE

## The code

The two files that define the `BIOSPort` and `EBIOSPort` classes are `BIOSPORT.H` and `BIOSPORT.CPP`. Both files are listed in their entirety in Figures 6-2 and 6-3. The code for the two classes defined here is fairly easy to follow, with the help of the BIOS function definitions given previously.

The most important thing to know when using these classes is which specific functions are *not* supported by the BIOS. Unfortunately, the list is fairly long.

*Functions not support by either class:*
```
SoftwareOverrunError()
XonXoffHandshaking()
RtsCtsHandshaking()
DtrDsrHandshaking()
Peek()
FlushRXBuffer()
FlushTXBuffer()
RXSpaceFree()
TXSpaceUsed()
```

*Functions only supported by class EBIOS:*
```
Dtr()
Rts()
Break()
```

These two classes make good use of an often-mentioned C++ feature: inheritance. Since the input, output, and status functions are identical for the `BIOSPort` and `EBIOSPort` classes, it makes sense to derive `EBIOSPort` directly from `BIOSPort`. `EBIOSPort` then has to have its own private implementations of a few new functions, and the `write_settings()` and `read_settings()` functions, but it shares several other functions with its parent class.

## Inheritance

One of the interesting things to note in this class is the use of inheritance. While all of the classes in this book have been derived from the `RS232` class, they did not inherit any usable code. `RS232` is an abstract class that doesn't actually do anything on its own.

In this case, class `EBIOSPort` inherits all of the methods and data from the `BIOSPort` class. One of the interesting problems to overcome here lies in the area of initialization. Since the `EBIOSPort` supports different baud rates and parities, it needs its own version of `write_settings()`, which has to be called in the constructor. It also has the ability to read the current state of DTR and RTS, so it has a `read_settings()` function, which `BIOSPort` doesn't.

When constructing an object of a derived class, the C++ compiler generates code to first construct an instance of the parent class. This means that when the `EBIOSPort` constructor is called, an instance of `BIOSPort` will have already been created. We don't want to execute the constructor code since it works completely differently in each of the two classes.

To get around this problem, I created a protected version of the default constructor, `BIOSPort::BIOSPort( void )`. This is the constructor that the compiler will call by default when creating an instance of `BIOSPort`. This constructor doesn't attempt to initialize any of the settings, which means the port will still be uninitialized when the `EBIOSPort` constructor gets called.

The void `BIOSPort` constructor is set as `protected` simply for safety reasons. Calling this constructor will create a `BIOSPort` object that is in a dangerous state. Because the port has not actually been initialized, there is no telling what would happen if it was inadvertently used. By making it `protected`, we insure that it can only be used by a derived class, which will presumably know that it is dealing with a dangerously uninitialized object.

```
// ******************* START OF BIOSPORT.H *********************

// This header file has all of the definitions and prototypes
// needed to use the BIOSPort and EBIOSPort classes. This file
// should be included by any module that needs to access either
// of the classes.

#ifndef _BIOSPORT_DOT_H
#define _BIOSPORT_DOT_H
```

```cpp
#include <dos.h>
#include "rs232.h"

class BIOSPort : public RS232
{
    protected :
        int line_status;
        int first_debug_output_line;
        RS232Error write_settings( void );
        virtual int read_buffer( char *buffer,
                                 unsigned int count );
        virtual int write_buffer( char *buffer,
                                  unsigned int count = -1 );
        virtual int read_byte( void );
        virtual int write_byte( int c );
        BIOSPort( void );

    public :
        BIOSPort( enum RS232PortName port_name,
                  long baud_rate = UNCHANGED,
                  char parity = UNCHANGED,
                  int word_length = UNCHANGED,
                  int stop_bits = UNCHANGED,
                  int dtr = SET,
                  int rts = SET,
                  int xon_xoff = DISABLE,
                  int rts_cts = DISABLE,
                  int dtr_dsr = DISABLE );
        virtual ~BIOSPort( void );
        virtual RS232Error Set( long baud_rate = UNCHANGED,
                                int parity = UNCHANGED,
                                int word_length = UNCHANGED,
                                int stop_bits = UNCHANGED );
        virtual int TXSpaceFree( void );
        virtual int RXSpaceUsed( void );
        virtual int Cd( void );
        virtual int Ri( void );
        virtual int Cts( void );
        virtual int Dsr( void );
```

```
            virtual int ParityError( int clear = UNCHANGED );
            virtual int BreakDetect( int clear = UNCHANGED );
            virtual int FramingError( int clear = UNCHANGED );
            virtual int HardwareOverrunError( int clear = UNCHANGED );
            virtual int FormatDebugOutput( char *buffer = 0,
                                           int line_number = -1 );
};

class EBIOSPort : public BIOSPort
{
    protected :
        RS232Error write_settings( void );
        void read_settings( void );
        int first_debug_output_line;
        int break_on;

    public :
        EBIOSPort( enum RS232PortName port_name,
                   long baud_rate = UNCHANGED,
                   char parity = UNCHANGED,
                   int word_length = UNCHANGED,
                   int stop_bits = UNCHANGED,
                   int dtr = SET,
                   int rts = SET,
                   int xon_xoff = DISABLE,
                   int rts_cts = DISABLE,
                   int dtr_dsr = DISABLE );
        ~EBIOSPort( void );
         virtual RS232Error Set( long baud_rate = UNCHANGED,
                                 int parity = UNCHANGED,
                                 int word_length = UNCHANGED,
                                 int stop_bits = UNCHANGED );
        virtual int Break( long milliseconds = 300 );
        virtual int Dtr( int setting = UNCHANGED );
        virtual int Rts( int setting = UNCHANGED );
        virtual int FormatDebugOutput( char *buffer = 0,
                                       int line_number = -1 );
};
```

```
#endif // #ifndef _BIOSPORT_DOT_H

// ********************* END OF BIOSPORT.H ***********************
```

**Listing 6-1. BIOSPORT.H, the header file for the two BIOS classes.**

```
// ******************** START OF BIOSPORT.CPP ********************
//
// This file contains all of the code used by the BIOSPort and
// EBIOSPort classes.
//

#include <stdio.h>
#include <ctype.h>
#include "rs232.h"
#include "biosport.h"
#include "_8250.h"

// The BIOSPort constructor doesn't have very much work to do. It
// sets all the saved settings to invalid values, since none of
// them can be accessed. It has to set up the debug output, then
// set all of the port settings, and then return. Note that there
// is no way to detect an error when attempting to access a BIOS
// port, so the constructor always succeeds.

BIOSPort::BIOSPort( RS232PortName port,
                    long baud_rate,
                    char parity,
                    int word_length,
                    int stop_bits,
                    int dtr,
                    int rts,
                    int xon_xoff,
                    int rts_cts,
                    int dtr_dsr )
{
    port_name = port;
    error_status = RS232_SUCCESS;
```

```
    first_debug_output_line = RS232::FormatDebugOutput();
    debug_line_count = FormatDebugOutput();
    saved_settings.BaudRate = -1L;
    saved_settings.Parity = '?';
    saved_settings.WordLength = -1;
    saved_settings.StopBits = -1;
    saved_settings.Dtr = -1;
    saved_settings.Rts = -1;
    saved_settings.XonXoff = -1;
    saved_settings.RtsCts = -1;
    saved_settings.DtrDsr = -1;
    settings.Adjust( baud_rate,
                     parity,
                     word_length,
                     stop_bits,
                     dtr,
                     rts,
                     xon_xoff,
                     rts_cts,
                     dtr_dsr );
    write_settings();
    line_status = 0;
}

// The void constructor is called by the inherited class EBIOSPort
// when it is being constructed. Since EBIOSPort will initialize all
// the settings, this constructor just initializes the debug output.
// Note that this constructor is protected, since it doesn't create
// a properly initialized port that could be used as an object by
// itself.

BIOSPort::BIOSPort( void )
{
    first_debug_output_line = RS232::FormatDebugOutput();
    debug_line_count = FormatDebugOutput();
}

// There is no BIOS function to close a port, so the destructor
// doesn't have to do anything.
```

# SERIAL COMMUNICATIONS: A C++ DEVELOPER'S GUIDE

```cpp
BIOSPort::~BIOSPort( void )
{
}

// The write_settings function is fairly limited when it comes to
// options. There are lots of opportunities for errors here.
// Note that if the constructor attempts an invalid setting, the
// error code never gets returned to the calling program, since
// the constructor doesn't return a value.

RS232Error BIOSPort::write_settings( void )
{
    union REGS r;
    RS232Error status = RS232_SUCCESS;
    r.x.dx = port_name;
    r.h.ah = 0;
    r.h.al = 0;
    switch ( toupper( settings.Parity ) ) {
        case 'E' : r.h.al |= 0x18; break;
        case 'O' : r.h.al |= 0x08; break;
        default  : settings.Parity = 'N';
                   status = RS232_ILLEGAL_PARITY_SETTING;
        case 'N' : r.h.al |= 0x00; break;
    }
    switch ( settings.StopBits ) {
        case 1 : r.h.al |= 0; break;
        default : settings.StopBits = 2;
                  status = RS232_ILLEGAL_STOP_BITS;
        case 2 : r.h.al |= 4; break;
    }
    switch ( settings.WordLength ) {
        case 5 : r.h.al |= 0; break;
        case 6 : r.h.al |= 1; break;
        case 7 : r.h.al |= 2; break;
        default : settings.WordLength = 8;
                  status = RS232_ILLEGAL_WORD_LENGTH;
        case 8 : r.h.al |= 3; break;
    }
    switch ( settings.BaudRate ) {
```

```c
            case 110L     : r.h.al |= 0x00; break;
            case 150L     : r.h.al |= 0x20; break;
            case 300L     : r.h.al |= 0x40; break;
            case 600L     : r.h.al |= 0x60; break;
            case 1200L    : r.h.al |= 0x80; break;
            case 2400L    : r.h.al |= 0xa0; break;
            case 4800L    : r.h.al |= 0xc0; break;
            default       : settings.BaudRate = 9600L;
                            status = RS232_ILLEGAL_BAUD_RATE;
            case 9600L    : r.h.al |= 0xe0; break;
        }
        int86( 0x14, &r, &r );
        if ( settings.Dtr != -1 ) {
            settings.Dtr = -1;
            status = RS232_DTR_NOT_SUPPORTED;
        }
        if ( settings.Rts != -1 ) {
            settings.Rts = -1;
            status = RS232_RTS_NOT_SUPPORTED;
        }
        if ( settings.RtsCts != -1 ) {
            settings.RtsCts = -1;
            status = RS232_RTS_CTS_NOT_SUPPORTED;
        }
        if ( settings.DtrDsr != -1 ) {
            settings.DtrDsr = -1;
            status = RS232_DTR_DSR_NOT_SUPPORTED;
        }
        if ( settings.XonXoff != -1 ) {
            settings.XonXoff = -1;
            status = RS232_XON_XOFF_NOT_SUPPORTED;
        }
        return status;
}

// If the data ready bit is set in the UART LSR, this routine calls
// the BIOS function to read the character. Otherwise it returns
// a timeout. Even if the data ready bit is set, this routine is
// still vulnerable to hanging up in a several second delay if the
// incoming DSR line is not set.
```

```cpp
int BIOSPort::read_byte( void )
{
    union REGS r;

    if ( error_status < 0 )
        return error_status;
    r.h.ah = 3;
    r.x.dx = port_name;
    int86( 0x14, &r, &r );
    line_status |= r.h.ah;
    if ( r.h.ah & LSR_DATA_READY ) {
        r.h.ah = 2;
        r.x.dx = port_name;
        int86( 0x14, &r, &r );
        line_status |= r.h.ah;
        if ( ( r.h.ah & 0x80 ) == 0 )
            return( r.h.al );
    }
    return( RS232_TIMEOUT );
}

// This function also uses a standard BIOS function call. It is
// also vulnerable to a delay if DSR or CTS are not set.

int BIOSPort::write_byte( int c )
{
    union REGS r;

    if ( error_status < 0 )
        return error_status;
    r.x.dx = port_name;
    r.h.ah = 0x01;
    r.h.al = (char) c;
    int86( 0x14, &r, &r );
    line_status |= r.h.ah;
    if ( r.h.ah & 0x80 )
        return RS232_TIMEOUT;
    return RS232_SUCCESS;
}
```

## THE BIOS AND EBIOS DRIVERS

```
RS232Error BIOSPort::Set( long baud_rate,
                         int parity,
                         int word_length,
                         int stop_bits )
{
    settings.Adjust( baud_rate,
                     parity,
                     word_length,
                     stop_bits,
                     UNCHANGED,
                     UNCHANGED,
                     UNCHANGED,
                     UNCHANGED,
                     UNCHANGED );
    return write_settings();
}

// The next four routines all execute the BIOS call that reads
// in the MSR. The appropriate bit is then masked out, and the
// result is returned to the calling routine.

int BIOSPort::Cd( void )
{
    union REGS r;

    if ( error_status < RS232_SUCCESS )
        return error_status;
    r.x.dx = port_name;
    r.h.ah = 3;
    int86( 0x14, &r, &r );
    line_status |= r.h.ah;
     return ( r.h.al & MSR_CD ) != 0;
}

int BIOSPort::Ri( void )
{
    union REGS r;

    if ( error_status < RS232_SUCCESS )
```

```cpp
        return error_status;
    r.x.dx = port_name;
    r.h.ah = 3;
    int86( 0x14, &r, &r );
    line_status |= r.h.ah;
    return ( r.h.al & MSR_RI ) != 0;
}

int BIOSPort::Cts( void )
{
    union REGS r;

    if ( error_status < RS232_SUCCESS )
        return error_status;
    r.x.dx = port_name;
    r.h.ah = 3;
    int86( 0x14, &r, &r );
    line_status |= r.h.ah;
    return ( r.h.al & MSR_CTS ) != 0;
}

int BIOSPort::Dsr( void )
{
    union REGS r;

    if ( error_status < RS232_SUCCESS )
        return error_status;
    r.x.dx = port_name;
    r.h.ah = 3;
    int86( 0x14, &r, &r );
    line_status |= r.h.ah;
    return ( r.h.al & MSR_DSR ) != 0;
}

// The four routines that check line status bits operate almost
// identically to the modem status routines.  The only difference
// is that the line status bits are accumulated in a private data
// member, so instead of just checking the bit in the LSR, these
// routines have to check the current state ORed with the cumula-
```

## THE BIOS AND EBIOS DRIVERS

```
// tive state. In addition, each of the routines has the option of
// either leaving the bit set, or clearing it after reading it.

int BIOSPort::ParityError( int reset )
{
    union REGS r;
    int status;

    if ( error_status < RS232_SUCCESS )
        return error_status;
    r.x.dx = port_name;
    r.h.ah = 3;
    int86( 0x14, &r, &r );
    line_status |= r.h.ah;
    status = ( line_status & LSR_PARITY_ERROR ) != 0;
    if ( reset != UNCHANGED && reset != 0 )
        line_status &= ~LSR_PARITY_ERROR;
    return status;
}

int BIOSPort::BreakDetect( int reset )
{
    union REGS r;
    int status;

    if ( error_status < RS232_SUCCESS )
        return error_status;
    r.x.dx = port_name;
    r.h.ah = 3;
    int86( 0x14, &r, &r );
    line_status |= r.h.ah;
    status = ( line_status & LSR_BREAK_DETECT ) != 0;
    if ( reset != UNCHANGED && reset != 0 )
        line_status &= ~LSR_BREAK_DETECT;
    return status;
}

int BIOSPort::FramingError( int reset )
{
```

```cpp
    union REGS r;
    int status;

    if ( error_status < RS232_SUCCESS )
        return error_status;
    r.x.dx = port_name;
    r.h.ah = 3;
    int86( 0x14, &r, &r );
    line_status |= r.h.ah;
    status = ( line_status & LSR_FRAMING_ERROR ) != 0;
    if ( reset != UNCHANGED && reset != 0 )
        line_status &= ~LSR_FRAMING_ERROR;
    return status;
}

int BIOSPort::HardwareOverrunError( int reset )
{
    union REGS r;
    int status;

    if ( error_status < RS232_SUCCESS )
        return error_status;
    r.x.dx = port_name;
    r.h.ah = 3;
    int86( 0x14, &r, &r );
    line_status |= r.h.ah;
    status = ( line_status & LSR_OVERRUN_ERROR ) != 0;
    if ( reset != UNCHANGED && reset != 0 )
        line_status &= ~LSR_OVERRUN_ERROR;
    return status;
}

// The formatted debug output for BIOSPort is sparse. It prints out
// two lines of information that dump the states of the MSR and LSR.

int BIOSPort::FormatDebugOutput( char *buffer, int line_number )
{
    if ( buffer == 0 )
        return( first_debug_output_line + 2 );
```

## THE BIOS AND EBIOS DRIVERS

```
        if ( line_number < first_debug_output_line )
            return RS232::FormatDebugOutput( buffer, line_number );
        switch( line_number - first_debug_output_line ) {
            case 0 :
                sprintf( buffer,
                        "Derived class: BIOSPort   "
                        "RI: %2d  CD: %2d  CTS: %2d  DSR: %2d",
                        Ri(), Cd(), Cts(), Dsr() );
                break;
            case 1 :
                Ri();
                sprintf( buffer,
                        "Parity Err: %d   "
                        "Break Det: %d   "
                        "Overrun Err: %d   "
                        "Framing Err: %d",
                        ( line_status & LSR_PARITY_ERROR ) ? 1 : 0,
                        ( line_status & LSR_BREAK_DETECT ) ? 1 : 0,
                        ( line_status & LSR_OVERRUN_ERROR ) ? 1 : 0,
                        ( line_status & LSR_FRAMING_ERROR ) ? 1 : 0 );
                break;
            default :
                return RS232_ILLEGAL_LINE_NUMBER;
        }
        return RS232_SUCCESS;
}
// The read_buffer routine is set up to continue reading in data
// as long as the data ready bit is set in the LSR. With a true
// BIOS, this means that it will generally only read in a single
// byte before returning to the Read() routine. It is up to the
// calling program to make sure a time value is set up so that
// multiple bytes can be read in. Note that a BIOS  emulation system
// will usually be able to feed in an entire buffer with a single
// call.

int BIOSPort::read_buffer( char *buffer, unsigned int count )
{
    union REGS rin;
    union REGS rout;
```

```c
        ByteCount = 0;
        if ( error_status < 0 )
            return error_status;
        rin.x.dx = port_name;
        while ( count > 0 ) {
            rin.h.ah = 3;
            int86( 0x14, &rin, &rout );
            line_status |= rout.h.ah;
            if ( ( rout.h.ah & LSR_DATA_READY ) == 0 )
                break;
            rin.h.ah = 2;
            int86( 0x14, &rin, &rout );
            line_status |= rout.h.ah;
            if ( rout.h.ah & 0x80 )
                break;
            *buffer++ = rout.h.al;
            count--;
            ByteCount++;
        }
        *buffer = '\0';
        if ( count > 0 )
            return RS232_TIMEOUT;
        else
            return RS232_SUCCESS;
}
// Like read_buffer(), the write_buffer routine will usually only
// be able to write a single byte when using a true BIOS
// implementation. It is up to the caller to invoke Write() with
// a long enough time delay to be able to send the entire buffer.
// A BIOS emulation system will usually be able to take in the
// entire buffer with one call to the write_buffer().

int BIOSPort::write_buffer( char *buffer, unsigned int count )
{
    union REGS rin;
    union REGS rout;

    rin.x.dx = port_name;
    ByteCount = 0;
```

## THE BIOS AND EBIOS DRIVERS

```
        if ( error_status < 0 )
            return error_status;
        while ( count > 0 ) {
            rin.h.ah = 3;
            int86( 0x14, &rin, &rout );
            line_status |= rout.h.ah;
            if ( ( rout.h.ah & LSR_THRE ) == 0 )
                break;
            rin.h.ah = 1;
            rin.h.al = (char) *buffer++;
            int86( 0x14, &rin, &rout );
            if ( rout.h.ah & 0x80 )
                break;
            line_status |= rout.h.ah;
            buffer++;
            count--;
            ByteCount++;
        }
        if ( count > 0 )
            return RS232_TIMEOUT;
        else
            return RS232_SUCCESS;
}

// If the THRE bit is set, there is room for one byte, if clear,
// there is room for 0 bytes.
int BIOSPort::TXSpaceFree( void )
{
    union REGS r;

    if ( error_status < RS232_SUCCESS )
        return error_status;
    r.x.dx = port_name;
    r.h.ah = 3;
    int86( 0x14, &r, &r );
    line_status |= r.h.ah;
    if ( r.h.ah & LSR_THRE )
        return 1;
    else
```

```cpp
        return 0;
}

// If the data ready bit is set, there is one byte present in the
// buffer, else 0.

int BIOSPort::RXSpaceUsed( void )
{
    union REGS r;

     if ( error_status < RS232_SUCCESS )
        return error_status;
    r.x.dx = port_name;
    r.h.ah = 3;
    int86( 0x14, &r, &r );
    line_status |= r.h.ah;
    if ( r.h.ah & LSR_DATA_READY )
        return 1;
    else
        return 0;
}

// EBIOSPort has a few extra functions above and beyond BIOSPort.
// It has the ability to read in the old state of DTR and RTS,
// and can send a break signal. It also has a few extra baud rates
// and other line settings.

EBIOSPort::EBIOSPort( RS232PortName port,
                     long baud_rate,
                     char parity,
                     int word_length,
                     int stop_bits,
                     int dtr,
                     int rts,
                     int xon_xoff,
                     int rts_cts,
                     int dtr_dsr )
{
    port_name = port;
```

```
        error_status = RS232_SUCCESS;

        first_debug_output_line = BIOSPort::FormatDebugOutput();
        debug_line_count = FormatDebugOutput();
        read_settings();
        saved_settings = settings;
        settings.Adjust( baud_rate,
                         parity,
                         word_length,
                         stop_bits,
                         dtr,
                         rts,
                         xon_xoff,
                         rts_cts,
                         dtr_dsr );
        break_on = 0;
        write_settings();
        line_status = 0;
}

EBIOSPort::~EBIOSPort( void )
{
}
// The only additional information that I have to offer with this
// output routine is the setting of the break flag, which will
// usually be clear.

int EBIOSPort::FormatDebugOutput( char *buffer, int line_number )
{
    if ( buffer == 0 )
        return( first_debug_output_line + 1 );
    if ( line_number < first_debug_output_line )
        return BIOSPort::FormatDebugOutput( buffer, line_number );
    switch( line_number - first_debug_output_line ) {
        case 0 :
            sprintf( buffer,
                     "Derived class: EBIOSPort   "
                     "Break flag: %2d",
                     break_on );
```

```
                break;
        default :
            return RS232_ILLEGAL_LINE_NUMBER;
    }
    return RS232_SUCCESS;
}

// There are exactly two settings that I can read here:  the state
// of Dtr and Rts.  It isn't much, but I read them both in and
// set the rest of the values to be invalid.

void EBIOSPort::read_settings( void )
{
    union REGS r;

    r.x.dx = port_name;
    r.h.ah = 5;
    r.h.al = 0;
    int86( 0x14, &r, &r );
    settings.Dtr = ( ( r.h.bl & 0x1 ) != 0 );
    settings.Rts = ( ( r.h.bl & 0x2 ) != 0 );
    settings.BaudRate = -1L;
    settings.Parity = '?';
    settings.WordLength = -1;
    settings.StopBits = -1;
    settings.XonXoff = -1;
    settings.RtsCts = -1;
    settings.DtrDsr = -1;
}

// Since write_settings() uses a different function for the EBIOS,
// it has a few extra settings to support.

RS232Error EBIOSPort::write_settings( void )
{
    union REGS r;
    RS232Error status = RS232_SUCCESS;

    r.x.dx = port_name;
```

## THE BIOS AND EBIOS DRIVERS

```c
    r.h.ah = 4;
    if ( break_on )
        r.h.al = 1;
    else
        r.h.al = 0;
    switch ( toupper( settings.Parity ) ) {
        case 'E' : r.h.bh = 1; break;
        case 'O' : r.h.bh = 2; break;
        default  : settings.Parity = 'N';
                   status = RS232_ILLEGAL_PARITY_SETTING;
        case 'N' : r.h.bh = 0; break;
    }
    switch ( settings.StopBits ) {
        case 1 : r.h.bl = 0; break;
        default : settings.StopBits = 2;
                  status = RS232_ILLEGAL_STOP_BITS;
        case 2 : r.h.bl = 1; break;
    }
    switch ( settings.WordLength ) {
        case 5 : r.h.ch = 0; break;
        case 6 : r.h.ch = 1; break;
        case 7 : r.h.ch = 2; break;
        default : settings.WordLength = 8;
                  status = RS232_ILLEGAL_WORD_LENGTH;
        case 8 : r.h.ch = 3; break;
    }
    switch ( settings.BaudRate ) {
        case 110L   : r.h.cl = 0x00; break;
        case 150L   : r.h.cl = 0x01; break;
        case 300L   : r.h.cl = 0x02; break;
        case 600L   : r.h.cl = 0x03; break;
        case 1200L  : r.h.cl = 0x04; break;
        case 2400L  : r.h.cl = 0x05; break;
        case 4800L  : r.h.cl = 0x06; break;
        default     : settings.BaudRate = 9600L;
                      status = RS232_ILLEGAL_BAUD_RATE;
        case 9600L  : r.h.cl = 0x07; break;
        case 19200L : r.h.cl = 0x08; break;
    }
```

```
        int86( 0x14, &r, &r );
        r.x.dx = port_name;
        r.h.ah = 5;
        r.h.al = 1;
        r.h.bl = (unsigned char) ( ( settings.Dtr ) ? 1 : 0 );
        r.h.bl |= ( settings.Rts ) ? 2 : 0;
        int86( 0x14, &r, &r );
        if ( settings.RtsCts != -1 ) {
            settings.RtsCts = -1;
            status = RS232_RTS_CTS_NOT_SUPPORTED;
        }
        if ( settings.DtrDsr != -1 ) {
            settings.DtrDsr = -1;
            status = RS232_DTR_DSR_NOT_SUPPORTED;
        }
        if ( settings.XonXoff != -1 ) {
            settings.XonXoff = -1;
            status = RS232_XON_XOFF_NOT_SUPPORTED;
        }
        return status;
}

// EBIOSPort can set Dtr and Rts, BIOSPort can't.

int EBIOSPort::Dtr( int setting )
{
    if ( setting != UNCHANGED ) {
        settings.Dtr = ( setting != 0 );
        write_settings();
    }
    return ( settings.Dtr != 0 );
}

int EBIOSPort::Rts( int setting )
{
    if ( setting != UNCHANGED ) {
        settings.Rts = ( setting != 0 );
        write_settings();
    }
```

## THE BIOS AND EBIOS DRIVERS

```cpp
    return ( settings.Rts != 0 );
}

int EBIOSPort::Break( long milliseconds )
{
    long timer;

    if ( error_status < RS232_SUCCESS )
        return error_status;
    timer = ReadTime() + milliseconds;
    break_on = 1;
    write_settings();
    while ( ReadTime() < timer )
        IdleFunction();
     break_on = 0;
    write_settings();
    return RS232_SUCCESS;
}

RS232Error EBIOSPort::Set( long baud_rate,
                           int parity,
                           int word_length,
                           int stop_bits )
{
    settings.Adjust( baud_rate,
                     parity,
                     word_length,
                     stop_bits,
                     UNCHANGED,
                     UNCHANGED,
                     UNCHANGED,
                     UNCHANGED,
                     UNCHANGED );
    return write_settings();
}
```

**Listing 6-2. BIOSPORT.CPP, the code for the two BIOS classes.**

# SERIAL COMMUNICATIONS: A C++ DEVELOPER'S GUIDE

## Testing the BIOS classes

Building a version of `TEST232` to test these two classes requires the usual steps. First, modify the definition of `FILES` in `TEST232.MAK` to look like this:

```
FILES = biosport.obj
```

This will cause the make system to compile and link the code for this class in with the rest of the code needed for `TEST232.EXE`.

The second step is the usual modification to the source of `TEST232.CPP`. In this case, I modify the switch statement that creates the new `RS232` objects to look like this:

```
switch ( i ) {
  case 0 :
   Ports[ i ] = new BIOSPort( port_names[ i ], 9600, 'N', 8, 1 );
   break;
  default :
   Ports[ i ] = new EBIOSPort( port_names[ i ], 9600, 'N', 8, 1 );
}
```

Note that with the two port configuration of `TEST232.EXE`, this will open COM1 as a `BIOSPort` and COM2 as an `EBIOSPort`. Figure 6-4 shows a screen shot illustrating the program running in this configuration.

One additional modification you need to make to `TEST232.EXE` is to add the appropriate include line to bring `BIOSPORT.H` and all its definitions into the file. The list of header files should look like this:

```
#include "portable.h"
#include <stdio.h>
#include <stdlib.h>
#include <string.h>
#include <conio.h>
#include <ctype.h>
#include "rs232.h"
#include "textwind.h"
#include "biosport.h"
```

# THE BIOS AND EBIOS DRIVERS

```
bF60433000                          xxxxxxxxxxxxxxxxxxxxxxxxxxxxxx
r1001111171012000
r3000111010000000
OK



at



OK


Base class: RS232  COM1    Status: Success
Byte count:    0   Elapsed time:      0  TX Free:    1  RX Used:    0
Saved port:   -1,?,-1,-1  DTR,RTS: -1,-1 XON/OFF,RTS/CTS,DTR/DSR: -1,-1,-1
Current port: 1200,N,8,1  DTR,RTS: -1,-1 XON/OFF,RTS/CTS,DTR/DSR: -1,-1,-1
Derived class: BIOSPort   RI: 0  CD: 0   CTS: 1  DSR: 1
Parity Err: 0   Break Det: 0   Overrun Err: 1  Framing Err: 0
```

**Figure 6-3. A Screen Shot from TEST232.EXE.**

Figure 6-3 illustrates one of the perils with the BIOS port drivers. The system running `TEST232.EXE` in fact only had a port on COM1, so COM2 should never have even been opened. But since the BIOS doesn't have an error return for a missing port, the constructor executes successfully, and we are left with an object that is going to operate incorrectly. You can see an example of that incorrect operation in the screen shot. COM2 is erroneously returning input characters, which are displayed on the screen in a continuous line.

In addition, there is no good way to determine whether a given configuration supports EBIOS. So a port opened with the `EBIOSPort` constructor may operate incorrectly when in fact a port exists. About the only rule of thumb you can count on here is that all PS/2 systems will have the Extended BIOS. Other systems or emulation software may or may not.

This leaves us with a fairly dangerous set of `RS232` objects. While they may be our only choice for access of COM ports under many configurations, we are going to be extremely dependent on proper configuration of the software by end users. If the end users don't understand their setup, these objects will work poorly or not at all.

353

CHAPTER 7

# The FOSSIL Driver

FOSSIL is an acronym for "Fido-Opus-Seadog Standard Interface Layer." The first FOSSIL was developed in an attempt to define a level of standardization missing from the IBM PC serial interface design. The IBM PC BIOS support for serial ports is simply not up to the task of serious serial communications. Early pioneers in the IBM PC BBS world had to implement custom versions of serial interface code that dealt directly with the PC hardware.

## BBS Drivers

While most BBS authors successfully implemented their own serial interfaces, the BBS approach still created numerous problems. First, the BBS authors wanted to concentrate on interesting tasks, such as providing good user interfaces or developing nationwide mail networks. Instead, they often found themselves debugging system hardware problems for the vast array of machines BBS system operators were attempting to bring up.

An even more serious problem related to door programs and external protocols. A door program is an external program that can be executed by a user logged in on a BBS. By giving a BBS the ability to call external programs, the BBS author opens the doors to a wide variety of support programs written by enterprising programmers. Popular BBS programs, such as today's PCBoard, have literally hundreds of door programs available, performing tasks ranging from mail delivery to games to callback verifiers.

External protocols are another feature useful for BBS authors. If a new file transfer protocol such as ZMODEM becomes popular, an external protocol driver allows a BBS to add support for that protocol without modifying the BBS code. Without external protocol programs, every time a BBS author or user wanted to add a new file transfer protocol, they would be required to alter the BBS source code. External door programs such as Chuck Forsberg's DSZ.COM made new protocols available much more quickly than would have been possible if every BBS system had to be modified.

In the early 1980s, door programs and external protocols were not easy to implement. Once again, even for the simplest external program, the programmer had to sit down and write that same serial interface code.

### The solution

The early BBS implementors decided to do what IBM or Microsoft should have done, which was to define a set of system services for the PC serial port. The FOSSIL specification was the result. A FOSSIL driver can be implemented as a device driver, a TSR, or even part of the system BIOS. It is simply a piece of software that provides access to the serial ports on a PC using a set of extensions to the BIOS INT 14H services.

By placing the interrupt-driven serial support in a standalone driver, the BBS writer no longer had to devote substantial amounts of code to supporting serial hardware. Even better, external door programs and protocol drivers could now take advantage of the same driver, making their lives much simpler. Once the BBS program opens a port and configures it, the door program doesn't even have to worry about setting the baud rate or handshaking options.

The early definition of FOSSIL envisioned a future in which BBS programs could run on virtually any hardware and O/S built on Intel 80x86 platform. By building a FOSSIL driver for a particular computer, all existing BBS software would work without changes.

In practice, building FOSSIL drivers for each platform has been somewhat successful. Several good FOSSIL drivers are available for standard PCs. In addition, noncompatible computers such as the DEC Rainbow were able to run BBS software once an appropriate FOSSIL driver was developed. In addition, FOSSIL drivers for standard PCs have been quick to take advantage of features such as 16550 FIFO buffering. Waiting for every door and BBS program to take advantage of the same thing might have taken years.

### The FOSSIL Specification

The FOSSIL specification, release 5, defines the complete interface between the application program and the serial interface hardware. You can find the

# THE FOSSIL DRIVER

document describing the entire interface on several on-line services; it is also available on most Opus BBS systems.

The FOSSIL interface defines a very complete set of functions for talking to serial hardware. The only major functions that we can't implement in the `RS232` class are direct control of the RTS line, and DTR/DSR handshaking. This is a considerable improvement over the simple interface provided by the IBM PC BIOS.

In addition to the serial port interface, the FOSSIL definition includes support for a few other basic system services, such as keyboard input, screen output, and timer tick support. These are not relevant for the `FOSSIL` class defined here. Curious readers can look up the specification.

### Function 0 : Initialize port (BIOS)

This function is identical to IBM BIOS function 0, with one exception. The FOSSIL spec supports 19,200 and 38,400 bps initialization. To do so, they replaced the port settings for 110 and 150 baud with those two values. See Chapter 6 on the BIOS driver for a complete definition of the bit settings.

*Input registers:*
- AH : Set to 0, the function value
- AL : Broken down into four bit fields. See Chapter 6 for details on BIOS function 0.
- DX : The port number, starting at 0 for COM1

*Return values:*
- AH : The current line status
- AL : Set to the reflect the modem status value.

### Function 1: Transmit a single byte

This function is identical to the INT 14H BIOS function to transmit a byte. The primary difference here is that the character does not get immediately transmitted. Instead, it is placed into the queue of characters waiting to be transmitted as TX interrupts occur.

*Input registers:*
- AH : Set to 1, the function value
- AL : The character to be transmitted
- DX : The port number, starting at 0 for COM1

*Return values:*
- AH : The current line status
- AL : Set to the reflect the modem status value

### Function 2: Get a received character

This function is used to read in an input character from the received character buffer. It is designed to be compatible with INT 14H BIOS function 2, which tries to read a character in from the UART receiver buffer. Because this routine waits for a character instead of returning immediately on an empty buffer, `class FOSSIL` uses an alternate function for reading data.

*Input registers:*
- AH : Set to 2, the function value
- DX : The port number, starting at 0 for COM1

*Return values:*
- AH : Timeout error if bit 7 is set, else the current line status
- AL : The character read in

### Function 3: Read status registers

This function is compatible with INT 14H BIOS function 3. It simply reads in the current status of the modem status register and the line status register, and returns the results.

*Input registers:*
- AH : Set to 3, the function value
- DX : The port number, starting at 0 for COM1

## THE FOSSIL DRIVER

*Return values:*

    AH :     The port line status

    AL :     The port modem status

### Function 4: Open serial port

This function addresses a major oversight in the original PC BIOS. It is called to open a serial port before any other services are required. The Open Serial Port function notifies the FOSSIL device driver that the port is about to be used, which allows it to allocate system resources, such as memory buffers. It also lets the FOSSIL lock out other processes from using the port in a multitasking environment. The other useful feature provided by this function is the ability to cause the open request to fail. If the FOSSIL device driver is installed, and the appropriate COM port is available, the success code is returned. If the driver isn't installed or the port isn't present, the application program is informed of the failure. Notifying the program of failure prevents application programs from attempting to work with hardware that is nonexistent or is engaged with another program.

*Input registers:*

    AH :     Set to 4, the function value

    DX :     The port number, starting at 0 for COM1

*Return values:*

    AX :     Set to 0x1954 if successful

    BL :     Maximum function number supported by this FOSSIL driver

    BH :     FOSSIL revision supported

### Function 5: Close port

This function is every bit as useful as function 4. It allows the system to reallocate resources and disable the serial hardware after an application is no longer using the port. This function is sorely missing from the IBM PC BIOS. While the BIOS itself may not need this function, many systems that perform BIOS emulation would benefit greatly from this function. For example, a program implementing modem access across a network doesn't have any way to let the modem server know that it is done with a modem when the program exits. FOSSIL function 5 gives the application that capability.

*Input registers:*
- AH : Set to 5, the function value
- DX : The port number, starting at 0 for COM1

*Return values*
None.

### Function 6: Control DTR

This function gives the application the ability to raise or lower DTR. IBM added this capability to the Extended BIOS, which became available after FOSSIL was already implemented. Because of this, the function number and parameters are not compatible with the Extended BIOS.

In addition, it is important to note that the FOSSIL spec does not offer a function to control RTS. It is automatically asserted when the port is opened and will only change if RTS/CTS handshaking is on.

*Input registers:*
- AH : Set to 6, the function value
- AL : Set to 1 to raise DTR, 0 to lower DTR
- DX : The port number, starting at 0 for COM1

*Return values:*
Nothing.

### Function 8: Flush the TX buffer

This function doesn't return until all of the characters in the TX buffer have been transmitted. The function isn't used in `class FOSSIL` since it takes away our ability to do other processing in the idle function. It also offers the possibility of long delays should the transmitter be blocked due to a handshaking event.

# THE FOSSIL DRIVER

*Input registers:*
    AH :    Set to 8, the function value
    DX :    The port number, starting at 0 for COM1

*Return values:*
    Nothing.

### Function 9: Purge the input buffer

This function lets the application program throw out all the characters presently pending in the RX buffer. Since the BIOS doesn't have an input buffer, it doesn't have an analogous function.

*Input registers:*
    AH :    Set to 9, the function value
    DX :    The port number, starting at 0 for COM1

*Return values:*
    Nothing.

### Function 0x0a: Purge the output buffer

This function lets the application program throw out all the characters presently pending in the TX buffer. Once again, since the BIOS doesn't have an output buffer, it doesn't have an analogous function. Note that this function differs from function 8 in that none of the characters presently residing in the TX buffer will be transmitted when this function is called.

*Input registers:*
    AH :    Set to 0x0a, the function value
    DX :    The port number, starting at 0 for COM1

*Return values:*
    Nothing.

### Function 0x0b: Transmit with no wait

This function adds a single character to the output buffer. Unlike function 1, it will not wait indefinitely if the TX buffer is presently full. Instead, it returns immediately with an error flag, so the application program can continue processing. This function is used by `class FOSSIL` instead of function 1, since it offers additional flexibility.

*Input registers:*

    AH :    Set to 0x0b, the function value
    AL :    The character to be added to the transmit buffer
    DX :    The port number, starting at 0 for COM1

*Return values*

    AX :    Set to 1 if the character was added to the buffer, 0 if it wasn't.

### Function 0x0c: Single character peek

This function is called to peek one character ahead in the RX buffer. While it would be nice to be able to peek ahead an arbitrary number of bytes, as is possible in `class PC8250`, this is a big improvement over the BIOS, which offers no peek function.

*Input registers:*

    AH :    Set to 0x0c, the function value
    DX :    The port number, starting at 0 for COM1

*Return values:*

    AH :    Set to 0 if a character was read, 0xff if not
    AL :    The next character in the buffer if AH is set to 0

### Function 0x0f: Select flow control

This function allows the application program to select which handshaking options to use. The FOSSIL driver supports RTS/CTS flow control, as well as independent XON/XOFF flow control for the transmitter and receiver. The

# THE FOSSIL DRIVER

`RS232 class` does not support split handshaking, so only bidirectional flow control is used by `class FOSSIL`.

*Input registers:*
- AH : Set to 0x0f, the function value
- AL : Flow control bits
  - bit 0: Enable XON/XOFF reception to stop the transmitter
  - bit 1: Enable RTS/CTS flow control
  - bit 2: Must be set to 0
  - bit 3: Enable XON/XOFF transmission when the RX buffer passes the high water mark.
- DX : The port number, starting at 0 for COM1

*Return values:*
None.

### Function 0x18: Read a buffer

This is a function that is sorely missing from the BIOS interface. It allows a block of data to be read in from the port all at once. This is generally much more efficient than reading in a single byte at a time, as the BIOS forces us to do. Once again, this function might not be useful to the BIOS itself, but software that emulates the BIOS interface would have benefitted greatly from a function like this. Note that this function reads in as many characters as possible, then returns immediately.

*Input registers:*
- AH : Set to 0x18, the function value
- CX : The number of characters requested
- DX : The port number, starting at 0 for COM1
- ES : Segment of the buffer that is to receive the data
- DI : Offset of the buffer

*Return values:*
    AX :    The count of characters actually transferred.

### Function 0x19: Write a buffer

This function is the converse of function 24. It allows a block of data to be transferred to the TX buffer with a single call. This is usually much more efficient than sending the characters one at a time. This function will attempt to place as many characters as possible in the TX buffer, then return immediately.

*Input registers:*
    AH :    Set to 0x19, the function value
    CX :    The number of characters to be sent
    DX :    The port number, starting at 0 for COM1
    ES :    Segment of the buffer that contains the data to be sent
    DI :    Offset of the buffer

*Return values:*
    AX :    The count of characters actually transferred.

### Function 0x1a: Break control

This function is used to either set or clear a breaking condition on a port. This is another function that was added to the Extended BIOS after the FOSSIL definition, which is why the FOSSIL driver is not compatible.

*Input registers:*
    AH :    Set to 0x1a, the function value
    AL :    Set to 1 to start breaking, 0 to stop
    DX :    The port number, starting at 0 for COM1

*Return values:*
    None.

# THE FOSSIL DRIVER

### *Function 0x1b: Get FOSSIL driver information*

This is a general-purpose function that returns information about the presently installed FOSSIL driver. The block of data returned from the driver has the following structure:

```
struct fossil_struct {
    short int structure_size;
    short int revision;
    char FAR *fossil_name;
    short int input_buffer_size;
    short int input_bytes_available;
    short int output_buffer_size;
    short int output_bytes_available;
    char screen_width;
    char screen_height;
    char baud_rate_id;
}
```

These fields should be fairly self-explanatory. Not all of them are used by `class FOSSIL`, but many of them are. Some, such as the `fossil_name` element, are helpful in a general sense and are printed with the debug output.

*Input registers:*

    AH :     Set to 0x1b, the function value
    CX :     Size in bytes of the buffer that will receive the data
    DX :     The port number, starting at 0 for COM1
    ES :     Segment of the buffer that is to receive the data
    DI :     Offset of the buffer

*Return values:*

    AX :     The count of bytes actually sent to the user buffer.

### Sources

Given the well-crafted FOSSIL specification, the next logical question is: Where are all these wonderful FOSSIL device drivers? Since the FOSSIL driver is used only on BBS systems, that is the logical place to start looking.

The most reliable source of a FOSSIL driver is one of the larger on-line services. CompuServe has several FOSSIL drivers located in the IBMBBS conference. If you browse through the files in the IBMBBS library, looking for files with the keyword "FOSSIL," you will find several available for immediate download.

Probably the best known FOSSIL driver for IBM PCs under MS-DOS is X00.SYS by Ray Gwinn. Another popular driver is BNU by David Nugent. Both are available in the IBMBBS forum. Both drivers are fully featured, and can be loaded as device drivers from your CONFIG.SYS file or as TSRs from the command line. Both have some excellent debugging features that can help during the development process.

If you don't want to invest the time and money to download these drivers from CompuServe, you can usually find several different drivers on well-stocked BBS systems. Opus systems will almost always have at least one or two drivers on their system, as well as the FOSSIL Level 5 document that amounts to the official "standard."

### Why bother?

Admittedly the FOSSIL interface is nice and thorough, but you still have to ask yourself if there is good reason to support it. There is. The FOSSIL driver is still very popular in the BBS community and you may find yourself forced to use it if you write door programs or external protocol drivers. A really good implementation of either program ought to support both the FOSSIL driver and the standard PC8250 class.

You may even find a FOSSIL driver useful for software other than BBS programs. For example, if you are writing code that is designed to work under a multitasking O/S such as DESQview or Windows, you will often have to worry that your Interrupt Service Routine may be swapped out of memory or moved to a different location in memory. By loading a FOSSIL before your multitasking software is started, you eliminate this problem.

# THE FOSSIL DRIVER

## The Source Code

The source code shown here implements class FOSSIL. This class implements nearly every virtual function included in the base class, RS232. The only missing functions are:

```
DtrDsrHandshaking()
Cts()
SoftwareOverrunError()
```

There just aren't any hooks in the FOSSIL specification to let us implement these missing functions. However, the functionality we get from the FOSSIL driver is an order of magnitude ahead of the BIOSPort class.

Class FOSSIL is derived from the BIOSPort class. It can take advantage of nine functions in the BIOSPort class. The four-line status and the four-modem status functions are identical, as is the read_byte() function. The rest of the functionality for this class had to be built from scratch. It makes sense to take advantage of the previously written functions, as well as the two lines of debug output available from the BIOSPort class. If the code has already been written, we might as well take advantage of it.

```
// ******************** START OF FOSSIL.H ********************

// This header file has all the definitions and prototypes needed
// to use the FOSSIL class. This file should be included by any
// module using that specific class.

#ifndef _FOSSIL_DOT_H
#define _FOSSIL_DOT_H

#include <dos.h>
#include "rs232.h"
#include "biosport.h"

// Note that the FOSSIL class is derived from BIOSPort. BIOSPort
// provides 9 virtual functions that work properly with a FOSSIL
// driver. This is a good example of code reuse.
```

# SERIAL COMMUNICATIONS: A C++ DEVELOPER'S GUIDE

```cpp
class FOSSIL : public BIOSPort
{
    protected :
        int first_debug_output_line;
        RS232Error write_settings( void );
        virtual int read_buffer( char *buffer,
                                 unsigned int count );
         virtual int write_buffer( char *buffer,
                                   unsigned int count = -1 );
        virtual int write_byte( int c );
        FOSSIL( void );

    public :
        FOSSIL( enum RS232PortName port_name,
                long baud_rate = UNCHANGED,
                char parity = UNCHANGED,
                int word_length = UNCHANGED,
                int stop_bits = UNCHANGED,
                int dtr = SET,
                int rts = SET,
                int xon_xoff = DISABLE,
                int rts_cts = DISABLE,
                int dtr_dsr = DISABLE );
        virtual ~FOSSIL( void );
        virtual RS232Error Set( long baud_rate = UNCHANGED,
                                int parity = UNCHANGED,
                                int word_length = UNCHANGED,
                                int stop_bits = UNCHANGED );
        virtual int TXSpaceFree( void );
        virtual int RXSpaceUsed( void );
        virtual int FormatDebugOutput( char *buffer = 0,
                                       int line_number = -1 );
        virtual int RXSpaceFree( void );
        virtual int TXSpaceUsed( void );
        virtual int Break( long milliseconds = 300 );
        virtual int XonXoffHandshaking( int setting = UNCHANGED );
        virtual int RtsCtsHandshaking( int settings = UNCHANGED );
        virtual int Dtr( int settings = UNCHANGED );
        virtual int Peek( void *buffer, unsigned int count );
```

```
            virtual int FlushRXBuffer( void );
            virtual int FlushTXBuffer( void );
};

#endif // #ifndef _FOSSIL_DOT_H

// *********************** END OF FOSSIL.H ***********************
```

**Listing 7-1. FOSSIL.H, the header file for class FOSSIL**

```
// ******************* START OF FOSSIL.CPP *******************
//
// This file contains all of the code used by the FOSSIL class.
//

#include <stdio.h>
#include <string.h>
#include <ctype.h>
#include "rs232.h"
#include "fossil.h"
#include "_8250.h"

// The following two structures and constructor code are here to
// support the fossil_info class. The single constructor for this
// class executes FOSSIL function 0x1b, which loads the fossil
// information block into the fossil_struct structure. The
// contents of struct fossil_struct are stored in their own
// separate structure to guarantee proper offsets and packing of
// all data members.

struct fossil_struct {
    short int structure_size;
    short int revision;
    char FAR *ident;
    short int input_buffer_size;
    short int input_bytes_available;
    short int output_buffer_size;
    short int output_bytes_available;
};
```

# SERIAL COMMUNICATIONS: A C++ DEVELOPER'S GUIDE

```cpp
class fossil_info : public fossil_struct {
    public :
        fossil_info( int port_number );
};

fossil_info::fossil_info( int port_number )
{
    union REGS r;
    struct SREGS s;

    r.x.dx = port_number;
    r.x.cx = sizeof( fossil_struct );
    s.es = (unsigned int)((long)(void FAR *)&structure_size >> 16);
    r.x.di = (unsigned int) (long) (void FAR *) &structure_size;
    r.h.ah = 0x1b;
     int86x( 0x14, &r, &r, &s );
}

// The FOSSIL constructor looks similar to the BIOSPort constructor.
// It differs in just a couple respects. First, the port open
// function provided by the FOSSIL driver lets us detect when
// the port isn't present or the driver isn't loaded. This gives
// this constructor an error exit. Second, one of the data members
// in the saved_settings is initialized to 1, which is where it
// always is when the FOSSIL driver is installed.

FOSSIL::FOSSIL( RS232PortName port,
                long baud_rate,
                char parity,
                int word_length,
                int stop_bits,
                int dtr,
                int rts,
                int xon_xoff,
                int rts_cts,
                int dtr_dsr )
{
```

```
    union REGS r;

    port_name = port;
    error_status = RS232_SUCCESS;

    first_debug_output_line = BIOSPort::FormatDebugOutput();
    debug_line_count = FormatDebugOutput();
    r.h.ah = 4;
    r.x.dx = port_name;
    r.x.bx = 0;
    int86( 0x14, &r, &r );
    if ( r.x.ax != 0x1954 ) {
        error_status = RS232_PORT_NOT_FOUND;
        return;
    }
    saved_settings.BaudRate = -1L;
    saved_settings.Parity = '?';
    saved_settings.WordLength = -1;
    saved_settings.StopBits = -1;
    saved_settings.Dtr = -1;
    saved_settings.Rts = -1;
    saved_settings.XonXoff = -1;
     saved_settings.RtsCts = -1;
    saved_settings.DtrDsr = -1;
    settings = saved_settings;
    settings.Dtr = 1;
    settings.XonXoff = 0;
    settings.RtsCts = 0;
    settings.Adjust( baud_rate,
                     parity,
                     word_length,
                     stop_bits,
                     dtr,
                     rts,
                     xon_xoff,
                     rts_cts,
                     dtr_dsr );
    write_settings();
    line_status = 0;
```

```cpp
}

// Unlike the BIOSPort destructor, the FOSSIL driver actually has a
// function call that lets the FOSSIL driver know that the port is
// no longer in use.

FOSSIL::~FOSSIL( void )
{
    union REGS r;

    if ( error_status == RS232_SUCCESS ) {
        r.x.dx = port_name;
        r.h.ah = 5;
        int86( 0x14, &r, &r );
    }
}

// The FOSSIL version of write_settings is nearly the same as the
// BIOSPort version. It has additional code to set DTR and the
// two handshaking options.

RS232Error FOSSIL::write_settings( void )
{
    union REGS r;
    RS232Error status = RS232_SUCCESS;

    r.x.dx = port_name;
    r.h.ah = 0;
    r.h.al = 0;
    switch ( toupper( settings.Parity ) ) {
        case 'E' : r.h.al |= 0x18; break;
        case 'O' : r.h.al |= 0x08; break;
        default  : settings.Parity = 'N';
                   status = RS232_ILLEGAL_PARITY_SETTING;
        case 'N' : r.h.al |= 0x00; break;
    }
```

# THE FOSSIL DRIVER

```c
    switch ( settings.StopBits ) {
        case 1  : r.h.al |= 0; break;
        default : settings.StopBits = 2;
                  status = RS232_ILLEGAL_STOP_BITS;
        case 2  : r.h.al |= 4; break;
    }
    switch ( settings.WordLength ) {
        case 5  : r.h.al |= 0; break;
        case 6  : r.h.al |= 1; break;
        case 7  : r.h.al |= 2; break;
        default : settings.WordLength = 8;
                  status = RS232_ILLEGAL_WORD_LENGTH;
        case 8  : r.h.al |= 3; break;
    }
    switch ( settings.BaudRate ) {
        case 19200L : r.h.al |= 0x00; break;
        case 38400L : r.h.al |= 0x20; break;
        case 300L   : r.h.al |= 0x40; break;
        case 600L   : r.h.al |= 0x60; break;
        case 1200L  : r.h.al |= 0x80; break;
        case 2400L  : r.h.al |= 0xa0; break;
        case 4800L  : r.h.al |= 0xc0; break;
        default     : settings.BaudRate = 9600L;
                      status = RS232_ILLEGAL_BAUD_RATE;
        case 9600L  : r.h.al |= 0xe0; break;
    }
    int86( 0x14, &r, &r );
// Set up DTR
    r.x.dx = port_name;
    r.h.ah = 6;
    r.h.al = (unsigned char) settings.Dtr;
    int86( 0x14, &r, &r );
// Set up handshaking
    r.x.dx = port_name;
    r.h.ah = 0x0f;
    r.h.al = 0;
    if ( settings.RtsCts )
        r.h.al |= 2;
    if ( settings.XonXoff )
```

```cpp
        r.h.al |= 9;
    int86( 0x14, &r, &r );

    if ( settings.Rts != -1 ) {
        settings.Rts = -1;
        status = RS232_RTS_NOT_SUPPORTED;
    }
    if ( settings.DtrDsr != -1 ) {
        settings.DtrDsr = -1;
        status = RS232_DTR_DSR_NOT_SUPPORTED;
    }
    return status;
}

// The FOSSIL debug output adds the fossil ID from the fossil
// data structure, and a couple of buffer counts not found in
// the BIOSPort class.

int FOSSIL::FormatDebugOutput( char *buffer, int line_number )
{

    if ( buffer == 0 )
        return( first_debug_output_line +  2 );
    if ( line_number < first_debug_output_line )
        return BIOSPort::FormatDebugOutput( buffer, line_number );
    fossil_info port_data( port_name );
    switch( line_number - first_debug_output_line ) {
        case 0 :
            sprintf( buffer,
                    "Derived class: FOSSIL  "
                    "TX Used: %5u  RX Free: %5u",
                    TXSpaceUsed(),
                    RXSpaceFree() );
            break;
        case 1 :
            strcpy( buffer, "FOSSIL Id: " );
            {
                for ( int i = 0 ; i < 60 ; i++ )
                    buffer[ i+ 11 ] = port_data.ident[ i ];
```

# THE FOSSIL DRIVER

```
                buffer[ i + 11 ] = '\0';
            }
            break;
        default :
            return RS232_ILLEGAL_LINE_NUMBER;
    }
    return RS232_SUCCESS;
}

RS232Error FOSSIL::Set( long baud_rate,
                       int parity,
                       int word_length,
                       int stop_bits )
{
    settings.Adjust( baud_rate,
                     parity,
                     word_length,
                     stop_bits,
                     UNCHANGED,
                     UNCHANGED,
                     UNCHANGED,
                     UNCHANGED,
                     UNCHANGED );
    return write_settings();
}

// This function uses the FOSSIL version of the single character
// output function, since it returns immediately, unlike the BIOS
// function.

int FOSSIL::write_byte( int c )
{
    union REGS r;

    if ( error_status < 0 )
        return error_status;
    r.x.dx = port_name;
    r.h.ah = 0x0b;
    r.h.al = (char) c;
```

```
        int86( 0x14, &r, &r );
        if ( r.x.ax )
            return RS232_SUCCESS;
        return RS232_TIMEOUT;
    }

    // The read_buffer and write_buffer functions take advantage of the
    // dedicated FOSSIL functions that transfer blocks of data with
    // a single function call.

    int FOSSIL::read_buffer( char *buffer, unsigned int count )
    {
        union REGS r;
        struct SREGS s;

        ByteCount = 0;
        if ( error_status < 0 )
            return error_status;

        r.x.dx = port_name;
        r.h.ah = 0x18;
        r.x.cx = count;
        s.es = (unsigned int) ( (long) (void FAR *) buffer >> 16 );
        r.x.di = (unsigned int) (long) (void FAR *) buffer;
        int86x( 0x14, &r, &r, &s );
        ByteCount = r.x.ax;
        buffer[ ByteCount ] = '\0';
        if ( ByteCount != count )
            return RS232_TIMEOUT;
        return( RS232_SUCCESS );
    }

    int FOSSIL::write_buffer( char *buffer, unsigned int count )
    {
        union REGS r;
        struct SREGS s;
```

## THE FOSSIL DRIVER

```
    if ( error_status < RS232_SUCCESS )
        return error_status;

    r.x.dx = port_name;
    r.x.cx = count;
    r.h.ah = 0x19;
    s.es = (unsigned int) ( (long) (void FAR *) buffer >> 16 );
    r.x.di = (unsigned int) (long) (void FAR *) buffer;
    int86x( 0x14, &r, &r, &s );
    ByteCount = r.x.ax;
    if ( ByteCount != count )
        return RS232_TIMEOUT;
    return RS232_SUCCESS;
}

// The following four functions all get their data from the
// fossil_info data structure. The data is loaded automatically
// by the fossil_info constructor.

int FOSSIL::TXSpaceFree( void )
{
    if ( error_status < RS232_SUCCESS )
        return error_status;

    fossil_info port_data( port_name );

    return( port_data.output_bytes_available );
}

// Ray Gwinn's driver, X00.SYS, doesn't return exactly the numbers
// expected here, so I adjust them if the FOSSIL driver turns out
// to be his.

int FOSSIL::TXSpaceUsed( void )
{
    if ( error_status < RS232_SUCCESS )
        return error_status;

    fossil_info port_data( port_name );
```

```cpp
        if ( port_data.ident[ 0 ] == 'R' &&
             port_data.ident[ 1 ] == 'a' &&
             port_data.ident[ 2 ] == 'y' )
            return( port_data.output_buffer_size -
                    port_data.output_bytes_available - 1 );

        return( port_data.output_buffer_size -
                port_data.output_bytes_available );
}

int FOSSIL::RXSpaceUsed( void )
{
    if ( error_status < RS232_SUCCESS )
        return error_status;

    fossil_info port_data( port_name );

    return( port_data.input_buffer_size -
            port_data.input_bytes_available );
}

int FOSSIL::RXSpaceFree( void )
{
    if ( error_status < RS232_SUCCESS )
        return error_status;

    fossil_info port_data( port_name );

    return( port_data.input_bytes_available );
}

// The FOSSIL driver adds a dedicated Break function, which is
// missing from the BIOS specification.

int FOSSIL::Break( long milliseconds )
{
    long timer;
    union REGS r;
```

## THE FOSSIL DRIVER

```
        if ( error_status < RS232_SUCCESS )
            return error_status;
        timer = ReadTime() + milliseconds;
        r.h.ah = 0x1a;
        r.h.al = 1;
        r.x.dx = port_name;
        int86( 0x14, &r, &r );
        while ( ReadTime() < timer )
            IdleFunction();
        r.h.ah = 0x1a;
        r.h.al = 0;
        r.x.dx = port_name;
        int86( 0x14, &r, &r );
        return RS232_SUCCESS;
    }

    // The two handshaking commands don't really do any work, they just
    // modify the data structure and then let write_settings() perform
    // FOSSIL function calls necessary to make the actual changes.

    int FOSSIL::XonXoffHandshaking( int setting )
    {
        if ( error_status < RS232_SUCCESS )
            return error_status;
        if ( setting != UNCHANGED ) {
            settings.XonXoff = ( setting != 0 );
            write_settings();
        }
        return settings.XonXoff;
    }

    int FOSSIL::RtsCtsHandshaking( int setting )
    {
        if ( error_status < RS232_SUCCESS )
            return error_status;
        if ( setting != UNCHANGED ) {
            settings.RtsCts = ( setting != 0 );
            write_settings();
        }
```

```cpp
        return settings.RtsCts;
}


// The FOSSIL driver has a unique function for setting DTR.
// Unfortunately, it doesn't offer a similar function for RTS.

int FOSSIL::Dtr( int setting )
{
    if ( error_status < RS232_SUCCESS )
        return error_status;
    if ( setting != UNCHANGED ) {
        settings.Dtr = ( setting != 0 );
        write_settings();
    }
    return settings.Dtr;
}


// The FOSSIL driver can only peek ahead a single byte, and we use
// that function here.

int FOSSIL::Peek( void *buffer, unsigned int count )
{
    union REGS r;

    if ( error_status < RS232_SUCCESS )
        return error_status;
    ByteCount = 0;
    if ( count ) {
        r.h.ah = 0x0c;
        r.x.dx = port_name;
        int86( 0x14, &r, &r );
        if ( r.h.ah == 0 ) {
            *(char *)buffer = r.h.al;
            ByteCount = 1;
        }
    }
    return RS232_SUCCESS;
}
```

## THE FOSSIL DRIVER

```cpp
// The two flush functions have special FOSSIL commands to get the
// job done.

int FOSSIL::FlushRXBuffer( void )
{
    union REGS r;

    if ( error_status < RS232_SUCCESS )
        return error_status;
    r.h.ah = 10;
    r.x.dx = port_name;
    int86( 0x14, &r, &r );
    return RS232_SUCCESS;
}

int FOSSIL::FlushTXBuffer( void )
{
    union REGS r;

    if ( error_status < RS232_SUCCESS )
        return error_status;
    r.h.ah = 9;
    r.x.dx = port_name;
    int86( 0x14, &r, &r );
    return RS232_SUCCESS;
}

// ******************** END OF FOSSIL.CPP ************************
```

**Listing 7-2. FOSSIL.CPP, the source code for class FOSSIL.**

### Building TEST232.EXE

To modify `TEST232.CPP` to work properly with the new `FOSSIL` class you must make just a couple of changes. First, add a single include file to the list of includes so that the header file `FOSSIL.H` is used. The resulting list should look like this:

```
#include "portable.h"
#include <stdio.h>
#include <stdlib.h>
#include <string.h>
#include <conio.h>
#include <ctype.h>
#include "rs232.h"
#include "textwind.h"
#include "biosport.h"
#include "fossil.h"
```

Note that `BIOSPORT.H` still has to be included as well, since class `FOSSIL` is derived from class `BIOSPort`.

The second modification I made to `TEST232.CPP` instructed it to open every port as a FOSSIL port. The resulting code at the start of main() looked like this:

```
switch ( i ) {
    default :
        Ports[ i ] = new FOSSIL( port_names[ i ],
                                9600, 'N', 8, 1 );
}
```

When this code executes, it will attempt to open both test ports as `FOSSIL` ports. If the `FOSSIL` constructor returns an error, the port won't be opened.

The final step necessary to create a custom version of `TEST232.EXE` is to edit the makefile, `TEST232.MAK`. The `FILES` definition line should be modified to look like this:

```
FILES = BIOSPORT.OBJ FOSSIL.OBJ
```

# THE FOSSIL DRIVER

```
OK
atdt 250-3778

CARRIER 9600
PROTOCOL: LAP-M

COMPRESSION: V.42BIS

CONNECT 9600
```

```
Base class: RS232   COM1    Status: Success
Byte count:      0  Elapsed time:        0  TX Free:    511  RX Used:      0
Saved port:     -1,?,-1,-1  DTR,RTS: -1,-1  XON/OFF,RTS/CTS,DTR/DSR: -1,-1,-1
Current port:   9600,N,8,1  DTR,RTS:  1,-1  XON/OFF,RTS/CTS,DTR/DSR:  0, 0,-1
Derived class: BIOSPort  RI:  0  CD:  1  CTS:  1  DSR:  1
Parity Err: 0  Break Det: 0  Overrun Err: 0  Framing Err: 0
Derived class: FOSSIL   TX Used:    0  RX Free:    512
FOSSIL Id: Ray Gwinn's double aught buckshot driver, X00 V1.24



Toggle XON/XOFF handshaking returns: 0
```

**Figure 7-1. A screen shot from TEST232.EXE**

### A Test Run

Figure 7-1 shows a screen shot from `TEST232.EXE`. It is being run in conjunction with a version of `X00.SYS`, a popular MS-DOS FOSSIL driver. The exact version of the FOSSIL driver can be determined by noting the bottom line of the debug output.

The actual performance of a FOSSIL driver is dependent on the driver itself. I have noticed tremendous variations in the speed of drivers, the memory space they occupy, and even whether they correctly implement all FOSSIL features. You will have to experiment a bit to determine which ones will work best for you.

CHAPTER 8

# The Microsoft Windows Driver

Since the release of version 3.0, Microsoft Windows has clearly become the desktop graphical user interface (GUI) of choice in the IBM-compatible world. While most users seem to be enamored with the easy to-use-interface, C programmers have had to deal with the difficulties in learning a complex API and a new set of programming tools.

Because of the flexibility of C++, communications programmers don't have to get too wrapped up in the never-ending arguments over whether Windows is a gift from the gods or an abomination. To them, it is just another platform to support with another class. Since the O/S dependent portions of communications code have been virtualized, adding support for Windows is just another chapter in this book.

## Windows Programming

Programmers have had to make some major adjustments in order to start developing applications for Microsoft Windows. There are two major conceptual hurdles to conquer, and they are both fairly difficult for programmers trained to write conventional software under MS-DOS.

The first difficulty new Windows programmers encounter is shifting their point of view to an event-driven programming system. Most learned to write programs that go out and seek events, such as user input. Under MS-Windows, the events seek the programs out.

The second difficulty for new Windows programmers is adjusting to the GUI. Simple C I/O statements such as `printf()` no longer work under MS-Windows. Instead, programmers have to learn the intricacies of menus and dialog boxes, and learn about writing to the screen using bit-mapped proportional fonts.

In this chapter, I am going to bypass these difficulties, and concentrate solely on the communications aspects of Windows programming. Fortunately, control of the communications ports under MS-Windows is fairly straightforward. Windows has a set of new functions that you have to learn, but applying them doesn't take a major paradigm shift.

### The MS-Windows device driver

Although Windows is often put down as not being a real "operating system," it sure seems like one when it comes to talking to hardware. The techniques used in Chapter 3 to talk to the UART directly in the `PC8250` class just won't work under Windows. Communicating directly with the hardware is always discouraged, and frequently impossible. Instead, Windows wants you to talk to the RS-232 ports via a device driver.

Using a device driver has some disadvantages. Developers are constrained by the limitations of both the driver API and the driver implementation. However, the benefits of a well-designed driver should outweigh the disadvantages. The most important benefit of the driver is that it provides a standard interface that can be used to communicate with all sorts of different hardware. The `WindowsPort` class developed in this chapter can talk just as easily to an intelligent DigiBoard as a standard PC COM1. All that is needed in each case is a vendor provided device driver.

An even bigger advantage of using a device driver should be found as Windows evolves into Windows NT. There aren't any communications programs available for NT as of this writing, but presumably they should be relatively easy to port from their Windows counterparts.

### The communications API

The communications API consists of a set of 17 function calls. While these functions are designed to also support a few basic operations on printer ports, for the most part they are oriented strictly towards RS-232 operations. In addition to these function calls, the communications API is heavily dependent on a pair of structures—the DCB and COMSTAT structures. The Windows Comm API functions:

## THE MICROSOFT WINDOWS DRIVER

```
BuildCommDCB()
ClearCommBreak()
CloseComm()
EnableCommNotification()
EscapeCommFunction()
FlushComm()
GetCommError()
GetCommEventMask()
GetCommState()
OpenComm()
ReadComm()
SetCommBreak()
SetCommEventMask()
SetCommState()
TransmitCommChar()
UngetCommChar()
WriteComm()
DCB structure
COMSTAT structure
```

Note that the definitions of these functions are those used in MS-Windows 3.1. For the most part, the same function set was supported in Windows 3.0. A few structure elements have changed, but the function set is essentially identical.

Note that nearly all of the functions in the communications group of the Windows API take an integer argument named `idComDev` as their first argument. This is the port identifier returned by Windows when the port is first opened with the `OpenComm()` call.

**int BuildCommDCB( LPSTR lpszDef, DCB FAR *lpdcb )**

This function is used to build a Device Control Block (DCB). The DCB (explained in detail later in this chapter) contains all of the user controllable settings for the port, which includes the standard parity, baud rate, etc. This function takes an input string of the form "COM1:9600,N,8,1," and fills in the DCB settings with the appropriate values. The port can then be set to those values by calling the `SetCommState()` command.

This function may be of some use to programmers who are setting up the port based on keyboard input. I won't use it in the `WindowsPort` class, as I want to have more comprehensive control over the port.

This function returns a 0 if successful, a -1 if an error occurs.

**int ClearCommBreak( int idComDev )**

The Windows API supports break signaling in a fairly rudimentary fashion. `SetCommBreak()` puts the port into a breaking condition, and this function clears the breaking condition. The single parameter is the port ID returned from the `Open-Comm()` function. This function returns a 0 if successful, -1 if there is an error.

The `WindowsPort` class calls this function in the virtual `Break` function.

**int CloseComm( int idComDev )**

This function closes the port and makes it available for other programs running under Windows. The single argument is the port ID returned from the `Open-Comm()` function. The function returns a 0 if successful and a -1 on error.

The `WindowsPort` class calls this function as part of its destructor.

**BOOL EnableCommNotification( int idComDev,**
                            **HWND hwnd,**
                            **int cbWriteNotify,**
                            **int cbOutQueue )**

This function was introduced as part of the API in Windows 3.1. This function sets up the port identified by the `idComDev` parameter to generate WM_COMMNO-TIFY events to be sent to the window identified by `hwnd`. There are three types of events that can be generated. CN_RECEIVE and CN_TRANSMIT events are generated when a specified amount of activity occurs on the input or output buffers. CN_EVENT events are used to track events such as incoming parity errors, breaks, or modem status line changes.

While this is a step towards letting programmers convert their communications applications to a strictly event-driven paradigm, there are still a few missing pieces

## THE MICROSOFT WINDOWS DRIVER

in the notification system. Because of this, the `WindowsPort` class doesn't take advantage of these events.

This function returns a zero when it fails, a non-zero when it succeeds.

**LONG EscapeCommFunction( int idComDev, int nFunction )**

This function is used to handle a few miscellaneous things that aren't covered elsewhere in the Windows API. The `nFunction` argument determines what function is actually performed on the specified port. The argument values used in the `WindowsPort` class are:

```
CLRDTR :    Drops DTR on the specified port.
CLRRTS :    Drops RTS on the specified port.
SETDTR :    Sets DTR on the specified port.
SETRTS :    Sets RTS on the specified port.
```

These functions all return a zero if the function is successful, and a value less than zero when it fails.

**int FlushComm( int idComDev, int fnQueue )**

This function is used to flush either the input or output buffers for the port specified by the `idComDev` parameter. If the `fnQueue` argument is zero, the transmit buffer is flushed. If non-zero, the receiver buffer is flushed. This function is used to implement the `FlushRXQueue()` and `FlushTXQueue()` virtual functions in the `WindowsPort` class.

A return value of zero indicates success. A return value less than zero indicates an invalid device was specified. A return greater than zero indicates an error on the specified device.

**int GetCommError( int idComDev, COMSTAT FAR *lpStat )**

This function returns the current status of the given port. The return value is a mask consisting of various bit settings, defining things such as line status flags, software buffer overruns, and transmit timeouts.

The `COMSTAT` structure returned by this function returns an additional status byte with more information about handshaking, plus a count indicating how many characters are present in both the transmit and receive buffer.

`GetCommError()` is called by the `WindowsPort` class member functions whenever an error occurs, or an error status check is requested. Most of the flags returned directly by this function are ORed into a cumulative line status word, which can be cleared when the status function is called.

The error codes relevant to the `WindowsPort` class are:

| | |
|---|---|
| CE_BREAK | An incoming break was detected. |
| CE_CTSTO | A CTS timeout occurred while transmitting a character. This error will only occur when CTS pacing is enabled in the DCB structure. |
| CE_DSRTO | A DSR timeout occurred while transmitting a character. This error will only occur when DSR pacing is enabled in the DCB structure. |
| CE_FRAME | An incoming framing error was detected. |
| CE_MODE | This error is returned when either the port handle is invalid, or an invalid mode is requested. |
| CE_OVERRUN | A hardware overrun error was detected. |
| CE_RLSDTO | A CD timeout occurred while transmitting a character. This error will only occur when CD pacing is enabled in the DCB structure. |
| CE_RXOVER | This bit is set when a software receive buffer overrun error occurs. |
| CE_RXPARITY | An incoming parity error was detected. |

## THE MICROSOFT WINDOWS DRIVER

CE_TXFULL               The TX buffer was full when a character transmission was attempted.

**UINT GetCommEventMask( int idComDev, int fnEvtClear )**

The Comm Event Mask is a word that is maintained by the Windows device driver. It is used to keep track of line status events, such as an incoming break signal, changes in the modem status lines, etc. The events that are to be monitored by this word are selected by the setup function SetCommEventMask().

During the function call, any of the bits can be cleared after it is read. The bits to be cleared are selected in the fnEvtClear bit mask.

This function isn't used by the WindowsPort class. All of the events that could be detected using this function are detected in other ways.

**int GetCommState( int idComDev, DCB FAR *lpdcb )**

GetCommState() is called to request that the device driver load the current state of the requested port into a DCB structure. The DCB data contains all of the user definable items, including things such as the baud rate, parity, and other line settings. The exact details of the DCB contents will be detailed later in this section.

The WindowsPort class calls this function in the read_settings() member function. This is called in the constructor to initialize the DCB.

This function returns a zero when it's successful, less than zero when it fails.

**int OpenComm( LCSTR lpszDevControl,**
              **UINT cbInQueue,**
              **UINT cbOutQueue )**

This is the function used under Windows to open a communications port (or a printer port). The first parameter contains a string with the port name, such as COM1. The next two parameters are used to specify the size of the input and output buffers.

When successful, this function returns an integer ID greater than or equal to zero. In the event of an error, one of several possible error returns less than zero is given.

This function is used in the constructor to open the port. If the function returns an error code, the Windows error code is translated to an RS232 class error code and is stored in the `error_status` member, which flags the object as unusable to the rest of the member functions.

The error returns that can come back from this function are:

| | |
|---|---|
| IE_BADID | A bad or invalid device was selected. |
| IE_BAUDRATE | A bad or invalid baud rate was selected. |
| IE_BYTESIZE | A bad or invalid word length was selected. |
| IE_DEFAULT | The default parameters are invalid. |
| IE_HARDWARE | The hardware is in use by another program, and can't be opened. |
| IE_MEMORY | A memory allocation error occurred when trying to reserve buffer space for the device. |
| IE_NOPEN | The device is not open. |
| IE_OPEN | The device has already been opened. |

**`int ReadComm( int idComDev, void FAR *lpvBuf, int cbRead )`**

`ReadComm()` is used in the `WindowsPort` class to read both single bytes and blocks of data. The three parameters are what you would expect: a port ID, a buffer pointer, and a count of bytes requested.

The return code from this function is a little complicated. The function always returns the count of bytes read in. If an error occurred, the count of bytes is negated

## THE MICROSOFT WINDOWS DRIVER

and a negative number is returned. The actual error code for the read function then can be retrieved using the `GetCommError()` function. Since it isn't possible to distinguish an error when a count of 0 is returned, the programmer should <u>always</u> call `GetCommError()` when that value is encountered.

**`int SetCommBreak( int idComDev )`**

This function is used in tandem with `ClearCommBreak()` to issue break signals from the given port. This function is called to put the port into a breaking condition. The program then has to idle for a period of time, and clear the breaking condition. After that, the port is ready to resume its normal function.

A successful break initiation causes a zero to be returned. An error condition causes a return of less than zero.

**`UINT FAR* SetCommEventMask( int idComDev, UINT fuEvtMask )`**

This function is called to cause Windows to begin recording certain error and status events in a word in the driver. The events that the program wants to monitor for are specified in the bit mask parameter. Typical events include changes in modem status lines and incoming line status errors.

The `WindowsPort` class calls this function, but it has a slightly back-handed reason for doing so. All of the events that can be accessed with the event mask are recorded using the `GetCommError()` function, so the event mask isn't needed for that. However, the event mask gives us an undocumented way to get some other information that is not available using the Windows API.

Looking through the Windows API for communications functions, you will find that most of the virtual functions defined in class `RS232` are fairly easy to implement. The one serious omission is the absence of functions to read the current state of the incoming modem status lines. While the event mask lets you see when the status lines *change* state, we don't have a way to directly read them.

Some early pioneers of communications programming under Windows dug around a little bit and found that the communications driver stored a copy of the 8250 Modem Status Register at a fixed location 35 bytes after the event mask word. Word spread, and enough programmers began using this feature that it has become an unacknowledged feature of the API. Until new functions are added to directly support reading these lines, it is likely that Microsoft and other device driver developers will be forced into continuing to support this feature.

The `WindowsPort` constructor reads in the event mask, then forms a far pointer to the modem status register, which is used anytime one of the lines is read in.

The communications port bits that can be set or cleared as part of the event mask are:

| | |
|---|---|
| `EV_BREAK` | This flag is used to detect incoming breaks. |
| `EV_CTS` | An event will be generated when CTS changes state. |
| `EV_CTSS` | When the event occurs, this bit will either be set or cleared to indicate the state of CTS during the last modem status event. |
| `EV_DSR` | An event will occur when DSR changes state. |
| `EV_ERR` | This bit is used to enable events on line status errors. |
| `EV_RING` | This bit is either set or cleared to indicate the state of the incoming RI bit during the last modem status event. |
| `EV_RLSD` | This bit is used to enable events caused by the CD line changing state. |
| `EV_RLSDS` | This bit is either set or cleared to indicate the state of the incoming RI bit during the last modem status event. |
| `EV_RXCHAR` | This bit is used to generate an event any time a new incoming character is detected. |

## THE MICROSOFT WINDOWS DRIVER

EV_RXFLAG                  This bit is set to generate an event anytime the special event character is received. The event character can be specified in the DCB structure.

EV_TXEMPTY                This bit is used to generate an event whenever the transmitter goes empty.

**int SetCommState( const DCB FAR * lpdcb )**

This function is used to set the port's parameters to the values specified in the DCB. This basically sets all of the port parameters that are under the user's control. This function is called in the `write_settings()` virtual function to configure the port.

This function returns a zero when it succeeds, or a negative number when it fails.

**int TransmitCommChar( int idComDev, char chTransmit )**

This function is used to transmit a single character out of the specified port. It returns a zero when successful, a negative number when it fails.

The `WindowsPort` class uses the more versatile `WriteComm()` function to support output in both the `write_byte()` and `write_buffer()` functions.

**int UngetCommChar( int idComDev, char chUnget )**

This function is used to stuff a character back into the receive buffer after it has been read. Note that the buffer can only absorb a single character, so this function cannot be called more than once consecutively. This function is not used by the `WindowsPort` class.

`UngetCommChar()` returns a zero on success, a value less than zero on failure.

```
int WriteComm( int idComDev,
               const void FAR *lpvBuf,
               int cbWrite )
```

WriteComm() is the function used by both write_byte() and write_buffer() to send data out to the port. The three arguments to this function define the port, a pointer to the data to be sent, and a count of bytes to be written. Like the ReadComm() function, WriteComm() returns a count of bytes whether or not an error occurs. If an error occurs during writing, the byte count is negated. A negative or zero byte count means the caller needs to check for an actual error code with GetCommError().

WriteComm() has an unusual way of handling requests for more data than it can presently handle. If there is not enough room in the TX buffer for the entire block of data to be transmitted, WriteComm() will blithely write over existing data in the buffer until the output is complete. Because of this, it is important to only request an output count less than or equal to the current space available in the output buffer.

**struct DCB**

The DCB structure is used by the SetCommState() and GetCommState() functions to read and write the current settings of the comm port. This is done via the long list of data elements in this structure, which are defined below:

| | |
|---|---|
| BYTE Id | This contains the integer ID returned from the OpenComm() function. This value is used throughout the Comm API functions to identify the port. |
| UINT BaudRate | This is the current baud rate for the port. Some values that are too large to fit in an unsigned int have special constants that have an upper byte of 0xff. |

## THE MICROSOFT WINDOWS DRIVER

`BYTE ByteSize`  The current word length setting for the UART.

`BYTE Parity`  The current parity setting for the UART. Unfortunately, instead of using easy-to-remember characters, such as are used in class `RS232`, this value must be set to one of several defined constants.

`BYTE StopBits`  The number of stop bits to be used by the UART.

`UINT RlsTimeout`  This setting specifies the maximum amount of time that the driver will wait for the CD signal to become true during transmission. The value is expressed in milliseconds. This setting, along with the next two settings, is always left at zero by the `WindowsPort` class.

`UINT CtsTimeout`  The maximum amount of time the driver will wait for the CTS signal to be asserted.

`UINT DsrTimeout`  The maximum amount of time the driver will wait for the DSR signal to be asserted.

`UINT fBinary`  This bitflag determines whether the port is in binary (raw) mode. When in nonbinary mode, the port will register an End of File when the EOF character is received. The `WindowsPort` class always operates in binary mode.

`UINT fRtsDisable`  If this bitflag is set, the RTS signal is disabled and will remain low. This setting is not used by the `WindowsPort` class to control RTS. Instead, the escape function is invoked with the set/clear RTS function.

| | |
|---|---|
| UINT fParity | If this bit is set, parity checking is enabled. When this bit is set, parity errors will be detected and reported. |
| UINT fOutxCtsFlow | If this bitflag is set, CTS will be used to control the port's transmission. This is used by the `WindowsPort` class to implement RTS/CTS flow control. |
| UINT fOutxDsrFlow | This bit is used to implement the transmit half of DTR/DSR flow control. |
| UINT fDtrDisable | This bit is used to disable DTR for the duration of the setting. The `WindowsPort` class uses an escape function to control DTR, so this bit will always be clear. |
| UINT fOutX | This bit is used to enable XON/XOFF control of the transmitter. |
| UINT fInX | This bit is used to enable XON/XOFF control in the `WindowsPort` receiver. This causes the port to issue an XOFF character when the receiver passes the high-water mark. |
| UINT fPeChar | It is possible to cause the windows driver to replace characters that were received with bad parity with a special flag character. This bitflag controls that feature. This bit is always clear in the `WindowsPort` class. |
| UINT fNull | This flag specifies that null (`'\0'`) characters are to be discarded. |

## THE MICROSOFT WINDOWS DRIVER

| | |
|---|---|
| `UINT fChEvt` | This flag is used to enable events once a special event character has been received. This feature is not used by the `WindowsPort` class. |
| `UINT fDtrflow` | This flag is used to cause the receiver to use DTR to control the flow of data coming into the receiver buffer. |
| `UINT fRtsflow` | This flag is used to cause the receiver to use RTS to control the flow of data coming into the receiver buffer. |
| `char XonChar` | This byte contains the XON character used by both the receiver and transmitter for flow control. |
| `char XoffChar` | This byte contains the XOFF character used by both the receiver and transmitter for flow control. |
| `UINT XonLim` | This specifies the minimum number of characters allowed in the receiver before an XON is issued. |
| `UINT XoffLim` | This byte specifies the high-water mark in the RX buffer. When there is only room for this number of characters remaining, an XOFF will be issued to stop input. |
| `char PeChar` | If the `fPeChar` flag is set, this character will be substituted for any incoming characters that were received with a parity error. |
| `char EofChar` | If the port is not in Binary mode, this character will be treated as an EOF character. |
| `char EvtChar` | If the `fChEvt` flag is set, the receipt of this incoming character will generate an event flag. |

**struct COMSTAT**

The `COMSTAT` structure is filled in by the `GetCommError()` function. It contains three data members:

BYTE status

> The status byte has a set of flags that keep track of a few things related to the transmitter.

    CSTF_CTSHOLD

> If this flag is set, it indicates that the transmitter is waiting for the CTS line to go high before transmitting a character.

    CSTF_DSRHOLD

> This flag is used to indicate that the transmitter is waiting for DSR to go high before transmitting a character.

    CSTF_RLSDHOLD

> This flag indicates that the transmitter is waiting for CD to go high before transmitting a character.

    CSTF_XOFFHOLD

> This flag indicates that the transmitter is holding while waiting for an XON to be received.

    CSTF_XOFFSENT

> This flag indicates that an XOFF character has been sent to the remote end. Under certain configurations, the Windows device driver can halt transmission immediately after sending an XOFF character. This is because there are some systems that will treat any character following an XOFF as if it were an XON. This is an unusual configuration, and isn't supported directly by the `WindowsPort` class.

    CSTF_EOF

> This flag indicates that the EOF character has been received.

## THE MICROSOFT WINDOWS DRIVER

CSTF_TXIM               When this flag is set, it means there is still a character waiting to be transmitted.

UINT cbInQue            This structure element indicates how many characters are currently in the receiver buffer.

UINT cbOutQue           This structure element indicates how many characters are currently in the transmit buffer.

**Putting it together**

The Windows communications API matches up very well with the member functions in the RS232 class. The only function that can't be implemented using straightforward API calls is the RS232::Peek() virtual function, which looks into the input buffer. In theory, this could be hacked together using the UngetCommChar() function (which won't work properly with Windows 3.1). In practice this has enough difficulties to make it not worth attempting.

Listing 8-1 shows the header file that defines the WindowsPort class. A quick look at the header file shows that this is a very generic class definition. The only place it deviates too much from the norm is in the addition of a few additional private data members:

```
int line_status;
char FAR * modem_status_register;
DCB saved_dcb;
DCB dcb;
```

The two DCB structures are used in conjunction with the settings and saved_settings members defined as part of the base class. With many of the other classes we have used so far, the settings argument was enough to keep track of all the information needed to define the port. The Windows communications port has quite a few other attributes that are stored in the DCB, so we keep a copy of the current DCB. In addition, the original settings of the port are stored in a DCB so that it can be restored with its original settings when the port closes.

**401**

The `modem_status_register` is a pointer to the undocumented copy of the UART's MSR in the driver's data area. This pointer is used anytime the modem status functions, such as `Cts()`, are called.

The `line_status` structure element is used to accumulate the status bits returned from the `GetCommError()` function. Any time that error function is called, the resulting bits are ORed into the `line_status` word, so that they can be checked by one of the line status functions such as `HardwareOverrunError()`. The line status bits are optionally cleared when the status functions are invoked.

Note that the `line_status` structure element also accumulates the software buffer overflow error bit, which isn't strictly a line status error.

```
// ******************* START OF WINPORT.H *******************

// This file contains the definitions and declarations
// necessary to use the WindowsPort class.

#ifndef _MSWINCOM_DOT_H
#define _MSWINCOM_DOT_H

#include "rs232.h"
#include "_8250.h"

// New error codes defined for the WindowsPort class.

enum WindowsPortError {
        WINDOWS_PORT_DEFAULT_PARAMETERS = RS232_NEXT_FREE_ERROR,
        WINDOWS_PORT_NOT_OPEN,
        WINDOWS_PORT_ALREADY_OPEN,
        WINDOWS_PORT_HANDSHAKE_LINE_IN_USE,
        WINDOWS_PORT_NEXT_FREE_ERROR,
        WINDOWS_PORT_NEXT_FREE_WARNING = RS232_NEXT_FREE_WARNING };

// The WindowsPort class declaration looks similar to most of the
// other classes. It has nearly complete support for all of the
// virtual functions in the RS232 class.
```

## THE MICROSOFT WINDOWS DRIVER

```cpp
class WindowsPort : public RS232
{
    private :
        int first_debug_output_line;
        int handle;
        int line_status;
        char FAR * modem_status_register;
        DCB saved_dcb;
        DCB dcb;
        void read_settings( void );
        RS232Error write_settings( void );
        RS232Error translate_windows_error( int error );
        virtual int read_buffer( char *buffer,
                            unsigned int count );
        virtual int write_buffer( char *buffer,
                            unsigned int count = -1 );
        virtual int read_byte( void );
        virtual int write_byte( int c );

    public :
        WindowsPort( enum RS232PortName port_name,
                    long baud_rate = UNCHANGED,
                    char parity  = UNCHANGED,
                    int word_length = UNCHANGED,
                    int stop_bits = UNCHANGED,
                    int dtr = SET,
                    int rts = SET,
                    int xon_xoff = DISABLE,
                    int rts_cts = DISABLE,
                    int dtr_dsr = DISABLE );
        virtual ~WindowsPort( void );
        virtual RS232Error Set( long baud_rate = UNCHANGED,
                            int parity = UNCHANGED,
                            int word_length = UNCHANGED,
                            int stop_bits = UNCHANGED );
        virtual int TXSpaceFree( void );
        virtual int RXSpaceUsed( void );
        virtual int Break( long milliseconds = 300 );
        virtual int SoftwareOverrunError( int clear = UNCHANGED );
```

```cpp
        virtual int Cd( void );
        virtual int Ri( void );
        virtual int Cts( void );
        virtual int Dsr( void );
        virtual int ParityError( int clear = UNCHANGED );
        virtual int BreakDetect( int clear = UNCHANGED );
        virtual int FramingError( int clear = UNCHANGED );
        virtual int HardwareOverrunError( int clear = UNCHANGED );
        virtual int XonXoffHandshaking( int setting = UNCHANGED );
        virtual int RtsCtsHandshaking( int setting = UNCHANGED );
        virtual int DtrDsrHandshaking( int setting = UNCHANGED );
        virtual int Dtr( int setting = UNCHANGED );
        virtual int Rts( int setting = UNCHANGED );
        virtual int RXSpaceFree( void );
        virtual int TXSpaceUsed( void );
        virtual int FlushRXBuffer( void );
        virtual int FlushTXBuffer( void );
        virtual char * ErrorName( int error );
        virtual int FormatDebugOutput( char *buffer = 0,
                                      int line_number = -1 );
};

#endif // #ifndef _MSWINCOM_DOT_H

// ******************* END OF WINPORT.H *******************
```

**Listing 8-1. WINPORT.H**

The code that implements the `WindowsPort` class is shown in Listing 8-2. The virtual functions are all constructed using very straightforward calls to the Windows API.

```cpp
// ******************* START OF WINPORT.CPP *******************

// This file contains the source code that implements the
// WindowsPort class.

#include <windows.h>
#include <ctype.h>
```

## THE MICROSOFT WINDOWS DRIVER

```c
#include "winport.h"

#define INPUT_BUFFER_SIZE 1024
#define OUTPUT_BUFFER_SIZE 1024

// The WindowsPort constructor opens the port using the MS-Windows
// function call OpenComm(). It then does the standard reading of
// the existing settings, saving them, and then writing the new
// settings. Note that we acquire a pointer to the internal driver
// byte that has the Modem Status Lines.

WindowsPort::WindowsPort( RS232PortName port,
                          long baud_rate,
                          char parity,
                          int word_length,
                          int stop_bits,
                          int dtr,
                          int rts,
                          int xon_xoff,
                          int rts_cts,
                          int dtr_dsr )
{
    char name[ 15 ];

    port_name = port;
    error_status = RS232_SUCCESS;
    line_status = 0;

    first_debug_output_line = RS232::FormatDebugOutput();
    debug_line_count = FormatDebugOutput();

    wsprintf( name, "COM%d", port_name + 1 );
    handle = OpenComm(name, INPUT_BUFFER_SIZE, OUTPUT_BUFFER_SIZE );
    if ( handle < 0 ) {
        error_status = translate_windows_error( handle );
        return;
    }
    modem_status_register = (char FAR *) SetCommEventMask(handle, 0 );
    modem_status_register += 35;
```

```
        read_settings();
        saved_settings = settings;
        saved_dcb = dcb;
        settings.Adjust( baud_rate,
                         parity,
                         word_length,
                         stop_bits,
                         dtr,
                         rts,
                         xon_xoff,
                         rts_cts,
                         dtr_dsr );
        write_settings();
}


// The destructor restores the previous settings, then closes the
// port using the Windows call,

WindowsPort::~WindowsPort( void )
{
    if ( error_status == RS232_SUCCESS ) {
        settings = saved_settings;
        dcb = saved_dcb;
        write_settings();
        CloseComm( handle );
    }
}


// The set function looks much like the Set function for all the
// other RS232 derivatives seen in the book. It just adjusts the
// current port settings, then calls write_settings() to do the
// dirty work.

RS232Error WindowsPort::Set( long baud_rate,
                             int parity,
                             int word_length,
                             int stop_bits )
{
        settings.Adjust( baud_rate,
```

## THE MICROSOFT WINDOWS DRIVER

```
                    parity,
                    word_length,
                    stop_bits,
                    UNCHANGED,
                    UNCHANGED,
                    UNCHANGED,
                    UNCHANGED,
                    UNCHANGED );
    return write_settings();
}

// read_settings() does most of its work on the DCB associated with
// the current port. All of the settings that it can figure out
// are found in the DCB. The current settings of RTS and DTR can't
// be found, so they are set to -1, indicating that they are
// unknown.

void WindowsPort::read_settings( void )
{
    int status;
    RS232Error error;

    status = GetCommState( handle, &dcb );
    if ( status < 0 ) {
        error = translate_windows_error( status );
        if ( error >= RS232_ERROR )
            error_status = error;
        return;
    }
    if ( ( dcb.BaudRate & 0xff00 ) == 0xff00 )
        switch( dcb.BaudRate ) {
            case CBR_110    : settings.BaudRate = 110;     break;
            case CBR_300    : settings.BaudRate = 300;     break;
            case CBR_600    : settings.BaudRate = 600;     break;
            case CBR_1200   : settings.BaudRate = 1200;    break;
            case CBR_2400   : settings.BaudRate = 2400;    break;
            case CBR_4800   : settings.BaudRate = 4800;    break;
            case CBR_9600   : settings.BaudRate = 9600;    break;
            case CBR_14400  : settings.BaudRate = 14400;   break;
```

```cpp
                    case CBR_19200  : settings.BaudRate = 19200;   break;
                    case CBR_38400  : settings.BaudRate = 38400L;  break;
                    case CBR_56000  : settings.BaudRate = 56000L;  break;
                    case CBR_128000 : settings.BaudRate = 128000L; break;
                    case CBR_256000 : settings.BaudRate = 256000L; break;
                    default         : settings.BaudRate = -1;      break;
        } else
            settings.BaudRate = dcb.BaudRate;
        switch ( dcb.Parity ) {
            case NOPARITY    : settings.Parity = 'N'; break;
            case ODDPARITY   : settings.Parity = 'O'; break;
            case EVENPARITY  : settings.Parity = 'E'; break;
            case MARKPARITY  : settings.Parity = 'M'; break;
            case SPACEPARITY : settings.Parity = 'S'; break;
            default          : settings.Parity = '?'; break;
        }
        settings.WordLength = dcb.ByteSize;
        switch ( dcb.StopBits ) {
            case ONESTOPBIT   : settings.StopBits = 1; break;
            case ONE5STOPBITS :
            case TWOSTOPBITS  : settings.StopBits = 2; break;
            default           : settings.StopBits = -1; break;
        }
        settings.Rts = -1;
        settings.Dtr = -1;
        settings.XonXoff = dcb.fOutX;
        settings.RtsCts = dcb.fRtsflow;
        settings.DtrDsr = dcb.fDtrflow;
}

// write_settings() does almost everything it needs to do by
// modifying the DCB and then calling SetCommState(). Setting
// RTS and DTR is done by sending an escape function to the
// driver.

RS232Error WindowsPort::write_settings( void )
{
    int set_status;
    RS232Error status = RS232_SUCCESS;
```

## THE MICROSOFT WINDOWS DRIVER

```c
if ( settings.BaudRate <= 19200L )
    dcb.BaudRate = (int) settings.BaudRate;
else if ( settings.BaudRate == 38400L )
    dcb.BaudRate = CBR_38400;
else
    status = RS232_ILLEGAL_BAUD_RATE;
switch ( toupper( settings.Parity ) ) {
    case 'N' : dcb.Parity = NOPARITY; break;
    case 'E' : dcb.Parity = EVENPARITY; break;
    case 'O' : dcb.Parity = ODDPARITY; break;
    case 'M' : dcb.Parity = MARKPARITY; break;
    case 'S' : dcb.Parity = SPACEPARITY; break;
    default : status = RS232_ILLEGAL_PARITY_SETTING; break;
}
switch ( settings.WordLength ) {
    case 8 : dcb.ByteSize = 8; break;
    case 7 : dcb.ByteSize = 7; break;
    case 6 : dcb.ByteSize = 6; break;
    case 5 : dcb.ByteSize = 5; break;
    default : status = RS232_ILLEGAL_PARITY_SETTING; break;
}
switch ( settings.StopBits ) {
    case ONESTOPBIT     : dcb.StopBits = 1; break;
    case ONE5STOPBITS   :
    case TWOSTOPBITS    : dcb.StopBits = 2; break;
    default : status = RS232_ILLEGAL_STOP_BITS; break;
}
if ( settings.Rts == 0 )
    EscapeCommFunction( handle, CLRRTS );
else if ( settings.Rts == 1 )
    EscapeCommFunction( handle, SETRTS );
if ( settings.Dtr == 0 )
    EscapeCommFunction( handle, CLRDTR );
else if ( settings.Dtr == 1 )
    EscapeCommFunction( handle, SETDTR );
dcb.fOutX = dcb.fInX = ( settings.XonXoff != 0 );
dcb.fOutxCtsFlow = dcb.fRtsflow = ( settings.RtsCts != 0 );
dcb.fOutxDsrFlow = dcb.fDtrflow = ( settings.DtrDsr != 0 );
```

```cpp
        set_status = SetCommState( &dcb );
        if ( set_status == 0 )
            return status;
        return translate_windows_error( set_status );
}

// The Windows port driver sends back its own error codes in
// certain stituations. This function translates them to their
// class RS232 equivalents.

RS232Error WindowsPort::translate_windows_error( int error )
{
    switch ( error ) {
        case IE_BADID     : return RS232_PORT_NOT_FOUND;
        case IE_BAUDRATE  : return RS232_ILLEGAL_BAUD_RATE;
        case IE_BYTESIZE  : return RS232_ILLEGAL_WORD_LENGTH;
        case IE_DEFAULT   :
            return (RS232Error) WINDOWS_PORT_DEFAULT_PARAMETERS;
        case IE_HARDWARE  : return RS232_PORT_IN_USE;
        case IE_MEMORY    : return RS232_MEMORY_ALLOCATION_ERROR;
        case IE_NOPEN     : return (RS232Error)
                                    WINDOWS_PORT_NOT_OPEN;
        case IE_OPEN      : return (RS232Error)
                                    WINDOWS_PORT_ALREADY_OPEN;
        default           : return RS232_ERROR;
    }
}

// The ReadComm() does all the work necessary to implement this
// function.

int WindowsPort::read_byte( void )
{
    int result;
    unsigned char c;
    COMSTAT comstat;

    if ( error_status < 0 )
        return error_status;
```

# THE MICROSOFT WINDOWS DRIVER

```cpp
    result = ReadComm( handle, &c, 1 );
    if ( result > 0 )
        return (int) c;
    line_status |= GetCommError( handle, &comstat );
    return RS232_TIMEOUT;
}

// Before calling WriteComm(), I check to be sure there is room
// for a new character in the output queue. Once that is
// determined, WriteComm() does the rest of the work.

int WindowsPort::write_byte( int c )
{
    int result;
    COMSTAT comstat;

    if ( error_status < 0 )
        return error_status;
    line_status |= GetCommError( handle, &comstat );
    if ( comstat.cbOutQue == OUTPUT_BUFFER_SIZE )
        return RS232_TIMEOUT;
    result = WriteComm( handle, &c, 1 );
    if ( result > 0 )
        return RS232_SUCCESS;
    line_status |= GetCommError( handle, &comstat );
    return RS232_TIMEOUT;
}

// The read_buffer() routine is slightly more complicated than
// read_byte(), but it still calls ReadComm() to do most of the
// work. It just has to take into account the possibility that
// an incomplete read may take place.

int WindowsPort::read_buffer( char *buffer, unsigned int count )
{
    int result;
    COMSTAT comstat;

    ByteCount = 0;
```

```
    if ( error_status < 0 )
        return error_status;
    result = ReadComm( handle, buffer, (int) count );
    if ( result > 0 )
        ByteCount = result;
    else {
        ByteCount = -result;
        line_status |= GetCommError( handle, &comstat );
    }
    if ( ByteCount < count )
        return RS232_TIMEOUT;
    else
        return RS232_SUCCESS;
}

// Like read_buffer(), this routine is basically just an extension
// of its single-byte sibling. However, it has to take into account
// the possibility that a partial buffer write may occur.

int WindowsPort::write_buffer( char *buffer, unsigned int count )
{
    int result;
    COMSTAT comstat;
    unsigned int buffer_space;

    ByteCount = 0;
    if ( error_status < 0 )
        return error_status;
    line_status |= GetCommError( handle, &comstat );
    buffer_space = OUTPUT_BUFFER_SIZE - comstat.cbOutQue;
    if ( buffer_space > count )
        result = WriteComm( handle, buffer, count );
    else
        result = WriteComm( handle, buffer, buffer_space );
    if ( result > 0 )
        ByteCount = result;
    else {
        ByteCount = -result;
        line_status |= GetCommError( handle, &comstat );
```

## THE MICROSOFT WINDOWS DRIVER

```cpp
    }
    if ( ByteCount < count )
        return RS232_TIMEOUT;
    return RS232_SUCCESS;
}

// This function has a dedicated Windows API call to do its work.

int WindowsPort::FlushRXBuffer( void )
{
    int status;

    if ( error_status < RS232_SUCCESS )
        return error_status;
    status = FlushComm( handle, 1 );
    if ( status != 0 )
        return translate_windows_error( status );
    return RS232_SUCCESS;
}

// The COMSTAT structure returned from GetCommError contains
// the information we need to determine how the space in both
// the TX and RX buffers is presently being used.

int WindowsPort::TXSpaceFree( void )
{
    COMSTAT comstat;

    if ( error_status < RS232_SUCCESS )
        return error_status;
    line_status |= GetCommError( handle, &comstat );
    return OUTPUT_BUFFER_SIZE - comstat.cbOutQue;
}

int WindowsPort::RXSpaceUsed( void )
{
    COMSTAT comstat;

    if ( error_status < RS232_SUCCESS )
```

```cpp
        return error_status;
    line_status |= GetCommError( handle, &comstat );
    return comstat.cbInQue;
}

// The Windows API function takes care of sending the break.

int WindowsPort::Break( long milliseconds )
{
    long timer;

    if ( error_status < RS232_SUCCESS )
        return error_status;
    SetCommBreak( handle );
    timer = ReadTime() + milliseconds;
    while ( ReadTime() < timer )
        IdleFunction();
    ClearCommBreak( handle );
    return RS232_SUCCESS;
}

// The four Modem Status routines all take advantage of directly
// peeking at the MSR byte inside the driver. They just mask off
// the bit they are interested in, and return a logical result to
// the calling routine.

int WindowsPort::Cd( void )
{
    if ( error_status < RS232_SUCCESS )
        return error_status;
    return ( *modem_status_register & MSR_CD ) != 0;
}

int WindowsPort::Ri( void )
{
    if ( error_status < RS232_SUCCESS )
        return error_status;
    return ( *modem_status_register & MSR_RI ) != 0;
}
```

## THE MICROSOFT WINDOWS DRIVER

```cpp
int WindowsPort::Cts( void )
{
    if ( error_status < RS232_SUCCESS )
        return error_status;
    return ( *modem_status_register & MSR_CTS ) != 0;
}

int WindowsPort::Dsr( void )
{
    if ( error_status < RS232_SUCCESS )
        return error_status;
    return ( *modem_status_register & MSR_DSR ) != 0;
}

// The four line status routines and the software overrrun error
// detect routine all get their information from the
// Windows API function GetCommError(). It returns all the line
// status bits, rearranged by Windows just for fun.

int WindowsPort::SoftwareOverrunError( int clear )
{
    COMSTAT comstat;
    int return_value;

    if ( error_status < RS232_SUCCESS )
        return error_status;
    line_status |= GetCommError( handle, &comstat );
    return_value = ( ( line_status & CE_RXOVER ) != 0 );
    if ( clear != UNCHANGED && clear != 0 )
        line_status &= ~CE_RXOVER;
    return return_value;
}

int WindowsPort::ParityError( int reset )
{
    COMSTAT comstat;
    int return_value;
```

```cpp
        if ( error_status < RS232_SUCCESS )
            return error_status;
        line_status |= GetCommError( handle, &comstat );
        return_value = ( ( line_status & CE_RXPARITY ) != 0 );
        if ( reset != UNCHANGED && reset != 0 )
            line_status &= ~CE_RXPARITY;
        return return_value;
}

int WindowsPort::BreakDetect( int reset )
{
    COMSTAT comstat;
    int return_value;

    if ( error_status < RS232_SUCCESS )
        return error_status;
    line_status |= GetCommError( handle, &comstat );
    return_value = ( ( line_status & CE_BREAK ) != 0 );
    if ( reset != UNCHANGED && reset != 0 )
        line_status &= ~CE_BREAK;
    return return_value;
}

int WindowsPort::FramingError( int reset )
{
    COMSTAT comstat;
    int return_value;

    if ( error_status < RS232_SUCCESS )
        return error_status;
    line_status |= GetCommError( handle, &comstat );
    return_value = ( ( line_status & CE_FRAME ) != 0 );
    if ( reset != UNCHANGED && reset != 0 )
        line_status &= ~CE_FRAME;
    return return_value;
}

int WindowsPort::HardwareOverrunError( int reset )
{
```

## THE MICROSOFT WINDOWS DRIVER

```
    COMSTAT comstat;
    int return_value;

    if ( error_status < RS232_SUCCESS )
        return error_status;
    line_status |= GetCommError( handle, &comstat );
    return_value = ( ( line_status & CE_OVERRUN ) != 0 );
    if ( reset != UNCHANGED && reset != 0 )
        line_status &= ~CE_OVERRUN;
    return return_value;
}

// All of the handshaking functions rely on write_settings() to do
// the dirty work of actually changing the settings. They then
// return the current setting to the caller.

int WindowsPort::XonXoffHandshaking( int setting )
{
    if ( error_status < RS232_SUCCESS )
        return error_status;
    if ( setting != UNCHANGED ) {
        settings.XonXoff = ( setting != 0 );
        write_settings();
    }
    return( settings.XonXoff );
}

int WindowsPort::RtsCtsHandshaking( int setting )
{
    if ( error_status < RS232_SUCCESS )
        return error_status;
    if ( setting != UNCHANGED ) {
        settings.RtsCts = ( setting != 0 );
        write_settings();
    }
    return( settings.RtsCts );
}

int WindowsPort::DtrDsrHandshaking( int setting )
```

```cpp
{
    if ( error_status < RS232_SUCCESS )
        return error_status;
    if ( setting != UNCHANGED ) {
        settings.DtrDsr = ( setting != 0 );
        write_settings();
    }
    return( settings.DtrDsr );
}

// Setting DTR and RTS is done with a Windows API Escape code.

int WindowsPort::Dtr( int setting )
{
    if ( error_status < RS232_SUCCESS )
        return error_status;
    if ( setting != UNCHANGED ) {
        if ( settings.DtrDsr == 1 )
            return WINDOWS_PORT_HANDSHAKE_LINE_IN_USE;
        else {
            if ( ( settings.Dtr = setting ) == 1 )
                EscapeCommFunction( handle, SETDTR );
            else
                EscapeCommFunction( handle, CLRDTR );
        }
    }
    return settings.Dtr;
}

int WindowsPort::Rts( int setting )
{
    if ( error_status < RS232_SUCCESS )
        return error_status;
    if ( setting != UNCHANGED ) {
        if ( settings.RtsCts == 1 )
            return WINDOWS_PORT_HANDSHAKE_LINE_IN_USE;
        else {
            if ( ( settings.Rts = setting ) == 1 )
                EscapeCommFunction( handle, SETRTS );
```

## THE MICROSOFT WINDOWS DRIVER

```
            else
                EscapeCommFunction( handle, CLRRTS );
        }
    }
    return settings.Rts;
}

// All the information needed to perform the following functions is
// found in the COMSTAT function returned by GetCommError().


int WindowsPort::RXSpaceFree( void )
{
    COMSTAT comstat;

    if ( error_status < RS232_SUCCESS )
        return error_status;
    line_status |= GetCommError( handle, &comstat );
    return INPUT_BUFFER_SIZE - comstat.cbInQue;
}

int WindowsPort::TXSpaceUsed( void )
{
    COMSTAT comstat;

    if ( error_status < RS232_SUCCESS )
        return error_status;
    line_status |= GetCommError( handle, &comstat );
    return comstat.cbOutQue;
}

// The Windows API provides a dedicated function to perform this
// task.

int WindowsPort::FlushTXBuffer( void )
{
    int status;
```

```
    if ( error_status < RS232_SUCCESS )
        return error_status;
    status = FlushComm( handle, 0 );
    if ( status != 0 )
        return translate_windows_error( status );
    return RS232_SUCCESS;
}

// The debug output includes a complete dump of the current DCB
// structure for the port, which describes virtually everything
// Windows knows about the port. The only thing left out here
// which could be interesting in the COMSTAT structure.

int WindowsPort::FormatDebugOutput( char *buffer, int line_number )
{
    if ( buffer == 0 )
        return( first_debug_output_line + 7 );
    if ( line_number < first_debug_output_line )
        return RS232::FormatDebugOutput( buffer, line_number );
    switch( line_number - first_debug_output_line ) {
        case 0 :
            wsprintf( buffer,
                    (LPSTR) "Derived class: WindowsPort  "
                    "Ri: %2d  Cts: %2d  Cd: %2d  Dsr: %2d  "
                    "RX Overrun: %d",
                    Ri(), Cts(), Cd(), Dsr(),
                    SoftwareOverrunError() );
            break;
        case 1 :
            wsprintf( buffer,
                    "TX Used: %5d   RX Free: %5d  "
                    "Parity Err: %d  Break: %d  "
                    "Overrun: %d  Framing Err: %d",
                    TXSpaceUsed(), RXSpaceFree(),
                    ParityError(),
                    BreakDetect(),
                    HardwareOverrunError(),
                    FramingError() );
            break;
```

```
        case 2 :
            wsprintf( buffer,
                    "DCB: RlsTimeout: %04x  CtsTimeout: %04x  "
                    "DsrTimeout: %04x  fBinary: %1d",
                    dcb.RlsTimeout,
                    dcb.CtsTimeout,
                    dcb.DsrTimeout,
                    dcb.fBinary );
            break;
        case 3 :
            wsprintf( buffer,
                    "DCB: fRtsDisable: %1d  fParity: %1d  "
                    "fOutxCtsFlow: %1d  fOutxDsrFlow: %1d",
                    dcb.fRtsDisable,
                    dcb.fParity,
                    dcb.fOutxCtsFlow,
                    dcb.fOutxDsrFlow );
            break;
        case 4 :
            wsprintf( buffer,
                    "DCB: fDtrDisable: %1d  fOutX: %1d  fInx: %1d  "
                    "fPeChar: %1d  fNull: %1d  fChEvt: %1d",
                    dcb.fDtrDisable,
                    dcb.fOutX,
                    dcb.fInX,
                    dcb.fPeChar,
                    dcb.fNull,
                    dcb.fChEvt );
            break;
        case 5 :
            wsprintf( buffer,
                    "DCB: fDtrflow: %1d  fRtsflow: %1d  XonChar: "
                                                         "%02x  "
                    "XoffChar: %02x  XonLim: %04x  XoffLim: %04x",
                    dcb.fDtrflow,
                    dcb.fRtsflow,
                    dcb.XonChar,
                    dcb.XoffChar,
                    dcb.XonLim,
                    dcb.XoffLim );
```

```cpp
                break;
            case 6 :
                wsprintf( buffer,
                            "DCB: PeChar: %02x  EofChar: %02x  EvtChar: %02x "
                            "TxDelay:  %04x",
                            dcb.PeChar,
                            dcb.EofChar,
                            dcb.EvtChar,
                            dcb.TxDelay );
                break;
            default :
                return RS232_ILLEGAL_LINE_NUMBER;
        }
        return RS232_SUCCESS;
}


char * WindowsPort::ErrorName( int error )
{
    if ( error < RS232_NEXT_FREE_ERROR && error >= RS232_ERROR )
        return RS232::ErrorName( error );
    if ( error < RS232_NEXT_FREE_WARNING && error >= RS232_WARNING )
        return RS232::ErrorName( error );
    if ( error >= RS232_SUCCESS )
        return RS232::ErrorName( error );
    switch ( error ) {
        case WINDOWS_PORT_DEFAULT_PARAMETERS :
            return "Default parameters in error";
        case WINDOWS_PORT_NOT_OPEN :
            return "Port not open";
        case WINDOWS_PORT_ALREADY_OPEN :
            return "Port already open";
        case WINDOWS_PORT_HANDSHAKE_LINE_IN_USE :
            return "Handshake line in use";
```

## THE MICROSOFT WINDOWS DRIVER

```
        default :
            return( "Undefined error" );
    }
}

// ******************* END OF WINPORT.CPP *******************
```

**Listing 8-2. WINPORT.CPP**

There is one additional file that needs to be created in order to build Windows programs. In the previous chapters, the O/S dependent code was contained in a file called `MSDOS.CPP`. The two functions that will change for Windows are now contained in `MSWIN.CPP`. The first is the idle function, which is called whenever one of the functions is waiting for input. Under MS-DOS, there really isn't anything to do in the idle function. Of course, the programmer could use the idle function for other activity, but it isn't essential.

Under MS-Windows, the idle function needs to be redefined. Since MS-Windows is a cooperative multitasking system, we need to give time back to the O/S. This is usually done with a loop that calls the Windows `PeekMessage()` function. Unfortunately, the exact format of this loop is going to vary slightly depending on how the Windows application is implemented. Because of this uncertainty, the generic function is still a "do-nothing" function in `MSWIN.CPP`:

```
while ( PeekMessage ( &msg, 0, 0, 0, PM_REMOVE ) ) {
    TranslateMessage ( &msg );
    DispatchMessage ( &msg );
}
```

The `ReadTime()` function makes a direct call to a Windows API function, which providentially returns the time in the exact format we need it.

```
// ********************* START OF MSWIN.CPP *********************
//
// This module contains OS specific routines. These routines are
// all defined for MS-Windows. When the target OS is MS-DOS, OS/2,
// or UNIX, different versions of these routines must be linked in.

#include <windows.h>
```

```
#include "rs232.h"

// This idle routine presently does nothing. A real windows program
// would need to service the message loop in its idle routine,
// probably with a call to PeekMessage().

int RS232::IdleFunction( void )
{
    return RS232_SUCCESS;
}

//
// ReadTime() returns the current time of day in milliseconds. It
// uses the Windows specific tick count function, instead of
// polling MS-DOS or the BIOS.
//

long ReadTime( void )
{
    return GetTickCount();
}

// ********************* END OF MSWIN.CPP *********************
```

**Listing 8-3. MSWIN.CPP**

## A Test Program

The standard test program used in the previous chapters is not going to help you under the Windows programming environment. `TEST232.CPP` is a useful program, but it makes heavy use of video BIOS services, which just won't work under Windows.

Many beginning Windows programmers are dismayed to find that writing even the simplest "Hello, world!" program can take hundreds of lines of boiler-plate code. The amount of code needed to create the Windows equivalent of `TEST232.CPP` would unfortunately run into at least 1,000 lines of C code, which is probably more than most readers want to try to digest.

## THE MICROSOFT WINDOWS DRIVER

In order to cut back on both overhead and complexity, I am going to take a shortcut for our Windows test program. Instead of writing a pure Windows application, I am going to use Borland's EasyWin package for all of the screen and keyboard I/O. Borland, Microsoft, and Zortech all provide similar packages which offer a certain amount of compatibility with the standard I/O functions from the C runtime library. None of the packages are compatible with one another, and all have serious shortcomings. Borland's looked like it offered the best hope of making a useful test program, so that is what I will use here.

```
// ******************* START OF TEST232W.CPP *******************

// This short test program is designed to test the WindowsPort
// class under MS-Windows. To avoid the lengthy process of writing
// a full Windows application, TEST232W.CPP uses Borland's EasyWin
// function set, which allows the use of standard I/O under
// Windows. The program normally acts as a simple terminal.
// Commands are accessed by pressing the Escape key.

#include <windows.h>
#include <stdio.h>
#include <conio.h>
#include <ctype.h>
#include <string.h>
#include "rs232.h"
#include "winport.h"

// Local function prototypes.

void DrawDump( RS232 *port );
void DrawHelp( void );
int HandleCommand( RS232 *port );

// Local data

int ReadingFlag = 1;
long NextDump = 0;
```

```
// main() sits in an infinite loop. The only exit from the loop
// is when HandleCommand() returns true, which will happen when the
// EXit command is given. In the first part of the loop, keyboard
// input is handled, either by being routed out the port, or by
// jumping to the command handler. Next, if the program is in
// Reading mode, input data is read from the port and displayed on
// the screen. Finally, if 500 milliseconds has elapsed since the
// last time the port status was dumped, it is done again.

main()
{
    int c;
    WindowsPort port( COM1 );

    for ( ; ; ) {
        if ( kbhit() ) {
            c = getch();
            if ( c == 27 ) {
                if ( HandleCommand( &port ) )
                    break;
            } else
                port.Write( c );
        }
        if ( ReadingFlag ) {
            c = port.Read();
            if ( c > 0 ) {
                if ( c == 13 )
                    gotoxy( 0, wherey() );
                else
                    putc( c, stdout );
            }
        }
        if ( NextDump < GetTickCount() ) {
            DrawDump( &port );
            NextDump = GetTickCount() + 500;
        }

    }
}
```

## THE MICROSOFT WINDOWS DRIVER

```c
    return 0;
}

// Since EasyWin under Borland doesn't let us open an extra window
// for the port status dump, I just format it and send it out to
// the Clipboard. This may or may not be legal with EasyWin, but
// it seems to work.

void DrawDump( RS232 *port )
{
    int i;
    char buffer[ 131 ];
    char far *clip;
    HGLOBAL hclip;

    hclip = GlobalAlloc( GPTR, 1000 );
    clip = GlobalLock( hclip );
    *clip = '\0';

    for ( i = 0 ;
          i < port->DebugLineCount() ;
          i++ ) {
        port->FormatDebugOutput( buffer, i );
        _fstrcat( clip, buffer );
        _fstrcat( clip, "\r\n" );
    }
    OpenClipboard( 0 );
    SetClipboardData( CF_TEXT, hclip );
    CloseClipboard();
}

// A quick reminder of what keyboard commands do what.

void DrawHelp( void )
{
    printf( "EX:   Exit\n" );
    printf( "DT:   Toggle DTR\n" );
    printf( "RT:   Toggle RTS\n" );
    printf( "RF:   Togge Reading Flag\n" );
```

427

```
    printf( "FT:   Flush TX buffer\n" );
    printf( "FR:   Flush RX buffer\n" );
    printf( "RB:   Read a buffer\n" );
    printf( "RC:   Read a character\n" );
    printf( "WS:   Write a string\n" );
    printf( "SE:   Set new port parameters\n" );
    printf( "RH:   Toggle RTS/CTS handshaking\n" );
    printf( "BR:   Send a Break signal\n" );
}

// The command handler. It reads in a two-character command from
// the keyboard and does something based on that. This is designed
// to be easy to extend with new commands.

int HandleCommand( RS232 *port )
{
    char buffer[ 81 ];
    int c1;
    int c2;
    int c;
    long baud;
    int sb;
    int wl;
    char parity;

    printf( "\nEnter 2 letter command (HE for help) : ");
    c1 = getch();
    if ( c1 == 27 ) {
        port->Write( 27 );
        return 0;
    }
    c2 = getch();
    putc( '\n', stdout );
    switch ( ( toupper( c2 ) << 8 ) + toupper( c1 ) ) {
        case 'HE' : DrawHelp(); break;
        case 'EX' : return 1;
        case 'DT' : port->Dtr( !port->Dtr() ); break;
        case 'RT' : port->Rts( !port->Rts() ); break;
        case 'RF' : ReadingFlag = !ReadingFlag; break;
```

## THE MICROSOFT WINDOWS DRIVER

```
        case 'FT' : port->FlushTXBuffer(); break;
        case 'FR' : port->FlushRXBuffer(); break;
        case 'WS' :
            port->Write("Test string: 123456789ABCDE"
                        "FGHIJKLMNOPQRSTUVWXYZ\n");
            printf( "ByteCount = %d  Elapsed Time=%ld\n",
                    port->ByteCount,
                    port->ElapsedTime );
            break;
        case 'RB' :
            port->Read( buffer, 80 );
            printf( "ByteCount = %d  Elapsed Time=%ld\n",
                    port->ByteCount,
                    port->ElapsedTime );
            printf( "Buffer: %s\n", buffer );
            break;
        case 'RC' :
            c = port->Read();
            printf( "Char = " );
            if ( c >= 0 )
                if ( isprint( c ) )
                    printf( "%c\n", c );
                else
                    printf( "<%d>", c );
            else
                printf( "%s\n", port->ErrorName( c ) );
            break;
        case 'SE' :
            printf( "Enter baud,parity,word length, stop bits: " );
            baud = wl = sb = parity = UNCHANGED;
            scanf( "%ld,%c,%d,%d", &baud, &parity, &wl, &sb );
            printf( "Set returns a %s\n",
                    port->ErrorName( port->Set( baud, parity, wl,
                                                 sb ) ) );
            break;
        case 'RH' :
            port->RtsCtsHandshaking( !port->RtsCtsHandshaking() );
            break;
```

```
        case 'BR' : port->Break( 500 ); break;
    }
    return 0;
}

// ******************* END OF TEST232W.CPP *******************
```

**Listing 8-4. TEST232W.CPP**

As you can see from the listing, an EasyWin program looks a lot like a standard MS-DOS program. The normal C functions like `printf()` and `getch()` do pretty much what you would expect them to do. Borland's package also gives you full access to the Windows API at the same time, which is essential for testing the `WindowsPort` class.

This program acts as a simple terminal emulator. It sits in a loop, routing keyboard output to the serial port, and sending the serial port input to the screen. Access to the

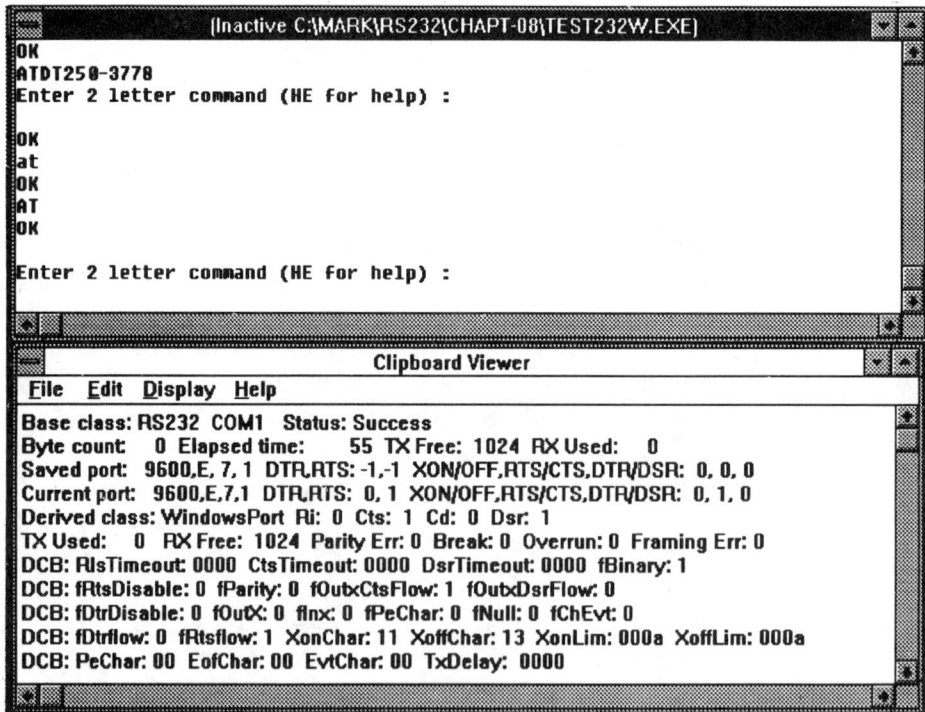

Figure 8-1. A screen shot from TEST232W.EXE

## THE MICROSOFT WINDOWS DRIVER

extended functions is achieved by pressing the escape key. At that point the usual sort of things can be done, such as toggling control lines, changing line settings, etc.

Figure 8-1 shows a screen shot from the test program. Like all the other test programs from earlier in the book, this one features a running status dump. With the DOS based programs it was easy to open a second text window and route the status output there. EasyWin doesn't give us that option, however. So instead, once every 500 milliseconds, `TEST232W.EXE` sends a status dump to the clipboard. The Windows 3.1 clipboard viewer treats the message as normal text and displays it without any trouble.

### Building TEST232W.EXE

Listing 8-5 shows the make file used to create the test program with Borland C++ 3.1. If you would prefer to use the environment, you only need to create a new project and add five files to it:

```
TEST232W.CPP
RS232.CPP
MSWIN.CPP
WINPORT.CPP
TEST232W.DEF
```

`TEST232W.DEF` is shown in Listing 8-6. While a DEF file is not strictly needed to create this project, the Borland Linker will issue a warning message if you don't supply one, so I use this generic version.

```
# ******************* START OF TEST232W.MAK ********************
#
# This is the make file use to create TEST232W.EXE, from Chapter 8.
# To create the executable, just type:
#
#              make -f test232w.mak
#

.cpp.obj:
  bcc -W -c {$< }
```

```
test232w.exe : mswin.obj test232w.obj winport.obj rs232.obj
            tlink /v/x/c/P-/Twe
c0ws+mswin+test232w+winport+rs232,\
            test232w,,mathws.lib+import.lib+cws.lib,test232w.def

# ******************** END OF TEST232W.MAK **********************
```

**Listing 8-5. TEST232W.MAK**

```
;******************* START OF TEST232W.DEF ********************

NAME            TEST232W
DESCRIPTION     'Test of WindowsPort RS232 Class'
EXETYPE         WINDOWS
CODE            PRELOAD MOVEABLE DISCARDABLE
DATA            PRELOAD MOVEABLE MULTIPLE
HEAPSIZE        16000
STACKSIZE       16000

;******************* END OF TEST232W.DEF **********************
```

**Listing 8-6. TEST232W.DEF**

## Summary

While it is certainly true that writing Windows applications can require a lot of education and work, Microsoft did a good job of supplying all the necessary communications tools. The Windows API fit neatly into the `RS232` class, doing better than any other interface except for the completely customized `PC8250` class.

Writing a great Windows communications application is still going to require a lot of work. But at least you can expect to find yourself on familiar ground when using the `WindowsPort` class.

CHAPTER 9

# Making Modems Usable

Probably nothing has been more of a hindrance to public acceptance of communications software than the ordinary desktop modem. This may seem like a contradiction; after all, what would communications software be *without* modems?

While it is true that modems are absolutely crucial to desktop communications, it is also true that the lack of standardization between various brands and models of modems has led to a virtual Tower of Babel for end users. In principle, it ought to be simple to buy a modem and a software package, install both of them, and immediately begin accessing on-line services like CompuServe.

In practice, nothing could be farther from the truth. Most first time users realize they are in trouble when their installation software gives them a prompt that looks like this:

```
Modem setup string? _
```

This seemingly simple question usually causes the first in a never-ending series of research sessions devoted to the investigation of DIP switch settings and the "AT" command set. Eventually, most users will thrash out a configuration that works for them, but even the slightest disturbance will break it, leading to yet another frustrating investigation.

In this industry, evolving standards are usually in a state of dynamic tension with innovation. To achieve mass acceptance, both hardware and software have to achieve a certain amount of uniformity, usually by adherence to official or "de facto" standards. This has proven to be true of computers, peripherals, operating systems, and even applications. Where, then, did modem manufacturers go wrong?

## The Hardware Standards

When it comes to hardware, modem manufacturers have done pretty well. The past 20 years have seen a steady progression of modem standards, starting with the AT&T standards of the 1960s and 1970s, and leading up to the CCITT standards in effect today.

Virtually every modem being sold for desktop users adheres to one of three standards:

V.22*bis*:   :   The inexpensive workhorse, provides 2,400 bps communications. The chipsets to make these modems are so inexpensive that they are becoming standard equipment on new systems, particularly notebook machines.

V.32   :   The 9,600 bps throughput of these modems has been eclipsed by their faster siblings.

V.32*bis*   :   14,400 bps modems, quickly becoming priced as commodities.

In addition, a new standard will be emerging in the near future for modems operating at 19,200 bps, or perhaps even 28,800 bps. This standard is presently a work in progress, referred to informally as V.fast.

The notable thing about these modems is that virtually all of the modems being produced today are able to communicate with one another. Regardless of the manufacturer, and the hardware used to build the modem, one V.32*bis* modem is able to connect to another without too much trouble. This is a tribute to the standardization process.

It is true that some manufacturers have achieved limited success selling nonstandard modems. US Robotics and Telebit both come to mind as examples of companies that have been fairly successful at this. There are two important facts to note about these renegade modems:

1. The nonstandard modems have usually been created in an attempt to break new ground in throughput. Modems such as the USR HST and the Telebit Trailblazer were sending data faster than their contemporary standards permitted. Once the standards caught up with technology, the non-standard modems were replaced with conventional ones.

2. The nonstandard modems could always fall back to slower speeds and talk to other modems that were adhering to the standard. So even though these modems deviated from the norm, they still offered a "safety net" for their owners.

In any case, when expressed as a fraction of the total market, the nonstandard modems are decidedly a rather small minority.

## The Software Standards

Today's modems are almost universally smart modems. This means that the modem has an onboard microprocessor, and communicates with the computer when off-line via the RS-232 interface. The "language" used to control the modem is usually referred to as the "AT Command Set."

The AT Command Set was introduced by the pioneer of desktop modems, Hayes. To say that Hayes was an overnight success might be an exaggeration, but after the introduction of the Smartmodem 300, Hayes quickly moved to a position of industry dominance.

The AT command set as introduced with the Smartmodem 300 provided a simple and convenient way for the modem to make phone calls. Before the introduction of smart modems, a user would typically make a dial-up connection by picking up the telephone and dialing the number for a remote modem. When the remote end picked up the call and began sending its answer tone, the user would put the handset into an acoustic coupler, whereupon his or her modem would respond to the answer tone, leading to a connection.

You can imagine how enjoyable this would be when repeated dozens of times a day, or when trying to get through to a perpetually busy number. When the unfortunate user of an old-fashioned dumb modem finally upgraded to the Hayes Smartmodem 300, making the phone call meant just typing in the characters "ATDT 555-

1212" followed by a carriage return. The modem would automatically go off-hook, dial the remote end, and wait for a carrier.

Even better than this was the fact that now the entire dialing process could be automated. If a dial-up number was perpetually busy, it was a simple matter to write a dialer program that could try it once very 15 seconds, around the clock. The possibilities were endless, even showing up in the movie "War Games."

All this was accomplished using the AT command set. The "AT" in the name refers to the fact that every command starts with the two characters "A" and "T." This is commonly referred to as the Attention sequence, although it isn't clear whether the name came before or after the use of the two letters.

Every AT command sent to the modem consists of the two letters, followed by a string of alphanumeric characters, and ending in a carriage return character. The original Smartmodem had a relatively small roster of commands the user could employ. Over succeeding generations, the command set grew, leading to what I consider to be the benchmark, which is the command set for the Smartmodem 2400.

Nearly every modem being sold today claims to be "Hayes Compatible." They are as long as the extent of Hayes compatibility means having a set of commands that all start with "AT." In point of fact, no modem manufacturer can resist tinkering with the command set. Usually this means adding a few new commands as an extension to the set. It often means tinkering with a few of the existing commands, and maybe even leaving out a few that aren't used very frequently.

If this sounds chaotic, it is. But fortunately, it *is* possible to identify a core set of commands that will work with every modem, and as long as you don't deviate from those, you can write software that works with every "Hayes compatible" modem. Later in this chapter, I will show that individual modems will have to have unique configuration and setup commands.

### The Smartmodem 2400 command set

All of the commands in this set start with the characters "AT," and are terminated with a carriage return character, `'\r'`, with one exception. In general, commands can be strung together by simply concatenating the command characters (minus the leading "AT"). For example, the three commands "ATZ," "ATE1," and "ATV1" could be combined and sent to the modem as "ATZE1V1." You can expect all modems to accept at least 40 characters per command, although most will accept more.

# MAKING MODEMS USABLE

The exception to the "AT" prefix rule is the Repeat command. By sending the unadorned string "A/" to the modem, with no trailing carriage return, the modem repeats the last command.

Many of these commands are somewhat irrelevant in the desktop context this book addresses. See the specifics on each command for a discussion of the usefulness of individual commands.

ATA  The Answer command. This causes the modem to go off-hook and begin emitting the answer tone. This is usually done in response to an incoming ring detect.

ATBn  If n is set to 0, this command selects the CCITT V.22 standard for 1,200 bps communications. A setting of 1 selects Bell 212A. The default for modems sold in the US is usually 1. Very few modems in use today use 1,200 bps communications, so this settings is not particularly useful.

ATDs  This is the dial command. The "s" stands for a dialing string. The dialing string consists of a string of digits to dial, mixed with dial string modifiers. The dialing modifiers are:

    P  Dial in Pulse mode. Pulse mode is usually the default setting for dialing.

    T  Dial in Tone mode. Since most people prefer to dial in tone mode, dialing strings typically start with "ATDT."

    ,  Pause during dialing. The length of the pause is determined by the contest of S register 8 (more about that later), and usually defaults to 2 seconds.

    !  Perform a hook flash. This is often necessary on PBX systems to access special phone system features.

    W  Wait for dial tone. Most PBX systems require you to dial a trunk access code, such as 9, and then wait for a second dial tone before dialing. The "W" dialing code gives you that capability.

| | |
|---|---|
| @ | Wait for silence. Some systems don't provide an access tone when you connect to them. When you specify that you want to wait for silence, it means the remote end should stop ringing and be silent for 5 seconds before dialing continues. |
| ; | Return to command mode after dialing. Normally the modem will wait for a connection after dialing. If the ";" is used to terminate the dialing string, the modem dials and then returns to command mode while the call is being processed. |
| S=n | The value n can be a number from 0 to 3. It refers to one of four dialing strings that have been stored in the modem. Since most modem dialing is done under program control, this feature is not particularly useful today. A communications program typically has access to a dialing directory containing hundreds of numbers. |

ATEn    This command controls the echoing of characters in command mode. A value for n of 0 disables echoing, 1 enables. Normally there is no reason to change the default, which is to echo characters.

ATHn    A value of 0 causes the modem go hang up. A value of 1 tells the modem to go off hook. We use the ATH0 command in this chapter's Modem class to break a connection.

ATIn    The different values of n produce various product ID codes, firmware checksums, etc. These are relatively useless for our purposes. They might be useful for debugging a suspected hardware problem in conjunction with the manufacturer's technical support department.

ATLn    This command adjusts the speaker's volume level, with n of 0 being the lowest volume, 3 being the highest. Note that many modems require volume adjustment to be done via an external potentiometer, so this command is not always effective.

ATMn  The Smartmodem 2400 has four different operating modes for the speaker. They are defined as follows:

0: The speaker is *always* off.
1: The speaker is on during dialing, and turns off when carrier is detected. This is the default setting. It is useful to be able to hear the modem during the dialing stage.
2: The speaker is *always* on. This can be quite noisy once carrier is attained.
3: The speaker is off during dialing, on while waiting for carrier, and off when carrier is attained.

ATOn  This command is used to return the modem to the online state when it is in command mode. The default value of n, 0, just returns the modem to the online state. A value of 1 causes the modem to go reinitiate the equalization retraining process.

ATQn  The ATQ command is used to enable or disable result codes. The normal result codes, such as "OK" and "RING" are returned by default, or when n=0. "ATQ1" disables result codes. The Modem class developed in this chapter will always depend on result codes being sent.

ATSr=n  The S registers are used to control various facets of the modem's behavior, such as the ring to answer on, the backspace character, escape character. The pertinent S registers will be discussed later in this chapter. This command is used to set register "r" to the value "n."

ATSr?  This command is used to display the value of register "r."

ATVn	The modem has the ability to display result codes in numeric form or verbose form. Verbose responses are the traditional English form, such as "CONNECT," "OK," and so on. Numeric codes are simple numbers, which are somewhat harder to translate. While it is somewhat more difficult for a program to deal with, verbose codes are used by the Modem class.

ATXn	This is yet another command that modifies the result code set. When n=0, the only message returned when a connection occurs is "CONNECT." With higher values of n, messages such as "CONNECT 2400" are returned. Unfortunately, the array of different message possibilities that can be returned with the various values of n is somewhat staggering. To avoid confusion, I will stick with the default value of n=4 and not tinker with the other possibilities.

ATYn	The default value of 0 disables the long break disconnect. A value of 1 enables the disconnect. When a break of greater than 1.6 seconds is received, and the disconnect is enabled, the modem will disconnect.

ATZn	The ATZ command performs a software reset of the modem. Optionally, a value of n can be passed to specify one of several profiles to set the modem to. The original Hayes Smartmodem had two profiles that could be called up with n=0 and n=1.

AT&Cn	By default, the Hayes Smartmodem kept the CD line high at all times. This is probably a bad thing for software that is trying to work effectively with the modem, because it makes it much more difficult to determine if and when a connection is actually present, and when it is broken. The Modem class in this chapter will use this command with n=1 to cause CD to accurately track the state of the carrier. n=0 is used to restore the default setting and keep CD high at all times.

AT&Dn    This command determines what action the modem takes when DTR drops from high to low. With the default setting of n=0, the modem ignores DTR. n=1 causes the modem to enter command mode when DTR drops. n=2 causes the modem to hang up and enter command mode when DTR drops. And finally, the most drastic action is taken when n=3. In this modem, the modem hangs up, resets all of its operating parameters, and enters command mode when DTR drops.

AT&F    This command restores the factory settings of the modem. This command is particularly useful, as it is really the only way to put the modem in a known state.

AT&Gn    This command selects one of several optional guard tones. It is typically not used in the United States.

AT&Jn    Some of the Hayes Smartmodems used this command to select different types of telephone line jacks. Very few manufacturers presently support this command.

AT&Pn    The make/break ratio in pulse dialing varies slightly between the various countries. The US uses the default value specified by n=0. The United Kingdom uses n=1.

AT&Qn    Some modems support synchronous operation, which can be selected with values of n other than the default of 0. This feature is used infrequently by those with specific hardware needs.

AT&Rn    This option determines how the modem uses the RTS line. Under the default value of n=0, CTS will track RTS. With n=1, CTS will always be high.

AT&Sn        With the default parameter of n=0, the modem will keep DSR high at all times. With n=1, DSR is low when in command mode, and high when online.

AT&Tn        This option is used to initiate one of many test procedures.

While this list of options may seem rather long, it is by no means comprehensive. However, it provides a good basis to start from, as most new modems will support this command set at a minimum.

In addition to the AT commands, there are two command sequences that don't start with AT and aren't terminated with a carriage return.

A\           Repeat the last command. This is the sole command that doesn't have an "AT" prefix or a carriage return terminator. This command is handy when it can be used to avoid reentering a long dialing string. It is not particularly useful when writing programs to control the modem.

+++          The escape sequence. An online modem can be commanded to drop back to command mode if it sees three consecutive occurrences of the escape sequence in the data stream. Note that Hayes requires a guard time of 1 second before and after the sequence where no other data is sent. This capability is part of the notorious Heatherington '302 patent held by Hayes, which most modem manufacturers seem to be willing to pay royalties for the privilege of using.

## The S registers

The Hayes modem maintains a bank of internal status registers, or S registers, that determine how many of the modem's functions operate. Like the AT command set, the set of S registers has been highly customized by various manufacturers. However, the basic set used by the Hayes Smartmodem 2400 has remained more or less inviolate.

The contents of the S register can be examined with the "ATSr?" command, and modified with the "ATSr=n" command.

**Table 9-1. The S Register definitions.**

| Register | Range | Default | Meaning |
| --- | --- | --- | --- |
| S0 | 0-255 | 0 | Ring to answer on. A value of 0 disables the auto answer capability of the modem. |
| S1 | 0-255 | N/A | Ring count. This is a count of the number of incoming rings on the line. |
| S2 | 7 bit ASCII characters | 0x2b, '+' | The escape character used to take the modem to command mode when it is on line. |
| S3 | 7 bit ASCII characters | 0x0d, CR | The character used by the modem as a carriage return. |
| S4 | 7 bit ASCII characters | 0x0a, LF | The character used by the modem as a line feed. |
| S5 | Non-printing ASCII control characters | 0x08, BS | The character used by the modem as a backspace |
| S6 | 0-255 | 2 | The number of seconds to wait before dialing, if blind dialing is enabled. |
| S7 | 0-255 | 30 | The number of seconds to wait for carrier after dialing is complete. |
| S8 | 0-255 | 2 | The number of seconds to pause when a comma is found in the dialing string. |
| S9 | 0-255 | 6 | The number of 100 millisecond units carrier must be active before being recognized as valid. |
| S10 | 0-255 | 14 | The number of 100 millisecond units that carrier must be low before the modem disconnects. |
| S11 | 50-255 | 70 | The DTMF dialing duration in milliseconds. |
| S12 | 20-255 | 50 | The escape code guard time in 20 millisecond units. A valid escape code (+++) must be surrounded by this much idle line time to be considered valid. |

## Today's Modems

The modems being sold to users today can generally be expected to follow the hardware and software standards shown above. However, today's modems have capabilities that have far surpassed those of the Smartmodem 2400, and those need to be taken into account as well.

Figures 9-1 and 9-2 show a couple of representative examples of modems in use today. The Practical Peripherals PM9600SA is a standard V.32 intelligent mode. The Intel modem is a SatisFAXtion Modem/400e. The Intel modem is a V.32*bis* modem that in addition has a Group 3 FAX capability.

The Intel modem is a good example of the top end of the line for modems being sold today. It supports V.32*bis* modulation, which allows throughput of up to 14,400 bps on standard telephone lines. It supports both MNP and CCITT error correction and data compression, allowing for fast and reliable connections. In addition, it has built in Group 3 FAX capabilities, allowing the modem to both send and receive FAXes.

Figure 9-1. The Practical Peripherals PM9600 SA.

# MAKING MODEMS USABLE

**Figure 9-2. Intel SatisFAXtion Modem/400e.**

Practical Peripherals has a complete line of modems, ranging from high end V.32*bis* FAX modems down to standard 2,400 baud units. The modem shown in Figure 9-2 is an example of a mid-line modem in today's market. The PM9600 SA has V.32 modulation, allowing a maximum throughput of 9,600 bps. It also supports V.42 error correction and V.42*bis* data compression, but does not have built in FAX capabilities. Modems with this sort of feature set will sell for somewhat less than the top of the line modems, allowing them to maintain a market presence.

The bottom end of today's market is represented by the inexpensive clone 2,400 baud modem, using V.22*bis* modulation. Since all V.32 and V.32*bis* modems will talk to 2,400 baud modems, these units are in no particular danger of being made obsolete. There extreme low price makes them a standard feature in many desktop clones and notebook systems being sold today.

While many of the better known manufacturers are shipping 2,400 baud modems with data compression and error correction options, the extreme low end units generally aren't equipped with this sort of firmware. So while you can expect to find these features in high-end and mid-line modems, you can't be so sure at the low end. Because of this, the `Modem` class being developed in this chapter needs to be able to work both with and without these features.

### Modem capabilities

The first step towards writing a useful modem class is to define a set of capabilities that can work with in a uniform way. For any given modem, the following need to be defined: a standard setup, a list of capabilities, and a way to recognize appropriate responses from the modem.

The `Modem` class defined in this chapter keeps this information about modems in a `ModemCapabilities` structure. This structure contains all the information necessary to write useful software that can interact with the modem:

```
struct ModemCapabilities {
    char *name;
    char *initialization_string;
    char *fail_strings;
    char *compression_strings;
    char *protocol_strings;
    long initial_baud_rate;
    int locked_baud_rate;
    int handshaking;
};
```

A typical entry for is shown below. This is for the Practical Peripherals 14400FX modem similar to the one pictured earlier in the chapter. This entry describes every thing the `Modem` class needs to know about the modem in order to work with it.

```
{ "Practical Peripherals 14400FX",
  "AT &F0 &C1 &D2 S95=44",
  "NO CARRIER\0ERROR\0NO DIALTONE\0BUSY\0NO ANSWER\0\0",
  "CLASS 5\0V.42BIS\0\0",
  "LAP-M\0ALT\0\0",
  57600L,
  1,
  1
}
```

## MAKING MODEMS USABLE

The test program in this chapter has three different modems defined in the `ModemCapabilities` database. When writing programs to use the `Modem` class, you might only have to define one or two modem types that are in use by your users. However, a commercial application needs to develop a more comprehensive list of modems. Unfortunately, there isn't a handy source that contains the programming information for all the different modems on the market today.

The various entries in the structure are defined here.

`char *name`

This is simply the name of the modem type being defined. In a typical application, a user would be able to pick a particular modem off a list composed of all the name entries available.

`char *initialization_string`

This is a simple string used to initialize the modem. The initialization string should put the modem into a well-defined state that allows it to work properly with the Modem class. The characteristics of the modem after initialization should include:

1. The modem should give verbose responses to commands. These help the user as much as the programmer. This should include the type of lengthy "CONNECT" messages typically produced using ATX4 or greater.
2. The modem should disconnect if DTR drops.
3. The CD line from the modem should accurately reflect whether the modem is connected to another modem.
4. If available, the modem should use whatever error correcting protocols are available to it, including MNP-4 and V.42 (LAP-M).
5. If available, the modem should also use whatever data compression protocols are available to it, including MNP-5 and V.42bis.
6. The modem should have RTS/CTS handshaking enabled, if available.
7. The modem should have a baud rate locked at a high rate, if available. If the baud rate isn't locked at a level considerably above that of the carrier, data compression won't be particularly useful.

## `char *fail_strings`

This string is a list of response strings that indicate a failure to connect to a remote end. The strings are separated by `'\0'` characters, with the final string being empty. These strings contain messages like "NO CARRIER" and "BUSY." This allows the Modem class to compensate for unusual messages that may be issued by various modems when trying to connect.

## `char *compression_strings`

This string is a list of response strings that indicate a connection was made using data compression. Most modems will issue a connect message the looks something like this when data compression is being used:

```
CONNECT /MNP
```

Since many modems support various sorts of data compression, they can potentially have more than one string indicating that compression takes place. This list of strings can handle as many as each modem can issue.

## `char *protocol_strings`

Just as with data compression, each modem has the potential to handle several sorts of error correcting protocols. This string gives the substrings to scan for when a connect message occurs. If any one of them is found to be a match, it can be assumed that the connection will have an error correcting protocol in place.

## `long initial_baud_rate`

This is the baud rate the Modem class should use to communicate with the modem initially. This value should be set as high as the modem can accommodate.

`int locked_baud_rate`

This boolean flag is used to indicate that the modem is configured to have a locked baud rate. This means that the modem will continue to communicate with the PC at a fixed baud rate, regardless of the speed of the connection. This is the normal state of affairs for any modem that supports either data compression or error correcting protocols. It also implies that the modem must support handshaking.

`int handshaking`

This boolean flag is used to indicate that the modem support RTS/CTS handshaking. Most modems today will have to use this to support advanced communications features.

### Creating a capability entry

Most modems come with a booklet that contains at least 30 or 40 pages describing the various programming options available to the end user. It might seem like a rather difficult job to come up with a new entry for each and every modem. Fortunately, most modems have some common features.

Nearly every modem sold today will support the "AT&F" option. This option is used to restore all modem settings to their factory defaults. The factory defaults are designed to mimic the Hayes standard as well as possible. Once at that starting point, it is simply a matter of scanning each option and seeing if a deviation from the default value is necessary.

Two variations that are usually needed are the two that make DTR and CD into useful control lines. These are usually accomplished with the "&C1" and "&D2" options.

Most modems by default will have their protocol and error compression capabilities enabled, which will usually implies both hardware handshaking and a locked baud rate.

Finally, you will generally want to find the best way to issue as much information as possible during negotiations and connection. The ATX commands are generally where this takes place.

## SERIAL COMMUNICATIONS: A C++ DEVELOPER'S GUIDE

**The Modem class**

Taking advantage of this information requires the use of the Modem class. This class is not particularly complex, but it will take care of the tasks that most communications programs are going to need. These include:

1. Initializing the modem and the port line parameters.
2. Dialing out and waiting for a connection. Once the connection is made, determining the parameters of the connection.
3. Alternatively, answering an incoming call and waiting for a connection.
4. Disconnecting when the call is complete.

All of these things are accomplished by the Modem class, using virtually every modem on the market today that advertises itself as being "Hayes compatible."

Listing 9-1 shows a listing of MODEM.H, the header file that contains the class definition for the Modem class. Any program wanting to take advantage of the class needs to include this file. The public interface to the class consists of 14 member functions and a constructor.

```
// ********************* START OF MODEM.H *********************

// This header file has all of the definitions and prototypes
// needed to use the Modem class. This file should be included
// by any module that uses the Modem class.

#ifndef _MODEM_DOT_H
#define _MODEM_DOT_H

#include "rs232.h"

enum ModemError {   MODEM_SUCCESS            = 0,
                    MODEM_NO_RESPONSE        = -100,
                    MODEM_NO_CONNECTION      = -101,
                    MODEM_DISCONNECT_FAILED  = -102,
                    MODEM_USER_ABORT         = -103 };

// This structure defines the layout of the modem capability
```

# MAKING MODEMS USABLE

```cpp
// database elements. At present, all of the definitions that
// can be used to define a particular brand or type of modem
// are stored in a static array in MODEM.CPP. A commercial
// application might store these off line in a datatbase.

struct ModemCapabilities {
    char *name;
    char *initialization_string;
    char *fail_strings;
    char *compression_strings;
    char *protocol_strings;
    long initial_baud_rate;
    int locked_baud_rate;
    int handshaking;
};

// The Modem class definition

class Modem {
    protected :
        RS232 *port;
        ModemCapabilities *modem_data;
        long local_baud_rate;
        int tone_dial;
        int protocol;
        int compressing;
        ModemError wait_for_response( void );
        ModemError wait_for_connection( void );
        long carrier_timeout;
        virtual void echo( char c ) { cout << c; }
        void read_line( char *buffer, int buf_size );

    public :
        Modem( RS232 &rs232_port, char *modem_name );
        ModemError Initialize( void );
        ModemError Answer( void );
        ModemError Dial( char *number );
        ModemError Disconnect( void );
        ModemError SendCommand( char * );
```

```
            int ReadRegister( int reg );
            virtual ModemError UserAbort( void );
            void PulseDial( void ){ tone_dial = 0; }
            void ToneDial( void ){ tone_dial = 1; }
            void SetCarrierTimeout( long length )
                            { carrier_timeout = length; }
            char *ErrorName( ModemError status );
            virtual void DumpState( void );
            int Protocol( void ){ return protocol; }
            int Compressing( void ){ return compressing; }};

#endif // #ifdef _MODEM_DOT_H

// ********************* END OF MODEM.H *********************
```

**Listing 9-1. MODEM.H**

### The public interface

The 14 functions and constructor that define the public interface are all relatively straightforward. You can use the descriptions in this section to help illuminate the code listing shown in Listing 9-2, which immediately follows.

```
Modem( RS232 &rs232_port, char *modem_name )
```

The constructor for an object of class Modem takes two arguments. First, it needs a reference to an RS232 port that is actually attached to the modem. Second, it needs the name of the type of modem that is being used. The name would normally be pulled out of a configuration file, or picked from a list of entries in a database.

The constructor initializes a couple of private data members, but doesn't actually manipulate the port or the modem. This is done when the program decides it is time, in the next member function, Initialize().

# MAKING MODEMS USABLE

**`ModemError Initialize( void )`**

This function has the job of initializing both the modem and the serial port. Initializing the modem consists of just sending the initialization string down and waiting for the appropriate response, usually an "OK" message. This function also turns on RTS/CTS handshaking, if the modem supports it, and sets the baud rate to the initial rate specified in the `ModemCapabilities` database entry.

**`ModemError Answer( void )`**

An incoming ring on the modem can be detected in one of two ways. First, the actual "RING" message can be read in on the serial port. This is probably the most reliable way to detect the ring. Second, the RI line from the UART can be monitored using calls to `RS232::Ri()`.

Once the ring is detected, this function can be called to cause the modem to go off-hook and attempt to answer the call. It will take care of sending the message, then waiting for the appropriate CONNECT or NO CARRIER message to be read in. It will also detect whether the call established an error correcting protocol, and whether it is using data compression.

If the modem doesn't support locked baud rates, the baud rate reported by the modem as part of the CONNECT message will be applied to the port using the `RS232::Set()` function, so that communications can begin immediately.

If the call was properly answered, `MODEM_SUCCESS` is returned from the function. Otherwise one of the `ModemError` status codes is returned.

**`ModemError Dial( char *number )`**

This function is almost the same as the `Answer()` function. Instead of going off-hook in response to an incoming ring, however, this function initiates the process by causing the modem to dial a digit string of the programmer's selection. It then goes through the same verification procedure while waiting for a response, and returns the same `ModemError` status codes.

**ModemError Disconnect( void )**

This function is called to break down a call in progress. Since the `Initialize()` function is supposed to set the modem up properly, all it should take to hang up is to drop the DTR line for a second. This function does that first, then checks to see if the modem has responded by disconnecting.

If the modem failed to disconnect when DTR was dropped (which may be the case for some modems that don't allow software control of this feature), the "+++" escape sequence is sent, followed by the ATH0 command. If this fails to disconnect the modem, about the only choice left is the power switch.

This modem returns either `MODEM_SUCCESS` or one of the other `Modem Error` codes.

**ModemError SendCommand( char * )**

This function is provided to give the programmer the ability to send strings to the modem and monitor for the proper receipt of the "OK" response code.

**int ReadRegister( int reg )**

This function sends the "ATSr?" command to the modem requesting that the modem provide the current contents of one of its status registers. The response is then read back from the modem and returned to the calling routine. If the value is less than zero, it indicates that an error occurred, and the return value should be translated to be of type `ModemErrror` for interpretation.

**virtual ModemError UserAbort( void )**

Many of the modem functions can take a long time. Functions such as `Modem::Dial()` may take 60 seconds or more to finish to completion. This virtual function is called periodically to check for a user-initiated abort. The base class definition just checks for incoming keystrokes, and aborts if the user has hit a key. Derived classes are free to implement their own abort procedures.

```
void PulseDial( void )
void ToneDial( void )
```

These two functions are used to set the default dialing type. They act by just modifying the `tone_dial` member to be either true or false.

```
void SetCarrierTimeout( long length )
```

By default, the `Dial()` and `Answer()` functions will wait 60 seconds for a connection to be established before timing out and returning a failure. This function allows the programmer to modify this time. The single parameter is the new time value, in milliseconds.

```
char *ErrorName( ModemError status )
```

This function translates `ModemError` status codes to ASCII strings, suitable for display to end users.

```
virtual void DumpState( void )
```

This function is used to print out the current status of the `Modem` object. It isn't as sophisticated as the status function used in the RS232 class. The function is defined as virtual to allow for derived class improvements.

```
int Protocol( void )
int Compressing( void )
```

These two functions are simply access functions that provide read-only access to protected member functions. The first is used to determine whether an error correcting protocol is in use in the current connection. The second indicates whether data compression is in effect.

## Protected members

The `Modem` class has a few protected data members and functions that are used internally to support various features of the class.

### RS232 *port

This is a pointer to the port that the modem is attached to. The `Modem` class doesn't need to be a friend to the `RS232` class, since it only uses the publicly available functions. However, it does need to keep a pointer to the port so that it can access the various functions and members assigned to the port.

### ModemCapabilities *modem_data

This is a pointer to the capability structure passed using the constructor. It is referred to at various points by many of the member functions.

### long local_baud_rate

The local baud rate is the rate that the modem changes to when either the `Dial()` or `Answer()` functions connect to another modem. If the modem is using a locked rate, this rate will be the same as the initial baud rate. Otherwise, it will be the rate that the modem indicated it was using in the CONNECT message.

### int tone_dial

This member is a boolean flag indicating whether or not the modem should always dial using tone mode.

### int protocol

When a connection is made, this boolean flag is set or cleared to indicate whether or not an error correcting protocol is in use.

```
int compressing
```

This boolean flag is used to indicate whether a data compression protocol is in effect for the current call.

```
ModemError wait_for_response( void )
```

Most modem functions require sending a command to the modem, then waiting for an "OK" response from the modem. This internal protected function is called to wait for that "OK" message. This is used whenever a command is sent to the modem to ensure that the modem actually received the message and responded to it.

```
ModemError wait_for_connection( void );
```

This function is called by both the `Dial()` and `Answer()` functions. It waits for the modem to indicate either that it has successfully answered an incoming call, or it has failed to establish carrier. This function will also scan all of the strings issued by the modem to check for the presence of data compression and error correcting protocols.

```
long carrier_timeout
```

The amount of time in milliseconds that the modem will wait for carrier when either dialing or answering.

```
virtual void echo( char c )
```

During any of the modem activity, there will normally be a lot of data being sent back and forth between the modem and the computer. An echo routine is provided to allow the user to see what is happening. By default, the base class defines the echo routine as just a simple output to `cout`. Derived classes are free to extend this as they wish.

# SERIAL COMMUNICATIONS: A C++ DEVELOPER'S GUIDE

**void read_line( char *buffer, int buf_size );**

This function is used internally to read in lines of response from the modem. It operates somewhat differently from the RS232::Read() function, in that it will timeout quickly if no data is coming in. As long as characters continue coming in at least once every half second, it will keep reading until an entire line has been assembled.

This function also echoes the input characters as they are read.

```
// ********************* START OF MODEM.CPP *********************

// This file contains all of the code for the Modem class. It should
// be compiled and linked with any program wanting to use the class.

#include <conio.h>
#include <string.h>
#include <stdlib.h>
#include <stdio.h>
#include <ctype.h>
#include "portable.h"
#include "rs232.h"
#include "modem.h"

// The modem capability database is used to define all of the
// attributes used by a particular brand of modem. These are
// stored in the application, which is practical when just a few
// are defined. A bigger database might have to be moved into a
// conventional file.

ModemCapabilities ModemDataBase[] = {
{ "Hayes Compatible",
  "AT &F &C1 &D2",
  "NO CARRIER\0ERROR\0NO DIALTONE\0BUSY\0NO ANSWER\0\0",
  "",
  "",
```

```
        2400L,
        0,
        0
    },
    { "Practical Peripherals 14400FX",
        "AT &F0 &C1 &D2 S95=44",
        "NO CARRIER\0ERROR\0NO DIALTONE\0BUSY\0NO ANSWER\0\0",
        "CLASS 5\0V.42BIS\0\0",
        "LAP-M\0ALT\0\0",
        57600L,
        1,
        1
    },
    { "Intel SatisFAXtion 400e",
        "AT &F",
        "NO CARRIER\0ERROR\0NO DIALTONE\0BUSY\0NO ANSWER\0\0",
        "COMP\0\0",
        "LAPM\0MNP\0REL\0\0",
        57600L,
        1,
        1
    },
    { ""
} };

// The modem constructor sets up the capability database for the
// modem of the particular name, but doesn't do much else. If the
// brand name modem is not found via an exact match, the generic
// Hayes compatible definition is used.

Modem::Modem( RS232 &rs232_port, char *modem_name )
{
    int i;

    port = &rs232_port;
    modem_data = &ModemDataBase[ 0 ];
    for ( i = 0 ; *ModemDataBase[ i ].name != '\0' ; i++ ) {
        if ( strcmp( modem_name, ModemDataBase[ i ].name ) == 0 ) {
            modem_data = &ModemDataBase[ i ];
```

```
                break;
        }
    }
    tone_dial = 1;
    carrier_timeout = 60000L;
}


// The usual translation routine is used to print out the error
// names in more descriptive form.

char *Modem::ErrorName( ModemError status )
{
    switch ( status ) {
        case MODEM_SUCCESS          : return "Success";
        case MODEM_NO_RESPONSE      : return "No Response";
        case MODEM_NO_CONNECTION    : return "No Connection";
        case MODEM_DISCONNECT_FAILED : return "Disconnect failed";
        case MODEM_USER_ABORT       : return "User abort";
        default                     : return "Unknown Error";
    }
}


// The initialization routine just has to send out the initializa-
// tion string, then wait for a response. It inserts an extra one
// second delay in this routine, because some modems need a little
// extra time to handle initialization.

ModemError Modem::Initialize( void )
{
    long delay_time;

    port->Set( modem_data->initial_baud_rate );
    port->RtsCtsHandshaking( modem_data->handshaking );
    port->Write( '\r' );
    delay_time = ReadTime() + 1000;
    while ( ReadTime() < delay_time )
        port->IdleFunction();
    port->Write( modem_data->initialization_string );
    port->Write( '\r' );
    return wait_for_response();
```

}

```
// This protected routine is used to read lines of data back from
// the modem, generally after a response to a command. It reads the
// characters in, echos them using the echo routine, and tries to
// assemble a complete line. A "\n" character is used to terminate
// the line, or a timeout.

void Modem::read_line( char *buffer, int buf_size )
{
    int c;

    for ( ; ; ) {
        c = port->Read( 500 );
        if ( c < 0 )
            break;
        echo( (char) c );
        *buffer++ = (char) c;
        if ( —buf_size <= 1 )
            break;
        if ( c == '\n' )
            break;
    }
    *buffer = '\0';
}

// This protected routine is used to wait for an "OK" message
// after a modem command is sent. If it doesn't get it within
// 2 seconds, an error is returned. Most commands going to the
// modem can expect an "OK" response. The two notable exceptions
// are the dialing and answer commands.

ModemError Modem::wait_for_response( void )
{
    long timeout;
    char buffer[ 81 ];
    ModemError status;

    timeout = ReadTime() + 2000;
```

```
    while ( ReadTime() < timeout ) {
        read_line( buffer, 81 );
        if ( strncmp( buffer, "OK", 2 ) == 0 )
            return MODEM_SUCCESS;
        if ( ( status = UserAbort() ) != MODEM_SUCCESS )
            return status;
    }
    return MODEM_NO_RESPONSE;
}

// During dialing, the Dial() routine has to scan the input stream
// for lots of different strings that can indicate various things
// about protocols, data compression, and connections. This command
// is used to scan for a list of strings stored in the format used
// by the modem capability database.

char *scan_strings( char *buffer, char *strings )
{
    char *p;

    while ( *strings ) {
        if ( ( p = strstr( buffer, strings ) ) != 0 )
            return p;
        strings += strlen( strings ) + 1;
    }
    return p;
}

// This routine is called by both the Answer and Dial routines.
// It has to scan the incoming lines of data not just for the
// "CONNECT" message, but also the protocol and compression strings
// as well. Additionally, if the baud rate is not locked, it has
// to detect the new baud rate on connection.

ModemError Modem::wait_for_connection( void )
{
    long timeout;
    char *connect;
    char buffer[ 81 ];
    ModemError status;
```

```
        compressing = 0;
        protocol = 0;
        timeout = ReadTime() + carrier_timeout;
        while ( ReadTime() < timeout ) {
            read_line( buffer, 81 );
            if ( scan_strings( buffer, modem_data->fail_strings ) )
                return MODEM_NO_CONNECTION;
            if (scan_strings(buffer,modem_data->compression_strings ) )
                compressing = 1;
            if ( scan_strings( buffer, modem_data->protocol_strings ) )
                protocol = 1;
            if ( ( connect = strstr( buffer, "CONNECT" ) ) != 0 ) {
                if ( !modem_data->locked_baud_rate ) {
                    local_baud_rate = atol( connect + 8 );
                    if ( local_baud_rate !=0 )
                        port->Set( local_baud_rate );
                } else
                    local_baud_rate = modem_data->initial_baud_rate;
                return MODEM_SUCCESS;
            }
            if ( ( status = UserAbort() ) != MODEM_SUCCESS )
                return status;
        }
        return MODEM_NO_CONNECTION;
}

// This routine dials and then has another routine do the hard work
// of waiting for a response.

ModemError Modem::Dial( char *dial_string )
{

    port->Write( "ATD" );
    if ( tone_dial )
        port->Write( 'T' );
    else
        port->Write( 'P' );
    port->Write( dial_string );
```

```cpp
    port->Write( '\r' );
    return wait_for_connection();
}

// This routine sends the answer command, then lets the other rou
// tine wait for success or failure.

ModemError Modem::Answer( void )
{
    port->Write( "ATA\r" );
    return wait_for_connection();
}

// Although all of the modems in the database are supposed to be
// set up so that dropping DTR causes a disconnect, some may slip
// through the net. If dropping DTR doesn't cause a disconnect, the
// escape sequence is sent, followed by a Hangup message.

ModemError Modem::Disconnect( void )
{
    long delay_time;

    port->Dtr( 0 );
    delay_time = ReadTime() + 1250;
    while ( ReadTime() < delay_time )
        port->IdleFunction();
    port->Dtr( 1 );
    port->Write( "AT\r" );
    if ( wait_for_response() == MODEM_SUCCESS ) {
        port->Set( modem_data->initial_baud_rate );
        return MODEM_SUCCESS;
    }
    port->Write( "+++" );
    delay_time = ReadTime() + 1250;
    wait_for_response();
    port->Write( "ATH0\r" );
    if ( wait_for_response() == MODEM_SUCCESS ) {
        port->Set( modem_data->initial_baud_rate );
        return MODEM_SUCCESS;
```

# MAKING MODEMS USABLE

```
    }
    return MODEM_DISCONNECT_FAILED;
}

// This routine gives the user an opportunity to abort during long
// sequences, such as dialing.

ModemError Modem::UserAbort( void )
{
    if ( !kbhit() )
        return MODEM_SUCCESS;
    getch();
    return MODEM_USER_ABORT;
}

// ReadRegister() not only asks for the register value, it then
// scans it in and converts it from ASCII to binary so it can be
// used by the program.

int Modem::ReadRegister( int reg )
{
    char buffer[ 81 ];
    long timeout;
    int value;
    ModemError status;

    sprintf( buffer, "ATS%d?\r", reg );
    port->Write( buffer );
    timeout = ReadTime() + 3000;
    value = (int) MODEM_NO_RESPONSE;
    while ( timeout > ReadTime() ) {
        read_line( buffer, 80 );
        if ( strncmp( buffer, "OK", 2 ) == 0 )
            break;
        if ( ( status = UserAbort() ) != MODEM_SUCCESS )
            return status;
        if ( isdigit( *buffer ) )
            value = atoi( buffer );
```

```cpp
    }
    return value;
}

// This is the generic routine to send a command of your choice. It
// assumes the command will get an OK message in return.

ModemError Modem::SendCommand( char *command )
{
    port->Write( command );
    port->Write( '\r' );
    return wait_for_response();
}

// This routine is generally only useful during debugging. It
// dumps the state of the Modem structure out to the screen.

void Modem::DumpState( void )
{
    char *p;

    cout << "\nModem Status:\n\n"
         << "Name:                 "
         << modem_data->name << '\n';
    cout << "Init string:          "
         << modem_data->initialization_string << '\n';
    cout << "Fail strings:         ";
    p = modem_data->fail_strings;
    while ( *p ) {
        cout << p;
        p += strlen( p ) + 1;
        if ( *p )
            cout << ", ";
    }
    cout << '\n';
    cout << "Compression strings:  ";
    p = modem_data->compression_strings;
    while ( *p ) {
        cout << p;
```

```cpp
            p += strlen( p ) + 1;
            if ( *p )
                cout << ", ";
        }
        cout << '\n';
        cout << "Protocol strings:     ";
        p = modem_data->protocol_strings;
        while ( *p ) {
            cout << p;
            p += strlen( p ) + 1;
            if ( *p )
                cout << ", ";
        }
        cout << '\n';
        cout << "Initial baud rate:    "
            << modem_data->initial_baud_rate << '\n';
        cout << "Baud rate locked:     "
            << (( modem_data->locked_baud_rate ) ? 'Y' : 'N') << '\n';
        cout << "Hardware handshaking: "
            << (( modem_data->handshaking ) ? 'Y' : 'N') << '\n';
        cout << "Dialing method:       "
            << (( tone_dial ) ? "Tone" : "Pulse" ) << '\n';
        cout << "Carrier timeout:      " << carrier_timeout << '\n';
        cout << "Connected:            "
            << (( port->Cd() ) ? 'Y' : 'N' ) << '\n';
        if ( !port->Cd() )
            return;
        cout << "Local baud rate:      " << local_baud_rate << '\n';
        cout << "Compressing:          "
            << (( compressing ) ? 'Y' : 'N' ) << '\n';
        cout << "Protocol:             "
            << (( protocol ) ? 'Y' : 'N' ) << '\n';
}

// ********************* END OF MODEM.CPP *********************
```

**Listing 9-2. MODEM.CPP**

## A Test Program

Listing 9-3 shows a listing for a short test program, TSTMODEM.CPP, that is used to test out some of the modem functions. It is just a small terminal emulator that has a special menu that exercises a few of the modem functions. Figure 9-3 is a screen shot showing the program in progress.

The menu for the test program can be accessed at any time by pressing the Escape key. The eight functions available from the menu provide the ability to exercise most of the functions in class Modem:

Answer: This function is used to invoke the Answer() command. It will wait for the amount of time specified in the carrier_timeout variable before giving up. The function prints out the results when it returns, either with a successful acquisition of carrier or a timeout.

Exit: Quit the TSTMODEM program and return to the O/S.

Dial: This invokes the Dial() function, which dials out to the hard-coded number specified in TSTMODEM.CPP. The result returned from the function is printed out afterwards. Remember that the default abort function lets you quit by just pressing any key.

Hangup: The Hangup() function is invoked by the this menu selection.

Initialize: This menu selection executes the Initialize() function. This function is also automatically called when the program starts up.

Product-Id: The SendCommand() function is called with "ATI0" as the command string by this menu selection. This just causes the modem to spit out a product ID code, which is not normally too meaningful. It just provides a way to test the SendCommand() member function with your modem.

## MAKING MODEMS USABLE

Read-regs: This menu selection uses the `ReadRegister()` command to read the contents of the first 10 S registers of the modem. It then prints them out.

Status: This command invokes the `DumpState()` member function, providing a snapshot of the state of the `Modem` objects. Figure 9-3 shows a screen shot immediately after this menu item is invoked.

**Figure 9-3. A Screen Shot from TSTMODEM.EXE**

```cpp
// ******************** START OF TSTMODEM.CPP ********************

// This short program is used to test the Modem class. It is a
// very simple terminal emulator that can accept just a few
// commands.

#include <ctype.h>
#include "rs232.h"
#include "pc8250.h"
#include "modem.h"

int handle_command( Modem &modem );

// The main routine just acts as a terminal emulator. It invokes
// a command handler if the escape key is pressed.

int main()
{
    int c;
    PC8250 port( COM1, 19200 );
    Modem modem( port, "Practical Peripherals 14400FX" );
    ModemError init;

    init = modem.Initialize();
    cout << "\nInitialization returned:   "
         << modem.ErrorName( init )
```

```
            << '\n';
    for ( ; ; ) {
        if ( kbhit() ) {
            c = getch();
            if ( c == 27 ) {
                if ( handle_command( modem ) )
                    break;
            } else
                port.Write( c );
        }
        if ( ( c = port.Read() ) > 0 )
            cout << (char) c;
        cout.flush(); // Needed by Zortech and Microsoft
    }
    return 0;
}

// The command handler is used to send various commands to the
// modem via the normal modem class. It prints a help prompt so you
// will know exactly what your choice of commands is.

int handle_command( Modem &modem )
{
    int c;
    int i;
    ModemError status;
    char *command;
    int registers[ 11 ];

    cout << "\nAnswer Exit Dial Hangup Initialize "
            "Product-ID Read-regs Status\n\nEnter command: ";
    c = getch();
    cout << (char) c << '\n';
    switch ( toupper( c ) ) {
        case 'A' :
            command = "Answer";
            status = modem.Answer();
            break;
        case 'D' :
```

## MAKING MODEMS USABLE

```cpp
            command = "Dial";
            status = modem.Dial( "1-214-250-3778" );
            break;
        case 'E' :
            return 1;
        case 'H' :
            command = "Hangup";
            status = modem.Disconnect();
            break;
        case 'I' :
            command = "Initialize";
            status = modem.Initialize();
            break;
        case 'P' :
            command = "Product ID code";
            status = modem.SendCommand( "ATI0" );
            break;
        case 'R' :
            for ( i = 1 ; i < 11 ; i++ )
                registers[ i ] = modem.ReadRegister( i );
            for ( i = 1 ; i < 11 ; i++ ) {
                cout << "Register " << i << " = ";
                cout << registers[ i ] << '\n';
            }
            return 0;
        case 'S' :
            modem.DumpState();
            return 0;
        default :
            cout << (char) 7; return 0;
    }
    cout << command << " returned: " << modem.ErrorName( status )
                                                        << '\n';
    return 0;
}

// ****************** END OF TSTMODEM.CPP *********************
```

**Listing 9-3. TSTMODEM.CPP**

```
First Name? Mark Nelson

Answer Exit Dial Hangup Initialize Product-ID Read-regs Status

Enter command: S

Modem Status:

Name:                    Practical Peripherals 14400FX
Init string:             AT &F0 &C1 &D2 S95=44
Fail strings:            NO CARRIER, ERROR, NO DIALTONE, BUSY, NO ANSWER
Compression strings:     CLASS 5, V.42BIS
Protocol strings:        LAP-M, ALT
Initial baud rate:       57600
Baud rate locked:        Y
Hardware handshaking:    Y
Dialing method:          Tone
Carrier timeout:         60000
Connected:               Y
Local baud rate:         57600
Compressing:             Y
Protocol:                Y

NO CARRIER
```

**Figure 9-3. A Screen Shot from TSTMODEM.EXE**

### Making TSTMODEM.CPP

Listing 9-3 shows a sample make file used to build the test program. Instructions on building for the various supported C++ compilers can be found in Appendix A. Note that if you want to use a different type of RS232 object, you can modify both the source code for TSTMODEM.CPP, then modify the FILES listing in the make file.

```
#CC = tcc -w
#CC = bcc -w
#CC = ztc -b
CC = cl /W4 /AL

FILES = pc8250.obj pcirq.obj queue.obj isr_8250.obj

.cpp.obj:
```

```
        $(CC) -c $<

tstmodem.exe : tstmodem.obj rs232.obj msdos.obj modem.obj
$(FILES)
           $(CC) tstmodem.obj rs232.obj msdos.obj
modem.obj $(FILES)
```

**Listing 9-4. TSTMODEM.MAK**

CHAPTER 10

# File Transfers and ZMODEM

For many people, the whole purpose of modems and communications software is to perform file transfers. The amount of new software posted everyday on BBS systems and information services is staggering, and many hobbyists are preoccupied with sampling as much of it as possible. BBS networks around the world transfer huge files full of e-mail every day. Commercial ventures move large files around the world to update remote databases and share information. All of this activity requires the use of file transfer protocols.

## XMODEM and YMODEM

In the late 1970s, modems were just beginning to break into the newly emerging desktop computer market. In response to a lack of established standards for transferring files, Ward Christensen developed what came to be known as the XMODEM file transfer protocol. Enhancements to XMODEM came quickly, resulting in a whole family of protocols, including YMODEM and XMODEM-1K.

The existence of standard protocols that could be used to move files around easily helped fuel the growth of telecommunications, and is responsible for the existence of online informations services, BBS systems, and so on.

XMODEM was not a carefully designed protocol, resulting from intensive research and experimentation. It was much closer to being a weekend project that was meant as a personal utility. Given this original purpose, it has held up as well over time. While it is certainly capable, XMODEM does have a few serious limitations. Among them:

- Protocol control characters aren't "packetized," making the protocol vulnerable to noise and single character errors. The ACK and NAK characters that are sent as responses to blocks aren't surrounded by framing and check characters, so a spurious ACK or EOT at the right time could lead a sender to falsely conclude that a successful transfer occurred.
- XMODEM requires a completely clear 8-bit channel. The channel needs to pass all control characters, including XON, XOFF, CR, and so on. Many older time-sharing systems, (such as some UNIX systems), are not able to meet this requirement. Their device drivers cause certain protocol characters to disappear.
- The short packet lengths used by the XMODEM family, either 128 or 1,024 bytes, result in inefficient use of the channel, since each packet has to be acknowledged before the next one is sent. This is particularly a problem over packet switched networks.

## Enter ZMODEM

In 1986, the packet switched network provider Telenet commissioned Chuck Forsberg of Omen Technology to develop a new file transfer program that could be used effectively over its network. The result was ZMODEM, which consisted of both a public domain program and a new protocol. The name ZMODEM might imply that it was a lineal descendant from XMODEM and YMODEM, but this is not really the case. ZMODEM is a completely new protocol that has very little in common with either of these earlier systems.

ZMODEM has several important characteristics that make it superior to other popular protocols:

- All transactions are protected by either a 16-bit or 32-bit CRC, which greatly reduces the possibility of false ACKs and NAKs.
- The protocol works properly over communications links that absorb some or all control characters, although an 8-bit channel is still required.

- Data is sent in a continuous stream of packets, without waiting for acknowledgments. The protocol only stops sending when the receiver interrupts to report an error. Sending data in a continuous stream drastically improves transmission throughput on packet-switched networks or buffered modems.
- ZMODEM labels data packets uniquely to assist in error recovery. The receiver always knows where a block of data is supposed to be stored in a file. This labeling also helps in file transfer recovery, which allows a user to restart an aborted transfer at the place where it was interrupted.

Because of these superior characteristics, ZMODEM has become one of the most popular protocol choices in use today. This popularity makes ZMODEM the natural choice to use as an illustrative example in this book.

**Why ZMODEM?**

Given a finite amount of space available in this book to discuss file transfer protocols, ZMODEM is the natural choice to make. XMODEM and YMODEM are considerably simpler, and should be relatively easy for a programmer to develop using the tools presented elsewhere in this book. They have been well-documented in various magazines and books before, so this book wouldn't be breaking any new ground covering them.

ZMODEM is somewhat more of a challenge to implement, because it is a much more complex protocol. However, it is not only clearly superior to other protocols, it also is available nearly universally. Many UNIX and other time-sharing machines that don't have XMODEM software available are able to support ZMODEM.

When Chuck Forsberg developed the ZMODEM program for Telenet, he published a set of programs that were placed into the public domain. These programs, commonly referred to as RZ and SZ, were able to transfer files using ZMODEM on a number of UNIX hosts, and were later adapted to VMS. This public domain code has been adapted here to work under MS-DOS, and has been converted to a more object-oriented architecture. While my implementation may look very different from the original RZ/SZ source, it is still driven by core code that is fundamentally identical to that originally published by Chuck Forsberg.

Omen Technology later released versions of RZ and SZ that incorporate proprietary ZMODEM enhancements, such as Run Length Encoding and Variable Length Headers. These extensions are not supported here, although ambitious programmers could certainly add them to the ZMODEM class without too much difficulty. Omen Technology additionally sells quite a few different communications programs targeted for various platforms. Professional-YAM is a package that is a consistent leader in efficient, albeit terse, communications software. Professional-YAM is supported for quite a variety of host machines and operating systems. DSZ is a ubiquitous MS-DOS shareware program that performs ZMODEM file transfers. The release of this program by Omen Technology allowed BBS operators whose software did not work with ZMODEM to begin using the protocol via external protocol hooks.

Both the complete specification for ZMODEM and the RZ/SZ programs are included with the source code for this book. More up-to-date versions of both are available from Omen Technology.

### An overview of ZMODEM

ZMODEM differs from XMODEM in that *all* information transferred between the sender and receiver is contained in packets, referred to in ZMODEM as "frames." Even simple protocol messages, such as acknowledgments, are bundled into packets, giving ZMODEM good protection against accidental protocol signals.

A ZMODEM frame has two components. Every frame starts with a "header," which identifies the frame type, and carries up to four bytes of information. The four bytes are arbitrarily referred to as ZF0 through ZF3 (at positions 3 through 0, respectively). A header can optionally be followed by a stream of "data subpackets," which are blocks of unadorned data.

Data subpackets can each contain up to 1,024 bytes of data, and are followed by a CRC value for authentication. There is no limit to the number of data subpackets that can be attached to a header, which means all of the data for a file can be sent in a single frame.

# FILE TRANSFERS AND ZMODEM

The 18 frame types defined for ZMODEM are defined in the next section. Following that is a an explanation of the methods and options used to encode and send the various frame types.

## ZMODEM frame types

ZRQINIT=0    This frame is sent by the ZMODEM sender when it starts up. It is a request for the receiver to send its ZRINIT frame, which will start the file transfer. The ZRQINIT frame header can be used to trigger an auto-download in a receiving program. This capability is demonstrated in the example program for this chapter.

ZRQINIT frames do not transmit any data subpackets. The header byte ZF0 will contain the constant ZCOMMAND if the sender is attempting to send a command to the receiver (this feature is not supported in the ZMODEM class developed here), otherwise it will contain a 0.

ZRINIT=1    This frame is sent by the receiver to indicate that it is ready to receive files from the sender. It can either be sent spontaneously, or in response to a ZRQINIT frame. This frame has four bytes of capability information packed into the header. The ZF0 and ZF1 have the following bits that can be set or cleared depending on the capabilities of the receiver:

    CANFDX=1    The receiver is capable of true full-duplex operation, meaning it can send and receive data simultaneously. We take this ability for granted in the desktop world, but it is by no means universal.

    CANOVIO=2    The receiver can receive data while writing to the disk. This capability is needed to take full advantage of ZMODEM's streaming nature.

CANBRK=4    The receiver can send a break signal.

CANRLE=8    The receiver can decode RLE frames. This capability is not supported in the Zmodem class used here.

CANLZW=16   The receiver can uncompress data sent in the UNIX compress format. This capability is not supported in the ZMODEM class used here.

CANFC32=32  The receiver can accept 32-bit CRCs.

ESCCTL=64   The receiver needs to see all control characters escaped, instead of just XON, XOFF, and a few others.

ZF2 and ZF3 contain the size of the receiver's input buffer. If this value is nonzero, it means the receiver can't work in full streaming mode. It will instead need to stop receiving while it writes data to disk.

ZSINIT=2    This frame can be optionally sent to the receiver by the sender after the ZRINIT frames is processed. It provides the receiver with some information regarding the sender's capabilities. Two bits are packed into ZF0:

TESCCTL=64  This bit is used to indicate that the transmitter expects *all* control characters to be escaped.

TESC8=128   This bit is used to indicate that the transmitter expects the eighth bit to escape. This capability is not fully implemented by ZMODEM, but is included in the specification for future enhancements.

The ZSINIT header is followed by a single data subpacket. This subpacket contains a null terminated attention string no more than 32 bytes long. This attention string is used to wake up the sender when an error occurs.

# FILE TRANSFERS AND ZMODEM

ZACK=3      This frame type is used to acknowledge ZSINIT and ZCHALLENGE frames, as well as data subpackets followed by the ZCRCQ or ZCRCW terminators. If the response is to a ZCHALLENGE frame, the four header flag bytes are filled with a copy of the four header bytes sent with the ZCHALLENGE header.

ZFILE=4      This is the frame type used to initiate the actual transfer of a file. This frame consists of a header followed by a single data subpacket. The subpacket contains the file information. The four header bytes are packed with various flags relating to the file about to be transfered. ZF0 contains the file conversion option, ZF1 contains an optional management option, ZF2 has the transport option, and ZF3 contains extended options.

This frame has the greatest number of options to consider, and requires the longest explanation. Most of the options here are idiosyncratic, and are rarely used. For our purposes, the important items transmitted in the ZFILE frame will be the file name, length, and, optionally, the date. The rest of the options are detailed here for completeness.

### ZF0 conversion option

ZF0 is set to one of the following values, which dictate the conversion method used when storing the file data.

ZCBIN=1      A binary transfer, data is stored with no conversion.

ZCNL=2      Convert the received end-of-line to use the local conventions. This option can be useful when sending ASCII files between UNIX and MS-DOS systems.

ZCRECOV=3   Recover from an interrupted file transfer. The receiver checks to see if the destination file is shorter than the file to be sent. If it is, the file transfer can be resumed at the point where it was aborted.

**ZF1 management option**

ZF1 is set to one of the following values.

ZMNEWL=1    Overwrite the destination file only if the source is newer or longer.
ZMCRC=2     Compare the CRC values of the source and destination. If the values are different, transfer the file. Otherwise skip the transfer.
ZMAPND=3    Append the source file to the destination.
ZMCLOB=4    Unconditionally write over the destination file if it exists.
ZMNEW=5     If the destination file exists, only overwrite it if the source is newer.
ZMDIFF=6    If the destination file exists, only overwrite it if the files have different lengths or dates.
ZMPROT=7    This option is the opposite of ZMCLOB. It tells the receiver to only transfer the file if the destination file does not exist.

**ZF2 transport option**

ZF2 is set to one of the following options.

ZTLZW=1     The data being sent has been processed via the UNIX compress program. This option is not supported in the ZMODEM class.

## FILE TRANSFERS AND ZMODEM

ZTRLE=3   The data has been compressed using Run Length Encoding. This part of the specification was superseded in later versions of ZMODEM by the creation of proprietary RLE frames.

The missing option 2 belongs to ZCRYPT, an encryption option that was defined in the original ZMODEM specification, but was never implemented.

### ZF3 extended options

ZF3 is a bit map with extended options conditionally set. The only option defined in the ZMODEM spec is the ZTSPARS option, which allows for special processing of "sparse files." This option is defined in the ZMODEM specification, but is rarely if ever supported.

### The data subpacket

The data subpacket that follows the ZFILE header contains information about the file about to be transferred. The following fields are found consecutively in the data frame:

| | |
|---|---|
| Filename: | The filename is a null terminated string. |
| Length: | The length of the file. |
| Date: | The date and time in UNIX format, seconds past January 1, 1970. A value of 0 is used to indicate that the date is unknown. |
| Mode: | The file mode bits, expressed in UNIX format. The mode is set to 0 for files sent from MS-DOS systems. |
| S/N: | A serial number for the transmitting program. |
| Files left: | The number of files remaining to be sent. |
| Bytes left: | The total number for bytes left for the transfer. |

Every field following the file name is optional. Most implementations support the file length and date, but generally no more.

`ZSKIP=5`        This is a nice simple frame. It is sent when the receiver elects to not receive a file the sender has specified in a `ZFILE` frame. It has no data stored in the four header bytes, and doesn't send any data subpackets.

`ZNAK=6`         This is used to indicate that the last header was invalid, for any number of reasons.

`ZABORT=7`       The receiver sends this frame to indicate that the session should be aborted. This frame is usually sent in response to a user initiated cancellation.

`ZFIN=8`         This frame is sent when the sender has no more files to transmit. The receiver responds with a `ZFIN` frame of its own before exiting. Note that an oddity of the ZMODEM specification has the sender issue the two characters `"OO"` after receiving the ZFIN sent by the receiver.

`ZRPOS=9`        This frame can be sent at any time by the receiving program. A 4-byte offset is packed into the 4 bytes of header information. The offset is a request to the receiver to start sending data from that particular position in the file. This can be sent at the start of the file transfer if a recovery is being attempted, or during a transfer if an error is detected in the incoming data stream.

`ZDATA=10`       The four header bytes of this frame contains the file offset for the data to follow. Any number of data subpackets can follow.

`ZEOF=11`	This indicates that all of the file data has been sent. The four header bytes contain the offset of the EOF mark. This option adds reliability to the protocol, protecting against the possibility of a premature EOF on the destination file.

`ZFERR=12`	The sender or receiver can send this if a read/write error occurs while accessing the file. Receiving this frame type causes the session to abort.

`ZCRC=13`	This frame is sent by the receiver to request the 32-bit CRC for the file that has been indicated with the `ZFILE` frame. The sender sends a `ZCRC` frame with the CRC-32 packed into the four header bytes.

`ZCHALLENGE=14`
	This frame is used by the sender to test challenge the receiver. A random number is packed into the four data bytes of the header. The receiver is then responsible for echoing the same four digits back in another `ZCHALLENGE` frame. It isn't entirely clear what the purpose of this frame is, but it is easy enough to implement, so it is usually supported.

`ZCOMPL=15`	This frame is sent by the receiver when a `ZCOMMAND` request has been fulfilled. The four header bytes contain a status code returned from the command.

`ZFREECNT=17`	The sender can request a count from the receiver of free space available on the default volume. The receiver responds with a `ZACK` frame with the free space in bytes packed into the four header bytes.

ZCOMMAND=18   This frame gives the sender the ability to send a command to the receiving system. If ZF0 is set to a 0, the receiver executes the command and returns a ZCOMPL frame when done. If ZF0 is set to ZCACK1, the receiver returns a ZCOMPL packet immediately.

**Header formats**

In principle, if you know the definitions of all of the frame types, and how they interact, you have enough know-how to perform ZMODEM file transfers. In practice, this doesn't give you quite enough information. You also need to know the low-level format used to create headers and data subpackets, as well the techniques used to encode various control characters.

A ZMODEM frame is composed of a header, optionally followed by a stream of data subpackets. The header itself is relatively simple. It has four basic components:

- A header-type byte, indicating which of the three possible header types is being used.
- A frame-type byte, indicating which of the 18 possible frame types is being encoded.
- The four data bytes.
- The header CRC.

Unfortunately for ZMODEM implementors, headers come in three different varieties. A ZMODEM header can be encoded as:

- A HEX header, which is encoded using only printable ASCII characters. If data subpackets follow this header, they will be sent in binary, not HEX.
- A 16-bit CRC binary header. The data subpackets following this header will also be sent in straight binary, for more efficient use of bandwidth.
- A 32-bit CRC binary header. Data subpackets will also be sent in binary, using a 32-bit CRC for reliability.

## FILE TRANSFERS AND ZMODEM

ZMODEM software would be considerably easier to implement if there were only a single header type to contend with, and it isn't entirely clear that these three types offer much more flexibility. But, it's too late to change the specification, so there end up being three different routines for sending a header, instead of just one.

### HEX headers

HEX headers are sent using printable ASCII characters, with the single exception of the ZDLE character (Control X, or ASCII 23). The format is shown below:

ZPAD ZPAD ZDLE B frame-type ZF3 ZF2 ZF1 ZF0 CRC-1 CRC-2 CR LF XON

The leading ZPAD character is defined as the '*'. The ZPAD ZPAD ZDLE sequence is used by the receiver to detect the start of a frame. The character B is used to identify a HEX header. After the "B" character, all of the characters until the trailing CR/LF/XON sequence are hex encoded, meaning a two character printable value is used for every byte instead of the pure binary values.

HEX headers are used exclusively by the receiver when responding to the sender. The sender also uses HEX headers for any frame that doesn't have any data subpackets following the header. The two forms of binary headers are normally used when data subpackets are included in the frame. However, even in that case, the sender can use HEX headers if desired, at some small expense of efficiency.

When a remote sender starts a ZMODEM transfer, it first sends a ZRQINIT frame to the receiver, asking for an ZRINIT frame. On an IBM-PC, this header shows up looking something like this:

**↑B00000000000000

The up-arrow is actually the ZDLE character as displayed using the IBM-PC character set. Not visible are the three trailing characters: a carriage return, line feed, and XON character. The XON character protects the remote end against being shut down by a spurious XOFF generated by noise. Note that this string is the one used by terminal programs to autodetect the start of a ZMODEM file transfer. The 16-bit CRC applies to just the frame type and the four flag bytes.

### 16- and 32-bit CRC Binary headers

HEX headers aren't the most efficient way to send our data. To package information more efficiently, ZMODEM senders use Binary headers. In Binary headers, the information is packaged as single binary characters instead of hex characters, subject to ZMODEM control character encoding.

The format for the two headers are shown below:

16 bit:   ZPAD ZDLE A frame-type ZF3 ZF2 ZF1 ZF0 CRC-1 CRC-2

32 bit:   ZPAD ZDLE C frame-type ZF3 ZF2 ZF1 ZF0 CRC-1 CRC-2 CRC-3 CRC-4

The 32-bit CRC offers slightly higher reliability at the expense of some efficiency. When data subpackets follow the header, the format of the subpackets are determined by the format of the header. Data subpackets following 16-bit binary headers (or optionally the HEX headers) will use 16-bit CRC checking. Data subpackets following 32-bit binary headers will use 32-bit CRC checking. The 32-bit CRC headers can only be used if the receiver sent the CANFC32 bit in the ZRINIT header. The 16- or 32-bit CRC values apply to the frame type and the position flags.

## Data Subpacket Formats

ZMODEM gains some of its greatest efficiency by virtue of the way it sends data subpackets. Immediately following the header, the ZMODEM sender can send as many data subpackets as it wishes. A data subpacket consists of up to 1,024 binary data characters, with some control characters encoded, followed by a ZDLE and a subpacket termination character.

There are four different subpacket termination characters, each of which has a slightly different purpose. All of them indicate that a 16- or 32-bit CRC value will immediately follow. The four different characters also have additional meanings:

## FILE TRANSFERS AND ZMODEM

ZCRCE (h)   This character signals the end of the data subpacket, and the end of the frame. When the receiver sees this at the end of a subpacket, it knows that it needs to start looking for a header next.

ZCRCG (i)   This character terminates the current subpacket, but indicates that there will be at least another subpacket to follow. The receiver needs to check the CRC value that follows and then start receiving a new subpacket.

ZCRCQ (j)   This character terminates the current subpacket, but not the frame. Unlike ZCRCE, however, the receiver has to do more than just verify the checksum of the subpacket. In addition, the receiver needs to send a ZACK frame to indicate that the subpacket was received successfully.

ZCRCW (k)   This character terminates both the subpacket and the frame. After verifying the CRC, the receiver can expect a new header to start the next frame. This termination character also indicates that the receiver needs to send a ZACK to verify the receipt of the subpacket and the frame.

During normal file transfer, a ZMODEM sender could just send the entire file contents in a series of data subpackets, using ZCRCG to terminate every subpacket except the last. The last subpacket could be terminated with a ZCRCW, which would cause the receiver to acknowledge correct receipt of the entire frame. After receiving a ZACK, the sender would be assured that all of the data was properly received.

Under many circumstances, however, the sender may want to elicit ZACK frames on a more regular basis. One good example is when the sender is transmitting through a sophisticated modem with a large internal buffer. Some of these modems can buffer up as much as 20K worth of data. If the data subpackets are all being sent through a modem like this, the sender can load up the modem and get far out-of-sync with the receiver. If an error occurs, and the receiver issues a ZNAK, it may have to wade through 20K of data before getting caught back up with the sender. This leads to inefficient error recovery.

To solve this problem, the ZMODEM sender can use a predefined window size to regulate the synchronization between the sender and receiver. By issuing a `ZCRCQ` terminator once per every 4K or so, the sender can then wait for an acknowledgment before advancing to the next 4K window.

### Encoding

When sending binary data, either as part of a header or a data subpacket, ZMODEM needs to encode certain characters that act as control characters to the transmission medium. The characters encoded this way are:

```
CAN  (ZDLE)
DLE              DLE  + 0x80
XON              XON  + 0x80
XOFF             XOFF + 0x80
```

In addition, ZMODEM accommodates a special Telenet escape sequence, @-CR-@, by escaping CR and CR + 0x80 if the previous character was a @. Finally, if the receiver needs it, <u>all</u> control characters can be escaped if the `TESCCTL` bit is set in the `ZRINIT` frame.

Escaped characters will all be specially encoded by sending first a `ZDLE`, then the character ORed with 0x40, converting them to printable characters. The ZMODEM receiver can then just check for incoming `ZDLE` characters, and if the following character is between 0x40 and 0x5f, it converts it to its original form by clearing the 0x40 bit.

If the character following the `ZDLE` is greater than 0x5f, it is normally one of the four subpacket termination characters. However, ZMODEM also has special encoding for the noncontrol `DEL` character, ASCII 0x7f. Since the terminal interfaces on many operating systems treats `DEL` as a backspace character, ZMODEM can encode both 0x7f and 0xff using a `ZDLE` escape sequence. In these cases, 0x7f is encoded as `ZDLE` followed by "l," and 0xff is encoded as `ZDLE` followed by "m." Our ZMODEM class doesn't have to encode these characters this way, but it does have to decode them if they are encountered in the input stream.

Finally, when reading data, ZMODEM ignores incoming XON and XOFF characters, since they can't occur naturally in the incoming data stream.

# FILE TRANSFERS AND ZMODEM

The `ZDLE` escape encoding used by ZMODEM can exact a heavy performance penalty on file transfers, and they represent perhaps the weakest point of the protocol. A file that contains data that must be heavily escaped can take substantially longer to transfer using ZMODEM as compared to another streaming protocol such as YMODEM-G.

## Odds and ends

ZMODEM has a couple of loose ends that don't fit naturally into the frame/header/subpacket hierarchy. One of the first oddities is that ZMODEM senders typically send a single ASCII test line ahead of their `ZRQINIT` frame. The text of this line is `"rz\r"`. On a system using a command line interface this line has the potential to start the RZ program if it has not already been invoked. While this is certainly not a good general-purpose way to wake up a receiver, it doesn't do any harm, so most implementations leave it in.

An even stranger convention is that of sending the `"OO"` string after the `ZFIN` frame is seen from the ZMODEM receiver. The ZMODEM specification says these characters stand for "Over and Out." The exact purpose of this Dick Tracy reference is never made clear, but once again, since it does no harm, most implementations leave it in place.

Finally, it is possible to abort a ZMODEM transfer with a simple string of five consecutive `CAN` characters. While this is not a legitimate ZMODEM frame, it does make sense to have it as an option. First of all, if a ZMODEM sender or receiver already thinks it is in the middle of receiving a data subpacket, it may ignore a `ZABORT` or `ZFIN` frame. However, it will recognize the five consecutive `CAN` characters, regardless of the state of its present input. Secondly, this is an easy sequence to type from the keyboard, allowing a manual abort of a ZMODEM transfer. Finally, the same sequence can be used to abort an XMODEM or YMODEM file transfer in progress, which gives it a nice universal touch.

| SENDER | | RECEIVER | |
|---|---|---|---|
| The sender requests that the receiver send its initialization parameters. | **ZRQINIT** | | |
| | | **ZRINIT** | The receiver responds with a frame that gives most of its capabilities. |
| The sender provides the name of the file to be transferred, along with some optional data regarding its length, date, and so on. | **ZFILE** | | |
| | | **ZRPOS** | The receiver requests the file data starting at a certain location. For a new file this would normally be location 0. |
| A single data frame containing all of the file's contents is sent. All data subpackets are terminated with ZCRCG, except the last which is terminated with ZCRCE. | **ZDATA** | | |
| Once all of the data has been sent, the end of file is indicated. | **ZEOF** | | |
| | | **ZRINIT** | The receiver indicates it is ready to start over with a new file. |
| The sender indicates that it wants to terminate the session. If the sender had more files to send here, it would send another ZFILE frame. | **ZFIN** | | |
| | | **ZFIN** | The receiver agrees, and the connection is broken. |

**Figure 10-1. The simplest ZMODEM file transfer**

## A file transfer

All of these frames get put together in a relatively straightforward manner to perform a file transfer. Despite the complexity of ZMODEM at the lowest level, it has an appealing simplicity from a high-level point of view. To send a single file requires just a total of nine frames. Each additional file adds just another four frames to the total.

Figure 10-1 shows the steps that are necessary to perform the most minimal possible file transfer. This might be exactly how you would want ZMODEM to operate for two computers that were directly connected and didn't have to contend with high error rates, and large buffer sizes.

ZMODEM transfers taking place using modems in somewhat noisy environments will be modified somewhat from this simple model. The place where the major change takes place is in the way the data subpackets are sent in the ZDATA frame. Instead of terminating every data subpacket with ZCRCG, a subpacket will be terminated with ZCRCQ every 4K or so.

Terminating subpackets with ZCRCQ provokes a ZACK response from the receiver. The sender can use this response to pace itself, insuring that it doesn't get too far ahead of the receiver by simply waiting for a ZACK before it sends another subpacket terminated with ZCRCQ.

Additional frames are sent if a CRC error occurs while reading a data subpacket. When an error occurs, the receiver issues a ZRPOS frame with an offset indicating where it would like the sender to resume. After sending the ZRPOS frame, the receiver then has to wait while data stacked up in the buffers is flushed. Eventually, a new ZDATA frame will start, and its position should match up with that most recently requested.

With the large number of frame types available in the ZMODEM specification, there are quite a large number of possible interactions in the model. Most of them are not explicitly defined in the specification, which means they are defined by default by the operation of the RZ and SZ programs. Fortunately, most programs that use ZMODEM for file transfers don't attempt to do much more than that shown in the simplest transaction from Figure 10-1.

### The FileTransfer class

While this book only has source code for a single file transfer protocol, it still makes sense to try and leave room for more possibilities in the high-level design. I did this by defining a high-level virtual base called FileTransfer. This base class defines most of the elements needed by all file transfers, and leaves the specific definitions to the derived classes.

```
class FileTransfer {
    protected :
        virtual void error( char *fmt, ... );
        virtual void status( char *fmt, ... );
        RS232 *port;
        FILE *file;
        long file_length;
        long byte_count;
        int file_count;
```

```
            char file_name[ 128 ];
            char buffer[ 1025 ];
        public :
            virtual int Send( char *files[] ) = 0;
            virtual int Receive( char *file ) = 0;
};
```

The public interface to the `FileTransfer` class is nice and simple. It has a single function called to send files, and another to receive files. The `Send()` function takes an array of file names as an argument, making it possible for file transfer protocols to send multiple files. Some protocols, such as XMODEM, will only be able to send a single file, but they will still be able use the file name array as an acceptable way to get the name. The `Receive()` function also takes a file name, allowing it to receive a file using protocols such as XMODEM, or perhaps an ASCII Capture mode. Protocols such as ZMODEM or Kermit that transfer file names along with data will simply ignore this argument.

The protected members of this class contain data elements and functions that are needed by virtually every protocol that could be derived from these classes.

```
virtual void error( char *fmt, ... )
virtual void status( char *fmt, ... )
```

These two functions are used by the derived class to provide status information to the user. The status routine should be called periodically, allowing an application program to update any progress information that is maintained for the file transfer. The error routine is called whenever some anomalous event takes place. The presumption here is that the application program will probably want to handle these two things differently.

Both of these functions are expected to be able to handle a variable number of arguments which will be formatted by one of the functions in the `printf` family.

```
RS232 *port
```

This is a pointer to the port where the file transfer will take place. The ZMODEM constructor takes this port as its only argument.

# FILE TRANSFERS AND ZMODEM

`FILE *file`

This is a pointer to the handle for the file currently being transferred, whether for input or output.

`long file_length`

This is the expected length of the file being transferred. In some cases, such as with an XMODEM receiver, the file transfer routines may not know what the expected file length is. In these cases, the length should be set to -1.

`long byte_count`

This is the current count of bytes that have been transferred.

`int file_count`

This is a count of the number of files that have been transferred so far.

`char file_name[ 128 ]`

This buffer contains a copy of the name of the file presently being transferred.

`char buffer[ 1025 ]`

This buffer holds a block of data that has either been read from the file in preparation for sending, or is being accumulated in preparation for being written to the file. None of the protocols being used here have a need for a buffer longer than this, although many can get by with less. It may be preferable to design the class so that this is a void pointer, and the actual size is determined when the constructor executes. Doing it this way just makes the class somewhat simpler.

### The Zmodem class

The `Zmodem` class is directly derived from the `FileTransfer` class. It makes use of all the protected elements in the base class, and has its own virtual functions to implement the `Send()` and `Receive()` routines. It has a single constructor, which takes an `RS232` port object as its only argument.

Using the `Zmodem` class is very simple. After opening a port, the `Zmodem` object can be constructed at any time. Once it exists, a simple call to `Send()` can be made by creating an array of file names to send, and the transfer routine takes over. `Receive()` is called with a nominal argument of 0, since the file name is transferred with each file.

The virtual `status()` and `error()` routines as defined in this class both send their output directly to `stdout`. A production quality program would want to create derived versions of these functions that use a windowed interface to present the information in a more friendly fashion.

### The Test Program

The test program for this class, `TESTZM.CPP`, creates a simple `PC8250` object that should work with most PC communications ports, then acts as a simple terminal emulator. A short menu can be accessed with the Escape key, offering you the option to Send files, Receive files, or exit. The program also will autodetect the start of a Zmodem download, so you can normally start your receive by just starting the download from the remote end.

```
// ********************* START OF TESTZM.CPP *********************

// This is the test program for the Zmodem file transfer class. It
// is a simple terminal emulator that has a menu accessed via the
// Escape key. The Send function just sends a couple of predefined
// files. The Receive function will accept whatever the remote end
// sends.

#include <stdio.h>
#include <string.h>
#include <ctype.h>
#include "rs232.h"
```

# FILE TRANSFERS AND ZMODEM

```
#include "pc8250.h"
#include "zmodem.h"
#include "ascii.h"

int main()
{
    int c;
    char *files[] = { "TESTZM.EXE", "ZMODEM.H", 0 };
    PC8250 port( COM1, 38400L, 'N', 8, 1 );
    Zmodem *zmodem;

    port.XonXoffHandshaking( 1 );
    zmodem = new Zmodem( &port );
    setbuf( stdout, 0 );
    for ( ; ; ) {
        if ( kbhit() ) {
            c = getch();
            if ( c == 27 ) {
                printf( "\n(Escape Receive Send) Command: " );
                c = getch();
                printf( "\n" );
                switch( toupper( c ) ) {
                    case 'R' :
                        printf( "Starting to receive...\n" );
                        zmodem->Receive( 0 );
                        printf( "\nReceive complete\n" );
                        break;
                    case 'S' :
                        printf( "Starting to send...\n" );
                        zmodem->Send( files );
                        printf( "\nSend complete\n" );
                        break;
                }
                if ( c == 27 || toupper( c ) == 'E' )
                    break;
            } else
                port.Write( c );
        }
        c = port.Read();
```

```
            if ( c == CAN ) {
                char buf[ 21 ];
                port.Read( buf, 20, 500 );
                if ( strnicmp( buf, "B00000000000000\r\n", 17 ) == 0 )
                    zmodem->Receive( 0 );
                else {
                    putc( CAN, stdout );
                    for ( int i = 0 ; buf[ i ] ; i++ )
                        putc( buf[ i ], stdout );
                }
            } else if ( c > 0 )
                putc( c, stdout );
        }
        return 0;
}

// ******************* END OF TESTZM.CPP **********************
```

**Listing 10-1. The ZMODEM test program**

Listing 10-2 shows the make file to use to build this program. As with all the other make files, you need to be sure that the compiler line you will use in the first four lines of the file has the leading "#" removed. Once that is accomplished, you can build the file by typing:

```
        make -f testzm.mak
```

If you are using Microsoft C++ 7.0, you need to enter:

```
        nmake -f testzm.mak
```

```
# ******************* START OF TESTZM.MAK *********************
#
# This is the make file use to create TESTZM.EXE, from Chapter 10.
# To create the executable, just type:
#
#              make -f testzm.mak
#
```

# FILE TRANSFERS AND ZMODEM

```
#CC = tcc -w
CC = bcc -w
#CC = ztc -b
#CC = cl /W4 /AL

FILES = pc8250.obj isr_8250.obj queue.obj pcirq.obj

.cpp.obj:
   $(CC) -c $<

testzm.exe : testzm.obj zmodem.obj crc.obj rs232.obj msdos.obj
         $(FILES) $(CC) testzm.obj zmodem.obj crc.obj rs232.obj
         msdos.obj $(FILES)

# ********************* END OF TESTZM.MAK *********************
```

**Listing 10-2. TESTZM.MAK, the make file for testing ZMODEM**

## The CRC Classes

This chapter skipped very lightly over the subject of CRC calculations. Rather than get into a detailed discussion of the techniques needed to develop CRC values, I will instead present source code that supports both the 16-bit and 32-bit CRCs used by ZMODEM. Incidentally, the 16-bit CRC calculation used here is identical to the one used for both XMODEM and YMODEM, so this code may be useful elsewhere.

Listing 10-3 shows the header file for the two CRC classes, `CRC16` and `CRC32`. Each class has a single constructor, which sets the CRC to an initial value. Each class has two other public functions: `update()`, which updates the CRC to account for a new data byte, and `value()`, which returns the current CRC value. The `update()` function takes advantage of the inline function ability of C++. Since the `update()` function will normally be called repeatedly in a tight loop, it is an excellent candidate for inlining.

The CRC functions here use a table look-up method, which should be relatively efficient. The coefficient tables used to calculate the CRC values are initialized when the first CRC object is created, and are left in place for the duration of the program.

# SERIAL COMMUNICATIONS: A C++ DEVELOPER'S GUIDE

```
// *********************** START OF CRC.H ************************
//
// This header file contains the definitions for the two CRC
// classes, Crc16 and Crc32.
//

#ifndef _CRC_DOT_H
#define _CRC_DOT_H

// The two CRC objects create 16- and 32-bit CRC values using the
// polynomials used by ZMODEM. The calculations are table driven,
// with the table being initialized by the constructor at runtime.
// The constructor assigns an initial value to the crc, and then
// it is updated on a character by character basis.

class Crc32 {
    private :
        static unsigned long table[ 256 ];
        static int initialized;
        unsigned long crc;
    public :
        Crc32( unsigned long init_value );
        void update( int c );
        unsigned long value( void ){ return crc; }
};

inline void Crc32::update( int c )
{
    crc = table[ ( (int) crc ^ ( c & 0xff ) ) & 0xff ] ^
          ( ( crc >> 8 ) & 0x00FFFFFFL );
}

class Crc16 {
    private :
        static unsigned short table[ 256 ];
        static int initialized;
        unsigned short crc;
    public :
        Crc16( unsigned short init_value );
        void update( int c );
```

# FILE TRANSFERS AND ZMODEM

```cpp
                unsigned short value( void ){ return crc; }
};

inline void Crc16::update( int c )
{
    crc = (unsigned short)
            ( table[ (( crc >> 8 ) & 0xff ) ] ^
              ( crc << 8 ) ^ ( c & 0xff ) );
}

#endif // #ifndef _CRC_DOT_H

// ********************* END OF CRC.H **************************
```

**Listing 10-3. CRC.H**

```cpp
// ******************* START OF CRC.CPP ***********************
//
// This file contains the supporting code for the two CRC classes,
// Crc16 and Crc32.
//

#include "portable.h"
#include "crc.h"

unsigned long Crc32::table[ 256 ];
int Crc32::initialized = 0;

Crc32::Crc32( unsigned long init_value )
{
    if ( !initialized ) {
        int i;
        int j;
        unsigned long coeff;

        for ( i = 0; i < 256 ; i++ ) {
            coeff = i;
            for ( j = 0; j < 8; j++ ) {
                if ( coeff & 1 )
                    coeff = ( coeff >> 1 ) ^ 0xEDB88320L;
```

```cpp
                else
                    coeff >>= 1;
            }
            table[ i ] = coeff;
        }
        initialized = 1;
    }
    crc = init_value;
}

unsigned short Crc16::table[ 256 ];
int Crc16::initialized = 0;

Crc16::Crc16( unsigned short init_value )
{
    if ( !initialized ) {
        int i;
        int j;
        int k;
        int crc;

        for ( i = 0 ; i < 256 ; i++ ) {
            k = i << 8;
            crc = 0;
            for ( j = 0 ; j < 8 ; j++ ) {
                if ( ( crc ^ k ) & 0x8000 )
                    crc = ( crc << 1 ) ^ 0x1021;
                else
                    crc <<= 1;
                k <<= 1;
            }
            table[ i ] = (unsigned short) crc;
        }
        initialized = 1;
    }
    crc = init_value;
}
// ********************* END OF CRC.CPP *********************
```

**Listing 10-4. CRC.CPP, supporting code for the CRC classes**

# FILE TRANSFERS AND ZMODEM

## Source Code

The Zmodem source code is shown below. The three files listed are ZMODEM.H, _ZMODEM.H, and ZMODEM.CPP. The first header file is the public definitions file, which needs to be included by any module that will create a Zmodem object. The second header file contains constants and definitions used internally. Finally, the C++ file contains all of the code to implement the Zmodem class.

```
// *************** START OF ZMODEM.H ************************

// This header file has the class definitions needed for an
// application program to perform Zmodem file transfers.
// The Zmodem class is derived from the virtual base class
// FileTransfer. The public interface to the Zmodem class
// consists of just three functions: a constructor, and
// functions to send and receive files.

#ifndef _ZMODEM_DOT_H
#define _ZMODEM_DOT_H

class FileTransfer {
    protected :
        virtual void error( char *fmt, ... );
        virtual void status( char *fmt, ... );
        RS232 *port;
        FILE *file;
        long file_length;
        long byte_count;
        int file_count;
        char file_name[ 128 ];
        char buffer[ 1025 ];

    public :
        virtual int Send( char *files[] ) = 0;
        virtual int Receive( char *file ) = 0;
};

const int ZMAXHLEN = 16;    // Max header information length
const int ZATTNLEN = 32;    // Max length of attention string
```

```cpp
class Zmodem : public FileTransfer {
    private :
        int WakeUpSender( void );
        int ReceiveFiles( void );
        int ReceiveSingleFile( void );
        void SendHexHeader( int len, int type, char *hdr );
        void SendBinaryHeader(int length, int type, char * header);
        int ReadHeader( char *header );
        int ReadDataFrame( char *buf, int length );
        int ReadDataFrameCRC32( char *buf, int length );
        int ReadDataFrameCRC16( char *buf, int length );
        void SendAttentionString( void );
        void AckZFIN( void );
        int OpenInputFile( char *data );
        void PackLongIntoHeader( long header_data );
        long UnpackHeaderIntoLong( char *header );
        void SendHexEncodedChar( int c );
        void SendEncodedChar( int c );
        void SendChar( int c ) { port->Write( (char) c, 30000L ); }
        void SendZFIN( void );
        int ReadHexHeaderCRC16( char *header );
        int ReadBinaryHeaderCRC16( char *header );
        int ReadBinaryHeaderCRC32( char *header );
        int ReadEncodedByte( void );
        int ReadUnencodedByte( void );
        int ReadHexByte( void );
        int ReadChar( long timeout );
        int GetRinitHeader( void );
        int SendSingleFile( char *name );
        int SendFileContents( void );
        void SendDataFrame(char *buffer, int length, int frameend);
        int SyncWithReceiver( int flag );
        int receiver_wants_crc32;
        int current_frame_uses_crc32;
        long received_file_position;
        long transmitted_file_position;
        long last_sync_position;
        long last_reported_position;
```

## FILE TRANSFERS AND ZMODEM

```
        unsigned int receiver_buffer_length;
        int file_at_eof;
        int wake_up_sender_header_type;
        int Rxcount;
        char received_header[ ZMAXHLEN ];
        char transmitted_header[ ZMAXHLEN ];
        char attention_string[ ZATTNLEN + 1 ];
        int last_char_sent;

    public :
        Zmodem( RS232 *rs232_port );
        int Send( char *files[] );
        int Receive( char *file );
};

#endif // #ifdef _ZMODEM_DOT_H

// ********************* END OF ZMODEM.H *********************
```

**Listing 10-5. ZMODEM.H**

```
// ****************** START OF _ZMODEM.H *********************

// This header file has various constants used by the Zmodem class.

#ifndef __ZMODEM_DOT_H
#define __ZMODEM_DOT_H

const int ZPAD       = '*';  // ZPAD starts every header
const int ZDLE       = 24;   // The general purpose escape code
const int ZBIN       = 'A';  // Starts a binary CRC-16 frame
const int ZHEX       = 'B';  // Starts a hex CRC-16 frame
const int ZBIN32     = 'C';  // Starts a binary CRC-32 frame
const int ZMAXSPLEN = 1024;  // Max subpacket length

// These constants define all the various frame types
const int ZRQINIT   = 0;    // Request for receiver init frame
const int ZRINIT    = 1;    // A receiver init frame
```

# SERIAL COMMUNICATIONS: A C++ DEVELOPER'S GUIDE

```cpp
const int ZSINIT     = 2;    // A sender init frame
const int ZACK       = 3;    // General purpose Acknowledge frame
const int ZFILE      = 4;    // File name and data
const int ZSKIP      = 5;    // Skip the incoming file
const int ZNAK       = 6;    // General purpose Not Acknowledge
const int ZABORT     = 7;    // Abort session
const int ZFIN       = 8;    // Session is complete
const int ZRPOS      = 9;    // Request to start sending from an
                             // address
const int ZDATA      = 10;   // Start of a data frame
const int ZEOF       = 11;   // End of file
const int ZFERR      = 12;   // Fatal Read or Write error D
const int ZCRC       = 13;   // Request for CRC value of a file
const int ZCHALLENGE = 14;   // Challenge frame
const int ZCOMPL     = 15;   // Request is complete
const int ZCAN       = 16;   // Remote end canceled
const int ZFREECNT   = 17;   // Request for free bytes on filesystem
const int ZCOMMAND   = 18;   // Command from sending program
const int ZSTDERR    = 19;   // Output to stderr data follows

// Escape sequences in binary data

const int ZCRCE      = 'h';  // CRC next, frame ends, header follows
const int ZCRCG      = 'i';  // CRC next, frame continues nonstop
const int ZCRCQ      = 'j';  // CRC next, frame conts., expect ZACK
const int ZCRCW      = 'k';  // CRC next, ZACK expected, end of
                             // frame
const int ZRUB0      = 'l';  // Translate to rubout, 0x7f
const int ZRUB1      = 'm';  // Translate to rubout, 0xff

// ReadDataFrame() return values

const int GOTFLAG    = 0x100;
const int GOTCRCE    = ZCRCE | GOTFLAG;   // ZDLE-ZCRCE received
const int GOTCRCG    = ZCRCG | GOTFLAG;   // ZDLE-ZCRCG received
const int GOTCRCQ    = ZCRCQ | GOTFLAG;   // ZDLE-ZCRCQ received
const int GOTCRCW    = ZCRCW | GOTFLAG;   // ZDLE-ZCRCW received
const int GOTCAN     = CAN   | GOTFLAG;   // CAN*5 seen
```

## FILE TRANSFERS AND ZMODEM

```
// Byte positions within header array

const int ZF0          = 3;           // Position 0 in the flags array
const int ZF1          = 2;
const int ZF2          = 1;
const int ZF3          = 0;
const int ZP0          = 0;           // Low order 8 bits of position
const int ZP1          = 1;
const int ZP2          = 2;
const int ZP3          = 3;

// Bit Masks for ZRINIT flags byte ZF0

const int CANFDX       = 0x01; // Rx can send and receive true full
                               // duplex
const int CANOVIO      = 0x02; // Rx can receive data during disk I/O
const int CANBRK       = 0x04; // Rx can send a break signal
const int CANRLE       = 0x08; // Receiver can decode RLE
const int CANLZW       = 0x10; // Receiver can uncompress
const int CANFC32      = 0x20; // Receiver can use 32 bit CRC
const int ESCCTL       = 0x40; // Receiver expects ctl chars to be
                               // escaped
const int ESC8         = 0x80; // Receiver expects 8th bit to be
                               // escaped

// Miscellaneous constants

const int OK                 =  0;
const int ERROR              = -1;
const int TIMEOUT            = -2;
const int GARBAGE_COUNT      = -3;

#endif // #ifdef __ZMODEM_DOT_H

// ********************* END OF _ZMODEM.H *********************
```

**Listing 10-6.** _ZMODEM.H

# SERIAL COMMUNICATIONS: A C++ DEVELOPER'S GUIDE

```cpp
// ******************** START OF ZMODEM.CPP *******************

// This file contains all of the source code needed to support
// Zmodem file transfers. This code is directly derived from the
// public domain code released by Chuck Forsberg and Omen Technology.
// The Zmodem enhancements published by Omen Technology, including
// variable headers and run length encoding are not supported here.
// The Omen Technology code is available with the source code
// for this book for the curious.

#include <stdio.h>
#include <stdlib.h>
#include <string.h>
#include <stdarg.h>
#include "rs232.h"
#include "crc.h"
#include "ascii.h"
#include "zmodem.h"
#include "_zmodem.h"

// The two notification routines belong to the base class. There
// isn't any reason to override them in a derived class such as
// Zmodem, but a specific application may want to develop its own
// virtual functions to replace these.

void FileTransfer::error( char *fmt, ... )
{
   va_list argptr;

   va_start( argptr, fmt );
   vprintf( fmt, argptr );
   putc( '\n', stdout );
   va_end( argptr );
}

void FileTransfer::status( char *fmt, ... )
{
   va_list argptr;

   va_start( argptr, fmt );
```

## FILE TRANSFERS AND ZMODEM

```
    vprintf( fmt, argptr );
    putc( '\n', stdout );
    va_end( argptr );
}

// The Zmodem constructor only has to initialize a few variables.

Zmodem::Zmodem( RS232 *rs232_port )
{
    port = rs232_port;
    file_count = 0;
    file_name[ 0 ] = '\0';
    file_length = -1L;
    file = 0;
    receiver_buffer_length = 16384;
    wake_up_sender_header_type = ZRINIT;
}

// The public Send functionsends a batch of files one at a time
// via the SendSingleFile function. When a normal completion
// occurs, it is flagged with a ZFIN frame.

int Zmodem::Send( char *files[] )
{
    PackLongIntoHeader( 0L );
    SendHexHeader(4, ZRQINIT, transmitted_header);
    GetRinitHeader();
    byte_count = -1;
    while ( *files ) {
        if ( SendSingleFile( *files ) == ERROR )
            return ERROR;
        files++;
    }
    SendZFIN();
    return OK;
}

// This function is used *everywhere*, and benefits from being
// declared as inline.
```

```c++
inline int Zmodem::ReadChar( long timeout )
{
    int c = port->Read( timeout );
    return ( c < 0 ) ? TIMEOUT : c;
}


// This is the worker routine that transmits a single file.

int Zmodem::SendSingleFile( char *name )
{
    int c;
    unsigned long crc_value;
    long lastcrcrq = -1;
    int length;

    file = fopen( name, "rb" );
    if ( file == NULL) {
        error( "Failed to open %s", name );
        return OK;
    }
    file_at_eof = 0;
    fseek( file, 0, SEEK_END );
    file_length = ftell( file );
    fseek( file, 0, SEEK_SET );
    length = sprintf( buffer, "%s%c%u 0 0 0 0", name, 0,
                    file_length );

    for ( ; ; ) {
        PackLongIntoHeader( 0L );
        SendBinaryHeader( 4, ZFILE, transmitted_header );
        SendDataFrame( buffer, length, ZCRCW );
again:
        c = ReadHeader( received_header );
        switch ( c ) {
            case ZRINIT:
                while ( ( c = ReadChar( 5000L ) ) > 0 )
                if ( c == ZPAD )
                    goto again;
```

```c
            /* **** FALL THRU TO **** */
        default:
            continue;
        case ZCAN:
        case TIMEOUT:
        case ZABORT:
        case ZFIN:
            return ERROR;
        case ZCRC:
            if ( received_file_position != lastcrcrq ) {
                Crc32 crc( 0xFFFFFFFFL );
                lastcrcrq = received_file_position;
                fseek( file, 0L, SEEK_SET );
                while ( ( ( c = getc( file ) ) != EOF ) && --
                    lastcrcrq ) crc.update(c );
                crc_value = ~crc.value();
                fseek( file, 0L, SEEK_SET );
                lastcrcrq = received_file_position;
            }
            PackLongIntoHeader( crc_value );
            SendBinaryHeader( 4, ZCRC, transmitted_header );
            goto again;
        case ZSKIP:
            fclose( file );
            return OK;
        case ZRPOS:
            if (fseek( file,received_file_position,SEEK_SET) )
                return ERROR;
            last_sync_position = ( byte_count =
                                transmitted_file_position =
                                last_reported_position =
                                received_file_position) -1;
            return SendFileContents();
        }
    }
}
int Zmodem::SendFileContents( void )
{
```

# SERIAL COMMUNICATIONS: A C++ DEVELOPER'S GUIDE

```
    int c;
    int e;
    int n;
    int junkcount;
    int newcnt;

    junkcount = 0;

start_read:
    newcnt = receiver_buffer_length;
    PackLongIntoHeader( transmitted_file_position );
    SendBinaryHeader( 4, ZDATA, transmitted_header );
    do {
        n = fread( buffer, 1, 1024, file );
        if ( n < 1024 )
            file_at_eof = 1;

        if ( file_at_eof )
            e = ZCRCE;
        else if ( junkcount > 3 )
            e = ZCRCW;
        else if ( byte_count == last_sync_position )
            e = ZCRCW;
        else if ( receiver_buffer_length && ( newcnt -= n ) <= 0 )
            e = ZCRCW;
        else
            e = ZCRCG;
        SendDataFrame( buffer, n, e );
        byte_count = transmitted_file_position += n;
        if ( e == ZCRCW )
            goto waitack;
        while ( port->RXSpaceUsed() ) {
            switch ( ReadChar( 100 ) ) {
                case CAN:
                case ZPAD:
                    c = SyncWithReceiver( 1 );
                    if ( c == ZACK )
                        break;
                    SendDataFrame( buffer, 0, ZCRCE );
```

## FILE TRANSFERS AND ZMODEM

```
                    goto gotack;
                case XOFF:
                case XOFF | 0x80 :
                    ReadChar( 10000L );
                default:
                    junkcount++;
            }
        }
    } while ( !file_at_eof );
    for ( ; ; ) {
        PackLongIntoHeader( transmitted_file_position );
        SendBinaryHeader( 4, ZEOF, transmitted_header );
        switch ( SyncWithReceiver( 0 ) ) {
            case ZACK:
                continue;
            case ZRPOS:
                goto start_read;
            case ZRINIT:
                return OK;
            case ZSKIP:
                fclose( file );
                return c;
            default:
                fclose( file );
                return ERROR;
        }
    }

//Backchannel processing

waitack:
    junkcount = 0;
    c = SyncWithReceiver( 0 );
gotack:
    switch ( c ) {
        default:
        case ZCAN:
            fclose( file );
            return ERROR;
```

```
            case ZSKIP:
                fclose( file );
                return c;
            case ZACK:
            case ZRPOS:
                break;
            case ZRINIT:
                return OK;
        }
        while ( port->RXSpaceUsed() ) {
            switch ( ReadChar( 100 ) ) {
                case CAN:
                case ZPAD:
                    c = SyncWithReceiver( 1 );
                    goto gotack;
                case XOFF :
                case XOFF | 0x80 :
                    ReadChar( 10000L );
            }
        }
        goto start_read;
}

// If all goes well, the public receive function just calls
// WakeUpSender(), then ReceiveFiles(). If both of those
// do what they are supposed to do, a batch of files will
// have been properly transferred.

int Zmodem::Receive( char *rfile )
{
    static char CancelString[] = {
        CAN, CAN, CAN, CAN, CAN, CAN, CAN, CAN, CAN, CAN,
        BS,  BS,  BS,  BS,  BS,  BS,  BS,  BS,  BS,  BS };

    UNUSED( rfile );
    switch ( WakeUpSender() ) {
        case 0      :
        case ZCOMPL : return OK;
        case ERROR  : break;
```

## FILE TRANSFERS AND ZMODEM

```
            default   : if ( ReceiveFiles() == OK )
                          return OK;
    }
    port->Write( CancelString, sizeof CancelString, 30000L );
    if ( file )
        fclose( file );
    return ERROR;
}

// This is the general purpose receiver function. It calls the
// ReceiveSingleFile function repeatedly as long as the wakeup
// function keeps receiving ZFILE frames.

int Zmodem::ReceiveFiles( void )
{
    int return_status ;

    for ( ; ; ) {
        switch ( return_status = ReceiveSingleFile() ) {
            case ZEOF:
            case ZSKIP:
                switch ( WakeUpSender() ) {
                    case ZCOMPL:
                        return OK;
                    default:
                        return ERROR;
                    case ZFILE:
                        break;
                }
                continue;
            default:
                return return_status;
            case ERROR:
                return ERROR;
        }
    }
}

// Some data used various places in the class
```

# SERIAL COMMUNICATIONS: A C++ DEVELOPER'S GUIDE

```c++
static char *Zendnames[] = { "ZCRCE", "ZCRCG", "ZCRCQ", "ZCRCW" };

static char *frametypes[] = {
    "No Response to Error Correction Request",
    "No Carrier Detect",
    "TIMEOUT",
    "ERROR",
    "ZRQINIT",  "ZRINIT",   "ZSINIT",   "ZACK",     "ZFILE",
    "ZSKIP",    "ZNAK",     "ZABORT",   "ZFIN",     "ZRPOS",
    "ZDATA",    "ZEOF",     "ZFERR",    "ZCRC",     "ZCHALLENGE",
    "ZCOMPL",   "ZCAN",     "ZFREECNT", "ZCOMMAND", "ZSTDERR"
};

// This function is used when receiving files. It sends out the
// initial frame and waits for a response from the sender. If
// things go properly it will get the file data subpacket and
// return ZFILE. If the sender has no more files it will send a
// ZFIN, which is handled here.

int Zmodem::WakeUpSender( void )
{
    int c;
    int n;

    for ( n = 0 ; n < 16 ; n++ ) {
        PackLongIntoHeader( 0L );
        transmitted_header[ ZF0 ] =
                CANFC32 | CANFDX | CANOVIO | CANBRK;
        SendHexHeader( 4,
                wake_up_sender_header_type, transmitted_header );
        if ( wake_up_sender_header_type == ZSKIP )
            wake_up_sender_header_type = ZRINIT;
        for ( int try_again = 1 ; try_again ;  ) {
            switch ( ReadHeader( received_header ) ) {
                case ZRQINIT :
                case ZEOF    :
                case TIMEOUT :
                default      :
                    try_again = 0;
```

# FILE TRANSFERS AND ZMODEM

```
                break;
            case ZFILE   :
                wake_up_sender_header_type = ZRINIT;
                c = ReadDataFrame( buffer, 1024 );
                if ( c == GOTCRCW )
                    return ZFILE;
                SendHexHeader( 4, ZNAK, transmitted_header );
                break;
            case ZSINIT  :
                if (ReadDataFrame( attention_string, ZATTNLEN )
                        == GOTCRCW ) {
                    PackLongIntoHeader( 1L );
                    SendHexHeader(4, ZACK, transmitted_header);
                } else
                    SendHexHeader(4, ZNAK, transmitted_header);
                break;
            case ZCOMPL  :
                 break;
            case ZFIN    :
                AckZFIN();
                return ZCOMPL;
            case ZCAN    :
                return ERROR;
            }
        }
    }
    return 0;
}

// This is the workhorse routine that reads a single file from the
// sender. It reads in headers until it gets a ZDATA header, then
// it switches over to reading data subpackets until it gets one
// of the end of supbacket codes.

int Zmodem::ReceiveSingleFile( void )
{
```

```c
    int c;
    int error_count;
    long rxbytes;

    if ( OpenInputFile( buffer ) == ERROR )
        return wake_up_sender_header_type = ZSKIP;
    error_count = 0;
    rxbytes = 0L;
    for ( ; ; ) {
        PackLongIntoHeader( rxbytes );
        SendHexHeader( 4, ZRPOS, transmitted_header );
nxthdr:
        switch ( c = ReadHeader( received_header ) ) {
            default:
                error( "ReceiveSingleFile: ReadHeader returned "
                                        "%d", c );
                return ERROR;
            case ZNAK:
            case TIMEOUT:
                if ( ++error_count >= 20 ) {
                    error("ReceiveSingleFile: ReadHeader returned "
                                        "%d", c );
                    return ERROR;
                }
            case ZFILE:
                ReadDataFrame( buffer, 1024 );
                continue;
            case ZEOF:
                if ( UnpackHeaderIntoLong( received_header ) !=
                                        rxbytes )
                    goto nxthdr;
                if ( fclose( file ) != 0 ) {
                    wake_up_sender_header_type = ZFERR;
                    error( "ReceiveSingleFile: fclose() returned "
                                        "error" );
                    return ERROR;
                }
                return c;
            case ERROR:
```

```
            if ( ++error_count >= 20 ) {
                error("ReceiveSingleFile: ReadHeader returned "
                                            "%d", c );
                return ERROR;
            }
            SendAttentionString();
            continue;
        case ZSKIP:
            fclose( file );
            status( "ReceiveSingleFile: Sender SKIPPED file" );
            return c;
        case ZDATA:
            if ( UnpackHeaderIntoLong( received_header ) !=
                                            rxbytes ) {
                if ( ++error_count >= 20 )
                    return ERROR;
                SendAttentionString();
                continue;
            }
moredata:
            switch ( c = ReadDataFrame( buffer, 1024 ) ) {
              case ZCAN:
                error( "ReceiveSingleFile: ReadData returned "
                                            "%d", c );
                return ERROR;
              case ERROR:
                if ( ++error_count >= 20 ) {
                    error( "ReceiveSingleFile: ReadData "
                                            "returned %d", c );
                    return ERROR;
                }
                SendAttentionString();
                continue;
              case TIMEOUT:
                if ( ++error_count >= 20 ) {
                    error( "ReceiveSingleFile: ReadData "
                                            "returned %d", c );
                    return ERROR;
                }
```

```
                            continue;
                        case GOTCRCW:
                            error_count = 0;
                            fwrite( buffer, 1, Rxcount, file );
                            rxbytes += Rxcount;
                            PackLongIntoHeader( rxbytes );
                            SendHexHeader( 4, ZACK, transmitted_header );
                            SendChar( XON );
                            goto nxthdr;
                        case GOTCRCQ:
                            error_count = 0;
                            fwrite( buffer, 1, Rxcount, file );
                            rxbytes += Rxcount;
                            PackLongIntoHeader( rxbytes );
                            SendHexHeader( 4, ZACK, transmitted_header );
                            goto moredata;
                        case GOTCRCG:
                            error_count = 0;
                            fwrite( buffer, 1, Rxcount, file );
                            rxbytes += Rxcount;
                            goto moredata;
                        case GOTCRCE:
                            error_count = 0;
                            fwrite( buffer, 1, Rxcount, file );
                            rxbytes += Rxcount;
                            goto nxthdr;
                    }
                }
            }
#ifdef _MSC_VER
    return 0;  // MSC 7.0 generates an error w/o this line,
               // although it can never be reached
#endif
}

// This routine just has to decide whether to send the binary
// header using CRC-16 or CRC-32. After that it just spits out the
// data.
```

```cpp
void Zmodem::SendBinaryHeader( int length, int type, char *header )
{
    int i;
    Crc32 crc32( 0xFFFFFFFFL );
    unsigned long crc32val;
    Crc16 crc16( 0 );

    status( "SendBinaryHeader: %d %s %lx",
            length,
            frametypes[ type + 4 ],
            UnpackHeaderIntoLong( header ) );
    SendChar( ZPAD );
    SendChar( ZDLE );
    if ( receiver_wants_crc32 ) {
        SendChar( ZBIN32 );
        SendEncodedChar( type );
        crc32.update( type );
        for ( i = 0; i < length; i++ ) {
            crc32.update( 0xff & header[ i ] );
            SendEncodedChar( header[ i ] );
        }
        crc32val = ~crc32.value();
        for ( i = 0 ; i < 4 ; i++ ) {
            SendEncodedChar( (int) crc32val );
            crc32val >>= 8;
        }
    } else {
        SendChar( ZBIN );
        SendEncodedChar( type );
        crc16.update( type );
        for ( i = 0 ; i < length ; i++ ) {
            SendEncodedChar( header[ i ] );
            crc16.update( header[ i ] & 0xff );
        }
        crc16.update( 0 );
        crc16.update( 0 );
        SendEncodedChar( crc16.value() >> 8 );
        SendEncodedChar( crc16.value() );
    }
```

}

```cpp
// Sending the hex header involves no decisions whatsoever.

void Zmodem::SendHexHeader( int len, int type, char *header )
{
    int n;
    Crc16 crc( 0 );

    status( "SendHexHeader: %d %s %lx", len,
            frametypes[type + 4], UnpackHeaderIntoLong( header ) );
    SendChar( ZPAD );
    SendChar( ZPAD );
    SendChar( ZDLE );
    SendChar( ZHEX );
    SendHexEncodedChar( type );
    crc.update( type );
    for ( n = 0 ; n < len ; n++ ) {
        SendHexEncodedChar( header[ n ] );
        crc.update( 0xff & header[ n ] );
    }
    crc.update( 0 );
    crc.update( 0 );
    SendHexEncodedChar( crc.value() >> 8 );
    SendHexEncodedChar( crc.value() );
    SendChar( CR );
    SendChar( LF | 0x80 );
    if ( type != ZFIN && type != ZACK )
        SendChar( XON );
}

// Reading in headers and data subpackets is a relatively difficult
// job. The next four routines combine to read in headers. The
// first routine dispatches one of the next three, depending on
// what the header type is.

int Zmodem::ReadHeader( char *header )
{
    int c;
    int n;
```

## FILE TRANSFERS AND ZMODEM

```
    int cancount;
    Settings settings;

    port->ReadSettings( settings );
    n = 1400;
    n += ( settings.BaudRate > 19200L ) ? 19200 : (int)
                            settings.BaudRate;

startover:
    cancount = 0;
again:
    switch ( c = ReadChar( 10000L ) ) {
        case TIMEOUT:
            goto finished;
        case CAN:
gotcan:
            if ( ++cancount >= 5 ) {
                c = ZCAN;
                goto finished;
            }
            switch ( c = ReadChar( 100 ) ) {
                case TIMEOUT:
                    goto again;
                case ZCRCW:
                switch ( ReadChar( 100 ) ) {
                    case TIMEOUT:
                        c = ERROR;
                        goto finished;
                    default:
                        goto agn2;
                }
                default:
                    break;
                case CAN:
                    if ( ++cancount >= 5 ) {
                        c = ZCAN;
                        goto finished;
                    }
```

```
                        goto again;
                }
        default:
agn2:
                if ( --n == 0 ) {
                    c = GARBAGE_COUNT;
                    goto finished;
                }
                goto startover;
        case ZPAD | 0x80:       /* This is what we want. */
        case ZPAD:
                break;
    }
    cancount = 0;
splat:
    switch ( c = ReadUnencodedByte() ) {
        case ZPAD:
            goto splat;
        case TIMEOUT:
            goto finished;
        default:
            goto agn2;
        case ZDLE:          /* This is what we want. */
            break;
    }

    c = ReadUnencodedByte();
    switch ( c ) {
        case ZBIN32:
            current_frame_uses_crc32 = 1;
            c = ReadBinaryHeaderCRC32( header );
            break;
        case TIMEOUT:
            goto finished;
        case ZBIN:
            current_frame_uses_crc32 = 0;
            c = ReadBinaryHeaderCRC16( header );
            break;
        case ZHEX:
```

```
                current_frame_uses_crc32 = 0;
                c = ReadHexHeaderCRC16( header );
                break;
            case CAN:
                goto gotcan;
            default:
                goto agn2;
        }
        received_file_position = header[ ZP3 ] & 0xff;
        received_file_position <<= 8;
        received_file_position += header[ ZP2 ] & 0xff;
        received_file_position <<= 8;
        received_file_position += header[ ZP1 ] & 0xff;
        received_file_position <<= 8;
        received_file_position += header[ ZP0 ] & 0xff;
finished:
        switch ( c ) {
            case GOTCAN:
                c = ZCAN;
            /* **** FALL THRU TO **** */
            case ZNAK:
            case ZCAN:
            case ERROR:
            case TIMEOUT:
            case GARBAGE_COUNT:
                error( "Got %s", frametypes[ c + 4 ] );
            /* **** FALL THRU TO **** */
            default:
                if ( c >= -4 && c <= 22 )
                    error( "ReadHeader: %s %lx",
                            frametypes[ c + 4 ],
                            received_file_position );
                else
                    error( "ReadHeader: %d %lx", c,
                            received_file_position );
        }
        return c;
}
```

```cpp
// At this point most of the hard work has been done. The next
// three routines just read in the type of header and the data
// associated with it, then check to see if the CRC is correct.

int Zmodem::ReadBinaryHeaderCRC16( char *header )
{
    int c;
    int i;
    Crc16 crc( 0 );
    int header_type;

    if ( ( c = ReadEncodedByte() ) & ~0xff )
        return c;
    header_type = c;
    crc.update( c );

    for ( i = 0 ; i < 4 ; i++ ) {
        if ( ( c = ReadEncodedByte() ) & ~0xff )
            return c;
        crc.update( c );
        header[ i ] = (char) c;
    }
    if ( ( c = ReadEncodedByte() ) & ~0xff )
        return c;
    crc.update( c );
    if ( ( c = ReadEncodedByte() ) & ~0xff )
        return c;
    crc.update( c );
    if ( crc.value() & 0xFFFF ) {
        error( "Bad CRC" );
        return ERROR;
    }
    return header_type;
}

int Zmodem::ReadBinaryHeaderCRC32( char *header )
{
    int c;
    int i;
```

## FILE TRANSFERS AND ZMODEM

```
    Crc32 crc( 0xFFFFFFFFL );
    int header_type;

    if ( ( c = ReadEncodedByte() ) & ~0xff )
        return c;
    header_type = c;
    crc.update( c );

    for ( i = 0 ; i < 4 ; i++ ) {
        if ( ( c = ReadEncodedByte() ) & ~0xff )
            return c;
        crc.update( c );
        header[ i ] = (char) c;
    }
    for ( i = 0; i < 4 ; i++ ) {
        if ( ( c = ReadEncodedByte() ) & ~0xff )
            return c;
        crc.update( c );
    }
    if ( crc.value() != 0xDEBB20E3L ) {
        error( "Bad CRC" );
        return ERROR;
    }
    return header_type;
}

int Zmodem::ReadHexHeaderCRC16( char *header )
{
    int c;
    Crc16 crc( 0 );
    int i;
    int header_type;

    if ( ( c = ReadHexByte() ) < 0 )
        return c;
    header_type = c;
    crc.update( c );

    for ( i = 0 ; i < 4 ; i++ ) {
```

```
        if ( ( c = ReadHexByte() ) < 0 )
            return c;
        crc.update( c );
        header[ i ] = (char) c;
    }
    if ( ( c = ReadHexByte() ) < 0 )
        return c;
    crc.update( c );
    if ( ( c = ReadHexByte() ) < 0 )
        return c;
    crc.update( c );
    if ( crc.value() & 0xFFFF ) {
        error( "Bad CRC" );
        return ERROR;
    }
    switch ( c = ReadChar( 100 ) ) {
        case CR :
        case CR | 0x80 :
            ReadChar( 100 );
    }
    return header_type;
}

// The next three routines are used to read in binary data
// subpackets. This code is somewhat simpler than the code
// used to read in a header, mostly because there are fewer
// things to go wrong.

int Zmodem::ReadDataFrame( char *buffer, int length )
{
    if ( current_frame_uses_crc32 )
        return ReadDataFrameCRC32( buffer, length );
    else
        return ReadDataFrameCRC16( buffer, length );
}

int Zmodem::ReadDataFrameCRC32( char *buffer, int length )
{
    int c;
```

# FILE TRANSFERS AND ZMODEM

```c
    Crc32 crc( 0xFFFFFFFFL );
    char *end;
    int d;

    Rxcount = 0;
    end = buffer + length;
    while ( buffer <= end ) {
        if ( ( c = ReadEncodedByte() ) & ~0xff ) {
crcfoo:
            switch ( c ) {
                case GOTCRCE:
                case GOTCRCG:
                case GOTCRCQ:
                case GOTCRCW:
                    d = c;
                    c &= 0xff;
                    crc.update( c );
                    if ( ( c = ReadEncodedByte() ) & ~0xff )
                        goto crcfoo;
                    crc.update( c );
                    if ( ( c = ReadEncodedByte() ) & ~0xff )
                        goto crcfoo;
                    crc.update( c );
                    if ( ( c = ReadEncodedByte() ) & ~0xff )
                        goto crcfoo;
                    crc.update( c );
                    if ( ( c = ReadEncodedByte() ) & ~0xff )
                        goto crcfoo;
                    crc.update( c );
                    if ( crc.value() != 0xDEBB20E3L ) {
                        error( "Bad CRC" );
                        return ERROR;
                    }
                    Rxcount = (int) ( length - (end - buffer) );
                    error( "ReadDataFrameCRC32: %d %s",
                        Rxcount, Zendnames[ d - GOTCRCE & 3 ] );
                    return d;
                case GOTCAN:
                    error( "Sender Canceled" );
```

```
                    return ZCAN;
                case TIMEOUT:
                    error( "TIMEOUT" );
                    return c;
                default:
                    error( "Garbled data subpacket" );
                    return c;
            }
        }
        *buffer++ = (char) c;
        crc.update( c );
    }
    error( "Data subpacket too long" );
    return ERROR;
}

int Zmodem::ReadDataFrameCRC16( char *buffer, int length )
{
    int c;
    Crc16 crc( 0 );
    char *end;
    int d;

    Rxcount = 0;
    end = buffer + length;
    while ( buffer <= end ) {
        if ( ( c = ReadEncodedByte() ) & ~0xff ) {
crcfoo:
            switch ( c ) {
                case GOTCRCE:
                case GOTCRCG:
                case GOTCRCQ:
                case GOTCRCW:
                    crc.update( (d = c) & 0xff );
                    if ( ( c = ReadEncodedByte()) & ~0xff )
                        goto crcfoo;
                    crc.update( c );
                    if ( ( c = ReadEncodedByte() ) & ~0xff )
                        goto crcfoo;
```

## FILE TRANSFERS AND ZMODEM

```cpp
                crc.update( c );
                if ( crc.value() & 0xFFFF ) {
                    error( "Bad CRC");
                    return ERROR;
                }
                Rxcount = (int) ( length - ( end - buffer ) );
                error( "ReadDataFrame: %d    %s",
                       Rxcount, Zendnames[ d - GOTCRCE & 3 ] );
                return d;
            case GOTCAN:
                error( "Sender Canceled" );
                return ZCAN;
            case TIMEOUT:
                error( "TIMEOUT" );
                return c;
            default:
                error( "Garbled data subpacket" );
                return c;
            }
        }
        *buffer++ = (char) c;
        crc.update( c );
    }
    error( "Data subpacket too long" );
    return ERROR;
}

// The attention string processor has to process a couple of
// special characters used to sleep and send breaks.

void Zmodem::SendAttentionString()
{
    int i = 0;
    int c;
    long timer;

    while ( port->TXSpaceUsed() > 0 )
        port->IdleFunction();
    while ( ( c = attention_string[ i++ ] ) != 0 ) {
```

```cpp
            switch ( c ) {
                case 0xde :
                    timer = ReadTime() + 1000L;
                    while ( ReadTime() < timer )
                        port->IdleFunction();
                    break;
                case 0xdd :
                    port->Break();
                    break;
                default:
                    SendChar( c );
            }
        }
    }

// This function is called by the receiver before exiting.

void Zmodem::AckZFIN( void )
{
    int n;

    status( "AckZFIN" );
    PackLongIntoHeader( 0L );
    for ( n = 0 ; n < 4 ; n++ ) {
        port->FlushRXBuffer();
        SendHexHeader( 4, ZFIN, transmitted_header );
        switch ( ReadChar( 10000L ) ) {
            case 'O':
                ReadChar( 120 );    /* Discard 2nd 'O' */
                status( "AckZFIN complete" );
                return;
            case TIMEOUT:
            default:
                break;
        }
    }
}
```

# FILE TRANSFERS AND ZMODEM

```c
// This utility routine has to scan the incoming data subpacket for
// the file name and length.

int Zmodem::OpenInputFile( char *data )
{
    strcpy( file_name, data );
    if (sscanf(data + strlen(data) + 1, "%ld", &file_length) < 1 )
        file_length = -1L;
    file = fopen( file_name, "wb" );
    if ( !file )
        return ERROR;
    return OK;
}

// File position values are longs packed into a four byt header.
// The following two routines are resposible for packing and
// unpacking the data.

void Zmodem::PackLongIntoHeader( long header_data )
{
    transmitted_header[ ZP0 ] = (char) header_data;
    transmitted_header[ ZP1 ] = (char) ( header_data >> 8 );
    transmitted_header[ ZP2 ] = (char) ( header_data >> 16 );
    transmitted_header[ ZP3 ] = (char) ( header_data >> 24 );
}

long Zmodem::UnpackHeaderIntoLong( char *header )
{
    long l;

    l = header[ ZP3 ] & 0xff;
    l = ( l << 8 ) | ( header[ ZP2 ] & 0xff );
    l = ( l << 8 ) | ( header[ ZP1 ] & 0xff );
    l = ( l << 8 ) | ( header[ ZP0 ] & 0xff );
    return l;
}

// Hex headers need to send data in hex format.
```

```cpp
void Zmodem::SendHexEncodedChar( int c )
{
    static char *digits = "0123456789abcdef";

    SendChar( digits[ ( c & 0xF0 ) >> 4 ] );
    SendChar( digits[ c & 0xF ] );
}

// This routine handles all the escape sequences necessary to send
// control characters.

void Zmodem::SendEncodedChar( int c )
{
    if ( c & 0x60 )
        SendChar( last_char_sent = c );
    else {
        switch ( c &= 0xff ) {
            case CR :
            case CR | 0x80 :
                if ( ( last_char_sent & 0x7f ) != '@' ) {
                    SendChar( last_char_sent = c );
                    break;
                } // else fall through
            case ZDLE :
            case DLE :
            case XON :
            case XOFF :
            case DLE | 0x80 :
            case XON | 0x80 :
            case XOFF | 0x80 :
                SendChar( ZDLE );
                c ^= 0x40;
                SendChar( last_char_sent = c );
                break;
            default:
                SendChar( last_char_sent = c );
        }
    }
}

// Read a byte, taking into account escape sequences, and checking
```

# FILE TRANSFERS AND ZMODEM

```
// for the 5*CAN abort sequence.

int Zmodem::ReadEncodedByte( void )
{
    int c;

    for ( ; ; ) {
        c = ReadChar( 10000L );
        if ( c == ZDLE )
            break;
        switch ( c ) {
            case XON :
            case XON | 0x80 :
            case XOFF :
            case XOFF | 0x80 :
                break;
            default:
                return c;
        }
    }
    for ( ; ; ) {
        if ( ( c = ReadChar( 10000L ) ) < 0 )
            return c;
        if ( c == CAN && ( c = ReadChar( 10000L ) ) < 0 )
            return c;
        if ( c == CAN && ( c = ReadChar( 10000L ) ) < 0 )
            return c;
        if ( c == CAN && ( c = ReadChar( 10000L ) ) < 0 )
            return c;
        switch ( c ) {
            case CAN:
                return GOTCAN;
            case ZCRCE:
            case ZCRCG:
            case ZCRCQ:
            case ZCRCW:
                return c | GOTFLAG;
            case ZRUB0:
                return 0x7f;
```

```cpp
                case ZRUB1:
                    return 0xff;
                case XOFF :
                case XOFF | 0x80 :
                case XON :
                case XON | 0x80 :
                    break;
                default:
                    if ( ( c & 0x60 ) ==  0x40 )
                        return ( c ^ 0x40 );
                    else
                        return ERROR;
        }
    }
}

// This routine reads a raw data byte, throws out the parity bit
// and ignores handshaking characters.

int Zmodem::ReadUnencodedByte( void )
{
    int c;

    for ( ; ; ) {
        if ( ( c = ReadChar( 10000L ) ) < 0 )
            return c;
        switch ( c &= 0x7f ) {
            case XON:
            case XOFF:
                continue;
            default:
                return c;
        }
    }
}

// When reading Hex headers, hex values need to be converted to a
// usable format.

int Zmodem::ReadHexByte( void )
```

## FILE TRANSFERS AND ZMODEM

```
{
    int c;
    int n;

    if ( ( c = ReadUnencodedByte() ) < 0 )
        return c;
    n = c - '0';
    if ( n > 9 )
        n -= ( 'a' - ':' );
    if ( n & ~0xF )
        return ERROR;
    if ( ( c = ReadUnencodedByte( )) < 0 )
        return c;
    c -= '0';
    if ( c > 9 )
        c -= ( 'a' - ':' );
    if ( c & ~0xF )
        return ERROR;
    c += ( n << 4 );
    return c;
}

// The sender needs to get the RINIT frame before it can start
// sending the file. This routine takes care of that.

int Zmodem::GetRinitHeader( void )
{
    int i;

    for ( i = 0 ; i < 10 ; i++ ) {
        switch ( ReadHeader( received_header ) ) {
            case ZCHALLENGE: /* Echo receiver's challenge number */
                PackLongIntoHeader( received_file_position );
                SendHexHeader( 4, ZACK, transmitted_header );
                continue;
            case ZCOMMAND:           /* They didn't see our ZRQINIT */
                PackLongIntoHeader( 0L );
```

# SERIAL COMMUNICATIONS: A C++ DEVELOPER'S GUIDE

```
                SendHexHeader( 4, ZRQINIT, transmitted_header );
                continue;
            case ZRINIT:
                receiver_wants_crc32 = received_header[ ZF0 ] &
                                            CANFC32;
                receiver_buffer_length =
                        ( received_header[ ZP0 ] & 0xff ) +
                        ( ( received_header[ ZP1 ] & 0xff ) << 8 );
                return OK;
            case ZCAN:
            case TIMEOUT:
                return ERROR;
            case ZRQINIT:
                if ( received_header[ ZF0 ] == ZCOMMAND )
                    continue;
            default:
                SendHexHeader( 4, ZNAK, transmitted_header );
                continue;
        }
    }
    return ERROR;
}

// This routine sends a data subpacket, which is used here to send
// file names and file data.

void Zmodem::SendDataFrame(char *buffer, int length, int frameend)
{
    Crc32 crc32( 0xFFFFFFFFL );
    unsigned long crc32val;
    Crc16 crc16( 0 );
    int i;

    status( "SendDataFrame: %d %s",
            length, Zendnames[ frameend - ZCRCE & 3 ] );
    if ( receiver_wants_crc32 ) {
        for ( i = 0 ; i < length ; i++ ) {
            SendEncodedChar( buffer[ i ] );
```

```
            crc32.update( buffer[ i ] & 0xff );
        }
        SendChar( ZDLE );
        SendChar( frameend );
        crc32.update( frameend );
        crc32val = ~crc32.value();
        for ( i = 0 ; i < 4 ; i++ ) {
            SendEncodedChar( (int) crc32val );
            crc32val >>= 8;
        }
    } else {
        for ( i = 0 ; i < length ; i++ ) {
            SendEncodedChar( buffer[ i ] );
            crc16.update( buffer[ i ] & 0xff );
        }
        SendChar( ZDLE);
        SendChar( frameend);
        crc16.update( frameend );
        crc16.update( 0 );
        crc16.update( 0 );
        SendEncodedChar( crc16.value() >> 8 );
        SendEncodedChar( crc16.value() );
    }
    if ( frameend == ZCRCW )
        SendChar( XON );
}

// The sender sends a ZFIN frame just before exiting.

void Zmodem::SendZFIN( void )
{
    for ( ; ; ) {
        PackLongIntoHeader( 0L );
        SendHexHeader( 4, ZFIN, transmitted_header );
        switch ( ReadHeader( received_header ) ) {
            case ZFIN:
                SendChar( 'O');
                SendChar( 'O');
            case ZCAN:
```

```cpp
            case TIMEOUT:
                return;
        }
    }
}

int Zmodem::SyncWithReceiver( int flag )
{
    int c;

    for ( ; ; ) {
        c = ReadHeader( received_header );
        switch ( c ) {
            case ZCAN:
            case ZABORT:
            case ZFIN:
            case TIMEOUT:
                return ERROR;
            case ZRPOS:
                if (fseek(file, received_file_position, SEEK_SET) )
                    return ERROR;
                file_at_eof = 0;
                byte_count = last_reported_position
                    = transmitted_file_position =
                                    received_file_position;
                last_sync_position = received_file_position;
                return c;
            case ZACK:
                last_reported_position = received_file_position;
                if ( flag || transmitted_file_position ==
                            received_file_position )
                    return ZACK;
                continue;
            case ZRINIT:
            case ZSKIP:
                fclose( file );
                return c;
            case ERROR:
```

```
            default:
                SendBinaryHeader( 4, ZNAK, transmitted_header );
                continue;
        }
    }
}

// ******************** END OF ZMODEM.CPP ********************
```

**Listing 10-7. ZMODEM.CPP**

CHAPTER 11

# Terminal Emulation

One of the first questions that beginning communications programers often ask is "How do I clear the screen of a caller logged in to my BBS?" These hypothetical programmers will usually have learned how to create nice-looking screens for their programs using run time library functions such as `clrscr()`, `gotoxy()`, and `textcolor()`. These same programmers then find out, much to their dismay, that these functions don't work properly when used for the interface code in a communications program.

The reason for this is fairly simple, but it does require a little understanding of the hardware involved. Most display devices, ranging from DEC VT-100 terminals to IBM PC VGA Monitors, save the contents of the display in a specialized piece of hardware referred to as a "frame buffer." In text modes on the PC, the frame buffer is just a block of memory that has two bytes for each character on the screen. One byte per character contains the actual display value of the character, in 8-bit IBM ASCII. The second byte for each character contains the display attribute.

On the PC, all I have to do to clear the screen is step through display memory, setting each character to an ASCII blank, and each attribute to simple white-on-black. Thus, a simple version of `clrscr()` could be written to look like this:

```
void clrscr( void )
{
    char far *screen = (char far *) 0xb8000000L;

    for ( int row = 0 ; row < 25 ; row++ )
        for ( int col = 0 ; col < 80 ; col++ ) {
            *screen++ = ' ';
            *screen++ = 0x07;
        }
}
```

All this routine does is write out blanks with a normal display attribute to every position on the screen. It is extremely fast, and is easy to implement, which is why most C and C++ compilers come with a routine that accomplishes the same thing.

Getting this same thing to happen across an RS-232 communications link is considerably more difficult, however. If I want to clear the screen on a PC hooked up to my BBS via modem, I can't just create a far pointer that lets me directly access the frame buffer on the remote system. Instead, I have to rely on traditional protocols to let me accomplish something similar.

## Escape Sequences

In the days before desktop computers, most interactive computing was done via remote terminals attached to time-shared computers. These remote terminals had the same problem as our BBS programmer: the main computer didn't have any way to directly address memory on the terminal, and thus had no way to write to different areas all over the screen quickly and easily.

Hardware and firmware designers quickly developed protocols to overcome this difficulty. When designing the RS-232 interface between the computer and the terminal, designers added a protocol that let programmers step outside the traditional ASCII display characters to send "terminal control sequences." A terminal control sequence is just a special set of input that sends a display or formatting command to the terminal.

For example, one early display terminal was the DEC VT-52. A programmer who wanted to clear an area on the screen of a VT-52 could send the two-character sequence ESC J. This command told the VT-52 to clear everything from the cursor to the end of the screen. Another sequence could be used to home the cursor immediately before this command, resulting in a completely clear screen with just a few characters.

In order to distinguish these commands from normal display data, the commands were frequently prefaced with the ASCII ESC (Escape) character, 0x1b. The Escape code would not show up as part of a normal display sequence, so it provides an unambiguous way to distinguish special command sequences. Since so many terminal manufacturers used control sequences that started with the Escape character, these sequences have come to be known generically as "Escape Sequences."

# TERMINAL EMULATION

## Terminal Intelligence Quotients

Early terminals that responded to control sequences were dubbed "smart terminals," to distinguish them from "dumb terminals," which could only display text. A dumb terminal acted as nothing much more than a fully electronic teletype, able to print at the bottom line of the screen and scroll text upwards as it progressed.

Today every terminal sold is a smart terminal, so this usage is not as meaningful as it was at one time.

## Tower of Babel

Over the past 25 years or so, manufacturers of display terminals have deemed it appropriate to create a unique and proprietary set of Escape sequences to control their particular terminals. An example of the confusion this causes can be seen by looking at the `termcap` file shipped with most UNIX systems. The `termcap` file futilely attempts to define all the possible sequences for any terminal that could conceivably be connected to a UNIX system. The result is a file containing several 100K of cryptic runes that works often, but not always.

In a perhaps futile attempt to cut down on this confusion, the American National Standards Institute (ANSI) has created a specification known as ANSI X3.64, "Additional Controls for Use with American National Standard Code for Information Interchange." This specification defines a set of Escape Sequences that can be used to handle most of the commands needed by ASCII display terminals.

ANSI X3.64 includes commands such as:

- Cursor movement
- Setting horizontal and vertical tabs
- Delete character/line
- Insert character/line
- Define protected areas

ANSI X3.64 really can't claim much success in the world of ASCII display terminals. Some manufacturers have adopted ANSI-like command sets for the terminals, and others offer it as a secondary command set. But for the most part, developers still have to contend with the same Tower of Babel that existed 15 years ago. The only difference today is that there are more dialects to master..

## ANSI.SYS

IBM and Microsoft created a device driver called `ANSI.SYS` that supports a very limited subset of the ANSI X3.64 command set. This driver would allow software that was written to work with display terminals to run on the IBM PC with no fundamental changes. In practice, it has been used mostly as an accessory to `.BAT` files, allowing batch file programmers to create flashy screens in what are otherwise simple programs.

While ANSI.SYS may not have been particularly useful for communications programmers, it did have one unintended side effect. By defining a standard for terminal Escape sequences used on the PC, it gave the same communications programmers a standard to which they could program. Since the actual set of commands is so short and simple, it began finding its way into both shareware such as Procomm and Telix, as well as commercial programs such as Crosstalk.

The official definition of the command set used by ANSI.SYS can be found in the *IBM DOS Technical Reference Manual*. For the most part, the commands conform to those in the official standard, although there is some variation. It is important to recognize that this is a very limited subset of the official specification. Software written for terminals that conform more closely to the specifications, such as DEC's VT-100, will often have trouble with the more limited IBM version.

### ANSI.SYS Escape sequences

The official specification for ANSI X3.64 gives a common format that all ANSI command sequences should follow. Each command starts with an ASCII ESC code, 0x1b, which serves notice that an Escape sequence has started. An optional "[" character immediately follows most of the commands, although not all. Immediately following that is a set of 0 or more numeric parameters, separated by semicolons. Finally, a one- or two-character command set terminates the command.

# TERMINAL EMULATION

**Table 11-1. The components of an ANSI command sequence.**

| | |
|---|---|
| ESC | All commands start with the Escape code |
| "[" | Used with most, but not all commands |
| Parameter | A number composed of ASCII digits "0" through "9" |
| ";" | The separator used between parameters |
| Command prefix | An optional prefix between " " and "/" (0x20 and 0x2f) can precede the command character. |
| Command | Normally the command character lies in the range between ASCII "@" and "~" (0x40 and 0x7e). |

The IBM version of ANSI.SYS modifies this sequence somewhat. First of all, normal ANSI parameters are always ASCII representations of decimal numbers. For example, a typical cursor positioning command might look like this:

```
ESC[23;1H
```

Simple C code to issue this command might look like this:

```
printf( "\x1b[%d;%dH", row, column );
```

IBM and Microsoft extended the parameter definition to allow for the use of character strings as parameters. This means that in addition to normal numeric parameters, an ANSI input parser also has to be able to accommodate quoted strings, that might look like this:

```
ESC[0;68;"dir";13p
```

This sequence, which is quoted directly from the IBM manual, redefines function key F10 to issue the DIR command followed by a carriage return.

In addition, IBM and Microsoft completely broke with specification for the definition of the Set Mode and Reset Mode commands. These functions completely deviate from the standard mode, and have to be parsed for individually.

The following sequences are supported by ANSI.SYS as shipped with MS-DOS and IBM-DOS:

**Cursor position:**     ESC[#;#H     -or-
                         ESC[#;#f

This command moves the cursor to the row and column specified in the first two parameters. The default for each of the two parameters is 1, so one or both can be omitted. The row and column numbers used by ANSI.SYS are 1 based, which means the upper left-hand corner of the screen is row 1, column 1.

**Cursor up:**     ESC[#A

This command moves the cursor up by the number of rows specified by the numeric parameter. If the parameter is not given, it defaults to 1. The cursor won't try to move past the first row on the screen.

**Cursor down:**     ESC[#B

This command moves the cursor down by the number of rows specified by the numeric parameter. If the parameter is not given, it defaults to 1. The cursor won't try to move down past the last row on the screen.

**Cursor right:**     ESC[#C

This command moves the cursor right by the number of columns specified by the numeric parameter. If the parameter is not given, it defaults to 1. The cursor won't try to move past the last column on the screen.

**Cursor left:**     ESC[#D

This command moves the cursor left by the number of columns specified by the numeric parameter. If the parameter is not given, it defaults to 1. The cursor won't try to move past the first column on the screen.

**Device status request:**   ESC[6n

This command causes ANSI.SYS to issue a cursor position report, which has the format:

ESC[#;#R

The two numeric parameters in the cursor position report give the current row and column of the cursor. This command is frequently used as a way to determine if a PC is performing ANSI emulation.

**Save cursor position:**   ESC[s

This command saves the current row and column of the cursor. The cursor can be restored to the saved position with the next command, Restore Cursor Position.

**Restore cursor position:**   ESC[u

This command restores the cursor row and column to the position saved previously with the Save Cursor Position command.

**Erase screen:**   ESC[2J

This command is used to erase the entire display. The cursor is returned to position 1,1 after the screen is erased.

**Erase to end of line:**   ESC[K

This command erases all positions from the cursor to the end of the current row. The cursor position isn't modified.

```
Set colors:        ESC[#;...;#m
```

This command is used to set custom display colors on the screen. Any number of color commands can be combined into a single escape sequence. The numeric parameters defined for this command are:

| | |
|---|---|
| 0  | Reset color to white on black |
| 1  | Set foreground color to high intensity |
| 4  | Turn on underline (only meaningful on a monochrome display) |
| 5  | Set the blinking attribute |
| 7  | Reverse video |
| 8  | Invisible attribute |
| 30 | Set the foreground color to black |
| 31 | Set the foreground color to red |
| 32 | Set the foreground color to green |
| 33 | Set the foreground color to yellow |
| 34 | Set the foreground color to blue |
| 35 | Set the foreground color to purple |
| 36 | Set the foreground color to cyan |
| 37 | Set the foreground color to white |
| 40 | Set the background color to black |
| 41 | Set the background color to red |
| 42 | Set the background color to green |
| 43 | Set the background color to yellow |
| 44 | Set the background color to blue |
| 45 | Set the background color to purple |
| 46 | Set the background color to cyan |
| 47 | Set the background color to white |

## TERMINAL EMULATION

**Set Mode:**        ESC[=#h  -or-
                     ESC[?7h

This command sets the video to one of the 7 predefined BIOS video modes, or optionally turns on character wrapping at the end of the line. The mode commands are defined as follows:

| | |
|---|---|
| 0 | Set mode to 40 x 25 black and white |
| 1 | Set mode to 40 x 25 color |
| 2 | Set mode to 80 x 25 black and white |
| 3 | Set mode to 80 x 25 color |
| 4 | Set mode to 320 x 200 color |
| 5 | Set mode to 320 x 200 black and white |
| 6 | Set mode to 640 x 200 black and white |
| 7 | Enable wrap at the end of line |

Note that this command, and Reset Mode, which follows, have a syntax that deviates from standard ANSI and will require special parsing. The default value of the numeric parameter is 0.

**Reset Mode:**      ESC[=#l  -or-
                     ESC[?7l

This command behaves identically to Set Mode, except it will disable wrap at the end of line if the numeric parameter is 7.

**Keyboard Key Reassignment:**        ESC[#;#;...#p

ANSI.SYS can redefine keyboard output for any key. This is the function that required the extension of the ANSI specification to allow for quoted strings. The syntax of this command is straightforward. The key to be redefined is specified using either the first or the first two parameters. Standard ASCII keys are defined using a single numeric parameter, extended function keys are defined using a 0 in the first parameter followed by a scan code in the second. The remaining parameters in the list are concatenated to form a single string which is the new definition.

For example, an escape sequence to redefine function key F1 to sound a beep would look like this:

```
ESC[0;59;"echo ";7;13p
```

Redefining the Z key on the keyboard to perform the same function would take a command like this:

```
ESC[90;"echo ";7;13p
```

**Keyboard sequences**

ANSI.SYS doesn't have anything to say about keyboard sequences. The `AnsiTerminal` class developed here does perform translation of keystrokes, compatible with existing ANSI X3.64 terminals.

Table 11-2. AnsiTerminal keyboard translations

| | | | | | | | | |
|---|---|---|---|---|---|---|---|---|
| Left Arrow | ESC[D | | | Home | ESC[H | | | |
| Right Arrow | ESC[C | | | End | ESC[F | | | |
| Up Arrow | ESC[A | | | PgUp | ESC[I | | | |
| Down Arrow | ESC[B | | | PgDn | ESC[G | | | |
| Insert | ESC[L | | | | | | | |
| F1 | ESC[M | Shift F1 | ESC[Y | Ctrl F1 | ESC[k | Alt F1 | ESC[w |
| F2 | ESC[N | Shift F2 | ESC[Z | Ctrl F2 | ESC[l | Alt F2 | ESC[x |
| F3 | ESC[O | Shift F3 | ESC[a | Ctrl F3 | ESC[m | Alt F3 | ESC[y |
| F4 | ESC[P | Shift F4 | ESC[b | Ctrl F4 | ESC[n | Alt F4 | ESC[z |
| F5 | ESC[Q | Shift F5 | ESC[c | Ctrl F5 | ESC[o | Alt F5 | ESC[@ |
| F6 | ESC[R | Shift F6 | ESC[d | Ctrl F6 | ESC[p | Alt F6 | ESC[[ |
| F7 | ESC[S | Shift F7 | ESC[e | Ctrl F7 | ESC[q | Alt F7 | ESC[\ |
| F8 | ESC[T | Shift F8 | ESC[f | Ctrl F8 | ESC[r | Alt F8 | ESC[] |
| F9 | ESC[U | Shift F9 | ESC[g | Ctrl F9 | ESC[s | Alt F9 | ESC[^ |
| F10 | ESC[V | Shift F10 | ESC[h | Ctrl F10 | ESC[t | Alt F10 | ESC[_ |

# TERMINAL EMULATION

## A Terminal Class

The terminal class needs to perform a simple task. It needs to filter data going in both directions, to and from the RS-232 port. Keyboard input that is being sent to the RS-232 port needs to be translated to escape (or other) sequences. RS-232 input needs to have Escape sequences filtered out and translated into screen activity.

The definition of the `Terminal` class is shown below. With this virtual base class it is extremely simple to write a short program that performs terminal emulation. The example program for this chapter, TESTERM.CPP, uses a derived class, `AnsiTerminal`, to actually perform terminal emulation.

```
// ***************** START OF TERMINAL.H *******************
//
// This header file contains the definitions for the base class
// Terminal. It is a virtual base class, so it can't be cons-
// tructed. The derived class AnsiTerminal is used in this book.

#ifndef _TERMINAL_DOT_H
#define _TERMINAL_DOT_H

#include "portable.h"
#include "rs232.h"
#include "textwind.h"

class Terminal {
    protected :
        RS232 *port;
        TextWindow *window;
    public :
        Terminal( RS232 &p, TextWindow &w )
                            { port = &p; window = &w; }
        virtual int ReadPort( void ) = 0;
        virtual void Display( int c ) = 0;
        virtual void WriteKey( int c ) = 0;
        virtual ~Terminal( void ){ ; }
};

#endif // #ifndef _TERMINAL_DOT_H
```

Listing 11-1. TERMINAL.H

The three functions that the `Terminal` class needs to perform take care of all the basic terminal emulation functions. While more sophisticated classes might need additional public features, nothing needs to be added to get a fully functioning program. The public functions defined by the base class are defined below.

```
Terminal( RS232 &p, TextWindow &w )
```

This is the constructor for the base class. While the base class cannot be instantiated by itself, any derived class should call this constructor before entering its constructor. All this constructor does is set up the internal protected pointers to an `RS232` port object and a `TextWindow` object.

While the `RS232` object should be fairly familiar by this point, the `TextWindow` object is a member of a class that hasn't been discussed yet in this book. `TextWindow` is just a very simple class developed for handling screen I/O with some of the test programs in this book. It simply uses the PC BIOS to create windows, put data on the screen, insert and delete lines, and so on. It will be presented later in this chapter with little or no discussion, and is also used in the standard test program presented in Appendix A. `TextWindow` could easily be replaced by a more sophisticated class, as long as it supports all the required member functions, such as `Clear()`, `Goto()`, `SetPosition()`, and so on.

```
int ReadPort( void )
```

A very simple terminal program that doesn't perform any sort of emulation would probably read characters in directly from the RS-232 port using a call to `RS232::Read()`. When performing terminal emulation, this strategy begins to have problems. The normal display data coming in from the port will be interspersed with escape sequences, and the terminal program would have to filter those out and act on them.

The virtual function `ReadPort()` relieves the emulation program of having to worry about this. Instead of directly calling the `Read()` function, the terminal program calls `Terminal::ReadPort()`. This function reads data in from the RS-232 port, and actively filters out terminal escape sequences. The escape sequences are translated into function calls that operate on the screen,

# TERMINAL EMULATION

while normal display characters are passed back to the calling program.

The nice part about `ReadPort()` is that the base class describes virtually nothing about the internal workings of this function. This leaves the derived class free to implement its filtering function however works best for it, while maintaining a nice simple interface to the calling program.

`int Display( int c )`

For the `AnsiTerminal` class, this function is a simple inline piece of code that writes a character directly out to the screen. However, other `Terminal` classes may need to perform different processing here, which can be accomplished by developing a more sophisticated virtual function. A good example of this might be the VT-52 terminal. This terminal can be set into graphics mode, in which normal ASCII characters are translated into a different character set used for drawing lines, boxes, and so on. This could be accomplished easily with a simple version of `Display()`.

`void WriteKey( int c )`

Most `Terminal` classes will want to translate IBM PC extended keys into different sequences, such as the ANSI escape sequences documented here. The `WriteKey()` function is responsible for taking as input a standard key code, and writing out whatever sequence is necessary to the RS-232 port.

Some terminals have more complicated keyboard mapping systems than that found in the `AnsiTerminal` class, allowing for different key mappings to be selected by terminal escape sequences. In addition, it would be relatively simple to allow for user controlled remapping of the keyboard using this function.

## A Test Program

`TESTTERM.CPP` is the listing for the program that is used to test the `AnsiTerminal` class. There are a couple of interesting things to note about this program. One striking feature is the relative simplicity of a program that has to deal with three complex classes. Another point to note is that the program operates on base classes only, which means that replacing either the port type or the terminal emulation is simply a matter of changing the constructor.

# SERIAL COMMUNICATIONS: A C++ DEVELOPER'S GUIDE

```cpp
// *************** START OF TESTTERM.CPP ********************

// This test program implements a simple IBM ANSI terminal
// emulator.With a properly designed class, a terminal emulator
// amounts to just a few lines of code, since all of the
// work here is being done by the AnsiTerminal object. Note
// that the Terminal and RS232 objects are both pointers to
// the base class, not the derived class. This shows how terminal
// emulation can be performed without knowing anything
// about the emulation code, or the display class.

#include "rs232.h"
#include "pc8250.h"
#include "ascii.h"
#include "terminal.h"
#include "ansiterm.h"
#include "textwind.h"

main()
{
    TextWindow window( 0, 0, 80, 25 );
    RS232 *port = new PC8250( COM1, 19200, 'N', 8, 1 );
    Terminal *terminal = new AnsiTerminal( *port, window );
    int c;

    window << "Press F10 to exit...\n";
    port->RtsCtsHandshaking( 1 );
    for ( ; ; ) {
        c = terminal->ReadPort();
        if ( c < 0 && c != RS232_TIMEOUT )
            break;
        if ( c >= 0 )
            terminal->Display( c );
        c = window.ReadKey();
        if ( c == F10 )
            break;
        if ( c != 0 )
            terminal->WriteKey( c );
    }
```

# TERMINAL EMULATION

```
        delete terminal;
        delete port;
        return 0;
}

// *************** END OF TESTTERM.CPP *******************
```

**Listing 11-2. TESTTERM.CPP**

In `TESTTERM.CPP`, all of the interpretation of escape sequences is being done in the derived class member function `ReadPort()`. Any escape sequences in the input stream are pulled out by this function and acted on immediately. Normal characters are passed through to `TESTTERM.CPP`, which then immediately displays them.

## Class AnsiTerminal

Implementation of the `AnsiTerminal` class is fairly painless. The most difficult piece of code in the entire class is the parser, which breaks incoming escape sequences down into a list of parameters. Once the incoming escape sequence has been broken down, the individual routines that execute each of the ANSI command sequences are very simple.

```
// ****************** START OF ANSITERM.H ******************
//
// This is the public definition for the AnsiTerminal class.
// It has just three public functions, as well as a construc
// tor and a destructor.

#ifndef _ANSITERM_DOT_H
#define _ANSITERM_DOT_H

#include "portable.h"
#include "terminal.h"

class AnsiTerminal : public Terminal {
    private :
```

```cpp
            void parse( void );
            int parse_ansi_string( void );
            void position_cursor( void );
            void cursor_move( int row_dir, int col_dir );
            void cursor_position_report( void );
            void erase_in_display( void );
            void erase_in_line( void );
            void save_position( void );
            void restore_position( void );
            void set_color( void );
            void set_mode( void );
            char *ansi_parms[ 16 ];
            int parm_count;
            int saved_row;
            int saved_col;
            char **keys;
            char **extended_keys;
        public :
            AnsiTerminal( RS232 &p, TextWindow &w );
            virtual ~AnsiTerminal( void );
            virtual int ReadPort( void );
            virtual void Display( int c ){ *window << c; }
            virtual void WriteKey( int c );
};

#endif   // #ifdef _ANSITERM_DOT_H

// ******************* END OF ANSITERM.H *******************
```

**Listing 11-3. ANSITERM.H**

The listing above shows ANSITERM.H, the header file with the class definition for the AnsiTerminal class. In addition to the four virtual functions defined by the base Terminal class, AnsiTerminal has a constructor, plus a fairly lengthy list of private data and function members. These members are described below, followed by a listing of the code supporting the class.

# TERMINAL EMULATION

```
char *ansi_parms[ 16 ]
int parm_count
```

These two data members are used when parsing the input escape sequence. The constructor allocates a set of character arrays, and places pointers to them in the `ansi_parms[]` pointer array. During parsing, each incoming parameter is stored in an element of the array, starting at position 0. The `parm_count` index always points to the element of the array currently being accessed. When the parser returns, the last parameter should be the ANSI command character, which can be accessed in `ansi_parms[parm_count]`.

```
int saved_row
int saved_col
```

These two members support the ANSI commands to save and restore the current cursor position. When the command to save the position is received, the cursor position is written into these two data members. When the command to restore the cursor position is received, it is read out of the two data members and used to update the screen.

```
char **keys
char **extended_keys
```

These two 256 element arrays contain the list of keyboard translations. Standard key sequences representing "normal" IBM ASCII keystrokes are stored in the `keys[]` array. Extended keys, which are referenced by a scan code, are stored in the `extended_keys[]` array. Most of the keys have a null pointer in their key translation array, in which case just the normal ASCII code is sent.

The `AnsiTerminal` class doesn't support the key redefinition command, but having these two arrays in place makes it a fairly simple matter to add support for this function.

# SERIAL COMMUNICATIONS: A C++ DEVELOPER'S GUIDE

**virtual int ReadPort( void )**

This public virtual function normally just reads in the current value from the RS232 port, and returns whatever it read to the calling program. The exception occurs when the incoming character is an ASCII ESC code. If this is the case, it marks the beginning of an incoming Escape sequence. The incoming sequence is handled by the parse() function, and the command is acted on. Finally, the value RS232_TIMEOUT is returned to the calling program, indicating no character was received.

**void parse( void )**

This member function is called when an incoming ESC is detected. Its job is to read in the rest of the Escape sequence, parse it, and execute the command requested by the remote end.

In reality, this routine doesn't do too much work on its own. As soon as it is called, it invokes parse_ansi_string() to break the incoming sequence down into a list of usable parameters. Once that routine returns, the rest of parse() executes the appropriate member function based on a big switch statement. The real work is all done elsewhere.

**int parse_ansi_string( void )**

This routine has the hardest job of any function in the AnsiTerminal class. It has to take that incoming string of characters and break it down into a list of parameters stored in the ansi_parms[] array, so they can be successfully processed by other routines.

This routine operates as a simple state machine, which is always in one of four states:

READY_TO_READ:  The state machine starts here, when it is ready to read in the first character of an upcoming parameter. It returns to this state every time it reads in the ";" character used to separate parameters.

# TERMINAL EMULATION

Reading a non-numeric character other then the double quote (") in this position signals the end of an ANSI Escape sequence.

READING_DIGITS: Once the first digit in a numeric parameter has been read in, the parser moves to this state. It stays in this state until it reads the ";" character indicating another parameter is coming, or some other non-numeric character, which should be the command parameter.

READING_STRING: Once the initial " character is read in, indicating the start of a quoted string, the parser moves to this state and stays there until the trailing " character is found.

DONE_WITH_STRING: The trailing quote character puts the parser in this state, where it then waits for either the ";" indicating another parameter is coming, or a non-numeric command character.

**void position_cursor( void )**

Escape sequences "H" and "f" invoke this member function. It converts the two parameters in `ansi_parms[]` to row and column coordinates, then uses the `TextWindow::SetPosition()` function to position the cursor. If either of the row or column parameters is missing, the value of 1 is used as the default. Note that the row and column address parameters passed by the Escape sequence are 1 based, instead of 0 based as the `TextWindow` class expects, so some additional conversion is done.

**void cursor_move( int row_dir, int col_dir )**

This member function is used to support the four cursor movement commands generated by Escape sequences "A," "B," "C," and "D." The two direction parameters should be set to 1, 0, or -1 to indicate the direction of movement for the row and column.

This function checks the `ansi_parms[]` array to see if a value was passed, in which case it is used as the distance to travel measured in rows or columns. If no value was passed, the distance defaults to 1. It relies on the `SetPosition()` command to avoid trying to move outside the current bounds of the window.

**void cursor_position_report( void )**

When the "ESC[6n" command is received, IBM's version of ANSI.SYS sends a cursor position report, which is in the form "ESC[#;#R," where the two numeric parameters are the row and column. This function takes care of sending the cursor position report, getting the current row and column using the `TextWindow::GetPosition()` command, then formatting the string and sending it out the `RS232` port.

**void erase_in_display( void )**

The ANSI command to erase some or all of the display actually has three different modes, depending on the parameter that is sent in the "ESC[#J" command. IBM ANSI.SYS only recognizes a parameter value of 2, which is used to clear the entire screen. `AnsiTerminal` accomplishes this by calling `TextWindow::Clear()`, followed by `TextWindow::SetPosition()` to home the cursor.

**void erase_in_line( void )**

Like the previous command, the ANSI specification gives several possible parameters that can be passed with "ESC[#K" command. The version supported by IBM ANSI.SYS is called when the parameter is either not present or set to 0. This command erases the current line from (and including) the cursor position to the end of the line. Since the `TextWindow` class doesn't have a member function to do this,

# TERMINAL EMULATION

it is accomplished by first reading the cursor position with `TextWindow::GetPosition()`, then getting the width of the line with `TextWindow::GetDimensions()`. The line is filled with blanks using the insertion operator, "<<," then the cursor position is restored with `TextWindow::SetPosition()`.

**void save_position( void )**

The "ESC[s" command is an extension of the ANSI specification that is unique to ANSI.SYS. All this command does is read the current cursor position by calling `TextWindow::GetPosition()`, and storing it in the member data elements `saved_row` and `saved_col`.

**void restore_position( void )**

Like the previous command, the "ESC[u" command is unique to ANSI.SYS. This command restores the settings stored previously in `saved_row` and `saved_col` by calling `TextWindow::SetPosition()`.

**void set_color( void )**

The code to execute this command is somewhat more complicated than any of the previous commands. First, instead of having a single parameter, this command can have any number of numeric parameters strung together. Second, there are 21 possible parameters, each of which modifies the screens current display attribute.

The `set_color()` command accomplishes this by executing a loop that starts with the first parameter and works through the list in `ansi_parms[]`. The loop terminates when it reaches the value of `parm_count`, which is the index for the ANSI command value, and is one past the last parameter.

Each parameter in the list is processed by first retrieving the current display attribute with a call to `TextWindow::GetAttribute()`. The attribute is then modified, either by changing the foreground color, the background color, or replacing it with an entirely new attribute. All this is accomplished by a large `switch` statement that does the job in a very straightforward manner. Finally, the new attribute is set using the `TextWindow::SetAttribute()` command.

```
void set_mode( void )
```

The "ESC[=#h" and "ESC[=#l" commands are used to set new video modes. ANSI.SYS will change the display into various video modes, such as 40 by 25 text mode, and 320 by 200 graphics mode. In addition, a parameter value of 7 is used to set and reset end of line wrap mode.

The implementation of the two mode commands in `AnsiTerminal` doesn't support any of the mode values except 7, which controls wrap mode. This accomplishes its task by calling the `TextWindow::SetWrap()` function.

```
AnsiTerminal( RS232 &p, TextWindow &w )
```

The constructor for an object of type `AnsiTerminal` first calls the base class constructor, which takes care of assigning the `TextWindow` and `RS232` pointers that are used by the class. Next, it takes care of setting up the output screen, by calling the `Clear()`, `Goto()`, and `SetWrap()` members of class `TextWindow`.

Once the output screen has been set up, the next thing the constructor does is allocate the memory used in the `ansi_parms[]` array, as well as the two key code translation arrays. Finally, the two key code translation arrays are initialized with their default values.

```
virtual ~AnsiTerminal( void )
```

The `AnsiTerminal` destructor frees the memory allocated for the three arrays used during the emulation, and then exits.

```
virtual void Display( int c )
```

The `Display()` routine is used to display normal characters that make it through the escape sequence filtering. For ANSI emulation, this is nice and simple. The characters are just output to the `TextWindow` using the insertion operator.

# TERMINAL EMULATION

**`virtual void WriteKey( int c )`**

This function checks to see if the key is one of the extended key codes or a standard ASCII code. Depending on which it is, a translation is looked up from one of the two key code translation tables. If a translation exists, it is sent. If no translation exists, and the key is a standard ASCII key , the key value is sent. Extended keys aren't sent if no translation exists.

```
// ****************** START OF ANSITERM.CPP *****************

// This file contains all the code to support the AnsiTerminal
// class, which is a terminal emulation class that supports
// the IBM PC ANSI.SYS control sequences.

#include <stdio.h>
#include <stdlib.h>
#include <string.h>
#include "portable.h"
#include "textwind.h"
#include "terminal.h"
#include "ansiterm.h"

// These two defines can be used to help debug the terminal
// emulation class. DEBUG is used to split the screen and pro
// vide a bottom window that displays escape sequences as they
// are parsed. KEYBOARD_FAKE lets you input escape sequences
// from the keyboard.

//#define KEYBOARD_FAKE
//#define DEBUG

#ifdef DEBUG
TextWindow *debug_window;
#endif

// This is a list of keyboard mappings that are defined when
// the emulator first starts. These key mappings can be
// remapped dynamically, although this class does not support
```

```c
// the feature. These values are loaded into the mapping
// arrays when the constructor executes.

struct key_strings {
    int key_value;
    char *translation;
} initial_key_translations[] = { { LEFT,        "\x1b[D" },
                                 { RIGHT,       "\x1b[C" },
                                 { UP,          "\x1b[A" },
                                 { DOWN,        "\x1b[B" },
                                 { HOME,        "\x1b[H" },
                                 { END,         "\x1b[H" },
                                 { PGUP,        "\x1b[I" },
                                 { PGDN,        "\x1b[G" },
                                 { INSERT,      "\x1b[L" },
                                 { F1,          "\x1b[M" },
                                 { F2,          "\x1b[N" },
                                 { F3,          "\x1b[O" },
                                 { F4,          "\x1b[P" },
                                 { F5,          "\x1b[Q" },
                                 { F6,          "\x1b[R" },
                                 { F7,          "\x1b[S" },
                                 { F8,          "\x1b[T" },
                                 { F9,          "\x1b[U" },
                                 { F10,         "\x1b[V" },
                                 { SHIFT_F1,    "\x1b[Y" },
                                 { SHIFT_F2,    "\x1b[Z" },
                                 { SHIFT_F3,    "\x1b[a" },
                                 { SHIFT_F4,    "\x1b[b" },
                                 { SHIFT_F5,    "\x1b[c" },
                                 { SHIFT_F6,    "\x1b[d" },
                                 { SHIFT_F7,    "\x1b[e" },
                                 { SHIFT_F8,    "\x1b[f" },
                                 { SHIFT_F9,    "\x1b[g" },
                                 { SHIFT_F10,   "\x1b[h" },
                                 { CONTROL_F1,  "\x1b[k" },
                                 { CONTROL_F2,  "\x1b[l" },
                                 { CONTROL_F3,  "\x1b[m" },
                                 { CONTROL_F4,  "\x1b[n" },
```

```
                    { CONTROL_F5,   "\x1b[o"  },
                    { CONTROL_F6,   "\x1b[p"  },
                    { CONTROL_F7,   "\x1b[q"  },
                    { CONTROL_F8,   "\x1b[r"  },
                    { CONTROL_F9,   "\x1b[s"  },
                    { CONTROL_F10,  "\x1b[t"  },
                    { ALT_F1,       "\x1b[w"  },
                    { ALT_F2,       "\x1b[x"  },
                    { ALT_F3,       "\x1b[y"  },
                    { ALT_F4,       "\x1b[z"  },
                    { ALT_F5,       "\x1b[@"  },
                    { ALT_F6,       "\x1b[["  },
                    { ALT_F7,       "\x1b[\\" },
                    { ALT_F8,       "\x1b[]"  },
                    { ALT_F9,       "\x1b[^"  },
                    { ALT_F10,      "\x1b[_"  },
                    { 0,            0         }
                };

// The constructor sets up the pointers to the port and the
// TextWindow objects. It puts the window in a predefined
// state, allocates the memory for the ansi string parsing
// storage, then initializes the key maps. If the DEBUG macro
// is turned on, the screen is split and a second debug
// text window is opened.

AnsiTerminal::AnsiTerminal( RS232 &p, TextWindow &w ) :
                    Terminal( p, w )
{
    int key;
    char *translation;

    window->Clear();
    window->Goto();
    window->SetWrap( 1 );
    saved_row = 0;
    saved_col = 0;
    for ( int i = 0 ; i < 15 ; i++ )
        ansi_parms[ i ] = new char[ 81 ];
```

```cpp
        ansi_parms[ 15 ] = 0;
        keys = new char *[ 256 ];
        extended_keys = new char *[ 256 ];
        for ( i = 0 ; i < 256 ; i++ ) {
            if ( keys )
                keys[ i ] = 0;
            if ( extended_keys )
                extended_keys[ i ] = 0;
        }
        for ( i = 0; initial_key_translations[ i ].translation !=
                                                    0 ; i++ ) {
            key = initial_key_translations[ i ].key_value;
            translation = initial_key_translations[ i ].translation;
            if ( extended_keys && key > 256 )
                extended_keys[ ( key >> 8 ) & 0xff ] = translation;
            else if ( keys )
                keys[ key ] = translation;
        }
#ifdef DEBUG
    Set43LineMode( 1 );
    debug_window = new TextWindow( 25, 0, 80, 18 );
    debug_window->SetWrap( 1 );
#endif
}

// ReadPort filters port input for the end application. If it
// sees the first character of an escape sequence, it gets
// parsed, and the application never sees it. Normal charac
// ters get passed straight back to the application. Note that
// if the KEYBOARD_FAKE macro is defined, input comes from the
// keyboard instead of the port.

int AnsiTerminal::ReadPort( void )
{
    int c;
```

# TERMINAL EMULATION

```
#ifdef KEYBOARD_FAKE
    while ( ( c = window->ReadKey() ) == 0 )
        ;
    if ( c == F10 )
        return RS232_ERROR;
#else
    c = port->Read();
#endif
    if ( c == ESC ) {
        parse();
        return RS232_TIMEOUT;
    }
    return c;
}

// The destructor for an AnsiTerminal objects just has to free
// up the memory allocated for the ANSI parser. If DEBUG is
// turned on, the screen is restored to 25 line mode. This
// routine has to cope with the differences in "delete" in
// different versions of C++.

AnsiTerminal::~AnsiTerminal( void )
{
    for ( int i = 0 ; i < 15 ; i++ )
#ifdef DELETE_ARRAY
        delete[] ansi_parms[ i ];
    delete[] keys;
    delete[] extended_keys;
#else
        delete ansi_parms[ i ];
    delete keys;
    delete extended_keys;
#endif
#ifdef DEBUG
    Set43LineMode( 0 );
#endif
}
```

```
// This is the actual parser that reads in ANSI strings. It
// is just a fairly simple state machine, that sits in a loop
// reading in characters until it detects the end of an ANSI
// sequence. When it is done, the ansi_parms[] array holds a list
// of numeric and quoted strings, and parm_count is the index
// to the last valid string. Error handling is nonexistent, if
// anything odd happens the routine just returns with a failure.

int AnsiTerminal::parse_ansi_string( void )
{
    int index;
    enum { READY_TO_READ,
           READING_DIGITS,
           READING_STRING,
           DONE_WITH_STRING } scan_state;
    int c;

    parm_count = 0;
    index = 0;

    for ( int i = 0 ; i < 15 ; i++ )
        if ( ansi_parms[ i ] != 0 )
            memset( ansi_parms[ i ], 0, 81 );
#ifdef KEYBOARD_FAKE
    while ( ( c = window->ReadKey() ) == 0 )
        ;
#else
    c = port->Read( 200 );
#endif
    if ( c != '[' )
        return 0;

    scan_state = READY_TO_READ;
    for ( ; ; ) {
        if ( index >= 80 || ansi_parms[ parm_count ] == 0 )
            return 0;
#ifdef KEYBOARD_FAKE
        while ( ( c = window->ReadKey() ) == 0 )
            ;
```

```
#else
        c = port->Read( 1000 );
#endif
        if ( c < 0 )
            return 0;
        switch ( scan_state ) {
          case READY_TO_READ:
             if(parm_count == 0 && ( c == '=' || c == '?'))
                ansi_parms[ parm_count++ ][ 0 ] = (char) c;
             else if ( c == '"' ) {
               scan_state = READING_STRING;
               ansi_parms[ parm_count ][ index++ ] = (char) c;
             } else if ( c >= '0' && c <= '9' ) {
                ansi_parms[ parm_count ][ index++ ] = (char) c;
                scan_state = READING_DIGITS;
             } else if ( c == ';' ) {
                parm_count++;
                index = 0;
             } else {
                ansi_parms[ parm_count ][ index ]=(char) c;
                 return 1;
             }
             break;
          case READING_DIGITS :
             if ( c == ';' ) {
                parm_count++;
                index = 0;
                scan_state = READY_TO_READ;
             } else if ( c >= '0' && c <='9' )
                ansi_parms[ parm_count ][ index++ ] = (char) c;
             else {
                ansi_parms[ ++parm_count ][ 0 ] = (char) c;
                 return 1;
             }
             break;
          case READING_STRING :
             if ( c == '"' )
                 scan_state = DONE_WITH_STRING;
             ansi_parms[ parm_count ][ index++ ] = (char) c;
```

```cpp
                    break;
            case DONE_WITH_STRING :
                if ( c == ';' ) {
                    parm_count++;
                    index = 0;
                    scan_state = READY_TO_READ;
                } else {
                    ansi_parms[ ++parm_count ][ 0 ] = (char) c;
                     return 1;
                }
                break;
        }
    }
}

// This routine is the high-level controller for the terminal
// emulation class. It calls parse_ansi_string() to break the
// escape sequence down into usable components, then dispatches
// the appropriate member function to do the work. If DEBUG is
// switched on, the escape sequence is dumped out to the debug
// window.

void AnsiTerminal::parse( void )
{
    if ( parse_ansi_string() ) {
#ifdef DEBUG
        debug_window->Goto();
        DisplayAttribute att = debug_window->GetAttribute();
        debug_window->SetAttribute( att ^ 0x77 );
        *debug_window << "ESC [ ";
        for ( int i = 0 ; i <= parm_count; i++ )
            *debug_window << "<" << ansi_parms[ i ] << ">";
        *debug_window << "  ";
        window->Goto();
#endif
        switch( ansi_parms[ parm_count ][ 0 ] ) {
            case 'A' : cursor_move( -1, 0 ); break;
            case 'B' : cursor_move( 1, 0 ); break;
            case 'C' : cursor_move( 0, 1 ); break;
```

## TERMINAL EMULATION

```
                case 'D' : cursor_move( 0, -1 ); break;
                case 'H' : position_cursor(); break;
                case 'J' : erase_in_display(); break;
                case 'K' : erase_in_line(); break;
                case 'f' : position_cursor(); break;
                case 'l' : set_mode(); break;
                case 'h' : set_mode(); break;
                case 'm' : set_color(); break;
                case 'n' : cursor_position_report(); break;
                case 's' : save_position(); break;
                case 'u' : restore_position(); break;
            }
        }
}

// ESC[#;#f and ESC[#;#H
//
// These two commands have the same effect, which is to position
// the cursor at a location specified by the two numbers,
// which are a row and column sequence. One or both parameters
// can be omitted, in which case the default value of 1 is
// used. Note that row and column numbers in ANSI are 1 based,
// while the TextWindow class numbers are 0 based.

void AnsiTerminal::position_cursor()
{
    int row;
    int col;

    if ( parm_count > 0 )
        row = atoi( ansi_parms[ 0 ] );
    else
        row = 1;
    if ( parm_count > 1 )
        col = atoi( ansi_parms[ 1 ] );
    else
        col = 1;
    window->SetPosition( row - 1, col - 1 );
}
```

# SERIAL COMMUNICATIONS: A C++ DEVELOPER'S GUIDE

```
// ESC[#A   Cursor up
// ESC[#B   Cursor down
// ESC[#C   Cursor right
// ESC[#D   Cursor left
//
// These four commands are all handled with this member function.
// The single numeric parameter defaults to 1 if it is omitted.
// Any movement outside the screen bounds is ignored by the
// TextWindow functions, so this routine doesn't have to worry
// about it.

void AnsiTerminal::cursor_move( int row_dir, int col_dir )
{
    int offset;
    int row;
    int col;

    if ( parm_count > 0 )
        offset = atoi( ansi_parms[ 0 ] );
    else
        offset = 1;
    window->GetPosition( row, col );
    row += offset * row_dir;
    col += offset * col_dir;
    window->SetPosition( row, col );
}


// ESC[6n   Device Status Report
//
// This command is handled by issuing a Cursor Position Report
// sequence, ESC[#;#R, whith the two numeric parameters being
// the row and column number. Note that handling the command
// this way is somewhat idiosynchratic to the PC.

void AnsiTerminal::cursor_position_report( void )
{
    int row;
    int col;
    char temp[ 40 ];
```

```cpp
    if ( parm_count != 1 )
        return;
    if ( strcmp( ansi_parms[ 0 ], "6" ) != 0 )
        return;
    window->GetPosition( row, col );
    sprintf( temp, "%c[%d;%dR", ESC, row + 1, col + 1 );
    port->Write( temp );
}

// ESC[2J   Erase in display
//
// The official ANSI version of this command will erase some
// or all of the display, depending on the value of the numeric
// parameters.The IBM PC version only supports parameter 2,
// which erases the entire display. The cursor is homed as part
// of this command.

void AnsiTerminal::erase_in_display( void )
{
    if ( parm_count != 1 )
        return;
    if ( strcmp( ansi_parms[ 0 ], "2" ) != 0 )
        return;
    window->Clear();
    window->SetPosition( 0, 0 );
}

// ESC[K   Erase in line
//
// This is another ANSI command that is only partially supported
// by IBM ANSI. When no numeric parameter is given, the
// line is erased from the cursor position to the end of the line.

void AnsiTerminal::erase_in_line( void )
{
    int row;
    int col;
    int width;
    int height;
    int i;
```

```cpp
        if ( parm_count != 0 )
            return;
        window->GetPosition( row, col );
        window->GetDimensions( width, height );
        for ( i = col ; i < width; i++ )
            *window << ' ';
        window->SetPosition( row, col );
    }

    // ESC[s   Save Cursor Position
    //
    // This command saves off the current cursor position for
    // later restoration. This is an IBM extension to the ANSI
    // standard.

    void AnsiTerminal::save_position( void )
    {
        if ( parm_count != 0 )
            return;
        window->GetPosition( saved_row, saved_col );
    }

    // ESC[u   Restore Cursor Position
    //
    // Another IBM extension to the ANSI standard. This command
    // restores the previously saved cursor position.

    void AnsiTerminal::restore_position( void )
    {
        if ( parm_count != 0 )
            return;
        window->SetPosition( saved_row, saved_col );
    }

    // ESC[#;#;...;#m   Set Graphics Rendition
    //
```

# TERMINAL EMULATION

```cpp
// This command sets the current display attributes to various
// attributes. Multiple command parameters can be stringed
// together in unlimited combinations. This implementation is
// limited to 14 parameters.

void AnsiTerminal::set_color( void )
{
    int command;
    int att;

    for ( int i = 0 ; i < parm_count ; i++ ) {
        command = atoi( ansi_parms[ i ] );
        att = window->GetAttribute();
        switch( command ) {
            case 0  : att = NORMAL_ATTRIBUTE;            break;
            case 1  : att = att | 8;                     break;
            case 5  : att = att | 0x80;                  break;
            case 7  : att = REVERSE_ATTRIBUTE;           break;
            case 8  : att = INVISIBLE_ATTRIBUTE;         break;
            case 30 : att = ( att & 0xf0 ) | 0x00;       break;
            case 31 : att = ( att & 0xf0 ) | 0x04;       break;
            case 32 : att = ( att & 0xf0 ) | 0x02;       break;
            case 33 : att = ( att & 0xf0 ) | 0x0e;       break;
            case 34 : att = ( att & 0xf0 ) | 0x01;       break;
            case 35 : att = ( att & 0xf0 ) | 0x05;       break;
            case 36 : att = ( att & 0xf0 ) | 0x03;       break;
            case 37 : att = ( att & 0xf0 ) | 0x07;       break;
            case 40 : att = ( att & 0x0f ) | 0x00;       break;
            case 41 : att = ( att & 0x0f ) | 0x40;       break;
            case 42 : att = ( att & 0x0f ) | 0x20;       break;
            case 43 : att = ( att & 0x0f ) | 0x60;       break;
            case 44 : att = ( att & 0x0f ) | 0x10;       break;
            case 45 : att = ( att & 0x0f ) | 0x50;       break;
            case 46 : att = ( att & 0x0f ) | 0x30;       break;
            case 47 : att = ( att & 0x0f ) | 0x70;       break;
        }
        window->SetAttribute( att );
    }
}
```

```
// ESC[=#h   ESC[=#l    Set/Reset Mode
// ESC[=h    ESC[=l
// ESC[=0h   ESC[=0l
// ESC[?7h   ESC[?7l
//
// This command is used to change the current video mode. The
// TextWindow class used here doesn't support changing modes,
// so most versions of this command aren't supported. The single
// exception is the last version, which turns on-/offline wrap.

void AnsiTerminal::set_mode( void )
{
    if ( parm_count != 2 )
        return;
    if ( strcmp( ansi_parms[ 0 ], "?" ) != 0 &&
         strcmp( ansi_parms[ 0 ], "=" ) != 0 )
        return;
    if ( strcmp( ansi_parms[ 1 ], "7" ) != 0 )
        return;
    switch( ansi_parms[ 2 ][ 0 ] ) {
        case 'h' : window->SetWrap( 1 ); break;
        case 'l' : window->SetWrap( 0 ); break;
    }
}

// Writing a key to the serial port is done by checking to see
// if a translation is defined. If not, the key itself is sent
// out, otherwise the translation is sent.

void AnsiTerminal::WriteKey( int key )
{
    char *translation;

    if ( extended_keys && key > 256 ) {
        translation = extended_keys[ ( key >> 8 ) & 0xff ];
        if ( translation != 0 )
            port->Write( translation );
    } else {
        if ( keys )
```

```
            translation = keys[ key ];
        else
            translation = 0;
        if ( translation != 0 )
            port->Write( translation );
        else
            port->Write( key );
    }
}

// ***************** END OF ANSITERM.CPP ******************
```

**Listing 11-4. ANSITERM.CPP**

## Debugging Hooks

Debugging terminal emulation code can be difficult. There are two problems in particular. First of all, as the escape codes are transmitted from the remote terminal, they are deliberately filtered out of the input stream, so they aren't visible to the programmer during debugging. Because of this, it is difficult to tell whether or not the emulation code is responding properly to escape sequences, since you can't see what sequences are being received.

Secondly, it can be difficult to convince a remote system to send the exact sequences you want to test. For example, you may never be able to get your local BBS to send the "ESC[s" sequence needed to save the cursor row and position.

These two problems are handled by providing special debugging code inside the `AnsiTerminal` class. Two special macros enable the debugging code when they are defined.

The first macro is called `DEBUG`. When `DEBUG` is defined, by virtue of a preprocessor `#define` statement in `ANSITERM.CPP`, some extra code is enabled. This code has the effect of opening up a debug window that displays ANSI Escape sequences as they are parsed.

The `DEBUG` code accomplishes this by putting the screen into 43 line mode when the `AnsiTerminal` constructor is called, and creating a second text window that occupies the bottom half of the screen. The top 25 lines are still used for normal terminal emulation. During the parsing of input data, the Escape sequences are displayed in the debug window.

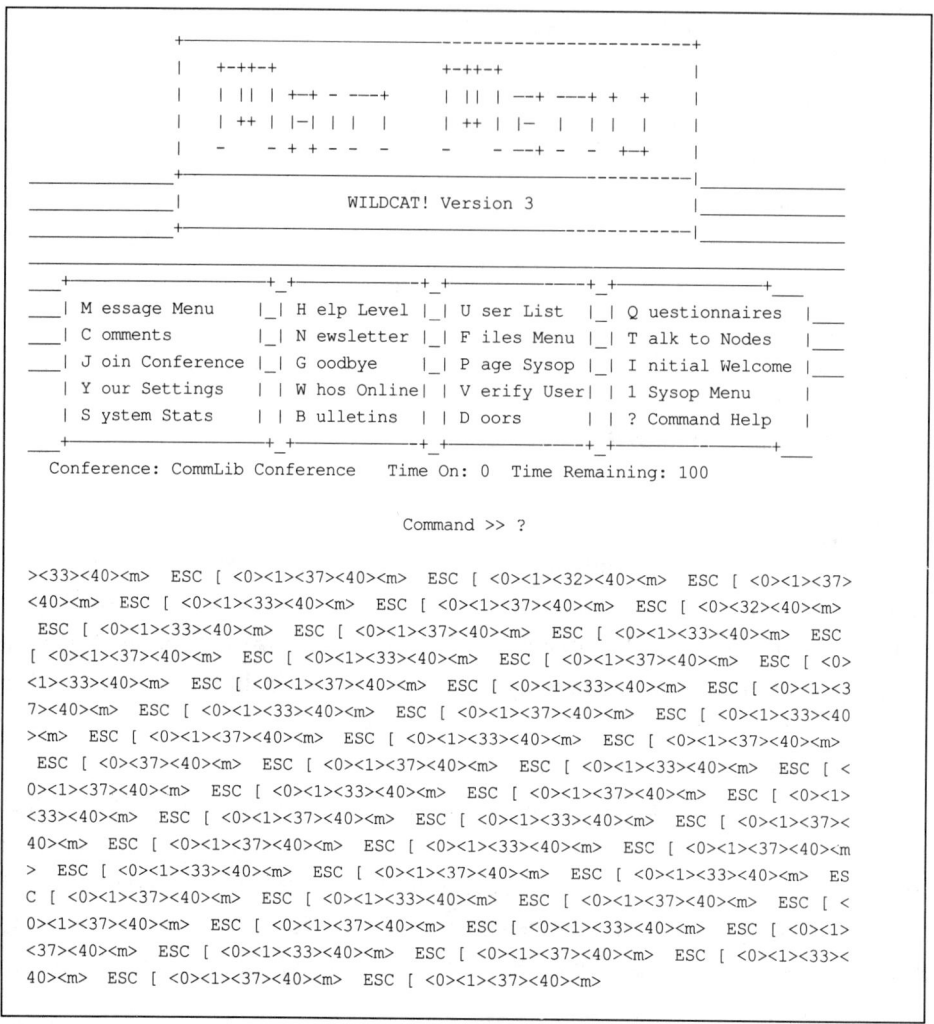

**Figure 11-1. A sample screen with DEBUG turned on**

The debug output is shown in Figure 11-1. During the course of a BBS session, scores of escape sequences are shown in the debug window. While this may seem somewhat overwhelming, it is usually fairly easy to spot simple problems with a complete output dump such as this. Working on more complicated problems may require modification of the code that displays the escape sequences. For example, this code could be modified to show only certain sequences, or perhaps to filter other sequences out.

The second macro used to help during the debugging process is called KEYBOARD_FAKE. The name of the macro describes exactly what it does: it allows you to fake escape sequences using keyboard input. When the KEYBOARD_FAKE macro is turned on, input that normally comes from the RS232 port instead is read in from the keyboard. In this way, you can input whatever escape sequences you want to test without struggling to convince a remote system to send them to you over an RS-232 link.

### The TextWindow class

Although the Terminal class depends on the TextWindow class for access to the screen, this chapter hasn't spent much time discussing it. This book is about RS-232 programming, so screen output is just a necessary evil. Clearly, a serious application would need to use a good screen interface package. The constructor for AnsiTerminal expects to be passed a reference to an already created TextWindow object, which it can use freely throughout the duration of the AnsiTerminal object's life.

The TextWindow functions used by AnsiTerminal are listed below. Ideally, these functions should probably be converted to virtual functions that belong to a base class. In that way the terminal emulation classes would call virtual functions to perform display operations without any prior knowledge of how the TextWindow class works. Instead, terminal emulation code would use a virtual API defined for a base class. Programmers could then implement terminal emulation using any one of several derived display classes.

**TextWindow& operator<<( int c )**

This is the basic insertion operator for the class. All it does is display characters on the screen, updating the cursor position accordingly.

**void Clear( void )**

This function clears the entire `TextWindow` object, which may or may not occupy the entire screen.

**int SetPosition( int row, int col )**

This function sets the cursor position to the row and column specified as arguments to the function. Note that the row and column are zero based, and the positioning is relative to the `TextWindow` object, not to absolute positions on the screen.

**void GetPosition( int &rol, int &col )**

`GetPosition()` is used to read the current position of the row and column. This function is used to handle the ANSI command used to save the current cursor position.

**void GetDimensions( int &width, int &height )**

This function returns the width and height of the `TextWindow` object. The only place this information is used in the `AnsiTerminal` class is when clearing from the current cursor position to the end of the line.

**void SetAttribute( int a )**

This function accepts IBM PC display attributes as its single argument. That attribute then becomes the one used to display all the characters subsequently displayed in the `TextWindow`. It is also the attribute used when either the entire object or part of it is displayed.

# TERMINAL EMULATION

**`DisplayAttribute GetAttribute( void )`**

`AnsiTerminal` needs to be able to read in the current attribute. Many of the ANSI commands that modify the attribute only affect the foreground or background color, so you need to have a copy of the current attribute in order to make that modification.

**`void SetWrap( int setting )`**

The ANSI command that sets modes can either clear or set the end of line wrap flag.

**`void Goto( void )`**

The `Goto()` function is used to select the particular `TextWindow` object. If multiple `TextWindow` objects are present on the screen, this moves the focus for keyboard input to the particular object. In addition, if an overlapping window class was being used, this might bring the selected object to the top if was previously obscured.

**`int ReadKey( void )`**

This function reads in a key from the keyboard. If no key is present in the keyboard buffer, it returns a 0. Extended keys are returned with a 0 in the low byte and the extended IBM keyboard scan code in the upper byte.

The source code for the `TextWindow` class is shown below. These source files are also used in the `TEST232.CPP` test file listed in the Appendix.

```
// **************** START OF TEXTWIN.H *********************
//
// Text windows are used by utility and test programs to provide
// a convenient set of display functions under MS-DOS.

#ifndef _TEXTWIN_DOT_H
#define _TEXTWIN_DOT_H
```

```c
#include <dos.h>
#include <conio.h>
#include "portable.h"
#include "ascii.h"

enum DisplayAttribute { NORMAL_ATTRIBUTE = 0x07,
                        REVERSE_ATTRIBUTE = 0x70,
                        INVISIBLE_ATTRIBUTE = 0 };

// The TextWindow class is a very limited display class that
// uses the BIOS for all of its input and output. It supports
// just a few basic operations, but these are enough for test
// and demonstration programs.

class TextWindow {
    protected:
        static int count;
        unsigned char start_row;
        unsigned char start_col;
        unsigned char width;
        unsigned char height;
        int border;
        unsigned char row;
        unsigned char col;
        int wrap;
        DisplayAttribute attribute;
        unsigned int *save_buffer;
        void write_char( unsigned char c );
        void write_repeated_chars( unsigned char c, int count );
        void position( int r, int c );
        void save_window();
        void save_border();
        void restore_window();
        void restore_border();
    public :
        TextWindow( int r, int c, int w, int h );
        ~TextWindow();
        TextWindow& operator<<( char c );
        TextWindow& operator<<( int c );
```

# TERMINAL EMULATION

```cpp
        TextWindow& operator<<( char *s );
        void Clear( void );
        void AddBorder( void );
        void DisplayTitle( char *title );
        void Scroll( unsigned char line_count );
        int SetPosition( int row, int col );
        void GetPosition( int &rol, int &col );
        void GetDimensions( int &width, int &height );
        void SetAttribute( int a ) { attribute =
                                    (DisplayAttribute) a; }
        DisplayAttribute GetAttribute( void ) { return attribute; }
        void SetWrap( int setting ){ wrap = setting; }
        void Goto( void );
        int ReadKey( void );
};

// A couple of simple access routines that are short enough to
// inline.

inline void TextWindow::GetPosition( int &r, int &c )
{
    r = row;
    c = col;
}

inline void TextWindow::GetDimensions( int &w, int &h )
{
    w = width;
    h = height;
}

// This class provides a very handy way to save a cursor posi
// tion and restore it later.

class SaveCursor {
    protected :
        unsigned char row;
        unsigned char col;
    public :
```

```cpp
        SaveCursor();
        ~SaveCursor();
};

inline SaveCursor::SaveCursor( void )
{
    union REGS r;

    r.h.ah = 3;
    r.h.bh = 0;
    int86( 0x10, &r, &r );
    row = r.h.dh;
    col = r.h.dl;
}

inline SaveCursor::~SaveCursor( void )
{
    union REGS r;

    r.h.ah = 2;
    r.h.dh = row;
    r.h.dl = col;
    r.h.bh = 0;
    int86( 0x10, &r, &r );
}

// PopupWindow is a class derived from TextWindow. It is
// almost identical, except for the fact that it saves the
// underlying text when created and restores it when destroyed.

class PopupWindow : public TextWindow {
    protected :
        SaveCursor saved_cursor;
    public :
        PopupWindow( int r, int c, int w, int h );
};

// A couple of handy support routines
```

# TERMINAL EMULATION

```c
int Menu( char *menu[] );
int ReadLine( char *prompt, char *buffer, int length );
void Set43LineMode( int control );

// Keyboard definitions for codes returned from ReadKey()

const int F1           = 0x3b00;
const int F2           = 0x3c00;
const int F3           = 0x3d00;
const int F4           = 0x3e00;
const int F5           = 0x3f00;
const int F6           = 0x4000;
const int F7           = 0x4100;
const int F8           = 0x4200;
const int F9           = 0x4300;
const int F10          = 0x4400;
const int ALT_F1       = 0x6800;
const int ALT_F2       = 0x6900;
const int ALT_F3       = 0x6a00;
const int ALT_F4       = 0x6b00;
const int ALT_F5       = 0x6c00;
const int ALT_F6       = 0x6d00;
const int ALT_F7       = 0x6e00;
const int ALT_F8       = 0x6f00;
const int ALT_F9       = 0x7000;
const int ALT_F10      = 0x7100;
const int CONTROL_F1   = 0x5e00;
const int CONTROL_F2   = 0x5f00;
const int CONTROL_F3   = 0x6000;
const int CONTROL_F4   = 0x6100;
const int CONTROL_F5   = 0x6200;
const int CONTROL_F6   = 0x6300;
const int CONTROL_F7   = 0x6400;
const int CONTROL_F8   = 0x6500;
const int CONTROL_F9   = 0x6600;
const int CONTROL_F10  = 0x6700;
const int SHIFT_F1     = 0x5400;
const int SHIFT_F2     = 0x5500;
const int SHIFT_F3     = 0x5600;
```

```cpp
const int SHIFT_F4   = 0x5700;
const int SHIFT_F5   = 0x5800;
const int SHIFT_F6   = 0x5900;
const int SHIFT_F7   = 0x5a00;
const int SHIFT_F8   = 0x5b00;
const int SHIFT_F9   = 0x5c00;
const int SHIFT_F10  = 0x5d00;
const int UP         = 0x4800;
const int DOWN       = 0x5000;
const int LEFT       = 0x4b00;
const int RIGHT      = 0x4d00;
const int HOME       = 0x4700;
const int END        = 0x4f00;
const int PGUP       = 0x4900;
const int PGDN       = 0x5100;
const int INSERT     = 0x5200;
const int DELETE     = 0x5300;

const int ALT_A = 0x1e00;
const int ALT_B = 0x3000;
const int ALT_C = 0x2e00;
const int ALT_D = 0x2000;
const int ALT_E = 0x1200;
const int ALT_F = 0x2100;
const int ALT_G = 0x2200;
const int ALT_H = 0x2300;
const int ALT_I = 0x1700;
const int ALT_J = 0x2400;
const int ALT_K = 0x2500;
const int ALT_L = 0x2600;
const int ALT_M = 0x3200;
const int ALT_N = 0x3100;
const int ALT_O = 0x1800;
const int ALT_P = 0x1900;
const int ALT_Q = 0x1000;
const int ALT_R = 0x1300;
const int ALT_S = 0x1f00;
const int ALT_T = 0x1400;
const int ALT_U = 0x1600;
```

```
const int ALT_V = 0x2f00;
const int ALT_W = 0x1100;
const int ALT_X = 0x2d00;
const int ALT_Y = 0x1500;
const int ALT_Z = 0x2c00;

#endif  // #ifdef _TEXTWIN_DOT_H

// ****************** END OF TEXTWIN.H ********************
```

**Listing 11-5. TEXTWIN.H**

```
// *************** START OF TEXTWIN.CPP ********************
//
// This file contains all of the code needed to support the
// Text Windows used for example programs in this book. These
// are "quick-and-dirty" text windows, using the BIOS for most
// of the work.

#include <stdlib.h>
#include <string.h>
#include <dos.h>
#include <conio.h>
#include <ctype.h>
#include <bios.h>
#include "textwind.h"

// This static data member keeps track of how many windows are
// open. When the count drops to zero, cleanup work can be done.

int TextWindow::count = 0;

// write_char uses the BIOS function to write the current
// character using the window attribute. This function is a
// protected member function, and is used by the << operator.

inline void TextWindow::write_char( unsigned char c )
{
```

```cpp
    union REGS r;

    r.h.ah = 9;
    r.h.al = c;
    r.h.bl = attribute;
    r.h.bh = 0;
    r.x.cx = 1;
    int86( 0x10, &r, &r );
}

// This protected function uses the BIOS parameter to write a
// single character repeatedly. This is much faster than writing
// individual characters in a loop. It is used when writing
// the border and clearing the screen.

inline void TextWindow::write_repeated_chars( unsigned char c,
                                                 int count )
{
    union REGS r;

    r.h.ah = 9;
    r.h.al =  c;
    r.h.bl =  attribute;
    r.x.cx = count;
    r.h.bh = 0;
    int86( 0x10, &r, &r );
}

// This protected member function positions the cursor at the
// desired position relative to the text window. The protected
// function doesn't check for validity of the row and column
// values. It also doesn't set the row and column data members.

inline void TextWindow::position( int r, int c )
{
    union REGS rin;

    r += start_row;
    c += start_col;
```

```c
        rin.h.ah = 2;
        rin.h.dh = (unsigned char) r;
        rin.h.dl = (unsigned char) c;
        rin.h.bh = 0;
        int86( 0x10, &rin, &rin );
}

// This public member function positions the cursor in a
// window. It also stores the new position in the row and column
// data members.

int TextWindow::SetPosition( int r, int c )
{
    union REGS rin;

    if ( r < 0 || c < 0 )
        return 0;
    if ( r >= (int) height || c >= (int) width )
        return 0;
    row = (unsigned char) r;
    col = (unsigned char) c;
    r += start_row;
    c += start_col;
    rin.h.ah = 2;
    rin.h.dh = (unsigned char) r;
    rin.h.dl = (unsigned char) c;
    rin.h.bh = 0;
    int86( 0x10, &rin, &rin );
    return 1;
}

// This public member function positions the cursor in the
// current location of the window defined by *this.

void TextWindow::Goto( void )
{
    union REGS rin;

    rin.h.ah = 2;
```

```cpp
        rin.h.dh = (unsigned char) ( row + start_row );
        rin.h.dl = (unsigned char) ( col + start_col );
        rin.h.bh = 0;
        int86( 0x10, &rin, &rin );
}

// This public function uses the BIOS to scroll a text window.

inline void TextWindow::Scroll( unsigned char line_count )
{
    union REGS r;

    r.h.ah = 6;
    r.h.al = line_count;
    r.h.ch = start_row;
    r.h.cl = start_col;
    r.h.dh = (unsigned char) ( start_row + height - 1 );
    r.h.dl = (unsigned char) ( start_col + width - 1 );
    r.h.bh = attribute;
    int86( 0x10, &r, &r );
}

// This routine writes a formated character to the output
// window. Special processing is performed for the CR, LF, and
// BS keys.

TextWindow& TextWindow::operator<<( char c )
{
    switch ( c ) {
        case '\r' :
            col = 0;
            break;
        case '\n' :
            col = 0;
        row += 1;
            break;

        case '\b' :
            if ( col > 0 )
```

```
                    col--;
                break;
            default :
                position( row, col );
                write_char( c );
                col++;
                if ( col >= width ) {
                    if ( wrap ) {
                        col = 0;
                        row++;
                    } else
                        col--;
                }
        }
        if ( row >= height ) {
            row = (unsigned char) ( height - 1 );
            Scroll( 1 );
        }
        position( row, col );
        return *this;
}

// This routine writes a formated string to the output
// window. Special processing is performed for the CR, LF, and
// BS keys.

TextWindow& TextWindow::operator<<( char *s )
{
    unsigned char c;

    while ( ( c = *s++ ) != '\0' ) {
        switch ( c ) {
            case '\r' :
                col = 0;
                break;
            case '\n' :
                col = 0;
                row += 1;
                break;
```

```cpp
                case '\b' :
                    if ( col > 0 )
                        col--;
                    break;
                default :
                    position( row, col );
                    write_char( c );
                    col++;
                    if ( col >= width ) {
                        if ( wrap ) {
                            col = 0;
                            row += 1;
                        } else
                            col--;
                    }
                    break;
            }
            if ( row >= height ) {
                row = (unsigned char) ( height - 1 );
                Scroll( 1 );
            }
            position( row, col );
    }
    return *this;
}

TextWindow& TextWindow::operator<<( int c )
{
    return operator<<( (char) c );
}

// The only constructor for a text window just defines the
// starting row and column, and the width and height.
// Constructing a window doesn't actually draw anything on the
// screen.

TextWindow::TextWindow( int r, int c, int w, int h )
{
    count++;
```

# TERMINAL EMULATION

```cpp
    start_row = (unsigned char ) r;
    start_col = (unsigned char ) c;
    width = (unsigned char) w;
    height = (unsigned char) h;
    border = 0;
    save_buffer = 0;
    attribute = NORMAL_ATTRIBUTE;
    row = 0;
    col = 0;
    wrap = 0;
}

// The destructor for a text window restores any saved data
// that was under the window. It also repositions the cursor
// if the last window was just closed.

TextWindow::~TextWindow( void )
{
    if ( save_buffer ) {
        restore_window();
        if ( border )
            restore_border();
#ifdef DELETE_ARRAY
        delete[] save_buffer;
#else
        delete save_buffer;
#endif
    }
    count--;
    if ( count == 0 ) {
        start_row = 0;
        start_col = 0;
        position( 23, 0 );
    }
}

// Clearing the window is easy.

void TextWindow::Clear( void )
```

**595**

```cpp
{
    Scroll( 0 );
}

// This function writes the border out around the window. If
// a save buffer has been established, the data under the
// border is saved.

void TextWindow::AddBorder( void )
{
    unsigned char r;
    SaveCursor a;

    if ( save_buffer && border == 0 )
        save_border();
    border = 1;
    position( -1, -1 );
    write_char( 218 );
    position( -1, width );
    write_char( 191 );
    position( height, -1 );
    write_char( 192 );
    position( height, width );
    write_char( 217 );
    for ( r = 0 ; r < height ; r++ ) {
        position( r, -1 );
        write_char( 179 );
        position( r, width );
        write_char( 179 );
    }
    position( -1, 0 );
    write_repeated_chars( 196, width );
    position( height, 0 );
    write_repeated_chars( 196, width );
}

// The title just gets displayed on top of the border.

void TextWindow::DisplayTitle( char *s )
```

# TERMINAL EMULATION

```
{
    int col = 0;

    if ( ( strlen( s ) + 2 ) > width )
        return;
    if ( !border )
        AddBorder();
    SaveCursor save_it;
    position( -1, col++ );
    write_char( 180 );
    while ( *s ) {
        position( -1, col++ );
        write_char( *s++ );
    }
    position( -1, col );
    write_char( 195 );
}


// Popup windows save the area under the window. This function
// function saves the main window, another one saves the border
// area.

void TextWindow::save_window( void )
{
    union REGS rpos;
    union REGS rread;
    union REGS rout;
    int i;
    SaveCursor save_it;

// Allocate enough space for the window plus the border. To
// simplify the storage issues, I treat the save buffer as the
// screen array followed by a border array. The border array
// will have weird indexing, but the screen array won't.

    if ( save_buffer == 0 )
        save_buffer = new unsigned int[ ( width + 2 ) *
                                        ( height + 2 ) ];
    if ( save_buffer ) {
```

```
        i = 0;
        rpos.h.ah = 2;
        rpos.h.bh = 0;
        rread.h.ah = 8;
        rread.h.bh = 0;
        for ( rpos.h.dh = start_row ;
              rpos.h.dh < (unsigned char) ( start_row + height ) ;
              rpos.h.dh++ )
            for ( rpos.h.dl = start_col ;
                  rpos.h.dl < (unsigned char)(start_col + width) ;
                  rpos.h.dl++ ) {
                int86( 0x10, &rpos, &rout );
                int86( 0x10, &rread, &rout );
                save_buffer[ i++ ] = rout.x.ax;
            }
    }
}

// When a popup window is destroyed, the area under it is
// restored. This function restores the text under the window,
// but doesn't do anything about the border.

void TextWindow::restore_window( void )
{
    union REGS rpos;
    union REGS rwrite;
    union REGS rout;
    int i;
    SaveCursor save_it;

    if ( !save_buffer )
        return;
    i = 0;
    rpos.h.ah = 2;
    rpos.h.bh = 0;
    rwrite.h.ah = 9;
    rwrite.h.bh = 0;
    rwrite.x.cx = 1;
```

```c
        for ( rpos.h.dh = start_row ;
              rpos.h.dh < (unsigned char) ( start_row + height ) ;
              rpos.h.dh++ )
            for ( rpos.h.dl = start_col ;
                  rpos.h.dl < (unsigned char) ( start_col + width ) ;
                  rpos.h.dl++ ) {
                int86( 0x10, &rpos, &rout );
                rwrite.h.al = (unsigned char) save_buffer[ i ];
                rwrite.h.bl = (unsigned char)(save_buffer[ i++ ] >> 8);
                int86( 0x10, &rwrite, &rout );
            }
    }

// When a popup window is saved, the border has to be saved as
// well. The main window is saved in a standard row by column
// order in the save buffer. The border area is stored some
// what more haphazardly, right here.

void TextWindow::save_border( void )
    {
    union REGS rpos;
    union REGS rread;
    union REGS rout;
    int i;
    SaveCursor save_it;

    if ( save_buffer == 0 )
        return;
    i = width * height;
    rpos.h.ah = 2;
    rpos.h.bh = 0;
    rread.h.ah = 8;
    rread.h.bh = 0;
    for ( rpos.h.dl = (unsigned char) ( start_col - 1 );
          rpos.h.dl < (unsigned char) ( start_col + width + 1 ) ;
          rpos.h.dl++ ) {
        rpos.h.dh = (unsigned char) ( start_row - 1 );
        int86( 0x10, &rpos, &rout );
```

```
            int86( 0x10, &rread, &rout );
            save_buffer[ i++ ] = rout.x.ax;
            rpos.h.dh = (unsigned char) ( start_row + height );
            int86( 0x10, &rpos, &rout );
            int86( 0x10, &rread, &rout );
            save_buffer[ i++ ] = rout.x.ax;
        }
        for ( rpos.h.dh = start_row ;
              rpos.h.dh < (unsigned char) ( start_row + height ) ;
              rpos.h.dh++ ) {
            rpos.h.dl = (unsigned char) ( start_col - 1 );
            int86( 0x10, &rpos, &rout );
            int86( 0x10, &rread, &rout );
            save_buffer[ i++ ] = rout.x.ax;
            rpos.h.dl = start_col;
            rpos.h.dl += width;
            int86( 0x10, &rpos, &rout );
            int86( 0x10, &rread, &rout );
            save_buffer[ i++ ] = rout.x.ax;
        }
}

// This protected function restores the border in the same odd
// order that it was saved.

void TextWindow::restore_border( void )
{
    union REGS rpos;
    union REGS rwrite;
    union REGS rout;
    int i;
    SaveCursor save_it;

    if ( save_buffer == 0 )
        return;
    i = width * height;
    rpos.h.ah = 2;
    rpos.h.bh = 0;
    rwrite.h.ah = 9;
```

# TERMINAL EMULATION

```
        rwrite.h.bh = 0;
        rwrite.x.cx = 1;
        for ( rpos.h.dl = (unsigned char) ( start_col - 1 );
              rpos.h.dl < (unsigned char) ( start_col + width + 1 ) ;
              rpos.h.dl++ ) {
            rpos.h.dh = (unsigned char) ( start_row - 1 );
            int86( 0x10, &rpos, &rout );
            rwrite.h.al = (unsigned char) save_buffer[ i ];
            rwrite.h.bl = (unsigned char) ( save_buffer[ i++ ] >> 8 );
            int86( 0x10, &rwrite, &rout );
            rpos.h.dh = (unsigned char) ( start_row + height );
            int86( 0x10, &rpos, &rout );
            rwrite.h.al = (unsigned char) save_buffer[ i ];
            rwrite.h.bl = (unsigned char) ( save_buffer[ i++ ] >> 8 );
            int86( 0x10, &rwrite, &rout );
        }
        for ( rpos.h.dh = start_row;
              rpos.h.dh < (unsigned char) ( start_row + height ) ;
              rpos.h.dh++ ) {
            rpos.h.dl = (unsigned char) ( start_col - 1 );
            int86( 0x10, &rpos, &rout );
            rwrite.h.al = (unsigned char) save_buffer[ i ];
            rwrite.h.bl = (unsigned char) ( save_buffer[ i++ ] >> 8 );
            int86( 0x10, &rwrite, &rout );
            rpos.h.dl = (unsigned char) ( start_col + width );
            int86( 0x10, &rpos, &rout );
            rwrite.h.al = (unsigned char) save_buffer[ i ];
            rwrite.h.bl = (unsigned char) ( save_buffer[ i++ ] >> 8 );
            int86( 0x10, &rwrite, &rout );
        }
}

// A popup window is just like a text window except that it
// has an automatic save buffer and save cursor. The construc
// tor doesn't do anything except make a text window and then
// save it.

PopupWindow::PopupWindow( int r, int c, int w, int h )
        : TextWindow( r, c, w, h )
```

```cpp
{
    save_window();
}

// This internal utility routine hides the cursor by moving it
// off the screen. It is used when in the menu code.

inline void hide_cursor( void )
{
    union REGS r;
    r.h.ah = 2;
    r.h.dh = 25;
    r.h.dl = 0;
    r.h.bh = 0;
    int86( 0x10, &r, &r );
}

int Menu( char *menu[] )
{
    int items;
    int maxlen;
    int length;
    int i;
    int c;
    int selection;

    items = 0;
    maxlen = 0;
    while ( ( length = strlen( menu[ items ] ) ) != 0 ) {
        items++;
        if ( length > maxlen )
            maxlen = length;
    }
    if ( items == 0 )
        return -1;
    PopupWindow w( 5, 25, maxlen + 2, items );
    w.Clear();
    w.AddBorder();
    for ( i = 0 ; i < items ; i++ ) {
```

```
        w.SetPosition( i, 1 );
        w << menu[ i ];
}
selection = 0;
for ( ; ; ) {
    w.SetAttribute( REVERSE_ATTRIBUTE );
    w.SetPosition( selection, 1 );
    w << menu[ selection ];
    hide_cursor();
    while ( ( c = w.ReadKey() ) == 0 )
        ;
    w.SetAttribute( NORMAL_ATTRIBUTE );
    w.SetPosition( selection, 1 );
    w << menu[ selection ];
    switch ( c ) {
        case 27 : //Escape
            return( -1 );
        case 13 : // CR
            return( selection );
        case HOME :
            selection = 0;
            break;
        case END :
            selection = items - 1;
            break;
        case DOWN :
            if ( selection < ( items - 1 ) )
                selection++;
            break;
        case UP :
            if ( selection > 0 )
                selection--;
            break;
        default :
            for ( i = ( selection + 1 ) % items ;
                  i != selection ;
                  i = ( i + 1 ) % items ) {
                if ( toupper( c ) ==
                              toupper( menu[ i ][ 0 ] ) ) {
```

```
                    selection = i;
                    break;
                }
            }
            break;
        }
    }
#ifdef _MSC_VER
    return -1;  // To pass /W4 under Microsoft, not really necesary
#endif
}

int ReadLine( char *prompt, char *buffer, int length )
{
    int c;
    int count;

    PopupWindow w( 5, 10, 60, 1 );
    w.Clear();
    w.AddBorder();
    w << prompt << ' ';
    count = 0;

    for ( ; ; ) {
        while ( ( c = w.ReadKey() ) == 0 )
            ;
        switch ( c ) {
            case ESC :
                return 0;
            case CR :
                buffer[ count ] = '\0';
                return 1;
            case BS :
                if ( count > 0 ) {
                    count--;
                    w << BS;
                    w << ' ';
                    w << BS;
                }
```

# TERMINAL EMULATION

```
                    break;
                default :
                    if ( c >= ' ' && c <= 0x7f ) {
                        if ( count < length ) {
                            buffer[ count++ ] = (char) c;
                            w << c;
                        }
                    }
            }
        }
#ifdef _MSC_VER
    return -1;  // To pass /W4 under Microsoft, not really necesary
#endif
}

// ReadKey returns a 0 if no key is ready. The _bios_keybrd()
// routine under Borland C++ has trouble if a Ctrl-Break has
// been pressed, so I replace it with the equivalent int86()
// function call for that compiler only.

int TextWindow::ReadKey( void )
{
#ifdef __TURBOC__
    union REGS r;
    r.h.ah = 1;
    int86( 0x16, &r, &r );
    if ( r.x.flags & 0x40 )   // Test for the zero flag
        return 0;
    r.h.ah = 0;
    int86( 0x16, &r, &r );
    if ( r.h.al != 0 )
        return r.h.al;
    else
        return r.x.ax;
#else  // #ifdef __TURBOC__
    int c;

// Under Borland C, this function will never return true if
// CTRL-BREAK has been pressed, effectively closing the keyboard.
```

```cpp
        if ( _bios_keybrd( _KEYBRD_READY ) == 0 )
            return 0;
        c = _bios_keybrd( _KEYBRD_READ );
        if ( ( c & 0xff ) == 0 )     // A normal ASCII key
            return c;
        else
            return c & 0xff;         // A function or other extended key
#endif // #ifdef __TURBOC__ ... #else
}
// This is an unsophisticated way to change to 43-line mode,
// or 50-line mode on a VGA. Note that it doesn't disable EGA
// corsor emulation, so if you try to change the cursor size,
// strange things might happen. All this routine does to
// change modes is select the appropriate size font, 8x8 for
// 43-line mode, else 8x14 or 8x16.

void Set43LineMode( int control )
{
    union REGS r;

    if ( control ) {
        r.h.ah = 0x11;
        r.h.al = 0x12;
        r.h.bl = 0;
        int86( 0x10, &r, &r );
    } else {
        r.h.ah = 0x14;   // Change to 11 for EGA
        r.h.al = 0x12;
        r.h.bl = 0;
        int86( 0x10, &r, &r );
        r.h.ah = 0;
        r.h.al = 3; // Change to 2 for BW80
        int86( 0x10, &r, &r );
    }
}
// ***************** END OF TEXTWIND.CPP *******************
```
**Listing 11-6. TEXTWIND.CPP**

## Making the test program

The test program for this chapter, TESTTERM.CPP, can be created using the make file shown below. Just like the make files used in the previous chapters, you just need to remove the comment prefix from the line containing the commands for your particular compiler.

```
# This is the make file for the terminal emulation test program.
# Just remove the leading comment line from your compiler, then
# execute:
#          Borland and Zortech:  make -ftestterm.mak
#
#          Microsoft:            nmake -ftestterm.mak
#

#CC = tcc -w
#CC = bcc -w
#CC = ztc -b
#CC = cl /W4 /AL

FILES = pc8250.obj isr_8250.obj queue.obj ansiterm.obj pcirq.obj

.cpp.obj:
   $(CC) -c $<

testterm.exe : testterm.obj rs232.obj textwind.obj msdos.obj
                                                        $(FILES)
              $(CC) testterm.obj rs232.obj textwind.obj msdos.obj
                                                        $(FILES)
```

**Listing 11-7. TESTTERM.MAK, the make file for the test program**

APPENDIX A

# TEST232.EXE

## A General Purpose Test Program

Most of the classes derived from `class RS232` can be tested using a text-based program under MS-DOS. Rather than writing a unique test program for each new class, most of the chapters in this book have used a common test program to exercise the various member functions of each class.

`TEST232.CPP` is a general-purpose C++ program that can simultaneously test up to four `RS232` ports. Each port is associated with a single text window on the screen. An additional window is opened at the bottom of the screen to display either a help screen or the debug information for the class. The screen is placed into 43 line mode to help accommodate all this information. The `TextWindow` class presented in Chapter 11 is used for screen input and output.

Slight variations to the program are described in each chapter. This basically consists of modifications to include different header files, different numbers of ports, and use different constructors to open the ports. Once all the ports have been opened, operation of `TEST232.CPP` is the same for all port types.

## Operations

`TEST232` is designed to let you test out all of the member functions in a class. By letting each text window connected to a port act as a simple terminal emulator, you can test the basic operation of a port by simply typing in characters and watching for any response. By hooking up a modem you should see characters echoed on the screen in response to the modem.

Not all of the member functions are as easy to test as the simple read and write functions. `TEST232` tries to provide the basic mechanism for testing these functions with a set of quick access functions that you can get to via function keys. When `TEST232` first comes up, a function key menu is displayed in the bottom half of the windows.

Figure A-1 shows a screen shot taken from a TEST232. This particular configuration is taken from Chapter 4, when the program is configured to test 4 Micro Channel ports simultaneously. The top portion of the screen contains four small terminal emulation screens, each of which is attached to a single port. The bottom half of the screen is a help window, which gives a brief description of what each of the function keys is doing.

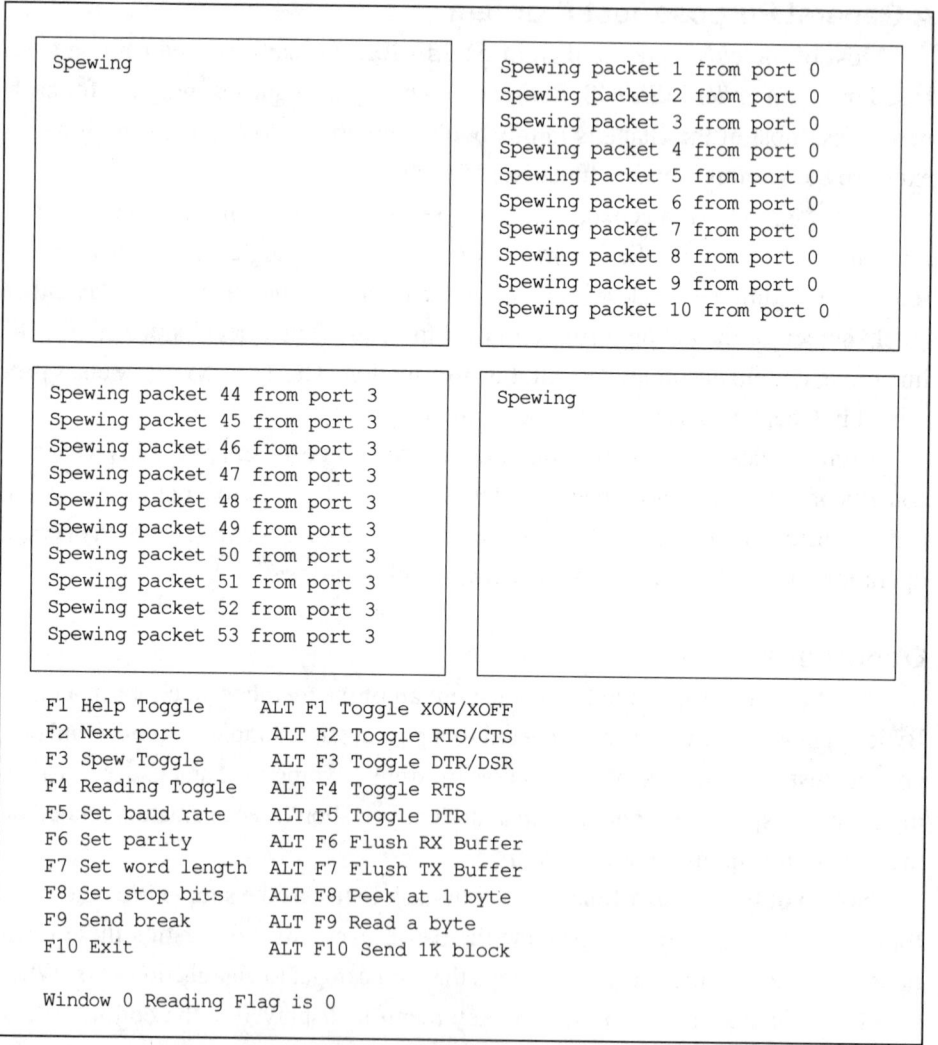

Figure A-1. TEST232.EXE with a help screen

# APPENDIX A: TEST232.EXE

Although all of the function keys are in use in this particular version of TEST232, it would be a relatively simple matter to add a new column of function keys that were invoked with the Shifted function keys. There is room for a whole new column of descriptions on the help screen, and adding the new functions is just a matter of extending the `switch` statement that is called upon keyboard input.

The very last line in Figure A-1 shows the program's status line. Whenever one of the function keys is pressed to execute a function, the result of the function is displayed in this status line. This lets you know immediately when an error occurs as the result of execution of a member function.

## Function Descriptions

The function keys currently have the following definitions:

### F1 - Help toggle

While it is convenient to have the definitions of the help keys displayed on the bottom of the screen, it is perhaps even more useful to have the status dump for a port on the screen. Function key F1 toggles the help screen. Removing the help screen puts the status display for the current Focus Window on the screen. The Focus Window is the window that currently is receiving keyboard input.

Figure A-2 shows a screen shot from TEST232 after pressing the F1 key. The bottom half of the screen now shows the status output from the first port. The help screen can be recalled at any time by just pressing F1 again.

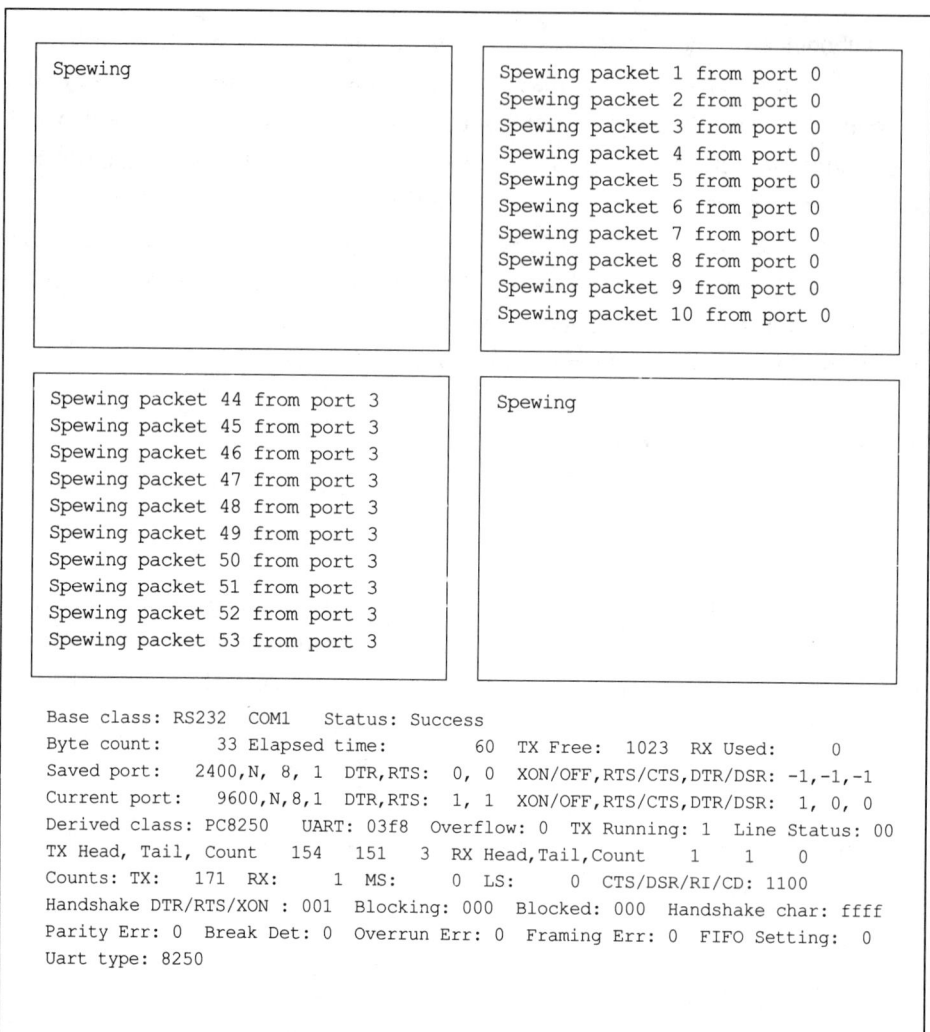

Figure A-2. TEST232.EXE with a status screen

### F2 - Move focus to the next port

TEST232 always has a single window that is considered the Focus Window. This window should have a cursor in it, and its port will receive any keystrokes generated by the user while the program is running. To change to the next focus window, the user just presses the F2 key, and the cursor will move to the next window. The sequence rolls over from the last window to the first window.

APPENDIX A: TEST232.EXE

### F3 - Spew toggle

`TEST232` has the useful ability to "spew" on any given port. When a port is in spewing mode, it continually sends lines of text with the format:

```
"Spewing packet %d from port %d"
```

There are a couple of useful applications for this. First, by using a simple null modem cable, it is possible to connect two ports together, either on the same or different computers, and use the spewing messages to exercise the RS-232 line. Any missed or erroneous characters are visible immediately due to the nature of the output.

Secondly, handshaking testing can be done using the spewing port. Toggling the "Reading" flag (see the F4 definition, next) can be used to force handshaking activity on a port that is spewing.

Function key F3 toggles the spewing flag for the currently focused port. Figure A-2 shows a spewing configuration on a MicroChannel machine. In this particular case, COM1 and COM2 are connected together, and COM3 and COM4 are connected.

### F4 - Toggle reading flag

Each port has a "Reading" flag that indicates whether or not it is currently reading input from the RS-232 line. Toggling this flag will prevent the port from reading any input data, which lets you do several things. First, it can be used to force handshaking activity. Secondly, it can be used to load the input buffer with predefined sequences designed to test some of the input functions. The input functions can then be executed in an attempt to read in a block or a string. Note that this program doesn't presently have function keys dedicated to reading strings or buffers, but they could be added quite simply.

Function key F4 is used to toggle the reading flag for the current focus port.

**F5 - Set baud rate**
**F6 - Set parity**
**F7 - Set word length**
**F8 - Set stop bits**

These four function keys are used to modify the line parameters for the currently focused port. After pressing the function key, a data entry box pops up to ask you what the new parameter setting should be. After minimal parsing, the new rate is applied to the port using the `RS232::Set()` member function. The current settings will be displayed in the status window, and the return code from the `Set()` command will be displayed on the bottom line of the display.

```
ati 3
PM14400FXSA Version 1.12c (c) Practical Peripherals 1992

OK        New baud rate
```

**F9 - Send break**

This command sends a break using the default time value for `RS232::Break()`. The status code returned is displayed on the bottom of the status window.

**F10 - Exit**

This command closes all the ports, restores the screen to 25-line mode, and exits.

**ALT F1 - Toggle XON/XOFF handshaking**
**ALT F2 - Toggle RTS/CTS handshaking**
**ALT F3 - Toggle DTR/DSR handshaking**

These three function keys are used to set and reset the three possible handshaking modes for the currently defined port. Once handshaking is enabled, you can easily use F3 and F4 to set up sequences that should test the handshaking abilities of the `RS232` driver.

# APPENDIX A: TEST232.EXE

### ALT F4 - Toggle RTS
### ALT F5 - Toggle CTS

These two commands toggle the outbound control lines. These can also be used to test handshaking, by manually starting and stopping a remote port or modem that is using hardware handshaking.

### ALT F6 - Flush RX Buffer
### ALT F7 - Flush TX Buffer

These two function keys can be used to test the two Flush functions. With a status display on the screen you should be able to see an immediate indication as to whether the function was successful or not.

### ALT F8 - Peek at 1 byte

If the reading flag for a port is turned off, you can accumulate characters in the input buffer, then test the peek function using `ALT-F8`. This will show the count of characters that have been peeked at, then show the status and the character itself in the status output line.

### ALT F9 - Read a byte

Just as with the previous peek function, you can read bytes out of the input buffer one at a time if they have been allowed to accumulate.

### ALT F10 - Send a 1K block

This command allocates a 1K block, fills it with the character A, then sends it out of the focused port. It allocates 2.5 seconds to get the job done. At lower baud rates some drivers will not be able to send that many characters in 2.5 seconds, and may return errors.

# SERIAL COMMUNICATIONS: A C++ DEVELOPER'S GUIDE

## The Source Code

```cpp
// ******************** START OF TEST232.CPP ********************
//
// This test program is used to test various RS232 classes.
//

#include "portable.h"
#include <stdio.h>
#include <stdlib.h>
#include <string.h>
#include <conio.h>
#include <ctype.h>
#include "rs232.h"
#include "textwind.h"
#include "pc8250.h"

// The window count can range from 1 to 4.  The window_parms array
// will be modified depending on the value of WINDOW_COUNT.

#define WINDOW_COUNT 1

void HandleCommand( int key );
void DrawHelp( void );
void DrawDump( void );

TextWindow *Windows[ 4 ] = { 0, 0, 0, 0 };
RS232 *Ports[ 4 ] = { 0, 0, 0, 0 };
RS232 *Port = 0;
RS232PortName port_names[ 4 ] = { COM1, COM2, COM3, COM4 };
int window_parms[ 4 ][ 4 ] = {
#if ( WINDOW_COUNT == 1 )
                              { 1,  1, 78, 10 },
#else
                              { 1,  1, 38, 10 },
#endif
                              { 1, 41, 38, 10 },
                              { 13, 1, 38, 10 },
                              { 13, 41, 38, 10 } };
```

# APPENDIX A: TEST232.EXE

```c
int Spewing[ 4 ] = { 0, 0, 0, 0 };
long SpewCount[ 4 ] = { 0L, 0L, 0, 0 };
int Reading[ 4 ];

TextWindow *UserWindow;
TextWindow *StatusLine;
int FocusWindow = -1;
int Done = 0;
int Helping = 1;
long NextStatusUpdate = 0;

int main()
{
    int i;
    int c;
    char buffer[ 81 ];

#if ( WINDOW_COUNT > 2 )
    Set43LineMode( 1 );
    TextWindow *temp = new TextWindow( 0, 0, 80, 43 );
    UserWindow = new TextWindow( 24, 0, 80, 12 );
    StatusLine = new TextWindow( 36, 0, 80, 1 );
#else
    TextWindow *temp = new TextWindow( 0, 0, 80, 25 );
    UserWindow = new TextWindow( 12, 0, 80, 12 );
    StatusLine = new TextWindow( 24, 0, 80, 1 );
#endif
    temp->Clear();
    delete temp;
    UserWindow->Clear();
    StatusLine->Clear();

    for ( i = 0 ; i < WINDOW_COUNT ; i++ ) {
        switch ( i ) {
            default :
                Ports[ i ] = new PC8250( port_names[ i ],
                                9600, 'N', 8, 1, 1, 1 );
        }
```

```cpp
            if ( Ports[ i ]->ErrorStatus() == RS232_SUCCESS ) {
                Windows[ i ] = new TextWindow(window_parms[ i ][ 0 ],
                                              window_parms[ i ][ 1 ],
                                              window_parms[ i ][ 2 ],
                                              window_parms[ i ][ 3 ] );
                Windows[ i ]->Clear();
                Windows[ i ]->AddBorder();
                Windows[ i ]->SetPosition( 0, 0 );
                if ( FocusWindow == -1 )
                    FocusWindow = i;
                Reading[ i ] = 1;
            } else {
                *StatusLine << "\nError opening port "
                            << itoa( i, buffer, 10 )
                            << "   status = "
                            << Ports[ i ]->ErrorName(
                                    Ports[ i ]->ErrorStatus() )
                            << ".  Hit any key to continue...";
                while ( Windows[ FocusWindow ]->ReadKey() == 0 )
                    ;
                *StatusLine << '\n';
            }
        }
        DrawHelp();
        Port = Ports[ FocusWindow ];
        while ( FocusWindow != -1 && !Done ) {
            c = Windows[ FocusWindow ]->ReadKey();
            if ( c > 255 ) {
                HandleCommand( c );
                Windows[ FocusWindow ]->Goto();
            } else if ( c != 0 )
            Port->Write( c );
            for ( i = 0 ; i < WINDOW_COUNT ; i++ ) {
                if ( Spewing[ i ] && Ports[ i ]->TXSpaceUsed() == 0 ) {
                    sprintf( buffer,
                             "Spewing packet %ld from port %d\r\n",
                             SpewCount[ i ]++,
                             i );
                    Ports[ i ]->Write( buffer );
                }
```

# APPENDIX A: TEST232.EXE

```cpp
            if ( Reading[ i ] ) {
                Ports[ i ]->Read( buffer, 80 );
                if ( Ports[ i ]->ByteCount > 0 ) {
                    *Windows[ i ] << buffer;
                    if ( i != FocusWindow )
                        Windows[ FocusWindow ]->Goto();
                }
            }
        }
        if ( !Helping ) {
            if ( ReadTime() > NextStatusUpdate ) {
                DrawDump();
                NextHelpUpdate = ReadTime() + 500;
            }
        }
    }
    for ( i = 0 ; i < WINDOW_COUNT ; i++ ) {
        if ( Windows[ i ] )
            delete Windows[ i ];
        delete Ports[ i ];
    }
    Set43LineMode( 0 );
    return 0;
}

void HandleCommand( int c )
{
    char buffer[ 11 ];
    RS232Error status;
    int result;

    *StatusLine << '\n';
    switch ( c ) {
        case F1 :
            Helping = !Helping;
            UserWindow->Clear();
            if ( Helping )
                DrawHelp();
            return;
        case F2 :
```

```cpp
            do
                FocusWindow = ++FocusWindow % WINDOW_COUNT;
            while ( Windows[ FocusWindow ] == 0 );
            Port = Ports[ FocusWindow ];
            if ( !Helping )
                UserWindow->Clear();
            Windows[ FocusWindow ]->Goto();
            return;
        case F3 :
            Spewing[ FocusWindow ] = !Spewing[ FocusWindow ];
            Windows[ FocusWindow ]->AddBorder();
            if ( Spewing[ FocusWindow ] )
                Windows[ FocusWindow ]->DisplayTitle( "Spewing" );
            return;
        case F4 :
            Reading[ FocusWindow ] = !Reading[ FocusWindow ];
            *StatusLine << "Window "
                        << itoa( FocusWindow, buffer, 10 );
            *StatusLine << " reading flag is "
                        << itoa( Reading[ FocusWindow ], buffer, 10 );
            return;
        case F5 :
            ReadLine( "New baud rate:", buffer, 10 );
            status = Port->Set( atol( buffer ) );
            *StatusLine << "Set baud rate to "
                        << ltoa( atol( buffer ), buffer, 10 )
                        << " returns status of: ";
            break;
        case F6 :
            ReadLine( "New parity:", buffer, 10 );
            status = Port->Set( UNCHANGED, buffer[ 0 ] );
            *StatusLine << "Set parity to "
                        << buffer[ 0 ]
                        << " returns status of: ";
            break;
        case F7 :
            ReadLine( "New word length:", buffer, 10 );
            status = Port->Set( UNCHANGED, UNCHANGED, atoi( buffer ) );
            *StatusLine << "Set word length to "
                        << itoa( atoi( buffer ), buffer, 10 )
```

# APPENDIX A: TEST232.EXE

```
                    << " returns status of: ";
    break;
case F8 :
    ReadLine( "New stop bits:", buffer, 10 );
    status = Port->Set( UNCHANGED,
                        UNCHANGED,
                        UNCHANGED,
                        atoi( buffer ) );
    *StatusLine << "Set stop bits to "
                << itoa( atoi( buffer ), buffer, 10 )
                << " returns status of: ";
    break;
case F9 :
    status = (RS232Error) Port->Break();
    *StatusLine << "SendBreak returns: ";
    break;
case F10 :
    Done = 1;
    return;
case ALT_F1 :
    result = Port->XonXoffHandshaking();
    status = (RS232Error) Port->XonXoffHandshaking
                                          ( !result );
    *StatusLine << "Toggle XON/XOFF handshaking returns: ";
    if ( status >= 0 ) {
        *StatusLine << itoa( status, buffer, 10 );
        return;
    }
    break;
case ALT_F2 :
    result = Port->RtsCtsHandshaking();
    status = (RS232Error) Port->RtsCtsHandshaking
                                          ( !result );
    *StatusLine << "Toggle RTS/CTS handshaking returns: ";
    if ( status >= 0 ) {
        *StatusLine << itoa( status, buffer, 10 );
        return;
    }
    break;
case ALT_F3 :
```

```cpp
            result = Port->DtrDsrHandshaking();
            status = (RS232Error) Port->DtrDsrHandshaking
                                                    ( !result );
            *StatusLine << "Toggle DTR/DSR handshaking returns: ";
            if ( status >= 0 ) {
                *StatusLine << itoa( status, buffer, 10 );
                return;
            }
            break;
        case ALT_F4 :
            status = (RS232Error) Port->Rts( !Port->Rts() );
            *StatusLine << "Toggle RTS returns: ";
            if ( status >= 0 ) {
                *StatusLine << itoa( status, buffer, 10 );
                return;
            }
            break;
        case ALT_F5 :
            status = (RS232Error) Port->Dtr( !Port->Dtr() );
            *StatusLine << "Toggle Dtr returns: ";
            if ( status >= 0 ) {
                *StatusLine << itoa( status, buffer, 10 );
                return;
            }
            break;
        case ALT_F6 :
            status = (RS232Error) Port->FlushRXBuffer();
            *StatusLine << "Flush RX Buffer returns: ";
            break;
        case ALT_F7 :
            status = (RS232Error) Port->FlushTXBuffer();
            *StatusLine << "Flush TX Buffer returns: ";
            break;
        case ALT_F8 :
            status = (RS232Error) Port->Peek();
            *StatusLine << "Peek count: "
                        << itoa( Port->ByteCount, buffer, 10 )
                        << " ";
            if ( status >= 0 ) {
                if ( Port->ByteCount > 0 ) {
```

```
                    *StatusLine << "Char: ";
                    if ( isprint( status ) )
                        *StatusLine << (char) status;
                    else
                        *StatusLine << '<'
                                    << itoa( status, buffer, 16 )
                                    << '>';
                }
                return;
            }
            *StatusLine << "Status: ";
            break;
        case ALT_F9 :
            status = (RS232Error) Port->Read();
            if ( status >= 0 ) {
                *Windows[ FocusWindow ] << (char) status;
                return;
            }
            *StatusLine << "Read character returns: ";
            break;
        case ALT_F10 :
            {
                void *p = malloc( 1024 );
                if ( !p )
                    return;
                memset( p, 'A', 1024 );
                status = (RS232Error) Port->Write( p, 1024, 2500 );
                free( p );
            }
            *StatusLine << "Write 1K ByteCount: "
                        << itoa( Port->ByteCount, buffer, 10 )
                        << "  Elapsed Time: ";
            *StatusLine << ltoa( Port->ElapsedTime, buffer, 10 )
                        << "  Status: ";
            break;
        default :
            return;
    }
    *StatusLine << Port->ErrorName( status );
}
```

```
void DrawDump( void )
{
    int i;
    char buffer[ 81 ];

    UserWindow->SetPosition( 0, 0 );
    for ( i = 0 ;
          i < Port->DebugLineCount() ;
          i++ ) {
        Port->FormatDebugOutput( buffer, i );
        if ( i != 0 )
            *UserWindow << '\n';
        *UserWindow << buffer;
    }
    Windows[ FocusWindow ]->Goto();
}

void DrawHelp( void )
{
    UserWindow->Clear();
    UserWindow->SetPosition( 0, 0 );
    *UserWindow << "F1 Help Toggle      ALT F1 Toggle XON/XOFF\n";
    *UserWindow << "F2 Next port        ALT F2 Toggle RTS/CTS\n";
    *UserWindow << "F3 Spew Toggle      ALT F3 Toggle DTR/DSR\n";
    *UserWindow << "F4 Reading Toggle   ALT F4 Toggle RTS\n";
    *UserWindow << "F5 Set baud rate    ALT F5 Toggle DTR\n";
    *UserWindow << "F6 Set parity       ALT F6 Flush RX Buffer\n";
    *UserWindow << "F7 Set word length  ALT F7 Flush TX Buffer\n";
    *UserWindow << "F8 Set stop bits    ALT F8 Peek at 1 byte\n";
    *UserWindow << "F9 Send break       ALT F9 Read a byte\n";
    *UserWindow << "F10 Exit            ALT F10 Send 1K block\n";
    Windows[ FocusWindow ]->Goto();
}

// ******************* END OF TEST232.CPP *******************
```

**Listing A-1. TEST232.CPP**

# APPENDIX A: TEST232.EXE

## Building TEST232.EXE

A make file for TEST232.EXE is shown in Listing A-2. The make file can be adapted to work with the current versions of Zortech, Microsoft, and Borland C++ compilers. As shown, it has been configured for Borland C++, by removing the leading # character from in front of the "CC" definition for Borland C++.

```
# This is the make file for the RS232 class test program.
# Just remove the leading comment line from your compiler, then
# execute:
#           Borland and Zortech:  make -ftest232.mak
#
#           Microsoft:            nmake -ftest232.mak
#

#CC = tcc -w
CC = bcc -w
#CC = ztc -b
#CC = cl /W4

FILES = pc8250.obj queue.obj isr_8250.obj pcirq.obj

.cpp.obj:
  $(CC) -c $<

test232.exe : test232.obj rs232.obj textwind.obj msdos.obj $(FILES)
        $(CC) test232.obj rs232.obj textwind.obj msdos.obj
                                                              $(FILES)
```

**Listing A-2. TEST232.MAK, the make file for TEST232.EXE**

This same test program is used with several other test classes. In order to use other RS232 classes, two things need to be done. First, the include files and setup portions of TEST232.CPP need to be modified to reflect a different device driver. For example, to test DigiBoards, I modify the list of include files to look like this:

```
#include "portable.h"
#include <stdio.h>
#include <stdlib.h>
#include <string.h>
#include <conio.h>
#include <ctype.h>
#include "rs232.h"
#include "textwind.h"
#include "digi.h"
```

With the DigiBoard driver, I will be working with four ports at once, so I also modify the `WINDOW_COUNT` macro to reflect that:

```
// The window count can range from 1 to 4.  The window_parms
// array will be modified depending on the value of
// WINDOW_COUNT.

#define WINDOW_COUNT 4
```

The final two changes needed when working with a new driver concern the list of ports to be opened. The `port_names[]` array is used to name all the ports, and it will generally have to be modified to accurately reflect the names of the ports you want to open. A sample version is shown below:

```
RS232PortName port_names[ 4 ] = { COM5, COM6, COM7, COM8 };
```

# APPENDIX A: TEST232.EXE

Finally, the actual creation of the RS232 objects needs to be changed to create new versions of the correct derived class. The code below shows that.

```
for ( i = 0 ; i < WINDOW_COUNT ; i++ ) {
    switch ( i ) {
        default :
            Ports[ i ] = new DigiBoard( port_names[ i ],
                                  9600, 'N', 8, 1, 1, 1
);
    }
```

## Conclusion

When creating or modifying new derived classes, it is absolutely essential that you have a general purpose test program that lets you exercise all the code paths in the new driver. TEST232 does the job, and in addition is easily extensible to include other functions.

# APPENDIX B

# Sources

**Altex Electronics, Inc.**
**11342 IH-35 North**
**San Antonio, TX 78233**
**800-531-5369**

Altex carries a complete line of communications equipment, including the BocaBoard. They have several low cost breakout boxes and cable systems.

**Arnet Corporation**
**618 Grassmere Park Drive**
**Nashville, Tennessee 37211**
**800-377-6686**

Arnet makes a complete line of intelligent and standard multiport boards for the IBM PC architecture.

**BBS Callers Digest**
**701 Stokes Rd.**
**Medford, New Jersey 08055**
**800-822-0437**

BBS Callers Digest and Boardwatch Magazine are the two leading magazines exclusively devoted to covering the on-line world, including information services, BBSs, networks, and so on.

**Blaise Computing, Inc.**
**819 Bancroft Way**
**Berkeley, California 94710**
**800-333-8087**

Blaise makes C and Pascal communications libraries.

**Boardwatch Magazine**
7586 West Jewell Ave.
Denver, Colorado 80232
800-933-6038

BBS Callers Digest and Boardwatch Magazine are the two leading magazines exclusively devoted to covering the on-line world, including information services, BBSs, networks, and so on.

**Channel 1 BBS**
PO Box 338
Cambridge, MA 02238-0338
617-864-0100 (Voice)
617-354-8873 (BBS)

Channel 1 is one of the largest commercial BBS systems in the country. It features an enormous selection of files, public forums, Interment access, and various other features.

**C User's Journal**
1601 W. 23rd Street
Suite 200
Lawrence, KS 66046
913-841-1631

C User's Journal is a popular programming magazine.

**Clark Development Co.**
PO Box 571365
Murray, UT 84157-1365
800-356-1686 (Voice)
801-261-1686 (International)
801-261-8976 (BBS)

Clark Development Co. is the producer of PCBoard, one of the world's most popular BBS programs.

# APPENDIX B: SOURCES

**CompuServe**
PO Box 20212
Columbus, OH 43220-9988
800-524-3388 (Voice)
614-457-0802 (International)

Compuserve is the leading on line information service.

**Datatran Corporation**
355 Yuma Street
Denver, Colorado 80223
303-778-0870

Datatran makes a variety of RS-232 breakout boxes, as well as the Datatracker DT-5 shown in this book.

**Digi International, Inc.**
6400 Flying Cloud Drive
Eden Prairie, MN 55344
612-943-9020

Digi International is the leading supplier of intelligent and non-intelligent multiport boards. They have a wide range of products geared towards every size application.

**Dr. Dobb's Journal**
411 Borel Ave.
San Mateo, CA 94402
800-456-1215
303-447-9330

DDJ is a popular programming magazine, and frequently features articles relating to hardware interfacing.

**Greenleaf Software**
16479 Dallas Parkway #570
Dallas, TX 75248
800-523-9830
214-248-2561

Greenleaf makes communications libraries for both C and C++ programmers.

**Intel Corporation**
**PC Enhancements Division**
5200 N.E. Elam Young Parkway
Hillsboro, Oregon 97124
800-538-3373
503-629-7354 (International)

Intel's line of SatisFAXtion modems have an extremely comprehensive set of advanced features, making them technology leaders in this area. Their modems are available through normal retail channels.

**JDR Microdevices**
2233 Samaritan Drive
San Jose, CA 95124
800-538-500
408-559-1200 (International)

JDR carries a wide variety of computer equipment. Most germane to readers of this book is that they carry an inexpensive dual port RS-232 card that can be equipped with 16550 UARTs instead of standard 16450s.

**Magna Carta Software**
PO Box 475594
Garland, TX 75047-5594
214-226-6909

Magna Carta makes the C Communication Toolkit, a C library for communications programming

# APPENDIX B: SOURCES

**Mustang Software**
PO Box 2264
Bakersfield, CA 93303
805-395-02223 (Voice)
805-395-0650 (BBS)

Mustang makes the Wildcat! BBS, an easy to use and popular system.

**National Semiconductor**
2900 Semiconductor Drive
Santa Clara, CA 95052

National makes the 8250 and 16550 UART chips that are standard equipment in IBM compatible PCs.

**Practical Peripherals**
375 Conejo Ridge Avenue
Thousand Oaks, CA 91361
818-991-8200

Practical Peripherals sells a complete line of modems and fax/modems. Their modems are available through retail channels at very competitive prices.

**Programmer's Connection**
7249 Whipple Avenue NW
North Canton, OH 44720
800-336-1166
216-494-3781

Programmer's Connection carries a complete line of software for programmers, including communications libraries.

**Programmer's Paradise**
1163 Shrewsbury Ave
Shrewsbury, NJ 07702
800-445-7899

Programmer's Paradise carries a complete line of software and some hardware for programmers. You should have a copy of their catalog and one from Programmer's Connection on your bookshelf.

**South Mountain**
76 S. Orange Ave.
Suite 3
South Orange, NJ 07079
800-451-6174
201-762-6965

South Mountain makes a communications programming library for C programmers.

**Specialized Products Company**
3131 Premier Drive
Irving, TX 75063
800-866-5353

Specialized Products carries an extremely large line of communications and test equipment. Their catalog is a worthwhile reference all in itself.

APPENDIX C

# Source Code

| File Name | Location | Description |
|---|---|---|
| ansiterm.cpp | Chapter 11 | All of the source code for the AnsiTerminal class is found in this file. It needs to be compiled and linked with any program that is using this class. |
| ansiterm.h | Chapter 11 | The AnsiTerminal class is defined here. Any module referencing AnsiTerminal will need to include this file. |
| ascii.h | Chapter 3 | Some commonly used ASCII character definitions. |
| biosport.cpp | Chapter 6 | The code to support class BIOSPort is all found in this file. This file needs to be compiled and linked in with any program using the BIOSPort class. |
| biosport.h | Chapter 6 | The definition of class BIOSPort is found in this header file. Any module that accesses this class will need to include BIOSPORT.H. |
| boca.cpp | Chapter 4 | The interrupt service routine for the BocaHandler class is found in this file. Any program written to use a BocaBoard will need to include this module in its project. |

| File Name | Location | Description |
|---|---|---|
| boca.h | Chapter 4 | The header file needed to create a BocaHandler object. A program that is using one of these multiport boards needs to include this header file. |
| crc.cpp | Chapter 10 | The supporting code for the two CRC classes is found in this module. |
| crc.h | Chapter 10 | This header file defines the Crc32 and Crc16 classes, which are both used by the Zmodem class. |
| digi.cpp | Chapter 5 | The member functions for class DigiBoard. This module needs to be compiled and linked in with any program that is going to use intelligent DigiBoards. |
| digi.h | Chapter 5 | The DigiBoard class is defined here. Any program that wants to open ports on an intelligent DigiBoard needs to include this header file. |
| fossil.cpp | Chapter 7 | The code that implements all of the functions supporting the FOSSIL class is found here. This module will need to be compiled and linked with any program that is going to use the FOSSIL class. |
| fossil.h | Chapter 7 | The FOSSIL class is defined in this header file. Any C++ module that wants to access the FOSSIL class will need to include this header file. |
| isr_8250.cpp | Chapter 3 | The source code for the PC8250 interrupt service routine. |

# APPENDIX C: SOURCE CODE

| File Name | Location | Description |
|---|---|---|
| mca.cpp | Chapter 4 | This file contains the MicroChannel interrupt handler. This handler is used in conjunction with the PC8250 class ISR. |
| mca.h | Chapter 4 | The header file that contains the definitions needed to use the MicroChannel interrupt handler for class PC8250. |
| modem.cpp | Chapter 9 | The code for the Modem class. This module should be compiled and linked with any program using the Modem class. |
| modem.h | Chapter 9 | The header file that contains the definition of class Modem and related items. This header file must be included by any program using the Modem class. |
| msdos.cpp | Chapter 2 | A few of the functions in the RS232 class have different versions depending on whether the target system is MS-DOS or Windows. The MS-DOS versions of these functions are found in this file, with the Windows versions appearing in MSWIN.CPP. |
| mswin.cpp | Chapter 8 | The O/S specific functions in the RS232 class are confined to this module. This file contains the MS Windows versions of these functions. |
| pc8250.cpp | Chapter 3 | This file contains all of the member functions used by the PC8250 class. |

| File Name | Location | Description |
|---|---|---|
| `pc8250.h` | Chapter 3 | The header file that needs to be included by any program that is going to create objects of the `PC8250` class. |
| `pcirq.cpp` | Chapter 3 | This is the MS-DOS interrupt manager. It takes care of hooking and unhooking interrupts for the `PC8250` class ISR, as well as the control break handers. |
| `pcirq.h` | Chapter 3 | The header file that needs to be included by any module that wants to use the MS-DOS interrupt manager. |
| `portable.h` | Chapter 2 | This header file contains a number of macro definitions that assist in writing portable code. Macros used in this book such as `CLI()`, `OUTPUT()`, and `INTERRUPT` are defined differently here, depending on which compiler is being used. |
| `queue.cpp` | Chapter 3 | The code for the member functions of `class Queue` that aren't defined as being inline. |
| `queue.h` | Chapter 3 | The header file for the `Queue` class used by the `PC8250` member functions and ISR. Most of the member functions in this class are inline, with the function body found here. |
| `rs232.cpp` | Chapter 2 | This module contains the definitions of non virtual member functions used in `class RS232`. It needs to be compiled and linked with any program using a class derived from `RS232`. |

# APPENDIX C: SOURCE CODE

| File Name | Location | Description |
|---|---|---|
| `rs232.h` | Chapter 2 | The definitions for `class RS232`. This header file needs to be included by any module that references this class. |
| `terminal.h` | Chapter 11 | This header file contains the definition for the `Terminal` class, which is the base class that `AnsiTerminal` is derived from. |
| `test232.cpp` | Appendix A | This is the general purpose test program used to test most of the classes in the book. |
| `test232.mak` | Appendix A | The make file used to create TEST232.EXE. |
| `test232w.cpp` | Chapter 8 | This is the test program used under Microsoft Windows to test the `WindowsPort` class. Note that this program is specific to the Borland C++ compiler. |
| `test232w.def` | Chapter 8 | The definition file used to link TEST232W.CPP. |
| `test232w.mak` | Chapter 8 | The make file used to create TEST232W.EXE. |
| `testterm.cpp` | Chapter 11 | This is the test program used to exercise the terminal emulation class developed in Chapter 11. |
| `testterm.mak` | Chapter 11 | The make file used to create TESTTERM.EXE. |
| `testzm.cpp` | Chapter 10 | This is the test program used to exercise the ZMODEM class. |
| `testzm.mak` | Chapter 10 | The make file used to create TESTZM.EXE. |

| File Name | Location | Description |
|---|---|---|
| textwind.cpp | Chapter 11 | The source code that implements the TextWindow class is all found in this file. It needs to be compiled and linked with any module using this class. |
| textwind.h | Chapter 11 | This file contains the definitions for the general purpose TextWindow class that is used for terminal emulation. It is also used by the TEST232 program to exercise most of the MS-DOS based RS232 derived classes. |
| tstmodem.cpp | Chapter 9 | The test program for class Modem. |
| tstmodem.mak | Chapter 9 | The make file for building TSTMODEM.EXE. |
| winport.cpp | Chapter 8 | The code supporting the WindowsPort class is found in this C++ module. It needs to be linked in with any program using the class. |
| winport.h | Chapter 8 | The definition of the WindowsPort class is found here. A Windows program that is going to access this prototype needs to include this header file. |
| zmodem.cpp | Chapter 10 | The code that implements the Zmodem class is all found in this file. It needs to be compiled and linked into any program using class Zmodem to perform file transfers. |
| zmodem.h | Chapter 10 | This file contains the definition of the Zmodem class. Any program that is going to use the class to perform file transfers needs to include this header file. |

# APPENDIX C: SOURCE CODE

| File Name | Location | Description |
|---|---|---|
| _8250.h | Chapter 3 | This file has the definitions for all the registers and bit masks used in the 8250 family of UARTs. It is used extensively by the member functions and ISR of the PC8250 class. |
| _msdos.h | Chapter 2 | The prototype for a function called Bus() is kept here. It is used internally by the PC8250 class to determine whether the system has a MicroChannel or ISA bus. |
| _pc8250.h | Chapter 3 | A private header file used by the PC8250 class and its ISR code to define common structures. |
| _zmodem.h | Chapter 10 | This header file contains constants and definitions used internally by the Zmodem class. |

# Glossary

**Abstract base class.** This is a class whose member functions are all pure virtual. The abstract base class cannot be instantiated by itself. Only those classes derived from the abstract base class can be created and used to perform useful work. This terminology is not part of the C++ standard, it is part of the jargon that has grown around the language.

**ANSI.** The American National Standards Institute. The primary technical standards body in the United States.

**ANSI C.** A shorthand term for the ANSI Standard for the C Programming Language. This standard was published in February, 1990, as Standard X3.159-1989.

**ASCII.** The American Standard Code for Information Interchange. This standard is officially defined as ANSI Standard X3.4. This seven bit specification has become the universally accepted standard way of exchanging text data.

**Bits Per Second (bps).** A commonly used measure of signaling speed. Usually this figure is used to indicate total throughput capability of a medium.

**CCITT.** An international standards body, chartered by the United Nations. The CCITT is primarily concerned with standards in the area of telecommunications, and is the dominant body setting standards for today's generation of modems. Its French name is commonly translated to mean "Consultative Committee for International Telephone and Telegraph."

**CD (Carrier Detect).** The commonly used name for the Received Line Signal Detect (RLSD) signal used in RS-232 communications. A DCE asserts the RLSD line when it establishes a connection with another modem, indicating the circuit is ready to use.

**DCE.** Data Communications Equipment. The original RS-232 specification had a world view where every piece of data communications equipment was either a DTE (Data Terminal Equipment), or a DCE (Data Communications Equipment). In the simplest terms, a DCE device is a modem, and a DTE device is a terminal.

**DTE.** Data Terminal Equipment. This designation is part of the RS-232 specification. A DTE is a device that connects to a DCE and uses it to communicate with a DTE at some remote location. A DTE is usually a terminal or a PC acting as a terminal via terminal emulation software.

**DSR.** An abbreviation for Data Set Ready, an RS-232 signal generated by a DCE. DSR is generally used to indicate that a modem is powered up and ready to receive and send data. It is infrequently used as a handshaking line in conjunction with DTR.

**DTR.** An abbreviation for Data Terminal Ready, an RS-232 signal generated by a DTE. DTR is usually used to indicate that a terminal is powered up and ready to send and receive data. It is infrequently used as a handshaking line in conjunction with DSR.

**DigiBoard.** A multiport board made by DigiBoard, Inc. This company makes many different varieties of boards. Some come with on board processors and are referred to as "Intelligent Boards".

**Electronic Industries Association (EIA).** A group composed of companies involved in the electronics industry. While the EIA is involved in many activities, it is mentioned in this book because of its sponsorship of the RS-232 standard. The EIA is can be reached at:

> Electronic Industries Association,
> 2001 Eye Street NW
> Washington, DC 20006

**Flow Control.** See "handshaking".

**FOSSIL.** FOSSIL is an acronym for "Fido/Opus/Seadog Standard Interface Layer". FOSSIL drivers were developed to provide a device independent programming standard BBS programmers could use to access communications hardware.

# GLOSSARY

**Full duplex.** A full duplex communications channel allows simultaneous communications in both directions. This is the predominant type of communications channel in use by desktop machines today.

**Half duplex.** A half duplex channel allows communications to go in either direction, but not simultaneously. This requires the two modems at either end of the line to cooperate using some sort of protocol to determine who is allowed to transmit at any given time.

**Handshaking.** In general, handshaking can be the exchange of signals between communicating entities. In this book, I use the term handshaking to mean the process by which a receiver throttles a transmitter to avoid buffer overflow.

**Hardware handshaking.** Hardware handshaking consists of using the RTS/CTS or DTR/DSR signal pairs to throttle transmission. A receiver can block transmission of additional characters by dropping a control line until the receiver buffer has been emptied down to a predetermined point.

**High water mark.** When using software or hardware handshaking, the high water mark refers to a specific point in the input buffer. When the input buffer fills up past this point, the RS-232 driver will attempt to block any further incoming data through the use of handshaking.

**ISO.** The International Standards Organization. The ISO is another standards body sanctioned by the United Nations.

**LAPM.** V.42 modems use LAPM as their preferred method of error control. LAPM stands for Link Access Protocol for Modems.

**Low water mark.** When using software or hardware handshaking, the low water mark refers to a specific point in the input buffer. When the input buffer is emptied below this point, the RS-232 driver will remove any blocking that has prevented the reception of incoming data.

**Marking.** Digital communications lines are historically referred to as being in either a 'marking' or 'spacing' state, dating back to the days of telegraphy. A 1 bit is referred to as a marking bit, and a 0 is a spacing bit.

**MNP-4, MNP-5.** MNP stands for Microcom Network Protocol. Microcom, Inc. is a compnay that established a set or proprietary protocols for their modems. MNP-4 and MNP-5 are the two best known protocols, and are widely licensed by other modem manufacturers. MNP-4 is used to provide an error free connection between two modems. MNP-5 is used to perform data compression on the transmitted data stream. These standards will probably be eventually superceded by V.42 and V.42*bis*.

**Modem.** In general, a modem (short for modulator/demodulator) is a device that converts serial data to a format that can be transmitted over dialup or leased phone lines, and converts data received from the phone lines back to serial data.

**Multiport board.** RS-232 multiport boards are boards equipped with multiple RS-232 ports. In the desktop PC world, these boards usually have 4, 8, or 16 ports. These boards are divided into two categories. Intelligent boards have an on board processor and memory to move much of the processing off the PC motherboard. Non-intelligent boards just have UARTs and glue circuitry, which means the PC has to handle interrupts for all the UARTs.

**Null modem cable.** A Null modem cable is a special cable used to connect two DTE devices together directly without a modem. It routes RS-232 signals properly so that both devices have inputs connected to outputs and outputs connected to inputs.

**Overrun Error.** A hardware error caused when the UART receives another incoming byte before the CPU has read the last one.

**Parity bit.** A parity bit is an extra bit that is added to a data byte being transmitted. Usually the parity bit is set to a 0 or 1 in order to force the data byte to have an odd or even number of set data bits, hence the terms "Odd parity" and "Even parity". This extra bit allows the receiver to detect any single bit error.

**Pure virtual function.** In C++, a pure virtual function is a function defined as 0 in a base class. The presence of a pure function in a class means that the class cannot be instantiated. In this book, class RS232 has several pure virtual functions, which

## GLOSSARY

means only classes derived from RS232 can be instantiated.

**RLSD.** See CD, Carrier Detect.

**RTS.** One of the six modem control lines supported on the IBM PC standard communications port. RTS is generally paired up with CTS to provide RTS/CTS hardware handshaking.

**RS-232-C.** The best known EIA standard relating to low speed asynchronous communications.

**Spacing.** Digital communications lines are historically referred to as being in either a 'marking' or 'spacing' state, dating back to the days of telegraphy. A 1 bit is referred to as a marking bit, and a 0 is a spacing bit.

**Software handshaking.** Software handshaking refers to the process of using the XON/XOFF character pairs to disable then reenable the transmission of characters from a transmitter. The receiver issues an XOFF when it is in danger of having its buffer overflow. It issues an XON to resume transmission when the buffer has been emptied.

**Start bit.** This is the first bit issued when a UART wants to send a data byte. The start bit will unambiguously tell the receiver that a set of data bits is to follow. This is normally a space, or 0 bit.

**Stop bit.** This bit is normally issued by a UART to follow the data byte. This bit is usually a mark, or 1 bit, and is used to separate consecutive characters and to help with resynchronization.

**UART.** Universal Asynchronous Receiver/Transmitter. A UART is normally a single chip dedicated to converting bytes to and from a serial data stream that can travel on RS-232 data lines.

**Unicode.** Unicode is a recently approved standard that replaces traditional 7 bit ASCII with a 16 bit standard for character transmission, storage, and display. Unicode gives good coverage to most international alphabets, including Asian languages, and is expected to come into wide use rapidly.

**V.22, V.22***bis***.** This CCITT standard specifies the format for 1200 and 2400 bps modems used over dialup telephone lines. V.22*bis* modems probably represent the majority of installed modems in the field today, although they will eventually be displaced by faster models.

**V.24.** This CCITT Recommendation is the sister standard to the EIA's RS-232-C. While it defines a few additional circuits above and beyond the 25 defined by RS-232-C, they are essentially identical.

**V.32, V.32***bis***.** These CCITT standards specify the formats for 9600 and 14,400 bps modems used over dialup telephone lines. These modems represent the current standard for communications applications.

**V.42.** This CCITT specification dictates the protocol used to provide an error free connection between two modems. V.42 implicitly supports MNP-4 when necessary, although its normal mode of operation is LAPM.

**V.42***bis***.** This is the CCITT specification for data compression for modems. V.42*bis* represents a substantial improvement over its predecessor, MNP-5, in that it can compress up to 4:1, and can disable compression when necessary.

**Virtual functions.** In C++, a virtual function is a function that is called by way of a function pointer. Virtual functions in a base class will point to different functions depending on which derived class is used to instantiate the base class.

**XON/XOFF.** XON/XOFF handshaking is a form of software handshaking. The name comes from the fact that the XOFF character is used to throttle transmission, and the XON character is used to restart it.

**ZMODEM.** ZMODEM is a widely use file transfer protocol which improves on many of the deficiencies found in XMODEM and YMODEM.

# Index

(THRE) interrupt, 137
9- to 25-pin adapter, 29
25-pin D-Subminiature, 16
8250, 33, 34, 133, 149
8250 compatibility, 273
8259 interrupt controller, 152, 158, 240, 258
16450, 34
16550, 34, 37, 136, 149, 156, 257, 356
_8250.H, 169
_interrupt function type modifier, 229
_PC8250.H, 169, 176, 178
_ZMODEM.H, 505

## A

abstract class, 5, 70
acoustic coupler, 435
AddPort (), 265
America On Line, 55
ANSI C, 8, 11, 67
Apple Macintosh, 22
Arnet, 260
ASCII, 13
ASCII.H, 169
AT command set, 44

## B

baud, 20
baud rate divisor, 141
BBS, 355
  detect, 91
  systems, 54
Bell 103, 42
Bell 212, V.22, 42
Bimodem, 53
Binary headers, 488
BIOS, 21, 33, 133, 152, 323, 356
  initialize port, 324
  input character, 326
  output character, 325
  readstatus, 326
BIOSPORT.CPP, 351
BIOSPORT.H, 334
BIOSPort::~BIOSPort (), 334, 335, 336
BIOSPort::BreakDetect (), 341
BIOSPort::Cd (), 339
BIOSPort::Cts (), 340
BIOSPort::Dsr (), 340
BIOSPort::FormatDebugOutput (), 342
BIOSPort::FramingError (), 341
BIOSPort::HardwareOverrunError (), 342

BIOSPort::ParityError (), 341
BIOSPort::read_buffer (), 343
BIOSPort::read_byte (), 338
BIOSPort::Ri (), 339
BIOSPort::RXSpaceUsed (), 346
BIOSPort::Set (), 339
BIOSPort::TXSpaceFree (), 345
BIOSPort::write_buffer (), 344
BIOSPort::write_byte (), 338
BIOSPort::write_settings (), 336
bits per second, 20
Blast, 53
BNU, 366
Boca Research, 257
BOCA.CPP, 264
boca_isr (), 266
BocaBoard, 257
BocaHandler, 261
BocaHandler::AddPort (), 263
BocaHandler::BocaHandler (), 263
BocaHandler::~BocaHandler (), 263
BocaHandler::DeletePort (), 264
Borland, 9
Break Detect, 139, 147
break bit, 143
break signal, 143
breakout boxes, 57
BuildCommDCB (), 387
Bus (), 132

## C

C libraries, 55
C++ features, 4
cable-making equipment, 61
cabling, 23
cabling kit, 62
Carrier Detect (CD), 18, 22, 91, 138
CCITT, 46
CCITT Recommendation V.24, 12
CE_BREAK, 390
CE_CTSTO, 390
CE_DSRTO, 390
CE_FRAME, 390
CE_MODE, 390
CE_OVVERUN, 390
CE_RLSDTO, 390
CE_RXOVER, 390
CE_RXPARITY, 390
CE_TXFULL, 391
Christensen, Ward, 475
CLASS CRC16, 500
CLASS CRC32, 500
class
    BIOSport, 332
    DigiBoard, 271, 296
    EBIOSport, 333
    file transfer, 493
    FOSSIL, 368
    fossil_info (), 370
    Handler, 162, 209
    Modem, 451
    PC8250, 163

# INDEX

RS232, 70, 72, 114
   settings, 114
   WindowsPort, 403
ClearCommBreak (), 388
CloseComm 90, 388
CLRDTR, 389
CLRRTS, 389
CompuServe Information Service (CIS), 55, 433
CompuServe Quick-B, 53
ConnectToIRQ (), 229, 238, 240, 253
CONSTAT, 386
Control-Break, 240
Control-C, 240
count, 93
CRC.CPP, 501
Crosstalk, 53
CTS, 138

## D

Data Communications Equipment (DCE), 12
Data Ready, 147
Data Set Ready (DSR), 22
Data Terminal Equipment (DTE), 12
Data Terminal Ready (DTR), 22
Datatracker DT-5, 57
DCB, 386
DCE, 14
DEC Rainbow, 356
DeletePort (), 266

DESQView, 217, 269, 366
device independent RS-232 function cells, 66
DIGI.CPP, 319
DIGI.H, 300
DigiBoard, 260
DigiBoard API, 275
   character ready flag, 287
   clear RX buffer, 289
   clear TX buffer, 289
   drop a port's handshake lines, 285
   extended port control, 281
   extended port initialization, 280
   get a port's parameters, 286
   get board information, 283
   get buffer count, 290
   get buffer sizes, 288
   get RX free space, 288
   get TX free space, 289
   initialize port, 277
   input a single character, 279
   output a single character, 278
   peek, 290
   raise handshake lines, 290
   read and modem status, 279
   read buffer, 288
   set BIOS pacing option, 293
   set handshaking, 289
   set water marks, 289
   write buffer, 288
DigiBoard interface, 275
DigiBoard::Break (), 309

DigiBoard::BreakDetect (), 312
DigiBoard::Cd (), 310
DigiBoard::Cts (), 311
DigiBoard::DigiBoard (), 298
DigiBoard::~DigiBoard (), 302
DigiBoard::Dsr (), 311
DigiBoard::Dtr (), 314
DigiBoard::DtrDsrHandshaking (), 314
DigiBoard::ErrorName (), 319
DigiBoard::FlushRXBuffer (), 317
DigiBoard::FormatDebugOutput (), 317
DigiBoard::FramingError (), 312
DigiBoard::HardwareOverrunError (), 313
DigiBoard::ParityError (), 311
DigiBoard::PeekBuffer (), 315
DigiBoard::read_buffer (), 308
DigiBoard::read_byte (), 307
DigiBoard::read_settings (), 303
DigiBoard::Ri (), 310
DigiBoard::Rts (), 314
DigiBoard::RtsCtsHandshaking (), 314
DigiBoard::RXSpaceFree (), 316
DigiBoard::RXSpaceUsed (), 316
DigiBoard::Set (), 309
DigiBoard::TXSpaceFree (), 316
DigiBoard::TXSpaceUsed (), 315
DigiBoard::valid_port (), 306
DigiBoard::write_buffer (), 308
DigiBoard::write_byte (), 307
DigiBoard::wrote_settings (), 305
DigiBoard::XonXoffHandshaking (), 313
DisconnectFromIrq (), 211, 229, 238

distinctive ring, 23
Divisor Latch Access Bit, 143
door program, 355
DOS device driver, 275
double buffering, 135
DSR, 138
DSZ.COM, 355, 478
DTE, 14
DTR, 144
DTR/DSR handshaking, 178
dual-port RAM, 272
dumb modems, 44

# E

EBIOS, 323
EBIOSPort::Break (), 351
EBIOSPort::Dtr (), 350
EBIOSPort::EBIOSPort (), 346
EBIOSPort::~EBIOSPort (), 347
EBIOSPort::read_settings (), 348
EBIOSPort::Rts (), 350
EBIOSPort::Set (), 351
EBIOSPort::write_settings (), 348
edge-trigger mode, 152, 245
EIA, 12
EnableCommNotification (), 388
enum
    DigiBoardError, 299
    ModemError, 450
    RS232Error, 76, 122
    RS232PortName, 112
    WindowsPortError (), 402

# INDEX

error codes, 77
error status, 77
EscapeCommFunction (), 389
EV_BREAK, 394
EV_CTS, 394
EV_CTSS, 394
EV_DSR, 394
EV_ERR, 394
EV_RING, 394
EV_RLSD, 394
EV_RLSDS, 394
EV_RXCHAR, 394
EV_RXFLAG, 395
EV_TXEMPTY, 395
event mask word, 393
Extended BIOS, 278
    initialize port, 327
    read modem control register, 328
    write modem control register, 328

## F

FIFO, 150
FIFO Enable bit, 150
File Transfer::error (), 494
File Transfer::status (), 494
file transfers, 50
flow control, 47
FlushComm (), 389
FlushRXQueue (), 389
FlushTXQueue (), 389
Forsberg, Chuck, 355, 476

FOSSIL, 355
    Level 5 document, 366
    specification, 356
FOSSIL API,
    break control, 364
    close port
    control DTR, 360
    flush TX buffer, 360
    get a received character, 358
    get driver information, 365
    initialize byte, 357
    open serial port, 359
    purge RX buffer, 361
    purge TX buffer, 361
    read buffer, 363
    read status register, 358
    set flow control, 362
    single character peek, 362
    transmit byte, 357
    transmit with no wait, 362
    write buffer, 364
FOSSIL.CPP, 381
FOSSIL.H, 369
FOSSIL::Break (), 378
FOSSIL::Dtr (), 380
FOSSIL::FlushRXBuffer (), 381
FOSSIL::FlushTXBuffer (), 381
FOSSIL::FormatDebugOutput (), 374
FOSSIL::~FOSSIL (), 372
FOSSIL::FOSSIL (), 370
FOSSIL::Peek (), 380
FOSSIL::read_buffer (), 376
FOSSIL::RtsCtsHandshaking (), 379
FOSSIL::RXSpaceFree (), 378

FOSSIL::RXSpaceUsed (), 378
FOSSIL::Set (), 375
FOSSIL::TXSpaceFree (), 377
FOSSIL::TXSpaceUsed (), 377
FOSSIL::write_buffer (), 376
FOSSIL::write_byte (), 375
FOSSIL::write_settings (), 372
FOSSIL::XonXoffHandshaking (), 379
fossil_info::fossil_info (), 370
Framing Error, 139, 147
full-duplex, 41
function pointers, 67, 69

## G

gender changer, 30
GEnie, 55
GetCommError (), 389, 390
GetCommEventMask (), 391
GetCommState (), 391

## H

half-duplex, 41
handle_modem_status_interrupt (), 171
handle_rx_interrupt (), 172
handle_tx_interrupt (), 172
Handler, 245, 248, 249
Handler::DeletePort (), 211
hardware flow control, 48
hardware overrun error, 37
Hayes ESP card, 157
HEX headers, 487
high-level API, 273

HookVector (), 235
Huffman coding, 45

## I

I/O bus, 134
IE_BADID, 392
IE_BAUDRATE, 392
IE_BYTESIZE, 392
IE_DEFAULT, 392
IE_HARDWARE, 392
IE_MEMORY, 392
IE_NOPEN, 392
IE_OPEN, 392
inheritance, 4, 5
INT 1BH, 240
INT 14H, 71
INT 14H BIOS interface, 275
INT 23H, 240
int86(), 276
Int DisconnectFromIRQ (), 240
intelligent dispatcher, 66
International Organization for Standardization (ISO), 14
Interrupt ID Register, 139, 169
Interrupt manager package, 229
Interrupt Service Routine (ISR), 139
interrupt chaining, 246
interrupt enable register, 137
ISA bus, 245, 271
ISO 10646, 14
ISR, 157
isr_8250 (), 210
ISR_8250.CPP, 169, 175

# INDEX

isr_data:: ms_int_count, 166
isr_data::blocked, 166
isr_data::blocking, 166
isr_data::handshaking, 166
isr_data::line_status, 166
isr_data::modem_status, 167
isr_data::overflow, 165
isr_data::rx_int_count, 165
isr_data::RXQueue, 167
isr_data::send_handshake_char, 166
isr_data::tx_int_count, 166
isr_data::tx_running, 165
isr_data::TXQueue, 167
isr_data::uart, 165
isr_data::uart_type, 165

## J
jump_start (), 174, 212, 220

## K
Kermit, 52

## L
laptop computers, 154
level-triggered, 245
Line Control Register (LCR), 36, 141
line monitors, 59
line status handler, 181
Line Status Interrupt (LSI), 139, 140
Line Status Register (LSR), 146

locked DTE, 47
Loopback bit, 145
LZW, 47

## M
Macintosh Cabling, 31
mandatory virtual functions, 87
Mark parity, 142
MCA,CPP, 252
MCA.H, 249, 250
MicroChannel, 160
MicroChannelHandler::AddPort (), 252
MicroChannelHandler::DeletePort (), 252
MicroChannelHandler::MicroChannel-Handler (), 251
MicroChannelHandler::~MicroChan-nelHandler (), 251
Microcom, Inc., 45
Microsoft, 9
Microsoft Windows, 385
Mini 8-pin connector, 32
MNP-4, 44
MNP-5, 45
modem, 433
   class, 450
   control register, 144
   status interrupt, 138, 140, 153
   status interrupt handler, 178
Modem Control Register (MCR), 36
Modem Status Register (MSR), 148

MODEM.CPP, 467
MODEM.H, 452
Modem::Answer (), 453, 464
Modem::carrier_timeout, 457
Modem::Compressing (), 455
Modem::compressing, 457
Modem::Dial (), 453, 463
Modem::Disconnect (), 454, 464
Modem::DumpState (), 455, 466
Modem::echo (), 457
Modem::ErrorName (), 455, 460
Modem::Initialize (), 453, 460
Modem::local_baud_rate, 456
Modem::Modem (), 452
Modem::modem_data, 456
Modem::port, 456
Modem::Protocol (), 455
Modem::protocol, 456
Modem::PulseDial (), 455
Modem::read_line (), 458, 461
Modem::ReadRegister (), 454, 465
Modem::SendCommand (), 454, 466
Modem::SetCarrierTimeout (), 455
Modem::tone_dial, 456
Modem::ToneDial (), 455
Modem::UserAbort (), 454, 465
Modem::wait_for_connection (), 457, 461
Modem::wait_for_response (), 457, 461
ModemCapabilities, 446
motherboard timing, 153
MS-DOS, 385
MSDOS.CPP, 93, 109, 132
MSDOS.H, 109, 131
MSWIN.CPP, 424
multiport boards, 38
multitasking, 39

## N

notebook, 154
Novell NASI, 72
null modem adapter, 30
Null Modem Cable, 26

## O

OpenComm (), 391
Opus BBS, 54, 357
OS/2, 39
OUT1, 36, 144
OUT2, 36, 144
Overrun Error, 139, 147

## P

packet-switched networks, 52
Parity Errors, 139, 147
parity bits, 142
PBX, 23
PC BIOS, 71
PC to Modem cable, 25
PC8250, 88, 103, 107, 160, 248, 323
PC8250.CPP, 182, 208
PC8250.H, 164
PC8250::Break (), 197, 217
PC8250::BreakDetect (), 199, 218

# INDEX

PC8250::Cd (), 198, 217
PC8250::check_rx_handshaking (), 188, 212
PC8250::check_uart (), 187, 211
PC8250::Cts (), 198, 217
PC8250::Dsr (), 198, 217
PC8250::Dtr (), 203, 221
PC8250::DtrDsrHandshaking (), 202, 220
PC8250::ErrorName (), 208, 222
PC8250::fifo_setting, 168
PC8250::first_debug_output_line, 107, 168
PC8250::FlushRXBuffer (), 191, 214
PC8250::FlushTXBuffer (), 205, 222
PC8250::FormatDebugOutput (), 205, 222
PC8250::FramingError (), 199, 218
PC8250::handler, 168
PC8250::HardwareOverrunError (), 200, 218
PC8250::interrupt_number, 168
PC8250::irq, 168
PC8250::isr_data, 168
PC8250::ParityError (), 198, 218
PC8250::PC8250 (), 182, 209
PC8250::~PC8250 (), 187, 211
PC8250::PeekBuffer (), 204, 222
PC8250::read_buffer (), 190, 213
PC8250::read_byte (), 189, 212
PC8250::read_settings (), 194, 215
PC8250::Ri (), 198, 217
PC8250::Rts (), 204, 221

PC8250::RtsCtsHandshaking (), 201, 220
PC8250::RXSpaceFree (), 205, 216
PC8250::RXSpaceUsed (), 197, 216
PC8250::Set (), 196, 215, 216
PC8250::set_uart_address_and_irq (), 186, 211
PC8250::SoftwareOverrunError (), 200, 218
PC8250::TXSpaceFree (), 197, 216
PC8250::TXSpaceUsed (), 205, 216
PC8250::write_buffer (), 191, 214
PC8250::write_byte (), 190, 213
PC8250::write_settings (), 192, 215
PC8250::XonXoffHandshaking (), 201, 219
PC8250_HANDSHAKE_LINE_IN_USE, 221
PC8250_UART_NOT_FOUND, 103
PC8250Error, 104, 161
PCBoard, 54
PCIRQ.CPP, 168, 240
PCIRQ.H, 230
pinouts, 16
polled-mode output, 37
polling loop, 138
portable, 11
PORTABLE.H, 109, 112
procedural programming, 4
Procomm, 546
Prodigy, 55
protected data members, 81
pure function, 70

## Q

Queue, 224
Queue.CPP, 227
Queue.H, 227
Queue::Clear (), 226, 299
Queue::FreeCount (), 226, 228
Queue::Head (), 229
Queue::Insert (), 225, 228
Queue::InUseCount (), 217, 226, 228
Queue::Peek (), 227, 228
Queue::Queue (), 225, 228
Queue::Remove (), 212, 226, 228
Queue::Tail (), 229
Queue::FreeCount (), 217

## R

RBBS, 54
RD, 19
ReadComm (), 392
ReadLine (), 604
ReadTime(), 131
receive buffer register, 135
Receive Data Available (RDA) interrupt, 137, 141
receive interrupt handler, 180
Received Data register, 36
reset mode, 551
restore cursor position, 549
RestoreKeyboardBreak (), 237
Ring Indicator (RI), 23, 62, 138
RJ-11, 258
RJ-45, 62
RS-232 Standard, 11

RS-232-C, 12
RS-422, 31
RS232 _ILLEGAL_PARITY-SETTING, 89
RS232 Byte-Count, 78
RS232 class, 65
RS232 ElapsedTime, 78
RS232 SUCCESS, 77
RS232, 330
RS232.CPP, 96, 100, 109, 130
RS232.H, 72, 109, 103, 117
RS232:: debug_line_count, 106
RS232:: ErrorName(), 102, 106
RS232:: FlushRXBuffer(), 102, 215
RS232:: FlushTXBuffer(), 102
RS232:: FormatDebugOutput(), 106
RS232:: port_name, 82
RS232::Break(), 98, 128
RS232::BreakDetect(), 91
RS232::ByteCount, 86, 87
RS232::Cd(), 90
RS232::Cts(), 90
RS232::debug_line-count, 84, 97
RS232::DebugLineCount(), 97
RS232::Dsr(), 90
RS232::Dtr(), 100, 129
RS232::DtrDsrHandshaking(), 99, 129
RS232::ElapsedTime, 87, 92, 94, 96
RS232::error_status, 84, 96
RS232::ErrorName, 118
RS232::ErrorStatus(), 84, 96
RS232::FlushRXBuffer (), 117, 128
RS232::FormatDebugOutput(), 84, 120
RS232::Framing Error(), 91

# INDEX

RS232::HardwareOverrunError(), 91
RS232::IdleFunction(), 93, 95, 99, 105, 131
RS232::ParityError(), 91
RS232::Peek(), 96, 101, 118, 129
RS232::Read(), 85, 87, 92, 93, 122, 125, 126, 212
RS232::read_buffer(), 85
RS232::read_byte(), 86
RS232::Ri(), 90
RS232::~RS232(), 98
RS232::Rts(), 100, 129
RS232::RtsCtsHandshaking(), 99, 128, 129
RS232::RXSpaceFree(), 101, 128
RS232::RXSpaceUsed(), 90
RS232::Set(), 88
RS232::settings
RS232::SoftwareOverrunError(), 99, 128
RS232::TXSpaceFree(), 90
RS232::TXSpaceUsed(), 101, 128
RS232::Write(), 85, 87, 94, 95, 123, 124
RS232::write_buffer(), 85
RS232::write_byte(), 86
RS232::XonXoffHandshaking(), 99, 128
RS232:ReadSettings(), 96
RS232:saved_settings, 82
RS232_ILLEGAL_BAUD_RATE, 89
RS232_ILLEGAL_STOP_BITS, 89
RS232_ILLEGAL_WORD_LENGTH, 89
RS232_NO_TERMINATOR, 94
RS232_NOT_SUPPORTED, 98
RS232_TIMEOUT, 78, 79, 96
RS232PortName, 82, 209
RTS, 144
RTS/CTS handshaking, 21, 47, 178, 449
RZ/SZ, 477

# S

S registers, 442
save cursor position, 549
semaphore, 274
set colors, 550
set mode, 551
Set43LineMode (), 606
SetCommBreak (), 393
SetCommEventMask (), 393
SetCommState (), 387, 395
settings, 82
settings::adjust (), 129, 216
signal ground, 23
smart modems, 44
smart terminals, 545
software flow control, 48
Space parity, 142
StarGate, 260
status register, 259
stop bits, 142
struct COMSTAT, 400
struct DCB, 396
struct isr_data_block, 162
struct ModemCapabilties, 451

659

## T

TD, 19
Telepath, 55
Telix, 546
termcap file, 545
TERMINAL.H, 553
Terminal::Display (), 555
Terminal::ReadPort (), 554
Terminal::Terminal (), 554
Terminal::WriteKey (), 555
TEST232.CPP, 240, 253, 609, 616
TEST232.EXE, 242, 266, 352, 382
TEST232.MAK, 352, 625
TEST232W.CPP, 430
TEST232W.DEF, 432
TEST232W.MAK, 432
TESTERM.CPP, 556
TESTSZM.MAK, 498
TESTTERM.MAK, 607
TESTZM.CPP, 494
TEXTWIN.CPP, 589
TEXTWIN.H, 583
TextWindow, 554
TextWindow::clear (), 582
TextWindow::DisplayTitle (), 596
TextWindow::GetAttribute, 583
TextWindow::GetDimensions (), 582, 585
TextWindow::GetPosition, 582, 591
TextWindow::GetPosition (), 585
TextWindow::Goto, 583, 591
TextWindow::operator<< (), 582, 592
TextWindow::ReadKey (), 583, 605
TextWindow::Scroll, 592
TextWindow::SetAttribute (), 582
TextWindow::SetPosition (), 582
TextWindow::SetWrap, 583
TextWindow::~TextWindow (), 595
TextWindow::Textwindow (), 594
transmit holding register, 136, 141
Transmit Holding Register Empty, 147
TransmitCommChar (), 395
Transmitter Empty, 148
TrapKeyboardBreak (), 237
TSTMODEM.CPP, 471
TSTMODEM.MAK, 473
TX interrupt handler, 179

## U

UART chip, 33
UART scanning, 248
UARTs, 11
UNCHANGED, 79, 89
UngetCommChar (), 395
UnHookVector, 236
Unicode, 14
UNIX, 39
UNUSED, 80

## V

V.22*bis*, 42, 434
V.32, 43, 434
V.32*bis*, 37, 43, 434
V.42*bis*, 37, 46
V.fast, 43
virtual functions, 4, 5, 69, 70

# INDEX

void boca_isr (), 262
void isr_8250 (), 170
voltmeter, 63

## W

Wildcat!, 54
Windows, 366
WindowsPort, 386
WindowsPort::Break (), 414
WindowsPort::BreakDetect (), 416
WindowsPort::Cd (), 414
WindowsPort::Cts (), 415
WindowsPort::Dsr (), 415
WindowsPort::Dtr (), 418
WindowsPort::DtrDsrHandshaking (), 417
WindowsPort::error_status, 392
WindowsPort::ErrorName (), 422
WindowsPort::FlushRXBuffer (), 413
WindowsPort::FlushTXBuffer (), 419
WindowsPort::FormatDebugOutput (), 420
WindowsPort::FramingError (), 416
WindowsPort::HardwareOverrun-
   Error (), 416
WindowsPort::ParityError (), 415
WindowsPort::read_buffer (), 411
WindowsPort::read_byte (), 410
WindowsPort::read_settings (), 407
WindowsPort::Ri (), 414
WindowsPort::Rts (), 418
WindowsPort::RtsCtsHandshaking (), 417
WindowsPort::RXSpaceFree (), 419
WindowsPort::RXSpaceUsed (), 413
WindowsPort::Set (), 406
WindowsPort::TXSpaceFree (), 413
WindowsPort::TXSpaceUsed (), 419
WindowsPort::WindowsPort (), 405
WindowsPort::~WindowsPort (), 406
WindowsPort::write_buffer (), 395, 396, 412
WindowsPort::write_byte (), 395, 396, 411
WindowsPort::write_settings (), 408
WindowsPort::XonXoffHandshaking (), 417
WindowsPortSoftwareOverrunError (), 415
WINPORT.CPP, 423
WINPORT.H, 404
wired OR, 159
WriteComm (), 396

## X

X00.SYS, 383
Xenix, 39
XICONFIG.EXE, 277
XIDOS5.SYS, 275
XIDOSCFG.EXE, 292
XMODEM, 51, 457
XMODEM-1K, 51
XMODEM-1K-G, 51

XON/XOFF, 47, 286
  flow control, 49, 50
  handshaking, 180
  protocol, 48

# Y
YMODEM, 51, 457

# Z
ZABORT, 484
ZCHALLENGE, 485
ZCOMMAND, 486
ZCOMPL, 485
ZCRC, 485
ZDATA, 484
ZEOF, 485
ZFERR, 485
ZFIN, 484
ZFREECNT, 485
ZMODEM, 52, 457
  frame, 486
  header, 486
ZMODEM.CPP, 508
Zmodem::Receive (), 514
Zmodem::Send (), 509
Zmodem::Zmodem (), 509
ZNAK, 484
Zortech/Symantec, 9
ZRINIT, 479
ZRPOS, 484
ZRQINIT, 479
ZSKIP 484